Why Is Math
So Hard for
Some Children?

+ + + + + + + + + + + + + + + + +

Why Is Math So Hard for Some Children?

+ + + + + + + + + + + + + + +

The Nature and Origins of Mathematical Learning Difficulties and Disabilities

edited by

Daniel B. Berch, Ph.D.
National Institute of Child Health and Human Development
National Institutes of Health
Bethesda, Maryland

and

Michèle M.M. Mazzocco, Ph.D.
Johns Hopkins University School of Medicine
Baltimore, Maryland

with invited contributors

·P A U L·H·
BROOKES
PUBLISHING CO®

Baltimore • London • Sydney

Paul H. Brookes Publishing Co.
Post Office Box 10624
Baltimore, Maryland 21285-0624

www.brookespublishing.com

Typeset by Integrated Publishing Solutions, Grand Rapids, Michigan.
Manufactured in the United States of America by
The Maple-Vail Book Manufacturing Group, York, Pennsylvania.

Some individuals described in this book are composites, pseudonyms, or
fictional accounts. Actual individuals' names have been changed and
identifying details have been altered when necessary to protect their
confidentiality.

The following were written by a U.S. Government employee within the
scope of his official duties and, as such, shall remain in the public domain:
The introductions to Sections I–VI.

The opinions and assertions contained herein are the private opinions
of the authors and are not to be construed as official or reflecting the
views of the U.S. Government.

Library of Congress Cataloging-in-Publication Data

Why is math so hard for some children? : the nature and origins of
mathematical learning difficulties and disabilities / edited by Daniel B. Berch,
Michèle M.M. Mazzocco; with invited contributors.
    p.   cm.
Includes index.
ISBN-13: 978-1-55766-864-6 (hardcover)
ISBN-10: 1-55766-864-7 (hardcover)
1. Mathematical ability—Study and teaching.   2. Mathematics—Study
and teaching.   3. Learning disabilities—Education.   I. Berch, Daniel B.
II. Mazzocco, Michèle M.M.   III. Title.
QA11.2.W525 2007
510.71—dc22
    2007004667

British Library Cataloguing in Publication data are available
from the British Library.

Contents

About the Editors

Daniel B. Berch, Ph.D., Associate Chief, Child Development and Behavior Branch, National Institute of Child Health and Human Development, National Institutes of Health, 6100 Executive Boulevard, Room 4B05, Bethesda, MD 20892

Dr. Berch directs a funding program in Mathematics and Science Cognition and Learning—Development and Disorders, in addition to fulfilling his administrative duties as Associate Branch Chief. Dr. Berch came to the Washington D.C. area in 1997 on an Executive Branch Science Policy fellowship sponsored by the Society for Research in Child Development/American Association for the Advancement of Science. He was subsequently appointed Senior Research Associate at the U.S. Department of Education, advising the Assistant Secretary for Educational Research and Improvement on technical and policy matters pertaining to educational research. In his prior academic career, Dr. Berch was Director of Research for the Department of Psychology at the University of Cincinnati, where he also chaired the University's Institutional Review Board and served as Research Coordinator for the University Affiliated Cincinnati Center for Developmental Disorders. He has published an assortment of journal articles dealing with children's numerical cognition, mathematical learning disabilities, and spatial information processing. Dr. Berch is a fellow of the American Psychological Association's Division of Experimental Psychology and is currently serving as an ex officio member of the U.S. Department of Education's National Mathematics Advisory Panel, which will advise the administration on the best use of scientifically based research to advance the teaching and learning of mathematics.

Michèle M.M. Mazzocco, Ph.D., Associate Professor of Psychiatry and Behavioral Sciences, Johns Hopkins University School of Medicine; Director, Math Skills Development Project, Kennedy Krieger West Campus, Kennedy Krieger Institute, 3825 Greenspring Avenue, Painter Building, Baltimore, MD 21211

Dr. Mazzocco serves as Associate Professor of Population and Family Health Sciences, Johns Hopkins Bloomberg School of Public Health, in addition to her other positions at the Johns Hopkins University School of Medicine and the Kennedy Krieger Institute. She completed her doctoral training in experimental psychology at Arizona State University and a postdoctoral fellowship at the University of Colorado Health Sciences Center. Prior to that training, Dr. Mazzocco spent time as a classroom teacher while working toward a master's degree in early childhood education. As such, she is interested in applying findings from her research to the classroom and other applied settings. Dr. Mazzocco's research interests concern typical and atypical development in childhood. In 1997, she initiated and developed a longitudinal research program on mathematical ability and disability during the elementary and middle school years, which was in its 10th year at the time of this book's publication. Dr. Mazzocco has published more than 70 articles and chapters related to aspects of child development, including mathematical ability and disability, and she teaches courses in child development and learning disabilities.

About the Contributors

Mark H. Ashcraft, Ph.D., Professor of Psychology, University of Nevada, Las Vegas, 4505 South Maryland Parkway, MS 5030, Las Vegas, NV 89154. Dr. Ashcraft teaches psychology at the University of Nevada, Las Vegas. He received his doctorate in psychology from the University of Kansas in 1975. He was Professor of Psychology at Cleveland State University from 1975 to 2005. Dr. Ashcraft has authored more than 30 articles and chapters on mathematical cognition.

Rebecca Bull, Ph.D., Senior Lecturer, School of Psychology, University of Aberdeen, William Guild Building, Aberdeen, Scotland AB24 2UB, United Kingdom. Dr. Bull completed her doctorate at the University of St. Andrews in 1997. Her research interests include mathematical cognition in deaf and hearing children and adults and the interaction of working memory and executive functioning with social and academic skills.

Brian Butterworth, Ph.D., Professor of Cognitive Neuropsychology, Institute of Cognitive Neuroscience, University College, London, 17 Queen Square, London, England WC1N 3AR, United Kingdom. In addition to his work in cognitive neuropsychology at University College, London, Dr. Butterworth was the founding editor of the academic journal *Mathematical Cognition*. He taught at Cambridge University for 8 years and is a professorial fellow at the University of Melbourne, Australia. He was elected Fellow of the British Academy in 2002. Dr. Butterworth is currently working with colleagues on the neuroscience and genetics of mathematical abilities and is developing screening tools and interventions for use in schools.

Jennifer Byrd-Craven, M.S., Graduate Research Assistant, University of Missouri, 210 McAlester Hall, Columbia, MO 65207. Ms. Byrd-Craven received her master of science in clinical neuropsychology in 2001 from the University of Texas–Tyler, and is working toward a 2007 doctorate from the University of Missouri–Columbia at the time of this book's publication. Her research interests include cognitive development and individual differences in stress response during development.

Benjamin Clarke, Ph.D., Research Associate, Pacific Institutes for Research, 1600, Millrace Drive, Suite 111, Eugene, OR 97404. In addition to his work at the Pacific Institutes for Research, Dr. Clarke is a project director on an Institute of Education Sciences field grant to develop, field test, and validate a kindergarten mathematics curriculum and assessment system. He received his doctorate in psychology in 2002 from the University of Oregon. Dr. Clarke has also worked on the external evaluation team for Oregon Reading First, as an associate for the Western Region Reading First Technical Assistance Center, and as a researcher investigating the teaching of reading comprehension with first-grade students.

Margarete Delazer, Ph.D., Professor of Neuropsychology, Clinical Department of Neuropsychology, Innsbruck Medical University, Anichstrasse 35, Innsbruck 6020, Austria. Dr. Delazer teaches and works as a clinical neuropsychologist at the Department of Neurology. Dr. Delazer has performed several research projects on number processing and arithmetic. These studies include neuropsychological single case and group studies, as well as studies using functional magnetic resonance imaging.

Chris Donlan, Ph.D., Senior Lecturer, University College, London, Chandler House, 2 Wakefield Street, London, England WC1N 1PF, United Kingdom. Prior to his work at University College in London, Dr. Donlan was a teacher in special education for 10 years before receiving a doctorate in psychology and developing a research program exploring the role of language in mathematical development.

Linda Ewing-Cobbs, Ph.D., Professor of Pediatrics, Children's Learning Institute, University of Texas Health Science Center, 7000 Fannin, Suite 2401, Houston, TX 77030. In addition to teaching pediatrics, Dr. Ewing-Cobbs is Director of the Dan L. Duncan Neurodevelopmental Clinic at the University of Texas Health Science Center in Houston. She is the principal investigator on several grants funded by the National Institutes of Health that examine developmental cognitive and executive processes as well as neuroimaging factors that influence academic skill development and functional academic performance in children who sustain traumatic brain injuries and of children with developmental learning differences.

Jack M. Fletcher, Ph.D., Distinguished University Professor, Department of Psychology, University of Houston, Medical Center Annex, 2151 West Holcombe Boulevard, Suite 222, Houston, TX 77204-5053. For more than 30 years, Dr. Fletcher, a child neuropsychologist, has conducted research on many issues related to reading, learning disabilities, and dyslexia, including definition and classification, neurobiological correlates, and intervention. He was the 2003 recipient of the Samuel T. Orton award from the International Dyslexia Associations and a co-recipient of the Albert J. Harris award from the International Reading Association in 2006.

Douglas Fuchs, Ph.D., Nicholas Hobbs Professor of Special Education and Human Development, Vanderbilt University, Peabody College Box 328, Nashville, TN 37203. In addition to his teaching duties, Dr. Fuchs co-directs the Kennedy Center Reading Clinic at Vanderbilt University. He conducts programmatic research on response-to-intervention as a method for identifying children with learning disabilities and on reading instructional methods for improving outcomes for students with learning disabilities.

Lynn S. Fuchs, Ph.D., Nicholas Hobbs Professor of Special Education and Human Development, Vanderbilt University, Peabody College Box 328, Nashville, TN 37203. Dr. Fuchs also co-directs the Kennedy Center Reading Clinic at Vanderbilt University. She conducts programmatic research on assessment methods for enhancing instructional planning and on instructional methods for improving reading and math outcomes for students with learning disabilities.

David C. Geary, Ph.D., Curators' Professor, Department of Psychological Sciences, 210 McAlester Hall, University of Missouri, Columbia 65207. Dr. Geary received his doctorate in developmental psychology in 1986 from the University of California at Riverside and from there, held faculty positions at the University of Texas at El Paso and the University of Missouri. Dr. Geary served as Chair of the Department of Psychological Sciences from 2002 to 2005 and as the University of Missouri's Middlebush Professor of Psychological Sciences from 2000 to 2003, and is now Curators' Professor. Dr. Geary was recently appointed to the National Mathematics Advisory Panel, a group convened to advise the administration on the best use of scientifically based research to advance the teaching and learning of mathematics.

Russell M. Gersten, Ph.D., Professor of Special Education, University of Oregon R.G. Research Group, 2525 Cherry Avenue, Suite 300, Signal Hill, CA 90755. Dr. Gersten is a nationally recognized expert in both quantitative and qualitative research and evaluation methodologies with an emphasis on translating research into classroom practice. Increasingly, he has served as an expert in the area of mathematics research. Dr. Gersten was recently appointed to the National Mathematics Advisory Panel, a group convened to advise the administration on the best use of scientifically based research to advance the teaching and learning of mathematics.

Herbert P. Ginsburg, Ph.D., Jacob Schiff Professor of Psychology and Education, Teachers College of Columbia University, 525 West 120th Street, New York, NY 10027. Dr. Ginsburg's research interests include the development of mathematical thinking (with particular attention to young children and disadvantaged populations) and the assessment of cognitive function. He has conducted basic research on the development of mathematical thinking and has developed mathematics curricula for young children, tests of mathematical thinking, and video workshops to enhance teachers' understanding of students' learning of mathematics.

Sharon Griffin, Ph.D., Associate Professor of Education and Psychology, Hiatt Center for Urban Education, Clark University, 950 Main Street, Worcester, MA 01610. Dr. Griffin is the author of *Number Worlds: A Prevention/Intervention Math Program,* a member of the Mathematical Sciences Education Board at the National Research Council, and the recipient of several research awards to apply the findings of cognitive science to educational practice.

Steven A. Hecht, Ph.D., Associate Professor, Florida Atlantic University–Davie, 2912 College Avenue, Davie, FL 33314. Dr. Hecht is an applied cognitive developmental psychologist. His research includes a focus on identifying and describing children with math difficulties and disabilities. This research has practical implications for making math less difficult for some children.

Mary K. Hoard, Ph.D., Research Specialist, University of Missouri, 200 South 6th Street, Columbia, MO 65207. Dr. Hoard received her doctorate in developmental psychology in 2005 from the University of Missouri–Columbia. She has been a senior research specialist in the Department of Psychological Sciences at the University of Missouri since 2001, coordinating a research program on children's mathematical development.

Derek R. Hopko, Ph.D., Associate Professor and Licensed Psychologist, University of Tennessee, Knoxville, 307 Austin Peay Building, Knoxville, TN 37996-0900. Dr. Hopko graduated from West Virginia University in 2000 and completed his residency and post-doctoral training at the University of Texas Medical School in Houston. Dr. Hopko's research and clinical interests involve the behavioral assessment and treatment of individuals with mood and anxiety disorders. Dr. Hopko conducts treatment outcome research as it pertains to the relative efficacy of interventions to treat clinical depression, also addressing co-existent medical conditions that may be involved in the etiology and maintenance of depressive syndromes.

Nancy C. Jordan, Ed.D., Professor, University of Delaware, School of Education, 113 Willard Hall, Newark, DE 19716. Dr. Jordan received her doctorate in education from Harvard University and did post-doctoral work at the University of Chicago. She is the principal investigator for a developmental study of mathematics disabilities funded by the National Institute of Child Health and Human Development (NICHD), and is the director of the Children's Math Project, also funded by NICHD. She is the author or co-author of many articles on math learning difficulties.

Jeremy A. Krause, Department of Psychology, University of Nevada, Las Vegas, 4505 Maryland Parkway, MS 5030, Las Vegas, NV 89154. Mr. Krause is a doctoral candidate in psychology at the University of Nevada, Las Vegas. His research focus is on mathematical cognition.

Alex López-Rolón, M.A., Marie Curie Research Fellow, Laboratory of Cognitive Neurology and Neuropsychology, Department of Neurology, Innsbruck Medical University, Anichstrasse 35, Innsbruck 6020, Austria. Mr. López-Rolón is a psychologist working for the Austrian chapter of a trans-European research network on numeracy and brain development. He is a former scholar of the Ministry of Education of Japan and winner of a Teaching Excellence Award from the Japanese Educational Pictures Association.

Michael McCloskey, Ph.D., Professor, Department of Cognitive Science, Johns Hopkins University, 327 Krieger Hall, 3400 North Charles Street, Baltimore, MD 21218. Dr. McCloskey's research focuses on issues of mental representation and computation in the areas of spatial cognition and lexical processing. He studies cognitive deficits in children and adults with brain damage or learning disabilities, with the aim of gaining insight into normal cognitive representations and processes, how these are instantiated in the brain, and how they are disrupted when the brain is damaged or fails to develop normally.

Melissa M. Murphy, Ph.D., Johns Hopkins University School of Medicine, Kennedy Krieger Institute, 3825 Greenspring Avenue, Painter Building, Baltimore, MD 21211. Dr. Murphy is a post-doctoral fellow in developmental psychology at the Johns Hopkins University School of Medicine, Department of Psychiatry and Behavioral Science. She is actively involved in research at the Math Skills Development Project at the Kennedy Krieger Institute. Her research interests include characterizing math learning disability as well as exploring the relationship between language and cognition in both typical and atypical development.

Lara Nugent, M.A., Research Specialist, Department of Psychological Sciences, University of Missouri, 200 South 6th Street, Columbia, MO 65207. Ms. Nugent received her master's degree in cognitive psychology in 1997 from the University of Missouri–Columbia, while studying learning, memory, and attention with Dr. Nelson Cowan and Dr. Mike Stadler. She has helped to coordinate a research program on the development of children's mathematical skills with Dr. David C. Geary at the University of Missouri since 2004.

Sandra Pappas, Ph.D., Project Director, Teachers College, Columbia University, Human Development Office, Box 118, 525 West 120th Street, New York, NY 10027. The goal of Dr. Pappas's research efforts has been to expand the definition of mathematical competence to include both strategic and metacognitive abilities. The main focus of her empirical work has been to identify techniques that can be used within the classroom to promote the identification of mistakes, adapting strategies based on the demands of the task, and awareness and expression of thinking. The premise underlying her research is that efforts toward increasing students' metacognitive abilities will lead to improved performance over time not just in mathematics, but across multiple academic domains.

Stephen A. Petrill, Ph.D., Professor, The Ohio State University, 1787 Neil Avenue, Columbus, OH 43210. Dr. Petrill completed his doctorate at Case Western Reserve University. He studies gene environment processes and the development of reading and math ability. His scholarly interests include autism and other developmental disabilities.

Robert Plomin, Ph.D., Director and Research Professor, Institute of Psychiatry, King's College, Post Office Box P080, De Crespigny Park, London, England SE5 8AF, United Kingdom. Dr. Plomin is MRC Research Professor of Behavioral Genetics at the Institute of Psychiatry in London and Director of the Social, Genetic and Developmental Psychiatry Centre. His current research includes a study of 10,000 pairs of twins born in England during 1994–1996, which focuses on developmental problems in language, cognition, and adjustment. He is senior author of *Behavioral Genetics* (5th ed.), the major textbook in the field of genetics (Worth Publishers, in press) as well as author of a dozen other books. He has published more than 600 papers and chapters.

Vivian Reigosa, Ph.D., Senior Research Associate, Cuban Center for Neuroscience, Avenue 25, #15202, Cubanacan Playa, Ciudad Habana 11600, Cuba. In addition to teaching, Dr. Reigosa serves as Head of the Department of Brain Development at the Cuban Center for Neuroscience, where she has been on staff since 1988. Dr. Reigosa received her doctorate in psychology from Havana University in Havana, Cuba. She has published articles in the areas of language disorders diagnosis and reading disabilities. Dr. Reigosa's research is currently focused on the brain and developmental dyscalculia.

Susan M. Rivera, Ph.D., Assistant Professor, Department of Psychology, University of California, Davis, 202 Cousteau Place, Davis, CA 95618. Dr. Rivera specializes in neurocognitive development. Her work includes the study of individuals who are typically developing as well as individuals with neurodevelopmental disorders such as autism and fragile X syndrome. Dr. Rivera's investigations focus on several aspects of "parietally mediated" cognitive functioning, including arithmetic reasoning, so-called *dorsal stream functioning*, biological motion perception, and multisensory integration. She uses several different techniques in her research including eye-tracking, event-related potentials (ERP), and functional magnetic resonance imaging (fMRI).

James M. Royer, Ph.D., Research Professor of Psychology, University of Massachusetts–Amherst, 135 Hicks Way, Amherst, MA 01003. Dr. Royer is a Research Professor of Psychology at the University of Massachusetts–Amherst. He is also the director of the Laboratory for the Assessment and Training of Academic Skills. Dr. Royer completed his doctoral work in educational psychology at the University of Illinois, Urbana. His research interests are mathematical cognition and literacy.

Ruth S. Shalev, M.D., Director, Zusman Pediatric Neurology Unit, Shaare Zedek Medical Center, POB 3235, Jerusalem 91031, Israel. Dr. Shalev serves as Professor of Pediatric Neurology at the Ben Gurion University of the Negev, Israel, in addition to serving as head of pediatric neurology at Zedek Medical Center. Her scientific work has focused on the epidemiology and demographic features of developmental dyscalculia as well as on clinical aspects of cognitive disorders in children and adolescents.

Tony J. Simon, Ph.D., Associate Professor, Department of Psychiatry and Behavioral Sciences, University of California–Davis, MIND Institute, 2825 50th Street, Room 2341, Sacramento, CA 95817. Dr. Simon is a pediatric cognitive neuroscientist. His research focuses on the neural basis of cognitive impairments seen in genetic disorders that produce mental retardation, developmental disability, and psychopathology. Building on his influential theory of the foundations of numerical competence, Dr. Simon investigates how dysfunction in specific neurocognitive processing systems, such as attention and spatial cognition, can generate a range of cognitive and behavioral impairments. His goal is to develop remedial intervention programs that will minimize such disability. Dr. Simon's current projects center on studies of visuospatial and numerical cognition in children with chromosome 22q11.2 deletion syndrome, also known as DiGeorge syndrome and velocardiofacial syndrome.

H. Lee Swanson, Ph.D., Professor of Educational Psychology, Graduate School of Education, University of California–Riverside, Sproul Hall 2127, Riverside, CA 92521. Dr. Swanson holds a doctorate from the University of New Mexico and did post-doctoral work at the University of California, Los Angeles. He is the editor of the *Journal of Learning Disabilities*. Major teaching interests include information processing and individual differences and learning disabilities.

Joseph K. Torgesen, Ph.D., Russell and Eugenia Morcom Chair of Psychology and Education, Department of Psychology, Florida State University, Tallahassee, FL 32306. Dr. Torgesen has been conducting research involving students with reading and learning disabilities for more than 30 years. He serves as Director of the Florida Center for Reading Research and was appointed by President George W. Bush to serve on the National Board of Education Sciences in 2004.

Kevin J. Vagi, Ph.D., NIH Postdoctoral Fellow, Training in Mental Retardation/Developmental Disabilities Project, Department of Psychology, University of Miami, 352 Fred C. and Helen Donn Flipse Building, 5665 Ponce de Leon Boulevard, Coral Gables, FL 33146. Dr. Vagi's work, funded by National Institutes of Health/National Institute of Child Health and Human Development (NIH/NICHD), examines risk factors that contribute to the prevalence of developmental disabilities, with particular emphasis on secondary analyses of large-scale data sets. He is working on a project that will determine the impact of certain environmental toxins (e.g., lead, mercury) on the development of academic failure and mental retardation.

Rena Walles, M.S., Graduate Research Assistant, University of Massachusetts, Amherst, 135 Hicks Way, Amherst, MA 01003. Ms. Walles received her bachelor's degree in psychology from Saint Anselm College in 2002. She is a graduate student at the University of Massachusetts, where she received her master of science degree in 2005 and proposed her doctoral dissertation in August 2006.

Laura Zamarian, M.S., Psychologist, Department of Psychology, University of TriesteVia Sant'Anastasio, 12 Trieste 36134, Italy. Ms. Zamarian holds a position in cognitive neuropsychology at the University of Trieste. She engages in clinical and scientific collaboration with the Department of Cognitive Neurology and Neuropsychology at Innsbruck Medical University. Her main topics of interest are number processing and calculation abilities in patients with brain damage and healthy and pathological aging.

Sydney S. Zentall, Ph.D., Professor of Special Education, Department of Educational Studies, Purdue University, 100 North University Street, BRNG Hall, West Lafayette, IN 47906. Dr. Zentall has published widely in both psychology and education in the area of attention deficit hyperactivity disorder (ADHD) and has been the recipient of grants from the National Institute of Mental Health and the Office of Special Education. In 1995, she was inducted into the ADD Hall of Fame by Children and Adults with Attention Deficit/Hyperactivity Disorder (CHADD). She is the past president of the Division for Research of the Council for Exceptional Children.

Foreword
The Birth of a New Discipline

The fact that some people have great difficulties learning mathematical concepts, procedures, and facts—difficulties that go well beyond what would be expected from their general intelligence or competence in other aspects of life—has been known for at least a century. Neurologists noted the phenomenon near the turn of the 20th century, and it has received sporadic attention ever since. However, as noted in Gersten, Clarke, and Mazzocco's introductory chapter to this volume, the amount of attention devoted to mathematical difficulties trails far behind the amount devoted to the parallel phenomenon of dyslexia. Searches by these authors of the ERIC and PubMed databases yielded quantitative evidence of the magnitude of the discrepancy. For example, searches of ERIC that used a variety of reasonable descriptors for each type of disability yielded the following ratios of articles on reading disabilities to articles on math disabilities: for the period 1966–1975, 100:1; for 1976–1985, 36:1; for 1986–1995, 22:1; and for 1996–2005, 14:1. Although the ratio has decreased over time, the discrepancy remains startling.

The reasons for the discrepancy are not hard to understand. Most people view reading as more important than math, and in some ways, an argument can be made for this view. Poor reading skills clearly pose serious problems for success in almost every aspect of adult life. However, inferior mathematical skill is far more injurious than is commonly recognized. It is not just that lack of mathematical proficiency rules out high-level jobs in engineering and science or that mathematical proficiency in high school is positively related to adult income. In Chapter 19, the final chapter in this volume, McCloskey provides a particularly interesting list of certain aspects of mathematical thinking that are crucial in typical adults' everyday lives:

- Understanding whole numbers, fractions, percentages, and ratios—crucial for time and money management, including everything from balancing a checkbook to making decisions about income taxes to comparing terms on mortgages and car payments

- Understanding spatial relations—crucial for reading maps

- Understanding functions—crucial for understanding how home heating costs vary with thermostat settings, how diabetic symptoms vary with exercise and consumption of sweets, and so forth

- Understanding data displays, probability, variability, and chance—crucial for targeting how much money to set aside for retirement, for choosing among alternative investments, and for evaluating the statements of politicians and advocacy groups about public policy

Now consider some occupational applications of mathematical thinking:

- Setting prices for jobs to be done
- Estimating discounts on the spot while negotiating sales deals
- Using spreadsheet programs to monitor revenues and expenditures
- Projecting resource needs for the future

McCloskey also provides numerous examples of how occupations that usually are thought of as not requiring mathematical skills—forklift operator, gas station attendant, manufacturing worker, and so forth—actually do require them for the employee to be successful and at times, even safe.

> I worked for Nabisco. As a mixer, you had to know the correct scale and formulas. I kept messing up. I lost my job . . . If you don't know math, you can't succeed. (Curry, Schmitt, & Waldron, 1996, p. 63)

As McCloskey also points out, many non-occupational activities also require math skills: gardening (e.g., buying the right amount of fertilizer and grass seed), quilting (e.g., buying the right amount of materials of different colors), cooking (e.g., measuring ingredients for recipes), home repair projects (e.g., buying the right amount of carpet), and so forth to name only a few. And consider the following, poignant testament to the personal cost of mathematical disabilities:

> For as long as I can remember, numbers have not been my friend (Blackburn, 2006).

Volume editors Daniel B. Berch and Michèle M.M. Mazzocco have provided an invaluable obstetrical service in helping to bring into this world a new discipline of mathematical disabilities. To the best of my knowledge, this is the first book that has brought together a wide variety of perspectives and data on the phenomenon. The approach is multidisciplinary, including evidence from neurology; neuroscience; epidemiology; behavior genetics; cognitive, developmental, and educational psychology; and math education and special education. As would be expected in the early days of any new field, especially one that is sufficiently complex to demand insights from all of these disciplines, the amount that is known is dwarfed by the amount that is unknown. However, the forthrightness with which the authors face difficult questions and the progress they are making toward answering them are impressive. Consider some of the basic questions that they raise and that provide unifying themes across chapters:

What defines mathematical disabilities? As discussed in chapters by Mazzocco (Chapter 2), by Shalev (Chapter 3), and by Geary and colleagues (Chapter 5), no clear biological marker of mathematics disabilities has been identified. Math disability clearly has a genetic basis: The substantial heritability reported by

Petrill and Plomin (Chapter 14), and the elevated rates of mathematical disabilities among blood relatives described by Gersten and colleagues (Chapter 1) at-
test to this fact. However, for now at least, the presence of such disabilities in
any individual can only be defined in terms of behavior.

But which behaviors are definitional? Knowledge of facts? Knowledge of
procedures? Conceptual understanding? The speed and accuracy of performance? The quality of strategies and choices among strategies? Moreover, should
math disabilities be defined in terms of composite variables (e.g., 2 years below
grade level on an achievement test) or in terms of specific processes (e.g., 2 years
below grade level in conceptual understanding or in knowledge of arithmetic
facts)?

A different type of definitional question involves whether it is most useful
to define mathematics disabilities relative to other children (e.g., the bottom N
percent), relative to other competencies (e.g., at least 1 standard deviation
below what would be expected from the child's IQ score), or in combined terms
(e.g., meeting both of the above criteria). Yet another set of definitional questions concerns whether children whose home and school environments place
them at risk for mathematical problems should be grouped together with children whose environments are supportive but who do equally poorly in math.
All of these definitional questions are crucial for answering many other questions, including the following:

Which children have math disabilities? How stringent a criterion should be set
for inclusion in this category? As Swanson states in his commentary to Part I,
Section III, some studies set criteria sufficiently stringent that only 4% of children
are classified as having mathematics disabilities, whereas other studies set criteria sufficiently inclusive that 48% of children are included. Investigators who
adopt the most inclusive criteria tend to refer to *mathematical difficulties* rather
than to *mathematical disabilities*; it remains unclear whether the two reflect different degrees of the same problem or whether they reflect different problems.

As Geary and colleagues note, the reason for the highly variable thresholds
is that research has not yet identified qualitative behavioral discontinuities that
separate children with and without mathematical disabilities. Shalev reviews
epidemiological studies across several countries that converge on a prevalence
of roughly 6%, but it is unclear whether this conclusion is based on pragmatic
and economic factors (how many children can be given special education in the
society) or on scientific and educational considerations. Royer and Walles
(Chapter 16) find that more boys than girls meet criteria for math disabilities, as
do more children from low-income than middle-income backgrounds and more
African American and Latino children than White or Asian children, but again,
the reasons for the discrepancies remain unclear. Without either biological
markers or qualitative discontinuities in mathematical behavior, establishing
nonarbitrary criteria for mathematics disabilities remains a challenging issue.

What is the structure of mathematics disabilities? Individual differences in
knowledge of mathematical concepts, procedures, and facts almost always correlate positively with each other. They also correlate positively with a wide
range of other abilities, including reading proficiency and general intelligence.
Children with math disabilities are thus not only worse at retrieval of arithmetic

facts but also at understanding mathematical concepts, executing relevant procedures, choosing among alternative strategies, understanding the language of story problems, understanding the instructions of teachers and textbooks, and so forth. These pervasive relations make theory construction both easier and harder—easier because there is no dearth of relations to focus on as the key ones, and harder because any reasonably simple theoretical structure must ignore important relations.

Among the promising developments reviewed in this volume are several theoretical proposals regarding the structure of mathematical thinking in general and mathematical disabilities in particular. Geary and colleagues emphasize the roles of three processes: working memory functioning, phonological processing, and visuospatial thinking. In Chapter 4, Butterworth and Reigosa suggest that in addition to general cognitive processes such as working memory, domain specific, modular representations of numbers play an important role. The roles of two underlying problems—poor fact retrieval and poor number sense—are emphasized by Jordan in Chapter 6; by Barnes, Fletcher, and Ewing-Cobbs in Chapter 10, and by Bull in her commentary to Part II, Section III.

Reflecting general trends in cognitive science, research on the neural substrate provides an increasingly important source of theoretical insights regarding mathematical performance and disabilities. In Chapter 13, Simon and Rivera focus on the brain circuitry underlying mathematical performance. They emphasize the role of several parietal areas, especially the inferior parietal sulcus and angular and supramarginal gyri, but they also note that prefrontal, cingulate, insula, precuneus, and temporal areas are often involved. The degree to which this circuitry is specific to mathematical processing remains controversial at this point, as does the degree to which mathematical disabilities reflects problems in one or more of these brain areas, but the rate of progress in this area is heartening.

How can findings with children and adults who are typical learners be used to understand the performance of children with mathematical disabilities? There is widespread agreement among the authors that insights from studies of typical learners' mathematical performance provide a useful base for analyzing and improving the performance of children with mathematics disabilities. There is much less agreement, however, as to what the relevant insights are. Some investigators, including Butterworth and Reigosa, Geary and colleagues, and Swanson, emphasize weaknesses in basic information processes such as working memory, phonological processing, and visuospatial representation. Other investigators, such as Jordan (Chapter 6); Hecht, Vagi, and Torgesen (Chapter 7); and Ginsburg and Pappas (Commentary on Part III), emphasize weaknesses in conceptual understanding and number sense. All of the investigators are struck by the children's poor mastery of number facts, but the investigators vary considerably in their explanations of the phenomena.

A noteworthy characteristic of this volume is that it does not limit itself to the cognitive aspects of mathematical disabilities—it also addresses social and emotional influences. Royer and Walles note the important role of motivation and how it often suffers when children make the transition to middle school. In Chapter 15, Ashcraft, Krause, and Hopko note how math anxiety interferes with many people's ability to solve math problems, and thus adversely affects their grades, test scores, and likelihood of taking future math courses. Ashcraft and colleagues also present evidence that math anxiety is stable over time, separate from general anxiety, and unrelated to intelligence, and that it works in large part by interfering with working memory functioning. Its sources, however, remain a mystery.

How can findings on the mathematical functioning of other atypical populations best be utilized? Children with a variety of primary diagnoses also encounter difficulty with mathematics. This volume includes chapters on the mathematical difficulties of children with specific language impairments (Donlan, Chapter 8), Turner and fragile X syndromes (Mazzocco, Murphy, and McCloskey, Chapter 9), spina bifida (Barnes, Fletcher, and Ewing-Cobbs, Chapter 10), attention deficit hyperactivity disorder (Zentall, Chapter 11), and traumatic brain injuries (Zamarian, López-Rólon, and Delazer, Chapter 12).

The research provides a sobering lesson for anyone who suspects that identifying the neural substrate of mathematical cognition will provide a royal road to theoretical progress. Consider the neuropsychological findings discussed by Zamarian and colleagues. Double dissociations have been observed in which addition and subtraction were preserved but multiplication was not; the reverse has been observed as well. In other cases, multiplication and addition were preserved but subtraction was not; the opposite has been observed, too. Thus, there is no single "arithmetic module" that subsumes all operations. Cases also have been reported in which certain classes of problems within a single operation have been preserved but others have not—tie problems have been preserved but non-tie problems have not, multiplying by 0 and 1 have been preserved but other problems have not, and so forth. Again, the relations have gone in both directions. Conceptual and procedural knowledge have shown similar double dissociations, as have approximate and exact calculation, and strategies and factual knowledge. And this list of dissociations is limited to whole number arithmetic, a small part of mathematics in general. Thus, although the study of intact and impaired brains is almost certain to make important contributions to theoretical progress eventually, the road will be neither straight nor fast.

How can research be applied to helping children with math disabilities? This volume includes several impressive efforts to help children with poor math skills. In Chapter 17, Griffin describes highly encouraging results with her Number Worlds curriculum for improving the numerical understanding of preschoolers and early elementary school students from low-income backgrounds. Among the principles that underlie this curriculum are aligning instruction with the natural developmental sequence of understandings, providing hands-on games and activities, encouraging communication about mathematical concepts, and engaging children's emotions and imaginations as well as their thinking. At the end of the curriculum, the low-income children's performance matched or exceeded the performance of children from upper-middle income backgrounds and children from Japan.

Fuchs and Fuchs (Chapter 18) use schema construction theory to similar good effect. By teaching rules for solving problems, categories for classifying problems that can be solved in similar ways, and the goal of relating novel problems to familiar ones, teachers produce not only learning of the instructed problems but impressive transfer as well. The gains are present in both typical populations and in children with mathematical disabilities. The success of these theory-based instructional efforts is perhaps the best evidence to date of the promise of the research described in this book.

Robert S. Siegler, Ph.D.
Teresa Heinz Professor of
Cognitive Psychology
Carnegie Mellon University
Pittsburgh, Pennsylvania

REFERENCES

Blackburn, J. (2006). *Damn the three times table.* Retrieved September 7, 2006, from Dyscalculia and Dyslexia Interest Group web site: http://ddig.lboro.ac.uk/documents/Jess_dyscalculia.doc

Curry, D., Schmitt, M.J., & Waldron, S. (1996). *A framework for adult numeracy standards: The mathematical skills and abilities adults need to be equipped for the future.* Adult Numeracy Network. Author.

Preface

Although reading skills are acknowledged by virtually everyone to be crucial for leading a productive life in modern society, the importance of acquiring basic math skills for functioning effectively in the 21st century is only beginning to be recognized by the general public. In their 1996 book, *Teaching the New Basic Skills: Principles for Educating Children to Thrive in a Changing Economy* (Free Press), Richard J. Murnane and Frank Levy observe that the "basic" math skills that are needed in the average American workplace are actually those that ought to be acquired by the ninth grade, ". . . yet many American students graduate from high school without mastering them." Ten years later (February 9, 2006), U.S. Secretary of Education Margaret Spellings, in testimony before the U.S. Senate Committee on Health, Education, Labor and Pensions, stated that ". . . almost half of our 17-year-olds do not have the basic understanding of math needed to qualify for a production associate's job at a modern auto plant."

Certainly, large numbers of students, even at the middle school level, have not acquired the basic skills they need in preparation for succeeding at high school level math. A teacher in the Washington D.C. area attested to precisely this state of affairs in a letter to *The Washington Post* several years ago:

> Many of the seventh graders I teach have a poor sense of numbers. They don't understand that adding two numbers results in a larger number, that multiplication is repeated addition, that 5 × 6 is larger than 5 × 4, or that one-quarter is smaller than one-half. This lack of basic math facts detracts from their ability to focus on the more abstract operations required in math at a higher level. (Sheridan, 2004)

Despite renewed efforts to strengthen the math skills of students in the United States and in many other countries, what is often overlooked is that any given approach to mathematics instruction will not be equally effective for all children. For some children who do not initially show improvement through standard pedagogical methods, the learning difficulties they experience will diminish within a year or two; such students may be most suitably considered as having a *developmental delay* in acquiring basic math skills. However, other children who do not respond well to established educational methods may more appropriately be characterized as having a mathematical learning *disability*. Although the lay public is generally familiar with the idea that some children can be classified as having a *reading* disability, they are much less likely to be aware of the fact that a child can possess a learning disability in *mathematics*. Moreover, as many adults who have succeeded in the workplace nevertheless acknowledge that math was a challenging subject for them in school, they may find it hard to understand that some children experience such severe and enduring impairments in math that prevailing instructional practices frequently fail to mitigate these problems.

Furthermore, comparatively little information on mathematical learning disabilities has been made available to special educators, let alone to the general public. One way to demonstrate the relative lack of the availability of any kind of information on this topic is to examine the number of web sites and other Internet sources devoted to mathematical learning disabilities as compared with reading disabilities (RD). At the time of this writing (October 30, 2006), when we "Googled" the phrase *reading disability*, it yielded 331,000 hits, and *math disability*—10,400 or only 3.1% of the RD hits (*dyslexia* produced 24,300,000 hits, whereas *dyscalculia* yielded only 260,000 hits or 1.1% of the dyslexia hits).

There are some hopeful signs that data related to mathematical learning disabilities is slowly beginning to reach a wider audience, however. For example, over the past 2 years, the National Center for Learning Disabilities in New York has been expanding their information base to include the topic of learning disabilities (LD) related to math. In 2005, they formed a roundtable of experts in this field to advise them on the nature of the research base, and they have since added math and LD information to their web site (http://www.ncld .org). However, the creation of such a forum naturally begs the question as to how much we actually do know about math LD and whether this knowledge is indeed founded on a rigorous and replicable evidence base. Establishing a robust research base is imperative if we truly expect to be able answer the question posed in the title of the present volume: "Why is math so hard for some children?" First, both the nature and origins of mathematical learning disabilities must be ascertained. Moreover, before seriously considering implementing remedial approaches on a broad scale, educators and professionals in the field must, at the very least, be able to define precisely what they mean by *mathematical learning disability*, and then develop both reliable and valid measures for identifying children with such a disorder.

These are just some of the complex issues addressed in this book, which consists of the first comprehensive and multidisciplinary examination of the study of mathematical learning difficulties and disabilities, including the historical foundations of this emerging field, current theoretical conceptions and research methods, the latest empirical findings, and descriptions of research-based instructional interventions. Multiple perspectives on this rapidly evolving area are presented, drawing on such disparate fields as cognitive and developmental psychology, educational psychology, neuropsychology, cognitive neuroscience, behavioral genetics, and special education.

The first section in Part I of this volume presents a historical overview of the field, followed by a detailed examination of issues pertaining to the definition and identification of math disabilities. The final chapter in this section examines what is currently known about the prevalence of this disorder worldwide. In Section II of Part I, both elementary and higher order cognitive processing deficits are reviewed, followed by an account of differences in numerical and arithmetic processing skills between children with math disabilities only and those with co-morbid math and reading disabilities. Then difficulties with fractions are elucidated, focusing especially on problems in mentally representing the meaningful aspects of fraction symbols.

Part II begins with a section on neuropsychological factors in math disabilities. The first chapter in this section assesses the role of language in mathematical learning by examining the mathematical deficits of children with specific language impairments. This is followed by several different chapters that include reviews and appraisals of numerical and arithmetic deficits associated with various neurodevelopmental abnormalities, including fragile X syndrome, Turner syndrome, spina bifida/myelomeningocele, and attention deficit hyperactivity disorder (ADHD), as well as deficits attributable to brain damage in children and adults. Section IV of Part II outlines the exciting contributions that neuroimaging and quantitative genetic approaches are beginning to make to our understanding of mathematical disabilities.

Section V of Part III addresses issues concerning sources of individual differences that may influence math performance, including math anxiety, motivation, gender, and cultural factors. The final section includes chapters that describe recent findings regarding interventions for young children who are at risk for developing math difficulties, effective instructional interventions for mitigating math problem-solving difficulties in school-age children, and how individuals with mathematical learning disabilities are frequently disadvantaged when it comes to meeting the quantitative demands of everyday life. Although numerous intervention programs are being designed for children who struggle with mathematics, the chapters in this section exemplify a more recently emerging trend toward developing evidence-based practices.

We hope this book will appeal not only to researchers working in the area of learning disabilities but also to special educators, mathematics educators, and clinicians whose practice includes children with learning disabilities or academic difficulties and to educational policy makers and even some parents of children with mathematical learning disabilities. Although several of the topics covered in this volume (e.g., cognitive neuroscience and behavioral genetics) entail some rather complex concepts and methodological approaches, these ideas are generally presented in a manner that should make them accessible to a wide-ranging audience. The chapter authors have tried to achieve this objective by carefully defining some of the foundational principles and assumptions guiding their work and by providing mini-tutorials, where appropriate. In addition, the brief descriptions at the beginning of each of the six sections have been designed to introduce the general reader to some of the basic concepts they will encounter in the ensuing chapters.

At the very least, we hope that this volume will bring to light the progress being made in this important field. Moreover, the recognition that mathematical learning disabilities do indeed exist, that their nature and origins are beginning to yield to scientific study, and that valid diagnostic and remedial tools are in the process of being developed should provide the reader with a useful guide as to what can be accomplished in the future. We dedicate our book to those working to achieve progress in this field, and, more important, to the children who are experiencing and enduring the effects of a mathematical learning disability as well as those who have yet to be diagnosed. They deserve no less.

Daniel B. Berch

Michèle M.M. Mazzocco

REFERENCES

Murnane, R.J., & Levy F. (1996). *Teaching the new basic skills: Principles for educating children to thrive in a changing economy.* New York: Free Press.
Sheridan, S.B. (2004, December 27). *The Washington Post.*

Acknowledgments

As perhaps only the editors of a collection of book chapters can appreciate, it takes the commitment and cooperation of a great many people to bring a project like this to fruition. First and foremost, I want to acknowledge our excellent and peerless slate of contributors for their willingness to share their considerable knowledge and expertise in a manner that makes the complicated conceptual issues and challenging methodological complexities associated with this nascent field accessible to a wide audience.

Thanks are also extended to the leadership at the National Institute of Child Health and Human Development (NICHD) of the NIH for strongly supporting not only the idea behind and preparation of this volume but also much of the research in the field of math disabilities, the results of which are evident throughout this volume. These individuals include Dr. Duane Alexander, NICHD Director, Dr. Yvonne Maddox, NICHD Deputy Director, and Dr. Anne Willoughby, Director of NICHD's Center for Research for Mothers and Children. In addition, I am particularly grateful to Dr. Peggy McCardle, Chief of NICHD's Child Development and Behavior Branch, for her encouragement and guidance during the formative stages of this venture as well as for her steadfast support in virtually every facet of my work at the Institute. And, I will always be indebted to Dr. G. Reid Lyon for initially bringing me to NICHD a decade ago to build a multidisciplinary funding program for research in mathematical cognition and learning disabilities.

My co-editor, Dr. Michèle M.M. Mazzocco, and I are also extremely grateful to Rebecca Lazo, Stephen Peterson, and Leslie Eckard of Paul H. Brookes Publishing Co. for their commitment to excellence, sage advice, and first-rate stewardship of this effort. Their astute guidance was of immense benefit in ensuring as smooth a series of transitions as possible from the initial concept all the way through to the production process. Furthermore, their collective excitement about this undertaking kept our own level of enthusiasm intact during times when it was difficult to envision the final product.

I would be remiss if I did not acknowledge Dr. Mazzocco for her unswerving dedication to this project, not to mention her wise counsel, thoughtful comments and criticisms, boundless energy, and the countless hours of hard work she has devoted to every phase of this endeavor—all during a time when she was simultaneously serving as the senior editor of another book. It is no exaggeration to say that the present volume would not have turned out half as well without her many invaluable contributions.

Finally, I am indebted to my parents, Saul and Faye, whose resolute faith in my abilities has always bolstered my confidence when I needed it most, and to Valerie, for her patience, support, and encouragement, especially during the final stages of this project.

D.B.B.

When I first began to explore the field of mathematical learning disability in the mid-1990s, the field was in its infancy. This was evident by the relatively small body of research published on the subject matter at the time, and by the explicit comments to this effect in the opening remarks of most of the work that then existed. During the last ten years, statements on the absence of research in this area have often reappeared in the literature, despite the growth that the field has witnessed. I believe that the work represented in this volume is testimony that the field has advanced beyond its infancy, even if it remains a relatively young field. The advances are apparent from the vast amount of expertise that the chapter authors have coalesced in so thoughtful and thorough a manner. I am deeply indebted to them for their contributions to this volume.

I am also grateful for the education, support, and guidance that have led me to the position of co-editor of this volume. First, I thank Dr. Daniel B. Berch for the opportunity to join him in this endeavor, and for the support and patience he offered me throughout this enriching process. I wish to acknowledge Dr. G. Reid Lyon, with whom my initial conversations about mathematical learning disabilities fostered the growth of my own research career. I also wish to acknowledge my colleagues David C. Geary and Michael McCloskey, with whom I've had the good fortune to seek counsel and collaboration throughout all phases of this research, and Research Coordinator Gwen F. Myers, for her outstanding commitment during the first 7 years of my longitudinal research. I am particularly grateful to the children who, each year for the last 9 years, have volunteered their time, effort, and opinions as participants in that research. They have been among my most powerful and dedicated teachers.

I am grateful to many others who have supported me on or up to this path, including my parents Marion and William who—among other things—nurtured my love for mathematics and science; my mentors Susan Somerville and Paul McHugh, who remain strong forces in my life and work; and especially my husband Michael, for his unwavering support for all my endeavors.

M.M.M.M.

Part I

Section I

Characterizing Learning Disabilities in Mathematics

"The greatest unsolved theorem in mathematics is why some people are better at it than others."
—Adrian Mathesis

*W*hy do some children experience persistent difficulties with learning mathematics, and *how* are these manifested in their performance? If we are to attempt to describe the nature and origins of children's mathematical learning difficulties and disabilities, it is necessary to first clarify what is meant by the terms used in the field. What is a mathematical learning disability? Does it differ from dyscalculia? When does a mathematical learning *difficulty* warrant the label *disability*? Can we say with absolute certainty that mathematical learning disabilities exist? If so, how often do these disabilities emerge among school-age children, and does this frequency differ across countries worldwide?

The use of these and related terms has varied throughout the brief history of mathematical learning disability (MLD) research. In Chapter 1, Gersten and colleagues describe how advances in our understanding of MLD represent a confluence of findings from the many disciplines that have contributed to this field during the last century. This historical perspective makes it possible to appreciate some of the sources of the inconsistencies in contemporary terminology. The authors also illustrate the paucity of research on MLD as compared with the considerably larger research literature pertaining to the topic of reading disability. Despite this discrepancy in research-based knowledge between these two areas, Gersten and colleagues underscore the rapid gains made in the MLD field during the past decade.

In Chapter 2, Mazzocco focuses specifically on terminology used in the field of MLD research, and claims that the inconsistent use of terms in research designs is a barrier to greater progress in the field. She seeks to establish a common language, to the extent possible, for the remaining chapters in this volume. By proposing boundaries for how terminology within this field is to be used, she also addresses the extent to which populations designated by specific terms overlap with one another. She reminds us that the need to establish a common, targeted consensus definition is currently one of the primary objectives of the field.

In Chapter 3, Shalev illustrates one of the most significant practical outcomes of an inconsistently used definition of MLD. She describes how prevalence rates (i.e., the proportion of existing cases in an entire population at a specified time) reported for mathematical learning disabilities vary as a function of the definitions used to classify children as having MLD. Through her review of prevalence studies conducted within many individual nations across the globe, Shalev provides the most up-to-date information available on the prevalence of MLD. In doing so, she establishes the magnitude of the issue by demonstrating the universality of MLD, indeed "the robustness of the phenomenon," as mathematical learning disabilities occur on a worldwide scale despite inconsistencies in the definitions used.

In view of the inconsistent use of terminology used in the field, a major objective of the chapters in this section is to establish a common language—not only for the subsequent chapters but also for the field. Efforts to reach a consensus definition of MLD are likely to be aided by an increasing awareness of both the sources and consequences of an imprecise definition.

Chapter 1

Historical and Contemporary Perspectives on Mathematical Learning Disabilities

Russell Gersten, Ben Clarke, and Michèle M.M. Mazzocco

+ +

Although the history of mathematical learning disability (MLD) is relatively short, any depiction of its history requires delving into the histories of medicine (particularly neurology), developmental psychology, cognitive science, mathematics education, special education, and even law. Indeed, each of these fields has contributed to the foundations of contemporary MLD research, including the areas of identification, diagnosis, and treatment of math disabilities. These multiple sources of information and the perspectives associated with each of these fields have given rise to the multidisciplinary field of MLD research and practice that exists today.

Despite the contribution of different disciplines to the domain of MLD research, a notable lack of communication exists across the various disciplines. This phenomenon is not unique to the field of MLD; it is present in any multidisciplinary field. A common language, or at least a common understanding across perspectives, can be facilitated by acknowledging the important contribution of each discipline to the foundation of future work. Consequently, in this chapter we review key contributions from neurology, developmental psychology, cognitive science and neuropsychology, and education and special education; we then briefly describe how the law

This research was supported in part by Grant Number S283B050034A from the Office of Elementary and Secondary Education of the U.S. Department of Education, awarded to Dr. Gersten, and NIH Grant HD 034061, awarded to Dr. Mazzocco. The authors wish to thank Elyse Hunt-Heinzen for her excellent contributions to data analysis and the preparation of this manuscript.

reflects these contributions in its mandates for children with MD. By synthesizing the contributions from these diverse sources, we hope to illustrate the solid foundation on which current MD research is building, even if its history has been comparatively short and sporadic.

Throughout its history, the terminology specific to what we now call *mathematics disability* has varied. For the most part, the intended meanings associated with different terms—for example, acalculia, dyscalculia, arithmetic disorder, specific learning disabilities in mathematics, or more recently, mathematics difficulties—have at times also been inconsistent. In this chapter, we use the term *mathematical learning disability* (MLD) even in instances in which another term may have been used initially due to the historical or clinical context in which it originated. We also describe definitions that have been put forth as the field developed, highlighting the diverse emphases that emerged during different historical periods.

Although some of the historical trends reviewed in this chapter are unique to the field of MLD, many are not. Some discussions reflect the history of learning disabilities as a broader field, others, the historical trends within the even broader field of child development. We make reference to these relationships where appropriate and also contrast them with the historical developments that have taken place within the well-established field of reading disability research.

HISTORICAL TRENDS

A comparison of the histories of MLD and reading disability (RD) illustrates that the field of MLD research has emerged as an active science rather recently. In terms of the sheer number of studies published in MLD and RD research, MLD has consistently received far less attention than RD. Although the number of published studies in MLD has begun to increase steadily, this relatively steep increase in attention to MLD is quite recent. Figures 1.1 and 1.2 demonstrate the discrepancy in the number of research studies conducted on RD versus MLD over the last 50 years and also how the ratio of studies of RD to MLD has declined from 100:1 to 14:1 since the 1950s. Figure 1.1a shows the number of research studies conducted on reading disability (RD) versus mathematical learning disability (MLD) from 1956 to 2005, based on an ERIC literature search, showing the relative frequency of studies conducted in these fields over time. The literature search for studies on RD included the key word terms *reading disorder, reading disability,* and *dyslexia.* The literature search for studies on MLD included the key word terms *acalculia, dyscalculia, mathematics disorder, mathematics disability, mathematics difficulties, arithmetic disorders,* and *mathematics disorders.* Figure 1.1b depicts the ratio of studies of RD versus MLD for each decade. Obviously, research devoted to RD still outnumbers studies on MLD, but there is some evidence that the interest in MLD research is steadily increasing.

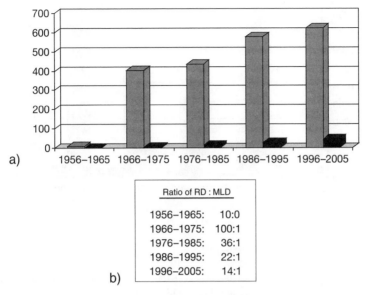

Figure 1.1. Figure 1.1. a) The number of research studies conducted on reading disability (RD) versus mathematical learning disability (MLD) from 1956 to 2005 (*Key:* ▓ = RD, ■ = MLD) and b) the ratio of studies of RD versus MLD for each decade from 1956–2005. *Source:* Educational Resources Information Center (ERIC) search.

A comparison of Figures 1.1 and 1.2 reveals comparable trends in studies carried out in education and medicine. We acknowledge that there is some overlap in the studies indexed in the education and medical databases (i.e., ERIC and PubMed). Nevertheless, the general trends are comparable across the two fields, because both datasets reveal a dramatic increase in the number of MLD studies indexed along with a striking decrease in the ratio of studies devoted to RD relative to MLD.

MEDICAL STUDIES AS THE FOUNDATION FOR RESEARCH ON MATHEMATICAL LEARNING DISABILITY

At first glance, it may appear implausible that the history of MLD research can be traced to the field of medicine. Yet, medical case studies, which are typically reports of individual patients with unique injuries and associated outcomes, have implications for specific aspects of biological function or development in the general population. Therefore, the relevance of medical case studies to MLD comes not from the rareness of individuals who are the subjects of such reports but from the unusual opportunities they offer to learn about brain function specific to mathematics. Individuals with specific brain lesions provide an "experiment in nature," from which it is possible to learn how mathematics-related skills are associated with distinct

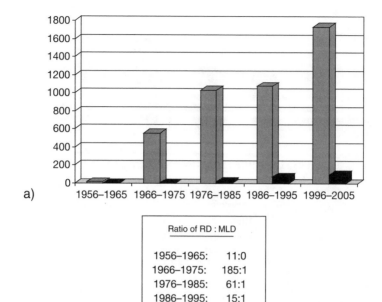

a)

b)

Ratio of RD : MLD	
1956–1965:	11:0
1966–1975:	185:1
1976–1985:	61:1
1986–1995:	15:1
1996–2005:	18:1

Figure 1.2. The number of research studies conducted on reading disability (RD) versus mathematical learning disability (MLD) from 1956 to 2005, using the same key word terms used for Figure 1.1 (*Key:* ▨ = RD, ■ = MLD). Note that the scale differs from that used in Figure 1.1; b) the ratio of studies of RD versus MLD for each decade. Source: National Library of Medicine and the National Institutes of Health: PubMed search.

neuroanatomical regions, as described in detail in Chapter 13. Indeed, with respect to MLD, the notion that a disability specific to mathematics could even exist initially emerged from medical case studies.

Among the first such case studies was a report by Lewandowsky and Stadelmann published in 1908. These neurologists demonstrated not only that mathematics ability was impaired because of a lesion to the brain's left hemisphere (within the posterior regions of the cortex, specifically) but also that this outcome was independent of any disruption to language function. This marked the beginning of viewing mathematics skills as potentially separate from overall cognitive ability. Moreover, Lewandowsky and Stadelmann described specific aspects of mathematics ability rather than mathematics as a unitary construct—a distinction with which we continue to grapple today (see Dowker, 2005, for a detailed treatment of this issue with respect to arithmetic abilities).

Additional case studies supported these conclusions, but it was not until 10 years later that Peritz (1918) proposed the notion of a "calculation center" within a specific left hemispheric region (the left angular gyrus). This notion was met with some controversy, as others believed that mathematics disability could result from disruption to one of several brain regions (e.g., the work of Luria, 1966). As this debate continued—or perhaps because of it—during the 1920s Swedish neurologist Salomon Henschen orchestrated the first systematic study of arithmetic disorders. It was Henschen who, in 1919, coined the term *acalculia*, or acquired disability of mathematics calculations. Note that this term preceded the term *dyscalculia*, or developmental mathematics disorder, by nearly 50 years, as described later in this chapter.

Henschen's case studies, and those of many others not reviewed here, demonstrated the complexity of mathematics as a cognitive construct and the challenges of localizing math ability to a single brain region or "calculation center." Although in support of the notion that mathematics and language functions were broadly independent of one another, he observed that some case study patients could read neither words nor numerals, whereas others had impairments in only one or the other ability. On the one hand, this observation appeared to run counter to the notion of math and language as independent functions; on the other, it was the type of observation that led Berger (1926) to propose that acalculia could be secondary to another, primary impairment. Thus, much like today's discussions of MLD, questions that emerged from the early medical case studies concerned the components of mathematics, the role of cognitive correlates, and the distinction between primary (direct) impairments in mathematics and impairments that are secondary to difficulties in other areas, such as language or spatial ability. The debate regarding the functional architecture of mathematics ability continues today within the broader and more diverse fields of clinical neuropsychology and cognitive science. This does not mean that medicine has taken a back seat to the study of MLD but instead reflects how the questions that are addressed today are both an extension and expansion of the foundation initially established in neurology.

Moreover, today's medical studies of MLD are limited neither to the specialty area of neurology nor to case studies. For example, the term *mathematics disorder* is included in the *Diagnostic and Statistical Manual (DSM-IV-TR)* developed by psychiatrists, having first appeared in the third edition (*DSM-III*; American Psychiatric Association, 1980). Furthermore, some of the most recent medical studies of MLD have addressed its incidence, such as the population-based study carried out by pediatricians (Barbaresi, Katusic, Collagin, Weaver, & Jacobsen, 2005; see also Chapter 3). Finally, in the branch of medicine referred to as the neural sciences—the field dedicated to uncovering "the mental processes by which we perceive, act, learn, and remember" (Kandel, Schwartz, & Jessell, 2000, p. 3)—scientists are addressing the mental processes involved in mathematical thinking as they continue to localize these processes to specific brain regions. It is worth noting that in the latest (fourth) edition of the "bible of neural sciences," *Principles of Neural Science* (Kandel et al., 2000), developmental dyslexia is indexed and described, whereas no such entry exists for developmental mathematics disorder or dyscalculia. However, Kandel and colleagues do address cognitive processes related to mathematics, such as working memory (see Chapter 5; Swanson & Siegel, 2001), even if the relationship to mathematics is not addressed.

MATH DISORDERS AS A NEUROPSYCHOLOGICAL PHENOMENON

The complexity of mathematics as a construct contributes to the lack of precision with which neural correlates of mathematics may be identified. From the perspective of the neural sciences—in which brain function is described at the microcellular level—even reading is sufficiently complex that "it is unlikely that there is a well-defined system in the brain dedicated to it . . . [and] dyslexia is probably a condition with several possible causes rather than a single syndrome" (Dronkers, Pinker, & Damasio, 2000, p. 1185). We would certainly expect no less from mathematics. So it is not surprising that the ongoing debates within neuropsychology and cognitive science are no longer focused on whether mathematics is linked to a single "calculation center," as proposed by Peritz in 1918, or is diffuse to the point that its disruption (i.e., dyscalculia) can result from "frontal, temporal, parietal, and temporoparietal lesions in the left hemisphere as well as in the right hemisphere . . ." (as reviewed by Kahn & Whitaker, 1991, p. 106). Instead, the questions driving these disciplines concern differentiation of aspects of mathematics behaviors, and more specifically, which cognitive processes and corresponding brain mechanisms lead to disabilities in these areas (e.g., see Chapters 4, 5, and 13).

A number of cognitive models have emerged as a result of these efforts (as described further in Chapter 12), such as the McCloskey (1992) model, which stipulates distinct Arabic versus verbal representation of calculations and further differentiates calculation comprehension and production. The research in this area borrows from the initial approach of single-patient studies, or multiple cases sometimes compared with individuals without any known disorders (e.g., McCloskey, 1992). Groups of patients or individuals having various syndromes may also be included in studies of these models (see Chapter 9). From these patient studies, models have been applied to groups of children with mathematics disability (e.g., Gross-Tsur, Manor, & Shalev, 1996). Although no consensus has been reached regarding the accuracy or "best fit" of any single model, nor with respect to the specific mathematics components responsible for the difficulties and disabilities observed in children who struggle with mathematics, this body of research suggests important caveats for oversimplifying the nature of MLD.

One neuropsychological tool available for studying models of mathematics disability is brain imaging. The historically recent advances in brain imaging techniques have led to significant progress beyond what was learned from the early single-patient studies. This is because it is no longer necessary to infer brain function from experiments in nature only (from lesions in specific regions); brain function can be imaged during specific cognitive tasks, including arithmetic (as discussed in more detail in Chapter 13). The more invasive imaging techniques of the 1980s, such as positron emission tomography (PET), have been replaced by functional magnetic resonance imaging (fMRI), a process carried out in an apparently harmless environment. Advances in these techniques include experimental paradigms that demonstrate different patterns of brain activation with different components of mathematics, such as exact (linguistic) and approximate (spatial) arithmetic (Dehaene, Spelke, Pinel, Stanescu, & Tsivkin, 1999), or two- versus three-operand calculations that differ in terms of working memory demands (Menon, Rivera, White, Glover, & Reiss, 2000). Of particular interest is evidence from studies regarding the role of the angular gyrus in arithmetic calculation, a proposal put forward by Peritz more than 80 years prior to these findings. Although the findings across studies and tasks have been inconsistent (e.g., as reviewed by Rickard et al., 2000), the imaging research supports the notion that distinct aspects of mathematics have corresponding differences in associated brain functions.

MATHEMATICAL LEARNING DISABILITY AS A HERITABLE TRAIT

A potential hereditary influence on math ability was observed as early as the mid-1900s (as reviewed by Barakat, 1951), and in 1974 Kosc described a threefold increase in MLD among family members of children with identified MLD, relative to the general population. Yet the empirically based genetic analyses of MLD did not appear until the 1990s. One approach to studies of heritability of the MLD was to investigate whether genetic influences contributed to the observed co-occurrence of MLD and reading disabilities (RD) (e.g., Knopik, Alarcón, & DeFries, 1997; Light & DeFries, 1995). A second approach was observed in the first published report of a twin study, in which Alarcón and colleagues (Alarcón, DeFries, Light, & Pennington, 1997) reported MLD heritability at .38, a rate comparable with that reported for RD.

Later, using family aggregation analyses, Shalev and colleagues (Shalev et al., 2001) reported a familial prevalence of MLD up to 10 times the prevalence observed in the general population. Large-scale studies of the heritability of MLD began only after 2000 (e.g., Oliver et al., 2004, as discussed in Chapter 14).

INSIGHTS GAINED FROM COGNITIVE PSYCHOLOGY

Kosc and the IQ–Achievement Discrepancy Model

More than 30 years ago, in a seminal paper on developmental dyscalculia (the then-current term for mathematics disabilities), Kosc (1970) attempted to synthesize current thinking on developmental dyscalculia and to postulate a specific working definition of the disorder. He defined it as

> A structural disorder of mathematical abilities that has its origin in a genetic or congenital disorder of those parts of the brain that are the direct . . . physiological substrate of the maturation of the mathematical abilities adequate to age, without a simultaneous disorder of general mental functions. (p. 192)

In other words, dyscalculia or MLD is limited to individuals with significant discrepancies between mathematical ability and their general intelligence or mental abilities.

According to Kosc, in order to meet diagnostic criteria for developmental dyscalculia, an impairment in mathematical abilities could *not* be accompanied by an impairment in general intelligence. This thinking almost exactly parallels that of leaders in the field of reading disabilities, such as Samuel Kirk and Barbara Bateman (Bateman, 1968). In fact, the conception of learning disabilities in reading and mathematics that Kosc, Kirk, and others espoused was written into the Education for All Handicapped Children Act of 1975 (PL 94-142). In the past decade, this definition of learning disabilities has been seriously and repeatedly challenged (Fletcher, Morris, & Lyon, 2003; Foorman & Francis, 1998), yet it continues to influence practice.

Kosc recognized that the literature on mathematical disorders was fragmented and that it reflected unclear categorizations of forms and types of dyscalculia. To reduce such fragmentation, Kosc (1970) proposed a classification system with six categories of performance difficulties: 1) verbally designating mathematical terms and relations, 2) manipulating real objects in accordance with the conventions of mathematics, 3) reading mathematical symbols, 4) manipulating mathematical symbols in writing, 5) carrying out mathematical operations, and 6) understanding mathematical ideas and in performing mental calculations.

Although the ideas underlying Kosc's definitions and subtypes of dyscalculia seem rather quaint, his clinical intuitions were prescient in that they led him to link problems in conceptual understanding of mathematics with problems in performing mental calculations. He also noted that a good deal of overlap existed between operational problems and conceptual problems. Furthermore, it should be pointed out that Kosc's six categories of performance difficulties correspond to the dissociations observed in medical case studies of acalculia described earlier.

However, in contrast to the acquired acalculias, Kosc emphasized the *developmental nature* of the disorder, indicating that research on MLD and children's cognitive development should be strongly linked. This is a tradition followed by many influential contemporary researchers, including David Geary (Geary, 2004) and Nancy Jordan (Jordan, Hanich, & Kaplan, 2003), to name just a few.

Kosc also stressed that forms of MLD have a strong link to hereditary or congenital impairments of the brain. In this respect, his thinking parallels that of contemporary theoreticians and researchers (e.g., Alarcón et al., 1997; Geary & Hoard, 2001) in two respects: 1) recognizing that there is a strong genetic component to MLD; and 2) appreciating that research on child development, especially the cognitive development of children who are typically developing, is crucial not only for understanding MLD but also for conceptualizing valid assessments and designing effective instructional interventions for this group of children.

In addition, Kosc recognized the role of instruction and its contribution to the acquisition of math knowledge and skills. He used the term *pseudo-dyscalculia* to refer to mathematical difficulties stemming from inadequate instruction. Furthermore, he noted that relevant mathematics instruction could help individuals with dyscalculia reach greater levels of mathematics achievement if it was effectively organized and permitted the individual to use compensatory skills. In this sense, his thinking parallels much of the contemporary thought on MLD. However, like most scientists of his era, Kosc's thinking about instructional approaches lacked precision.

Although Kosc's typology may appear overly complex to some, the theory that math-related disabilities could manifest themselves in different ways across individuals due to multiple domains of mathematics knowledge (e.g., number, algebra, and geometry) is an extension and expansion of the initial foundation set by neurology for contemporary research into math disabilities.

Interestingly, Kosc foreshadowed interest in instruction as a critical variable in diagnosing learning disabilities by noting the importance of the effectiveness of mathematics instruction *prior to classification of a learning disability.* The movement toward a Response-to-Intervention (RTI) model advocated for by a number of learning disabilities researchers (e.g., Fuchs, Mock, Morgan, & Young, 2003) has since been incorporated into federal legislation. It is important to recognize that as early as 1970, researchers in MLD were concerned with misclassification of students due to the poor quality of instruction they received in schools.

The Information Processing Era
of the 1980s: Focus on Automaticity

Several major breakthroughs in understanding MLD took place in the 1980s. Among them were the results from two sets of studies designed to apply insights from cognitive psychology to the systematic study of MLD. The two seminal research groups guiding this movement were led by Pellegrino and Goldman (1987) and Hasselbring and colleagues (Hasselbring et al., 1988), although many others have continued in this tradition.

The central finding that oriented this body of research is that the best *concurrent indicator* of MLD is difficulty in efficient retrieval of basic arithmetic combinations (also known as arithmetic facts), such as $5 + 2 = 7$ and $8 + 3 = 11$. Pellegrino and Goldman (1987) explained the importance of their finding by noting that students who cannot easily recall key number facts (e.g., $2 + 5 = 7$) spend so much energy computing these relatively simple combinations by finger counting that they have little in the way of "attentional resources" remaining to be allocated to the understanding of concepts being taught. Without facility and agility in retrieval of arithmetic combinations, students cannot really follow the logic of mathematical explanations as presented in traditional instruction, which assumes this facility has been aquired. As will be seen, attempts to develop effective problem-solving interventions for students with MLD have increasingly taken this difficulty into consideration.

By age 12, students who are typically achieving in mathematics tend to recall, on average, three times as many basic math combinations as do students with MLD (Hasselbring et al., 1988). This research revealed the devastating effects of a lack of fluent retrieval of basic number combinations on the ability to solve problems and to understand mathematical concepts. Not surprisingly, these researchers concluded that the most productive method for assisting students with MLD was to build automatic retrieval of basic combinations through extensive practice using well-designed sets of problems that were often computer-generated. This practice lasted approximately 10 minutes per day and often included some already learned facts in order to reduce frustration and continue to build automaticity.

These interventions were successful for most, but not all, of the students who needed assistance with fact retrieval automaticity. Hasselbring and colleagues (1988) noted that if students relied solely on counting fingers and did not even attempt to recall additional combinations from memory, the extended practice was not helpful. In contrast, if students did recall facts from memory, albeit slowly, it was found that extended drill and practice as brief as 4 weeks in duration often led to automatic retrieval of many new combinations. It was unclear whether this practice increased fluency or enhanced other aspects of mathematics performance as anticipated.

Insights from Information Processing and Cognitive Science Since the 1980s: Mathematics as a Complex Ability

Despite its importance for successful mathematics performance, math fact retrieval is only one component of mathematics that may be impaired in children with MLD. The information processing approach has led to the study of both cognitive abilities unique to mathematics cognition, such as recognizing numerosities, and those that are more domain general, such as memory ability and working memory (see Chapters 4 and 5, this volume). Therefore, since the 1970s there has been a shift from a focus on "central" skills (fact retrieval) to a broader approach, not unlike the earlier controversy over associating mathematics ability with a calculation center as opposed to viewing it as a set of complex and varied skills. The field of developmental psychology has provided an additional perspective on this debate.

INFLUENCES FROM DEVELOPMENTAL PSYCHOLOGY: THE WORK OF GEARY AND COLLEAGUES

Despite extraordinary progress in the understanding of reading disabilities during the 1970s and 1980s, advances in understanding the nature of MLD and effective instructional interventions for students with MLD were minimal until 1993. There is no clear external cause (e.g., a dramatic increase in federal research funding) for this dramatic turnaround, although one possible cause is the increased interest in mathematics that accompanied the publication of the National Council of Teachers of Mathematics (NCTM) Standards in 1989.

We believe, however, that the primary catalyst can be traced to advances in cognitive science. Much of the earlier work in MLD had focused heavily on automaticity and retrieval. Early cognitive science certainly was a major impetus behind the work of several researchers, such as Bransford, Hasselbring, Pellegrino, Goldman, and colleagues, on the retrieval of arithmetic facts. It became clear, however, that the study of MLD had to go beyond fact retrieval and well-designed curricula for enhancing this skill. In fact, Hasselbring and colleagues (1988) noted that a small but significant subgroup of students with MLD with whom they had worked actually failed to benefit from individualized, computerized practice in arithmetic facts.

In the early 1990s, Geary and colleagues embarked on a program of research to investigate the cognitive and performance patterns of students with math difficulties using an assessment battery that measured multiple aspects of mathematics performance and understanding. Their goal was to postulate cognitive mechanisms that explain performance patterns of children with MLD. Like most researchers, Geary began with the domain of arithmetic but structured his organizational framework so that it could be used to guide research across other domains, such as geometry and measurement.

The insights from schema theory and, in particular, the elegant research on counting strategies by Robert Siegler were, we believe, a major influence on the increase in the depth and breadth of MLD research. For example, Geary consistently mentioned Siegler's work on typical development of mathematics cognition as a guiding force behind his extensive programmatic research on MLD. Siegler's detailed descriptions of how young children develop increasingly efficient counting strategies provided a framework for thinking about the nature of MLD. Virtually all prior research and national standards on mathematics instruction and development involved use of the terms *procedural knowledge* and *conceptual knowledge* as two separate and distinct entities. However, one of the distinguishing features of Siegler's work was his consistent reminder of the interrelationships between the two. In his research, Siegler noted, for example, how what many would consider a routine arithmetic fact, 4 + 3 = 7, is, at some point in a child's life a challenging, even exciting mathematical problem to be solved, requiring conceptual understanding of underlying mathematical principles (see Siegle & Shrager, 1984, for a review). Thus, learning how to efficiently add 2 + 7— that is, by beginning with 7 and then counting on two more fingers—is a major advance in both a student's procedural proficiency in mathematics and the student's conceptual understanding (i.e., the emerging knowledge of commutativity.)

Among Geary's (1990) earliest published research in this area is a study in which he compared the strategies used by students with MLD with strategies used by proficient learners. Geary found, as he had hypothesized, that students with MLD not only made more errors in both recall of basic facts and counting of objects but also tended to rely on much more immature computational strategies.

An interesting sideline to the Geary (1990) study is the contrast between students with MLD who benefited from a remedial mathematics class and those who derived minimal benefit. Those who failed to benefit displayed immature strategies and tended to be inaccurate when retrieving facts from memory. In contrast, strategies used by students with MLD who benefited from instruction paralleled that of students of average ability. Geary hypothesized that this group of students did not, in fact, have MLD, but rather experienced *delays* in development of mathematics proficiency due either to inadequate instruction or entry into school with such limited knowledge of number that they were unable to benefit from traditional instruction. Note that the Geary (1990) study is one of the earliest applications of a Response-to-Intervention (RTI) model as a means of assessing students with MLD, even if that terminology was not used in his report.

The subsequent publication of Geary's seminal article (Geary, 1993) on the nature of MLD and the rich insights into the development of mathematical proficiency and understanding by Siegler and colleagues (Rittle-Johnson, Siegler, & Alibali, 2001; Shrager & Siegler, 1998) and Griffin and colleagues (Griffin, Case, & Siegler, 1994), as well as active efforts to support research on this topic by various funding agencies, have helped stimulate the slow but steady increase in serious empirical research in the field to emerge in the last 10 years, as illustrated in Figures 1.1 and 1.2.

Geary (2005) has demonstrated how findings from child development are critical for unpacking the cognitive problems associated with various types of MLD. He noted that "there is considerable potential to confuse difficulty in learning complex material with an actual cognitive disability . . ." (p. 306). He defined MLD as follows:

> A mathematics learning disability would be manifest as a deficit in conceptual or procedural competencies that define the mathematical domain, and these, in theory, would be due to underlying deficits in the central executive or in the information representation or manipulation (i.e., working memory) systems of the language or visuo-spatial domains. (Geary, 2004, p. 9)

Geary's line of research supports the existence of three types of MD. The first involves what he called "a straightforward deficit in the *ability* to retrieve facts from a semantics-based long-term memory network" (Geary, 2005, p. 306, italics added). Procedural difficulties in children with MLD are noted by a greater rate of counting errors and the use of immature strategies in solving simple arithmetic combinations. Working memory impairments in individuals with this type of MLD may hinder student performance by forcing an overreliance on strategies that require less demand on working memory, such as finger counting.

The second proposed type of MLD involves *disruptions* in retrieval due to the failure to inhibit irrelevant associations. For example, a student faced with the problem 4 + 8 might answer 5 or 9 simply because these are the most easily retrieved associations from simple counting. This type of MLD is typified by extreme *impulsivity* or lack of inhibition rather than the working memory problems experienced by individuals with the first type of MLD.

Geary (2005) posited a third area of cognitive impairment, one involving failures in visuospatial representations. Visuospatial measures have been found to be predictors of MLD (Fuchs, Compton, et al., in press) but to different degrees for different groups of children (Mazzocco, Bhatia, & Lesniak-Karpiak, 2006). It is also quite possible that these impairments play a larger role in students' math knowledge and achievement in Grades 4–9. During this time period there is an increased emphasis on intricate concepts involving rational numbers, and procedures in geometry are also covered.

Although Geary has provided a foundation for the notion of MLD sub-types and the importance of related skills, many competing definitions of MLD have emerged in the last 15 years (see Butterworth, 2005, for a review; see also Chapter 2) These include the notion of MLD as an impairment in the "number module," which is a selective capacity for understanding numbers (2005, p. 455). There may not yet be a consensus in MLD research, but cognitive psychology is moving the field toward fine-tuning the debates articulated years ago in medical case studies.

CONTRIBUTIONS FROM EDUCATIONAL PSYCHOLOGY

Relationship Between Reading Skill and MD

Among researchers whose perspective of mathematics is primarily that of an area of academic achievement, an intriguing question concerns the role of reading ability in the development of mathematics. In particular, for children with a mathematics disability, does the presence of reading skill mitigate mathematic difficulties, or conversely, does the absence of reading skill exacerbate mathematics difficulty? (For a review of the research investigating this topic, see Chapter 6.)

Among the most current research in this area is the work of Jordan and colleagues (Hanich & Jordan, 2001; Jordan, Kaplan, & Hanich, 2002). Their work builds on a history of research examining the link between reading and mathematics, first studied in depth by Rourke and colleagues beginning in the 1970s (although the foundation for the overall research question comes from the early work of Henschen, who observed the associations between math and language function, as discussed earlier in this chapter). Rourke and colleagues (1993) sought to determine whether children who exhibited specific patterns of performance strengths or weaknesses on the Wide Range Achievement Test (WRAT, Jastak & Jastak, 1965) reading, spelling, and arithmetic had predictable patterns on tests of neuropsychological function. Extensive work was done in analyzing the results of students who showed average academic performance in reading and spelling but low arithmetic performance and comparing them with the results of students who were low across all three academic subjects. Rourke, Finlayson, and Alan (1978) concluded that students who had poor academic skills across subjects had impairments in mathematics due to verbal deficiencies, whereas students who were only poor in mathematics had low mathematics performance due to visuospatial impairments. Rourke continued to study the neuropsychological functioning of these two subgroups across an array of different domains, such as motor and tactile-perceptual skills, and to develop theoretical models linking neuropsychological strengths and weaknesses to patterns of academic performance in reading and mathematics.

He also hypothesized that by examining patterns of neurological perform-ance, appropriate educational interventions could be designed. Although theoretically feasible, the history of designing aptitude by treatment inter-actions has limited empirical evidence within the field of educational re-search (Ysseldyke, 1973).

Jordan's Research on MD and MD/RD

In addition to Rourke's early work, Jordan's research has been influenced by the work of Dehaene, who demonstrated functionally distinct neuro-anatomical activation during "exact" versus "approximate" arithmetic. In a series of studies, Jordan and colleagues (Hanich & Jordan, 2001; Jordan et al., 2002) explored developmental trajectories of students characterized as having mathematics "difficulties." Their first longitudinal study involved grades 2–4, whereas the second study, which is ongoing, involved grades K–2. Several features distinguish this line of research. First, as just noted, these researchers studied a more inclusive sample of children than earlier researchers. Their reasoning was that, given the changing nature and face of mathematics instruction over the years of schooling, serious longitudinal research necessitates casting a comparatively wide net so that all students with potential MD are included in the sample.

Jordan and colleagues differentiated students with math difficulties who were adequate or even better than average in reading from those with difficulties in both mathematics and reading. They found that the trajec-tories of these groups differ in several ways. However, Jordan et al. (2003) found that many of these differences dissipated when they statistically con-trolled for IQ score, gender, ethnicity, and family income. (It is interesting to note how Jordan's important work complemented earlier studies of the potential genetic link between MD and RD. Light and DeFries (1995) found that influences from genetics and a shared environment both contribute to the covariance of these two academic difficulties.) The only difference that remained between the two groups of students was in understanding the principles underlying basic arithmetic (i.e., commutativity and the inverse relationship between subtraction and addition). This difference favored the group with math difficulties only.

This finding of two distinct subgroups of students with MD has been replicated independently in research conducted by Fletcher (2005) and Fuchs and Fuchs (2002). Fletcher noted that, in his own replication of Jor-dan's findings based on a sample of 7- to 13-year-olds, the MD/RD and MD groups were nonoverlapping populations but had overlapping distri-butions. In addition, Fletcher found that both types of MD groups had overlapping distributions with measures of attentional problems. Thus, he reasoned that the best early screening battery for MD should also include reading and attentional measures.

CONTRIBUTIONS FROM SPECIAL EDUCATION

The Impact of Special Education Legislation on MD

The research and theories of Kosc and Rourke played an important role in special education legislation. In 1975, Congress passed and President Ford signed the Education for All Handicapped Children Act (EHA). This law called for free and appropriate public education for all children with disabilities, including children with specific learning disabilities in academic areas such as reading, writing, and mathematics. Congress reauthorized the law in 1990, renaming it the Individuals with Disabilities Education Act (IDEA); several amendments to this act have since been passed. The legislation altered the shape of public education in the United States and continues to exert a powerful influence on most aspects of education. The impact on students with MD has been profound.

The concept of learning disability was relatively new at the time EHA was authorized. For that reason, EHA provided specific criteria for determining which students had LD. Until recently, the 1975 criteria remained in place. The two specific criteria were as follows:

> The child does not achieve commensurate with his or her age and ability levels in one or more of the areas listed . . . *if provided with learning experiences appropriate for the child's age and ability levels;* and the (multidisciplinary) team finds that a child has a severe discrepancy between achievement and intellectual ability in one or more of the following areas. (34 C.F.R. 300.541[a], cited in Herr & Bateman, 2003, emphasis added)

In addition, increased emphasis has been placed on providing services in the least restrictive environment; that is, whenever possible, students are to be provided with instruction in a regular classroom and have access to the general curriculum through appropriate instructional materials and strategies.

Among the areas listed were "mathematics calculation" and "mathematics reasoning." In the first 2 years after the passage of EHA, the major emphasis was on determination of the discrepancy between IQ and mathematics achievement. However, frustration with the IQ-discrepancy model has become widespread (Fletcher et al., 2003), and in the regulations accompanying the Individuals with Disabilities Education Improvement Act (IDEA) of 2004 (PL 108-446, 34 CFR Parts 300 & 30), the emphasis was placed squarely on the first criterion—a child performing at levels well below where he or she should be performing based on provision of appropriate learning experiences.

The legal shifts have been reflected in the increased emphasis of MD research on interventions that succeed with students within general classroom settings (e.g., Bottge & Hasselbring, 1993; Fuchs et al., 1997; Fuchs, Roberts, Fuchs, & Bowers, 1996; Woodward, Monroe, & Baxter, 2001; Woodward & Montague, 2002). We briefly discuss this body of research in the concluding sections of this chapter.

Instructional Intervention Research

With rare exception, there has been little overlap between fundamental research on the nature and development of MLD and instructional intervention research (the exception being the interventions to build fluency in retrieving basic number combinations conducted in the late 1980s). Or rather, intervention research has been influenced by crosscurrents in the fields of special education and mathematics education. These include behavior analysis, direct/explicit instruction, cognitive behavior modification, peer-mediated instruction, the 1989 NCTM standards, the cognitive strategy instruction models used in reading research, and situated learning. Some of the interventions have focused on the importance of building bridges between the concrete and the abstract as a cornerstone of solid mathematics instruction for students with LD (Butler, Miller, Crehan, Babbitt, & Pierce, 2003). However, few, if any, of these capitalize on the research base concerning characteristics of children with MLD (see Fuchs, Fuchs, & Prentice, 2004 for a notable exception). Consequently, we have chosen not to examine the history of these types of instructional interventions in this chapter. However, contemporary research on instructional intervention approaches with MLD students is covered in Chapter 18.

FUTURE DIRECTIONS

We conclude with a brief review of what we see as other contemporary movements in the field of MLD. In terms of basic and fundamental research, we see renewed interest in the concept of working memory, its influence, and its potential to play a pivotal role in explaining and understanding MLD (Swanson & Siegel, 2001). We also see renewed interest in the visuospatial component of MLD. The importance of these variables may grow as longitudinal research begins to explore mathematical development well beyond third grade, and with measures of word problems and problem solving, even in batteries given to kindergartners and first graders (Fuchs & Fuchs, 2002; Jordan, Kaplan, Olah, & Locuniak, 2006; Mazzocco & Myers, 2003). Another trend is a slow but steady increase in instructional interventions that address teaching concepts pertaining to topics such as ratios, proportions, and fractions.

One of the few research studies to merge the work on diagnostic categories with intervention research since Geary's initial study (1990) is a recent study by Fuchs and colleagues (2004), in which differential effects of an intervention were observed in students with MD only versus students with both MD and RD. It is likely that numbers of intervention studies that examine differential effectiveness of instructional approaches on subsets of students will increase, especially as the field begins to include studies of interventions that work for students with relatively severe disabilities in mathematics.

Note that although the initial studies described above focused on individuals with a demonstrated disability in mathematics, the advances in understanding MD may also emerge from research on individuals without mathematics difficulties. Thus a historical perspective on research in MD must include the gains related to the study of mathematics ability within the fields of developmental and educational psychology. We continue to see more of this kind of synergy. For example, researchers have developed and evaluated a wide array of approaches for teaching number concepts and operations to preschool children. These interventions are strongly rooted in insights from developmental and cognitive psychology (Clements & Sarama, in press; Ramani & Siegler, 2005).

A major theme in this chapter has been that advances in MD have almost invariably emerged from either multidisciplinary or transdisciplinary endeavors. Often, when researchers in a certain field appear to face a perplexing problem, solutions arise from related disciplines (Cline, 1965). At times, for example, when the field of special education research reached the limits of exploring the instructional implications of findings on lack of automaticity with mathematics facts, innovations from research on strategy use tended to reinvigorate the field. Clearly, such transdisciplinary work should—and will—continue.

REFERENCES

Alarcón, M., DeFries, J.C., Light, J.G., & Pennington, B.F. (1997). A twin study of mathematics disability. *Journal of Learning Disabilities, 30*, 617–623.

American Psychiatric Association. (1980). *Diagnostic and statistical manual of mental disorders* (3rd ed.). Washington, DC: Author.

Barakat, M.K. (1951). A factorial study of mathematical abilities. *The British Journal of Psychology, Statistical Section, 4*, 137–156.

Barbaresi, W.J., Katusic, S.K., Collagin, R.C., Weaver, A.L., & Jacobsen, S.J. (2005). Math learning disorder: Incidence in a population-based birth cohort, 1976–82, Rochester, Minn. *Ambulatory Pediatrics, 5*, 281–289.

Bateman, B. (1968). The efficacy of an auditory and a visual method of first grade reading instruction with auditory and visual learners. In H.K. Smith (Ed.), *Perception and reading* (pp. 105–112). Newark, DE: International Reading Association.

Berger, H. (1926). Über rechenstörungen bei herderkrankungen des großhirns. *Archiv fur Psychaitrie und Nervenkrankheiten, 78*, 238–263.

Bottge, B.A., & Hasselbring, T.S. (1993). A comparison of two approaches for teaching complex, authentic mathematics problems to adolescents in remedial math classes. *Exceptional Children, 59*, 556–566.

Butler, F.M., Miller, S.P., Crehan, K., Babbitt, B., & Pierce, T. (2003). Fraction instruction for students with mathematics disabilities: Comparing two teaching sequences. *Learning Disabilities Research & Practice, 18*, 99–111.

Butterworth, B. (2005). Developmental dyscalculia. In J.I.D. Campbell (Ed.), Handbook of mathematical cognition (pp. 455–467). New York: Psychology Press.

Clements, D.H., & Sarama, J. (in press). Effects of a preschool mathematics curriculum: Summary of research on the building blocks project. *Journal for Research in Mathematics Education.*

Cline, B.L. (1965). *Men who made a new physics.* Chicago, IL: The University of Chicago Press.

Dehaene, S., Spelke, E., Pinel, P., Stanescu, R., & Tsivkin, S. (1999). Sources of mathematical thinking: Behavioral and brain-imaging evidence. *Science, 284,* 970–974.

Dowker, A. (2005). *Individual differences in arithmetic: Implications for psychology, neuroscience and education.* Hove, UK: Psychology Press.

Dronkers, N.F., Pinker, S., & Damasio, A. (2000). Language and the aphasias. In E.R. Kandel, J.H. Schwartz, & T.M. Jessell (Eds.), *Principles of neural sciences* (4th ed., pp. 1169–1187). New York, NY: McGraw-Hill.

Education for All Handicapped Children Act of 1975, Pub. L. No. 94-142, 20 U.S.C. §§ 1400 *et seq.*

Fletcher, J.M. (2005). Predicting math outcomes: Reading predictors and comorbidity. *Journal of Abnormal Psychology, 38,* 308–312.

Fletcher, J.M., Morris, R.D., & Reid Lyon, G. (2003). Classification and definition of learning disabilities: An integrative perspective. In H. Lee Swanson, K.R. Harris, & S. Graham (Eds.), *Handbook of learning disabilities* (pp. 30–56). New York, NY: The Guilford Press.

Foorman, B.R., & Francis, D.J. (1998). The role of instruction in learning to read: Preventing reading failure in at-risk children. *Journal of Educational Psychology, 90,* 37–55.

Fuchs, L.S., Compton, D., Fuchs, D., Paulsen, K., Bryant, J.D., & Hamlett, C.L. (2005). The prevention, identification, and cognitive determinants of math difficulty. *Journal of Educational Psychology, 97,* 493–513.

Fuchs, L.S., & Fuchs, D. (2002). Mathematical problem solving profiles of students with mathematics disabilities with and without co-morbid reading disabilities. *Journal of Learning Disabilities, 35,* 563–574.

Fuchs, L. S., Fuchs, D., Compton, D. L., Powell, S. R., Seethaler, P. M., Capizzi, A. M., Schatschneider, C., & Fletcher, J. M. (2006). The cognitive correlates of third-grade skill in arithmetic, algorithmic computation, and arithmetic word problems. *Journal of Educational Psychology, 98,* 29–43.

Fuchs, L.S., Fuchs, D., Karns, K., Hamlett, C.L., Katzaroff, M., & Dutka, S. (1997). Effects of task-focused goals on low-achieving students with and without learning disabilities. *American Educational Research Journal, 34,* 513–543.

Fuchs, L.S., Fuchs, D., & Prentice K. (2004). Responsiveness to mathematical problem-solving instruction: Comparing students at risk of mathematics disability with and without risk of reading disability. *Journal of Learning Disabilities, 37,* 293–306.

Fuchs, D., Mock, D., Morgan, P., & Young, C. (2003). Responsiveness to intervention: Definitions, evidence and implications for the learning disabilities construct. *Learning Disabilities Research & Practice, 18,* 157–171.

Fuchs, D., Roberts, P.H., Fuchs, L.S., & Bowers, J. (1996). Reintegrating students with learning disabilities into the mainstream: A two-year study. *Learning Disabilities Research & Practice, 11,* 214–229.

Geary, D.C. (1990). *A componential analysis of an early learning deficit in mathematics.* Journal of Experimental Child Psychology, 363–383.

Geary, D.C. (1993). Mathematical disabilities: Cognitive, neuropsychological, and genetic components. *Psychological Bulletin, 114,* 345–362.

Geary, D.C. (2004). Mathematics and learning disabilities. *Journal of Learning Disabilities, 37,* 4–15.

Geary, D.C. (2005). Role of cognitive theory in the study of learning disability in mathematics. *Journal of Learning Disabilities, 38,* 305–307.

Geary, D.C., & Hoard, M.K. (2001). Numerical and arithmetical deficits in learning-disabled children: Relation to dyscalculia and dyslexia. *Aphasiology, 15,* 635–647.

Griffin, S.A., Case, R., & Siegler, R.S. (1994). Rightstart: Providing the central conceptual prerequisites for first formal learning of arithmetic to students at risk for school failure. In K. McGilly's (Ed.), *Classroom lessons: Integrating cognitive theory and classroom practice* (pp. 24–49). Cambridge, MA: MIT Press.

Gross-Tsur, V., Manor, O., & Shalev, R.S. (1996). Developmental dyscalculia: Prevalence and demographic features. *Developmental Medicine and Child Neurology, 38,* 25–33.

Hanich, L., & Jordan, N. (2001). Performance across different areas of mathematical cognition in children with learning disabilities. *Journal of Educational Psychology, 93,* 615–626.

Hasselbring, T., Sherwood, R., Bransford, J., Fleenor, K., Griffith, D., & Goin, L. (1988). Evaluation of a level-one instructional videodisc program. *Journal of Educational Technology Systems, 16,* 151–169.

Henschen, S.E. (1919). Uber sprach-, musik-, und rechenmechanismen und ihre lokalisationen im grobhirn. *Zeitschrift fur die gesamte Neurologie und Psychiatrie, 52,* 273–298.

Herr, C.M., & Bateman, B.D. (2003). Learning disabilities and the law. In H.L. Swanson, K.R. Harris, and S. Graham (Eds.), *Handbook of learning disabilities* (pp. 57–73). New York: The Guilford Press.

Individuals with Disabilities Education Improvement Act (IDEA) of 2004, PL 108-446, 20 U.S.C. §§ 1400 *et seq.*

Jastak, J.F., & Jastak, S.R. (1965). The Wide Range Achievement Test. Wilmington, DE: Guidance Associates.

Jordan, N., Hanich, L., & Kaplan, D. (2003). A longitudinal study of mathematical competencies in children with specific mathematics difficulties versus children with co-morbid mathematics and reading difficulties. *Child Development, 74,* 834–850.

Jordan, N., Kaplan, D., & Hanich, L. (2002). Achievement growth in children with learning difficulties in mathematics: Findings of a two-year longitudinal study. *Journal of Educational Psychology, 94,* 586–597.

Jordan, N., Kaplan, D., Olah, L.N., & Locuniak, M.N. (2006). Number sense growth in kindergarten: A longitudinal investigation of children at risk for mathematics difficulties. *Child Development, 77,* 153–175.

Kahn, H.J., & Whitaker, H.A. (1991). Acalculia: An historical review of localization. *Brain and Cognition, 17,* 102–115.

Kandel, E.R., Schwartz, J.H., & Jessell, T.M. (2000). *Principles of neural science* (4th ed.). New York: McGraw-Hill.

Knopik, V.S., Alarcón, M., & DeFries, J.C. (1997). Comorbidity of mathematics and reading deficits: Evidence for a genetic etiology. *Behavior Genetics, 27*(5), 447–453.

Kosc, L. (1970). Psychology and psychopathology of mathematical abilities. *Studia psychologica, 12,* 159–162.

Kosc, L. (1974). Developmental dyscalculia. *Journal of Learning Disabilities, 7,* 164–177.

Lewandowsky, M., & Stadelmann, E. (1908). Uber einen bemerkenswerten fall von hirnblutung und uber rechenstorungen bei herderkrankung des gehirns. *Journal fur Psychologie und Neurologie, 11,* 249–265.

Light, J.G., & DeFries, J.C. (1995). Comorbidity of reading and mathematics disabilities: Genetic and environmental etiologies. *Journal of Learning Disabilities, 28,* 96–106.

Luria, A.R. (1966). *Higher cortical functions in man* (2nd ed.). New York: Basic Books.

Mazzocco, M.M.M., Bhatia, N. S., & Lesniak-Karpiak, K. (2006). Visuospatial skills and their association with performance in girls with fragile X or Turner syndrome. *Child Neuropsychology, 12*, 87–110.

Mazzocco, M.M.M., & Myers, G.F. (2003). Complexities in identifying and defining mathematics learning disability in the primary school-age years. Annals of Dyslexia, 53, 218–253.

McCloskey, M. (1992). Cognitive mechanisms in numerical processing: Evidence from acquired dyscalculia. *Cognition, 44*, 107–157.

Menon, V., Rivera, S.M., White, C.D., Glover, G.H., & Reiss. A.L. (2000). Dissociating prefrontal and parietal activation during arithmetic processing. *NeuroImage 12*, 357–365.

National Council of Teachers of Mathematics. (1989). *Curriculum and evaluation standards for school mathematics*. Reston, VA: Author.

Oliver, B., Harlaar, N., Thomas, M.E., Kovas, Y., Walker, S.O., Petrill, S.A., et al. (2004). A twin study of teacher-reported mathematics performance and low performance in 7 year olds. *Journal of Educational Psychology, 96*, 504–517.

Pellegrino, J.W., & Goldman, S.R. (1987). Information processing and elementary mathematics. *Journal of Learning Disabilities, 20*, 23–32.

Peritz, G. (1918). Zur Pathopsychologie des Rechnens [On the pathopsychology of calculation]. *Dtsch Z Nervenheilkd 61*, 234–340.

Ramani, G.R., & Siegler, R.S. (2005, April). *It's more than just a game: Effects of children's board game play on the development of numerical estimation*. Poster presented at the biennial meeting of the Society for Research in Child Development, Atlanta, GA.

Rickard, T.C., Romero, S.G., Basso, G., Wharton, C., Flitman, S., & Grafman, J. (2000). The calculating brain: An fMRI study. *Neuropsychologia, 38*, 325.

Rittle-Johnson, B., Siegler, R., & Alibali, M. (2001). Developing conceptual understanding and procedural skill in mathematics: An iterative process. *Journal of Educational Psychology, 93*, 346–362.

Rourke, B.P. (1993). Arithmetic disabilities, specific or otherwise: A Neuropsychological perspective. *Journal of Learning Disabilities, 26*, 214–226.

Rourke, B.P., Finlayson, M., & Alan, J. (1978). Neuropsychological significance of variations in patterns of academic performance: Verbal and visual-spatial abilities. *Journal of Abnormal Child Psychology, 6*, 121–133.

Shalev, R.S., Manor, O., Kerem, B., Ayali, M., Badichi, N., Friedlander, Y., et al. (2001). Developmental dyscalculia is a familial learning disability. *Journal of Learning Disabilities, 34*, 59–65.

Shrager, J., & Siegler, R.S. (1998). SCADS: A model of children's strategy choices and strategy discoveries. *Psychological Science, 9*, 405–422.

Siegler, R.S., & Shrager, J. (1984). Strategy choices in addition and subtraction: How do children know what to do? In C. Sophian (Ed.), *Origins of cognitive skills (pp. 229–293)*. Mahwah, NJ: Lawrence Erlbaum Associates.

Swanson, H.L., & Siegel, L. (2001). Learning disabilities as a working memory deficit. *Issues in Education: Contributions from Educational Psychology, 7*, 1–48.

Woodward, J., Monroe, K., & Baxter, J. (2001). Enhancing student achievement on performance assessments in mathematics. *Learning Disabilities Quarterly, 24*, 33–46.

Woodward, J., & Montague, M. (2002). Meeting the challenge of mathematics reform for students with LD. *Journal of Special Education, 36*, 89–101.

Ysseldyke, J.E. (1973). Diagnostic-prescriptive teaching: The search for aptitude-treatment interactions. In L. Mann & D.A. Sabatino (Eds.), *The first review of special education* (pp. 5–32). New York: Grune & Stratton.

Chapter 2

Defining and Differentiating Mathematical Learning Disabilities and Difficulties

Michèle M.M. Mazzocco

+ +

In *The Phantom Tollbooth*, Norton Juster's account of the fanciful travels undertaken by a boy named Milo, the boy confesses to an animated Dodecahedron,[1]

> "I'm not very good at [math] problems."
> "What a shame," the Dodecahedron replied, "they're so very useful."
> (1961/1989, p. 174)

That math is indeed "very useful" and thus important is acknowledged by educators, psychologists, and policymakers, and, evidently even in children's literature and in theater (Peterson, 2002). Experts in the fields of education, psychology, and public policy also agree that some individuals are "not very good at math," even if there is disagreement regarding whether such math *difficulties* are attributable to an underlying *disability*. If we are to study, understand, and remediate mathematical learning disabilities (MLD), we must first define this term as a construct. However, for reasons discussed in this chapter, defining MLD is no easy task.

This chapter is a summary of the challenges to defining MLD. Although I do not present an exhaustive list of the definitions used by researchers and

---

Preparation of this chapter was supported by NIH grant HD R01 03461. The author thanks Daniel Berch for discussion and comments on an earlier draft.
[1]A solid shape having 12 pentagonal faces, with 3 faces meeting at each of twenty vertices, resulting in 30 edges.

practitioners, I illustrate the diversity of contemporary definitions by reviewing some of the criteria used across research studies to classify a child
as having MLD. Although researchers have agreed on some MLD criteria,
the lack of a more rigorous standardization of criteria impedes the ability to
aggregate and synthesize findings across studies. Thus, despite the solid
knowledge base that has been achieved in this field (and that is reflected
in this book), more substantial progress in understanding MLD would be
facilitated by establishing standardized criteria. Efforts to do so require
agreement on consistently used terminology; therefore, establishing this
terminology is a logical starting point in moving toward a consensus definition of MLD.

DEFINING MATHEMATICAL LEARNING DISABILITY:
CLARIFYING THE TERMINOLOGY

The task of defining MLD begins with resolving the differences reflected
by terms used to refer to it or to related constructs. Some of the most commonly used terms in the field are *mathematical*[2] *disabilities, mathematical learning disabilities, mathematical difficulties,* and *dyscalculia.*

The term *disability* suggests a biologically based disorder; a disability
in *learning* mathematics further implies a disorder characterized by specific
cognitive deficits. From this perspective, the terms *mathematical disability*
and *mathematical learning disability* (MLD) are variations of the same construct. Likewise, MLD and dyscalculia are typically used to refer to the
same intended population, as both imply an inherent disability rather than
one caused predominantly by environmental factors (but see Chapter 4 and
below). Thus three of these four commonly used terms refer to the same
population, and are not differentiated further in this chapter. For the sake
of simplicity, I use only the term *MLD* when referring to this construct
throughout the remainder of this chapter.

If we accept that *MLD, mathematical disability,* and *dyscalculia* are synonymous, we need only differentiate MLD from *mathematical difficulties.*
The latter term has been explicitly defined by some researchers as referring
to children whose poor mathematics achievement results from any one of a
number of potential causes (e.g., Gersten, Jordan, & Flojo, 2005; Hanich,
Jordan, Kaplan, & Dick, 2001; Jordan, Kaplan, Nabors Oláh, & Locuniak,
2006), with no reference to a presumed biological basis. Although this

---

[2]Adding to this complexity, the terms *mathematics* and *mathematical* are often used inconsistently and interchangeably to refer to these types of difficulties or disabilities. Consequently, throughout this volume the terms *mathematical* and *mathematics* are considered synonymous when referring to
either MLD or difficulties with mathematics. Another layer of complexity arises from the fact that
mathematical disabilities are at times specified as disabilities (or difficulties) in *arithmetic.* In this chapter, I do not address this level of specification by differentiating between arithmetic and mathematical
disabilities.

distinction between MLD and mathematical difficulties is not shared by all researchers—particularly in cases where MLD and dyscalculia are contrasted—disagreement about this issue likely arises from the inappropriate use of the term MLD to refer to children with mathematical difficulties, as described below.

The term *mathematical difficulties* represents a broader construct than does MLD. It includes children with below average to low average performance on tests of math achievement (Gersten et al., 2005). Thus it follows that the term *mathematical difficulties* differs from the term *MLD* because, as most researchers would agree, many children with low average performance in math do not have a mathematical disability. The term *mathematical difficulties* implies the presence of relatively poor mathematics achievement because poor achievement serves as the primary criterion for classifying children with mathematical difficulties in a research study. Typically, *low average performance* is operationalized as a standardized math achievement test score that falls below a cutoff point of approximately the 35th percentile. This cutoff value seems high when contrasted with the reported 6% (approximately) prevalence rate of MLD in the general population (see Chapter 3), but it enables researchers to study a larger group of children who struggle with mathematics than would be possible using a stricter criterion (see Geary & Hoard, 2005, for a more detailed discussion of the discrepancy between the cutoff value and prevalence rate).

Although there are additional reasons for applying either a more inclusive or more restrictive approach in studies of MLD (described later in this chapter), there are consequences to simultaneously adopting *both* of these approaches (and their associated yet distinct terms) when studying or describing one population (i.e., either children with MLD or children with mathematical difficulties). One consequence to adopting both approaches is that two groups of children are actually the subject of discussion and inquiry when only one of the populations is the implied target of interest. Although this may appear rather obvious, these two groups are in fact often treated as one, or are at least combined in discussion and generalizations made about MLD across research studies. On the one hand, combining these groups is logical because there is no measurable boundary separating children with MLD from those with mathematical difficulties. This is one reason why the present volume is dedicated to both mathematical difficulties and MLD. On the other hand, combining these two different groups is problematic for drawing any conclusions about either group.

The degree to which combining MLD and mathematical difficulties is problematic depends on the extent to which the two groups overlap. *Some* overlap clearly exists, because many if not most children with MLD are likely to exhibit poor mathematics achievement and will thus meet the criterion for mathematical difficulties. However, the overlap is only partial because not all children with mathematical difficulties will have a disability (i.e., MLD) despite the fact that, by definition, all children with mathematical difficulties have poor math achievement. Lack of overlap occurs in cases in which difficulty with math is attributable to socio-cultural or other environmental causes (Jordan et al., 2006; Chapter 16) rather than to an inherent weakness in mathematical cognition. Another reason for only partial overlap of these two groups is that not all children with MLD will meet the criterion for mathematical difficulties (i.e., poor math achievement) because some children with MLD may surmount their inherent difficulties by compensating for deficient or delayed skills in mathematical cognition. Over time, children who compensate for their MLD may eventually perform above the low average range in mathematics achievement; consequently, they will not qualify as having mathematical difficulties because they will not actually "fail" mathematics in the conventional sense. Instead, they may achieve proficiency with laborious struggles. Thus, a primary distinction between mathematical difficulties and MLD is that only the latter is defined (in part) on the basis of its biological origins.

What remains unclear concerning the distinction between MLD and mathematical difficulties is the degree of overlap between these groups and the extent to which the groups differ on specific, measurable characteristics. In certain circumstances—such as when selecting which group(s) to address in this book—a benefit to combining these two groups of children is the ability to recognize multiple influences on whether children will achieve age-appropriate levels of mathematics proficiency. In other circumstances— such as when attempting to establish a definition of MLD—attending to what differentiates these two groups is of greater benefit than is combining the two. In other words, progress toward defining MLD requires reconciling the inconsistencies in terminology used across the many disciplines that are involved in MLD research and further requires acknowledging group differences in samples of children from across studies.

BARRIERS TO DEFINING MATHEMATICAL LEARNING DISABILITY (MLD)

Barriers that Are Not Specific to Mathematics

Although some barriers to defining MLD are specific to difficulties with mathematics, other impediments exist that interfere with efforts to define broader categories of disorders that include MLD.

One barrier to defining MLD concerns the nature of disorders identified behaviorally versus biologically, even when a biological basis is presumed (as is the case with MLD). Another pertains to the vagueness of the construct of a "learning disability," and a third relates to the research practices that involve highly variable criteria used to define MLD, despite the shared intent among most researchers to study the same construct. None of these barriers is unique to MLD.

Mathematical Learning Disability as a Behaviorally Defined Disorder At the most inclusive level, MLD is a behaviorally defined disorder. Determination of its presence is based on observable and measurable performance on mathematics-related tasks, even if unobserved mental processes are inferred. As a consequence, MLD—like *any* terminology reflecting a behaviorally defined disorder—is an obscure term lacking distinct boundaries. Clearly, there are individuals for whom the *absence* of MLD is absolutely certain, such as children consistently and efficiently outperforming all of their age and grade mates on math tests; for other individuals, the *presence* of MLD is equally evident, such as an eighth grader with average intelligence who has struggled with single-digit arithmetic for all 9 years of schooling. At issue, however, are those individuals for whom establishing the presence or absence of MLD is more problematic. This is the same kind of dilemma faced when seeking to determine the presence of any of a number of behaviorally defined disorders, such as autism, conduct disorder, social phobia, obsessive compulsive disorder, or learning disability. The solution to this dilemma involves reaching a consensus definition.

A consensus definition of a disorder is typically based on a set of criteria established by expert groups. For example, a widely accepted source of established criteria for behavioral disorders is the *Diagnostic and Statistical Manual of Mental Disorders (DSM)*, published by the American Psychiatric Association. First published in 1952, the most recent revision of this document, the revised fourth edition *(DSM-IV-TR)*, was published in 2000. The frequency with which such revisions occur—indeed, the fact that revisions occur at all—reflects the emerging and dynamic nature of behavioral conditions for which there is no single, known biological marker. Thus, one barrier to defining MLD is that, as a behavioral condition, it is subject to evolving criteria that are influenced by findings of contemporary research studies. As a consequence, to adequately define MLD requires a familiarity with the most recent research findings from a broad range of disciplines (as reviewed in Chapter 1).

Mathematical Learning Disability as One Category of Learning Disability Subordinate to the broader classification of behaviorally defined conditions is the term *learning disability* (LD),[3] which is included in the *DSM-IV* as "Learning Disorders, formerly Academic Skills Disorders" (American Psychiatric Association, 1994, p. 46).

---

[3]Although the term *learning disability* is more inclusive in some European cultures, in this chapter and volume the term excludes children with mental retardation.

As has been discussed extensively over the last four decades, there are limits to the usefulness of LD definitions. Even recent reviews of the topic reflect how "LD definitions fail to provide substantive insight into the nature of the condition" (Kavale & Forness, 2000, p. 239). Indeed, some researchers consider the construct of LD to be "among the most problematic classifications because of the vagaries and antagonisms surrounding its definition" (Mather & Roberts, 1994, p. 49). MLD inherits the problematic aspects of this classification.

On the one hand, one could despair that, as a specific type of LD, MLD is subject to the fate of perpetual uncertainty. From a more optimistic perspective, one could consider MLD—which has a less comprehensive research base than LD in general or than reading disability (RD)—as a beneficiary of the successful attempts to overcome that uncertainty. Researchers of RD specifically, and of LD more broadly defined, have moved toward a more precise definition, and some expert groups have even published a consensus definition (Consensus Project, 2002). Thus, even if LD remains an obscure term, research efforts have provided a solid basis on which to selectively omit some of the criteria that previously interfered with accurately determining LD status in children, as briefly summarized below. That is, in part via a process of elimination, we move closer to defining MLD if we attend to what MLD is not.

A thorough review of a historical or contemporary account of defining LD is beyond the scope of this chapter, and each has been provided elsewhere in greater detail (e.g., Hallahan & Mock, 2003; Fletcher, Morris, & Lyon, 2003; respectively). Among the most significant and replicated findings are the numerous reports of how often discrepancy-based definitions of LD fail to identify children with LD. Criteria for a discrepancy-based definition typically require that an academic achievement test score fall "significantly" below that of an IQ test score (with inconsistent criteria for quantifying a "significant" discrepancy). Historically, these criteria have been applied to defining MLD as a form of LD (as discussed in Chapter 1).

Although some children who meet these criteria may indeed have LD, others with LD may not meet the criteria; this is particularly problematic if the skills that underlie a child's LD influence the child's outcome on IQ tests such that a large discrepancy in scores is unlikely. This limitation has been the subject of much debate regarding the definition and measurement of LD in general (e.g., Siegel, 1989), of RD specifically (e.g., Fletcher et al., 1998; Siegel & Smythe, 2005), and more recently of MLD (Mazzocco, 2005; Mazzocco & Myers, 2003). Thus as we move toward a consensus definition of MLD, it is helpful to refine previous standards. Although the field may still be without a consensus definition of MLD, sufficient grounds exist on which to conclude that a discrepancy in IQ and academic test performance should not be one of its defining features.

Does Mathematical Learning Disability Parallel RD in the Nature or Number of Core Deficits?   Within the field of LD research, investigators have examined whether differences between children with LD and those without LD are quantitative or qualitative. Quantitative differences reflect differences in degree with respect to the same form of a behavior, such as slower processing of letter sounds in children with RD than in children with average reading ability. Qualitative changes represent different forms of skills or behaviors, such as a child's reading words by sight and memorization rather than by decoding the phonological sequence of letters in a printed word. Despite solid evidence that LD typically represents quantitative rather than qualitative differences relative to children without LD (as discussed by Fletcher et al., 2003), there is insufficient evidence to support generalizing these findings to MLD. That is, assumptions based on the potentially inaccurate (and thus far untested) hypothesis that MLD will parallel RD with respect to its developmental nature may hinder explorations of alternative hypotheses.

Consider, for example, that children with RD have deficits in reading skills that are linked to well-established core deficits. Researchers of RD have been able to report *which* deficits are core to RD or *how* these core deficits are manifested in children (National Reading Panel, 2000). For MLD, the degree to which core deficits are well-established or agreed on by most researchers is not comparable to the level of agreement present among RD researchers. Although potential core deficits of MLD have been identified in children with MLD (see Chapters 4, 5, and 6), it remains unclear which of these will have a principal role in defining MLD (and mathematical difficulties). Moreover, the deficits that differentiate children with RD from their peers are on a continuum of ability levels; that is, the groups do not differ on the basis of different forms of skills or behaviors. In contrast, some (but not all) characteristics of MLD appear qualitative (versus quantitative) in nature; for example, children with MLD have different forms of behaviors than children without MLD, such as using immature finger counting strategies rather than mental calculations or fact retrieval during paper-and-pencil calculation exercises (Geary, 1990). Thus, at least some of the group differences between children with MLD and those without are not quantitative.

One result of assuming that quantitative differences predominate in comparisons of children with and without MLD is the wide range of cutoff scores used to identify children in different research studies, as mentioned earlier (and as reflected in many of the studies presented throughout this book). Cutoff scores used in research have ranged from 10% to 45%, despite researchers' intentions to study the same population (i.e., children with MLD). Caution is warranted when interpreting findings within or across studies as applying solely to children with MLD, when in reality the results most likely describe both children with MLD and those with mathematical difficulties. This caution applies not only to the researcher but also to anyone utilizing such findings.

Should researchers be faulted for their inconsistent definitions of MLD? Of course not, since no consensus definition has yet been reached. Nor has a universally agreed-on working definition been established. Until a working definition is available, researchers will continue to provide a clear rationale for the criteria used in their study, whether their purpose is to assess the characteristics of a broader group of students (for mathematical difficulties) or to avoid having children with MLD slip through the cracks if a more stringent set of criteria is used (as discussed by Geary, Hamson, & Hoard, 2000).

Drawing conclusions across studies may be a barrier to pinpointing the characteristics of children with MLD. That is, if the study sample includes a more diverse group of children with mathematical difficulties, the group characteristics may mask the unique characteristics of children with MLD—if it is true that unique characteristics comprise the MLD profile. Careful interpretation of a study's findings involves attending to the composition of participant samples and the generalizations drawn from the findings. It is the responsibility not only of the researcher *but also of individuals interpreting researchers' findings* (other researchers, policymakers, educators, and clinicians) to attend to these details when drawing inferences from or making generalizations about studies of children with MLD or math difficulties.

Barriers that Are Specific to Mathematics

In addition to the barriers shared between defining LD and other broad classifications, defining MLD is challenged further by the complexities associated with school mathematics and the variety of cognitive skills required for achieving mathematical proficiency. As the school years progress, mathematical content becomes increasingly more difficult. Indeed, some argue that mathematics in general is inherently difficult. Abilities specific to math and those related to its supporting cognitive domains (such as language and memory skills) may influence mathematics achievement and performance, but they do so to different degrees depending on the mathematics skill in question.

Mathematical Learning Involves a Wide Variety of Skills Mathematics includes a broad range of domains, each of which may require skills ranging from very basic, such as counting and enumeration, to higher order reasoning skills, such as those used in analytic geometry or algebraic topology. Children with MLD may have deficits in any of a number of basic math skills. But deficiencies in math may also be evident in mathematical principles (Geary et al., 2000; Hanich et al., 2001); mathematical procedures, such as regrouping; and even in strategies used during problem solving, such as finger counting. A definition of MLD must take into account these various sources of difficulty and the full range of possible manifestations, such as deficient basic skills, immature strategies, slowed response time, inaccurate calculation, or poor recognition of mathematics principles.

In light of the many skills involved within and across the mathematical domains, there are many sources of potential difficulty for children with MLD. These distinct mathematical abilities may also be differentiated in most children and adults, and in some cases the skills may have different developmental trajectories (as will be discussed). An understanding of abilities in mathematical cognition and of their developmental patterns can be valuable in determining the possible areas in which things may go wrong for a child with MLD. For example, some children may have relatively slower fact retrieval skills than their age mates, and others may be less efficient at solving word problems. The questions researchers face regarding potential impairments concern whether performance on specific measures of mathematical cognition are weaker in children with MLD (e.g., slower and/or less accurate) than in children without this condition, whether math skills that differentiate groups of children differ with respect to form of skill (e.g., retrieving math fact solutions versus calculating), whether the differences that emerge are primary (core) deficits, and whether different sets of skills delineate subgroups of children with MLD who have either a set of distinctive underlying impairments or a different manifestation of the same impairments.

These are complex questions that cannot be answered from any one study, in view of the number of potential skills to be addressed and because of the potential number of subgroups, if subtypes of MLD are identified. Thus, to define MLD, it is necessary to determine *which* of these mathematical abilities is prone to deficiency or difficulty in children with MLD. But it is also important to determine *how* the developmental trajectory for mathematics skills differs among children with and without MLD, particularly in view of the changes in mathematical skills required over time—either because of maturation or as a function of the increases in demands of the school curriculum (or both, as these are presumed to be related).

Mathematical Skills Increase in Complexity over the School-Age Years
The changing nature of mathematics skills introduced in school speaks to the need for developmentally appropriate indicators of MLD for children of different ages. Although this is also true for the case of reading disability, two important distinctions between MLD and RD lead to a more straightforward measurement of the latter: knowledge of early markers of RD and minimal changes in the nature of skills related to core deficits over time.

The early indicators of RD (such as poor rhyming performance) typically precede weak decoding ability that may not be as evident until the child demonstrates failure at sounding out words (as reviewed by Vellutino & Fletcher, 2005). Yet this principal core deficit in decoding *is* evident in primary school and remains a core deficit of reading over time. It is unknown whether researchers will uncover a parallel, early emerging, and stable deficit for children with MLD. Proposals for broad skills such as number sense will likely lead in the right direction (e.g., Dehaene, 1997; Gersten & Chard, 1999), but at present such constructs are almost as broadly defined as MLD is (Berch, 2005). Whereas the basic processes in reading remain stable over the school-age years (once established in primary school)—even if the reading demands change—additional mathematical concepts and procedures are continually introduced over time. Thus, curriculum changes in mathematics are not parallel to minimal changes needed over time in the most basic reading skills.

Changes in mathematical skills expectations over time have implications for when MLD is first manifested. My colleagues and I have found that although most children who met strict criteria for MLD by third grade had met those criteria in kindergarten (65%), another 20% failed to meet these criteria until second grade (Mazzocco & Myers, 2003). It is unclear whether the children first identified in second grade would have been identified sooner had more developmentally appropriate measures been administered earlier in their primary school years. Determination of the appropriate measures for early identification rests on knowledge of the early markers of MLD. That is, although researchers refer to "late emerging" LD in cases in which children are not identified until later than are most children with LD, the disability is present even if researchers and practitioners lack sufficient knowledge to detect it at an earlier age. It is also unclear how late in the school-age years MLD may first emerge as a measurable manifestation of disability; in other words, it is unknown at what ages or grades "late emerging" (or "late manifesting") MLD will first become evident to teachers, clinicians, and researchers.

In addition to the variability in how MLD is manifested, variability exists both in the ways that typically developing children learn and perform mathematics and the levels of performance exhibited at any given age or grade level. These individual differences in mathematical cognition skills (see Dowker, 2005) may be quantitative or qualitative (as discussed earlier for children with LD). Attention to the growth trajectories may inform us whether cognitive skills in children with MLD represent an impairment, a delay, or an individual difference model, which may in turn vary according to the mathematical skills that are examined. Individual differences may influence the choice to cease formal mathematics education after completion of courses required by schools or school districts (such as first-year algebra) or to pursue mathematics education through high school or university studies. Sociocultural factors also influence these personal decisions (see Chapter 16). For instance, it is at the higher levels of mathematics (such as high school mathematics) that the gender differences in mathematical ability favoring boys are more often reported by researchers, but these differences appear to be affected at least partially by sociocultural factors.

At what level of mathematics is it appropriate to attribute performance difficulties to MLD or even to mathematical difficulties? In other words, it is unlikely we would attribute failure at higher level mathematics (e.g., linear algebra) to MLD, although MLD would likely affect not only level of higher mathematics proficiency but also opportunities, desire, or encouragement to pursue higher mathematics courses. The dynamic nature of mathematics education calls for researchers in the field to consider the appropriate levels at which performance difficulties reflect MLD or mathematical difficulties, particularly in light of how difficult mathematics becomes for many individuals at its highest levels.

Mathematics Is Difficult   Increasing curriculum demands represent only one of the many ways in which mathematics is inherently difficult (Geary, 1995). This inherent complexity is perceived even by young children who have no known learning difficulties. For example, my colleagues and I have found that even typically developing second graders make reference to math being "hard" when simply asked to define it. Although the majority of second graders in our study made only neutral comments about math, 35% made reference to math being difficult; in contrast, only 10% made reference to *reading* being difficult (Mazzocco & Noeder, 2006).

Developmental trajectories of various mathematical skills may reflect *which* skills are relatively more difficult than others for many children (not only those with MLD or mathematical difficulties), and which skills become less difficult at different ages for all children. For example, research on both MLD and typically developing students demonstrates the struggles experienced by many students striving to understand proportional reasoning and what is represented by fractions (see Chapter 7). Certainly, quality of instruction plays a role in the efficient mastery of these difficult concepts. It stands to reason that the absence of high-quality instruction cannot be a primary causal mechanism underlying MLD (although it can be a primary cause of mathematical difficulties). Thus, a definition of MLD should take into account the exclusion of cases in which poor mathematical achievement results from lack of adequate instruction, according to current trends in defining LD (reviewed in Chapter 1).

Mathematical Learning Disability as a Stable Trait over Time   When a new mathematical principle, concept, or procedure is introduced in a classroom lesson, the novelty of the material itself may be a source of difficulty for some children; those children may initially perform below average until the material is mastered. This is one of many reasons why a child may appear to meet performance criteria for MLD when assessed at only a single point in time. Related reasons, too numerous to list completely, include absence from school, midyear relocation to a new school, language of instruction, and characteristics of the curriculum or of the instructor. It is therefore not surprising that many children who meet MLD criteria during 1 school year demonstrate improvement over time. This is less problematic when MLD criteria are met over 2 consecutive years, in which sustained difficulty in mathematics is more likely (Geary, 1990). For example, my colleagues and I found that approximately 30% of primary-school-age children who met MLD criteria in one grade failed to meet these criteria a second time by third grade (Mazzocco & Myers, 2003). In fact, more than half (53%) of our study participants met criteria for MLD in at least one of their four annual assessments during their primary school years. This means that if a one-time definition were to have been adopted, our rate of false positives would have exceeded population estimates of approximately 6% by a factor of 9, despite the fact that the study participants represented a relatively random group of children. Thus, definitions of MLD must reflect its stability as a trait rather than a difficulty exhibited at only a single point in time.

DISABILITY VERSUS DIFFICULTY—WHEN DO DEFINITIONS MATTER?

> "Let's travel by miles," advised the Humbug; "it's shorter."
> "Let's travel by half inches," suggested Milo; "it's quicker."
> "But which road should we take?" asked Tock. "It must make a difference."
> (Juster, 1961/1989, pp. 171–172)

There are several situations when use of a specific definition of MLD or mathematical difficulties does indeed make a difference, by significantly influencing an important outcome. For instance, the definitions used in research may influence the prevalence estimates obtained for a given population and may further influence the comparisons of prevalence rates across studies, countries, or school districts (see Chapter 3). The use of a particular MLD definition can affect which children will or will not be eligible for special education services and which children will be assigned to the *MLD* or *Typically Achieving* groups in a research study. These outcomes may ultimately lead to different conclusions regarding characteristics of the population(s) we seek to describe. This means that it is essential that the populations studied are properly defined and acknowledged as representing either MLD or the broader construct of mathematical difficulties.

I have already explained that many researchers use an achievement test cutoff score rather than an IQ–achievement discrepancy-based formula to define MLD, and that the actual cutoff score used varies quite markedly across studies (as reviewed by Butterworth, 2005; and by Murphy, Mazzocco, Hanich, & Early, in press). In studies of MLD that employ a relatively lenient cutoff score (such as the 35th percentile), children with mathematical difficulties are likely to be included even if their difficulty does not meet the criteria for MLD. A lower cutoff score (e.g., the 10th percentile) may be used to avoid this outcome, but at the expense of having a small study sample and perhaps missing some children with MLD who fail to meet the cutoff score criterion. Does this difference matter? Evidence points to the fact that group characteristics corresponding to these different cutoff levels are not only quantitative (e.g., Garrett, Mazzocco, & Baker, 2006) but also qualitative (Mazzocco & Myers, 2003; Murphy et al., in press). For this reason the field may benefit from evaluations of three groups of children in most research studies: one group representing children with MLD, another group representing children without MLD who have age appropriate mathematical achievement, and an intermediate group representing children whose poor achievement in mathematics is not due to MLD (i.e., a group with mathematical difficulties).

Although we and others have adopted such an approach (e.g., Mazzocco & Myers, 2003; Murphy et al., in press), at issue is how to differentiate the three participant groups. In an applied setting such as in schools, the most recently recommended methods for differentiating LD and low achieving groups take into account whether a child's difficulties persist despite adequate environmental circumstances, such as standard quality instruction (see Fletcher et al., 2003, for overview; also Chapter 1). On the one hand, this approach may separate children with MLD from those whose poor achievement is secondary to poverty or low IQ score. On the other hand, it would be incorrect to believe that the mere presence of such risk factors negates the appropriateness of an MLD classification. This dilemma, sounding awfully familiar, brings us back to the challenges of defining LD. Nevertheless, in order to adequately define MLD, we must continue our efforts to differentiate characteristics of these children from the characteristics of children with mathematical difficulties.

DEFINING FEATURES OF MATHEMATICAL LEARNING DISABILITY

Characteristic Cognitive Skills that Influence Mathematical Ability

A wide range of cognitive abilities support successful mathematics, and efforts to define MLD include studies of such skills. For instance, in a recent review of their work on MLD, Geary and Hoard (2005, p. 264) concluded that MLD "can be understood as being related to a combination of disrupted function of the central executive, including attentional control and poor inhibition of irrelevant associations, or difficulties with information representation and manipulation in the language system. In theory, [MLD] can also result from compromised visuo-spatial systems. . . ." These skills are among those that Butterworth (2005) refered to as "domain-general cognitive abilities," although he found their causal role to be less significant to MLD than that reported by other researchers (see also Chapter 4). Indeed, Butterworth states that MLD "does not seem to be a consequence of impairments in domain-general or more basic cognitive abilities such as semantic memory, working memory, spatial abilities, or linguistic abilities" (p. 464). Despite this obvious disagreement in the relative importance attributed to supporting cognitive skills, clear evidence suggests that MLD is associated with less efficient working memory skills (see Chapter 5), a higher incidence of reading disability in some but not all children with MLD (see Chapter 6), language skills (see Chapter 8), and several additional neuropsychological correlates (see also Chapters 4, 12, and 13). Given the breadth of skills with which MLD is correlated, it is possible that these associations will reveal important subgroup differences among children with MLD (for further discussion, see commentary by Bull, this volume; also Dehaene, Piazza, Pinel, & Cohen, 2005; Geary, 1993).

Characteristic Abilities Specific to Mathematics

Some researchers propose that basic number processing difficulties are the core deficits that underlie MLD, rather than the supporting cognitive skills described previously. Although Geary and Hoard (2005) have reported that number processing skills are "near-normal" for children with MLD "at least for the processing of simple numbers (e.g., 3, 6)," Butterworth (2005) asserted that MLD is "a deficit in the capacity to represent and process numerosities" (p. 464; see also Chapter 4). Findings to date point to skills such as number sense as an important area of investigation for characterizing the cognitive skills of children with MLD (but see Berch, 2005, for a review of the complexity of this construct).

Compelling support is available that biological mechanisms are tied to basic number processing skills (see Chapters 13 and 14), and further evidence shows that different aspects of number processing are deficient to varying degrees in children with MLD or mathematical difficulties (Hanich et al., 2001; Landerl, Bevan, & Butterworth, 2004). Evidence also exists that these different number processing skills are linked with activation of specific brain regions (e.g., Dehaene et al., 2005). As most brain imaging studies of number processing to date have included only adults as participants, it would be an oversimplification to generalize these findings to children. The few studies with children have demonstrated some similarities in structure for certain number processing tasks and different developmental patterns in relative activation of specific brain regions with different number processing tasks (see Chapter 13). Whether it will emerge as a core deficit of MLD, as a primary manifestation of MLD, or as one of several impairments, difficulty with number processing appears to be a defining feature of MLD.

DOES SELF-AWARENESS OF DEFICITS MATTER?

Later in their conversation, the Dodecahedron asked Milo,

> "Don't you know anything at all about numbers?"
> "Well, I don't think they're very important," snapped Milo, too embarrassed to admit the truth.
> (Juster, 1961/1989, p. 177)

Having determined that skills in representing numerosity play a central, albeit undetermined, role in defining MLD, how likely is it that a child with MLD will be aware of these and other mathematical deficits? In other words, do children with MLD differ in terms of their knowledge about their own cognitive abilities? Such self-awareness, or metacognition, includes (but is not limited to) the ability to monitor completion of a mathematics task, knowledge about the steps and strategies used during the task, accurate prediction of future performance, and accurate appraisal of a completed task. As another complex, behaviorally defined trait, there is no consensus definition of metacognition (see Baker, 1994, for a discussion and review).

It is likely that some, but not all, children with MLD or mathematical difficulties will have poor metacognitive skills related to their performance. Some researchers have found that children with a learning disability (LD, but not necessarily MLD) give themselves higher ratings of self-understanding than their teachers report them to have. This suggests that children with LD have poor metacognitive skills. However, children with LD give themselves lower ratings than do their peers without LD when rating themselves (Meltzer, Roditi, Houser, & Perlman, 1998), suggesting at least some degree of accuracy in their metacognitive skills. Children who are more accurate on mathematical tasks are also more accurate in evaluating or predicting the correctness of their own solution, compared with children with poor math performance (Desoete, Roeyers, & Buysse, 2001; Lucangeli, Cornoldi, & Tellarini, 1997). My colleagues and I found that young children with MLD are as accurate as their peers when claiming not to know how to solve a given problem; however, they are less accurate than their peers both when predicting whether they can solve a given problem correctly and when evaluating their solutions to math problems, regardless of whether their solutions are accurate (Garrett et al., 2006). This has important implications for expecting children with MLD to benefit from "checking their work," or for expecting children with MLD to know when to ask others for help in completing mathematics tasks.

Likewise, attitudes about math and even math anxiety may impede mathematics learning or performance—and thus lead to mathematical difficulty in some instances. Because MLD is a biologically based condition, attitudes about mathematics are unlikely to constitute a predominant causal factor of this disability; nevertheless, attitudes may exacerbate the cognitive characteristics associated with MLD. Anxiety about math may result from one's awareness that mathematics is an area of pronounced difficulty, yet math anxiety in an otherwise cognitively capable individual may still decrease performance accuracy (see Chapter 11). This bidirectional relationship between math ability and attitudes about math represents another layer of complexity, including the role of sociocultural factors, in determining the correlates or manifestation of MLD or mathematical difficulties (see Chapter 16).

SUMMARY AND CONCLUSION

MLD is a biologically based, behaviorally defined condition for which no consensus definition currently exists. The lack of a consensus definition is not a reflection of lack of knowledge in the field. On the contrary, in the last decade the field of MLD research has laid a foundation for a new generation of research questions. The answers to these questions will inform ongoing efforts to define MLD.

Current definitions of MLD do not share a common single core deficit, nor do they share a common set of core deficits. From the research carried out to date, we know that children with MLD share many cognitive and behavioral characteristics. We also know that basic skills in mathematical cognition, such as the representation of numerosity, underlie some of the challenges experienced by children with MLD, and that other challenges may result from impairments in cognitive substrates that support mathematical performance. The lack of consensus as to which of these skills is primary or secondary, or the degree to which they are evident in different study samples, is due at least in part to the wide range of criteria used across studies to classify children as having MLD in terms of definitions and the tests used to measure math-related skills.

As a consequence of these varying criteria, different studies of "MLD" yield groups of children of diverse composition. For example, consider participants from two unrelated hypothetical studies: At one extreme, the participants from Study 1 are selected on the basis of having MLD. The children in this group will have inherent selective impairments (perhaps in basic mathematical cognition), and although most will have poor math achievement, some of these children will have achieved adequate proficiency in mathematics by exerting significant and sustained effort over time. Participants from Study 2 represent the other extreme. This group will be less selective than the MLD group but will still have some mathematical difficulties. All children in the second group will have poor mathematics achievement—specifically, all will score below the 35th percentile on a standardized mathematics test. Their poor achievement will result from a wide range of environmental factors rather than from an inherent disability in mathematics. They are more likely to have come from low socioeconomic backgrounds (Jordan et al., 2006). In summary, the children from each of these two overlapping groups will struggle with mathematics but to different degrees and possibly for different reasons.

The primary difference between the MLD and mathematical difficulties groups is the biological etiology of the former. But this does not imply that children with MLD are unresponsive to environmental influences, such as instructional interventions. Although standard, solid instruction may be insufficient to overcome the actual cognitive underpinnings of MLD, clearly, interventions can and must be developed (see Section VI) both for children with MLD and those with more heterogeneous difficulties in mathematics. At issue is identifying the correct intervention—or the intervention that targets the primary areas of cognitive weaknesses or impairments. Thus, defining MLD will enhance efforts to develop and test appropriate interventions.

An even wider array of factors may influence the manifestation of MLD or mathematical difficulties, including but not limited to ADHD (Chapter 11), math anxiety (Chapter 15), or cultural factors (Chapter 16). In view of this range of influences, it is not surprising that researchers of MLD vary with respect to the specific questions they address and their research approaches, which are in turn influenced by the discipline in which a researcher has been trained, such as medicine, psychology, neuroscience, or education. Yet across disciplines, researchers of MLD share an appreciation for the importance of mathematics in many aspects of everyday life (see Chapter 19). Their objective—direct or indirect—is to contribute to efforts to prevent and treat mathematical disabilities. Despite the barriers to defining MLD, incremental efforts to define it and to differentiate it from other forms of mathematical difficulties will make significant contributions toward this goal. At the heart of this goal is the fact that, regardless of how they are defined, MLD and mathematical difficulties threaten the academic and day-to-day success of millions of children worldwide.

> "It's very much like your trying to reach Infinity. You know that it's there, but you just don't know where—but just because you can never reach it doesn't mean that it's not worth looking for."
> (Juster, 1989, p. 197)

REFERENCES

American Psychiatric Association (1994). *Diagnostic and statistical manual of mental disorders* (4th ed.). Washington, DC: Author.

Baker, L. (1994). Fostering metacognitive development. In H. Reese (Ed.), *Advances in child development and behavior* (Vol. 25, pp. 201–239). San Diego: Academic Press.

Berch, D.B. (2005). Making sense of number sense: Implications for children with mathematical disabilities. *Journal of Learning Disabilities, 38*, 333–339.

Butterworth, B. (2005). Developmental dyscalculia. In J.I.D. Campbell (Ed.), *Handbook of mathematical cognition* (pp. 455–467). New York: Psychology Press.

Consensus Project (2002, August). *Definition Consensus Project* sponsored by the International Dyslexia Association and the National Institute of Child Health and Human Development.

Dehaene, S. (1997). *The number sense: How the mind creates mathematics*. Oxford and New York: Oxford University Press.

Dehaene, S., Piazza, M., Pinel, P., & Cohen, L. (2005). Three partial circuits for number processing. In J.I.D. Campbell (Ed.), *Handbook of mathematical cognition* (pp. 433–453). New York: Psychology Press.

Desoete, A., Roeyers, H., & Buysse, A. (2001). Metacognition and mathematical problem solving in grade 3. *Journal of Learning Disabilities, 34*, 435–449.

Dowker, A. (2005). *Individual differences in arithmetic*. East Sussex and New York: Psychology Press.

Fletcher, J.M., Francis, D.J., Shaywitz, S.E., Lyon, G.R., Foorman, B.R., Stuebing, K.K.K., et al. (1998). Intelligent testing and the discrepancy model for children with learning disabilities. *Learning Disabilities Research and Practice, 13*, 186–203.

Fletcher, J.M., Morris, R.D., & Lyon, G.R. (2003). Classification and definition of learning disabilities: An integrative perspective. In H. Lee Swanson, K.R. Harris, & S. Graham (Eds.), *Handbook of learning disabilities* (pp. 30–56). New York: Guilford Press.

Garrett, A.J., Mazzocco, M.M.M., & Baker, L. (2006). Development of the metacognitive skills of prediction and evaluation in children with or without math disability. *Learning Disabilities Research and Practice, 21*, 77–88.

Geary, D.C. (1990). A componential analysis of an early learning deficit in mathematics. *Journal of Experimental Child Psychology, 49*, 363–383.

Geary, D.C. (1993). Mathematical disabilities: Cognitive, neuropsychological, and genetic components. *Psychological Bulletin, 114*, 345–362.

Geary, D.C. (1995). Reflections of evolution and culture in children's cognition: Implications for mathematical development and instruction. *American Psychologist, 50*, 24–37.

Geary, D.C., Hamson, C.O., & Hoard, M.K. (2000). Numerical and arithmetical cognition: A longitudinal study of process and concept deficits in children with learning disability. *Journal of Experimental Child Psychology, 77*, 236–263.

Geary, D.C., & Hoard, M.K. (2005). Learning disabilities in arithmetic and mathematics. In J.I.D. Campbell (Ed.), *Handbook of mathematical cognition* (pp. 253–267). New York: Psychology Press.

Gersten, R., & Chard, D. (1999). Number sense: Rethinking arithmetic instruction for students with mathematical disabilities. *Journal of Special Education, 33*, 18–28.

Gersten, R., Jordan, N.C., & Flojo, J.R. (2005). Early identification and interventions for students with mathematical difficulties. *Journal of Learning Disabilities, 38*, 293–304.

Hallahan, D.P., & Mock, D.R. (2003). A brief history of the field of learning disabilities.

In H.L. Swanson, K.R Harris, & S. Graham (Eds.), *Handbook of learning disabilities* (pp. 16–29). New York: Guilford Press.

Hanich, L.B., Jordan, N.C., Kaplan, D., & Dick, J. (2001). Performance across different areas of mathematical cognition in children with learning disabilities. *Journal of Educational Psychology, 93,* 615–626.

Jordan, N.C., Kaplan, D., Nabors Oláh, L., & Locuniak, M.N. (2006). Number sense growth in kindergarten: A longitudinal investigation of children at risk for mathematics difficulties. *Child Development, 77,* 153–175.

Juster, N. (1989). *The phantom tollbooth.* New York: Knopf. (Original work published 1961).

Kavale, K.A., & Forness, S.R. (2000). What definitions of learning disability say and don't say. *Journal of Learning Disabilities, 33,* 239–256.

Landerl, K., Bevan, A., & Butterworth, B. (2004). Developmental dyscalculia and basic numerical capacities: A study of 8–9 year old students. *Cognition, 92,* 99–125.

Lucangeli, D., Cornoldi, C., & Tellarini, M. (1997). Mathematics and metacognition: What is the nature of the relationship? *Mathematical Cognition, 3,* 121–139.

Mather, N., & Roberts, R. (1994). Learning disabilities: A field in danger of extinction? *Learning Disabilities Research and Practice, 9,* 49–58.

Mazzocco, M.M.M. (2005). Challenges in identifying target skills for math disability screening and intervention. *Journal of Learning Disabilities, 38,* 318–323.

Mazzocco, M.M.M., & Myers, G.F. (2003). Complexities in identifying and defining mathematics learning disability in the primary school age years. *Annals of Dyslexia, 53,* 218–253.

Mazzocco, M.M.M. & Noeder, M. (manuscript in preparation). Changes in the attitudes in young children's definitions of "mathematics" and "reading" during the primary school-age years.

Meltzer, L., Roditi, B., Houser, R.F., & Perlman, M. (1998). Perceptions of academic strategies and competence in students with learning disabilities. *Journal of Learning Disabilities, 31,* 437–451.

Murphy, M.M., Mazzocco, M.M.M., Hanich, L., & Early, M.C. (in press). Cognitive characteristics of children with mathematics learning disability (MLD) varies as a function of the cut-off criterion used to define MLD. *Journal of Learning Disabilities.*

National Reading Panel (2000). *Teaching children to read: An evidence-based assessment of the scientific research literature on reading and its implications for reading instruction* (NIH Pub. No. 00-4769). Rockville, MD: National Institute of Child Health and Human Development.

Peterson, I. (2002). Drama in numbers. *Science News, 162* (25 & 26), 392–393.

Siegel, L.S. (1989). IQ is irrelevant to the definition of learning disability. *Journal of Learning Disabilities, 22,* 469–478.

Siegel, L.S., & Smythe, I.S. (2005). Reflections on research on reading disability with special attention to gender issues. *Journal of Learning Disabilities, 38,* 473–477.

Vellutino, F.R., & Fletcher, J.M. (2005). Developmental dyslexia. In M. Snowling & C. Hulme (Eds.), *The science of reading: A handbook* (pp. 362–378). Malden, MA: Blackwell Publishing.

Chapter 3

Prevalence of Developmental Dyscalculia

Ruth S. Shalev

+ +

K nowledge of the prevalence of learning disabilities in general, and dyscalculia in particular, has major clinical, educational, and public health ramifications. It provides information regarding demographic characteristics, risk factors, and comorbid conditions, thereby enabling a knowledgeable response to the needs of children with learning disabilities. Determining the prevalence of dyscalculia can also aid in assessing the efficacy of educational programs and instructional methods. For example, when the prevalence in a particular population surpasses the generally accepted estimate, it may allude to a problem specific to the environs. Furthermore, in many countries, educational interventions are mandated by law, with consequent budgetary implications. Therefore, generating reliable data on the prevalence of learning disabilities is far from being a theoretical issue. Rather, it is a necessity for those agencies responsible for providing medical services and special educational interventions.

Basic research principles need to be implemented when determining the prevalence of a learning disability. Of prime importance is the definition of *learning disability*, for which a consensus has not yet been reached and, therefore, is still a topic of ongoing debate. For example, Kosc, as early as 1974, defined dyscalculia as a specific, genetically determined learning disability in a child with typical intelligence. Later, the *Diagnostic and Statistical*

Parts of this chapter are similar to that in "Developmental Dyscalculia: Prevalence and Prognosis," by R.S. Shalev, J. Auerbach, O. Manor, and V. Gross-Tsur, 2000, *European Child & Adolescent Psychiatry 9*(II), 58 64, Steinkopff Verlag.

Manual of Mental Disorders-IV-TR (DSM-IV-TR), defined dyscalculia as a condition "when arithmetic performance is substantially below that expected for age, intelligence and education" (American Psychiatric Association, 2000). Both definitions may appear intuitively correct but need to be operationalized so that *learning disability* and *substantially* can be quantified as objective criteria.

Discrepancy criteria, either between intellectual aptitude and achievement or between school grade and achievement, have been used to quantify the degree of disability necessary for diagnosing dyscalculia. For the intellectual ability–achievement definition, a discrepancy of 1 to 2 standard deviations (*SD*) is considered reliable. Although useful, this definition has inherent weaknesses. First, both achievement and aptitude reflect achievement-specific determinants, so that assessment of natural ability versus actual achievement can never be realized (Van den Broeck, 2002). Second, this definition becomes less relevant for children at both ends of the intellectual spectrum. Thus, children with high intelligence but with normal, albeit mediocre, learning skills will be labeled as having a learning disability, and children with low intelligence and low learning achievement may be overlooked. For the school grade–achievement definition, a 2-year discrepancy between school grade and achievement is considered significant. However, this definition is not applicable for children in the first years of elementary school and is problematic for older adolescents and young adults.

When eligibility for educational services is an issue, the definitions require additional adjustment. For example, if the aptitude–achievement discrepancy definition is used, individuals without significant academic impairment may receive services at the expense of others whose needs are greater. Another approach is to differentiate between children with learning disabilities who readily respond to remediation and those who do not (Vellutino, Scanlon, & Lyon, 2000). A definition that protects those with academic underachievement, regardless of aptitude, may be necessary when targeting eligibility for special educational services (Gordon, Lewandowski, & Keiser, 1999). It is evident, therefore, that the ultimate goal of a particular prevalence study dictates which definition(s) are most appropriate, because they probably delineate slightly different groups of children.

Another pivotal issue in a prevalence study is the mathematics test used to establish presence of dyscalculia. A minimal requirement is to use at least one test, previously validated on the population to be sampled, that taps a wide range of numerical and arithmetic skills (Desoete, Roeyers, & DeClercq, 2004). Unfortunately, this principle has not always been implemented and, therefore, arithmetic batteries such as the Neuropsychological Test Battery for Number Processing and Calculation in Children (NU-CALC), which systematically assess multiple numerical skills are needed (von Aster, Weinhold Zulauf, & Horn, 2006). The theoretical basis for the NUCALC is the triple-code model of number cognition. It assesses counting, dictation of numbers, mental calculations, reading numbers, positioning of numbers on an analog scale, oral and written comparisons of number pairs, number and contextual estimation, and problem solving.

Another challenge in determining prevalence is the methodology by which the populations to be sampled are selected. Many epidemiological studies are only partially representative, because they do not include enough sectors of the school system, ethnic or socioeconomic fabric, and so forth. Also of importance is the age of the child at the time the diagnosis of dyscalculia was made. The younger the child, the greater the likelihood that the learning disability will remit, because at an early age, the difficulties often reflect a transient, developmental phenomenon rather than a bona fide learning disability (Shaywitz, Escobar, Shaywitz, Fletcher, & Makuch, 1992).

And finally, it is imperative to identify medical and environmental conditions that may masquerade as learning disabilities or exacerbate the difficulties of a child who is considered academically weak who does not have a learning disability. ADHD (Lindsay, Tomazic, Levine, & Accardo, 2001), mathematics anxiety (Faust, Ashcraft, & Fleck,1996), overcrowded classes (Ginsburg, 1997), mainstreaming of children of different capabilities, inadequate teaching methods, untested curricula (Miller & Mercer, 1997), emotional issues, family adversity, and environmental deprivation (Broman, Bien, & Shaughnessy, 1985) can all negatively affect the student who is struggling with academic demands.

In this chapter the epidemiological studies performed in Europe, North America, India, and Israel are reviewed. When perusing the study summaries, the reader should take note of the following points: the definition of learning disability used, the tool(s) employed to assess arithmetic knowledge, and the size of and method by which the population was chosen. Although each study offers useful information, the ones that are most informative include more than a thousand randomly chosen subjects tested on at least one standardized arithmetic battery, preferably at more than one time point. In view of the current lack of a known biological marker for dyscalculia, any given definition will affect prevalence by delineating a subgroup of children based on the orientation and criteria of the definition.

EPIDEMIOLOGICAL STUDIES

Slovakia: Kosc, 1974

The first epidemiological study of arithmetic disorders was conducted by Kosc and published in 1974. In this study, 199 boys and 176 girls in fifth grade (mean age 10.8 years) were randomly selected from 14 elementary school classes in Bratislava. The children were administered two group tests. The first (which was standardized following the study) assessed the children's ability to mathematically manipulate varying numbers of designed objects and solve simple geometrical problems. In the second, a nonstandardized test, children were required to solve addition, subtraction, multiplication, and division exercises; perform mathematical sequences; and interpret symbols. Children scoring below the 10th percentile on either or both of these tests (n = 66) were further studied to exclude those with other neurological or developmental deficits. The precise reasons for exclusion were not stated, but the ultimate result of this two-stage study showed that 24 of the 375 children had dyscalculia, yielding a prevalence of 6.4%. This study, the first of its kind, led to findings that were remarkably similar to those of subsequent studies.

United States

Badian, 1983 Until recently, the epidemiology of arithmetic disorders in North America attracted little attention; the first study was carried out by Badian in 1983, and 20 years passed before additional studies were published. In the 1983 study, Badian estimated the prevalence of children with poor calculation and reading skills among all (n = 1476) elementary school students (grades 1–8) in one small town. One third of the children were in first through third grade, a third were in fourth through sixth grade, and the remaining third were in seventh and eighth grades. The children were assessed using the Stanford Achievement Test (Madden, Gardner, Rudman, Karlsen, & Merwin, 1973) and identified as having a learning disability if they scored at or below the 20th percentile for arithmetic, reading, or both. Dyscalculia was diagnosed in 94 children (6.4%) and the boys:girls ratio was 2.2:1. A total of 72 (4.9%) of the children were poor readers, of whom 40 also had dyscalculia. Badian speculated that the intensive educational interventions administered to students with dyslexia may explain the relatively higher prevalence of dyscalculia in comparison with dyslexia.

Mazzocco and Myers, 2003 The importance of the tools used to assess arithmetic function was demonstrated in the a 2003 study by Mazzocco and Myers. These researchers studied the prevalence of dyscalculia in kindergarten children who were followed prospectively through third grade. The definition of learning disability was based on children's arithmetic scores as well as on persistence of poor arithmetic achievement for 2 or more years during primary school (i.e., Grades K–3). The arithmetic tests were the Key Math subtests, which assess math concepts and skills; the Test of Early Math Ability (TEMA-2) (Ginsburg & Baroody, 1990), which assesses mastery of mathematics-related concepts; and the Woodcock-Johnson Revised Math Calculations subtest, which measures paper-and-pencil calculations

(Woodcock & Johnson, 1989). Diagnostic criteria were KeyMath-Revised subtest score of <7, TEMA-2 scores of <86 or <10th percentile, Woodcock-Johnson score of <86, and discrepancy scores of >14 points between IQ score and the math test used. The participants were recruited from a suburban public school district and were representative of the full range of middle class socioeconomic categories. Of the 249 children enrolled, 209 completed the 4-year study from kindergarten through third grade. The percentage of these children who met at least one of the criteria for dyscalculia reached 45%; the range was 2%–45% for kindergarten children, 1%–9% for first graders, 1%–10% for second graders, and 5%–21% for third graders. The authors concluded that, among the various tests they used to define dyscalculia, the one most likely to co-occur with at least one other test was a TEMA-2 score below the 10th percentile. When the TEMA-2 score was used as the diagnostic tool, 63% (22/35) of children with dyscalculia in primary school still had dyscalculia in third grade. These two criteria yielded a prevalence of 9.6%; a single criterion yielded a prevalence as high as 45%. This study also demonstrated the value of using multiple time points to define dyscalculia and showed that dyscalculia was stable for the majority (but not all) of the children during the primary school years. Results from other studies (e.g., Koumoula et al., 2004, below) also reflect the instability of learning disability in primary school-age children (Silver, Pennett, Black, Fair, & Balise, 1999).

Barbaresi and Colleagues, 2005   The most definitive epidemiological study of dyscalculia was conducted by Barbaresi, Katusic, Colligan, Weaver, and Jacobsen (2005), who calculated the cumulative incidence of dyscalculia. Cumulative incidence is the summation of age-specific incidence rates, that is, the expected risk of being diagnosed with dyscalculia by a specific age. The medical and school records of all (n = 5718) children in a birth cohort born between 1976 and 1982 were thoroughly examined; 1509 were designated as candidates for learning disabilities. For each child within each calendar year, all IQ and achievement test scores were used to form pairs of ability and achievement measures. Arithmetic was assessed using either the Woodcock-Johnson test (Woodcock & Johnson, 1989) or the Wide Range Achievement Test (Jastak & Wilkinson, 1984); IQ was assessed with age-appropriate Wechsler scales. The authors then estimated the incidence of dyscalculia using three different definitions: the Minnesota regression formula ($y < 17.4 + 0.62x$); discrepancy formula (for kindergarten through grade 3, $y < x - 15$; for grades 4 through 6, $y < x - 19$; and for grades 7 through 12, $y < x - 23$); and low-achievement formula ($x > 80$ and $y < 90$) (x = full-scale IQ score and y = achievement standard score). In addition, socioeconomic status, medical conditions, and comorbid psychological and psychiatric conditions were recorded.

The cumulative incidence of dyscalculia in children up to 19 years was 5.9% (using the Minnesota regression formula), 9.8% (using the discrepancy formula) and 13.8% (using the low-achievement formula). It is noteworthy that the cumulative incidence was only 1.3%–2.1% for 7-year-old children, increased to 5.3%–11% at age 13, and remained relatively stable (5.9%–13.8%) until age 19. This stability suggests that for most children with dyscalculia, the diagnosis has been made by early adolescence.

Two additional findings emerged from this comprehensive study. First, boys were more likely to have dyscalculia than girls, with relative risk ratios from 1.6 to 2.2 boys for every 1 girl. This is in contrast to observations indicating equality for dyscalculia between the sexes. However, since the results of this study were based on meticulously obtained, detailed information from all 5,718 children in one district, the male preponderance may indeed reflect a genuine vulnerability of boys for learning disabilities, consistent with the preponderance of boys observed in Badian's study (1983). Second, the majority (57%–64%) of children with dyscalculia also had dyslexia; this fact alludes to common genetic underpinnings for both types of learning disabilities.

Germany

Two epidemiological studies on the prevalence of dyscalculia in third-grade elementary school students have been conducted in Germany.

Klaver, 1992   The first, published by Klauer (1992), estimated the prevalence of dyscalculia by using a score of at least 2 *SD* below the mean on the arithmetic subtest of a battery that also included reading and spelling. The 546 children who participated were randomly chosen from 26 representative mainstream classrooms in one city. The prevalence of dyscalculia was 4.4% and that of dyslexia 3.7%.

Hein, Bzufka, and Neumarker, 2000   The second German study, by Hein, Bzufka, and Neumarker (2000), appraised the epidemiological aspects of dyscalculia in both rural and urban populations. The rural component included 181 children (92 boys and 89 girls) from third-grade classes in four different schools. Using a standardized academic achievement test for arithmetic and language, dyscalculia was diagnosed if the child's score was below average in arithmetic and average or above in spelling. Of the 12 children (6.6%) who fulfilled these criteria, 9 underwent further neurological and neuropsychological testing: 4 were subsequently excluded because of low IQ scores and 3 because of adequate performance on a repeat arithmetic test. This two-stage diagnostic process substantially lowered the prevalence of dyscalculia from the original estimate of 6.6%.

In the urban population in the study, 182 third graders (100 boys and 82 girls, mean age 8.7 ± 0.7) underwent a standardized test of arithmetic skills containing primarily arithmetic exercises and a few word problems.

To exclude children whose overall performance was poor, a standardized test of spelling was administered and teacher reports of children's assessment of both arithmetic and spelling was used. Children were defined as having a specific learning disability in arithmetic if they scored < 25th percentile on the arithmetic subtest and ≥ 50th percentile for spelling. Out of 12 children (6.6%) who met these criteria, 10 were girls. Five children were available for a second stage analysis, which included IQ tests, NUCALC, neuropsychological tests, and a neurological examination. Dyscalculia as a specific learning disability (rather than secondary to inadequate teaching or visual, hearing, neurological, psychiatric, or other disorders) was verified in only one of these five children.

The results of this study underscore both the importance of the sample size and the need for verifying the diagnosis. Hein and colleagues (2000) clearly demonstrated that even when the sample consists of several hundred subjects, the affected cohort will hover at about 10–20 individuals, and following critical evaluation of each child, this figure becomes even smaller. Thus, a sample of several thousand individuals is required before solid conclusions can be drawn.

England: Lewis, Hitch, and Walker 1994

The inclusive survey carried out by Lewis, Hitch, and Walker (1994) encompassed all fifth graders ages 9–10 years in 51 urban and rural elementary schools in a single education district in England. The only exclusion criterion was mental retardation. Complete data were available for 1056 (497 girls and 559 boys) of 1206 children. The arithmetic test chosen, the Young's Group Mathematics Test (Young, 1971), is a calculation test (group administered). Reading and writing were assessed by the Young's Spelling and Reading Test (Young, 1976), which focuses on single word recognition and vocabulary skills, whereas the Raven's Colored Progressive Matrices (CPM) (Raven, 1965) was used to estimate general ability. Dyscalculia was defined when the score on the arithmetic test < 85 and the Raven CPM and reading test scores were ≥ 90. If the scores on both the reading and arithmetic tests were < 85 and Raven CPM ≥ 90, the children were classified as having both a reading and arithmetic disorder. Using the criteria, dyscalculia as an isolated learning disability was found in 1.3% of the population (7 boys and 7 girls), and a combined reading and arithmetic disorder was identified in 2.3% (11 and 13, respectively). Although the number of children diagnosed was relatively small, the boys:girls ratio for arithmetic disorder was 1:1. Results showing that children with atypical arithmetic skills could read normally and, conversely, that children with reading disabilities had typical arithmetic skills led the authors to conclude that dyscalculia is not secondary to dyslexia.

Israel: Gross-Tsur, Manor, and Shalev, 1996

The prevalence of dyscalculia in Israel is 6.5%, similar to that of other countries (Gross-Tsur, Manor, & Shalev, 1996). This figure was derived from a population of 3029 children attending fourth grade in the municipally run schools of Jerusalem. The children underwent two screening procedures. The first was a nonstandardized group-administered test geared to assessing arithmetic achievement in fourth grade. The 600 children who scored in the lowest 20% were re-studied in fifth grade using an individually administered standardized arithmetic test (Shalev, Manor, Amir, & Gross-Tsur, 1993). Dyscalculia was diagnosed if the score on the latter was ≤ the mean for children two grades younger in combination with an IQ score ≥ 80. Following this two-phase screening procedure, 188 children with dyscalculia were identified, yielding a prevalence of 6.5%. In order to further characterize this cohort, 140 children underwent neuropsychological assessments. The major results demonstrated that 25% had attention-deficit/hyperactivity disorder (ADHD) and 17% had a significant reading impairment. Children with the dual diagnosis of dyscalculia and dyslexia were more profoundly impaired on arithmetic skills than children with dyscalculia alone or dyscalculia and ADHD (Shalev, Manor, & Gross-Tsur, 1997). Among the children with dyscalculia, behavioral and emotional problems—as measured by the Child Behavior Checklist (CBCL; Achenbach & Edelbrock, 1983) were reported in as many as 30%, anxiety and depression in 8%, thought disorders in 10%, social problems in 22%, and externalizing problems in 14% (Shalev, Auerbach, Manor, & Gross-Tsur, 2000). A slightly higher prevalence of girls to boys (1.1:1.0) was noted. This finding, observed in other epidemiological studies, suggested that dyscalculia may have been unique among other learning disabilities for which a three-fold preponderance for boys was accepted as a general rule. However, the very recent and meticulously conducted study by Barbaresi and colleagues (2005) clearly demonstrated a male preponderance for dyscalculia. Previous results indicating a relative female prevalence in arithmetic disorders may have reflected gender-related environmental and social factors affecting the study of arithmetic.

India: Ramaa and Gowramma, 2002

This study included 1408 children in third grade (7–8 years old) and fourth grade (8–9 years old) from 11 primary schools in the city of Mysore. Prevalence of dyscalculia was determined from two different perspectives: as an isolated learning disability and regardless of any comorbid learning problem. In the first part of the study, 251 children underwent an individually administered arithmetic test that measured number concepts, fundamental operations, and arithmetic reasoning. Children were encouraged to keep working during the testing session, and the strategies they used were observed. Answers were assessed both qualitatively and quantitatively. Poor performance because of unfamiliarity of task (n = 118), lack of practice (n = 45), insufficient exposure to arithmetic (n = 23), or carelessness during the test or lack of perseverance (n = 25) were exclusionary criteria. Fifteen children, amounting to a prevalence of ~6% (15/251) were diagnosed with dyscalculia as an isolated learning disability. Of these, 9 were boys and 6 girls, yielding a gender ratio of 1.3:1.

In the second part of the study, 328 children referred by their teachers underwent an individually administered arithmetic test. Of this group, 162 were excluded because of abnormal sensory function, emotional or behavioral problems, mental retardation, additional help at home, or inordinate absence from school. Of the remaining 166 children, 78 met the 2-year age–grade discrepancy criterion for dyscalculia, generating a prevalence of 5.5% (78/1408). Among these 78 children, 51% had reading and writing problems, 18% had writing problems, and 30% had dyscalculia only.

Both methodological approaches used in this study yielded a dyscalculia prevalence of 5%–6%. Of note, the number of girls referred for problems with arithmetic was greater than the number of boys, whereas the number of boys actually diagnosed with dyscalculia was greater. This apparent discrepancy may be due to the multiple factors operative in the diagnostic process of dyscalculia, from referral to confirmation (Ramaa & Gowramma, 2002).

Greece: Koumoula and Colleagues, 2004

Participants in this study were 240 children (124 boys and 116 girls), ages 7–11 years, attending grades 2 through 5 in urban and rural elementary schools of diverse socioeconomic strata. To tap number concepts and arithmetic skills, the NUCALC battery was administered (von Aster et. al., 2006). The children also took the Wechsler Intelligence Scale for Children–III (WISC-III) (Wechsler, 1974) digit span subtest and a reading test; language and mathematic performance reports were obtained from the teachers. Using a z-score of < –1.5 to define dyscalculia, the prevalence was estimated to be 6.3%. Among the 15 children identified with dyscalculia, 7 also had dyslexia. Gender was not associated with either low or high achievement in calculation (Koumoula et. al., 2004).

Although the sampling methodology was comprehensive, the dyscalculia cohort was small and limited to children in the first grades of elementary school—a developmental phase during which the diagnosis of learning disabilities may be unstable (Koumoula et al., 2004). This caveat, however, is true for all of the prevalence studies performed on young elementary school children.

Belgium: Desoete and Colleagues, 2004

The prevalence of dyscalculia was studied in the Flemish population of Belgium using the following standardized arithmetic tests: the Revised Kortrijk Arithmetic test (Centrum voor Ambulante Revalidatic, 2005), which is a 60-item Belgian mathematic test assessing mental computation and number system knowledge; and the timed Arithmetic Number Facts test (De Vos, 1992), consisting of 200 arithmetic number fact problems (e.g., $5 \times 9 =$ ___). Dyscalculia was defined by three criteria: severity of the arithmetic problem (a score of ≥ 2 SD below the mean); discrepancy between performance and general ability; and the teacher's report that dyscalculia persisted despite appropriate remediation. Accordingly, dyscalculia was diagnosed in 2.3%, 7.7%, and 6.6% of second graders (662 boys and 661 girls), third graders (699 boys and 637 girls), and fourth graders (644 boys and 675 girls), respectively. The relatively low prevalence among second graders may be attributed to teachers' reluctance to categorize such young children as having a learning disability. The proportion of girls to boys hovered at approximately 1:1, with a slight preponderance for girls in the younger grades and for boys in the fourth grade.

The results of this study are particularly robust because the authors sampled a large population, determined the severity of arithmetic skills by using a combination of tests rather a single tool, and verified that the learning disability was not due to environmental factors but persisted in spite of appropriate educational interventions.

CONCLUDING REMARKS

Current estimates of the prevalence of dyscalculia are predicated on epidemiological studies, which screen sufficiently large and representative populations using standard methodologies and validated arithmetic batteries. The choice of the arithmetic test can be pivotal in an epidemiological study because large differences in prevalence may be dependent on the test employed. Another major obstacle in determining the prevalence of dyscalculia is the lack of consensus regarding its definition. Traditional definitions, based on criteria such as IQ score discrepancy and low achievement, have failed to capture the underlying construct of a learning disability because they reflect achievement parameters rather than actual aptitude (Francis et al., 2005). Yet another confounding factor is the instability of the diagnosis of learning disabilities in elementary school children, which approaches 80% for dyslexia (Shaywitz et al., 1992) and ranges from 35%–50% for dyscalculia (Mazzocco & Myers, 2003; Shalev et al., 2005). Thus, bona fide epidemiological studies require multiple assessments, at appropriate time intervals, in order to provide accurate estimates for the prevalence of dyscalculia (Desoete et al., 2004; Mazzocco & Myers, 2003).

To substantially add to the present state of knowledge regarding the prevalence of dyscalculia, a reliable, biologically based marker for this learning disability is necessary. Until then, perhaps, it would be wise to focus on other features of dyscalculia, such as its genetic basis, neuroanatomic and neuropsychological underpinnings, clinical characteristics, and remedial interventions.

REFERENCES

Achenbach, T.M., & Edelbrock, C. (1983). *Manual for the child behavior checklist and revised child behavior profile*. Burlington, VT: Queen City Printers.

American Psychiatric Association. (2000). *Diagnostic and statistical manual of mental disorders* (4th ed., Text rev.). Washington, DC: Author.

Badian, N.A. (1983). Dyscalculia and nonverbal disorders of learning. In H.R. Myklebust (Ed.), *Progress in learning disabilities* (pp. 235–264). New York: Grune & Stratton.

Barbaresi, W.J., Katusic, S.K., Colligan, R.C., Weaver, A.L., & Jacobsen, S.J. (2005). Math learning disorder: Incidence in a population-based birth cohort, 1976–1982, Rochester, Minn. *Ambulatory Pediatrics, 5*, 281–289.

Broman, S., Bien, E., & Shaughnessy, P. (1985). *Low achieving children: The first seven years*. Mahwah, NJ: Lawrence Erlbaum Associates.

Connolly, A.J. (1998). *The key math revised: A diagnostic inventory of essential mathematics manual*. Circle Pines, MN: American Guidance Service.

Desoete, A., Roeyers, H., & DeClercq, A. (2004). Children with mathematics learning disabilities in Belgium. *Journal of Learning Disabilities, 37*, 50–61.

Faust, M.W., Ashcraft, M.H., & Fleck, D.E. (1996). Mathematics anxiety effects in simple and complex addition. *Mathematical Cognition, 2*, 25–62.

Francis, D.J., Fletch, J.M., Stuebing, K.K., Lyon, G. Reid, Shaywitz, B.A., & Shaywitz, S.E. (2005). Psychometric approaches to the identification of LD: IQ and achievement scores are not sufficient. *Journal of Learning Disabilities, 38*, 98–108.

Ginsburg, H.P. (1997). Mathematics learning disabilities: A view from developmental psychology. *Journal of Learning Disabilities, 30*, 20–33.

Ginsburg, H.P., & Baroody, A.J. (1990). *Test of early mathematics ability* (TEMA–2) (2nd ed.).

Gordon, M., Lewandowski, L., & Keiser, S. (1999). The LD label for relatively well-functioning students: A critical analysis. *Journal of Learning Disabilities, 32*, 485–490.

Gross-Tsur, V., Manor, O., & Shalev, R.S. (1996). Developmental dyscalculia: Prevalence and demographic features. *Developmental Medicine and Child Neurology, 38*, 25–33.

Hein, J., Bzufka, M.W., & Neumarker, K.J. (2000). The specific disorder of arithmetic skills. Prevalence studies in a rural and an urban population sample and their clinico-neuropsychological validation. *European Child & Adolescent Psychiatry, 9*, II87–II/101.

Jastak, S., & Wilkinson, G.S. (1984). *Wide range achievement test revised: Administration manual*. Wilmington, DE: Jastak Associates.

Klauer, K.J. (1992). In Mathematik mehr leistungsschwache Madchen, im Lesen und Rechshreiben mehr leistungsschwache Junden? *Seitschrif f. Entwicklungspsychologie u. Padagogische Psychologie, 26*, 48–65.

Kosc, L. (1974). Developmental dyscalculia. *Journal of Learning Disabilities, 7*, 46–59.

Koumoula, A., Tsironi, V., Stamouli, V., Bardani, I., Siapati, S., Grahan, A., et al. (2004). An epidemiological study of number processing and mental calculation in Greek schoolchildren. *Journal of Learning Disabilities, 37*, 377–388.

Lewis, C., Hitch, G.J., & Walker, P. (1994). The prevalence of specific arithmetic difficulties and specific reading difficulties in 9- to 10-year-old boys and girls. *Journal of Child Psychology and Psychiatry, 35*, 283–292.

Lindsay, R.L., Tomazic, T., Levine, M.D., & Accardo, P.J. (2001). Attentional function as measured by a continuous performance task in children with dyscalculia. *Journal of Developmental and Behavioral Pediatrics, 22*, 287–292.

Madden, R., Garner, E., Rudman, H., Karlsen, B., & Merwin, J. (1973). *Stanford Achievement Test*. New York: Harcourt Brace Jovanovich.

Mazzocco, M.M.M., & Myers, G.F. (2003). Complexities in identifying and defining mathematics learning disability in the primary school-age years. *Annals of Dyslexia, 53*, 218–253.

Miller, S.P., & Mercer, C.L. (1997). Educational aspects of mathematics disabilities. *Journal of Learning Disabilities, 30*, 47–56.

Ramaa, S., & Gowramma, I.P. (2002). A systematic procedure for identifying and classifying children with dyscalculia among primary school children in India. *Dyslexia, 8*, 67–85.

Raven, J. (1965). *Raven's colored and standard progressive matrices*. San Antonio, TX: Harcourt Assessment.

Shalev, R.S., Auerbach, J., Manor, O., & Gross-Tsur, V. (2000). Developmental dyscalculia: Prevalence and prognosis. *European Child & Adolescent Psychiatry, 9*, II 58–II 64.

Shalev, R.S., Manor, O., Amir, N., & Gross-Tsur, V. (1993). Acquisition of arithmetic in normal children: Assessment by a cognitive model of dyscalculia. *Developmental Medicine and Child Neurology, 35*, 593–601.

Shalev, R.S., Manor, O., & Gross-Tsur, V. (1997). Neuropsychological aspects of developmental dyscalculia. *Mathematical Cognition, 3*, 105–120.

Shalev, R.S., Manor, O., & Gross-Tsur, V. (2005). Developmental dyscalculia: A prospective 6 year follow-up of a common learning disability. *Developmental Medicine & Child Neurology, 47*:121–125.

Shaywitz, S.E., Escobar, M.D., Shaywitz, B.A., Fletcher, J.M., & Makuch, R. (1992). Evidence that dyslexia may represent the lower tail of a normal distribution of reading ability. *New England Journal of Medicine, 324*, 145–150.

Silver, C.H., Pennett, H.D.-L., Black, J.L., Fair, G.W., & Balise, R.R. (1999). Stability of arithmetic disability subtypes. *Journal of Learning Disabilities, 32*(2), 108–119.

Van den Broeck, W. (2002). The misconception of the regression-based discrepancy operationalization in the definition and research of learning disabilities. *Journal of Learning Disabilities, 33*, 194–204.

Vellutino, F.R., Scanlon, D.M., & Lyon, G.R. (2000). Differentiating between difficult-to-remediate and readily remediated poor readers: More evidence against the IQ-achievement discrepancy definition of reading disability. *Journal of Learning Disabilities, 33*, 223–238.

von Aster, M.G. (2001). ZAREKI—Neuropsychologische Testbatterie fur Zahlenvararbeitung und Rechen bei Kindern. Lisse: Swets Test Services.

von Aster, M.G., Weinghold Zulauf, M., & Horn, R. (2006). Die Neuropsychologische Testbatterie fur Zahlenverarbeitung und Rechnen bei Kindern, Revidierte Version (ZAREKI-R) [Neuropsychological Testbattery for Number Processing and Calculation in Children]. Frankfurt: Harcourt Test Services.

Wechsler, D. (1974). *Wechsler Intelligence Scale for Children—Revised*. New York: Harcourt Assessment.

Young, D. (1971). *Group Mathematics Test*. London: Sevenoaks: Hodder & Stoughton.

Young, D. (1976). *SPAR (Spelling and Reading Tests)*. London: Sevenoaks: Hodder & Stoughton.

Section II

Cognitive and Information Processing Features

*"Can you do addition?" the
White Queen asked. "What's one
and one and one and one and
one and one and one and one
and one?" "I don't know,"
said Alice. "I lost count."*
—Lewis Carroll

Whether children are adding two numbers by counting on their fingers, attempting to recall basic multiplication facts, estimating the number of dots on a page, or solving a complex word problem, they can be considered to be engaged in acts of *cognitive processing*. These mental operations, performed on representations of the external world, include attention, inhibition, and retrieval, among others. One key cognitive construct treated in the chapters in this section is that of *working memory*, which can be characterized as the *workspace of the mind*. This limited capacity system simultaneously stores and processes information that it controls by means of a hypothesized *central executive*, and may also include both *domain-general* properties, which are applicable across a range of cognitive tasks, and *domain-specific* features, which apply to restricted content domains such as mathematical processing.

In Chapter, 4, Butterworth and Reigosa argue that domain-general explanations of the deficits exhibited by children with mathematical learning disabilities lack strong empirical support. Instead, they contend that math disabilities arise from deficits in a domain-specific brain system specialized for detecting and comparing small numerosities (e.g., several dots or objects). They suggest that this system functions as part of a "starter kit" for the subsequent understanding of numbers and arithmetic.

In Chapter 5, Geary, Hoard, Nugent, and Byrd-Craven examine several cognitive mechanisms that may be responsible for the use of developmentally immature problem solving-strategies and procedures by children with MLD. These authors conclude that poor outcomes are primarily attributable to deficient working memory and long-term memory systems, along with a delayed understanding of certain arithmetic concepts. Moreover, deficits in phonological skills and inhibitory mechanisms may contribute to difficulties in recalling arithmetic facts.

Jordan examines relationships between mathematical difficulties (MD) and reading disabilities (RD) in Chapter 6. Contrary to Geary's earlier findings that problems with number and fact retrieval may be related to a phonological processing difficulty, Jordan's own research shows that when required to retrieve arithmetic facts rapidly, children with RD perform better than do children with MD and those with co-morbid disabilities (MD+RD). Although the latter two subtypes generally exhibit similar functional profiles when processing numbers, the children with MD do much better in solving complex word problems. She concludes that children with math difficulties can catch up to their typically-achieving peers in such tasks because their *verbal strengths* can compensate for their weaknesses in number processing.

The reasons why children frequently experience difficulties when working with fractions are elucidated by Hecht, Torgesen and Vagi in Chapter 7. These authors conclude that such difficulties may be largely attributable to the inadequate conceptual understanding of fraction symbols. This conceptual knowledge turns out to be a key determinant of the variability in several kinds of performance outcomes such as fraction computation, estimation, and word problems. The limited research to date with MLD children suggests that their representation of the meaningful aspects of fraction symbols, especially knowledge of part–whole relationships, is even more poorly developed than that of their typically-achieving peers.

In his thoughtful commentary on the chapters in this section, Swanson points out that although some consensus exists that children with MLD experience difficulties in accessing numerical information (e.g., math facts) accurately and efficiently, there is disagreement concerning the primary cognitive mechanisms that underlie math disabilities. He concludes that as the construct of MLD and the criteria for its diagnosis continue to differ greatly across studies, research in this field ought to be viewed as being in its early stages.

Chapter 4

Information Processing Deficits in Dyscalculia

Brian Butterworth and Vivian Reigosa

\+ +

The aim of this chapter is to identify the central information processing impairments in children with developmental dyscalculia. We make a distinction here between the term *arithmetic learning difficulties* (ALD), which is often used to describe children performing in the lowest 30% (e.g., Geary, Hoard, & Hamson, 1999), and *developmental dyscalculia* (DD), for which prevalence estimates lie between 3.6% (Lewis, Hitch, & Walker, 1994) and 6.4% (Gross-Tsur, Manor, & Shalev, 1996). We use the term *ALD* to refer to samples defined by relatively low performance on standardized arithmetic tests, which is likely to include not only children with DD but also those with a wide range of other impediments to typical academic achievement, whereas *DD* is used here to denote a more severe and a more selective impairment.

If children with DD have a basic information processing impairment relative to children who are typically achieving, the first critical question is whether this impairment is domain general or domain specific. Put another way, what tools are in the "starter kit" that individuals bring to the task of learning arithmetic? On the one hand, it may be the case that the usual tools children bring to learn most school subjects will do equally well for learning arithmetic, and that if any of these are not working efficiently, children will encounter trouble—to a greater or lesser extent.

On the other hand, is a special tool needed for numbers? Certainly, special tools are not always necessary in other realms of life; for example, it is possible to insert a screw into a plank of wood without a screwdriver by using a pliers or a wrench. However, such an approach wouldn't be easy, it wouldn't be quick, and it wouldn't be the way that most people do it. By the same token, perhaps what should be looked for in individuals having difficulty doing arithmetic is not absolute inabilities but slow, difficult, and atypical ways of dealing with numbers.

An important methodological problem arises when trying to isolate information processing impairments in DD: The larger the proportion of the cohort used in a study, the more heterogeneous it is likely to be. This will mean that information processing impairments that affect school achievement generally, such as poor language skills (including dyslexia), low IQ, poor working memory, and behavioral problems, are likely to differentiate the average performance of children with DD from that of children who are typically achieving on tasks requiring a wide range of capacities, skills, and learning experiences.

This is precisely the case with mathematics. Even school arithmetic is complex, with a diverse collection of facts and procedures prescribed by the curriculum. In the UK, for example, the following are prescribed for school-year 4 (age 9 years) (National Curriculum Online, 2006):

- Use symbols correctly, including less than (<), greater than (>), equals (=).

- Round any positive integer less than 1000 to the nearest 10 or 100.

- Recognize simple fractions that are several parts of a whole, and mixed numbers; recognize the equivalence of simple fractions.

- Use known number facts and place value to add or subtract mentally, including any pair of two-digit whole numbers.

- Carry out column addition and subtraction of two integers less than 1000, and column addition of more than two such integers.

- Know by heart facts for the 2, 3, 4, 5 and 10 multiplication tables.

- Derive quickly division facts corresponding to the 2, 3, 4, 5 and 10 multiplication tables. Find remainders after division.

- Choose and use appropriate number operations and ways of calculating (mental, mental with jottings, pencil and paper) to solve problems.

Because even 9- and 10-year-olds have so many different kinds of facts and skills to acquire, it is not surprising that the reported indicators of dyscalculia are diverse. The following arithmetical characteristics are frequently cited (e.g., Butterworth, 2005; Geary, 1993):

- Poor memory for arithmetical facts (e.g., number bonds and multiplication tables)

- Reliance on immature strategies (e.g., adding and multiplying using fingers)

- Poor grasp of arithmetical procedures (e.g., borrowing and carrying)

- Poor grasp of arithmetical laws (e.g., commutativity of addition)

DOMAIN-GENERAL EXPLANATIONS

In a review of learning disabilities in arithmetic, Geary and Hoard (2005) listed the underlying cognitive systems of basic information processing that could be implicated in DD. There is the *central executive* responsible for attentional and inhibitory control of information processing; the *language system* for representing and manipulating information in arithmetical fact storage and retrieval; and the *visuospatial system*. However, Geary and Hoard did allow the possibility of ". . . a more modularized—independent of phonetic/semantic memory and working memory—cognitive system for the representation and retrieval of arithmetical knowledge, including arithmetic facts" (2005, p. 259).

GENERAL INTELLIGENCE

The simplest domain-general explanation, for both expert and layperson, lies in intelligence or reasoning ability. Nine-year-old children with DD have ascribed their inability to learn math to their own stupidity, and their more able classmates frequently stigmatize them for being stupid as well (Butterworth, 2005). However, very poor number skills can coexist with high cognitive ability. This is certainly true in cases of acquired dyscalculia (e.g., C.G. in Cipolotti, Butterworth, & Denes, 1991; D.R.C. in Warrington, 1982). Developmental cases have also been reported (e.g., "Charles" in Butterworth, 1999). More recently, we have studied B.D., an English major at a leading U.S. university with very rigorous entry requirements whose arithmetic skills were extremely poor. Here is an example of her ability in multiplication (Losiewicz & Rusconi, 2006):

Experimenter:	Can you please tell me the result of 9 times 4?
BD:	Yes, well, looks difficult.
	[Thinks and repeats aloud the problem for a couple of minutes]
	Now, I am very uncertain between 52 and 45 . . . I really cannot decide: It could be the first but could be the second as well.
Experimenter:	Make a guess then.
BD:	Okay . . . um . . . I'll say 47.
Experimenter:	Ok, I'll write down 47. But you can still change your answer, if you want. For example, how about changing it to 36?

BD: Um, no . . . it does not seem a better guess than 47, does
                       it? I'll keep 47.

Moreover, developmental studies typically use a lower IQ bound to exclude
children with poor general cognitive abilities. For example, Geary and colleagues (1999) and Shalev, Manor, and Gross-Tsur (1997) excluded children
with an IQ scores below 80; Landerl, Bevan, and Butterworth (2004) excluded children below the 50th percentile on an IQ measure; and Koontz
and Berch (1996) excluded children "below normal IQ" (their sample had
an average IQ score of 102). At the very least, this means that low general
cognitive ability in itself cannot be the explanation for information processing impairments in DD. At the same time, this approach excludes, by
definition, the possibility that children (or adults) who are low in general
intelligence can have DD. This means that additional effects of low cognitive ability on DD, if there are any, cannot be assessed.

Memory

Domain-general explanations have been offered for each of the characteristics of DD, more or less separately. "Poor memory for arithmetical facts" has
been explained by Geary and Hoard (2005) and Geary (1993) as a failure of
(semantic) memory. This should apply to all forms of factual or semantic
memory, but this has never been demonstrated in children with DD. In fact,
in neurological cases, numerical long-term memory (LTM) and other aspects of semantic LTM double dissociate. For example, I.H., who had semantic dementia, had an extremely poor memory for all facts (including
language facts), except for arithmetical facts (Cappelletti, Butterworth, &
Kopelman, 2001), whereas C.G. could remember almost nothing about
numbers despite excellent memory and language skills (Cipolotti et al.,
1991). Similarly, the use of immature strategies, such as finger counting, has
been explained in terms of an inability to use the age-appropriate memory
retrieval strategy. But what undergirds this impairment in the ability to remember arithmetical facts?

    Geary has offered two possibilities: 1) "a deficit in the ability to repre-
sent phonetic/semantic information in long-term memory" (Geary, 1993)
or 2) "a deficit in the ability to inhibit irrelevant information from entering
working memory during problem solving" (Geary & Hoard, 2005, p. 259).
These possibilities pose several problems. First, it has been known for a
very long time that phonetic and semantic coding in LTM behave very differently, are affected by different factors such as phonetic similarity in the
former case and semantic similarity in the latter case, and can dissociate in
neurological patients (see Baddeley, 1986, for a review). Second, Geary's
basic proposition that access to LTM depends on routing through working

memory is inconsistent with 35 years of research demonstrating the neural and functional independence of these systems (see 1996; McCarthy & Warrington, 1990, for a review). Third, finger counting in arithmetic gives rise to errors and delays in working memory and therefore prevents the efficient laying down of long-term memory. This means that finger arithmetic is both the consequence and the cause of poor memory for arithmetic facts.

Although the idea that impaired working memory could be the cause of DD has considerable plausibility given the apparent role of working memory (WM) in calculation, very little evidence supports this. What is needed is an independent measure of WM capacity and a correlation between its functioning in nonnumerical and numerical tasks. Typically, it is found that children and adults with an arithmetical impairment perform less well on both types of WM tasks. Siegel and Ryan (1989) found that children with DD did more poorly than controls on a working memory task involving counting and remembering digits but not on a nonnumerical working memory task. McLean and Hitch (1999) found no difference on a nonnumerical task testing phonological working memory (nonword repetition), suggesting that children with DD do not have reduced phonological working memory capacity in general, although they may have a specific difficulty with working memory for numerical information. Temple and Sherwood (2002) found no differences between groups on any of the working memory measures (forward and backward digit span, word span, and the Corsi blocks) and no correlation between measures of WM and measures of arithmetical ability.

In Landerl and colleagues's (2004) study of 9-year-olds, children with DD and children who were typically achieving were matched on span, so it was unlikely that a WM impairment could explain differences between groups.

Language

Language difficulties have also been cited as a possible cause of DD. In the triple code theory of Dehaene and colleagues, language itself is needed to construct concepts of exact numbers greater than 4 (Carey, 2004; Dehaene & Cohen, 1995). Apparent empirical support for this position comes from observed association between DD and dyslexia, often construed as arising from a deficit in phonological processing (Lewis et al., 1994).

However, studies of neurological patients have revealed a sharp dissociation between those with severe acalculia but spared language and those with severely defective language but spared calculation. An example of spared language can be found in the story of C.G., who performed typically on all language tests (though she could no longer read) but was only able to count to 4 and was quite unable to handle any task at all involving numbers larger than 4 (Cipolotti et al., 1991). It is much rarer to see individuals with calculation selectively spared despite defective language; however, I.H., described previously, was able to carry out single-digit and multidigit calculations almost flawlessly yet performed at chance at spoken word comprehension, suggesting he was guessing, and close to zero on most tests of naming (Cappelletti et al., 2001). This dissociation suggests that the language and number circuits in the adult brain are distinct.

Space

Another candidate for a domain-general information processing impairment in DD is spatial cognition. Rourke (1993) has argued that DD is essentially due to a defective representation of space. More specifically, Geary (1993) noted that "a disruption of the ability to spatially represent numerical information . . . appears to affect both functional skills (e.g., columnar alignment in complex arithmetic problems) and the conceptual understanding of the representations (e.g., place value)" (p. 346). The idea that space and number are cognitively related has had many supporters, and the role of the parietal lobes in both space and number has been noted by researchers for more than 60 years (e.g., Gerstmann, 1940). The spatial representation of numerical magnitudes in the form of a mental number line has frequently been proposed (e.g., Dehaene, Piazza, Pinel, & Cohen, 2003; Fias, Lammertyn, Reynvoet, Dupont, & Orban, 2003; Galton, 1880; Spalding & Zangwill, 1950), and it would seem plausible that deficits in spatial representation ability could affect a sense of numerical magnitude. However, even severe unilateral spatial neglect, in which the individual neglects one side of space, affects a number bisection task but leaves arithmetic entirely spared (Zorzi, Priftis, & Umiltà, 2002). Though being unable to maintain a mental representation of multidigit numbers in the correct columnar organization leads to spatial acalculia in individuals with neurological impairments (Hécaen, Angelergues, & Houillier, 1961), such a condition has been rarely, if ever, reported as an isolated symptom. To our knowledge, it has never been reported in children with DD and does not appear to affect the grasp of basic numerical concepts.

DOMAIN-SPECIFIC EXPLANATIONS FOR INFORMATION PROCESSING IMPAIRMENTS IN DEVELOPMENTAL DYSCALCULIA

The possibility of a domain-specific explanation was raised sharply by Koontz and Berch in 1996. They asked "whether the mathematical difficulties experienced by [arithmetic disabled] children may stem in part from slower and less efficient cognitive processing of numerical information at an even more basic level than has heretofore been examined" (p. 2).

Research suggests that infants are born with an ability to recognize small numerosities (Antell & Keating, 1983; Starkey & Cooper, 1980) and carry out mental manipulations on representations of them (e.g., Simon, Hespos, & Rochat, 1995; Wynn, 1992; Wynn, Bloom, & Chiang, 2002; see Gelman & Butterworth, 2005, for a review). Moreover, primates can learn numerosities and associate them with numerals (Matsuzawa, 1985), order numbers in a sequence quickly (Kawai & Matsuzawa, 2000), and select the numerically larger of two visual arrays of objects (Brannon & Terrace, 1998). It has recently been established that monkeys use parietal and pre-frontal brain areas homologous to those used by humans in a matching-to-numerosity task in which their neurons are coarsely "tuned" to particular numerosities up to about 5 (Nieder & Miller, 2003; Sawamura, Shima, & Tanji, 2002).

This evidence suggests that in human infants and primates there is a domain-specific mechanism for detecting, comparing, and manipulating "the numerosity parameter" of environmental stimuli (Dehaene et al., 2003), but that this is not just a useful skill each species has developed independently. The neurofunctional data imply that humans have inherited this from an ancestral version in the common ancestor to humans and monkeys, which in turn implies that genes exist in the human genome code for building a domain-specific brain system (presumably in the parietal lobes) that carries out simple numerical information processing, such as detecting and comparing numerosities. This capacity functions as part of the starter kit for understanding numbers and arithmetic. Selective impairments will arise, in this view, when the specialized capacity, or "number module" (Butterworth, 1999), fails to develop normally. I have called this "the defective number module hypothesis" (see Butterworth, 2005, for an elaboration of this hypothesis).

Probably the earliest attempt to assess whether children with arithmetic learning disabilities (ALD) had an impairment in this specialized capacity was a study of 9- to 10-year-olds by Koontz and Berch (1996). They used a variant of the Posner physical versus name identity matching, using numerals (2, 3) and dots. There were two tasks, physical matching and name matching (i.e., same numerical value), with a classical letter matching task as a comparison. This task does not depend on either education or intelligence. In one task, the participants had to say whether two stimuli, numbers or letters, were physically identical (e.g., 2–2 or A–A). In a second task, they had to say whether two stimuli (numerals, dots, or a mixture of these—e.g., 2 • •, have the same numerical value.

Although the children with ALD in this study appeared more error prone and slower than children who were typically achieving on all the tasks, the critical issue was whether they were slower to access mental representations of numbers from numerals and whether irrelevant numerical information would interfere with a physical matching judgment. When making a physical identity judgment on, for example, 2–3, children who were typically achieving were slowed by the incompatible numerical information, but the children with ALD were not, suggesting that children with ALD did not access the meaning of the numerals quickly enough to create interference. At the same time, children with ALD were slowed in the name identity judgment by incompatible physical features (numeral and dots) although the children who were typically achieving were not, suggesting that the children with ALD were attending to the more superficial aspects of the stimuli rather than their meanings. There was also the interesting finding that the children with ALD, unlike the children who were typically achieving, were counting three dots.

Interference effects had previously been found by Duncan and MacFarland (1980). They used a physical identity task with the numbers 1–9 to show that even kindergarten children who are typically achieving show an interference effect related to the "distance" between the numbers (with smaller distances causing more interference, indexed as greater slowing of the "no" response). This implied that these children, as well as older children and adults, accessed the numerical magnitude of numerals even when it was irrelevant to the task (indeed, it actually interfered with the task), suggesting that the process of deriving meaning from numerals is autonomous and automatic.

A similar logic underscored a study by Girelli, Lucangeli, and Butterworth (2000) of children who were typically developing. They used a different task to investigate the role of automatic activation of number meaning: the numerical Stroop task. Two tasks were employed: In one, children were asked to judge which of two numbers was physically larger (e.g., the 3 in 3 5); in the other, children were asked to judge which was numerically larger (e.g., the 5 in 3 5). Three conditions were used: congruent (3 5), incongruent (3 5), and neutral (3 3 for the physical task and 3 5 for the numerical task). In typical adults, a size congruity effect is routinely observed. That is, in the physical task there will be facilitation in the congruent condition (faster relative to neutral) and interference in the incongruent condition (slower relative to neutral); in the numerical task as well, congruence will facilitate and incongruence will interfere (e.g., Foltz, Poltrock, & Potts, 1984). This pattern would constitute evidence for rapid and automatic activation of the numerical meaning of the numerals. Neither of these effects emerged in first graders; they emerged only in third graders and older children. These findings strongly suggest that the automatization in number processing is achieved gradually as numerical skills progress, in a manner consistent with Logan's (1988) account of automaticity. A convergent additional finding was that the normal distance effect was exhibited on the numerical task, but an inverse numerical distance effect was present in the physical task. This suggests that the meaning of the numeral is fully processed even when task irrelevant, and presumably unattended, so that when the distance is great and the selection of the larger one is faster, it becomes more likely that the numerical decision will affect the physical decision, which is always significantly faster. (A study similar to this was carried out by Rubinsten, Henik, Berger, & Shahar-Shalev [2002], and an interesting discussion of the development of magnitude representations and a critical evaluation of both studies can be found in Noel, Rousselle, & Mussolin, 2005.)

Applying this logic to children with DD, along the lines pioneered by Koontz and Berch (1996), we reasoned that a deficit in accessing numerical magnitudes from numerals will be shown in children in two ways. First, and most important, children's physical judgments should be fundamentally different and unaffected by DD, and children with DD should present with slowed numerical judgments relative to children who were typically achieving. Second, children who are typically achieving should show a congruity effect in the physical task because the meanings of the numerals will have been activated, but the children with DD should not show this effect. In our study of 9-year-olds, the first predicted result was obtained; children with DD took much longer to decide which of two numbers was numerically greater, although they were just as fast as children in control groups on the physical judgment. However, in the physical task, we found no effect of congruity in either group (Landerl et al., 2004).

The Stroop task was used by Rubinsten and Henik (2005) to investigate automatic access to number meanings in adults with DD. (Curiously, these researchers failed to cite the earlier study by Landerl and colleagues (2004). They used only tasks in which numerical value was task irrelevant: physical size, relative height (e.g., ^{3} $_5$) or relative grayness (e.g., **3** 5). If the logic of Koontz and Berch (1996), Girelli and colleagues (2000), and Landerl and colleagues were followed, then the following predictions would be made:

- On each of these tasks, there should be no overall difference in reaction time (RT) between adults who are typically achieving and adults with DD because the task requires attention to a nonnumerical dimension. (Indeed, this is what Landerl and colleagues found.)

- On each task, adults who are typically achieving should show facilitation and/or interference but DD adults should not, or at least they should show very reduced effects of congruity. However, neither of these predictions was fulfilled. Adults with DD performed approximately 30% slower on these nonnumerical tasks, and there was no omnibus interaction between group and congruity condition. Looking at interactions with congruity in each task separately revealed group-by-congruity interactions for height and grayness but not for size, whereas both groups showed congruity effects. Why there should be differences between the tasks was not explained, nor was the overall slowness of the group with DD. Unfortunately, it is very difficult to interpret these findings because

Rubinsten and Henik did not say what criteria were used to identify DD. They reported using the age-standardized battery employed by Shalev and colleagues (2001), to which they added items (presumably not age standardized). They did not say which cutoff was used (Shalev and colleagues used the 25th percentile), or whether it is even possible to use such a criterion when part of the test is not standardized. It may be relevant that the adults with DD performed at normal levels on untimed simple addition and subtraction and on "complex addition."

Koontz and Berch (1996) found that their group with ALD tended to provide slower responses for tasks involving three dots than for two dots, whereas this discrepancy was not found for the typically achieving group. They suggested that perhaps subitizing is impaired in individuals with ALD. Landerl and colleagues (2004), using a standard dot estimation paradigm with vocal responses, found a hint of a difference in the subitizing range (one to three dots, after controlling for age and color-naming speed), and a trend for the counting range (4–10). However, a study of 260 5- and 6-year-olds found highly significant effects (Reeve & Reynolds, 2004). Using a mixture modeling analysis of RTs, Reeve and Reynolds found that the 5-year-olds could be separated into three groups, which they termed "fast subitizers," "slow subitizers," and "nonsubitizers." The fast and slow subitizers showed the classic RT change of slope at about four dots, whereas the nonsubitizers did not show it and were also much slower. Reeve and Reynolds found that the grouping by the slope of dot estimation speed predicted addition performance (in percent correct) at both 5 and 6 years, with the nonsubitizers being by far the worst. The lack of significant results in the Landerl and colleagues study may thus have been due to sample size (N = 28).

Reeve and colleagues (reported in Reeve, 2006) found that nonsubitizers differed from the other groups on a number comparison task; nonsubitizers were both slower to make the judgment and, more strikingly, failed to show a significant distance effect. Additional evidence also suggests a dissociation between enumeration and number comparison. Reigosa and colleagues (2006) found that some children who were poor at estimation (roughly equivalent to Reeve & Reynolds's [2004] nonsubitizers) still showed a typical distance effect, and those with an abnormal distance effect were typical at estimation. They tested a sample of 2932 8- and 11-year-olds on a dot estimation task and a numerical comparison task. Both tasks were computerized and item-timed. Indexes for Subitizing (IS = RT three dots – RT one dot) and Numerical Distance (IND = RT distance 1 – RT distance 4) were calculated. They found a group of children (typically achieving and ALD), good in subitizing and counting, who showed a typical distance effect in number comparison. They also found two groups of children with DD who showed double dissociation: One group had very poor subitizing but showed a normal distance effect, and the other group showed exactly the opposite pattern. Moreover, the correlation between both indexes in the overall sample was low and not significant. Future research may settle on a more refined hypothesis, in which DD may turn out to be the consequence of one or two basic numerical processing impairments.

THE GENETICS OF DOMAIN-SPECIFIC INFORMATION PROCESSING DEFICITS

Since the mid 1990s it has been established that females with Turner syndrome (TS) perform poorly on mathematical tasks (Rovet, Szekely, & Hockenberry, 1994; see Mazzocco & McCloskey, 2005, for a review). TS occurs in 1 in 2500 live female births. It is a chromosomal abnormality in which all, or a substantial part, of one of the two X chromosomes that are present in females is missing. In the X-monosomy variant, found in about 50% of all cases, there is a single X chromosome in all cells (45,X) rather than the two found in 46,XX females. Because it is typical for one of the two X chromosomes to be inactivated early in embryonic development, it is perhaps surprising that TS should have neurodevelopmental consequences. The TS phenotype is associated with distinctive physical characteristics, such as short stature and early atresia of the ovaries, which leads to chronically low production or absence of female sex hormones. Estrogen replacement therapy is normally instituted in adolescence. The cognitive phenotype of TS typically shows IQ score and verbal abilities in the normal range, but most individuals have relatively poor visuospatial skills (about 1 standard deviation *(SD)* below verbal abilities) (Mazzocco & McCloskey, 2005). Some individuals with TS show major impairments of visuospatial memory (Bishop et al., 2000) as well as other cognitive features, such as attention problems, motor impairments (clumsiness), and poor social skills (Skuse et al., 1997). Anatomical abnormalities have been found in the parietal lobes (Murphy et al., 1993), especially along the intraparietal sulci, which are the brain regions activated in most numerical tasks. In addition, there appear to be abnormal activations during numerical tasks as well (Molko et al., 2003).

On standard arithmetic tests, individuals with TS perform worse, on average, than controls, and they have a higher incidence of math disability, however defined (Mazzocco & McCloskey, 2005). However, for single-digit arithmetic, individuals with TS are usually as accurate as matched controls, although considerably slower (Bruandet, Molko, Cohen, & Dehaene, 2004; Butterworth et al., 1999). As is true of individuals with DD who do not have TS, relevant information processing impairments have been identified in individuals with TS. For example, they are slower on a dot estimation task (Bruandet et al., 2004; Butterworth et al., 1999). Bruandet and colleagues noted that they are slower even with two dots: "This suggested that many of the patients were counting within the range in which controls normally subitize. Indeed, the increase in response time from three to four dots was 237 ms in the patients, close to the value observed in the counting range, where it was only 72 ms in the controls, a significance difference" (p. 293).

Both Bruandet and colleagues (2004) and Butterworth and colleagues (1999) found a trend of group differences in number comparison, but not a significant effect, nor was there an interaction with distance. However, in a Stroop version of number comparison, individuals with TS were significantly slower than controls in the numerical task, although a normal congruity effect indicated that physical size interacted with the numerical judgment (Butterworth et al., 1999). A striking finding was that on the physical size judgment, no overall differences were found in RTs between individuals with TS and controls, but there was an interaction between congruity and group. Controls showed the usual congruity effect, but the individuals with TS did not. Taken together with the numerical task results, this indicates that individuals with TS are slower in accessing the meaning of numerals, which slows number comparison and reduces the effect of number meanings on the physical task.

Thus, in this particular subgroup of individuals with DD, these basic information processing problems can be readily identified. Other special populations with math disabilities also show impairments in tests of the specialized capacity (number module). For example, individuals with Williams syndrome (WS) and Down syndrome (DS) perform worse than age-matched controls on most arithmetical tasks, though individuals with DS can achieve ceiling on very simple tasks. Overall, individuals with WS perform worse on average than those with DS, and this reflects performance on the capacity tests. Individuals with WS do not show a normal distance effect on number comparison, whereas those with DS do, and individuals with WS are worse at estimating the number of dots in a display and in seriating (ordering by magnitude) dot displays (Paterson, Girelli, Butterworth, & Karmiloff-Smith, 2006).

SUBTYPING

One important issue is whether different types of information processing impairments lead to different types of DD. The issue of subtyping has typically been investigated in terms of comorbidity with other developmental disorders, such as dyslexia (e.g., Landerl et al., 2004; Lewis et al., 1994) or ADHD (Shalev et al., 1997), but there have also been theoretically driven approaches to subtyping, some of which focus on specific types of information processing.

In a series of pioneering studies, Temple and colleagues identified three forms of developmental disorder affecting different components of arithmetical skill, as defined in the model of McCloskey and colleagues (e.g., McCloskey & Lindemann, 1992; Sokol, McCloskey, Cohen, & Aliminosa, 1991). McCloskey differentiated input from output systems (numerals and words) and, within each system, lexical from syntactic processes. In one study, Temple (1989) identified a child with "digit dyslexia," which selectively affected processing of the lexical content of numbers but left intact the development of number syntax (e.g., errors included "six thousand, six hundred and seventy-two" for 9172; "fifty-eight" for 41; and "three" for 2, but not syntactic errors such as "twelve" for 2 or "six hundred and thirty" for 63). McCloskey also distinguished between memory for arithmetical facts and knowledge of arithmetical procedures.

Temple identified both selective impairments in fact retrieval and impairments in arithmetical processes (e.g., Temple, 1991). She also carefully assessed whether impairments in number facts could be explained in terms of domain-general factors, but she found no evidence that participants had weak short-term memory (STM) spans on any span measure or that STM spans related to arithmetical fact skills (Temple & Sherwood, 2002). In this study, Temple also looked at speed of access to lexical representations outside the realm of numbers. Though it was true that children with slow number fact retrieval overall were also slower in naming colors and objects, Temple was careful not to make the causal link. First of all, there was no systematicity in the relationship between naming and retrieval. One subgroup was as fast as controls on multiplication fact retrieval but slower on addition. Second, it was not clear that the individuals with DD were actually retrieving facts rather than trying to calculate the answers. She concluded that "the results are consistent with modular accounts, in which there is a specialized system for the storage and retrieval of arithmetical facts" (Temple & Sherwood, 2002).

CONCLUSIONS

One of the striking things about DD is that it can be highly selective. Individuals may show typical or even excellent performance on all school subjects apart from mathematics. Typical or superior IQ score does not preclude one from having it, and the common DD characteristic of poor memory for arithmetical facts is not necessarily part of a wider impairment in either LTM or WM. The evidence reviewed currently favors a domain-specific interpretation of DD and answers Koontz and Berch's (1996) prescient query: Is it true that "mathematical difficulties experienced by ALD children may stem in part from slower and less efficient cognitive processing of numerical information at an even more basic level than has heretofore been examined"? The answer is yes, and the basic levels referred to can be identified as the estimation and comparison of numerosities. The individuals with DD described here are not only poor in school arithmetic and on standardized tests of arithmetic, they are slower and less efficient at recognizing the numerosities of displays of objects (typically dots) and/or at comparing numerosities in a variety of number comparison tasks. This is in line with Butterworth's (2005) defective number-module hypothesis, which proposed that DD arises from an impairment in information processing mechanisms specialized for recognizing, representing, and mentally manipulating small numerosities. It is not yet known whether this impairment interacts with other cognitive impairments to create identifiable symptom-pictures or subtypes of dyscalculia; and it does not exclude the possibility that there are other causes of learning difficulties in mathematics, even selective learning difficulties.

These conclusions have practical implications. First, the diagnosis of DD can consist of simple tests of the basic capacities to estimate and compare numerosities; indeed, a screener for DD based on these principles is now widely used in the UK (Butterworth, 2003) and forms the basis of the Maximat test that is being used to carry out a very large scale cohort study of DD in Cuba, led by the Cuban Centre for Neuroscience. Second, it may have implications for intervention. If the basic capacities for understanding numerosities are weak, these should form the focus of a training strategy rather than rote learning of number bonds and other arithmetical facts. If it turns out that there are subtypes of DD due to interaction with other cognitive deficits, or due to domain-specific information processing impairments yet to be identified, new and appropriate interventions will need to be devised.

REFERENCES

Antell, S.E., & Keating, D.P. (1983). Perception of numerical invariance in neonates. *Child Development, 54*, 695–701.

Baddeley, A. (1986). *Working memory.* Oxford: Clarendon Press.

Bishop, D., Canning, E., Elgar, K., Morris, E., Jacobs, P., & Skuse, D. (2000). Distinctive patterns of memory function in subgroups of females with Turner syndrome: Evidence for imprinted loci on the X-chromosome affecting neurodevelopment. *Neuropsychologia, 38*(5), 712–721.

Brannon, E.M., & Terrace, H.S. (1998). Ordering of the numerosities 1 to 9 by monkeys. *Science, 282*, 746–749.

Bruandet, M., Molko, N., Cohen, L., & Dehaene, S. (2004). A cognitive characterization of dyscalculia in Turner syndrome. *Neuropsychologia, 42*, 288–298.

Butterworth, B. (1999). *The mathematical brain.* London: Macmillan.

Butterworth, B. (2003). Dyscalculia Screener. London: nferNelson Publishing Company Ltd.

Butterworth, B. (2005). Developmental dyscalculia. In J.I.D. Campbell (Ed.), *The Handbook of Mathematical Cognition* (pp. 455–467). Hove, UK: Psychology Press.

Butterworth, B., Cipolotti, L., & Warrington, E. K. (1996). Short-term memory impairments and arithmetical ability. *Quarterly Journal of Experimental Psychology, 49A*, 251–262.

Butterworth, B., Granà, A., Piazza, M., Girelli, L., Price, C., & Skuse, D. (1999). Language and the origins of number skills: Karyotypic differences in Turner's syndrome. *Brain & Language, 69*, 486–488.

Butterworth, B., Shallice, T., & Watson, F. (1990). Short-term retention of sentences without "short-term memory". In G. Vallar & T. Shallice (Eds.), *Neuropsychological impairments of short-term memory*. Cambridge: Cambridge University Press.

Cappelletti, M., Butterworth, B., & Kopelman, M. (2001). Spared numerical abilities in a case of semantic dementia. *Neuropsychologia, 39*, 1224–1239.

Carey, S. (2004). On the origin of concepts. *Daedulus*.

Cipolotti, L., Butterworth, B., & Denes, G. (1991). A specific deficit for numbers in a case of dense acalculia. *Brain, 114*, 2619–2637.

Dehaene, S., & Cohen, L. (1995). Towards an anatomical and functional model of number processing. *Mathematical Cognition, 1*, 83–120.

Dehaene, S., Piazza, M., Pinel, P., & Cohen, L. (2003). Three parietal circuits for number processing. *Cognitive Neuropsychology, 20*, 487–506.

Duncan, E., & MacFarland, C. (1980). Isolating the effects of symbolic distance and semantic congruity in comparative judgments: An additive factors analysis. *Memory and Cognition, 8*, 612–622.

Fias, W., Lammertyn, J., Reynvoet, B., Dupont, P., & Orban, G.A. (2003). Parietal representation of symbolic and nonsymbolic magnitude. *Journal of Cognitive Neuroscience, 15*, 47–56.

Foltz, G.S., Poltrock, S.E., & Potts, G.R. (1984). Mental comparison of size and magnitude: Size congruity effects. *Journal of Experimental Psychology: Learning, Memory, and Cognition, 10*, 442–453.

Galton, F. (1880). Visualised numerals. *Nature, 21*, 252–256.

Geary, D.C. (1993). Mathematical disabilities: Cognitive, neuropsychological, and genetic components. *Psychological Bulletin, 114*, 345–362.

Geary, D.C., & Hoard, M.K. (2005). Learning disabilities in arithmetic and mathematics: Theoretical and empirical perspectives. In J.I.D. Campbell (Ed.), *Handbook of mathematical cognition* (pp. 253–268). New York: Psychology Press.

Geary, D.C., Hoard, M.K., & Hamson, C.O. (1999). Numerical and arithmetical cognition: Patterns of functions and deficits in children at risk for a mathematical disability. *Journal of Experimental Child Psychology, 74*, 213–239.

Gelman, R., & Butterworth, B. (2005). Number and language: How are they related? *Trends in Cognitive Sciences, 9*(1), 6–10.

Gerstmann, J. (1940). Syndrome of finger agnosia: Disorientation for right and left, agraphia and acalculia. *Archives of Neurology and Psychiatry, 44*, 398–408.

Girelli, L., Lucangeli, D., & Butterworth, B. (2000). The development of automaticity in accessing number magnitude. *Journal of Experimental Child Psychology, 76*(2), 104–122.

Gross-Tsur, V., Manor, O., & Shalev, R.S. (1996). Developmental dyscalculia: Prevalence and demographic features. *Developmental Medicine and Child Neurology, 38*, 25–33.

Hécaen, H., Angelergues, R., & Houillier, S. (1961). Les variétés cliniques des acalculies au cours des lésions rétro-rolandiques: Approche statistique du problème. *Revue Neurologique, 105*, 85–103.

Kawai, N., & Matsuzawa, T. (2000) Numerical memory span in a chimpanzee. *Nature, 403*, 39–40.

Koontz, K.L., & Berch, D.B. (1996). Identifying simple numerical stimuli: Processing inefficiencies exhibited by arithmetic learning disabled children. *Mathematical Cognition, 2*(1), 1–23.

Landerl, K., Bevan, A., & Butterworth, B. (2004). Developmental dyscalculia and basic numerical capacities: A Study of 8-9 Year Old Students. *Cognition, 93,* 99–125.

Lewis, C., Hitch, G., & Walker, P. (1994). The prevalence of specific arithmetic difficulties and specific reading difficulties in 9- and 10-year old boys and girls. *Journal of Child Psychology and Psychiatry, 35,* 283–292.

Logan, G. (1988). Toward an instance theory of automatization. *Psychological Review, 91,* 295–327.

Losiewicz, B., & Rusconi, E. (2006). Unpublished data from study of high-functioning dyscalculias. University College London.

Matsuzawa, T. (1985). Use of numbers by a chimpanzee. *Nature, 315,* 57–59.

Mazzocco, M.M.M., & McCloskey, M. (2005). Math performance in girls with Turner or Fragile X syndrome. In J.I.D. Campbell (Ed.), *Handbook of mathematical cognition* (pp. 269–297). New York: Psychology Press.

McCarthy, R.A., & Warrington, E.K. (1990). *Cognitive neuropsychology: A clinical introduction.* London: Academic Press.

McCloskey, M., & Lindemann, A.M. (1992). Mathnet: Preliminary results from a distributed model of arithmetic fact retrieval. In J.I.D. Campbell (Ed.), *The nature and origins of mathematical skills* (pp. 365–409). Amsterdam: Elsevier.

McLean, J.F., & Hitch, G.J. (1999). Working memory impairments in children with specific arithmetical difficulties. *Journal of Experimental Child Psychology, 74,* 240–260.

Molko, N., Cachia, A., Rivière, D., Mangin, J.-F., Bruandet, M., Le Bihan, D., et al. (2003). Functional and structural alterations of the intraparietal sulcus in a developmental dyscalculia of genetic origin. *Neuron, 40,* 847–858.

Murphy, D.G.M., DeCarli, C., Haxby, J.V., Allen, G., White, B.J., Macintosh, A.R., et al. (1993). X-chromosome effects on female brain: A magnetic resonance imaging study of Turner's syndrome. *Lancet, 342,* 1197–1200.

National Curriculum Online. (2006). *Welcome to mathematics.* Retrieved Dec. 19, 2006 from http://www.nc.uk.net/webdav/harmonise?Page/@id=6004&Subject/@id=22

Nieder, A., & Miller, E.K. (2003). Coding of cognitive magnitude. Compressed scaling of numerical information in the primate prefrontal cortex. *Neuron, 37,* 149–157.

Noel, M.-P., Rousselle, L., & Mussolin, C. (2005). Magnitude representation in children: Its development and dysfunction. In J.I.D. Campbell (Ed.), *Handbook of mathematical cognition.* London: Psychology Press.

Paterson, S.J., Girelli, L., Butterworth, B., & Karmiloff-Smith, A. (2006). Are numerical impairments syndrome specific? Evidence from Williams syndrome and Down's syndrome. *Journal of Child Psychology & Psychiatry, 47*(2), 190–204.

Reeve, R.A. (2006). *Developmental dyscalculia: What develops?* Paper presented at the NUMBRA Summer School, Jyväskylä, Finland.

Reeve, R.A., & Reynolds, F. (2004). *The nature of young children's mathematical (dis)-abilities.* Paper presented at the International Society for Behavioral Development, Ghent, Belgium.

Reigosa, V. Estévez, N., Valdés-Sosa, M., Torres, R., Sanabria, & G., Recio, B. (2006). *Subtypes in developmental dyscalculia.* Paper presented at the NUMBRA Summer School, Jyväskylä, Finland.

Rourke, B.P. (1993). Arithmetic disabilities, specific and otherwise: A neuropsychological perspective. *Journal of Learning Disabilities, 26,* 214–226.

Rovet, J., Szekely, C., & Hockenberry, M.-N. (1994). Specific arithmetic calculation deficits in children with Turner syndrome. *Journal of Clinical and Experimental Neuropsychology, 16,* 820–839.

Rubinsten, O., & Henik, A. (2005). Automatic activation of internal magnitudes: A study of developmental dyscalculia. *Neuropsychology, 19,* 641–648.

Rubinsten, O., Henik, A., Berger, A., & Shahar-Shalev, S. (2002). The development of internal representations of magnitude and their association with Arabic numerals. *Journal of Experimental Child Psychology, 81,* 74–92.

Sawamura, H., Shima, K., & Tanji, J. (2002). Numerical representation for action in the parietal cortex of the monkey. *Nature, 415,* 918–922.

Shalev, R.S., Manor, O., & Gross-Tsur, V. (1997). Neuropsychological aspects of developmental dyscalculia. *Mathematical Cognition, 3*(2), 105–120.

Shalev, R.S., Manor, O., Kerem B., Ayali, M., Badichi, N., Friedlander Y., et al. (2001). Developmental dyscalculia is a familial learning disability. *Journal of Learning Disabilities, 34*(1), 59–65.

Siegel, L.S., & Ryan, E.B. (1989). The development of working memory in normally achieving and subtypes of learning disabled children. *Child Development, 60,* 973–980.

Simon, T.J., Hespos, S.J., & Rochat, P. (1995). Do infants understand simple arithmetic? A replication of Wynn (1992). *Cognitive Development, 10,* 253–269.

Skuse, D., James, R., Bishop, D., Coppin, B., Dalton, P., Aamodt-Leepre, R.G., et al. (1997). Evidence from Turner's syndrome of an imprinted X-linked locus affecting cognitive function. *Nature, 387*(6634), 705–708.

Sokol, S.M., McCloskey, M., Cohen, N.J., & Aliminosa, D. (1991). Cognitive representations and processes in arithmetic: Inferences from the performance of brain-damaged subjects. *Journal of Experimental Psychology: Learning, Memory, and Cognition, 17,* 355–376.

Spalding, J.M.K., & Zangwill, O.L. (1950). Disturbance of number-form in a case of brain injury. *Journal of Neurology, Neurosurgery and Psychiatry, 13,* 24–29.

Starkey, P., & Cooper, R.G., Jr. (1980). Perception of numbers by human infants. *Science, 210,* 1033–1035.

Temple, C.M. (1989). Digit dyslexia: A category-specific disorder in developmental dyscalculia. *Cognitive Neuropsychology, 6,* 93–116.

Temple, C.M. (1991). Procedural dyscalculia and number fact dyscalculia: Double dissociation in developmental dyscalculia. *Cognitive Neuropsychology, 8,* 155–176.

Temple, C.M., & Sherwood, S. (2002). Representation and retrieval of arithmetical facts: Developmental difficulties. *Quarterly Journal of Experimental Psychology, 55A,* 733–752.

Warrington, E. (1982). The fractionation of arithmetical skills: A single case study. *Quarterly Journal of Experimental Psychology, 34A,* 31–51.

Wynn, K. (1992). Addition and subtraction by human infants. *Nature, 358,* 749–751.

Wynn, K., Bloom, P., & Chiang, W.C. (2002). Enumeration of collective entities by 5-month-old infants. *Cognition, 83*(3), B55–B62.

Zorzi, M., Priftis, K., & Umiltà, C. (2002). Brain damage: Neglect disrupts the mental number line. *Nature, 417*(6885), 138–139.

Chapter 5

Strategy Use, Long-Term Memory, and Working Memory Capacity

David C. Geary, Mary K. Hoard, Lara Nugent, and Jennifer Byrd-Craven

+ +

Although there is overlap in the phenotypes (e.g., information retrieval from long-term memory) that define learning disabilities in different academic domains (e.g., reading, mathematics), and overlap in the genes that contribute to these phenotypes (Plomin & Kovas, 2005), the authors of chapters in this volume present evidence consistent with the view that aspects of mathematical learning disability (MLD) represent a learning disorder that has specific cognitive, behavioral, and potentially neurological profiles. The resistance of this disorder to remediation has been documented by a 6-year longitudinal study by Shalev, Manor, and Gross-Tsur (2005), which indicated that MLD has persistent negative effects on educational achievement and, through this, later occupational opportunities (Rivera-Batiz, 1992). Our approach is to focus on specific components of mathematical development that are well understood in children who are typically achieving and then use the attendant theoretical models and experimental methodologies to study children with MLD in an effort to better understand the cognitive and behavioral phenotypes that define this form of learning disability (LD).

One of the more thoroughly studied domains with children who are typically achieving is the computational procedures or strategies they use

Preparation of this chapter was supported, in part, by grants R01 HD38283 from the National Institute of Child Health and Human Development (NICHD) and R37 HD045914, co-funded by NICHD and the Institute of Educational Sciences.

to solve simple and complex arithmetic problems (Ashcraft, 1982; Carpenter & Moser, 1984; Geary, 1994; Siegler, 1996; Siegler & Shrager, 1984) and the cognitive mechanisms that contribute to these competencies and their development (Ashcraft, 2002; Bull, Johnston, & Roy, 1999; Delaney, Reder, Staszewski, & Ritter, 1998). Our goal in this chapter is to present an overview of strategy development and associated mechanisms in children who are typically achieving and compare and contrast these with patterns found for children with MLD. The findings have provided important insights into aspects of the behavioral phenotype (e.g., strategy choices) and cognitive mechanisms associated with MLD. In the first section, we describe the strategies used by children who are typically achieving and children with MLD during the solving of arithmetic problems. In the second section, we outline the potential contributions of working memory, long-term memory, and conceptual knowledge to differences in the arithmetical problem solving of typically developing children and children with MLD.

DEVELOPMENT OF ARITHMETICAL COMPETENCIES

In the first section, we describe the strategies and procedures used by children who are typically achieving to solve simple and complex addition problems. Although our focus is on addition, the same basic patterns—use of a mix of problem-solving strategies, which, with schooling and development, shifts to the use of more efficient strategies—are found for subtraction, multiplication, and division (Geary, 1994), and in fact most academic domains (Siegler, 1996). Because of this, contrasting the strategies children who are typically achieving and children with MLD use to solve addition problems may provide more general insights into the arithmetic and academic development of children with LD. On the basis of addition studies, for instance, we predicted that children with LD in other academic areas, such as spelling, would use the same types of approaches as children who are typically achieving (e.g., retrieval, use of dictionary) (Lemaire & Lecacheur, 2002) but show deficits in specific areas, such as in the ability to retrieve the correct spelling of words.

Children Who Are Typically Achieving

By the time they enter school, most children have a conceptual understanding of some features of arithmetic (Klein & Bisanz, 2000), and, based on their counting skills, they have in place basic procedures to solve simple addition and subtraction problems (Geary, 1994, 2006). The most frequently used counting-based strategies, as well as later emerging memory-based processes, are described in Table 5.1. The two most commonly used counting-based procedures, whether children use their fingers or not, are termed *sum*

Table 5.1.   Common counting-based strategies and memory-based processes used to solve addition problems

Strategy or process	Description
Counting-based strategies	
Finger counting	Child overtly or subtly counts using fingers.
Verbal counting	Child counts out loud or silently (lips may move).
Memory-based processes	
Fingers	Child looks at fingers without counting them and then speaks the answer; representing the addends with fingers can prime retrieval of the answer.
Decomposition	With no indication of counting, child states that the answer was obtained in steps. Child reconstructs the answer based on the retrieval of a partial sum. For instance, the problem 6 + 7 might be solved by retrieving the answer to 6 + 6 (i.e., 12) and then adding 1 to this partial sum.
Retrieval	With no indication of counting, child quickly states an answer associated in long-term memory with the presented problem, such as stating "Eight" when asked to solve 5 + 3. When queried, the child states, "Just knew it."

(or *counting-all*) and *min* (or *counting-on;* Fuson, 1982; Groen & Parkman, 1972). The min procedure involves stating the larger valued addend and then counting a number of times equal to the value of the smaller addend, such as counting *5, 6, 7, 8* to solve 5 + 3. The sum procedure involves counting both addends, starting from 1. Less commonly, children will state the smaller addend and then count the larger addend; this is called the *max procedure*. In theory, the use of counting procedures results in the development of long-term memory representations of basic facts; that is, an associative link is formed between the answer generated by means of counting and the two addends (Siegler & Shrager, 1984). Once formed, these long-term memory representations support the use of the memory-based problem-solving processes described in Table 5.1.

As thoroughly documented in Siegler's (1996) research, children use a mix of strategies and memory-based processes to solve any set of arithmetic problems, but with maturation the mix becomes increasingly dominated by use of decomposition (e.g., 6 + 7 = 6 + 6 + 1; see Table 5.1) and direct retrieval. Early in development, the mix is dominated by use of counting strategies and frequent use of the sum or max procedures. With schooling and development, children's strategy mix shifts so that they employ the min procedure in greater frequency when they finger-count and verbally count to solve the presented problem (Geary, Bow-Thomas, Liu, & Siegler, 1996; Siegler, 1987). The Y axis of Figure 5.1 shows that with these procedural shifts and with changes in the frequency with which the various strategies and processes are used during problem solving, children solve problems

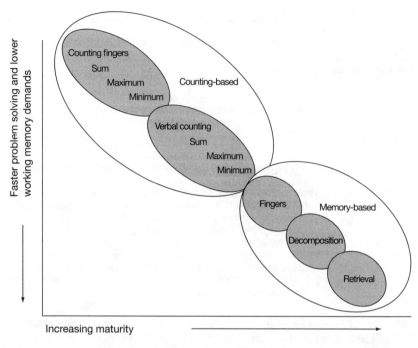

Faster problem solving and lower working memory demands

Increasing maturity

Figure 5.1. With development and schooling, children shift from the use of counting-based strategies to memory-based processes to solve simple addition problems. This shift results in faster problem solving and lower demands on working memory resources.

more quickly and with less reliance on working memory resources. The change in the efficiency of problem solving occurs because children use memory-based processes more frequently and because, with practice, it takes less time to execute each counting strategy and to retrieve information from long-term memory (Delaney et al., 1998; Geary et al., 1996; Lemaire & Siegler, 1995).

Children with Arithmetic Disability

When solving simple addition and subtraction problems (e.g., 4 + 3) and simple arithmetical word problems, children with MLD use the same types of strategies (e.g., verbal counting) as children who are typically achieving, but they differ in the strategy mix used and in the pattern of developmental change in this mix. A similar pattern is found whether children have comorbid disorders (e.g., reading disability [RD]) or only difficulties with mathematics, except that the pattern described below tends to be more pronounced for children with comorbid MLD and RD (MLD/RD) than for children with MLD only (Geary et al., 2000; Jordan & Montani, 1997, Russell

& Ginsburg, 1984). However, it is not yet known if a pattern of similar deficits or delays will emerge for other areas of mathematics in children with MLD/RD and children with MLD only (Fletcher, 2005). At least for the solving of simple addition and subtraction problems, a similar pattern for children with comorbid MLD and RD and children with MLD only has been found in the United States (Geary & Brown, 1991; Hanich, Jordan, Kaplan, & Dick, 2001; Jordan & Montani, 1997), Europe (Barrouillet, Fayol, & Lathulière, 1997; Ostad, 1997, 1998b, 2000; Svenson & Broquist, 1975), and Israel (Gross-Tsur, Manor, & Shalev, 1996). Basically, the problem-solving approaches found in children with MLD, whether or not they have comorbid RD, remain anchored for many years in the strategies and processes shown in the upper left quadrant of Figure 5.1.

In a recent cross-sectional study, Geary and colleagues (2004) compared the strategies used by children with MLD (with and without RD) to solve simple addition problems in first, third, and fifth grades and strategies used by their peers who are typically achieving. In all grades, children with MLD committed more counting errors and used the developmentally mature min procedure less frequently than did the children in the typically achieving groups. In keeping with the model of normal addition development shown in Figure 5.1, children in the typically achieving groups showed a shift through the elementary-school years in strategy use. First graders used finger counting to solve most of the problems and used verbal counting, retrieval, and decomposition to solve a few of the problems. Fifth graders used retrieval and decomposition to solve most of the problems but occasionally used verbal counting. The strategy mix of the typically achieving third graders was in between that of their first- and fifth-grade peers. For the groups of children with MLD, the across-grade differences were much less pronounced. Finger counting was common for the first graders (used to solve 80% of the problems), third graders (40% of the problems) and fifth graders (25% of the problems). Nonetheless, some differences were found. First-grade children with MLD rarely used memory-based processes, but their fifth-grade peers used these processes to solve almost half of the problems. The overall pattern replicated that found in earlier cross-sectional studies. During the course of the elementary school years, many children with MLD show a decrease in use of finger counting, an increase in use of verbal counting, and an improved ability to directly retrieve facts from long-term memory (Geary, Widaman, Little, & Cormier, 1987; Ostad, 1997).

The most consistent finding is that children with MLD differ from their peers who are typically achieving in the ability to use retrieval-based processes to solve simple addition and subtraction problems and simple arithmetical word problems (e.g., Barrouillet et al., 1997; Garnett & Fleischner, 1983; Geary, 1990, 1993; Hanich et al., 2001; Jordan et al., 2003; Jordan & Montani, 1997; Ostad, 1998b, 2000; Russell & Ginsburg, 1984). This is not to say that these children never correctly retrieve answers, but they show a persistent difference in the frequency of retrieval and in retrieval characteristics. When these children do retrieve arithmetic facts from long-term memory, they commit many more errors and sometimes show error and reaction time (RT) patterns that differ from those found with younger children who are typically achieving (Barrouillet et al., 1997; Fayol, Barrouillet, & Marinthe, 1998; Geary, 1990; Geary & Brown, 1991; Räsänen & Ahonen, 1995). The consistency of this pattern across time and across samples from different labs and different nations suggests that the memory retrieval deficits of children with MLD may reflect a cognitive disability. Several potential alternative explanations, such as a lack of exposure to arithmetic problems, a low confidence criterion, or low IQ score, have been ruled out (e.g., Geary et al., 2000), but other alternative explanations, such as poor motivation, mathematics anxiety, or attentional deficits, have not been assessed.

COGNITIVE MECHANISMS AND ARITHMETIC DEVELOPMENT

Several mechanisms have been hypothesized as underlying the group differences described previously in the mix of strategies used and developmental change in strategies for solving arithmetic problems. These mechanisms include working memory and long-term memory deficits, as well as immature conceptual knowledge (Geary, 1993, 2004), as we describe in the following sections.

Working Memory

Working memory is the ability to hold a mental representation of information in mind while simultaneously engaged in other mental processes. The most influential model of working memory is that developed by Baddeley and his colleagues; specifically, that working memory is composed of a central executive that is expressed as attention-driven control of information represented by one or more of three slave systems (Baddeley & Hitch, 1974; Baddeley, 1986, 2000). The slave systems are a language-based phonetic buffer, a visuospatial sketch pad, and an episodic buffer; debates regarding the nature of these components of working memory can be found in Miyake and Shah (1999). The focus here is on developmental change in the overall capacity of working memory in children who are typically achieving and same-age children with MLD, and on potential components of working memory that may distinguish these groups.

Children Who Are Typically Achieving　The overall capacity of working memory increases from preschool through the elementary school years. As an example, a standard working memory task is digit span, whereby the tester states a series of digits and the child repeats these as stated by the tester—forward digit span—or in reverse order—backward digit span. The forward digit span task appears to primarily involve the ability to passively represent number words in the phonological buffer. For this task, a typical preschool child can hold three to four number words in the phonological buffer, whereas a typical fourth grader can hold five to six number words (Kail, 1990). The mechanisms underlying this and related developmental changes appear to include an improved ability to use strategies, such as rehearsal, to keep the information active in the buffer (e.g., Kreutzer, Leonard, & Flavell, 1975), and changes in more fundamental systems that support more general age-related improvements in working memory capacity. The latter include one or some combination of an improved ability to control the focus of attention, increased speed of processing information represented in the slave systems, or slower decay of information represented in the slave systems (Cowan, Saults, & Elliott, 2002; Kail, 1991). On the basis of a review of this literature, Cowan and colleagues concluded that all of these fundamental components improve as part of normal development in childhood, and thus each contributes to the observed increase in overall working memory capacity.

Children with Mathematical Learning Disability   It has been well established that many children with MLD do not perform as well as their same-age peers on a variety of working memory tasks (Bull & Johnston, 1997; Bull et al., 1999; Geary, Hoard, Byrd-Craven, & DeSoto, 2004; Hitch & McAuley, 1991; McLean & Hitch, 1999; Siegel & Ryan, 1989; Swanson, 1993). Not yet known, however, is whether the performance of these children is largely due to deficits in the operation of the central executive system, one or more of the slave systems, or a combination. Of the working memory tasks used in this research, counting span is particularly relevant to understanding the processes underlying the solving of arithmetic problems (Hitch & McAuley, 1991; Siegel & Ryan, 1989). Counting span is the number of integers that can be accurately held in working memory; in this task, children must maintain representations of one or a series of numbers in working memory while engaged in the act of counting. Children are presented with a series of cards that contain target and sometimes distractor dots. The object of the task is to count the dots on each card and remember the associated number word while counting the dots on subsequent cards. These counting span items require holding representations of number words in the phonological buffer and maintaining these representations while performing the act of counting. Maintaining the representations in the buffer during counting engages the central executive.

As an illustration, we present the work of Geary and colleagues (2004). They compared groups of MD (with and without RD) and typically achieving first, third, and fifth graders on standardized achievement and IQ tests and on measures of counting span, counting knowledge (described below),

and the mix of strategies used to solve simple (e.g., 4 + 5) and more complex (e.g., 17 + 4) addition problems. At each grade level, children with MLD
scored lower than their peers who are typically achieving on the counting
span measure. Within each group, across-grade increases in counting span
occurred. For instance, the respective counting spans of first and fifth
graders who were typically achieving was 3.5 and 5.0. The respective
counting spans of first and fifth graders with MLD was 2.8 and 4.4. The pattern suggests that counting span and the component central executive and
phonological skills improve with age and schooling for children in both
groups, but that the deficit of children with MLD remains throughout the
elementary school years. Further analyses suggested that the magnitude of
the working memory deficit of children with MLD was equal to about one
year's growth in children who are typically achieving. In other words, it
appears as if children with MLD show developmental improvement in one
or several of the working memory processes that support counting span,
but remain about one year's worth of growth in overall working memory
capacity behind their peers who are typically achieving.

Working Memory and Group Differences　The relation between the overall working memory deficit of children with MLD and the earlier described
group differences in the developmental maturity and mix of strategies used
to solve addition problems was also assessed (Geary et al., 2004). During
the solving of simple addition problems and in comparison to same-grade
children who are typically achieving, first-grade children with MLD used
finger counting more frequently and verbal counting less frequently The
fifth-grade children with MLD relied on finger counting more frequently and
there were no strategy differences in third grade. The first grade children
with MLD also committed more finger-counting and retrieval errors than
did their peers who are typically achieving. An individual differences (combining children across the two groups) assessment revealed that for first
graders, lower counting span scores were associated with more finger counting, less verbal counting, and more finger-counting errors, above and beyond the influence of IQ score and counting knowledge. Counting span was
not independently related to use of finger counting in fifth grade. Controlling for the group difference in counting span eliminated the advantage of
children who are typically achieving for frequency of verbal counting and reduced their advantage for use of finger counting and finger-counting errors.
These results support the hypothesis that poor working memory resources
contribute to the more frequent finger counting and elevated counting errors
of children with MLD compared with their peers who are typically achieving
(Geary, 1990, 1993), especially during the early phases of skill acquisition.

　　During the solving of the more complex addition problems and in comparison to children who are typically achieving, first-grade children with
MD guessed more frequently, and fifth-grade children with MLD used finger

counting more frequently. The first-grade children with MLD also committed more finger-counting and decomposition (e.g., $17 + 5 = 15 + 5 = 20 + 2$) errors, and the third-grade children committed more decomposition errors. An individual differences analysis revealed that lower counting span scores were associated with more verbal counting errors in first grade and less use of decomposition in third and fifth grade. Because there was no overlap in the group-level strategy differences and those that emerged in the individual differences analyses, it must be concluded that the group differences in the strategy mix used to solve these more complex problems were not related to working memory (at least as measured by counting span) in a straightforward manner.

Another important question concerns how the mix of strategies used changes when solving more complex problems as opposed to simple ones and how this change might be influenced by working memory. For instance, the first graders who were typically achieving used verbal counting and direct retrieval more often to solve simple (e.g., $4 + 6$) than complex problems (e.g., $17 + 5$) and used finger counting more often to solve complex problems. The strategy shift across problem complexity was adaptive for these children, because even though finger counting takes longer, it is more likely to yield the correct answer when solving complex problems than is verbal counting or direct retrieval. The first-grade children with MLD did not show this adaptive strategy shift. Rather, in comparison to how they solved simple problems, they used finger counting less often and direct retrieval more often to solve complex problems. However, when they retrieved an answer it was almost always wrong, which indicates that they were guessing. Further analyses suggested that the ability to make an adaptive shift in the mix of problem solving strategies required strong working memory resources. The first-grade children with MLD may have frequently guessed to solve the complex problems because they did not have the working memory resources needed to execute the finger-counting strategy to solve these problems. The third-grade children with MLD did, however, make an adaptive shift across problem complexity and were very similar to the first graders who were typically achieving in this regard. The fifth-grade children with MLD, in turn, showed a pattern of strategy shifts similar to that found with typically achieving third graders. This pattern suggests a two-grade delay in the ability of children with MLD to make adaptive shifts in problem-solving strategies when switching from the solving of simple to more complex problems, and this delay may be related to their relatively poor working memory.

Long-Term Memory

Whereas working memory is the ability to explicitly and consciously hold a mental representation of information in mind while simultaneously engaged in other mental processes, long-term memory is represented by a more or less permanent store of information (e.g., word meanings). The store of information results through repeated exposure and can be accessed via attentional and working memory processes. The cognitive mechanisms underlying the representation of arithmetic facts in long-term memory are not fully understood but may involve, at least in part, aspects of the language system. Because the use of counting strategies typically engages the phonetic and semantic (e.g., understanding the quantity associated with number words) representational systems of the language domain, associations between addends and answers generated through counting using working memory should, in theory, become represented, at least in part, in the language system (Geary, 1993), and subsequently in long-term memory. Although not definitive, the work of Dehaene and his colleagues suggests that the retrieval of arithmetic facts is indeed supported by a system of language-related neural structures that appear to be engaged during incrementing processes, such as counting (Dehaene & Cohen, 1995, 1997). At the same time, counting is more likely to be used to solve addition problems than problems involving other arithmetic operations; thus, the cognitive and brain mechanisms supporting addition may differ in some respects from those that support the solving of subtraction, multiplication, and division problems (Pesenti, Seron, & Van Der Linden, 1994).

In any case, several components of Baddeley and Hitch's (1974) working memory model may contribute to the formation of these long-term memory representations when counting or other number-based incrementing is used for problem solving. Geary and colleagues hypothesized that for an association to be formed between problem addends and an answer generated by means of counting, the addends and the generated answer must be simultaneously active in the phonological buffer (Geary et al., 1991; Geary, Bow-Thomas, Fan, & Siegler, 1993). The quantity of numbers that can be active in the buffer is related in part to speed of counting. With a slow counting rate, the representation of the first addend is more likely to decay before the count is completed. Thus, even if the child generates the correct answer, this answer might not become strongly associated with the problem in long-term memory. This perspective implies that problems and answers generated by means of counting will become associated in long-term memory with greater difficulty when number words are articulated slowly. Independent of articulation speed, the same pattern could emerge if information decays quickly in the phonological buffer, if lapses in attention result in slowed articulation, or if irrelevant numerical associations enter working memory and compete with relevant representations for attentional focus (Conway & Engle, 1994; Cowan et al., 2002; Engle, 2002; Engle, Conway, Tuholski, & Shisler, 1995).

Children with Mathematical Learning Disability Difficulties in the formation of arithmetic-fact representations and/or in accessing these representations from long-term memory is a defining feature of MLD, but only a few studies have focused on the mechanisms noted previously that might underlie this retrieval deficit. Children with MLD sometimes perform poorly on tasks that assess speed of number articulation (Geary et al., 1991; Kirby & Becker, 1988) or speed of articulating nonnumber words (Bull & Johnston, 1997), but at other times they do not (Geary & Brown, 1991). One longitudinal study found that children with MLD/RD and children with MLD-only showed poor retrieval of addition facts relative to their peers who are typically achieving, but only the children with MLD/RD showed a slower speed of articulation (Geary et al., 1999; Geary et al., 2000). The articulation speed differences were found for familiar words but not unfamiliar nonwords. This pattern is consistent with the hypothesis that there are relatively low activation levels of phonetic representations of familiar words, including number words, when these are encoded into the phonological buffer (Gathercole & Adams, 1994). The low activation would slow speed of articulation and result in faster decay of information represented in the buffer, both of which would interfere with the formation of problem/answer associations in long-term memory.

Although we do not yet have definitive results, these findings are consistent with the hypothesis that the arithmetic-fact retrieval difficulties of at least some children with MLD result from a long-term memory activation/ retrieval deficit that involves aspects of the language system and that this same system may contribute to RD and the comorbidity of MLD and RD (Geary, 1993). Alternative explanations cannot be ruled out, however, because slow articulation speed might be due to fluctuations of attention rather than an atypical representation of information in the phonological buffer. Indeed, other evidence, including no articulation-speed deficits for children with MLD only, suggests at least one other source of the fact-retrieval deficit of children with MLD. This second form of retrieval deficit appears to involve the central executive; specifically, disruptions in the retrieval process due to difficulties in inhibiting irrelevant associations from entering working memory. This form of retrieval deficit was first discovered by Barrouillet and colleagues (1997), based on the memory model of Conway and Engle (1994), and was recently confirmed in our laboratory (Geary et al., 2000; see also Koontz & Berch, 1996). In the study by Geary and colleagues, one of the arithmetic tasks required children to use retrieval only—the children were instructed not to use counting strategies—to solve simple addition problems (see also Jordan & Montani, 1997). Children with MLD or MLD/RD, as well as children with RD only, committed more retrieval errors than did their peers who are typically achieving, even after IQ score was controlled for. The most common of these errors was a counting-string associate of one of the addends. For instance, common retrieval errors for the problem 6 + 2 were 7 and 3, the numbers following 6 and 2, respectively, in the counting sequence. Hanich and colleagues (2001) found a similar pattern, although the proportion of retrieval errors that were counting-string associates was lower than that found by Geary and colleagues (2000).

The pattern in these more recent studies (e.g., Geary et al., 2000) and that of Barrouillet and colleagues (1997) is in keeping with Conway and Engle's (1994) position that individual differences in working memory and retrieval efficiency are related, in part, to the ability to inhibit irrelevant associations. In this model, the presentation of a to-be-solved problem results in the activation of relevant information in working memory, including problem features—such as the addends in a simple addition problem—and information associated with these features. Problem solving is efficient when irrelevant associations are inhibited and prevented from entering working memory. Inefficient inhibition results in activation of irrelevant information, which functionally lowers working memory capacity. In this view, some children with MLD make retrieval errors, in part, because they cannot inhibit irrelevant associations from entering working memory. Once in working memory, these irrelevant associations either suppress or compete with the correct association for expression. These results suggest that the retrieval deficits of some children with MLD may result from deficits in the central executive and associated inhibitory mechanisms (Bull et al., 1999; Welsh & Pennington, 1988). The results also suggest that inhibitory mechanisms should be considered as potential contributors to the comorbidity of MD and ADHD in some children (Gross-Tsur et al., 1996).

In addition to the phonological and language system, long-term memory and working memory representations can be visuospatial or episodic (i.e., based on personal experience; Baddeley, 1986). Unfortunately, the episodic memory system of children with MLD has not been assessed, and their visuospatial memory system has only rarely been assessed. McLean and Hitch (1999) found evidence for poor executive functions for children with MLD, as well as poor performance on a task that assessed visuospatial memory, but other research groups have not found group differences on other spatial tasks (Geary et al., 2000; Morris et al., 1998). Despite these conflicting findings, the possibility of a visuospatial-based form of MLD should continue to be explored. It has been consistently found that magnitude comparison (Dehaene, Spelke, Pinel, Stanescu, & Tsivkin, 1999; Temple & Posner, 1998), mental number line (Zorzi, Priftis, & Umiltá, 2002), and many arithmetic tasks (Chochon, Cohen, van de Moortele, & Dehaene, 1999; Rivera, Reiss, Eckert, & Menon, 2005) engage areas of the parietal cortex that are anatomically very close to the visuospatial and posterior spatial-attentional systems.

In fact, Pinel, Piazza, Le Bihan, and Dehaene (2004) found that the brain regions that represent numerical magnitude also represent spatial magnitude (i.e., related size of objects), and Zorzi and colleagues (2002) found that individuals with injury to the right-parietal cortex showed deficits in spatial orientation and number line estimation. Dehaene and colleagues (1999) showed that adults' computational estimation may also be dependent on a similar parietal-spatial system that supports generation of a mental number line. In other words, any anatomical or functional deficits that influence the ability to represent visuospatial information in working memory or to form associations of these representations in long-term memory are likely to disrupt the learning of procedural and conceptual features of some areas in arithmetic and mathematics. It may be that these areas have not been well sampled in MLD studies. We are currently conducting research that will test the prediction that some children with MLD and with poor visuospatial memory will evidence deficits on tasks that are dependent on the ability to use a mental number line (Siegler & Opfer, 2003).

Conceptual Knowledge

Working memory represents the attentional and representational systems needed for the effective execution of procedures for arithmetical and mathematical problem solving, especially during the early phases of learning (Ackerman, 1988). Selection of one procedure or another to execute can be influenced by the child's conceptual understanding of the problem, however. In fact, the development of conceptual knowledge and procedural skills are interrelated, with conceptual knowledge influencing the selection of procedures and procedural execution offering an opportunity to make inferences about associated concepts (Ohlsson & Rees, 1991; Rittle-Johnson, Siegler, Alibali, 2001; Sophian, 1997). The conceptual knowledge of children with MLD has not been as systematically assessed as their skills in computational arithmetic, described above. The evidence that is available suggests that many children with MLD have a grade-appropriate understanding of many key concepts, such as commutativity and associativity (Russell & Ginsburg, 1984), but that they often differ from their peers who are typically achieving on measures of other concepts, such as counting knowledge (Geary, Bow-Thomas, & Yao, 1992), knowledge of place value, and the ability to estimate (Hanich et al., 2001).

It is most likely that different children with MLD have different patterns of strengths and weaknesses in their conceptual knowledge and procedural skills. In this section, we use counting concepts to illustrate how the conceptual knowledge of children with MLD may differ from that of their peers who are typically achieving and how this might influence the group differences described earlier in computational arithmetic, above and beyond the influences of working memory and long-term memory.

Counting Concepts in Children Who Are Typically Achieving The conceptual principles that guide counting behavior emerge during the preschool

Table 5.2.   Implicit counting principles and common but unessential features of counting

Implicit principles	
One-one correspondence	One and only one word tag (e.g., "one," "two") is assigned to each counted object.
Stable order	Order of the word tags must be invariant across counted sets.
Cardinality	The value of the final word tag represents the quantity of items in the counted set.
Abstraction	Objects of any kind can be collected together and counted.
Order-irrelevance	Items within a given set can be tagged in any sequence.
Unessential features	
Standard direction	Counting proceeds from left to right.
Adjacency	Consecutive count of contiguous objects.
Pointing	Counted objects are typically pointed at but only once.
Start at an end	Counting starts at one of the end points of an array of objects.

years, but it is debated as to whether these principles have an inherent basis (Gelman & Gallistel, 1978) or emerge through observation of the counting behavior of others and induction of regularities in this behavior (Briars & Siegler, 1984; Fuson, 1988). Also, of course, counting principles may emerge from a combination of inherent constraints and counting experience (Geary, 1995; Gelman, 1990). Gelman and Gallistel proposed that children's counting behavior is guided by five inherent and implicit principles that mature during the preschool years, as described in Table 5.2. During the preschool years, children's counting behavior and their description of counting suggest that knowledge of these implicit rules becomes more explicit and that the application of these principles during the act of counting becomes more stable and accurate.

Whether or not children experience inherent constraints, it is clear that they also make inductions about the basic characteristics of counting by observing standard counting behavior (Briars & Siegler, 1984; Fuson, 1988). These inductions may elaborate on and add to Gelman and Gallistel's (1978) counting rules. One result is children's belief that certain unessential features of counting are essential. By 5 years of age, many children not only know most of the essential features of counting described by Gelman and Gallistel but also believe that adjacency and start at an end are essential (see Table 5.2). Most children who are typically achieving understand Gelman and Gallistel's counting principles by the time they start first grade, but many children's beliefs about counting are still influenced by the observation of culture-specific counting procedures.

Counting Concepts in Children with Mathematical Learning Disability

Geary and colleagues (1992) contrasted the performance of first-grade children with MLD (with and without RD) and their peers who are typically achieving on tasks that assessed all of Gelman and Gallistel's (1978) basic principles and most of Briars and Siegler's (1984) unessential features of counting. The procedure involved asking the child to help a puppet learn how to count. The child watched the puppet count a series of objects. The puppet sometimes counted correctly and sometimes violated one of Gelman and Gallistel's counting principles or Briars and Siegler's unessential features of counting. The child's task was to determine if the puppet's count was "OK" or "Not OK and wrong." In this way, the puppet performed the procedural aspect of counting (i.e., pointing at and tagging items with a number word), leaving the child's responses to be based, for the most part, on his or her conceptual understanding of counting.

The results revealed that children with MLD differed from children who are typically achieving on two types of counting trials: pseudo-error and error. Pseudo-error trials involved counting, for instance, the first, third, fifth, and seventh items and then returning to the left-hand side of the array and counting the second, fourth, and sixth items. Technically the count was correct, but it violated the adjacency rule and the order-irrelevance principle. Error trials involved double-counting either the first or the last item. Children with MLD correctly identified these counts as errors when the last item was double-counted, suggesting they understood the one–one correspondence principle. Double counts were often labeled as incorrect when the first item was counted, suggesting that many children with MLD have difficulties holding information in working memory—in this case noting that the first item was double-counted—while monitoring the act of counting.

Follow-up studies that controlled for IQ score confirmed these findings (Geary et al., 1999; Geary et al., 2000). Longitudinally, children with MLD, regardless of their IQ score and reading achievement level, performed poorly on pseudo-error trials in first and second grade and on error trials (double-counting the first item in a series) in first grade. The pattern suggests that even in second grade, many children with MLD do not fully understand counting concepts, and in first grade many have difficulty holding information in working memory while monitoring the counting process (Hoard, Geary, & Hamson, 1999). A more recent cross-sectional study suggested that only a subset of children with MLD misunderstand pseudo-error trials, but this included some children with MLD in third and fifth grade (Geary et al., 2004).

For first graders, Geary and colleagues (1992) found that performance on pseudo-error trials was correlated ($r = .47$) with use of the min procedure when finger counting or when verbal counting was used to solve simple addition problems, and this explained the difference in use of min counting of children with MLD compared with their peers who are typically achieving. Ohlsson and Rees (1991) predicted that children's counting knowledge and skill at detecting counting errors would enable them to correct these miscounts and, thus, make fewer counting errors eventually. In support of this prediction, Geary et al. found that a combination of pseudo- and error-trial scores from the counting knowledge task was significantly related to the frequency of errors in finger counting and verbal counting while solving simple addition problems ($r = -.44$), and that this explained the group difference in the frequency of these errors.

A more recent study that controlled for IQ score and counting span largely confirmed these patterns and showed that counting-error detection was specifically related to the frequency of errors committed while using the verbal counting strategy to solve simple addition problems, whereas min usage while finger counting was specifically related to detection of pseudo-counting errors (Geary et al., 2004). These relations were found to contribute to the tendency described earlier of children with MLD to use the min procedure less often and commit more errors when using counting strategies to solve addition problems, in comparison with their peers who are typically achieving. In other words, many children with MLD do not fully understand counting at a conceptual level and this in turn contributes—above and beyond the influence of working memory and long-term memory—to some of their deficits in computational arithmetic.

SUMMARY AND CONCLUSION

An understanding of mathematical development in children who are typically achieving has provided a solid foundation for the study of the behavioral and cognitive phenotypes of children with MLD. During the past decade, research on children with MLD has expanded considerably and has yielded important insights into their strengths and weaknesses, especially in the area of computational arithmetic and supporting cognitive mechanisms. It is now understood that children with MLD use the same types of strategies (e.g., verbal counting), procedures (e.g., min), and memory processes (e.g., retrieval) as children who are typically achieving to solve addition and subtraction problems and related word problems (Geary et al., 2000; Geary et al., 2004; Hanich et al., 2001; Ostad, 2000). However, most children with MLD use a mix of problem-solving strategies that are more commonly used by younger children who are typically achieving, and they tend to commit more procedural and memory-based errors. Over the course of the elementary-school years, the procedural competencies of many children with MLD tend to improve, and thus their early deficits seem to represent a developmental delay at least for the solving of simple and moderately complex problems; the procedural skills of children with MLD as related to solving highly complex problems (e.g., 634 × 56) that require heavy working memory involvement have not been thoroughly studied (but see Russell & Ginsburg, 1984). At the same time, many children with MLD have difficulties retrieving basic arithmetic facts from long-term memory, a deficit that often does not show a substantive grade-to-grade improvement and thus may represent a cognitive difference (Jordan et al., 2003).

Researchers are beginning to understand some of the cognitive mechanisms that contribute to the delays and differences in computational arithmetic among children with MLD compared with children who are typically achieving. Among these mechanisms are potentially compromised working memory and long-term memory systems, and a delayed understanding of some arithmetical concepts. Cross-sectional studies have indicated that children with MLD have shorter working memory spans than their same-grade peers, although children in both groups show age-related and schooling-based improvements in working memory (Geary et al., 2004; McLean & Hitch, 1999; Swanson, 1993). Although these studies suggest that the group difference in overall working memory capacity—estimated by Geary and colleagues to be equivalent to one year of typical growth—appears to be stable during the elementary-school years, longitudinal studies are needed to fully understand the development of working memory competencies in children with MLD and how these changes may relate to developmental changes in computational arithmetic and other areas of mathematics. Additional research is also needed on the group differences and developmental trends in the components of working memory, specifically, the central executive (and subcomponents, such as attentional and inhibitory control) and the three slave systems.

At this time, it appears that poor overall working memory skills contribute to the use of developmentally immature problem-solving strategies (e.g., finger counting) and procedures (e.g., sum counting) and to more procedural errors by children with MLD, especially during the initial period of learning. The phonological buffer has been implicated in the difficulties children with MLD have in the ability to represent arithmetic facts in or retrieve them from long-term memory; specifically, poor activation of these facts when related information (e.g., problem addends) is encoded into the phonological buffer (Geary et al., 2000). However, a second form of retrieval deficit has also been identified and may involve the inhibitory mechanisms of the central executive (Barrouillet et al., 1997). With the solving of arithmetic problems, this deficit is manifested with the intrusion of irrelevant facts into working memory during problem solving, which interferes with the retrieval or expression of the correct answer.

In comparison to computational arithmetic, less is known about the conceptual knowledge of children with MLD. Studies have yielded mixed results, finding differences on some concepts for children with MLD and children who are typically achieving but no differences on other concepts (Geary et al., 1999; Hanich et al., 2001; Russell & Ginsburg, 1984). Although it is likely that different children with MLD have different patterns of strengths and weaknesses in their conceptual knowledge across arithmetical domains, many of these children are delayed in their understanding of counting concepts, especially in first grade (Geary et al., 1992; Geary et al., 2004). For instance, many of these children do not seem to understand Gelman and Gallistel's (1978) order-irrelevance principle or Briars and Siegler's (1984) adjacency rule (see Table 5.2). Their delayed understanding of this counting concept appears to contribute to their delayed use of the min procedure when counting strategies are used to solve addition problems. Moreover, it appears that the relation between counting knowledge and use of the min procedure is independent of the influence of working memory on the execution of these same procedures. In other words, working memory and conceptual knowledge appear to contribute in different ways to the development of computational arithmetic skills, and children with MLD may lag in the development of these skills because of poor working memory resources, poor conceptual knowledge, or some combination of these.

Despite these advances in our understanding of the arithmetical development of children with MLD, much remains to be accomplished. In comparison to simple arithmetic, relatively little research has been conducted on MLD children's ability to solve more complex arithmetic problems, and even less has been conducted in other mathematical domains. Nonetheless, it is very likely that the working memory deficits of many children with MLD interfere with their learning in more complex domains of mathematics and may even result in a wider performance gap between these children and their peers who are typically achieving. It remains to be seen whether conceptual deficits in counting and in other number-arithmetic domains are predictive of conceptual deficits in more complex areas of mathematics. Regardless, other areas in need of attention include the development of diagnostic instruments for MLD (Gersten et al., 2005); cognitive and behavioral genetic research on the comorbidity of MLD and other forms of LD and ADHD (Fletcher, 2005; Plomin & Kovas, 2005; Shalev et al., 2001); and, of course, the development of remedial techniques. If the progress over the past decade is any indication, then there should be significant advances in these areas in coming years.

REFERENCES

Ackerman, P.L. (1988). Determinants of individual differences during skill acquisition: Cognitive abilities and information processing. *Journal of Experimental Psychology: General, 117,* 288–318.

Ashcraft, M.H. (1982). The development of mental arithmetic: A chronometric approach. *Developmental Review, 2,* 213–236.

Ashcraft, M.H. (2002). Math anxiety: Personal, educational, and cognitive consequences. *Current Directions in Psychological Science, 11,* 181–185.

Baddeley, A.D. (1986). *Working memory.* Oxford: Oxford University Press.

Baddeley, A. (2000). The episodic buffer: A new component of working memory? *Trends in Cognitive Sciences, 4,* 417–423.

Baddeley, A.D., & Hitch, G.J. (1974). Working memory. In G.H. Bower (Ed.), *The psychology of learning and motivation: Advances in research and theory* (Vol. 8, pp. 47–90). New York: Academic Press.

Barrouillet, P., Fayol, M., & Lathulière, E. (1997). Selecting between competitors in multiplication tasks: An explanation of the errors produced by adolescents with learning disabilities. *International Journal of Behavioral Development, 21,* 253–275.

Bradley, L., & Bryant, P.E. (1983, February 3). Categorizing sounds and learning to read—A causal connection. *Nature, 301,* 419–421.

Briars, D., & Siegler, R.S. (1984). A featural analysis of preschoolers' counting knowledge. *Developmental Psychology, 20,* 607–618.

Bull, R., & Johnston, R.S. (1997). Children's arithmetical difficulties: Contributions from processing speed, item identification, and short-term memory. *Journal of Experimental Child Psychology, 65,* 1–24.

Bull, R., Johnston, R.S., & Roy, J.A. (1999). Exploring the roles of the visual-spatial sketch pad and central executive in children's arithmetical skills: Views from cognition and developmental neuropsychology. *Developmental Neuropsychology 15,* 421–442.

Carpenter, T.P., & Moser, J.M. (1984). The acquisition of addition and subtraction concepts in grades one through three. *Journal for Research in Mathematics Education, 15,* 179–202.

Chochon, F., Cohen, L., van de Moortele, P.F., & Dehaene, S. (1999). Differential contributions of the left and right inferior parietal lobules to number processing. *Journal of Cognitive Neuroscience, 11,* 617–630.

Conway, A.R.A., & Engle, R.W. (1994). Working memory and retrieval: A resource-dependent inhibition model. *Journal of Experimental Psychology: General, 123,* 354–373.

Cowan, H., Saults, J.S., Elliott, E.M. (2002). The search for what is fundamental in the development of working memory. *Advances in Child Development and Behavior, 29,* 1–49.

Dehaene, S. (1997). *The number sense: How the mind creates mathematics.* New York: Oxford University Press.

Dehaene, S., & Cohen, L. (1995). Towards an anatomical and functional model of number processing. *Mathematical Cognition, 1,* 83–120.

Dehaene, S., & Cohen, L. (1997). Cerebral pathways for calculation: Double dissociation between rote verbal and quantitative knowledge of arithmetic. *Cortex, 33,* 219–250.

Dehaene, S., Spelke, E., Pinel, P., Stanescu, R., & Tsivkin, S. (1999, May 7). Sources of mathematical thinking: Behavioral and brain-imaging evidence. *Science, 284,* 970–974.

Delaney, P.F., Reder, L.M., Staszewski, J.J., & Ritter, F E. (1998). The strategy-specific nature of improvement: The power law applies by strategy within task. *Psychological Science, 9,* 1–7.

Engle, R.W. (2002). Working memory capacity as executive attention. *Current Directions in Psychological Science, 11,* 19–23.

Engle, R.W., Conway, A.R.A., Tuholski, S.W., & Shisler, R.J. (1995). A resource account of inhibition. *Psychological Science, 6,* 122–125.

Fayol, M., Barrouillet, P., & Marinthe, C. (1998). Predicting arithmetical achievement from neuro-psychological performance: A longitudinal study. *Cognition, 68,* B63–B70.

Fletcher, J.M. (2005). Predicting math outcomes: Reading predictors and comorbidity. *Journal of Learning Disabilities, 38,* 308–312.

Foorman, B.R., Francis, D.J., Fletcher, J.M., Schatschneider, D., & Mehta, P. (1998). The role of instruction in learning to read: Preventing reading failure in at-risk children. *Journal of Educational Psychology, 90,* 37–55.

Fuson, K.C. (1982). An analysis of the counting-on solution procedure in addition. In T.P. Carpenter, J.M. Moser, & T.A. Romberg (Eds.), *Addition and subtraction: A cognitive perspective* (pp. 67–81). Mahwah, NJ: Lawrence Erlbaum Associates.

Fuson, K.C. (1988). *Children's counting and concepts of number.* New York: Springer-Verlag.

Garnett, K., & Fleischner, J.E. (1983). Automatization and basic fact performance of normal and learning disabled children. *Learning Disability Quarterly, 6,* 223–230.

Gathercole, S.E., & Adams, A.-M. (1994). Children's phonological working memory: Contributions of long-term knowledge and rehearsal. *Journal of Memory and Language, 33,* 672–688.

Geary, D.C. (1990). A componential analysis of an early learning deficit in mathematics. *Journal of Experimental Child Psychology, 49,* 363–383.

Geary, D.C. (1993). Mathematical disabilities: Cognitive, neuropsychological, and genetic components. *Psychological Bulletin, 114,* 345–362.

Geary, D.C. (1994). *Children's mathematical development: Research and practical applications.* Washington, DC: American Psychological Association.

Geary, D.C. (1995). Reflections of evolution and culture in children's cognition: Implications for mathematical development and instruction. *American Psychologist, 50,* 24–37.

Geary, D.C. (2004). Mathematics and learning disabilities. *Journal of Learning Disabilities, 37,* 4–15.

Geary, D.C. (2006). Development of mathematical understanding. In D. Kuhl & R.S. Siegler (Vol. Eds.), *Cognition, perception, and language: Vol. 2* (pp. 777–810). W. Damon (Gen. Ed.), *Handbook of child psychology* (6th ed.). New York: John Wiley & Sons.

Geary, D.C., Bow-Thomas, C.C., Fan, L., & Siegler, R.S. (1993). Even before formal instruction, Chinese children outperform American children in mental addition. *Cognitive Development, 8,* 517–529.

Geary, D.C., Bow-Thomas, C.C., Liu, F., & Siegler, R.S. (1996). Development of arithmetical competencies in Chinese and American children: Influence of age, language, and schooling. *Child Development, 67,* 2022–2044.

Geary, D.C., Bow-Thomas, C.C., & Yao, Y. (1992). Counting knowledge and skill in cognitive addition: A comparison of normal and mathematically disabled children. *Journal of Experimental Child Psychology, 54,* 372–391.

Geary, D.C., & Brown, S.C (1991). Cognitive addition: Strategy choice and speed-of-processing differences in gifted, normal, and mathematically disabled children. *Developmental Psychology, 27,* 398–406.

Geary, D.C., Brown, S.C, & Samaranayake, V.A. (1991). Cognitive addition: A short longitudinal study of strategy choice and speed-of-processing differences in normal and mathematically disabled children. *Developmental Psychology, 27,* 787–797.

Geary, D.C., Hamson, C.O., & Hoard, M.K. (2000). Numerical and arithmetical cognition: A longitudinal study of process and concept deficits in children with learning disability. *Journal of Experimental Child Psychology, 77,* 236–263.

Geary, D.C., Hoard, M.K., Byrd-Craven, J., & DeSoto, C.M. (2004). Strategy choices in simple and complex addition: Contributions of working memory and counting knowledge for children with mathematical disability. *Journal of Experimental Child Psychology, 88,* 121–151.

Geary, D.C., Hoard, M.K., & Hamson, C.O. (1999). Numerical and arithmetical cognition: Patterns of functions and deficits in children at risk for a mathematical disability. *Journal of Experimental Child Psychology, 74,* 213–239.

Geary, D.C., Widaman, K.F., Little, T.D., & Cormier, P. (1987). Cognitive addition: Comparison of learning disabled and academically normal elementary school children. *Cognitive Development, 2,* 249–269.

Gelman, R. (1990). First principles organize attention to and learning about relevant data: Number and animate-inanimate distinction as examples. *Cognitive Science, 14,* 79–106.

Gelman, R., & Gallistel, C.R. (1978). *The child's understanding of number.* Cambridge, MA: Harvard University Press.

Gelman, R., & Meck, E. (1983). Preschooler's counting: Principles before skill. *Cognition, 13,* 343–359.

Gersten, R., Jordan, N.C., & Flojo, J.R. (2005). Early identification and interventions for students with mathematics difficulties. *Journal of Learning Disabilities, 38,* 293–304.

Groen, G.J., & Parkman, J.M. (1972). A chronometric analysis of simple addition. *Psychological Review, 79,* 329–343.

Gross-Tsur, V., Manor, O., & Shalev, R.S. (1996). Developmental dyscalculia: Prevalence and demographic features. *Developmental Medicine and Child Neurology, 38,* 25–33.

Hanich, L.B., Jordan, N.C., Kaplan, D., & Dick, J. (2001). Performance across different areas of mathematical cognition in children with learning difficulties. *Journal of Educational Psychology, 93,* 615–626.

Hitch, G.J. & McAuley, E. (1991). Working memory in children with specific arithmetical learning difficulties. *British Journal of Psychology, 82,* 375–386.

Hoard, M.K., Geary, D.C., & Hamson, C.O. (1999). Numerical and arithmetical cognition: Performance of low- and average-IQ children. *Mathematical Cognition, 5,* 65–91.

Jordan, N.C., Hanich, L.B., & Kaplan, D. (2003). Arithmetic fact mastery in young children: A longitudinal investigation. *Journal of Experimental Child Psychology, 85,* 103–119.

Jordan, N.C., & Montani, T.O. (1997). Cognitive arithmetic and problem solving: A comparison of children with specific and general mathematics difficulties. *Journal of Learning Disabilities, 30,* 624–634.

Kail, R. (1990). *The development of memory in children* (third ed.). New York: W.H. Freeman.

Kail, R. (1991). Developmental change in speed of processing during childhood and adolescence. *Psychological Bulletin, 109,* 490–501.

Kirby, J.R., & Becker, L.D. (1988). Cognitive components of learning problems in arithmetic. *Remedial and Special Education, 9,* 7–16.

Klein, J.S., & Bisanz, J. (2000). Preschoolers doing arithmetic: The concepts are willing but the working memory is weak. *Canadian Journal of Experimental Psychology, 54,* 105–115.

Kreutzer, M.A., Leonard, C., & Flavell, J.H. (1975). An interview study of children's knowledge about memory. *Monographs of the Society for Research in Child Development, 40*(1, Serial No. 159).

Koontz, K.L., & Berch, D.B. (1996). Identifying simple numerical stimuli: Processing inefficiencies exhibited by arithmetic learning disabled children. *Mathematical Cognition, 2,* 1–23.

Lemaire, P., & Lecacheur, M. (2002). Applying the choice/no-choice methodology: The case of children's strategy use in spelling. *Developmental Science, 5,* 42–47.

Lemaire, P., & Siegler, R.S. (1995). Four aspects of strategic change: Contributions to children's learning of multiplication. *Journal of Experimental Psychology: General, 124,* 83–97.

McLean, J.F., & Hitch, G.J. (1999). Working memory impairments in children with specific arithmetic learning difficulties. *Journal of Experimental Child Psychology, 74,* 240–260.

Miyake, A., & Shah, P. (Eds.) (1999). *Models of working memory: Mechanisms of active maintenance and executive control.* Cambridge, United Kingdom: Cambridge University Press.

Morris, R.D., Stuebing, K.K., Fletcher, J.M., Shaywitz, S.E., Lyon, G.R., Shankweiler, D.P., et al. (1998). Subtypes of reading disability: Variability around a phonological core. *Journal of Educational Psychology, 90,* 347–373.

Ohlsson, S., & Rees, E. (1991). The function of conceptual understanding in the learning of arithmetic procedures. *Cognition and Instruction, 8,* 103–179.

Ostad, S.A. (1997). Developmental differences in addition strategies: A comparison of mathematically disabled and mathematically normal children. *British Journal of Educational Psychology, 67,* 345–357.

Ostad, S.A. (1998a). Comorbidity between mathematics and spelling difficulties. *Log Phon Vovol, 23,* 145–154.

Ostad, S.A. (1998b). Developmental differences in solving simple arithmetic word problems and simple number-fact problems: A comparison of mathematically normal and mathematically disabled children. *Mathematical Cognition, 4,* 1–19.

Ostad, S.A. (2000). Cognitive subtraction in a developmental perspective: Accuracy, speed-of-processing and strategy-use differences in normal and mathematically disabled children. *Focus on Learning Problems in Mathematics, 22,* 18–31.

Pesenti, M., Seron, X., & Van Der Linden, M. (1994). Selective impairment as evidence for mental organisation of arithmetical facts: BB, a case of preserved subtraction? *Cortex, 30,* 661–671.

Pinel, P., Piazza, D., Le Bihan, D., & Dehaene, S. (2004). Distributed and overlapping cerebral representations of number, size, and luminance during comparative judgments. *Neuron, 41,* 1–20.

Plomin, R., & Kovas, Y. (2005). Generalist genes and learning disabilities. *Psychological Bulletin, 131,* 592–617.

Räsänen, P., & Ahonen, T. (1995). Arithmetic disabilities with and without reading difficulties: A comparison of arithmetic errors. *Developmental Neuropsychology, 11,* 275–295.

Rittle-Johnson, B., Siegler, R.S., Alibali, M.W. (2001). Developing conceptual understanding and procedural skill in mathematics: An iterative process. *Journal of Educational Psychology, 93,* 346–362.

Rivera, S.M., Reiss, A.L., Eckert, M.A., & Menon, V. (2005). Developmental changes in mental arithmetic: Evidence for increased specialization in the left inferior parietal cortex. *Cerebral Cortex, 15,* 1779–1790.

Rivera-Batiz, F.L. (1992). Quantitative literacy and the likelihood of employment among young adults in the United States. *Journal of Human Resources, 27,* 313–328.

Rourke, B.P. (1993). Arithmetic disabilities, specific and otherwise: A neuropsychological perspective. *Journal of Learning Disabilities, 26,* 214–226.

Russell, R.L., & Ginsburg, H.P. (1984). Cognitive analysis of children's mathematical difficulties. *Cognition and Instruction, 1,* 217–244.

Shalev, R. S., Manor, O., & Gross-Tsur, V. (2005). Developmental dyscalculia: A prospective six-year follow-up, *Developmental Medicine and Child Neurology, 47,* 121–125.

Shalev, R.S., Manor, O., Kerem, B., Ayali, M., Badichi, N., Friedlander, Y., et al. (2001). Developmental dyscalculia is a familial learning disability. *Journal of Learning Disabilities, 34,* 59–65.

Shaywitz, B.A., Shaywitz, S.E., Blachman, B.A., Pugh, K.R., Fulbright, R.K., Skudlarski, P., et al. (2004). Development of left occipitotemporal systems for skilled reading in children after phonologically-based intervention. *Biological Psychiatry, 55,* 926–933.

Siegel, L.S., & Ryan, E.B. (1989). The development of working memory in normally-achieving and subtypes of learning disabled children. *Child Development, 60,* 973–980.

Siegler, R.S. (1987). The perils of averaging data over strategies: An example from children's addition. *Journal of Experimental Psychology: General, 116,* 250–264.

Siegler, R.S. (1988). Individual differences in strategy choices: Good students, not-so-good students, and perfectionists. *Child Development, 59,* 833–851.

Siegler, R.S. (1996). *Emerging minds: The process of change in children's thinking.* New York: Oxford University Press.

Siegler, R.S., & Opfer, J. (2003). The development of numerical estimation: Evidence for multiple representations of numerical quantity. *Psychological Science, 14,* 237–243.

Siegler, R.S., & Shrager, J. (1984). Strategy choice in addition and subtraction: How do children know what to do? In C. Sophian (Ed.), *Origins of cognitive skills* (pp. 229–293). Hillsdale, NJ: Erlbaum.

Sophian, C. (1997). Beyond competence: The significance of performance for conceptual development. *Cognitive Development, 12,* 281–303.

Svenson, O., & Broquist, S. (1975). Strategies for solving simple addition problems: A comparison of normal and subnormal children. *Scandinavian Journal of Psychology, 16,* 143–151.

Swanson, H.L. (1993). Working memory in learning disability subgroups. *Journal of Experimental Child Psychology, 56,* 87–114.

Temple, E., & Posner, M.I. (1998). Brain mechanisms of quantity are similar in 5-year-old children and adults. *Proceedings of the National Academy of Sciences USA, 95,* 7836–7841.

Zorzi, M., Priftis, K., & Umiltá, C. (2002, May 9). Neglect disrupts the mental number line. *Nature, 417,* 138.

Wagner, R.K., & Torgesen, J.K. (1987). The nature of phonological processing and its causal role in the acquisition of reading skills. *Psychological Bulletin, 101,* 192–212.

Welsh, M.C., & Pennington, B.F. (1988). Assessing frontal lobe functioning in children: Views from developmental psychology. *Developmental Neuropsychology, 4,* 199–230.

Chapter 6

Do Words Count?

Connections Between Mathematics and Reading Difficulties

Nancy C. Jordan

+ +

Mathematics learning requires diverse cognitive skills, even at the primary school level. Consider the following problems from two second-grade U.S. math textbooks: "Tim and Michelle both have birthdays in October. Michelle's is 5 days later than Tim's. If Tim's birthday is on October 9, what date is Michelle's birthday?" (Teaching Integrated Mathematics and Science, 2003) "In a mob of 41 kangaroos, 29 of them were adults. The rest were young kangaroos. A young kangaroo is called a joey. About how many kangaroos were joeys?" (Scott Foresman-Addison Wesley, 1999) Whether the child reads the problems or the teacher reads them to the child, the linguistic requirements of math word problems are obvious. In addition to performing a numerical operation, the child must understand the relevant lexicon and syntax, hold the verbal information in memory, and use the information to reach a solution. A second grader also might be asked to calculate a page of addition or subtraction number combinations in 1 minute, a task involving rapid number processing or automatic fact retrieval. Other second-grade math tasks include estimating parts of a whole (e.g., 1/3 of a juice glass), rounding to the nearest 10, solving written calculations with regrouping, recognizing congruent shapes, and reading clock faces and graphs. These activities involve nonverbal estimation, procedural learning, spatial reasoning, and attention, among other skills. Deficien-

---

This work was supported by a grant from the National Institute of Child Health and Human Development (R01 HD36672).

cies in reading and language might penalize children more on some math tasks (e.g., solving word problems) than on others (e.g., estimating quantities).

In light of the multiple skills involved in math performance, it is not surprising that children's mathematics difficulties, or disabilities, are poorly understood. Earlier studies tended to examine math-related skills in children who were classified as having a learning disability regardless of whether they had weaknesses in math, reading, or both (e.g., Montague, Applegate, & Marquard, 1993). Other studies identified children with math difficulties (MD*) without consideration of their performance in reading (Geary, 1990; Ostad, 1998, 1999; Russell & Ginsburg, 1984). Children with MD may or may not have concomitant difficulties in reading. It has been estimated that approximately one half to two thirds of children with MD also have reading difficulties (RD) (Barbaresi, Katusic, Colligan, Weaver, & Jacobson, 2005).

A number of researchers have focused on distinctions between children with math difficulties who are proficient in reading (MD only) and children with difficulties in reading as well as in math (MD/RD) (e.g., Badian, 1999; Jordan, Hanich, & Kaplan, 2003a, 2003b; Jordan & Montani, 1997; Rourke, 1993). The idea is that some math difficulties reflect a core deficit in language, one that is common to reading and math. The language deficits may or may not be accompanied by basic deficits in number. Other math difficulties may reflect specific numerical deficits (MD only) with intact language (Jordan & Hanich, 2003; Robinson, Menchetti, & Torgesen, 2002). The distinction between MD only and MD/RD is potentially important because the two classifications may represent different types of math difficulties with different developmental trajectories and outcomes (Fletcher, 2005).

The goal of this chapter is to examine connections between mathematics difficulties and reading difficulties. I attempt to clarify whether MD only and MD/RD have common origins or whether they represent qualitatively different types of math difficulties. I first look at studies that differentiate children with MD only from children with MD/RD, focusing on functional and cognitive characteristics, growth, and responsiveness to intervention. The studies come from my own research lab as well as from those of other math researchers (i.e., David Geary, Brian Butterworth, and Lynn Fuchs). Because I am interested in issues related to early identification and intervention, I concentrate on studies of children in early elementary school. I then examine key findings in the literature on early predictors of math achievement to identify the relative importance of number sense, reading, and other relevant variables. Reading difficulty, at least for studies examining primary-school populations, is typically defined as having weaknesses in decoding or recognizing written words. These read-

---

*In this chapter, MD refers to math difficulties; RD refers to reading difficulties.

ing skills rely heavily on phonological processes, a core deficit in RD (Chiappe, 2006).

I use the term *difficulties* rather than *disabilities* in our review and analyses. Referring to difficulties allows consideration of a wider group of children who may need special attention in school. Some studies in this review looked at populations of children performing in the low to below average range in reading or math (e.g., < 35th percentile); other studies restricted participants to children performing in the below average range (e.g., < 15th percentile, suggestive of a disability). Comparisons of children with math achievement in the low average range (15th to 30th percentile) versus the below average range (< 15th percentile) indicated that the two groups perform in a qualitatively similar fashion on number tasks, even though the latter group is more impaired in level of performance (Jordan & Hanich, 2003). Likewise, mild reading difficulties do not appear to be categorically distinct from severe difficulties, with the latter representing the low tail in a normal distribution (Shaywitz, Escobar, Shaywitz, Fletcher, & Makuch, 1992). Children at the lowest end of the spectrum both in reading and math (e.g., < 5th percentile) tend to have commensurately low IQ scores (Jordan & Hanich, 2003).

FUNCTIONAL PROFILES OF CHILDREN WITH MD, WITH AND WITHOUT RD

Recent research provides detailed comparisons of the functional profiles of children with MD only with the profiles of children with MD/RD, as well as contrasting groups of children with RD only and children with typical achievement. Such comparisons reveal similarities and differences among achievement groups in terms of numerical and supporting cognitive competencies and growth, which in turn help clarify the nature of the classifications (see Table 6.1 for a summary of results from several studies). Key findings are elaborated upon in the following paragraphs.

Geary, Hamson, and Hoard (2000) examined the pattern of number deficits in second-grade children with MD only ($n = 16$) and children with MD/RD ($n = 12$), along with comparison groups of children without MD. The groups without MD included children without difficulties in math or reading ($n = 26$) and children with RD only ($n = 14$). *Disabilities* was defined as performing below the 35th percentile on a standardized achievement test in both first and second grades. The mean math percentile score was 21 for the MD only group and 17 for the MD/RD group; the mean reading percentile score was 40 for MD only and 11 for MD/RD. Number comprehension, counting knowledge, addition strategies, working memory (digit span), spatial skills (mazes), and word articulation were assessed four times, in fall and spring of first and second grades. IQ score was controlled for in all of the analyses. Children in both MD groups performed worse

Table 6.1. Deficiencies in children with MD only, MD/RD, and RD only*

Skill	MD only	MD/RD	RD only
Counting	+	+	−
Number knowledge	+	+	−
Rapid fact retrieval	+	+	−
Number naming	+	+	−
Problem solving	−	+	−
Reliance on fingers	+	+	−
Digit span	−	+	−
Mazes (spatial skill)	−	−	−
Word articulation speed	−	+	+

Note: + = deficiency; − = no deficiency
*Compilation of results from several studies; see text for details.

than did their peers without MD in counting knowledge. There were no reliable group differences in number comprehension, but all groups performed at a ceiling level. On addition number combinations, both MD groups made more counting procedure and retrieval errors than the NA (typically achieving) and RD-only groups. Children with MD/RD made more counting and retrieval errors than did children with MD only. Both MD groups, however, did not decrease in finger counting from grades 1 to 2, in contrast to children without MD, who gradually relied less on their fingers. In terms of supporting cognitive competencies (above and beyond IQ score), the MD/RD group performed lower than the typically achieving group (but not lower than the MD-only group) on the digit span working memory task. No achievement group differences were found on the mazes spatial task. Children in both the MD/RD and RD groups had slow articulation speed for familiar words relative to the other groups, which seemed to be associated more with the reading difficulty than with math difficulty. Overall, Geary and colleagues comparisons of the various achievement subgroups suggest that children with MD only and children with MD/RD perform alike on basic number tasks, although the latter appear to be more deficient. There were no obvious number deficits found in children with RD only. Children with MD/RD and RD only showed weaknesses in word naming speed.

In a related study, Landerl, Bevan, and Butterworth (2004) studied small groups of 8- and 9-year-olds with dyscalculia (MD only, $n = 10$), dyslexia (RD only, $n = 10$), both dyscalculia and dyslexia, or double deficit (MD/RD, $n = 11$), and normal achievement ($n = 18$). These groups parallel the MD-only, MD/RD, and RD-only classifications, except that Landerl and colleagues defined dyscalculia as more than 3 standard deviations (SD) below the mean on a timed number-facts measure. Children with dyslexia performed below the 25th percentile on word reading. The groups did not differ in nonverbal IQ scores. Like those in Geary and colleagues (2000), participants were given a series of basic number tasks as well as tasks assessing supportive cognitive competencies. The number tasks included number reading and naming, number comparison (selecting the larger of two numbers), number writing, counting, and enumeration. Tests of supportive cognitive competencies included digit span (working memory) and mazes (spatial). Children with dyscalculia, regardless of the presence of RD, showed general deficits in number processing; this was not evident in supporting cognitive competencies, for which there were no group differences. Landerl and colleagues concluded, "Dyscalculia can best be defined as a deficit in the representation or processing of specifically numerical information" (p. 121). Interestingly, the patterns of performance of the two groups of children with dyscalculia were very similar, although the double deficit group (i.e., MD/RD) was slower and more error prone than the children with dyscalculia without RD. The findings do not support the theory of differential causes of MD/RD and MD only. Of course, it should be noted that the double deficit group showed relatively low performance on digit span, in keeping with the character of the Geary and colleagues (2000) MD/RD group, and the lack of significant results may have been due to the small sample size. Thus, replication of Landerl et al. findings is necessary.

The aforementioned research on children with MD, specific and otherwise, emphasized basic number skills and arithmetic computation. In our research lab, we looked at children's problem-solving skills as well as their basic calculation skills. We hypothesized that the abilities of children with MD would be uneven across areas of mathematical competence (Hanich, Jordan, Kaplan, & Dick, 2001; Jordan & Hanich, 2000; Jordan, Hanich, & Kaplan, 2003b; Jordan & Montani, 1997). Over a 16-month period, Jordan and colleagues (2003a) investigated the development of specific mathematical competencies in children with MD only ($n = 46$), MD/RD ($n = 42$), RD only ($n = 45$), and NA ($n = 47$). Consistent with Geary and colleagues (2000), difficulties were defined as performance at or less than the 35th percentile on a standardized achievement test. Jordan and colleagues looked at basic calculation, problem solving, and understanding of base-10 concepts. Children were assessed twice in second grade and twice in third grade; IQ score, gender, and income level were all controlled for. The achievement groups did not differ in rate of development between second and third grades. However, children with MD only had a reliable advantage over their MD/RD counterparts in areas of problem solving (e.g., solving arithmetic story problems and grasping arithmetic principles) but not in areas related to basic calculation (e.g., fast retrieval of facts and estimation) or place value. Children with MD only appeared to have consistent difficulties with calculation fluency. They performed as poorly as children with MD/RD when required to respond to number combinations quickly and relied on their fingers as much as children with MD/RD, even at the end of third grade. However, children with MD only used their fingers more accurately, indicating that they used better counting procedures than children with MD/RD, a finding also supported by Geary and colleagues (2000). Jordan and colleagues concluded that "deficiencies in fact retrieval, and by extension calculation fluency, are a defining feature of mathematics difficulties, specific or otherwise" (p. 847). They speculated that weaknesses in spatial representations related to numerical magnitudes (rather than weaknesses in verbal representations) underpin weaknesses in addition and subtraction fact retrieval. Children with MD might have difficulties imagining representations on a number line, a skill that is needed for performing addition and subtraction calculations. Of interest, however, skill with multiplication tables may depend more on verbal memory than does skill with addition and subtraction facts (Dowker, 2005).

Although it has been suggested that difficulties in reading (i.e., word decoding) and number fact retrieval share a core underlying deficit related to phonological processing (e.g., Geary, 1993; 1994), Jordan and colleagues's (2003a) data do not support this suggestion. In particular, children with RD only who were characterized by decoding weaknesses performed better than did children with MD only and MD/RD on a rapid fact retrieval task. In a subsequent study, Jordan and colleagues (2003b) found that third-grade children with poor arithmetic fact mastery performed as well in reading (on a measure of automatic word reading) as children with good fact mastery.

Children with MD only and RD only performed at about the same levels in problem solving (but slightly below children with typical achievement), indicating that children in these two groups use different pathways to solving problems; that is, children with RD only take advantage of their arithmetic strengths while children with MD exploit their reading strengths. However, the weakness of children with MD/RD in basic arithmetic combined with their reading deficits make achievement in most areas of math problematic. In fact, Jordan, Kaplan, and Hanich (2002) found that on a standardized test of math achievement, rate of growth for children with MD only was greater than that for children with MD/RD, even when controlling for IQ score and income level. In contrast, children with MD/RD and RD only achieved at about the same rate in reading, with both groups achieving more slowly than children without RD. Difficulties in reading have a negative influence on children's development in general mathematics achievement, but difficulties in math do not appear to affect the development of reading.

Fuchs and Fuchs (2002) provided further evidence that problem solving, rather than basic number and arithmetic skills, differentiates children with MD only from children with MD/RD. Participants were fourth graders with IQ scores in the average range ($n = 18$ MD only and $n = 22$ MD/RD).

Difficulties were defined as scoring at least 1.5 *SD* below the mean (or about the 10th percentile) on measures of computational and/or oral reading fluency. (The percentile cutoff along with the computational measure parallels the Landerl and colleagues [2004] criteria for dyscalculia.) When operational and problem-solving competence were separated on a set of complex story problems, children with MD only and MD/RD performed at about the same low level (compared with normative data involving children without MD) on basic arithmetic operations, but the MD-only group outperformed the MD/RD group on the problem-solving dimension. Problem solving included such skills as using correct problem-solving strategies and sorting relevant from irrelevant information; operations involved number facts and algorithms. Fuchs and Fuchs observed, " . . . in light of the semantic challenges associated with mathematics problem solving, regardless of whether the problems are accessed through reading or listening, the verbal performance deficits of comorbid students [i.e., MD/RD] along with their more pervasive disruptions of language may have contributed to the functional deficits we observed" (p. 572).

Overall, these works suggest that children with MD only and MD/RD have core deficits in numerical cognition or number sense, including number processing and basic arithmetic. These deficits appear to be relatively distinct from other cognitive competencies. The nature of the deficits does not seem to vary by MD group, although children with MD/RD show lower performance on number tasks than children with MD only. Children with MD, with or without RD, display difficulties in number knowledge, counting procedures, arithmetic operations, and computational fluency. What differentiates the MD only and MD/RD groups, even when IQ score is accounted for, is math problem solving, such as the ability to solve complex story problems, which is dependent on verbal as well as numerical skill. The potential for growth in math achievement or catching up to typically achieving peers is better for children with MD only, who can use their verbal strengths to compensate for their weaknesses with numbers.

RESPONSIVENESS TO INSTRUCTIONAL INTERVENTIONS

Responsiveness to interventions is another way of identifying and differentiating children with learning difficulties. A study by Fuchs and colleagues (Fuchs, Fuchs, & Prentice, 2004) suggested that children with MD only and children with MD/RD respond differently to instructional interventions. Participants were third graders with MD only ($n = 13$), MD/RD ($n = 32$), and RD only ($n = 27$), as well as a group of children who were not at risk ($n = 129$). The cutoff for difficulties (or "at risk for disability") was below the 25th percentile on a standardized achievement test. Within each group, about half of the children received a 16-week experimental intervention and the other half traditional instruction. All of the instruction was provided within the general education setting. The experimental intervention focused explicitly on concepts, computation, and labeling within the context of word problem solving. Instruction in transfer and self-regulated learning was provided. In general, children responded well to the experimental intervention relative to the response of the children in the control condition. When pretest and posttest scores were compared by group and math area, it was shown that the intervention responsiveness of the MD/RD group was lower than that of each of the other three achievement groups in conceptual understanding. In contrast, the children with MD only benefited from the intervention as much as their peers without MD. In the other two math areas (computation and labeling), the MD/RD, MD-only, and RD-only groups, respectively, made fewer gains than the NA group. These findings indicate that problem-solving interventions for children with MD only should focus more on explicit instruction in computation and labeling, whereas the intervention for children with MD/RD, who have more pervasive weaknesses, should include additional work in conceptual understanding. Fuchs and colleagues (2004) results clearly extend the work that describes functional profiles of children with MD only versus those with MD/RD, showing that intervention responsiveness varies according to achievement deficit patterns. Fuchs and colleagues speculated that the relatively poor intervention response of children with MD/RD

> May reside with a more pervasive set of underlying deficits associated with comorbidity, with each deficit contributing independently or synergistically to mathematics problem-solving dysfunction. Alternatively, and more simply, their poor response may be due to more serious math or reading functional deficits than students with MD only or RD only. (2004, p. 305)

EARLY PREDICTORS OF MATH ACHIEVEMENT

Although research on the validity of math proficiency screening is not as advanced as similar research in reading, a small but growing body of research on number sense in kindergartners and its predictability of future difficulties provides strong evidence that number sense can identify those likely to need support in math in primary school (Gersten, Jordan, & Flojo, 2005). This research supports the contention that children with MD have a core weakness in number sense that can be identified early and that number sense is predictive even when reading and other background variables are considered.

In our research lab, we are examining the development of number sense in young children and whether number sense predicts achievement in math. In the first phase of our longitudinal work, Jordan, Kaplan, Olah, and

Table 6.2.   Core number sense battery

Task	Areas Assessed
Counting skills (Geary, Bow-Thomas, & Yao, 1992)	Set enumeration; counting in sequence to 50; understanding of one-to-one correspondence, stable order, and cardinality principles.
Number knowledge (Griffin & Case, 1997)	Relationships between numbers (e.g., which is smaller, 8 or 6?) and magnitude comparisons (which number is closer to 5, 6 or 2?).
Nonverbal calculation (Levine, Jordan, & Huttenlocher, 1992; Huttenlocher, Jordan, & Levine, 1994)	Set transformations through adding or taking away objects that are hidden under a box. The child can see the initial set, which is then covered, and objects are added or taken away, but cannot see the final result. The child must indicate how many objects are under the box after the transformation.
Story problems (Jordan et al., 2003a)	Single-digit addition and subtraction problems embedded in "stories" with verbal referents (e.g., "Jill has 2 pennies. Jim gives her 1 more penny. How many pennies does Jill have now?").
Number combinations (Jordan et al., 2003a)	Single-digit addition and subtraction problems without verbal or physical referents (e.g., "How much is 2 and 1?").

Locuniak (2006) examined the development of number sense in 411 kindergartners over four time points while controlling for gender, age, and reading skill. Our number sense battery assessed counting skills and principles, number knowledge, number transformation, estimation, and number patterns—all areas that are directly related to learning primary-school math and math difficulties (Griffin & Case, 1997). A description of the core tasks is presented in Table 6.2. We examined children's level of performance at the end of kindergarten in addition to their rate of growth from the beginning to the end of kindergarten. Children received the same math curriculum throughout the school year. Because we were interested in high-risk children, children from low-income backgrounds were targeted. A factor analysis revealed two dimensions of the number sense battery, one dimension involving basic number skills (e.g., counting, number knowledge, and calculation in a nonverbal contest) and another involving more conventional arithmetic (e.g., story problems and number combinations involving simple calculations). Growth curve analyses revealed significant linear growth throughout kindergarten in most areas of number sense. Three distinct growth trajectories were found: children who ended kindergarten at a low level with flat growth throughout the year; children who ended kindergarten at a high level with relatively steep growth throughout the year; and children who ended kindergarten at a middle to high level with moderate growth.

The findings most relevant to the present discussion are those related to the predictor variables of reading and income level. Children from low-income families are most at risk for falling into an MD/RD group by second grade (Jordan, Kaplan, & Hanich, 2002). Reading proficiency at the end of kindergarten, assessed with a standardized measure of word-level fluency, was a strong predictor of performance on all number sense measures (but not of rate of growth). Regardless of whether kindergarten reading level reflects general verbal ability or early home experiences (Saxe et al., 1987), early reading difficulties should be viewed as a risk factor for math difficulties (Leppanen, Niemi, Aunola, & Nurmi, 2004). Children from low-income families showed weaker performance on most aspects of number sense than did children from middle-income families, although children from both income groups grew at similar rates. The exception was on arithmetic story problems, on which kindergarteners from low-income families not only performed more poorly than did middle-income families but also demonstrated much less growth from the beginning to the end of the year. In fact, children from low-income families were four times more likely to fall into a low performance/flat growth class than were their peers from middle-income families. Story problems required children to listen to a problem, understand its semantic and syntactic structure, and perform a simple number transformation involving addition or subtraction. In contrast, children in both income groups made comparable progress when asked to perform number transformations in a nonverbal context with visual referents.

Children who participated in Jordan and colleagues's (2006) study were tested on math achievement at the end of first grade. Preliminary analyses show that our number sense battery has strong predictive validity, even at the beginning of kindergarten, when children have had limited formal instruction in math. The correlation between performance on the number sense battery in the first month of kindergarten with math achievement in the last month of first grade (as measured by the Woodcock-Johnson III: Complete Battery [Tests of Achievement], Woodcock & Johnson, 1989) was .70. The correlation between the number sense battery at the end of kindergarten and math achievement at the end of first grade was .73. Although all of the kindergarten number sense subtests were positively and significantly correlated with first-grade math achievement, the ones that were most predictive (end of kindergarten) were number knowledge (.58), nonverbal calculation (.58), story problems (.58), and number combinations (.61). However, reading skill in kindergarten also was correlated with first-grade math achievement (.49). To determine the predictability of the number sense battery above and beyond other common predictors of achievement, we also performed a two-block regression analysis. The first block contained reading as well as measures of IQ and working memory; the second block contained the number sense battery at the end of kindergarten. We found that the number sense battery made a significant contribution to the variance in math achievement (i.e., an additional 12%, from 45% of the variance to 57%) when we accounted for the other variables. Reading, however, did not predict a significant amount of variance over and above number sense.

In summary, our number sense battery (Jordan et al., 2006), which includes core number skills, is strongly predictive of early math achievement. The findings are in keeping with other recent reports of early detectors of math difficulties (Gersten et al., 2005). Mazzocco and Thompson (2005) reported that the ability of kindergartners to read numbers, compare magnitudes of one-digit numbers, and perform simple mental calculations are strong predictors of learning disabilities in math in third grade. Speed of accessing number quantity information also appears to be important (Durand, Hulme, Larkin, & Snowling, 2005). Although basic reading proficiency is a strong predictor of math achievement, it does not predict math achievement above and beyond number sense. The added value of using early literacy measures to screen for math difficulties would be to pick up high-risk children who are likely to have MD/RD as opposed to MD only.

SUMMARY

Dividing children with MD according to their reading skill (typical versus delayed) provides important information for researchers, clinicians, and educators. Children with MD only as well as children with MD/RD show similar functional profiles with respect to number. Weak calculation fluency, a key characteristic of most math difficulties, reflects basic deficits in counting procedures and number knowledge. Although it has been suggested that there are children with MD/RD whose *primary* deficits are in phonological processing (Robinson et al., 2002), empirical research to date does not support this contention. Although reading skill predicts math achievement, number sense is a stronger predictor. Reading difficulties appear to aggravate rather than cause math difficulties. Compensatory mechanisms associated with reading and language strengths are less available to children with MD/RD than are those with MD only (Jordan et al., 2003a). Related to this issue, children with MD only show different growth trajectories in math achievement in primary school than children with MD/RD; children with MD only show steeper growth than children with MD/RD. Moreover, the two MD subgroups respond differently to instruction, with the MD/RD group needing more intense instruction in problem conceptualization.

It is important to note that low-income children are much more likely to fall into the MD/RD category, even when IQ score is considered in statistical analyses. Consequently, these children are at risk for relatively low growth in math achievement over time. Early intervention research should focus on developing basic number sense in both groups of MD children as well as on helping children with MD/RD develop and mobilize language-related skills to reason with numbers. Although the research gives us a good idea of the goals of early math intervention—namely, to develop foundational principles, counting strategies, and calculation fluency—the best way to build these skills is not clear and warrants investigation (Gersten et al., 2005).

REFERENCES

Badian, N.A. (1999). Persistent arithmetic, reading, or arithmetic and reading disability. *Annals of Dyslexia, 49,* 45–70.

Barbaresi, M.J., Katusic, S.K., Colligan, R.C., Weaver, A.L., & Jacobsen, S.J. (2005). Math learning disorder: Incidence in a population-based birth cohort, 1976–1982, Rochester, Minn. *Ambulatory Pediatrics, 5,* 281–289.

Chiappe, P. (2006). How reading research can inform mathematics difficulties: The search for the core deficit. *Journal of Learning Disabilities, 38,* 313–317.

Dowker, A. (2005). *Individual differences in arithmetic: Implications for psychology, neuroscience, and education.* Hove, UK, and NY: Psychology Press.

Durand, M., Hulme, C., Larkin, R., & Snowling, M. (2005). The cognitive foundations of reading and arithmetic skills in 7- to 9-year-olds. *Journal of Experimental Child Psychology, 91,* 113–136.

Fletcher, J.M. (2005). Predicting math outcomes: Reading predictors and comorbidity. *Journal of Learning Disabilities, 38,* 308–312.

Fuchs, L.S., & Fuchs, D. (2002). Mathematical problem-solving profiles of students with mathematics disabilities with and without comorbid reading disabilities. *Journal of Learning Disabilities, 35,* 564–574.

Fuchs, L.S., Fuchs, D., & Prentice, K. (2004). Responsiveness to mathematical problem-solving instruction: Comparing students at risk of mathematics disability with and without risk of reading disability. *Journal of Learning Disabilities, 37,* 293–306.

Geary, D.C. (1990). A componential analysis of an early learning deficit in mathematics. *Journal of Experimental Child Psychology, 49,* 363–383.

Geary, D.C. (1993). Mathematical disabilities: Cognitive, neuropsychological, and genetic components. *Psychological Bulletin, 114,* 345–362.

Geary, D.C. (1994). Mathematics and learning disabilities. *Journal of Learning Disabilities, 37,* 4–15.

Geary, D.C., Bow-Thomas, C., & Yao, Y. (1992). Counting knowledge and skill in cognitive addition: A comparison of normal and mathematically-disabled children. *Journal of Experimental Child Psychology, 54,* 372–391.

Geary, D.C., Hamson, C.O., & Hoard, M.K. (2000). Numerical and arithmetical cognition: A longitudinal study of process and concept deficits in children with learning disability. *Journal of Experimental Child Psychology, 77,* 236–263.

Gersten, R., Jordan, N.C., & Flojo, J.R. (2005). Early identification and interventions for students with mathematics difficulties. *Journal of Learning Disabilities, 38,* 293–304.

Griffin, S.A., & Case, R. (1997). Re-thinking the primary school math curriculum: An approach based on cognitive science. *Issues in Education, 3*(1), 1–49.

Hanich, L., Jordan, N.C., Kaplan, D., & Dick, J. (2001). Performance across different areas of mathematical cognition in children with learning difficulties. *Journal of Educational Psychology, 93*(3), 615–626.

Huttenlocher, J., Jordan, N.C., & Levine, S.C. (1994). A mental model for early arithmetic. *Journal of Experimental Psychology: General, 123*, 284–296.

Jordan, N.C., & Hanich, L.B. (2000). Mathematical thinking in second-grade children with different types of learning difficulties. *Journal of Learning Disabilities, 33*, 567–578.

Jordan, N.C., & Hanich, L.B. (2003). Characteristics of children with moderate mathematics deficiencies: A longitudinal perspective. *Learning Disabilities: Research and Practice, 18*(4), 213–221.

Jordan, N.C., Hanich, L.B., & Kaplan, D. (2003a). A longitudinal study of mathematical competencies in children with specific mathematics difficulties versus children with comorbid mathematics and reading difficulties. *Child Development, 74*(3), 834–850.

Jordan, N.C., Hanich, L.B., & Kaplan, D. (2003b). Arithmetic fact mastery in young children: A longitudinal investigation. *Journal of Experimental Child Psychology, 85*, 103–119.

Jordan, N.C., Huttenlocher, J., & Levine, S.C. (1992). Differential calculation abilities in young children from middle- and low-income families. *Developmental Psychology, 28*, 644–653.

Jordan, N.C., Kaplan, D., & Hanich, L.B. (2002). Achievement growth in children with learning difficulties in mathematics: Findings of a two-year longitudinal study. *Journal of Educational Psychology, 94*(3), 586–597.

Jordan, N.C., Kaplan, D., Olah, L.N., & Locuniak, M.N. (2006). Number sense growth in kindergarten: A longitudinal investigation of children at risk for mathematics difficulties. *Child Development, 77*, 153–175.

Jordan, N.C., & Montani, T.O. (1997). Cognitive arithmetic and problem solving: A comparison of children with specific and general mathematics difficulties. *Journal of Learning Disabilities, 30*, 624–634.

Landerl, K., Bevan, A., & Butterworth, B. (2004). Developmental dyscalculia and basic numerical capacities: A study of 8–9-year-old students. *Cognition, 93*, 99–125.

Leppanen, U., Niemi, P., Aunola, K., & Nurmi, J.E. (2004). Development of reading skills among preschool and primary school pupils. *Reading Research Quarterly, 39*(1), 72–93.

Levine, S.C., Jordan, N.C., & Huttenlocher, J. (1992). Development of calculation abilities in young children. *Journal of Experimental Child Psychology, 53*, 72–103.

Mazzocco, M.M.M., & Thompson, R.E. (2005). Kindergarten predictors of math learning disability. *Learning Disabilities Research and Practice, 20*, 142–155.

Montague, M., Applegate, B., & Marquard, K. (1993). Cognitive strategy instruction and mathematical problem-solving performance of students with learning disabilities. *Learning Disabilities Research and Practice, 29*, 251–261.

Ostad, S.A. (1998). Developmental differences in solving simple arithmetic word problems and simple number-fact problems: A comparison of mathematically normal and mathematically disabled children. *Mathematical Cognition, 4*, 1–19.

Ostad, S.A. (1999). Developmental progression of subtraction strategies: A comparison of mathematically normal and mathematically disabled children. *European Journal of Special Needs Education, 14*, 21–36.

Robinson, C.S., Menchetti, B.M., & Torgesen, J.K. (2002). Toward a two-factor theory of one type of mathematics disabilities. *Learning Disabilities Research & Practice, 17*(2), 81–89.

Rourke, B.P. (1993). Arithmetic disabilities specific and otherwise: A neuropsychological perspective. *Journal of Learning Disabilities, 26,* 214–226.

Russell, R.L., & Ginsburg, H.P. (1984). Cognitive analysis of children's mathematics difficulties. *Cognition and Instruction, 1,* 217–244.

Saxe, G.B., Guberman, S.R., Gearhart, M., Gelman, R., Massey, C.M., & Rogoff, B. (1987). Social processes in early number development. *Monographs of the Society for Research in Child Development, 52*(2).

Scott Foresman-Addison Wesley. (1999). *Math.* Menlo Park, CA: Addison Wesley Longman.

Shaywitz, S.E., Escobar, M.D., Shaywitz, B.A., Fletcher, J.M., & Makuch, R. (1992). Evidence that dyslexia may represent the lower tail of a normal distribution of reading ability. *The New England Journal of Medicine, 326,* 145–150.

Teaching Integrated Mathematics and Science (TIMS) Curriculum (2004). *Math trailblazers grade 2* (2nd ed.). Chicago, IL: Kendall/Hunt Publishing Company

Woodcock, R.W., & Johnson, M.B. (1989).*Woodcock–Johnson psychoeducational battery–revised.* Allen, TX: DLM.

Chapter 7

Fraction Skills and Proportional Reasoning

Steve A. Hecht, Kevin J. Vagi, and Joseph K. Torgesen

+ +

One of the most persistent problems for children with mathematical learning disabilities (MLD) is solving problems involving fractions (Algozzine, O'Shea, Crews, & Stoddard, 1987). For many of these children, this constitutes a major obstacle to their movement beyond basic math to more advanced topics in later elementary school and beyond (Hecht, 1998; Hecht, Close, & Santisi, 2003; Heller, Post, Behr, & Lesh, 1990; Loveless, 2003). Of course, many children without MLD also experience difficulties with fractions (Hope & Owens, 1987; Smith, 1995). For example, the fifth U.S. National Assessment of Educational Progress (NAEP) reported that only 53% of 7th graders and 71% of 11th graders could correctly subtract two "mixed" fractions with unlike denominators (e.g., $3\frac{1}{2} - 3\frac{1}{3} = $; see NAEP, 1990). More recently released items from the NAEP confirm that many children experience difficulty reasoning in this domain (National Center for Education Statistics, 2006). On the 1996 and 2005 NAEP, only 65% and 73% of 8th graders were able to correctly shade $\frac{1}{3}$ of a provided rectangle, respectively. On the 2003 NAEP, only 55% of the 8th graders tested could solve a word problem involving the division of one fraction quantity by another fraction (National Center for Education Statistics, 2006). The word problem was this: Jim has $\frac{3}{4}$ of a yard of string, which he wishes to divide into pieces, each $\frac{1}{8}$ of a yard long. How many pieces will he have?

Although difficulty with fractions is clearly not unique to students with MD, weaknesses in this area do constitute a very common feature of math disabilities, and thus it is useful to consider what is known about the proximal causes of difficulties with fractions. More clearly identifying the specific knowledge or processing weaknesses associated with surface-level math difficulties should help lead to a more coherent treatment of math disabilities themselves. Given the heterogeneity of students with MD (Geary, 1993), as well as the complexity of math learning itself, carefully describing distinct areas of math in which students with MD show weaknesses will help in discovering whether there are more fundamental cognitive or neurophysiological weaknesses underlying these difficulties (Chiappe, 2005; Robinson, Menchetti, & Torgesen, 2002; see also Torgesen, 1999, for a comparable argument in understanding reading disabilities). This will enable the development of a coherent account of the difficulties that children with MD are likely to encounter when solving problems involving different kinds of math skills (Chiappe, 2005; Robinson et al., 2002), such as fractions (Hecht, 1998).

Both theory and empirical evidence lead to the conclusion that poor performance on problems involving rational numbers may largely be traced to a separation between conceptual understanding of fractions and fraction problem solving (Hiebert & Wearne, 1986). Conceptual knowledge of fractions can be defined as the awareness of what fraction symbols mean and the ability to represent fractions in multiple ways. Four reports by the National Academies Press (Bransford, Brown, & Cocking, 2000; Donovan & Bransford, 2005; Kilpatrick, Swafford, & Findell, 2001; Pellegrino, Chudowsky, & Glaser, 2001) reviewed the major cognitive science perspectives that can provide researchers with some necessary elements for an information processing account of math skills. These reports stressed the necessity of working to obtain a body of coordinated, meaningful conceptual knowledge that reveals the logical structure of the discipline (e.g., fractions). In this chapter, we also emphasize the importance of acquiring relevant conceptual knowledge about fractional quantities and forming links between these understandings and the problem-solving process. The ability to conceptually understand numbers and operations is often cited in the mathematical cognition literature by the generic term referred to as *number sense* (Berch, 2005; Gersten & Chard, 1999; Robinson et al., 2002). It has been asserted that number sense is as important to mathematical learning as oral language skills, such as phonemic awareness, are to reading (Gersten & Chard, 1999). In the current context, a well-developed number sense for rational numbers is necessary for the child to effectively use meaningful understandings of fractional units during fraction problem solving.

In our attempt to explore the proximal causes of difficulties with math problems involving fractions, we first elaborate on a number of points concerning conceptual knowledge and why fraction skills are particularly difficult for some children. We next describe various ways that domain-specific conceptual knowledge is needed to solve fraction problems. Then, we examine selected empirical evidence pointing to links between conceptual knowledge and variability in the attainment of fraction skills.

CONCEPTUAL KNOWLEDGE AND
THE UNIQUE QUALITIES OF THE FRACTION UNIT

As a domain of math skills, fractions pose unique difficulties for learners. One of the major skills children must acquire in dealing with fractions is making sense of the fraction symbols (Stafylidou & Vosniadou, 2004). Fractions or rational number symbols have more varied and complex conceptual interpretations than children learn when performing whole number operations. Thus, working with fractions may be especially difficult. Kieren (1993) identified five common interpretations for fraction units: 1) part–whole, 2) measurement, 3) ratio, 4) quotient, and 5) operator, the first two of which are important to this chapter's discussion.

Part–whole and measurement interpretations are usually taught to children in the early elementary grades and constitute the bulk of basic fraction skills instruction (English & Halford, 1995). These interpretations are also part of the intuitive understandings many children develop, to some extent, with little or no formal instruction (Kieren, 1988; Sophian, Garyantes, & Chang, 1997). *Part–whole* means that fractions represent the parts of an entire object or set of objects indicated by the fraction symbols. For example, ½ can refer to a pie with half of it eaten, two pies with one of them eaten, and so on. *Measurement* refers to the fact that fractions are numbers that reflect cardinal size (Hecht, 1998). For example, fractions can be ordered from lowest to highest (e.g., ¼, ⅓, ½, ⅔) (Smith, Solomon, & Carey, 2005). Some educators consider part–whole and measurement conceptual understandings to be two aspects of one underlying fund of knowledge (e.g., see Behr, Lesh, Post, & Silver, 1983). One common thread among the various interpretations of fractions is that all of these understandings can pertain to how much of a quantity is present. Unfortunately, some children fail to attach meaning to fraction numerals (e.g., Hecht, 1998; Mack, 1993, 1995; Ni, 2000).

Once children have acquired conceptual knowledge about what fraction symbols mean, they can use that knowledge to solve fraction problems. However, links between conceptual knowledge and fraction problem solving can be difficult to establish when fraction operations contradict previous mathematical understandings that children have acquired from whole number instruction. Indeed, these seemingly contradictory understandings can actually interfere with proper execution of fraction procedures (e.g., see Mack, 1995; Ni & Zhou, 2005; Saxe, Taylor, McIntosh, & Gearhart, 2005). For example, multiplying two fractional quantities can yield a product that is smaller than each of the terms in the problem (e.g., $\frac{1}{2} \times \frac{1}{4} = \frac{1}{8}$). This contradicts whole number theory, which postulates that multiplication makes numbers larger (Stafylidou & Vosniadou, 2004). Also, some students overgeneralize whole number concepts by assuming that the value of a rational number gets larger if the denominator increases (Stafylidou & Vosniadou, 2004). Although these multiple conceptual understandings of fractions make rational numbers initially more complex to learn than whole numbers, children can benefit from acquiring conceptual knowledge about fractions. The richness in meanings derived from fraction symbols can actually support problem solving (Byrnes & Wasik, 1991; Hecht, 1998; Hecht et al., 2003; Hiebert, 1987).

CONCEPTUAL KNOWLEDGE AND FRACTION PROBLEM SOLVING

Conceptual knowledge of rational number units can aid students in selecting appropriate procedures for solving fraction computation problems (Hiebert & LeFevre, 1986). For example, a student is more likely to remember that $1/3 + 1/5$ requires converting the fraction to common denominators if the student forms a mental model of the part–whole interpretation of the fraction number units (e.g., pies with parts shaded). The student must also understand that the shaded parts identified by the fractions are of unequal size and therefore cannot be added together. A student who understands the measurement interpretation of fraction units can avoid the error of adding denominators in a problem (e.g., $1/2 + 1/5 = 2/7$), because the stated answer is smaller than the first term in the problem. Thus, meaningful understandings of fraction symbols can be used to detect or avoid procedural mistakes while solving fraction computation problems (Byrnes & Wasik, 1991; Hiebert, 1987). Clinical case studies using verbal protocol techniques have documented children's use of part–whole and measurement interpretations of fractions to select and to monitor the success of computation procedures (Mack, 1990; Streefland, 1993; see also Pitkethly & Hunting, 1996, for a review). Without sufficient conceptual knowledge, many students use memorized and often incorrect procedures to solve computation problems with fractions (Behr et al., 1983; Rittle-Johnson & Siegler, 1998).

Conceptual knowledge of fractions can also enhance the solving of fraction word problems. Translation of word problems into appropriate computations usually requires the construction of accurate mental models for the situations conveyed by the word problems (see e.g., Hegarty, Mayer, & Monk, 1995; Kintsch & Greeno, 1985; Stern, 1993). Students who rely on an inaccurate mental model for the situation conveyed by a word problem may be more likely to set up the wrong fraction computation problem to solve the word problem. Conceptual understandings of fractions may be used during the process of constructing mental models for fraction word problems. For example, it may be easier to construct an accurate mental model for the following real-world problem if the student has a firm understanding of the part–whole relationships conveyed by fractions: A cake recipe requires ¼ of a cup of butter for the filling and ⅓ of a cup of butter for the icing. How much butter is needed for the cake? (Hecht, 1998).

Finally, conceptual understandings are likely needed for estimation of fractions (Hecht, 1998; Hecht et al., 2003). Conceptual knowledge of the measurement interpretation of fractions should be associated with students' ability to convert fractional quantities into approximate whole number quantities (Behr & Post, 1986; Case & Sowder, 1990). For example, a student who understands that ⅟₉₉₉₉ and ⅟₉₉₉ are very small quantities is in a better position to consider the sum of these two fractional numbers as being closer to 1 than to 2 (Hecht; 1998). Students may also use their understanding of part–whole relations represented by fractions in order to translate fractional quantities into approximate whole number quantities. For example, ¹⁹⁄₁₀ can be represented as two circles with one completely shaded and the other almost completely shaded. The student could then consider ¹⁹⁄₁₀ to be about 2, because the part–whole interpretation for the fraction is approximately two circles that are shaded.

EMPIRICAL RELATIONS BETWEEN CONCEPTUAL KNOWLEDGE AND FRACTION PROBLEM SOLVING

One strategy that can be used to understand the deficits underlying the performance of children with MLD on fraction problems involves examining the fraction competencies in unselected samples of children (Hecht et al., 2003; Hecht, Torgesen, Wagner, & Rashotte, 2001). When this approach is combined with studies that compare children with MLD with children who are typical achievers, a clearer view of the factors that contribute to math disabilities emerges. Below, we summarize four studies that combine the two approaches in a relatively comprehensive analysis of relations among predictors and outcomes of fraction performance.

Byrnes and Wasik (1991)

Byrnes and Wasik (1991) investigated the association between fourth, fifth, and sixth graders' conceptual knowledge and their accuracy at solving addition and multiplication fraction computation problems involving unlike denominators (e.g., ⅓ + ⅕ = _____). The researchers assessed students' understanding of both the part–whole and measurement interpretations of fractions. In Experiment 1, the total score on the fraction concepts test significantly correlated with overall fraction computation accuracy across grades (r_{xy} = .50). Experiment 2 entailed another examination of the association between conceptual understanding and addition of fractions with unlike denominators. Fifth graders were tested immediately after receiving one training session designed to promote students' accuracy at adding fractions. Performance on each of the conceptual knowledge tasks significantly correlated with individual differences in fraction computation accuracy (overall r_{xy} = .55). Similar findings for relations between part–whole and measurement knowledge and fraction computation skills have been found in Chinese elementary school children as well (Ni, 2000). Byrnes and Wasik (1991) also found that fifth graders mastered conceptual knowledge before they mastered the procedures for solving fraction addition computation problems. They concluded that conceptual knowledge is necessary but not sufficient for acquiring skills in domains that involve using procedural knowledge (e.g., fraction computation). In these studies, general intellectual ability was not statistically controlled with respect to the correlations that were obtained between conceptual understanding and fraction computation skills. This leaves open the possibility that the associations are caused by their common dependence on general intellectual propensity to learn academic skills.

Hecht (1998)

Hecht (1998) provided evidence pointing to conceptual knowledge as a key determinant of variability in fraction computation, estimation, and word problem performance. A crucial feature of this study was the examination of unique relations between conceptual knowledge and fraction outcomes with other key factors controlled for, such as general intellectual ability. The study, which included 103 seventh and eighth graders, looked at both part–whole and measurement conceptual understandings about fractions in this age group.

The Hecht (1998) study was the first to provide strong quantitative evidence that conceptual knowledge *uniquely* contributes to variability in all three fraction outcomes. Conceptual knowledge uniquely accounted for approximately 5% of the variance in fraction computation skills, with procedural knowledge, simple arithmetic skills, reading of individual words, and vocabulary knowledge accounted for. Conceptual knowledge was strongly related to fraction estimation, uniquely accounting for about 33% of the variance. This result suggests that students are unable to estimate fraction computation answers without a firm understanding of the meaning of fraction symbols. Finally, conceptual knowledge uniquely accounted for approximately 6% of the variance in fraction word problem ability. Thus, students require an understanding of fractional quantities to select the appropriate procedures for solving fraction word problems.

A detailed error (bug) analysis revealed poor linkages between procedural knowledge and part–whole and measurement interpretations of fractions (Hecht, 1998). The mistakes were classified by inferring the kinds of strategies used to find the solution for incorrectly solved problems based on the nature of the mistakes made. Errors were classified into four major categories: procedural, wild guess (i.e., errors that cannot be explained in terms of faulty procedures or calculations [Hennessy, 1994]), no attempt (i.e., errors that occur when a student does not try to solve a given problem), or calculation error.

Of the 1,474 errors, approximately 82% involved a faulty procedure. Thirteen types of procedural errors were recorded. Wild guesses and no-attempts constituted approximately 14% of errors, and calculation errors occurred approximately 4% of the time. These results provide strong support for the conclusion that children who experience difficulties with fraction computation problems err primarily because they select incorrect procedures. These results also show that the difficulty level of fraction items is largely dependent on the complexity of the procedures required to solve these problems.

Hecht, Close, and Santisi (2003)

Hecht and his colleagues (2003) extended the findings from Hecht (1998) on the unique role of conceptual knowledge in a study of 105 fifth graders that found individual differences in fraction skills. Conceptual knowledge emerged as a unique correlate of variability in fraction computation, estimation, and word-problem skills, with classroom behavior, simple arithmetic skills, and working memory controlled for. Thus, converging empirical support is available, pointing to conceptual knowledge as a unique source of variance in all three types of fraction outcomes.

Hecht (in progress)

This in-progress research project is the first study to directly compare students with MD with students who are typically achieving in terms of cognitive abilities, classroom behavior, mathematical knowledge, and fraction skills outcomes. Research on MD is often based on children who score below either the 25th or 35th percentile on standardized math achievement tests (e.g., see Geary, 2005; Siegel & Ryan, 1989). With this criterion, based on the lowest 25th age-based percentile for the Math Calculation Cluster Score of the Woodcock Johnson III Tests of Achievement (Woodcock, McGrew, & Mather, 2000), 89 students with MLD and 171 fourth graders who were typically achieving have participated thus far. Students were tested in the spring of fourth grade and will be tested again in the spring of fifth grade.

Significant differences ($p < .05$ or smaller) between students with MLD and students who are typically achieving emerged on all fraction measures, as depicted in Table 7.1. Factual knowledge about simple arithmetic was indexed in terms of the percentage of problems that students, on average,

Table 7.1.   Mean levels of performance on fractions tests

	Score		
Type of computation	Students with MD	Students who are typically achieving	Cohen's *d*
Fraction computation (26)	4.6	9.8	1.4
Fraction estimation (12)	2.0	3.6	.6
Word problem solving (16)	4.6	8.8	1.3
Arithmetic retrieval use — addition (22)	6.3	11.04	.7
Arithmetic retrieval use — multiplication (22)	9.8	15.10	.8
Fraction size (22)	14.6	17.8	.8
Symbol picture (16)	8.1	12.3	1.3
Picture symbol (13)	4.0	9.7	1.8
Picture computation (13)	5.6	10.01	1.5

Source: Hecht, in progress.
Note: Mean total correct, except for arithmetic. Arithmetic expressed as total number of problems that were solved via the most efficient and least error-prone retrieval strategy. Maximum score possible in parentheses.

used retrieval to solve. Fraction size, symbol picture, picture symbol, and picture computation were used to measure both part–whole and measurement interpretations of fractions. For fraction size, students were asked to circle the largest fraction. Symbol picture involved converting a fraction symbol, such as ½, into a pictorial representation. Picture symbol involved changing a pictorial representation into a standard fraction symbol. Picture computation involved adding fractions together and supplying the answer in pictorial form, with the fraction terms in the addition problem represented in pictorial form.

Large differences (in terms of effect sizes) were obtained between students with MLD and typically achieving students for all measures except the fraction estimation task and arithmetic retrieval use. The latter two outcomes showed moderate differences between groups. Effect sizes (Cohen's standardized mean differences, *d*) are also presented, which should be interpreted as the difference in group means expressed in standard deviation units. For interpreting the effect sizes in Table 7.1, it should be noted that effect sizes of .80 or higher suggest large effects, those of .50–.79 suggest medium-sized effects, and those of .20–.49 reflect relatively small effects (Murphy & Myors, 1998). Of particular interest is that the effect sizes for the three tasks that measured part–whole knowledge about fractions were greater than 1, a very large effect size. Consistent with previous reports with older students, these data revealed substantial correlations (approximately the .50–.70 range) between measures of part–whole conceptual knowledge about fractions and fraction word problem solving and fraction computation (not depicted in Table 7.1).

The differences between the fraction test scores of students with MLD and students who are typically achieving were largely explainable by students' part–whole conceptual knowledge. Effect sizes for the fraction outcomes between groups were substantially reduced when differences in part–whole conceptual knowledge between students with MLD and students who were typically achieving were held constant. That is, the effect sizes were reduced for fraction computation (from 1.4 to .46), estimation (.60 to .09), and word problems (1.3 to .37) when a composite variable based on the conceptual knowledge tasks was held statistically constant. In all, these findings suggest that part–whole knowledge was an important reason for the differences in fraction outcomes between students with MLD and typically achieving students.

CONCLUSIONS

The recurrent theme in the work described here is that conceptual understandings about fractions and fraction problem solving are integrally related. Fractions appear to be particularly difficult for many children because of the unique conceptual characteristics of the fraction unit. The theoretical and empirical evidence suggests that, for many children, the difficulty in working with fractions is due to the poor representation of fraction-related semantic knowledge in long-term memory. Specifically, the representation of the meaningful aspects of rational numbers are less developed in children with MLD than they are in children who are typical achieving. This weakness in stimulus representation at the cognitive level provides some explanation for the particular difficulties that students with MLD have with fraction tasks (Donovan & Bransford, 2005; Ni, 2000). Conceptual knowledge about fractions may indeed be a domain-specific core deficit for children with MLD that affects fraction problem solving. However, there is no clear understanding of how difficulties in acquiring conceptual knowledge about fractions is related to other, domain-general characteristics of students with MLD identified in this book. A better understanding is needed of the ways children acquire links between conceptual knowledge about rational numbers and problem solving and also how specific instructional methods may play a role in establishing these links (e.g., see Baroody & Hume, 1991; Cramer et al., 2002; Donovan & Bransford, 2005; Kelly, Gersten, & Carnine, 1990; Perkins & Cullinan, 1985; Rittle-Johnson, Siegler, & Alibali, 2001).

REFERENCES

Algozzine, B., O'Shea, D., Crews, W., & Stoddard, K. (1987). Analysis of mathematics competence of LD adolescents. *The Journal of Special Education, 21,* 97–107.
Baroody, A.J., & Hume, J. (1991). Meaningful mathematics instruction: The case of fractions. *Remedial and Special Education, 12,* 54–68.

Behr, M., Post, T.R., & Silver, E.A. (1983). Rational number concepts. In R. Lesh & M. Landau (Eds.), *Acquisition of Mathematics Concepts and Processes* (pp. 91–126). New York: Academic Press.

Behr, M., & Post, T.R. (1986). Estimation and children's concept of rational number size. In H. Schoen & M. Zweng (Eds.), *Estimation and Mental Computation: 1986 NCTM Yearbook* (pp. 103–111). Reston, VA: National Council of Teachers of Mathematics.

Berch, D.B. (2005). Making sense of number sense: Implications for children with mathematical disabilities. *Journal of Learning Disabilities, 38,* 333–339.

Bransford, J.D., Brown, A.L., & Cocking, R.R. (Eds.). (2000). *How people learn: Brain, mind, experience, and school* (Expanded ed.). Washington, DC: National Academies Press.

Byrnes, J.P., & Wasik, B.A. (1991). Role of conceptual knowledge in mathematical and procedural learning. *Developmental Psychology, 27,* 777–786.

Case, R., & Sowder, J. (1990). The development of computational estimation: A neo-Piagetian analysis. *Cognition and Instruction, 7,* 79–104.

Chiappe, P. (2005). How reading research can inform mathematics difficulties: The search for the core deficit. *Journal of Learning Disabilities, 4,* 313–317.

Cramer, K.A., Post, T., & del Mas, R. (2002). Initial fraction learning by fourth- and fifth-grade students: A comparison of the effects of using commercial curricula with the effects of using the Rational Number Project Curriculum. *Journal for Research in Mathematics Education, 33,* 111–144.

Donovan, M.S., & Bransford, J.D. (2005). *How students learn: History, mathematics, and science in the classroom.* Washington, DC: National Academies Press.

English, L.D., & Halford, G.S. (1995). *Mathematics education: Models and processes.* Mahwah, NJ: Lawrence Erlbaum Associates.

Geary, D.C. (1993). Mathematical disabilities: Cognitive, neuropsychological, and genetic components. *Psychological Bulletin, 114,* 345–362.

Geary, D.C. (2005). Role of theory in study of learning difficulties in mathematics. *Journal of Learning Disabilities, 38,* 305–307.

Gersten, R., & Chard, D. (1999). Number sense: Rethinking arithmetic instruction for students with mathematics difficulties. *Journal of Learning Disabilities, 33,* 18–29.

Hecht, S., Close, L., & Santisi, M. (2003). Sources of individual differences in fraction skills. *Journal of Experimental Child Psychology, 86,* 277–302.

Hecht, S.A. (1998). Toward an information processing account of individual differences in fraction skills. *Journal of Educational Psychology, 90,* 545–559.

Hecht, S.A., Torgesen, J.K., Wagner, R.K., Rashotte, C.A. (2001). The relations between phonological processing abilities and emerging individual differences in mathematical computation skills: A longitudinal study from second- to fifth-grade. *Journal of Experimental Child Psychology, 79,* 192–227.

Hegarty, M., Mayer, R.E., & Monk, C.A. (1995). Comprehension of arithmetic word problems: A comparison of successful and unsuccessful problem solvers. *Journal of Educational Psychology, 87,* 18–32.

Heller, P.M., Post, T.R., Behr, M., & Lesh, R. (1990). Qualitative and numerical reasoning about fractions and rates by seventh- and eighth-grade students. *Journal for Research in Mathematics Education, 21,* 388–402.

Hennessy, S.A. (1994). The stability of children's mathematical behavior: When is a bug really a bug? *Learning and Instruction, 3,* 315–338.

Hiebert, J. (1987). *Conceptual and procedural knowledge: The case of mathematics.* Mahwah, NJ: Lawrence Erlbaum Associates.

Hiebert, J., & LeFevre, P. (1986). Conceptual and procedural knowledge in mathematics: An introductory analysis. In J. Hiebert (Ed.), *Conceptual and procedural knowledge* (pp. 1–27). Mahwah, NJ: Lawrence Erlbaum Associates.

Hiebert, J., & Wearne, D. (1986). Procedures over concepts: The acquisition of decimal number knowledge. In J. Hiebert (Ed.), *Conceptual and procedural knowledge* (pp. 199–223). Mahwah, NJ: Lawrence Erlbaum Associates.

Hope, J., & Owens, O. (1987). An analysis of the difficulty of learning fractions. *Focus on Learning Problems in Mathematics, 9,* 25–39.

Kelly, B., Gersten, R., & Carnine, D. (1990). Student error patterns as a function of curriculum design: Teaching fractions to remedial high school students and high school students with learning disabilities. *Journal of Learning Disabilities, 23,* 23–29.

Kieren, T.E. (1988). Personal knowledge of rational numbers: Its intuitive and formal development. In J. Hiebert & M. Behr (Eds.), *Number concepts and operations in the middle grades* (pp. 162–181). Reston, VA: National Council of Teachers of Mathematics.

Kieren, T.E. (1993). Rational and fractional numbers: From quotient fields to recursive understanding. In T. Carpenter, E. Fennema, & T. Romberg (Eds.), *Rational numbers: An integration of the research* (pp. 49–84). Mahwah, NJ: Lawrence Erlbaum Associates.

Kilpatrick, J., Swafford, J., & Findell, B. (2001). Adding it up: Helping children learn mathematics. Washington, DC : National Academies Press.

Kintsch, W., & Greeno, J.G. (1985). Understanding and solving word arithmetic problems. *Psychological Review, 92,* 109–129.

Loveless, T. (2003). Trends in math: The importance of basic skills. *Brookings Review, 21,* 40–43.

Mack, N.K. (1990). Learning fractions with understanding: Building on informal knowledge. *Journal for Research in Mathematics Education, 21,* 16–32.

Mack, N.K. (1993). Learning rational numbers with understanding: The case of informal knowledge. In T.P. Carpenter, E. Fennema, & T.A. Romberg (Eds.), *Rational numbers: An integration of research* (pp. 85–105). Mahwah, NJ: Lawrence Erlbaum Associates.

Mack, N.K. (1995). Confounding whole-number and fraction concepts when building on informal knowledge. *Journal for Research in Mathematics Education, 26,* 422–441.

Murphy, K.R., & Myors, B. (1998). *Statistical power analysis: A simple and general model for traditional and modern hypothesis tests.* Mahwah, NJ: Lawrence Erlbaum Associates.

National Assessment of Educational Progress (1990). *The Fifth National Mathematics Assessment.* Denver, CO: Author.

National Center for Education Statistics (2006). *NAEP questions.* Retrieved March 26, 2006, from http://nces.ed.gov/nationsreportcard/itmrls/

Ni, Y. (2000). How valid is it to use number lines to measure children's conceptual knowledge about rational number? *Educational Psychology, 20,* 139–152.

Ni, Y., & Zhou, Y.D. (2005). Teaching and learning fraction and rational numbers: The origins and implications of whole number bias. *Educational Psychologist, 40,* 27–52.

Pellegrino, J.W., Chudowsky, N., & Glaser, R. (Eds.). (2001). *Knowing what students know.* Washington, DC: National Academies Press.

Perkins, V., & Cullinan, D. (1985). Effects of direct instruction intervention for fraction skills. *Education & Treatment of Children, 8,* 41–50.

Pitkethly, A., & Hunting, R.P. (1996). A review of recent research in the area of initial fraction concepts. *Educational Studies in Mathematics, 30,* 5–38.

Rittle-Johnson, B., & Siegler, R.S. (1998). The relations between conceptual and procedural knowledge in learning mathematics: A review. In C. Donlan (Ed.), *The development of mathematical skill (pp. 75–110).* Hove, England: Psychology Press.

Rittle-Johnson, B., Siegler, R.S., & Alibali, M.W. (2001). Developing conceptual understanding and procedural skill in mathematics: An iterative process. *Journal of Educational Psychology, 93,* 346–362.

Robinson, C.S., Menchetti, B.M., & Torgesen, J.K. (2002). Toward a two-factor theory of one type of mathematics disabilities. *Learning Disabilities Research & Practice, 17,* 81–89.

Saxe, G.B., Taylor, E.V., McIntosh, C., & Gearhart, M. (2005). Representing fractions with standard notation: A developmental analysis. *Journal for Research in Mathematics Education, 36,* 137–157.

Siegel, L.S., & Ryan, E.B. (1989). The development of working memory in normally achieving and subtypes of learning disabled children. *Child Development, 60,* 973–980.

Smith, C.L., Solomon, G.E.A., & Carey, S. (2005). Never getting to zero: Elementary school students' understanding of the infinite divisibility of number and matter. *Cognitive Psychology, 51,* 101–140.

Smith, J.P. (1995). Competent reasoning with rational numbers. *Cognition and Instruction, 13,* 3–50.

Sophian, C., Garyantes, D., & Chang, C. (1997). When three is less than two: Early developments in children's understanding of fractional quantities. *Developmental Psychology, 33,* 731–744

Stafylidou, S., & Vosniadou, S. (2004). The development of students' understanding of the numerical value of fractions. *Learning and Instruction, 14,* 503–518.

Stern, E. (1993). What makes certain arithmetic word problems involving comparison of sets so difficult for children. *Journal of Educational Psychology, 85,* 7–23.

Streefland, L. (1993). Fractions: A realistic approach. In T.P. Carpenter, E. Fennema, & T.A. Romberg (Eds.), *Rational numbers: An integration of research* (pp. 289–304). Mahwah, NJ: Lawrence Erlbaum Associates.

Torgesen, J.K. (1999). Phonologically based reading disabilities: Toward a coherent theory of one kind of learning disability. In R.J. Sternberg & L. Spear-Swerling (Eds.), *Perspectives on learning disabilities* (pp. 231–262). New Haven: Westview Press.

Woodcock, R.W., McGrew, K.S., & Mather, N. (2000). *Woodcock-Johnson III: Complete Battery [Tests of Achievement].* Itasca, IL: Riverside Publishing.

Cognitive Aspects
of Math Disabilities

H. Lee Swanson

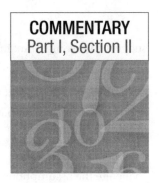

Cognitive psychologists have studied individual differences in mathematical cognition extensively during recent decades. This is because mathematical facility has been recognized as an important dimension of human intelligence for some time (e.g., Thurstone, 1938). Furthermore, it is hard not to overemphasize the importance of mathematical ability in a society that requires technical competence among its citizens, competence that, in turn, draws on high levels of mathematical literacy. Unfortunately, what is clear from a large range of studies on individual differences, reflected in the chapters by Butterworth and Reigosa (Chapter 4); Geary, Hoard, Nugent, and Byrd-Craven (Chapter 5); Jordan (Chapter 6); and Hecht, Torgesen, and Vagi (Chapter 7), is that a significant number of children demonstrate poor achievement in mathematics. As can be surmised from these chapters, the incidence of mathematical learning disabilities (MLD) may be as common as reading disabilities (RD). That is, several studies (Badian, 1983; Gross-Tsur, Manor, & Shalev, 1996) estimate that approximately 6%–7% of the school-age population has MLD. Although this figure may be inflated because of variations in definition, there is consensus that a significant number of children demonstrate poor achievement in mathematics. Given the prevalence of MLD in the general public school population, these chapters provide a much-needed overview of the cognitive mechanisms that underlie MD.

Before commenting on the issues raised in these chapters, however, a quick overview of the important points is necessary. Chapter 4 by Butterworth and Reigosa also focuses on the cognitive impairments in children with MLD (the authors prefer the term *developmental dyscalculia;* however, for consistency across this commentary I use the term *MLD*). They address the issue of whether MLD is domain general or domain specific. The authors indicate that poor number skills can coexist with high intellectual ability, but the role of IQ scores is unclear. This is because the majority of studies exclude children with lower IQ scores, and therefore the influence of IQ score on MLD cannot be adequately assessed. The authors further suggest that some domain-general explanations of MD, such as memory impairments, are suspect. More specifically, the authors challenge some of the conclusions reached by Geary and colleagues. Geary and colleagues suggest that children with MD have impaired ability to represent phonetic and semantic information in long-term memory as well as some difficulties in inhibiting irrelevant information in working memory (WM). However, Butterworth and Reigosa suggest that phonetic and semantic memory problems have been dissociated in the neuropsychological literature. They also challenge the assumptions that 1) access to long-term memory depends on WM, and 2) finger counting may be viewed as a means to control WM demands (or as a consequence or cause of poor memory for arithmetic facts). These authors suggest that, although WM has been considered a plausible explanation for difficulties in calculation, very little empirical evidence supports this account. They cite another one of their earlier studies (Landerl et. al., 2004) that matched children on span level and found that arithmetic problems were unrelated to WM. They also cite their earlier work (Girelli, Lucangeli, & Butterworth, 2000) showing that children with MLD took much longer than controls to decide which of two numbers was numerically greater, but these children performed comparably with children in control groups on physical judgments. This research suggests that children at risk for MLD are slower at subitizing numerical information (i.e., making rapid and accurate judgments of the numerosity of a small set of items). In general, Butterworth and Reigosa argue that MLD is due in part to a slower and less efficient cognitive processing of numerical information at a very basic level, such as recognizing numerical displays. Butterworth puts forth a defective number module hypothesis, which suggests that *MLD arises from mechanisms related to recognizing, representing and mentally manipulating numerosities.*

In Chapter 5, Geary and colleagues describe strategies and procedures used by children who are typically achieving to solve simple and complex addition problems. When children enter school, two common counting procedures are used: 1) counting with fingers and/or counting all of the numbers or 2) *counting on* one of the larger numbers. These counting procedures facilitate the development of memory representations for basic facts. Children who are typically achieving experience a gradual developmental shift during the elementary school years from using counting procedures to relying on arithmetic facts. Children with MLD, however, still rely more heavily on finger counting at the end of the elementary school years and therefore are less likely to use retrieval-based processes than their peers who are typically achieving. Thus, finger counting may be viewed as either a consequence or cause of poor memory for arithmetic facts. The authors indicate that difficulties in the formation of arithmetic facts or access to these representations from memory are a defining feature of MLD.

Chapter 5 reviews several studies showing that children with MLD do not perform as well as their same-age peers on WM tasks. However, the mechanisms that underlie these group differences in WM are still under investigation. Some studies suggest that problems in accessing numbers are attributable to difficulties in speed of processing (e.g., articulation speed). Other accounts suggest that these children have difficulty inhibiting irrelevant associations; that is, children with MLD make retrieval errors because they cannot inhibit irrelevant associations from entering working memory. Several other key points are brought out in Chapter 5, but these points are alluded to in our review of the chapters by Jordan and by Butterworth and Reigosa.

In Chapter 6, Jordan focuses on the links between reading difficulties (RD) and mathematical learning difficulties (MLD). The author indicates that children with MLD are not well understood based on the fact that in several studies, heterogeneous groups were used and reading performance was not controlled. Thus, there is a question as to whether the deficits exhibited by children with MLD are the same as those associated with RD. She argues that some authors have incorrectly assumed that MLD is related to language, which in turn suggests some commonality between math and reading. Jordan reviews studies (Geary, Hamson, & Hoard, 2000; Landerl, Bevan, & Butterworth, 2004) that indicate that children with either mathematical difficulties or mathematical disabilities showed general deficits in number processing, whether or not they had reading difficulties. The author primarily takes issue with Geary's earlier findings that the problems in number and fact retrieval may be related to a phonological processing difficulty. Her own research suggests that children with RD (i.e., with known phonological deficits) do better than those with MLD or comorbid math and reading difficulties (MLD+RD) on rapid fact retrieval. Overall, she concludes that children with MLD, as well as those with comorbid difficulties (MLD+RD) have core deficits in numerical cognition and number sense and show similar functional profiles with respect to numbers. Although reading skill predicts math achievement, number sense is a much stronger predictor. Jordan also notes that children from low income families are more likely to fall into the comorbid group even when IQ scores are controlled statistically. In general, she argues that both groups have difficulty in number knowledge, counting procedures, mathematical operations, and computational fluency. What differentiates the two is the ability to solve complex word problems.Children with MLD tend to grow in mathematical achievement and catch up to peers who are typically achieving because they can use their *verbal strengths* to compensate for their weakness in processing numbers. Thus, Jordan concludes that deficits in fact retrieval, and by extension—calculation and fluency—are the defining features in mathematical difficulties, specific or otherwise.

In Chapter 7, Hecht, Torgesen, and Vagi review their research that focuses on fractions and MD. Specifically, these researchers have found clear individual differences in the rate at which children acquire mathematical skills involving fractions. Fractions are difficult to study, however, especially from standardized tests, as these measures are actually composites of mathematical ability. Furthermore, it is difficult to link a child's performance on standardized tests to mathematical impairment because such measures overestimate the child's skills that have been acquired in some math domains and underestimate skills in others. The authors present a model of the kinds of knowledge that children need to know in order to successfully solve problems involving fractions. Their results show that knowledge reflects three correlated factors: procedural, factual, and conceptual. *Procedural knowledge* involves the child's awareness of processing steps; *conceptual understanding* enables children to connect meaning to a fraction symbol; and *factual knowledge* represents the memorization of facts. Intrinsic factors—such as WM—and extrinsic factors—such as formal instruction and practice—are also at play. Hecht and colleagues' results show that children who experience difficulty in solving fractions typically show errors in part–whole interpretations. That is, the faulty knowledge of whole numbers interferes with the proper execution of fraction procedures. For example, some children assume that the value of a rational number is larger even though the denominator increases. In a subsequent work, Hecht and colleagues (Hecht, Close, & Santisi, 2003) showed that mathematical knowledge, classroom behavior, and WM are uniquely correlated with fraction outcomes. However, they state that the dominant cause of incorrect performance on fraction computation problems by children who experienced math difficulty was procedural knowledge error.

PUTTING THOUGHTS TOGETHER

As the reader can tell, the authors disagree to some extent about the key cognitive mechanisms than underlie MLD. Furthermore, there is disagreement as to whether MLD and RD share a common disorder, whether retrieval of math facts can be dissociated from verbal ability, and whether WM plays a major role when compared to basic number processing. In synthesizing these chapters, I would like to make four general observations. I will then conclude with some observations based on a meta-analysis we (Swanson & Jerman, 2006) have recently completed on the published cognitive literature related to MLD.

Unclear Mechanisms

First, the primary cognitive mechanisms that separate MLD from RD are unclear. Some authors have suggested that memory representations for arithmetic facts are supported in part by the same phonological and semantic memory systems that support decoding and reading comprehension (for reviews, see Geary, 1993; Hecht, Torgesen, Wagner, & Rashotte, 2001). If this is the case, then one can argue that phonological processes that contribute to reading disorders are a source of math retrieval difficulties in children with MLD. Others challenge this assumption (Butterworth & Reigosa, chapter 4; Jordan, chapter 6). Unfortunately, there at least two reasons why it is difficult to determine from existing literature whether the cognitive processing of children with MLD is distinct from those with RD.

The first reason is that the operational criteria for defining MLD and RD, as well as the terminology, vary across studies (Butterworth and Reigosa outline these issues in Chapter 4). Variations in definitions and issues of comorbidity have raised questions about whether some of the processes associated with MLD include cognitive subprocesses specific to math or whether impairments affecting math extend to other domains, such as reading. When reviewing the studies, I found that the cutoff scores for defining MLD vary from the 48th percentile to the 8th percentile (see Chapter 2 for a more detailed discussion of this along with related issues). For example, Jordan and colleagues refer to children with math difficulties as children below the 35th percentile. Other studies have been more conservative, such as Koontz and Berch (1996), and have used the 25th percentile as a cutoff point in defining MLD. There are also issues related to terminology. Butterworth and Reigosa indicate that the diversity of terminology makes it difficult to identify children with MLD or, as the authors have termed it, *dyscalculia*. Jordan prefers to use the word *difficulty* rather than *disability*, which allows a higher cutoff score to define her sample. Thus, these definition gaps create a broad band for why individuals who perform poorly in math might have cognitive abilities that match those of individuals with RD.

A second difficulty in determining whether the cognitive processing of children with MLD is distinct from those with RD is that in many of these comparison studies I find that the classification procedures are not that distinct (orthogonal) from the comparison measure. For example, MLD and RD (and average achievers) are compared on computation and word problem solving measures when the classification measures of MLD (e.g., standardized tests) include similar mathematical operations. Thus, it is not surprising that many of the children with MLD are characterized as having primary impairments in calculation.

Third, different conclusions about primary mechanisms underlying MLD emerge because of sampling. For example, comparing cognitive development in children with neuropsychological findings in adults may lead to different conclusions. The majority of the authors refer to research suggesting that various kinds of cognitive deficits in children may reflect various forms of impairment related to neural structures. However, it is important to note that the majority of cognitive neuroscience research work on MLD has included adult rather than child samples. Certainly, even a casual review of the literature shows that MLD has been associated with brain structures, such as the left basal ganglia, thalamus, and the left parieto-occipito-temporal areas (e.g., Dehaene & Cohen, 1997). Damage to these regions may be associated with difficulties in accessing number facts. However, Butterworth and Reigosa (Chapter 4) place emphasis on some neurological evidence that the ability to understand numbers is dissociable from language (Cohen, Dehaene, Cochon, Lehericy, & Naccache, 2000) and semantic memory (Cappeletti, Butterworth, & Kopelman, 2001). When compared with the other authors who emphasize typical cognitive development (e.g., Geary et al., Chapter 5; Hecht et al., Chapter 7), however, we get a different picture. For example, based on the neurological evidence, both Butterworth and Crespo (Chapter 4) and Jordan (Chapter 6) suggest that MLD can be dissociated from language (e.g., semantic or phonological memory), whereas from the developmental literature, Geary and colleagues and Hecht and colleagues see a connection.

From a developmental perspective, Geary and colleagues and Jordan have found that procedural knowledge in children with MLD does improve over time. Nevertheless, the difficulty such children have with retrieving basic arithmetic facts from long-term memory does *not* improve over time. Geary and colleagues (Chapter 5) indicate that the mechanisms underlying this problem have been related to poor WM, either associated with the phonological system or the executive system, such as the inability to inhibit irrelevant information. In Chapter 6, Jordan indicates that the mechanisms that may underlie MLD are related to impairments in fact retrieval, and by extension, calculation and fluency. In contrast, Hecht and colleagues (Chapter 7) focus on the conceptual knowledge of children with MLD. They find that conceptual understanding about fractions is a consistent and important source of variability in fraction estimation, word problem solving, and fraction computation in children with MLD. In contrast, Butterworth and Reigosa suggest that the common assumption that poor memory for arithmetic facts is an underlying factor of MLD is incorrect. They put forward a domain-specific account of developmental dyscalculia based on evidence of slower and less efficient recognition of numerosities.

Because there is no consensus on subtypes of MLD, it is difficult to sort outcomes related to cognitive measures, and authors fail to delineate children with MLD that reflect a certain subtype. Not unlike the point made above, some of the diversity in findings and interpretations may be related to various subtypes of MLD under study. Butterworth and Reigosa indicate that there are different subtypes of MLD. Studies that include such subtypes may confound our general conclusions about the primary cognitive characteristics of MLD.

Fourth and finally, the components of memory that underlie MLD are unclear. Although the majority of studies cited in the aforementioned chapters suggest that children with MLD have memory impairments related to the accessing of number facts, the components related to these impairments are still under investigation. Some consensus can be found across the chapters that arithmetic facts in children with MLD are not retrieved quickly and/or accurately. To date, theories of the representation of arithmetic facts in long-term memory (e.g., distribution of associations model; Siegler & Shrager, 1984) indicate that performance on simple arithmetic depends on retrieval from long-term memory. The strength with which associations are stored, and hence, the probability of retrieving them correctly, depends in part on experience, with associations being formed each time an arithmetic problem is encountered regardless of whether the association is correct. Thus, the ability to utilize memory resources to temporarily store numbers when attempting to reach an answer is of significant importance in learning arithmetic. Poor recall of arithmetic facts, of course, leads to difficulties in executing calculation procedures and immature problem-solving strategies. The majority of studies cited in Chapter 5 (Geary and colleagues) suggest that children with MLD do not show the shift from direct counting procedures to a memory-based production of the solution. That is, these children do not remember that certain combinations of new numbers yield a particular result and have difficulty accessing facts from long-term memory (LTM), and therefore they have difficulty engaging in labor-intensive calculations. The research by Butterworth and Reigosa (Chapter 4) challenges many of these assumptions and suggests that the role of memory has been overstated.

PUTTING IT ALL TOGETHER

In summary, it is evident across these four chapters that there is a great deal of diversity in how the samples are defined, as well as in possible underlying problems of MLD. So this question emerges, given the diversity among the chapters: What are the primary cognitive impairments that underlie performance in children with MLD? I offer no simple answer to this question. However, in order to make some progress toward an answer, we (Swanson & Jerman, 2006) recently completed a quantitative synthesis of some of the published literature, comparing the cognitive functioning of children with MLD with that of 1) children who are typically achieving, 2) children with reading disabilities (RD), and 3) children with comorbid disabilities (MLD + RD). Before I discuss the results, it should be noted that our synthesis has its limitations (see Swanson & Jerman, 2006, for details on the article selection criteria). Two are most apparent. First and foremost, studies that either failed to report IQ scores or included children with below average IQ scores were deleted from our final selection. Thus, in line with the comments of Butterworth and Reigosa, we cannot address issues of the independence of IQ score (e.g., high versus low IQ score) from MLD. However, it was our assumption that studies that reported average IQ scores allowed us to focus on children whose general mental ability was not impaired. Second, in contrast to Jordan and others, we were unable to find clear-cut differences on cognitive measures between children with arithmetic and reading difficulties. This may be because (as stated earlier) studies that have examined MLD have used lenient selection criteria for classifying children as having a specific arithmetic impairment, and because in some cases poor arithmetic skills have been accompanied by relatively low reading skills. Therefore, it was difficult to determine whether results attributed to MLD are in fact due to arithmetic difficulties or whether they are outcomes related to generally poor academic skills that share the same process incorporating both reading and math skills.

In general, our most important finding was that the magnitude of effect sizes (ES) in overall cognitive functioning between MLD and average achievers was related primarily to verbal WM impairments when the effects of all other variables (e.g., age, IQ score, reading level, other cognitive domain categories) were partialed out. That is, IQ score and severity of math differences played little role in the outcomes related to the ESs of the cognitive variables. In general, our results are in line with the chapter by Geary and colleagues suggesting that MLD can be partly attributed to WM impairments.

Based on the four chapters reviewed here, along with our own meta-analysis of the literature, what can be concluded about the cognitive impairments that underlie MLD? Several possibilities are considered. First, I address the issue of whether verbal (semantic and/or phonological) memory impairments underlie MLD. Jordan's as well Butterworth and Reigosa's chapters suggest that Geary has overstated the importance of these memory processes. As indicated earlier, Landerl and colleagues (2004) have challenged the underlying assumptions that children with MLD have semantic memory impairments. These researchers argued that semantic memory has been confounded with numerical processing and that there is little evidence of nonnumerical semantic impairments in children with MLD. They also argued that semantic memory for numbers is mediated by a system different from a general memory system and that number knowledge is distinct from semantic memory. We found that when variables related to various classification measures and comparison measures (e.g., naming speed and problem solving) were partialed from the analysis, distinct processes related to verbal WM were related to the magnitude of the ESs. This suggests that impairments in a verbal memory system do play an important role. Whether this verbal memory system draws primarily from a phonological (or semantic) storage system is difficult to disentangle. Given that short-term memory (STM) taps a phonological system, and minimal group ES differences between children with MLD and average achievers emerged on word STM and digit STM, a system that involves processes other than phonological memory (e.g., executive processing of verbal material) is implicated.

Second, processes that underlie MLD can clearly be separated from processes that underlie RD. Based on the work of Jordan, we expected to see a clear differentiation between MLD and a comorbid group (MLD + RD) on measures of verbal problem solving. Jordan stated that verbal ability compensates for performance on problem-solving measures when compared to children with comorbid disabilities. We did not find this to be the case in our meta-analysis. In fact, the mean ES between children with MLD and children with MLD + RD was .13, and between children with MLD and children with RD only the mean ES was .10 on verbal problem solving. Our results suggest that children with RD and MLD were differentiated only on measures of naming speed and visuospatial WM. However, the magnitudes of these ESs were small.

Of course, the question emerges as to whether weak support for the notion that distinct processes separate children with MLD from those with RD means that both groups share a common set of mental resources. Some studies have documented that children with MLD perform poorly on very complex math tasks such as word problems, and that this is not necessarily due just to a numerical impairment but to both phonological and executive processing impairments (Swanson & Sachse-Lee, 2001). Thus, one could argue that the similarities between children with MLD and those with RD become much more reliable with greater manipulations of phonological information (a position consistent with Hecht et al., 2001). Phonological STM is believed to be composed of rehearsal components and phonological skills that are deficient in children with MLD and in children with RD. In our meta-analysis, we found that these two groups could *not* be differentiated on measures attributed to phonological memory (STM for digits and words). That is, the ESs between these two groups was .16 for STM-words and .03 for STM-digits. A further difficulty with the phonological explanation is that we found an advantage for RD in terms of naming speed, a measure assumed to tap phonological processing. Thus, although we do not discount the fact that RD and MLD children share similar impairments in phonological processing, some disadvantages emerged for children with MLD in memory areas not attributable to phonological skills (i.e., in visuospatial WM). We found a significant correlation between ESs related to math and reading on measures of verbal WM. Thus, we would argue that if a common processing impairment exists between these two groups, it is related to executive processes.

Focusing on variables independent of the classification variable, Landerl and colleagues (2004) compared children of different subtypes and found that those with MLD were considered typical on several tasks involving phonological STM, on accessing nonverbal information, and also on language and psychomotor abilities. They concluded that children with MLD were best defined in terms of impairments in processing numerical information. They also found that children with RD performed slightly similar to children in control groups on numerical processing tasks. Both children with MLD and those with RD were slower than controls in reciting number sequences, although unlike children with MLD, the number-naming trend in children with RD disappeared once general ability was controlled for. Although several studies (e.g., Landerl et al., 2004) have found that children with MLD differ more on measures that include numerical information than on other measures, we found in our meta-analysis that these tasks were comparable between the groups (e.g., ES for STM-numbers was .03). No doubt our findings did not tap all of the basics of numerical concepts, especially numerosity (i.e., dot counting, number comparison, and subitizing).

Finally, WM impairments may underlie MLD. Because verbal and visuospatial WM tasks were impaired in children with MLD as compared with average achievers, it appears that their memory impairments may operate outside a verbal system. This finding differs from other studies suggesting that WM impairments in children with MLD are domain specific. For example, Siegel and Ryan (1989) found that though children with MLD perform poorly on WM tests related to counting and remembering digits, they do not exhibit difficulties on nonnumerical WM tasks. A study by McClean and Hitch (1999) also suggested that children with MLD do not have general WM impairments but do have specific problems with numerical information. In contrast, Koontz and Berch (1996) tested children with and without MLD on digit and letter span tasks. They found that the children with MLD performed below average on both types of tasks, indicating a general WM difficulty. In contrast to both sets of findings just described, Temple and Sherwood (2002) found no difference between groups on any of the measures for forward and backward digit span, nor was there any correlation between memory and arithmetic ability. The review by Landerl and colleagues suggests that no convincing evidence exists that WM is a causal feature of math disabilities. Nevertheless, our results showed support for at least a verbal WM impairment when the influence of age, IQ score, and reading ability and related domain categories (e.g., STM-number information, naming speed) are partialed out. No doubt this conjecture will have to be tested in subsequent studies.

SUMMARY

In general, the chapters by Butterworth and Reigosa; Geary and colleagues; Jordan; and Hecht and colleagues reflect some of the best research on the topic of MLD and cognition. All of the chapters call for the accurate identification of children with MLD and note that there are clear confounds in the assessment of children with MLD. These confounds have resulted in part from the attribution of difficulties in math and reading acquisition to the same cognitive processes (i.e., phonological processes). In addition, the criterion for determining MLD has fluctuated from the 45th to the 8th percentile. In practice, these confounds have led to an inability to isolate the cognitive variables that underlie MLD. I do note some consensus, however, that children with MLD have difficulty in accurately and/or efficiently accessing numerical information such as math facts. Clearly, all four chapters suggest that identifying the cognitive as well as neural mechanisms underlying math disorders is only just emerging. As I have found, and as indicated by the authors of these chapters, the construct of MLD continues to vary tremendously across studies. There are different theoretical points represented, and the criteria for MLD qualification are not stable across studies. Thus, I would characterize research in the area of MLD as in the early developmental stages, and as such I would expect some disagreement regarding the role that certain processes play in MLD.

REFERENCES

Badian, N.A. (1983). Arithmetic and nonverbal learning. In H.R. Myklebust (Ed.), *Progress in learning disabilities* (Vol. 5, pp. 235–264). New York: Grune and Stratton.

Cappeletti, M., Butterworth, B., & Kopelman, M.D. (2001). Spared numerical abilities in a case of semantic dementia. *Neuropsychologia, 39*, 1224–1239.

Cohen, L., Dehaene, S., Cochon, F., Lehericy, S., & Naccache, L. (2000). Language and calculation within the parietal lobe: A cognitive, anatomical and fMRI study. *Neuropsychologia, 38*, 1426–1440.

Dehaene, S., & Cohen, L. (1997). Cerebral pathways for calculation: Double disassociation between rote verbal and quantitative knowledge of arithmetic. *Cortex, 33*, 2219–2250.

Geary, D.C. (1993). Mathematical disabilities: Cognitive, neuropsychological and genetic components. *Psychological Bulletin, 114*, 345–362.

Geary, D.C., Hamson, C.O., & Hoard, M.K. (2000). Numerical and arithmetical cognition: A longitudinal study of process and concept deficits in children with learning disability. *Journal of Experimental Child Psychology, 77*, 236–263.

Girelli, L., Lucangeli, D., & Butterworth, B. (2000). The development of automaticity in accessing number magnitude. *Journal of Experimental Child Psychology, 76*, 104–122.

Gross-Tsur, V., Manor, O., & Shalev, R.S. (1996). Developmental dyscalculia: Prevalence and demographic features. *Developmental Medicine and Child Neurology, 38*, 25–33.

Hecht, S.A., Close, L., & Santisi, M. (2003). Sources of individual differences in fraction skills. *Journal of Experimental Child Psychology, 86*, 277–302.

Hecht, S.A., Torgesen, J.K., Wagner, R., & Rashotte, C. (2001). The relationship between phonological processing abilities and emerging individual differences in mathematical computation skills: A longitudinal study of second to fifth grades. *Journal of Experimental Child Psychology, 79*, 192–227.

Koontz, K.L., & Berch, D.B. (1996). Identifying simple numerical stimuli: Processing inefficiencies exhibited by arithmetic learning disabled children. *Mathematical Cognition, 2*, 1–23.

Landerl, K., Bevan, A., & Butterworth, B. (2004). Developmental dyscalculia and basic numerical capacities: A study of 8–9 year old students. *Cognition, 93*, 99–125.

McLean, J.F., & Hitch, G.J. (1999). Working memory impairments in children with specific arithmetical difficulties. *Journal of Experimental Child Psychology, 74,* 240–260.

Siegel, L.S., & Ryan, E.B. (1989). The development of working memory in normally achieving and subtypes of learning disabled children. *Child Development, 60,* 973–980.

Siegler, R.S., & Shrager, J. (1984). Strategy choice in addition and subtraction: How do children know what to do? In C. Sophian (Ed.), *Origins of cognitive skill* (pp. 229–293). Mahwah, NJ: Lawrence Erlbaum Associates.

Swanson, H.L., & Jerman, O. (2006). Math disabilities: A selective meta-analysis of the literature. *Review of Educational Research, 76,* 249–274.

Swanson, H.L., & Sachse-Lee, C. (2001). Mathematical problem solving and working memory in children with learning disabilities: Both executive and phonological processes are important. *Journal of Experimental Child Psychology, 79,* 294–321.

Temple, C., & Sherwood, S. (2002). Representation and retrieval of arithmetical facts: Developmental difficulties. *Quarterly Journal of Experimental Psychology, 55A,* 733–752.

Thurstone, L.L. (1938). *Primary mental abilities Psychometric Monographs No. 1.*

Part II

Section III

Neuropsychological Factors

"We used to think that if we knew one, we knew two, because one and one are two. We are finding that we must learn a great deal more about 'and.'"
— N. Rose

I f impairments in the cognitive mechanisms described in Section II do in
fact underlie mathematical learning disabilities (MLD), then specific aspects of brain function or dysfunction must be related to how those processes are executed. Therefore, a more comprehensive understanding of
these cognitive mechanisms can be achieved through *neuropsychological*
studies of MLD, which are designed to identify the brain *functions* associated with cognitive processes linked to MLD. Specifically, the neuropsychological studies discussed in Section III provide an in-depth assessment of how cognitive mechanisms such as working memory, retrieval
skills, and visuospatial skills are associated with MLD.

In Chapter 8, Donlan's approach to neuropsychological studies of
MLD is to study a disorder for which the role of brain function is quite well
understood: specific language impairment (SLI). He demonstrates that children with SLI who exhibit deficits in the comprehension, production, or use
of language also display deficits in select aspects of mathematics, such as
calculation procedures and understanding number words. Donlan explains
that understanding the links between language and mathematical impairments can enhance our understanding of one model of MLD. That is, not all
children with MLD have language impairments, and not all children with
SLI have MLD; yet recognizing the association between these two disorders
allows researchers to expose one neuropsychological pathway to MLD.

In Chapter 9, Mazzocco, Murphy, and McCloskey adopt a different
neuropsychological approach to understanding pathways to MLD. Their
research methodology involves studying specific populations of children
whose known genetic disorders lead to deficits in the cognitive mechanisms that are proposed to underlie MLD, such as working memory, attention, or retrieval skills. For example, working memory deficits are commonly reported for children with fragile X syndrome, whereas children with
Turner syndrome are reported to have inefficient processing speed and retrieval skills. Mazzocco and colleagues hypothesize that individuals with
these two common but distinctly different disorders will exhibit dissimilar
manifestations of MLD, because for each group, MLD characteristics will
conform to the differences in brain function corresponding to each population's known associated cognitive deficits. Similarly, in Chapter 10, Barnes,
Fletcher, and Ewing-Cobbs adopt this approach to study children with
known aberrant brain development associated with spina bifida. By addressing the extent to which brain development is compromised and the
brain regions that are affected, these authors illustrate the relationship between specificity in brain dysfunction and mathematical disabilities.

Neuropsychological studies of MLD are not limited to research on
genetic disorders. In Chapter 11, Zentall focuses on the arithmetic difficulties experienced by children with attention-deficit/hyperactivity disorder
(ADHD). About one-third of children with ADHD are identified as having

MLD, and about one-fourth of children with MLD are also diagnosed as having ADHD. As we strive to understand how brain function underlies MLD, it is important to distinguish whether MLD is a direct or indirect consequence of other disorders that can affect learning more generally, such as ADHD. Toward this end, Zentall addresses why MLD in children with ADHD is not merely a symptom of ADHD.

The development of neuropsychological function is of primary interest in Chapters 8 through 11, wherein the manifestation of MLD is examined in the context of disorders that present in childhood. In Chapter 12, Zamarian, López-Rolón, and Delazer review studies of individuals whose initially intact mathematical abilities are interrupted by brain injury. They illustrate why examining the nature of impaired performance in adults with brain lesions allows neuropsychologists to gain important information about the cognitive architecture of mathematical thinking. Concomitantly, the study of individuals who experience traumatic brain injury during childhood informs us of the developmental aspects of brain function associated with mathematics (see Chapter 10 for a review of research in this area).

Considered together, the chapters in this section demonstrate how different pathways can lead to MLD and sometimes to different manifestations of MLD. In a commentary on these chapters, Bull addresses the notion that these manifestations may represent MLD subtypes, each of which may be based on associations between MLD and visual-spatial, working memory, or language-based skills. Although Bull focuses on the cognitive complexity of each of these three constructs, she also underscores that the interplay across domains must be considered in striving to understand the development of mathematical cognition during childhood.

REFERENCE

Rose, N. (1988). *Mathematical maxims and minims.* Raleigh, NC: Rome Press Inc.

Chapter 8

Mathematical Development in Children with Specific Language Impairments

Chris Donlan

+ +

Approximately 7% of 5- to 6-year-old children have specific language impairments (SLIs); that is, they have significant impairments in one or more areas of language despite scoring within or above the average range on tests of nonverbal ability (Bishop, 1997; Tomblin et al., 1997). The incidence of SLI in school-age children is high, and much research effort has been devoted to identifying the causal mechanisms of linguistic impairments. This research is particularly relevant to understanding problems with phonological memory (i.e., the storage and representation of speech sounds) and grammar (i.e., use of sentence structure and word endings to convey meaning) (Bishop, Adams, & Norbury, 2006; SLI consortium, 2004).

Because the label of SLI implies that children identified with it would only experience problems specific to language, one might reasonably expect mathematics to be an area of strength for these children. Consequently, it may seem surprising that children with SLI exhibit extremely poor mathematical attainments (Aram & Nation, 1980; Snowling, Adams, Bishop, & Stothard, 2001). The view that mathematical cognition is broadly independent of language is current and widespread (Gelman & Butterworth, 2005; Varley et al., 2005). If this view is correct, then the failure of children with SLI to perform well in math could be explained by obstacles in teaching or assessment rather than by mathematical disability. Under these circumstances, specialized teaching (Donlan & Hutt, 1991; Grauberg, 1998; Hutt,

1986) should allow students to develop their potential in a way that at least approximates the performance of their peers who are typically developing. A complicating factor here, as teachers and speech-language pathologists and therapists well know, is that individuals with SLI show many varied forms of language difficulties, and these frequently co-occur with other types of learning disabilities. Within any large group of children identified as having SLI, there will be individuals who have additional difficulties in key areas of development, such as motor coordination (Hill, 2001), visuo-spatial processing (Cowan, Donlan, Newton, & Lloyd, 2005), or attentional systems (Tirosh & Cohen, 1998).

According to Landerl, Bevan, and Butterworth (2004), it is the co-occurrence or comorbidity of developmental disorders that explains the commonly found association between reading difficulties and mathematical difficulties (Jordan, Hanich, & Kaplan, 2003). Landerl and colleagues studied 8- and 9-year-old children with specific impairments in reading or arithmetic and children with impairments in both areas. Similar patterns of broad-ranging, substantial impairments in basic number processing were found in the arithmetic-only and dual impairment groups but not in the reading-only group. These findings suggest that basic number processing impairments underlie arithmetic impairments and, of import, that reading impairments do not substantially influence number processing. The close relation between developmental disorders of reading and language (Bishop & Snowling, 2004) supports the extended interpretation that language and number are developmentally separable. Though acknowledging that the phonological aspects of some tasks (number naming and number sequence production) may have affected the performance of their group with reading impairments, Landerl and colleagues (2004) argued that basic number representation (as indicated, for example, by numerical magnitude comparison skills) was not compromised.

Thus, our task of examining the nature of mathematical development in children with SLI is a demanding one. We need to distinguish, if possible, the results of primary impairments (e.g., limited memory capacity) from those of secondary impairments (e.g., limited educational access). We also need to bear in mind the possibility that comorbid conditions may appear to be unitary, and therefore we must attempt to distinguish "pure" effects of SLI from the results of more complex causation.

Research into the nature of SLI is starting to unravel some of these issues. We know, for example, that the characteristic profile of language-specific impairment may persist into midlife (Clegg, Hollis, Mawhood, & Rutter, 2005). More boys than girls are affected, and genetic factors are known to be significant in causation. Twin studies (Bishop, 2002; Bishop et al., 2006) have consistently demonstrated high heritability for SLI. These studies show that impairments in phonological memory, as indicated by scores on a test of nonword repetition (Gathercole & Baddeley, 1996), are strong indicators of genetically transmitted language impairments. Other findings have identified further significant and independent heritability via scores on a test of grammatical morphology (English past-tense production) (Bishop et al., 2006). One interpretation of these findings is to view language as a complex process involving multiple, specialized systems (Hauser, Chomsky, & Fitch, 2002). The phonological memory system plays a key developmental role in the storage of speech-based information. The grammatical computation system supports developing knowledge and use of language structure. These and other systems must necessarily interact in development, but there may be independence among the genetic mechanisms on which they are based. According to Bishop and colleagues (2006), the patterns of genetic transmission underlying SLI are consistent with the view that language development draws on multiple specialized systems that are subject to independent genetic variability. This specialized systems framework provides a useful model for examining the general relation between language and mathematics and reviewing research on mathematical development in children with SLI.

LANGUAGE AND MATHEMATICAL COGNITION

This section examines evidence on the relation between language and mathematical thought from a range of research perspectives. The focus is on three key issues:

1. *Neural specialization:* A particular specialized systems framework may apply to mathematical cognition, entailing the interaction of linguistic and visuospatial systems. If such specialization operates in development, we may expect children with SLI to show differential performance across different areas of mathematical development.

2. *Learning of the sequence of number words:* This is a key element in mathematical development. The learning process is gradual and complex, involving the coordination of items within a structure of correspondences between speech sounds and numerical relations (e.g., "two, three, four, five" correspond to "twenty, thirty, forty, fifty," respectively). Such a process is likely to cause difficulties for children with SLI.

3. *Linguistic cues:* The grammatical systems within which quantifiers such as *some, a, one, two,* and so forth operate in combination with pluralization may facilitate the early development of number meanings. Children with SLI are likely to have difficulty acquiring these early grammatical relations. The influence of language on the later development of arithmetic concepts remains largely unstudied.

Evidence from Neuroscience

Neuroscientific research is examined in detail elsewhere in this book (see Chapter 13). However, of particular interest for this chapter is Dehaene's (1997) proposal that linguistic and visuospatial systems interact in the processing of numerical information. Supportive evidence includes a series of behavioral studies of bilingual adults (Spelke & Tsvikin, 2001) indicating the involvement of these two systems in the performance of arithmetic. Arithmetic training studies were given in one of the participants' languages based on problems such as "86 + 26 = 112 or 102?" Subsequent testing was carried out on similar problems, either in the same language as the training or in the nontrained language, and requiring either exact answers or merely approximate answers. Where exact answers were required, performance was better when testing used the same language as training. Where approximate answers were required, language had no effect on performance. Thus, it seems that the cognitive systems supporting arithmetic may be differentially language dependent. In line with this account, evidence from brain-imaging studies (Dehaene, Spelke, Pinel, Stanescu, & Tsivkin, 1999) identified increased activation in speech-related areas of the brain during performance of exact arithmetic. Increased activation in brain areas related to visuospatial processing was found during performance of approximate arithmetic.

Although these are important, not all researchers agree with the results. Case studies by van Harskamp, Rudge, and Cipolotti (2002) and Varley, Klessinger, Romanowski, and Siegal (2005) demonstrated that exact calculation skills can be retained despite extensive damage to language-related brain areas. Varley and colleagues (2005) also challenged the notion that the complex underlying structures of language and mathematics may be processed by common cognitive systems (Hauser et al., 2002). They studied three patients whose grammatical skills were severely impaired following brain damage. These individuals were able to generate solutions to complex equations, despite severe problems in comprehending reversible sentences.

To date, the main body of neuroscientific evidence concerning language and mathematical cognition is based on the mature adult brain. And as shown, evidence exists for neural specialization of linguistic and visuospatial systems that interact in mathematical cognition. If such specialization operates in development, children with SLI would be expected to show differential performance across different areas of mathematical development.

Cross-Cultural Studies

A fresh perspective on the relation between language and number is offered by studies of number processing in Amazonian cultures whose languages lack number words. Gordon (2004) studied the Piraha tribe, whose members have words for the concepts of *one, two,* and *many.* Across a range of concrete matching tasks (set sizes 1 to 10), accuracy fell dramatically for matching set sizes of greater than 3, although responses approximated target values across the range 1–9. Pica, Lemner, Izard, and Dehaene (2005) studied the Munduruku tribe, who have words for numbers from one through five, although numbers above two are used to refer to a range of quantities rather than a precise number. There was no evidence of use of numerals in a counting sequence. Approximate addition and comparison of large numbers of dots was performed identically to French controls. The findings of Gordon and Pica and colleagues are consistent with the view that the use of a number-word sequence in counting provides the necessary basis for exact number processing, whereas the system serving approximate number processing is independent of language.

The developmental role of the number-word sequence has been the focus of cross-linguistic studies exploring variation in the morphology of counting words, especially the differences between English (and some other European languages, such as French and Swedish) and East Asian languages (e.g., Chinese, Korean, Japanese). The variation in number words from 10 to 20 is especially interesting. English has a variety of word forms (e.g., eleven, twelve, thirteen, fourteen). Chinese is much more systematic (e.g., ten-one, ten-two, ten-three). Furthermore, the relation between the Chinese words and Hindu-Arabic notation is clear (ten-one/11, ten-two/12, ten-three/13), whereas the relation between the English words and Hindu-Arabic notation is obscure. Miura and colleagues (Miura, 1987; Miura & Okamoto, 2003) argued that children's understanding of the base-10 system of notation is enhanced by the transparent correspondence between East Asian number-word sequences and the Hindu-Arabic numeral system. In an authoritative review, Miller, Kelly, and Zhou (2005) demonstrated the clear advantage enjoyed by children in China over U.S. children in learning to produce the number-word sequence, especially the numbers in the teens; however, these authors also acknowledged the important role of social factors in the development of conceptual understanding (Towse & Saxton, 1998).

The two sets of evidence outlined here provide complementary support for the notion that culturally determined linguistic factors, especially the spoken number words, are crucially important for the development of number processing. Further support for this position comes from studies of Brazilian "street" children reported by Nunes, Schliemann, and Carraher (1993). These children had received little schooling, but were well practiced in practical calculation through experiences such as working in bars. Although they were able to calculate successfully in practical contexts, they were not able to perform formal written arithmetic. The children's superior performance in street math over math taught in school is explained, at least in part, by the use of oral versus written systems in street math. In one of the studies carried out by this team, when using spoken numbers, children were able to successfully compute problems for which they were unable to produce the corresponding Hindu-Arabic symbols.

The Role of Number Words in Mathematical Development

Intense research effort is being directed toward uncovering the ontogeny of mathematical skills and knowledge. Strong evidence points to the fact that infants in the first year of life are sensitive to exact numerosity in small arrays (e.g., Feigenson & Carey, 2005; Wynn, 1992) and to approximate numerosity in large arrays (e.g., Brannon, Abbott, & Lutz, 2004; Xu & Spelke, 2000), but it is also clear that in these early stages of development, a complex relation exists between representation of numerosity and representation of associated nonnumeric variables, such as cumulative surface area (Brannon et al., 2004; Clearfield & Mix, 2001). The pathways from early numerosity awareness to symbolic number processing are the subject of debate. A detailed proposal is presented by Carey (2004) in which linguistic factors play a crucial *bootstrapping* role; that is, they provide a framework that is central to the developmental process. Carey noted the gradual nature of acquisition of the initial items in the number-word sequence and suggested that children learn to identify sets of one, two, or three objects partly through their experience with number-relevant language, such as plural marking (e.g., "cars," houses") or use of the quantifiers *some* or *a* (Hodent, Bryant, & Houde, 2005). Subsequently, children's knowledge of the number-word sequence (initially acquired as a simple string of words without numerical meaning but with ordinal properties) is integrated with their representations of small sets of items. This combination provides the basis for a comprehensive system for symbolic representation of number.

An important examination of the logical basis of the bootstrapping principle is presented by Rips, Asmuth, and Bloomfield (in press). According to Carey (2004), knowledge of the number-word sequence allows the learner to move from early representations of small numerosities to a grasp of the ordinal properties of natural numbers. The critical argument made by Rips and colleagues is that a sequence of words per se is insufficient to support such conceptual development. Using an intriguing hypothetical example, Rips and colleagues demonstrated that knowledge of a limited sequence of words (which is all that is available to the young learner) does not entail understanding of the ordinal principle. Specifically, once the known sequence is exhausted, there is no "next," no implicit knowledge of the successor principle that defines the natural numbers. Only at a much later stage, dubbed by Rips and colleagues as *advanced counting*, is the learner able to construct the next term from any given point in the sequence, based on the correspondence between the structure of the number-word sequence and the properties of natural numbers.

If the bootstrapping account is insufficient to explain the early emergence of number concepts, what other resources are available to the learner? Suggestive findings from Brannon and van der Walle (2001) indicated that by 11 months old, infants may be able to detect ordinal relations between successive arrays of increasing or decreasing numerosities; if this is so, then the origins of the ordinal principle may lie not in the number-word sequence but in some earlier emerging nonverbal system. Sarnecka and Gelman (2004) argued that preschoolers show awareness of the general relation between number words and set size before they have mastered the mapping of specific number words to specific numerosities, indicating that number-sequence acquisition may build on preexisting ordinal knowledge.

Whatever its ontological basis, children's understanding of the principles underlying the use of the number sequence in object counting (Gelman & Gallistel, 1978) is influential in the development of formal mathematical skills. Geary, Hoard, Byrd-Craven, and DeSoto (2004) tested 7-year-olds (including a subgroup with mathematical disabilities [MD]) on a task that required monitoring of object counting. Variation in monitoring skills accounted for impairments in the development of arithmetic strategy found in the MLD group.

Lipton and Spelke's (2006) research highlighted the gradual and complex developmental process entailed in number-sequence learning in 5-year-olds. These researchers showed that, on the one hand, in a concrete context (numbers of objects in a jar), 5-year-olds understand the cardinal properties associated with specific number words, even when the words lie beyond a child's productive count range. On the other hand, knowledge of the number-word sequence is strongly associated with the ability to link specific number words to approximate numerosities. Children who failed to produce accurate sequences beyond 60 were also unable to map number words beyond 60 to numerically matching arrays of shapes, although they were successful in the same task with numbers within their count range. These findings suggest an important difference in the developmental processes supporting the following: 1) understanding the logic of number words and 2) mapping number words to approximate numerosities. The former is established when knowledge of number sequence is limited and can be applied to numbers outside of the productive range; the latter appears to be constrained within the productive list.

Language and School-Age Mathematics

Given the evidence reviewed so far, it is surprising that linguistic factors have received relatively little attention in research into the cognitive systems supporting conventional school mathematics. However, an important theoretical proposal by Huttenlocher and colleagues factors heavily into this issue. Huttenlocher, Jordan, and Levine (1994) proposed that, between the ages of 2 and 3, a general symbolic system develops through which the child is able to produce mental models representing the addition and subtraction of concrete objects (i.e., nonverbal calculation). Conventional verbal representations of such events (i.e., story problems) are only accessible at a later stage and are subject to variation according to social class, whereas nonverbal arithmetic is robust across social class (Jordan, Huttenlocher, & Levine, 1992). The proposal, then, is that general (i.e., nonspecialized) nonverbal systems provide the conceptual basis on which conventional (i.e., taught) verbal systems of arithmetic operate.

Jordan and colleagues went on to study school-age children with mathematical difficulties (MD), including groups with co-occurring reading difficulty (MD/RD). These studies are described in detail elsewhere in this book (see Chapter 6). Of importance for this chapter are the possible links among language, reading, and mathematical learning. Given the strength of evidence attributing children's reading difficulties to impairments in phonological processing (Snowling, 2000), and given the previously cited neuroscientific evidence concerning the involvement of linguistic systems in arithmetic, it might be plausible to propose that co-occurring difficulties in reading and math are traceable to common underlying impairments in phonological processing. Geary (1993) suggested that impoverished representation of phonological information in long-term memory may provide a common basis for poor word and arithmetic fact retrieval. However, Jordan and colleagues (2003) found no evidence to support such a view. Fact retrieval for addition and subtraction was similar in their MD and MD/RD groups and unimpaired in the RD only group.

Although they rejected the phonological deficit hypothesis, Jordan and colleagues (2003) drew attention to another important possible link between language and mathematical development based on the finding that their MD/RD group was less adept at solving story problems and had a poorer understanding of calculation principles than the MD-only group. Language comprehension, known to be associated with reading levels, is a necessary component of story problem solving and may also influence conceptual understanding of the principles of arithmetic (e.g., the commutative relation that holds within addition, the inverse relation between addition and subtraction). The brief discussion of these issues offered by Jordan and colleagues (2003) raises very important issues concerning the essential nature of arithmetic concepts. The extent to which language influences the development of these concepts is largely unexplored, although it is a central issue in mathematical development (Baroody, 2003; Bryant, 1995; Piaget, 1970). It is at least plausible to suggest that language, the core medium of teaching, should affect mathematical concepts. Relevant to these issues is the growing interest among linguists in the development of systems of quantification, which are central to communication about number and arithmetic (Breheny, Katsos, & Williams, in press; Guerts, 2003; Lidz & Musolino, 2002). The increasing popularity of experimental psycholinguistic studies in this area promises to facilitate collaborative work embracing the wider implications for mathematical development. Such undertakings are still in their infancy.

STUDIES OF CHILDREN WITH SPECIFIC LANGUAGE IMPAIRMENT

Preschoolers with Specific Language Impairment

In a pioneering study, Siegel, Lees, Allan, and Bolton (1981) used nonverbal techniques to compare number and quantity concepts in 26 children with SLI ages 3–5 years with those of a group of children who are typically developing. In the experimental tasks, participants were simply asked to select the correct item and were rewarded for doing so. Each task was composed of 25 stimuli, with a different configuration on each trial. A pass criterion of 9/10 consecutive correct responses was set. On tasks presenting perceptually explicit binary choices within which targets were distinguished on the basis of area (Task 1), number confounded with length (Task 2), and number confounded with density (Task 3), no difference was found between groups in the percentage of children reaching criterion. On three further tasks, however, in which choices were more complex (e.g., matching to sample on the basis of number confounded with length; matching to sample on the basis of number, with arrays randomly spaced), the control group significantly outperformed children with SLI. Siegel and colleagues (1981) proposed that language impairments may inhibit place holding in a sequence and thereby present a fundamental obstacle to number processing.

Fazio's Longitudinal Study

To date, the only longitudinal study of mathematical development has been carried out by Barbara Fazio. She has examined the mathematical progress of children with SLI assessed at ages 5, 7, and 9. Fazio compared 5-year-olds with SLI to children of the same age who were typically developing (age control group), and to younger children who were typically developing whose language skills broadly matched those of the SLI group (language control group). Fazio's sample was drawn from low-income families and may have been subject to the general effects of socioeconomic status (SES) on attainment. At the first time of measurement (1994), Fazio found that most of the 5-year-olds with SLI had severe impairments in the production of the number-word sequence and in object counting accuracy. These procedural impairments, however, were not matched at a conceptual level.

Fazio found that the SLI group showed a relatively strong grasp of counting principles in general and, in particular, of the principle that the final count word indicates the value of the set. This important finding suggested that SLI might impose less severe constraints on conceptual development than on procedural development.

Fazio (1996) followed up her original preschool sample after a 2-year interval. The impairment in production of the number-word sequence among children with SLI was still severe, continuing to match that of the language control group. Across a range of simple arithmetical tasks, the SLI group performed worse than did the students in the age control group but better than students in the language control group. All children tended to use their fingers and count in these tasks, but students in the age controls used the counting-on strategy more often and the counting-all strategy less often than did both other groups. These observations are especially important because the move to counting-on marks significant development in strategy use, one that appears to entail conceptual as well as procedural knowledge (Baroody, 1995; Nunes & Bryant, 1996). Fazio's prediction for the future was not positive. Based on the general theory that persistent impairments in phonological working memory underlie SLI (Bishop, North, & Donlan, 1996; Gathercole & Baddeley, 1996), Fazio suggested that number sequence and arithmetic fact learning may be substantially limited and predicted that these problems would present cumulative obstacles to both procedural and conceptual development.

Fazio's proposal is plausible. Phonological memory impairment is liable to affect vocabulary development in general (Jarrold, Baddeley, Hewes, Leeke, & Phillips, 2004). Insofar as phonological memory impairment affects the storage of serial order information, the processing of number words may be especially vulnerable. It is important to recall that the phonological processing impairments known to be associated with reading difficulty do not necessarily affect mathematical development (Jordan et al., 2003; Landerl et al., 2004). However, it is well established (Geary, 1993; Geary et al., 2004) that variance in counting span (i.e., a measure of concurrent object counting and storage totals) is strongly associated with mathematical development and mathematical difficulties, suggesting the possibility that working memory system(s) specialized for dealing with count-based information may cause mathematical difficulties and may overlap in some cases with constraints on phonological working memory.

Revisiting 10 children in her original SLI sample along with 11 members of the original age- and language-matched controls groups, Fazio (1999) tested participants' ability to perform written two-digit addition and subtraction with regrouping and two-digit multiplication and division under time-restricted and untimed conditions. The SLI group performed more poorly than controls in all tasks, showing particular difficulties in time-restricted conditions. Children with SLI were prone to making miscalcula-tions and were particularly poor in the direct retrieval of arithmetic facts. In all these ways, Fazio's prediction was borne out. However, she also observed that the SLI group had made slow but steady progress in mathe-matics over the 5-year period of observation. Their counting skills, originally severely restricted, now provided the primary means of calculation. In un-timed calculation and fact retrieval, their performance approximated that of the younger control group, which was originally matched for language level but now exceeded the levels of expressive and receptive language of the SLI group. Thus, measures of untimed calculation and arithmetic fact retrieval indicated broadly similar rates of mathematical development in the SLI group and younger controls, although rates of language develop-ment were significantly lower in the SLI group. What remains unclear is the rate of development of arithmetic concepts. Fazio (1999) concentrated on assessing calculation procedures and fact retrieval. The possibility that conceptual development may have developed at a different rate was not explicitly tested.

Pursuing the Specialized Systems Hypothesis

A series of studies by Donlan and colleagues (Donlan, 1998; 2003) was strongly influenced by the specialized systems hypothesis, focusing partic-ularly on the possibility that nonverbal systems supporting specific areas of mathematical development may be relatively unimpaired in children with SLI. Donlan (2003) exploited the nonverbal match-to-sample test format employed by Siegel and colleagues (1981), comparing 20 6-year-olds with SLI with 3 groups composed of typically developing children (4-year-olds, 5-year-olds, and 6-year-olds). The experimental task required participants to match arrays of items on the basis of number. Spatial arrangement of items was manipulated in order to distinguish matches based on numeros-ity from those based on perceptual comparison. The identity of items was also varied in order to provide a stringent test of participants' ability to rep-resent numerosity at an abstract level. Manipulation of set size introduced a further contrast. Low-number arrays containing two to five items were intended to be processed nonverbally. High-number arrays containing six to nine items were likely to require counting. Overall, the children in the SLI group outperformed the 4- and 5-year-olds in the control groups. They performed at a similar level to 6-year-old (same age) controls in the high-number perceptual condition but performed more poorly than 6-year-olds when spatial arrangement and item identity were varied. However, the pat-tern of performance of the SLI group indicated conceptual understanding in advance of younger controls (4- and 5-year-olds), who showed progres-sive decrements in performance across conditions. One interpretation of these findings is that early number concepts may develop at the typical rate in children with SLI but that procedural impairments associated with counting may present a substantial obstacle to further development.

Donlan, Bishop, and Hitch (1998) used a different experimental approach to examine basic concepts of number and quantity, exploiting the seminal work of Moyer and Landauer (1967). In this work the Symbolic Distance Effect (SDE), an inverse relation between stimulus difference and response time was found in the comparison of numerical magnitudes. SDE has been widely replicated (Dehaene, 1997), is present through development (Sekuler & Mierkiewicz, 1977), and is held to indicate that common processes underlie perceptual and symbolic (numerical) judgment (Dehaene, 1997; Moyer & Landauer, 1967). Donlan and colleagues (1998) assessed a group (n = 12) of 7-year-old children with SLI on single-digit magnitude judgments using a restricted number range (1–5) and compared performance on numeric (single digits and dot arrays) and nonnumeric stimuli (houses graded in size and animals graded in real-life size but presented as pictures with size held constant). A younger control group matched for receptive language skills was also tested. The children with SLI, overall, were not more accurate than children in the control groups. However, when the two children with SLI who failed to reach accuracy criterion were excluded from analysis, the SLI group showed faster reaction times than their language-matched peers on numeric as well as nonnumeric comparison tasks. Furthermore, both groups showed significant SDE. The results provided suggestive evidence that children with SLI represent the numerical magnitude as efficiently as they represent perceptual magnitude and that this ability may be unconstrained by language impairments.

Donlan and Gourlay (1999) carried out a more comprehensive study, testing children's ability to judge the relative magnitude of all single-digit pairs of integers and a selected sample of two-digit pairs. Performance on double-digits was taken as an indicator of implicit knowledge of a key concept underlying the place-value principle in Hindu-Arabic notation, namely that the place of nonunit digits in a multidigit numeral systematically modifies the magnitude represented.

In the Donlan and Gourlay (1999) study, 13 8-year-olds with SLI were compared with 13 8-year-olds matched for age and nonverbal IQ (Age Control or AC group) and with 12 younger children matched for language-comprehension level (LC group). Accuracy for single-digit judgments was achieved by 100% of AC children, 92% of the children with SLI, and 69% of LC children. The group latencies showed a clear pattern (SLI = AC < LC) with uniform symbolic distance effects for all groups. At a single-digit level, then, with the exception of one child, number representation in the SLI group appeared to be age-appropriate. The second experiment examined two-digit judgments (range of 10–99). Since the LC group had no formal school experience with two-digit numbers, only the AC and LC groups were tested.

A stringent accuracy criterion (85% correct) was achieved by 61% of children with SLI and 83% of AC children. There was no group effect on response time and no interaction between group and trial type.

Taken together, the studies reported in this section give some support to the view that specialized systems underlie the development of mathematical skills and, in particular, that nonverbal processes play a significant role in the development of number concepts, even when language development is impaired. However, the findings are by no means clear-cut, the sample sizes are small, and none of the studies brings together the range of mathematical tasks needed to explore the specialized systems hypothesis in a systematic way.

Verbal and Nonverbal Numerical Skills of Finnish Children with Specific Language Impairment

All of the studies reviewed previously and most of the literature in the areas of SLI and mathematical development concern English-speaking children. Given the importance of the number-word sequence in mathematical development, it is welcome to be able to consider evidence from language learners exposed to a different system. The Finnish number-word sequence has a structure that may be regarded as intermediate in its systematicity and in the transparency of its relation to the Hindu-Arabic system. Numbers 1–10 are represented by unique lexical items. The numbers 11–19 are represented in a structurally consistent manner, equivalent to "one-teen," "two-teen," and so on. From the number 20 on, as in East Asian languages, expressions equivalent to "two-ten-one," "two-ten-two," and so forth are used. Although the interesting contrast between Finnish and English has yet to be explored in this regard, bear in mind that the contrastive structure of the number-word sequences may have some influence on the process of development.

Koponen, Mononen, Räsänen, and Ahonen (2006) examined a substantial (N = 29) sample of 9- to 11-year-old-children with SLI to explore possible differences between verbal and nonverbal numerical skills. The criteria used to identify children with SLI were broadly similar to those used elsewhere (ICD-10, WHO, 1993) except that 7 of 29 individuals had scores of 80 or below on Raven's Coloured Progressive Matrices (Raven, 1993). Language test scores were indicative of significant expressive vocabulary and sentence comprehension impairments in most of the sample. A distinctive aspect of educational provision for children with SLI in Finland is the start of schooling a year early (at age 6). Despite their age (mean 10:3 years) and longer educational history, children in the SLI group were studying at the educational level of second-grade children (mean age 8:8). Control groups of typically developing children were composed of language-matched preschoolers (mean age 6:7) and groups of first (mean age 7:7), second (mean age 8:8), and third graders (mean age 9:7). The verbal test battery included number-sequence production tasks (including backward counting) and computer-based calculation (simple addition and subtraction) with key press responses. Nonverbal tasks were all administered by computer and included magnitude comparison for multidigit numbers, money-based transcoding requiring matching amounts stated in Hindu-Arabic numerals to collections of mixed units and composite units, and an estimation task requiring children to give numerical values to points between 10 and 1,000 on a vertical scale.

The SLI group outperformed the language controls on composite scores for both verbal and nonverbal numerical tasks (only on number-sequence production did the groups perform at the same level). In comparing children in the SLI group with children in the school-age control groups, no group difference was found in calculation accuracy; however, the response times of children in the SLI group were at a first-grade level and were significantly slower than the response times of children in the second- and third-grade groups. Nonverbal composite scores for children with SLI were at a first-grade level as well and were significantly below those in the second- and third-grade groups. Additional investigations were carried out in order to identify the extent of individual differences in mathematical performance by dividing the participants with SLI into subgroups according to performance levels on verbal (calculation) and nonverbal numerical batteries. Cutoff points were identified below which performance was considered to be impaired. A mean calculation-response time greater than 3 seconds was selected in order to distinguish participants using strategies other than retrieval. The nonverbal cutoff was defined as performance more than one standard deviation (SD) below the mean for second graders in multidigit magnitude comparison. According to these criteria, 12 children with SLI had difficulties in calculation and comparison, 8 had difficulties in calculation only, and the remaining 9 had no difficulties. To investigate possible mechanisms underlying individual differences in mathematical development in children with SLI, comparisons were made of the mean scores of the subgroup with calculation difficulties and the subgroup with comparison difficulties on tests of digit span, sentence comprehension, productive vocabulary, rapid serial naming, and Raven's Coloured Progressive Matrices (Raven, 1993). Only rapid naming reached significance, with the no-difficulty group tending to produce faster responses than the other groups. Supporting evidence for the importance of rapid naming came from high correlations between this measure and performance on addition and subtraction tasks.

The findings of Koponen and colleagues (2006) extend the knowledge in the field in several important ways. They emphasize the extent of individual differences in mathematical development in the SLI population. This issue has been raised before but has never been explored so comprehensively. For the first time, contrasting patterns of performance based on substantial variation in both verbal and nonverbal mathematical skills were revealed. Furthermore, the study invites renewed consideration of the definition of verbal and nonverbal skills. For example, the basis on which calculation (or fact retrieval) is described as a verbal skill is not clear. Children with SLI comprehensively outperformed language-matched controls in addition and subtraction, suggesting that instruction or maturation may be more important than language in accounting for calculation levels, or at least that the language impairments associated with SLI do not present unavoidable obstacles to developing calculation and retrieval skills. It is also important to bear in mind the possibility that number comparison, especially multidigit number comparison, may entail language-related processing. Koponen and colleagues pointed out that longer digit strings may require some sort of syntactic processing in order for children to derive magnitude representations.

Regardless of how these issues may be resolved, it seems clear that most children with SLI in Finland, as in the English-speaking countries in which other studies have been carried out, have significant difficulties with mathematics. An important parameter for comparison with the Finnish study was the educational level of the participants. Education level was estimated by noting the textbook used by each participant at the beginning of the study, and mapping this to the timeframe of the standard curriculum. On this measure, the mean of the SLI group matched that of children 12–22 months younger, whose school experience was 2 or 3 years less than that of the SLI group. Performance on the experimental tasks in the study exceeded predictions based on educational level for 9 of the 29 children in the SLI group, but the majority performed at or below the level predicted by their educational level, frequently showing weaknesses in calculation and comparison skills.

An important finding, in line with previous studies, is that the most severe mathematical impairment observed in the SLI group was in production of the number-word sequence; performance on this measure was at the same level as that of preschool language controls. Collaborative work is needed to establish whether the contrast between English and Finnish number-word sequences is reflected in the learning process of children with SLI, but it is at least clear that this is a persistent area of critical difficulty despite variation in linguistic structure.

The Number Talk Study

The largest and most comprehensive examination of mathematical skills in children with SLI is the Number Talk study, conducted by Donlan and colleagues in the UK (Cowan et al., 2005; Donlan, Cowan, Newton, & Lloyd, in press). The study set out to evaluate the relation between linguistic and cognitive systems and mathematical development in children with SLI. The team recruited a large, representative sample of children with SLI along with age- and language-matched controls. All participants were assessed on linguistic and cognitive skills and on a broad range of mathematical skills and knowledge. About 170 children participated in the study, evenly divided into three groups: SLI (mean age 8:2); controls matched for age, gender, nonverbal ability, and school location (AC); and younger controls (mean age 6:0) matched for language comprehension level, gender, and school location (LC).

The first analysis of the data (Cowan et al., 2005) evaluated group differences and factors influencing performance on a range of number-based skills. As has been repeatedly observed in other studies, the most severe impairment in the SLI group was in production of the number-word sequence, although the group also performed worse than age-matched controls on every other task. Children with SLI performed more poorly on a multidigit magnitude comparison than the AC group but better than the LC group, indicating the possible involvement of nonverbal processes. Where SLI performance approximated the level of the LC group (number-sequence production, basic calculation), language-related constraints may be inferred. The mean instructional level for children with SLI was lower than that for the AC group but exceeded that of the LC group.

Regression techniques were used to evaluate the effects of a range of predictors on variance in each number task. Widespread unique effects of language comprehension level and of nonverbal reasoning were found. Specifically, basic calculation scores showed independent effects of language comprehension, nonverbal reasoning, and working memory. Likewise, number-sequence production showed independent effects of language comprehension, nonverbal reasoning, and working memory, with a further unique contribution from educational level. Transcoding showed exactly the same pattern. Thus, a similar model with independent effects of language, nonverbal reasoning, and working memory, accounts for three key tasks: number-sequence production, transcoding, and basic calculation. Multidigit magnitude comparison, on the other hand, is significantly influenced by nonverbal reasoning and by working memory measures but not by language. The findings of Cowan and colleagues (2005) broadly confirm the findings of previous studies and break new ground in exploring the processes underlying mathematical difficulties in SLI. The widespread influence of language comprehension level, independent of memory span, is notable. The fact that a common model accounts for number-sequence production, transcoding, and basic calculation is intriguing. Magnitude comparison, on the other hand, shows no direct evidence of language levels. This evidence supports a specialized systems account of mathematical development in children with SLI.

A further study based on the Number Talk data (Donlan et al., in press) focuses on two important issues that recur throughout the literature on math and SLI: number-sequence production and conceptual development. The former is repeatedly observed to present the most significant impairment in children with SLI. It is unsurprising that this should be so, given the fact that phonological and grammatical processing impairments are defining problems for this population (Bishop et al., 2006). Learning the English number-word sequence may make demands on both systems, with the possible consequence that poor number-sequence knowledge operates as a core deficit undermining mathematical development in children with SLI. However, considerable evidence (Cowan et al., 2005; Donlan, 2003; Donlan et al., 1998; Donlan & Gourlay, 1999; Fazio, 1994) suggests that development of basic concepts of number and notation are not directly constrained by language impairments. The assessment of conceptual understanding in children with SLI has been somewhat limited. A novel element of the Number Talk study addresses this issue using a new task to assess children's understanding of arithmetic principles. The task entails having children verify addition and subtraction statements containing unfamiliar numerals. Within a role-play scenario, children acted for a "Martian" math teacher whose marking of pupils' homework was interrupted. In this way, understanding of principles or conceptual knowledge might be evaluated independent of procedural skills or impairments.

Donlan and colleagues (in press) compared performance of the Number Talk sample on key areas of basic number processing (number-sequence production, basic calculation, and multidigit magnitude comparison) as well as on the arithmetic principles task described above. The basic number tasks showed group effects as already reported (SLI = LC < AC for number-sequence production and basic calculation; LC < SLI < AC for multidigit magnitude comparison). However, on the test of arithmetic principles, the performance of the SLI group approximated that of the AC group, and the LC group performed significantly worse than each of the other groups. One explanation for these striking findings may lie in the fact that the Martian test of arithmetic principles is maximally symbolic because the "numerals" employed have no specific values. Work by Canobi (2005) supports this explanation. Canobi classified a subset of her sample of 7- to 9-year-olds who were typically developing as symbolic thinkers capable of abstract reasoning about addition and subtraction problems and more likely to demonstrate conceptual understanding in a symbolic rather than a concrete context. A symbolic preference of this sort may operate for children whose ability to manipulate actual numerals is significantly impaired.

It may be the case, then, that difficulty acquiring the spoken-number sequence constitutes a core deficit in SLI, inhibiting other aspects of basic number processing (see Donlan et al., in press, for further evidence). However, it also appears that many children with SLI are as capable as peers who are typically developing of grasping the logical principles underlying simple arithmetic.

CONCLUSIONS

Consistent findings emerging from the studies of children with SLI reviewed in this chapter include significant impairments in production of the number-word sequence and in basic calculation, calculation strategies, and fact retrieval. Impairments in numerical magnitude comparison are less substantial. A pattern whereby conceptual understanding appears to exceed procedural skill has been found in various studies for different tasks, including counting and basic calculation.

Taken together, these findings suggest a pattern of mathematical impairment that may be distinctive in children with SLI, although there are clear overlaps in the pattern found in children with MLD. Problems with calculation and fact retrieval are definitive of MLD (Geary, 1993). Production of the number-word sequence has not been a primary focus of studies of MLD, although there is some evidence of impairments in this area for such children with MLD (Hitch & McAuley, 1991). However, authoritative studies of children with MLD, or MLD (or MD)/RD, have found impairments in knowledge of counting and calculation principles (Geary, Hamson, & Hoard, 2000; Geary et al., 2004, Jordan et al., 2003), areas of apparent strength in children with SLI. Further study is needed to provide unequivocal evidence on this issue.

Individual differences in typical mathematical development are extremely wide-ranging (Dowker, 1998, 2005), but they may be even broader in children with SLI. One explanation for this could be the co-occurrence of SLI and other impairments. Landerl and colleagues (2004) proposed that the etiologies of co-occurring math and reading difficulties may be independent. Might it be the case that separately caused math and language difficulties co-occur in some but not all children with SLI? It is not possible to give a definitive answer to this question while causation remains only partially understood. What is known is that some children with SLI appear to have no difficulty in learning mathematics. Thus, if math difficulty represents comorbidity, then 70% to 80% percent of cases may be comorbid. However, this is only one of numerous possible explanations of the observed phenomenon.

An intriguing possibility is that specialized cognitive systems may interact in the development of both math and language (Bishop et al., in press; Hauser et al., 2002), and that particular areas of mathematical and linguistic development may follow more or less interactive developmental pathways. The possible independence of conceptual development in some children with SLI is especially interesting.

If efforts to uncover the developmental systems underlying mathematical development in children with SLI are to bear fruit, they must be tested through intervention. Very little is known yet about the ways in which instruction affects outcomes in this area. So far, a few studies have attempted to take into account instructional levels in order to clarify the interpretation of findings, but none has examined instruction per se. Urgent work is required to record the ways in which curriculum is differentiated for children with SLI and to measure the specific effects that such specialization might have. Most important, comparative studies are needed of theoretically motivated interventions both to advance understanding in the field and to enhance children's achievements.

REFERENCES

Aram, D.M., & Nation, J.E. (1980). Preschool language disorders and subsequent language and academic difficulties. *Journal of Communication Disorders, 13*, 159–170.

Baroody, A.J. (2003). The development of adaptive expertise and flexibility: The integration of conceptual and procedural knowledge. In A. Baroody & A. Dowker (Eds.), *The development of arithmetical concepts* (pp. 1–35). Mahwah, NJ: Lawrence Erlbaum Associates.

Bishop, D.V.M. (1983). *Test for the reception of grammar.* Manchester, UK: Author.

Bishop, D.V.M. (1997). *Uncommon understanding: Development and disorders of language comprehension in children.* Hove, UK: Psychology Press.

Bishop, D.V.M. (2002). The role of genes in the etiology of specific language impairment. *Journal of Communication Disorders, 35*, 311–328.

Bishop, D.V.M., Adams, C.V., & Norbury, C.F. (2006). Distinct genetic influences on grammar and phonological short-term memory deficits: Evidence from 6-year-old twins. *Genes, Brain and Behavior, 5*, 158–169.

Bishop, D.V.M., & Snowling, M.J. (2004). Developmental dyslexia and specific language impairment: Same or different? *Psychological Bulletin, 130*, 858–886.

Brannon, E., & van der Walle, G. (2001). The development of ordinal numerical competence in young children. *Cognitive Psychology, 43*, 53–81.

Brannon, E.M., Abbott, S., & Lutz, D.J. (2004). Number bias for the discrimination of large visual sets in infancy. *Cognition, 93*, B59–B68.

Breheny, R., Katsos, N., & Williams, J. (in press). Are generalized scalar implicatures generated by default? An on-line investigation into the role of context in generating pragmatic inferences. *Cognition.*

Bryant, P. (1995). Children and arithmetic. *Journal of Child Psychology and Psychiatry, 36*(1), 3–32.

Canobi, K.H. (2005). Children's profiles of addition and subtraction understanding. *Journal of Experimental Child Psychology, 92*, 220–246.

Carey, S. (2004). Bootstrapping and the origin of concepts. *Daedalus, 133*, 59–68.

Clearfield, M.W., & Mix, K.S. (2001). Amount versus number: Infants' use of area and contour length to discriminate small sets. *Journal of Cognition and Development, 2*, 243–260.

Clegg, J., Hollis, C., Mawhood, L., & Rutter, M. (2005). Developmental language disorders—A follow-up in later adult life. Cognitive, language and psychosocial outcomes. *Journal of Child Psychology and Psychiatry, 46*, 128–149.

Cowan, R., Donlan, C., Newton, E., & Lloyd, D. (2005). Number skills and knowledge in children with specific language impairment. *Journal of Educational Psychology, 97,* 732–744.

Dehaene, S. (1997). *The number sense: How the mind creates mathematics.* New York: Oxford University Press.

Dehaene, S., Spelke, E., Pinel, P., Stanescu, R., & Tsivkin, S. (1999). Sources of mathematical thinking: Behavioural and brain-imaging evidence. *Science, 284,* 970–929.

Donlan, C. (1998). Number without language? Studies of children with specific language impairments. In C. Donlan (Ed.), *The development of mathematical skills* (pp. 255–274). Hove, UK: Psychology Press.

Donlan, C. (2003). The early numeracy of children with specific language impairments. In A. Baroody & A. Dowker (Eds.), *The development of arithmetical concepts* (pp. 337–358). Mahwah, NJ: Lawrence Erlbaum Associates.

Donlan, C., Bishop, D.V.M., & Hitch, G.J. (1998). Magnitude comparisons by children with specific language impairments: Evidence of unimpaired symbolic processing. *International Journal of Language and Communication Disorders, 33,* 149–160.

Donlan, C., Cowan, R., Newton, E., & Lloyd, D. (in press). The role of language in mathematical development: Evidence from children with specific language impairment. *Cognition.*

Donlan, C., & Gourlay, S. (1999). The importance of nonverbal skills in the acquisition of place-value knowledge: Evidence from normally-developing and language-impaired children. *British Journal of Developmental Psychology, 17,* 1–19.

Donlan, C., & Hutt, E. (1991). Teaching maths to young children with language disorders. In K. Durkin & B. Shire (Eds.), *Language in mathematical education: Research and practice* (pp. 198–207). Milton Keynes: Open University Press.

Dowker, A. (1998). Individual differences in normal mathematical development. In C. Donlan (Ed.), *The development of mathematical skills* (pp. 275–301). Hove, UK: Psychology Press.

Dowker, A. (2005). *Individual differences in arithmetic: Implications for psychology, neuroscience and education.* Hove, UK: Psychology Press.

Fazio, B.B. (1994). The counting abilities of children with specific language impairment—A comparison of oral and gestural tasks. *Journal of Speech and Hearing Research, 37,* 358–368.

Fazio, B.B. (1996). Mathematical abilities of children with specific language impairment: A 2-year follow-up. *Journal of Speech and Hearing Research, 39,* 839–849.

Fazio, B.B. (1999). Arithmetic calculation, short-term memory, and language performance in children with specific language impairment: A 5-year follow-up. *Journal of Speech, Language, and Hearing Research, 42,* 420–431.

Gathercole, S.E., & Baddeley, A.D. (1996). *The Children's Test of Nonword Repetition.* London: Psychological Corporation.

Geary, D.C. (1993). Mathematical disabilities: Cognitive, neuropsychological and genetic components. *Psychological Bulletin, 114,* 345–362.

Geary, D.C., Hamson, C.O., & Hoard, M.K. (2000). Numerical and arithmetical cognition: A longitudinal study of process and concept deficits in children with learning disability. *Journal of Experimental Child Psychology, 77,* 236–263.

Geary, D.C., Hoard, M.K., Byrd-Craven, J., & DeSoto, M.C. (2004). Strategy choices in simple and complex addition: Contributions of working memory and counting knowledge for children with mathematical disability. *Journal of Experimental Child Psychology, 88,* 121–151.

Gelman, R., & Butterworth, B. (2005). Number and language: How are they related? *Trends in Cognitive Sciences, 9*(1), 6–10.

Gelman, R., & Gallistel, C.R. (1978). *The child's understanding of number.* Cambridge, MA: Harvard University Press.

Gordon, P. (2004). Numerical cognition without words: Evidence from Amazonia. *Science, 306,* 496–499.

Grauberg, E. (1998). *Elementary mathematics and language difficulties: A book for teachers, therapists and parents.* London: Whurr Publishers, Ltd.

Guerts, B. (2003). Reasoning with quantifiers. *Cognition, 86,* 223–251.

Hauser, M.D., Chomsky, N., & Fitch, W.T. (2002). The faculty of language: What is it, who has it and how did it evolve? *Science, 298,* 1569–1579.

Hick, R., Botting, N., & Conti-Ramsden, G. (2005). Cognitive abilities in children with specific language impairment: Consideration of visuo-spatial skills. *International Journal of Language & Communication Disorders, 40,* 137–149.

Hill, E. (2001). Non-specific nature of specific language impairments: A review of the literature with regard to concomitant motor impairments. *International Journal of Language and Communication Impairments, 36,* 149–171.

Hitch, G.J., & McAuley, E. (1991). Working memory in children with specific arithmetical learning difficulties. *British Journal of Psychology, 82,* 375–386.

Hodent, C., Bryant, P., & Houde, O. (2005). Language-specific effects on number computation in toddlers. *Developmental Science, 8,* 420–423.

Hutt, E. (1986). *Teaching language-disordered children: A structured curriculum.* London: Edward Arnold.

Huttenlocher, J., Jordan, N.C., & Levine, S.C. (1994). A mental model for early arithmetic. *Journal of Experimental Psychology: General, 123,* 284–296.

Jarrold, C., Baddeley, A.D., Hewes, A.K., Leeke, T.C., & Phillips, C.E. (2004). What links verbal short-term memory performance and vocabulary level? Evidence of changing relationships among individuals with learning disability. *Journal of Memory and Language, 50,* 134–148.

Jordan, N.C., Hanich, L.B., & Kaplan, D. (2003). A longitudinal study of mathematical competencies in children with specific mathematical difficulties versus children with comorbid mathematical and reading difficulties. *Child Development, 74,* 834–850.

Jordan, N.C., Huttenlocher, J., & Levine, S.C. (1992). Differential calculation abilities in young children from middle- and low-income families. *Developmental Psychology, 28,* 644–653.

Koponen, T., Mononen, R., Räsänen, P., & Ahonen, T. (2006). Basic numeracy in children with specific language impairment: Heterogeneity and connections to language. *Journal of Speech, Language, and Hearing Research, 49,* 58–73.

Landerl, K., Bevan, A., & Butterworth, B. (2004). Developmental dyscalculia and basic numerical capacities: A study of 8–9-year-old students. *Cognition, 93,* 99–125.

Lidz, J., & Musolino, J. (2002). Children's command of quantification. *Cognition, 84,* 113–154.

Lipton, J.S., & Spelke, E.S. (2005). Preschool children's mapping of number words to nonsymbolic numerosities. *Child Development, 76,* 978–988.

Lipton, J.S., & Spelke, E.S. (2006). Preschool children master the logic of number meanings. *Cognition, 98,* B57–B66.

Miller, K.F., Kelly, M., & Zhou, X. (2005). Learning mathematics in China and the United States: Cross-cultural insights into the nature and course of pre-school mathematical development. In J.I.D. Campbell (Ed.), *Handbook of mathematical cognition* (pp. 163–178). Hove, UK: Psychology Press.

Miura, I.T. (1987). Mathematics achievement as a function of language. *Journal of Educational Psychology, 79,* 79–82.

Miura, I.T., Okamoto, Y., Kim, C.C., Chang, C.M., Steere, M., & Fayol, M. (1994). Comparisons of children's cognitive representation of number: China, France, Japan, Korea, Sweden and the United States. *International Journal of Behavioural Development, 17,* 401–411.

Moyer, R.S., & Landauer, T. (1967). Time required for judgments of numerical inequality. *Nature, 215,* 1519–1520.

Nunes, T., & Bryant, P. (1996). *Children doing mathematics.* St. Louis: Blackwell Mosby.

Nunes, T., Schliemann, A.-L., & Caraher, D. (1993). *Street mathematics and school mathematics.* New York: Cambridge University Press.

Piaget, J. (1970). *Genetic epistemology.* New York: Columbia Press.

Pica, P., Lemer, C., Izard, V., & Dehaene, S. (2005). Exact and approximate arithmetic in an Amazonian indigene group. *Science, 306,* 499–503.

Pickering, S.J., & Gathercole, S.E. (2001). *Working memory test battery for children (WMTB-C).* London: The Psychological Corporation.

Raven, J.C. (1993). *Coloured Progressive Matrices* (Rev. ed.). Oxford: Oxford Psychologists Press.

Rips, L.J., Asmuth, J., & Bloomfield, A. (in press). Giving the boot to the boot strap: How not to learn the natural numbers. *Cognition.*

Sarnecka, B.W., & Gelman, S.A. (2004). Six does not just mean a lot: Preschoolers see number words as specific. *Cognition, 92,* 329–352.

Sekuler, R., & Mierkiewicz, D. (1977). Children's judgments of numerical inequality. *Child Development, 48,* 630–633.

Siegel, L.S., Lees, A., Allan, L., & Bolton, B. (1981). Non-verbal assessment of Piagetian concepts in preschool children with impaired language development. *Educational Psychology, 2,* 153–158.

Siegler, R.S., & Stern, E. (1998). Conscious and unconscious strategy discoveries: A microgenetic analysis. *Journal of Experimental Psychology: General, 127,* 377–397.

SLI Consortium. (2004). Highly significant linkage to SLI1 locus in an expanded sample of individuals affected by specific language impairment (SLI). *American Journal of Human Genetics, 94,* 1225–1238.

Snowling, M.J., Adams, J.W., Bishop, D.V., & Stothard, S.E. (2001). Educational attainments of school leavers with a preschool history of speech-language impairments. *International Journal of Language and Communications Disorders, 36,* 173–183.

Spelke, E., & Tsvikin, S. (2001). Language and number: A bilingual training study. *Cognition, 78,* 45–88.

Tirosh, E., & Cohen, A. (1998). Language deficit with an attention-deficit disorder: A prevalent co-morbidity. *Journal of Child Neurology, 13,* 493–497.

Tomblin, J.B., Records, N.L., Buckwalter, P., Zhang, X., Smith E., & O'Brien, M. (1997). Prevalence of specific language impairment in kindergarten children. *Journal of Speech, Language, and Hearing Research, 40,* 1245–1260.

Towse, J., & Saxton, M. (1998). Mathematics across national boundaries: Cultural and linguistic perspectives on numerical competence. In C. Donlan (Ed.), *The development of mathematical skills* (pp. 129–150). Hove, UK: Psychology Press.

van Harskamp, N.J., Rudge, P., & Cipolotti, L. (2002). Are multiplication facts implemented by the left supramarginal and angular gyri? *Neuropsychologia, 40,* 1786–1793.

Varley, R.A., Klessinger, N.J.C., Romanowski, C.A.J., & Siegal, M. (2005). Agrammatic but numerate. *Proceedings of the National Academy of Sciences, 102*(9), 3519.

World Health Organization. (1993). *The ICD-10 classification of mental and behavioural disorders: Diagnostic criteria for research* (pp. 142–143). Geneva: Author.

Wynn, K. (1992). Addition and subtraction in human infants. *Nature, 358,* 749–750.

Xu, F., & Spelke, E. (2000). Large number discrimination in 6-month-old infants. *Cognition, 74,* B1–B11.

Chapter 9

The Contribution of Syndrome Research to Understanding Mathematical Learning Disability

The Case of Fragile X and Turner Syndromes

Michèle M.M. Mazzocco, Melissa M. Murphy, and Michael McCloskey

+ +

How specific are difficulties in mathematics? Can we expect that all or most children with mathematical learning disability (MLD) will have the same *kinds* of difficulties with mathematics? Alternatively, does the manifestation of math difficulties vary across children? Is there a common primary deficit—or a common set of deficits—that underlies all of these mathematics difficulties? Or do the underlying causes of these difficulties differ across groups of children, such that each of several distinct cognitive characteristics leads to mathematics difficulty? Do the different profiles of cognitive characteristics explain the variability in the nature of children's MLD, or do they represent different pathways to the same MLD profile? Do these potential sources of variability differ in terms of their interaction with factors related to math achievement, such as math anxiety, in affecting mathematics ability or performance?

One approach to addressing these questions is to study neurodevelopmental disorders associated with poor mathematics achievement. In this chapter, we describe the usefulness of this approach for answering questions about MLD above and beyond those questions posed about the characteristics of individuals with such disorders. To exemplify this approach, we draw from the work on the cognitive phenotypes—or outward, observable characteristics—of individuals with fragile X or Turner syndrome. Our objective is to illustrate how syndrome research provides a model of the variability in cognitive skills observed across all people with MLD, how this variability may be explained by potential links between cognitive ability in math and ability in other cognitive or behavioral areas, and how different cognitive characteristics may lead to the same functional outcome: poor mathematics achievement.

WHY FOCUS ON FRAGILE X AND TURNER SYNDROMES TO STUDY MATHEMATICAL LEARNING DISABILITY?

There are many reasons to study fragile X and Turner syndromes as models of mathematical learning disability. First, both are relatively common disorders with a known genetic etiology occurring in approximately 1 in 2,000 to 9,000 live births (live *female* births for Turner syndrome; Crawford, Acuna, & Sherman, 2001; Davenport et al., in press; Rieser & Underwood, 1989). Thus, research on either disorder is directly applicable to a significant number of individuals, and participation in research on either syndrome is not limited to a small pool of available children within each respective population. Second, for both disorders there is a growing but well-established scientific literature on the cognitive phenotypes, including studies of associated math difficulties. Although it is unclear whether the math difficulties in girls[1] with either syndrome are primary deficits (i.e., caused directly by the syndrome) as opposed to deficits secondary to a broader underlying cognitive deficit (such as working memory), we can be confident that math difficulties observed among girls with either syndrome are not the result of an overall cognitive impairment, such as mental retardation. This confidence stems from the fact that research participation in many studies of math performance in people with these disorders is typically limited to girls without mental retardation, and many girls with either syndrome function in general classroom settings even when eligible for special education services. Finally, there is much variability both within and between these two populations in terms of the degree to which MLD (and other cognitive or behavioral difficulties) is evident and how MLD is manifested. We believe that this variability may help us to understand the associations between mathematics and other cognitive skills, and that these associations— or cognitive correlates—may shed light on factors that influence or account

---

[1]In our own studies of cognitive performance in people with fragile X (including mathematics achievement), we are interested in cognitive effects directly related to the fragile X mutation (described later in this chapter) versus indirect effects that result from mental retardation. For this reason, we include only females without mental retardation as participants in our studies. Thus, from this point forward, when referring to math performance in people with fragile X, we are referring primarily to females with fragile X without mental retardation.

for variation in mathematics ability in the general population. Thus, although other disorders are also associated with mathematics difficulties, a review of fragile X and Turner syndrome research provides a rich example of the benefits of this research approach.

CONTRIBUTIONS OF SYNDROME RESEARCH
TO UNDERSTANDING MATHEMATICAL LEARNING DISABILITY

In assessing the potential benefits of syndrome research, it is helpful to consider how phenotypes develop in children with developmental disorders. One model of phenotype development is the "three-level frameworks" proposed by Frith (2001). The first level in this model is the role of *biology*. When studying known genetic disorders, the specific biological contributions are more clearly defined than is the presence or absence of MLD: That is, even if there is a biological component to MLD, this component is not firmly established, particularly as MLD itself is subject to a wide range of defining criteria (as discussed in Chapters 2, 3, and 4). Level 2 in the model, *cognition*, is the internal processing influenced by both biology (e.g., genes, brain function) and environment (e.g., instruction, intervention, classroom influences), which in turn are influenced by the third level, *behavior* (e.g., attention in the classroom, performance on tests, poor math fact retrieval, arousal levels during test taking). The distinction between *cognition* and *behavior* is particularly relevant to work on syndrome phenotypes because initial phenotype studies are often based on standardized testing of broadly defined behaviors—such as poor mathematics scores and poor math achievement—for which associated or underlying cognitive deficits are inferred but not always specified (e.g., specific aspects of spatial, working memory, or number-sense deficits).

Indeed, at the broad level, many syndrome phenotypes may appear identical. This is the case for fragile X and Turner syndromes, both of which are associated with poor mathematics achievement, poor working memory and spatial skills, and spared verbal expression and reading skills. Once these general areas of deficits are identified for a given syndrome, it is possible to test theories of mathematics ability and potential underlying skills. It is at the level of these underlying skills that the differences may emerge across misleadingly "similar" phenotypes. If all syndrome groups conform to a single profile of mathematics and cognitive skills, then one model of MLD would suffice. In cases in which distinct differences emerge, syndrome phenotypes can serve as models of distinct pathways to mathematics disability, or perhaps of math disability subtypes. Studies of fragile X and Turner syndromes show sufficiently different profiles so as to implicate different routes to MLD.

FRAGILE X AND TURNER SYNDROMES AS MODELS
OF PATHWAYS TO MATHEMATICAL LEARNING DISABILITY

Before presenting information on mathematics in people with fragile X or Turner syndrome, we briefly review each disorder. The reader is referred elsewhere for more detailed summaries of fragile X (Cornish, Levitas, & Sudhalter, in press; Hagerman & Hagerman, 2002), or Turner syndrome (Davenport, Hooper, & Zegar, in press).

Fragile X Syndrome

Fragile X syndrome results from a mutation of a single gene located on the X chromosome (Verkerk et al., 1991). With an incidence of 1:4,000 to 1:9,000 live births (Crawford et al., 2001), fragile X is the leading known familial cause of mental retardation. The highly variable physical characteristics of the syndrome, such as a long face and protruding ears, do not occur among all people with the syndrome. Indeed, these features are also observed in many people in the general population. Thus, the physical characteristics of fragile X alone are not a reliable indication of its presence. Cognitive features, such as a family history of mental retardation, are among the characteristics considered when determining risk for fragile X.

Fragile X is an X-linked disorder, which is why it affects males (who have one X chromosome) more severely than females (who have two X chromosomes). Whereas approximately 50% of females with fragile X have mental retardation (Rousseau et al., 1994), nearly all males with fragile X have mental retardation (Bailey, Hatton, & Skinner, 1998). The females with fragile X who do not have mental retardation may have borderline to average levels of intellectual ability. This variability results in part from the random X inactivation, the process by which one of the two X chromosomes typically present in females is inactivated (Lyon, 1991), or essentially turned off. The inactivation process results in two populations of cells whereby either the maternally or paternally inherited X chromosome is inactive. In females, the percentage of *active* chromosomes that have the mutation can vary because the mutation will be on only one of the two X chromosomes. This variability in chromosome activation is associated with syndrome severity (Abrams et al., 1994).

Turner Syndrome

Turner syndrome occurs in approximately 1:2,000 to 1:5,000 live female births (Davenport et al., in press; Rieser & Underwood, 1989). It is sporadic in nature and thus generally does not run in families. Although the physical characteristics of Turner syndrome vary in frequency and severity, the most common feature—short stature—is evident in most people with this disorder (Sävendahl & Davenport, 2000). Turner syndrome results from either complete or partial loss of the second X chromosome that is typically present in a female. Therefore, Turner syndrome is diagnosed by karyotype analysis, or an analysis of an individual's complete set of chromosomes. The typical female karyotype has 46 chromosomes, including the two X chromosomes (46XX). When Turner syndrome results from total loss of an X chromosome, 45 intact chromosomes are present and the karyotype is referred to as 45X (Lippe, 1991). Other karyotypes are possible, including a partial versus total absence of an X chromosome, such that 46 chromosomes are present with one incomplete X chromosome. Girls with this karyotype have a milder outcome than do girls with the classic 45X karyotype (Temple & Carney, 1993). These and other variations in Turner syndrome karyotypes are discussed elsewhere in more detail (e.g., Ross, Roeltgen, Kushner, Wei, & Zinn, 2000).

The Existence and Persistence of Mathematical Learning Disability in Fragile X or Turner Syndrome

It is now well established that children with fragile X or Turner syndrome are at higher risk for poor math achievement, and that elevated risk for MLD is evident early in the primary school years. Even when using a conservative, low cutoff score (such as a standard score of 86) to define MLD, approximately 50% of girls with either syndrome meet criteria for MLD in kindergarten or first grade (Mazzocco, 2001). By the end of primary school, more than 75% of girls with either syndrome will have met criteria for MLD (Murphy, Mazzocco, Gerner, & Henry, 2006). Moreover, MLD is likely to persist in those in whom it emerges (Murphy et al., 2006). Indeed, poor math achievement continues through the school-age years for both fragile X (Mazzocco, 1998; Murphy & Mazzocco, in press) and Turner syndromes (Mazzocco, 1998; Murphy & Mazzocco, in press; Rovet, 1993). During the school-age years, math achievement is, on average, below grade and age expectations for girls with fragile X (Murphy & Mazzocco, in press) and two grades below age expectations for girls with Turner syndrome (Rovet, Szekely, & Hockenberry, 1994). Evidence across studies indicates the persistence of these deficits beyond the school years in that poor mathematics achievement has also been reported for adult women with fragile X (Bennetto, Pennington, Porter, Taylor, & Hagerman, 2001; Mazzocco, Pennington, & Hagerman, 1993) or Turner syndrome (Molko et al., 2003). Clearly, math difficulties are common and significant in both syndromes. What is less clear is whether the causes of poor math performance, or the nature of the math difficulties themselves, are different for individuals with fragile X than they are for those with Turner syndrome.

COGNITIVE CORRELATES AS INDICATORS OF
PATHWAYS TO MATHEMATICAL LEARNING DISABILITY

Correlational studies can address (but not definitely determine) whether associated skills underlie mathematics difficulties; of course, associations also implicate that mathematics difficulties themselves may influence performance in other areas. As an initial step toward addressing possible pathways to MLD, we first infer correlates of poor math achievement from earlier studies of the fragile X or Turner syndrome phenotypes and then test them against measures of mathematics performance.

Potential correlates of poor math achievement have been implicated by evidence of deficits in executive function and visuospatial skills for females with fragile X (Bennetto et al., 2001; Cornish et al., 2004; Cornish, Munir, & Cross, 1998; Kirk, Mazzocco, & Kover, 2005; Mazzocco et al., 1993) or Turner syndrome (Buchanan, Pavlovic, & Rovet, 1998; Haberecht et al., 2001; Kirk et al., 2005; Rovet & Netley, 1982; Tamm, Menon, & Reiss, 2003; Temple & Carney, 1995; Waber, 1979). Among the most robust of these findings from research on fragile X syndrome is evidence for deficits in executive function skills—deliberate, goal-oriented behaviors such as planning, organizing, and maintaining attention—which some researchers claim serve as a primary mechanism underlying poor performance on visuospatial tasks such as block-construction tasks (Bennetto et al., 2001), or even complex language comprehension tasks such as interpreting indirect speech (Simon, Keenan, Pennington, Taylor, & Hagerman, 2001). In contrast, the most robust finding from studies of Turner syndrome is the evidence for significant visuospatial difficulties. Considered together, these findings lead to the logical hypothesis that fragile X and Turner syndromes may serve as models of procedural and visuospatial subtypes of MLD, respectively.

CORRELATES AND CHARACTERISTICS OF
MATHEMATICS PERFORMANCE IN FRAGILE X OR TURNER SYNDROME

The proposed visuospatial subtype of MLD is the least thoroughly investigated (Geary, 1993), so we first focus on data from studies of Turner syndrome. As we indicate next, a test of the stated hypothesis is not straightforward and reflects the complexities inherent in seeking associations among constructs as complicated as mathematics, executive function, and visuospatial skills.

Is Turner Syndrome a Model of a Visual
Spatial Mathematical Learning Disability Subtype?

The co-occurrence of visuospatial and mathematics difficulties motivated some of the earliest explorations of the causes of poor math performance in girls with Turner syndrome (Rovet et al., 1994). As such, the earliest of these studies on arithmetic difficulties tested the hypothesis that visuospatial and math skills were correlated in girls with Turner syndrome (Rovet et al., 1994). This hypothesis was not supported by either an item analysis or correlations studies, leading Rovet and colleagues to conclude that visuospatial and mathematics skills are independent of each other, rather than related, in girls with Turner syndrome.

Our own research findings support Rovet's conclusions: We failed to find consistent, selective impairment on math items that have a strong visuospatial component, such as rank-ordering items according to height or volume, in primary-school-age girls with Turner syndrome (Murphy et al., 2006). Although we did find that geometry subtest scores on the KeyMath—Revised (Connolly, 1988) were significantly lower among kindergarteners with Turner syndrome relative to their peers without Turner syndrome (Mazzocco, 2001), this subtest did not differentiate between test scores of third graders with Turner syndrome from third-grade girls without Turner syndrome (Murphy et al., 2006). Moreover, correlations between various math scores (standardized scores of math achievement, math ability, and counting skills) and visuospatial reasoning scores were not correlated in younger girls (Mazzocco, Bhatia, & Lesniak-Karpiak, 2006) or 7- to 20-year-olds with Turner syndrome (Mazzocco, 1998). This research on Turner syndrome demonstrates that the co-occurrence of deficits in two areas of performance does not necessarily reflect a common cognitive deficit.

Thus, although there is some evidence to spatially oriented math difficulties in girls with Turner syndrome, the evidence is tentative at best, particularly in view of the aforementioned negative findings. Still, a spatial component of mathematics difficulty in this population cannot be ruled out because studies have not explored all aspects of mathematics nor all aspects of visuospatial skills, much less at different ages. Thus, although there is no compelling evidence of a predominant or widespread visuospatial math difficulty in Turner syndrome, the lack of such evidence may exemplify the complexity in the constructs of "math" and "spatial" skills. Indeed, while neuropsychologists propose and test these individual constructs (see Chapter 12), there is the recognition that the existence of potential, bidirectional relationships between each domain, such that none is a completely "pure" construct independent of influence from other cognitive domains. For example, even within the domain of working memory skills, differentiation is found in verbal versus spatial working memory in people with Turner syndrome (e.g., Buchanan et al., 1998; Haberecht et al., 2001).

Consider the finding that girls with Turner syndrome have relatively weak calculation skills compared with their peers on more complex (multi-digit) problems and the relatively frequent occurrence of procedural errors on these types of problems (e.g., Rovet et al., 1994; Temple & Marriott,

1998). The procedural errors include misaligning solutions during paper-and-pencil calculations that can be conceptualized as spatial errors (Mazzocco, 1998). Yet procedural errors may also reflect weak executive function skills, such as poor organization or inadequate tracking of the steps needed during complex problem solving (with complex defined as involving more than one step, versus single-digit arithmetic with solutions less than 10). Poor executive function skills may explain other errors seen with greater frequency in girls with Turner syndrome, such as neglecting to apply or complete a correct regrouping procedure (Rovet et al., 1994), relative to peers matched for age, grade, and verbal IQ score. Although it is unclear whether poor calculation on complex problems is associated with poor fact retrieval or working memory in girls with Turner syndrome, the evidence thus far fails to support the notion that Turner syndrome is a model of visuospatial MLD.

Characterizing Mathematics Performance in Girls with Turner Syndrome

If girls with Turner syndrome do not have a visuospatial MLD, is MLD in this group different from the MLD observed in the general population? To answer this question, we believe it is important to describe both the accurate, or spared, aspects of mathematics performance and the areas of deficiency.

Among individuals with Turner syndrome, poor mathematics performance is marked neither by inaccurate calculations overall nor by poor number sense (Bruandet, Molko, Cohen, & Dehaene, 2004; Murphy et al., 2006; Rovet et al., 1994; Temple & Marriott, 1998). Individuals with Turner syndrome show age-appropriate performance on tests of simple arithmetic, number comprehension, number production, rote or applied counting skills (Murphy et al., 2006), magnitude judgment accuracy, and estimation accuracy (Bruandet et al., 2004; Mazzocco, 2001; Murphy et al., 2006; Temple & Marriott, 1998).

The difficulty that is most consistently reported across studies of individuals with Turner syndrome is in speed of mathematics performance. This includes slower arithmetic fact retrieval and calculations (Bruandet et al., 2004; Molko et al., 2003; Rovet et al., 1994) relative to individuals without Turner syndrome, which may result in fewer problems attempted within a given time frame. Although slower response times are evident when problems include larger addends as opposed to smaller addends (Molko et al., 2003; Temple & Marriott, 1998), they also occur for magnitude judgments of very small item sets that are typically judged very quickly (i.e., subitized) rather than counted. Research indicates that women with Turner syndrome may actually count small sets of items, whereas other adults rapidly recognize the magnitude of small sets (Molko et al.,

2003). This may explain, rather than exemplify, the slow response times. That is, reliance on overt or covert counting requires more time than does retrieval of facts or quick judgments regarding amounts. Note that although this may differentiate girls with Turner syndrome from some other groups of individuals with MLD, evidence exists for a similar reliance on counting rather than subitizing from studies of MLD in the general population (e.g., Koontz & Berch, 1996), as reviewed by Butterworth and Reigosa in Chapter 4.

Similarly, poor retrieval skills have been observed among children with MLD in the general population and are more common when MLD co-occurs with reading disability (see Chapter 6). Yet, girls with Turner syndrome are not at risk for reading disability, and in fact, they typically have reading skills in or above the average range (e.g., Temple & Carney, 1996). Moreover, the slowed response time reported for the Turner syndrome phenotype is not limited to arithmetic tasks; slowed response relative to peers is also observed on measures of oral fluency, such as naming as many words as possible that share an initial letter (Temple, 2002). Maximum efficiency during oral fluency tasks requires an inherent organization in how words or names are retrieved, and thus, these tasks are believed to measure executive function skills. For example, if one was asked to name as many girls' names as possible within 1 minute, one could retrieve names randomly, which would take some time to think of each name. Or, one could use a more deliberate approach, such as retrieving names alphabetically or naming all the female students in one's classroom or on one's softball team, in which case cuing would facilitate word retrieval. The slower processing speed in girls with Turner syndrome may underlie their inefficient performance on tasks with working memory demands (Kirk et al., 2005), and it appears to underlie mathematics difficulties in this group as well. It is unknown how, or whether, these associations change with age or whether this association interacts with spatial components of mathematics in the later school years. Based on existing data regarding slow retrieval and procedural errors, executive function deficits appear to characterize mathematics difficulties in girls with Turner syndrome more so than spatial skills.

Characterizing Mathematics
Performance in Girls with Fragile X Syndrome

Executive function skills have also been reported as deficient in both children and adults with fragile X syndrome (Mazzocco, Hagerman, Cronister-Silverman, & Pennington, 1992). For this reason, in our early work we hypothesized that procedural errors would characterize the math difficulties observed in girls with this syndrome. Our earliest investigation failed to find higher rates of procedural errors in girls with fragile X relative to same-age peers or girls with Turner syndrome (Mazzocco, 1998). In fact, it was the girls in the Turner syndrome group that showed more errors of this type than girls with fragile X, as discussed previously.

Other group differences are implicated by fragile X phenotype research. In terms of performance strengths, girls with fragile X syndrome are as accurate as their same-age peers at reading and writing numbers and at rote-counting tasks such as counting aloud from 1, counting backwards, or skip counting (e.g., counting by tens; Murphy et al., 2006). In fact, performance by girls with fragile X *exceeds* the performance levels on reading numbers and rote counting observed in young children with MLD from the general population (Murphy et al., 2006). Performance times also do not differ from those of peers when judging the accuracy of solutions to arithmetic problems (Murphy & Mazzocco, in press).

Despite this relative strength in rote counting and performance speed, we (Murphy et al., 2006) have found that girls with fragile X are less accurate than are children with MLD on a variety of mathematics tasks, including tests of one-to-one correspondence—a very basic counting principle dictating that every item in a set is assigned one (and only one) number when counted. Moreover, we found that girls with fragile X have performance levels comparable to other children with MLD on other applied and conceptual counting skills, such as number constancy (i.e., recognizing that the quantity of a set does not change when the items in the set are merely rearranged, such as from a row to a circle), cardinality (i.e., understanding that the last number counted in the proper sequence indicates the quantity of the item set), or ordinal position (i.e., identifying the nth position in an array). Girls with fragile X, and children with MLD in general, have more difficulty on these applied and conceptual counting tasks than do same-age peers without MLD (Murphy et al., 2006).

This research on fragile X syndrome demonstrates that accurate rote counting does not implicate mastery of number sense. Even as young as kindergarten age, girls with fragile X have lower scores than same-age peers on test items that measure aspects of number comprehension and counting principles (Mazzocco, 2001), such as counting how many items are in a set or judging relative magnitudes (i.e., determining which of two sets has more), regardless of whether the sets are presented visually or verbally. Moreover, on verbal magnitude judgments, girls with fragile X also differ from girls with Turner syndrome (most of whom make accurate magnitude judgments, as discussed previously), but not from children from the general population who have MLD (Murphy et al., 2006). Children from all three groups—those with fragile X, Turner syndrome, and MLD—made more errors on mental number line judgments (e.g., determining whether 5 or 12 is closer to 8) relative to same-age peers (Murphy et al., 2006). Thus, some aspects of math difficulties appear only in girls with fragile X syndrome, other aspects appear only in girls with Turner syndrome, and others are commonly seen among many children with MLD.

What, if any, cognitive correlates are associated with these weak counting principles? Whereas we anticipated (and failed to find) visuospatial correlates of math skills among girls with Turner syndrome, correlates of visuospatial and mathematics skills proved to be stronger in girls with fragile X relative to girls with Turner syndrome or girls from the general population. These correlations were observed among kindergartners and first graders with fragile X, third graders, and both elementary and middle- or high-school-age girls (Mazzocco, 1998). For example, among girls with fragile X, the ability to distinguish individual shapes within a design and the ability to recall the correct location of items within an array were positively correlated with accurate identification of correct and incorrect counting procedures (Mazzocco et al., 2006). Scores on several visual perception and discrimination tasks were also positively correlated with paper-and-pencil math calculation skills. These correlations were not solely accounted for by IQ score because they failed to emerge for a same-age peer group matched on IQ score. In fact, these relationships also failed to emerge for girls with Turner syndrome matched on age and IQ score to girls with fragile X.

Although the evidence for spatial aspects of math performance is stronger among girls with fragile X than it is among girls with Turner syndrome, this does not establish the underlying causes of math difficulties. It is necessary to explore the hypothesis that executive function deficits contribute to the weak mathematics performance observed in girls with fragile X, and specifically the influence of working memory (see Chapter 5). Working memory loads for math tasks can vary in terms of number of sentences per word problem, number of operations required, or even the number of operands (e.g., $2 + 4 = 6$ versus $4 + 3 + 2 = 9$). Older (10- to 24-year-old) females with fragile X have been found to be as accurate as their same-aged peers at judging solutions to two-operand arithmetic problems but not when asked to judge three-operand problems (Rivera, Menon, White, Glaser, & Reiss, 2002). On the one hand, this finding suggests a relationship between working memory demands and performance that may be specific to fragile X; on the other hand, the two-operand problems may be subject to ceiling effects, given the older ages of the participants and the relative simplicity of the two-operand problems. Also, the two participant groups in this study had very different mean IQ scores, such that most participants in the fragile X group had IQ scores in the borderline to average range (70–108, based on a population average of 100), whereas all participants in the comparison group scored above 98 and up to 142. This wide of a difference makes it difficult to determine whether the working memory influences were specific to fragile X or to overall lower cognitive ability. In fact, in our own research with younger (8-year-olds) participants matched on IQ score, both the fragile X *and* an IQ-matched comparison group showed increased difficulty when working memory demands increased. Still, group differences did emerge when working memory demands were moderate, such that girls with fragile X made more errors than did girls in the comparison group despite taking the same amount of time to complete the task (Kirk et al., 2005). These findings suggest that working memory limitations in females with fragile X cannot be solely attributed to low full-scale IQ (FSIQ; Kirk et al., 2005), but it remains unclear whether these limitations contribute to the mathematical abilities and disabilities in this group. What is clear is that girls with fragile X have math difficulties that differ from both girls with Turner syndrome and children with MLD from the general population, and that both executive function and spatial skills may account for some of these difficulties.

Note that the emphasis of this chapter is on the group differences evident between fragile X and Turner syndromes, despite misleadingly similar global phenotypes. For instance, although both groups show executive function deficits, this finding should not be interpreted as reflecting a similarity between the groups, as differences between the fragile X and Turner syndrome groups did emerge in terms of the different aspects of executive function skills. These findings reflect not only important group differences but also the breadth and variation of the construct of *executive function skills* and the constructs of *math skills* and *spatial skills*.

COGNITION AND BEHAVIOR: MODELS OF DIFFERENT INTERACTIONS ACROSS GROUPS

To this point, we have presented important group differences in biology and cognition to exemplify two of the three levels of phenotype development. The third level concerns behaviors that may influence—and be influenced by—cognition, according to Frith's model. We limit this discussion to one behavioral characteristic that may influence math performance and that is discussed in detail in Chapter 15: math anxiety.

In Chapter 15, Ashcraft, Krause, and Hopko define math anxiety as "the negative emotional reaction some people experience when placed in situations that require mathematical reasoning or problem solving." Among the characteristics they associate with math anxiety are the following: 1) elevations in arousal level in response to mathematics tasks, 2) performance deficits apparent under timed but not untimed conditions, 3) accuracy traded for speed on arithmetic problems, and 4) slower and less accurate performance on calculations. To date, studies of fragile X and Turner syndrome have not explicitly explored the possible role of math anxiety in poor performance, but what little evidence exists suggests a relationship, especially in individuals with Turner syndrome.

Whereas anxiety, or at least social anxiety, is associated with fragile X (Lachiewicz & Dawson, 1994; Sobesky, Porter, Pennington, & Hagerman, 1995), it does not characterize Turner syndrome (McCauley, Feuillan, Kushner, & Ross, 2001). Yet indices of anxiety during cognitive tasks, specifically elevated heart rate relative to their peers during math and related cognitive tasks, has been reported among girls with Turner syndrome but not among girls with fragile X syndrome (Keysor, Mazzocco, McLeod, & Hoehn-Saric, 2002; Roberts, Mazzocco, Murphy, & Hoehn-Saric, 2006). Of interest is that performance on the math tasks themselves was more accurate among the girls with Turner syndrome—who showed more arousal—than in the group with fragile X syndrome. Also, girls with Turner syndrome had more difficulty than their peers on timed math achievement tests but not on untimed tests (Rovet et al., 1994), and they showed slow response times on arithmetic fact retrieval (Rovet et al., 1994; Temple & Marriott, 1998), especially as problem difficulty increased (Molko et al., 2003). Furthermore, both processing and working memory deficits are well documented among girls with Turner syndrome (Buchanan et al., 1998; Kirk et al., 2005; Tamm et al., 2003; Temple, Carney, & Mullarkey, 1996), and may place them at particular risk for math anxiety (see Chapter 15). Thus, the evidence for math anxiety is stronger in Turner syndrome than it is for fragile X syndrome on the basis that girls with Turner syndrome meet many of the criteria for math anxiety described above.

Ashcraft and colleagues (see Chapter 15) postulate that math anxiety diverts resources away from cognitive processing in order to manage the anxiety response, thereby placing demands on working memory above and beyond the task at hand. Moreover, they suggest that if memory resources are already limited, as may be the case in Turner syndrome, the effect of math anxiety could be further pronounced because of fewer resources available from which to draw. As such, math anxiety would interfere with the ability to solve problems accurately, to simultaneously learn from the process of problem solving, and to self-monitor response accuracy.

Despite evidence in favor of the contribution of math anxiety to the profile of deficits in Turner syndrome, unresolved questions remain. Ashcraft and colleagues report that research on math anxiety focuses on children in sixth grade and beyond because of the advanced nature of the math curriculum relative to earlier grades. Yet, specific difficulty in math distinguishes girls with Turner syndrome from their peers as early as kindergarten and early primary school (e.g., Mazzocco, 2001), suggesting that their difficulties may not be attributable to math anxiety, or that math anxiety (if present) emerges earlier in Turner syndrome than it does in the general population. An earlier emergence of math anxiety in Turner syndrome could reflect the relative difficulty of the primary and elementary school curriculum for girls with Turner syndrome compared with how difficult it is for the general population. This suggestion is supported by the higher rate of MLD in Turner syndrome relative to the general population and the corresponding poor performance on math achievement tests discussed previously (Mazzocco & McCloskey, 2005; Murphy et al., 2006; Rovet, 1993).

The hypothesis that math anxiety may contribute to poor math performance in Turner syndrome (rather than the reverse) would garner additional support if negative attitudes toward math and math anxiety were evident earlier than sixth grade in girls with Turner syndrome. Although empirical evidence documenting attitudes toward math in Turner syndrome is limited, analyses from our ongoing research indicate that a higher percentage of third graders with Turner syndrome (40%) reported disliking math than third graders from a normative group of children (13%). However, this difference is not specific to Turner syndrome; 53% of girls with fragile X and 30% of children with MLD from the general population also reported that they did not like math. These findings suggest that an inverse relationship between math performance and indices of math anxiety is evident earlier among children with MLD versus those without MLD. That is, whereas *later* emerging math anxiety may differentiate children with average versus above average mathematics ability (as reported by Ashcraft and colleagues), an early emerging dislike for mathematics—which may or may not evolve to conform to math anxiety—may reflect awareness of early difficulties in mathematics and differentiate those with below average math ability from those with average ability.

The nature of the relationship between math anxiety and performance may be reflected in this awareness of mathematics ability or metacognitive skills. Metacognition refers to knowledge of one's own cognition, including the online process of actively monitoring one's progress and the off-line processes of predicting performance level on a future task or evaluating performance levels on a completed task. Self-awareness of ability may further differentiate groups of children with MLD, including syndrome groups. For example, children with learning disabilities in general have poorer metacognition than their typically achieving peers (Vaidya, 1999), as indicated by higher self-ratings relative to teacher ratings (Meltzer, Roditi, Houser, & Perlman, 1998). The few studies of metacognition in children with MLD also indicate inaccurate prediction and evaluation of mathematics performance levels (Desoete, Roeyers, & Buysse, 2001; Garrett, Mazzocco, & Baker, 2006).

Metacognitive abilities have important implications for intervention strategies; telling a child to "check your work" will be ineffective if the child fails to recognize errors or fails to predict which problems are difficult and thus, need checking. Our research on metacognition in girls with fragile X or Turner syndrome is still in progress. However, from our work on physiological indices of arousal (Roberts et al., 2006), we have found that, relative to peers across both baseline and cognitive tasks (including mental arithmetic), physiological arousal is elevated among females with Turner syndrome but not among those with fragile X. As such, elevated levels of arousal may reflect heightened awareness of, or concern for, performance in Turner syndrome. However, there is no such indication of heightened awareness in girls with fragile X—despite the presence of mathematics difficulties in both groups.

CONTRIBUTION OF SYNDROME MODELS TO THE UNDERSTANDING OF THE BIOLOGICAL UNDERPINNINGS OF MATHEMATICAL LEARNING DISABILITIES

In addition to providing a model of MLD, syndrome research can inform us of possible biological mechanisms that account for some of the variation seen in mathematics ability in the general population. In this way, studies of specific syndromes are complementary to ongoing, traditional approaches to studying the genetics of MLD (reviewed in Chapter 14). For instance, consider the fact that the single X-chromosome gene is one that all human beings have, yet, when mutated, it leads to fragile X syndrome. Studies of atypical development in fragile X help us to learn about the function of this gene in all humans and animals. Similarly, all human beings have at least one X chromosome. It follows that, if by its absence, the second set of X chromosome genes gives rise to the features of Turner syndrome, its presence is responsible for some of the differences between individuals with and without Turner syndrome. Studies of Turner syndrome inform us of potential roles of X chromosome genes. Both syndromes can inform us of brain function, particularly through brain imaging research (see Chapters 4, 12, and 13).

It would be an oversimplification to conclude that all individuals within the populations studied fit into one performance profile. The data reviewed earlier are generalized across groups of individuals, and each group has its own degree of variability. In fact, variability is another source of potential differences between groups: Girls with Turner syndrome show more specific effects on math performance (less variability than girls with fragile X in terms of which math skills are deficient), whereas girls with fragile X have more widespread effects (many aspects of math performance appear difficult for this population).

Another oversimplification is the conclusion that all populations with X chromosome disorders, or that the genes on the X chromosome alone, are always associated with poor mathematical cognition. First, these and other disorders related to the X chromosome have qualitatively different phenotypes. Second, some disorders related to the X chromosome, such as Klinefelter syndrome, are not as clearly associated with math deficits. Klinefelter syndrome results from an extra X chromosome in a phenotypic male (XXY). Males with Klinefelter syndrome have significant language-based learning disorders, including reading disability, and they have executive function deficits in the absence of mental retardation (as reviewed by Geschwind, Boone, Miller, & Swerdloff, 2000). This disorder does not parallel Turner or fragile X in terms of math achievement and performance. Third, there are autosomal disorders (disorders related to genes on one of the 22 pairs of chromosomes that are not sex chromosomes) linked to poor math cognition, such as velocardiofacial syndrome (VCFS). VCFS results from a small deletion on chromosome 22; it affects intellectual development but does not always lead to mental retardation. However, even those without mental retardation have difficulty with math and multiple other areas of development and function (as reviewed by Simon, Burg, & Gothelf, in press). Some complex gene–environment interactions also lead to poor math ability, such as spina bifida (see Chapter 10). Finally, there are other known disorders in which poor math performance occurs in addition to mental retardation, such as in Down syndrome and Williams syndrome, making it difficult to differentiate primary and secondary effects. The study of these and other disorders can contribute to our understanding of the complexities of math disability phenotypes and heritability.

SYNDROME MODELS AND THE RELATIONSHIP BETWEEN MATHEMATICS ABILITY AND INTELLIGENCE

Phenotypes corresponding to genetic syndromes often include some degree of impairment in global intellectual ability, reflected in mean FSIQ scores that fall below the population average of 100. This lowering of FSIQ varies from slight to significant; the mean FSIQ score for girls with Turner syndrome is approximately 95, whereas the mean score for girls with fragile X syndrome is approximately 70. In many studies of fragile X, the mean IQ score is higher because of exclusion criteria applied to the study sample.

If the relationship between math performance and overall intellectual function were positively correlated (one increased with the other) and linear (both increased to comparable degrees at each interval), the math ability phenotypes corresponding to different genetic disorders would be expected to be quite comparable with one another, so long as IQ scores were similar. But this has not emerged from findings using IQ-matched groups (e.g., Mazzocco et al., 2006; Murphy & Mazzocco, in press). Also, any variation in math skills observed across disorders would be expected to reflect quantitative changes linked to level of IQ scores. Some evidence counters this linear relationship, just as some evidence indicates that there are math disorders in children whose diagnosis is not associated with significant lowering of IQ scores (e.g., Turner syndrome).

As mentioned earlier, girls with Turner syndrome have more specific math difficulties than girls with fragile X, despite having higher IQ scores on average; and girls with fragile X—but not girls with Turner syndrome—

have select skills (rote counting, reading numbers) that exceed performance levels observed in children with MLD from the general population, despite having lower IQ scores. This latter finding is consistent with the notion that children with low IQ scores can clearly learn some aspects of arithmetic. In fact, when given regular opportunities to engage in and practice computational problem solving, children with mental retardation learn commutativity principles, and although their IQ scores are not related to accuracy on commutativity judgments, amount of exposure to computational practice is positively correlated (Baroody, 1987). Thus, although there is certainly some correlation between math ability and IQ score, IQ alone is neither the cause of MLD nor the sole source of variability in math performance in syndrome groups or in the general population.

CONCLUSION

Returning to the questions posed at the beginning of the chapter, we reflect on the answers indicated by studies of neurodevelopmental disorders, specifically those answers associated with the study of fragile X and Turner syndromes.

How specific are difficulties in mathematics? Although math difficulties are likely to emerge in people with significant global impairment (such as mental retardation), children whose developmental disorder does not lead to mental retardation may also demonstrate specific challenges in mathematics. Math difficulties, broadly defined, can and do occur among individuals such as girls with Turner syndrome, who have average or above average academic achievement skills in other domains. The specificity of those math difficulties appear earlier in children with fragile X than they do in children with Turner syndrome, despite the fact that by the early school-age years, math difficulties appear to be more specific among girls with Turner syndrome than among girls with fragile X syndrome.

Can we expect that all or most children with MLD will have the same kinds of difficulties with mathematics? The evidence from research on Turner and fragile X syndromes clearly indicates that the answer to this question is no. This has important implications for how we characterize MLD as a construct, for how we differentiate mathematical learning disabilities from mathematical difficulties more broadly defined, and for the apparent lack of consensus sometimes observed among different studies of MLD (see Swanson's Commentary on Part I).

Is there a primary, common deficit—or a combination of deficits—that underlies these mathematics difficulties in different groups of children? Or do the underlying causes of mathematics difficulties differ such that distinct cognitive characteristics may each lead to mathematics difficulty? Clear differences emerge in the cognitive correlates of mathematics performance and in the overall cognitive profiles of children from the two groups examined in this chapter.

These differences have important implications for the likelihood—or unlikelihood—of a single core deficit for MLD.

Do the different cognitive characteristics explain the types or difficulties seen in children with MLD, or can these different cognitive factors lead to a similar difficulty seen in all children with MLD? Although there is not yet a definitive explanation for how distinct groups differ in math difficulties, it is clear from this syndrome research that not all MLD is created equal. Different profiles of mathematical strengths and weakness emerge, and these may reflect different cognitive profiles and pathways that lead to poor mathematics achievement. If all children with MLD had similar underlying characteristics, syndrome research would have implications for all (or at least most) individuals with MLD. It would be possible to carry out screening, diagnosis, and intervention research with an identified syndrome population and extend the findings to the population of children with MLD. Also, if there were similar characteristics underlying all MLD, it would suggest that MLD is a readily identifiable and treatable disorder.

Unfortunately, the evidence thus far fails to support the notion of children with MLD as a homogenous population. As models of MLD, fragile X and Turner syndromes demonstrate the kind and degree of variability that can be expected among children whose MLD is not associated with a genetic disorder.

REFERENCES

Abrams, M.T., Reiss, A.L., Freund, L.S., Baumgardner, T.L., Chase, G.A., & Denckla, M.B. (1994). Molecular-neurobehavioral associations in females with the fragile X full mutation. *American Journal of Medical Genetics, 51,* 317–327.

Bailey, D.B., Jr., Hatton, D.D., & Skinner, M. (1998). Early developmental trajectories of males with fragile X syndrome. *American Journal of Mental Retardation, 103,* 29–39.

Baroody, A.J. (1987). Problem size and mentally retarded children's judgment of commutativity. *American Journal of Mental Deficiency, 91,* 439–442.

Bennetto, L., Pennington, B.F., Porter, D., Taylor, A.K., & Hagerman, R.J. (2001). Profile of cognitive functioning in women with the fragile X mutation. *Neuropsychology, 15,* 290–299.

Bruandet, M., Molko, N., Cohen, L., & Dehaene, S. (2004). A cognitive characterization of dyscalculia in Turner syndrome. *Neuropsychologia, 42,* 288–298.

Buchanan, L., Pavlovic, J., & Rovet, J. (1998). A reexamination of the visuospatial deficit in Turner syndrome: Contributions of working memory. *Developmental Neuropsychology, 14,* 341–367.

Connolly, A. (1988). *KeyMath—Revised: A Diagnostic Inventory of Essential Mathematics.* Circle Pines, MN: American Guidance Service.

Cornish, K., Swainson, R., Cunnington, R., Wilding, J., Morris, P., & Jackson, G. (2004). Do women with fragile X syndrome have problems in switching attention? Preliminary findings from ERP and fMRI. *Brain and Cognition, 54,* 235–239.

Cornish, K.M., Levitas, A., & Sudhalter, V. (in press). Fragile X syndrome: The journey from genes to behavior. In M.M.M. Mazzocco & J.L. Ross (Eds.), *Neurogenetic developmental disorders: Manifestations and identification in childhood.* Cambridge, MA: MIT Press.

Cornish, K.M., Munir, F., & Cross, G. (1998). The nature of the spatial deficit in young females with fragile-X syndrome: A neuropsychological and molecular perspective. *Neuropsychologia, 36,* 1239–1246.

Crawford, D.C., Acuna, J.M., & Sherman, S.L. (2001). FMR1 and the fragile X syndrome: Human genome epidemiology review. *Genetics in Medicine, 3,* 359–371.

Davenport, M., Hooper, S., & Zegar, M. (in press). Turner syndrome throughout childhood. In M.M.M. Mazzocco & J.L. Ross (Eds.), *Neurogenetic developmental disorders: Manifestations and identification in childhood.* Cambridge, MA: MIT Press.

Desoete, A., Roeyers, H., & Buysse, A. (2001). Metacognition and mathematical problem solving in grade 3. *Journal of Learning Disabilities, 34,* 435–449.

Frith, U. (2001). What framework should we use for understanding developmental disorders? *Developmental Neuropsychology, 20,* 555–563.

Garrett, A.J., Mazzocco, M.M.M., & Baker, L. (2006). The development of offline metacognitive skills in children with and without math disability. *Journal of Learning Disabilities Research and Practice, 21,* 77–88.

Geary, D.C. (1993). Mathematical disabilities: Cognitive, neuropsychological, and genetic components. *Psychological Bulletin, 114,* 345–362.

Geschwind, D.H., Boone, K.B., Miller, B.L., & Swerdloff, R.S. (2000). Neurobehavioral phenotype of Klinefelter syndrome. *Mental Retardation and Developmental Disabilities Research Reviews, 6,* 107–116.

Haberecht, M.F., Menon, V., Warsofsky, I.S., White, C.D., Dyer-Friedman, J., Glover, G.H., et al. (2001). Functional neuroanatomy of visuo-spatial working memory in Turner syndrome. *Human Brain Mapping, 14,* 96–107.

Hagerman, R.J., & Hagerman, P.J. (2002). The fragile X premutation: Into the phenotypic fold. *Current Opinion in Genetics and Development, 12,* 278–283.

Keysor, C.S., Mazzocco, M.M., McLeod, D.R., & Hoehn-Saric, R. (2002). Physiological arousal in females with fragile X or Turner syndrome. *Developmental Psychobiology, 41,* 133–136.

Kirk, J.W., Mazzocco, M.M., & Kover, S.T. (2005). Assessing executive dysfunction in girls with fragile X or Turner syndrome using the Contingency Naming Test (CNT). *Developmental Neuropsychology, 28,* 755–777.

Koontz, K.L., & Berch, D.B. (1996). Identifying simple numerical stimuli: Processing inefficiencies exhibited by arithmetic learning disabled children. *Mathematical Cognition, 2,* 1–23.

Lachiewicz, A.M., & Dawson, D.V. (1994). Behavior problems of young girls with fragile X syndrome: Factor scores on the Conners' Parent's Questionnaire. *American Journal of Medical Genetics, 51,* 364–369.

Lippe, B. (1991). Turner syndrome. *Endocrinology and Metabolism Clinics of North America, 20,* 121–152.

Lyon, M.F. (1991). The quest for the X-inactivation centre. *Trends in Genetics, 7,* 69–70.

Mazzocco, M.M. (2001). Math learning disability and math LD subtypes: Evidence from studies of Turner syndrome, fragile X syndrome, and neurofibromatosis type 1. *Journal of Learning Disabilities, 34,* 520–533.

Mazzocco, M.M., Hagerman, R.J., Cronister-Silverman, A., & Pennington, B.F. (1992). Specific frontal lobe deficits among women with the fragile X gene. *Journal of the American Academy of Child and Adolescent Psychiatry, 31,* 1141–1148.

Mazzocco, M.M.M. (1998). A process approach to describing mathematics difficulties in girls with Turner syndrome. *Pediatrics, 102,* 492–496.

Mazzocco, M.M.M., Bhatia, N.S., & Lesniak-Karpiak, K. (2006). Visuospatial skills and their association with math performance in girls with fragile X or Turner syndrome. *Child Neuropsychology, 12*, 87–110.

Mazzocco, M.M.M., & McCloskey, M. (2005). Math performance in girls with Turner or fragile X syndrome. In J. Campbell (Ed.), *Handbook of Mathematical Cognition* (pp. 269–297). New York: Psychology Press.

Mazzocco, M.M.M., Pennington, B.F., & Hagerman, R.J. (1993). The neurocognitive phenotype of female carriers of fragile X: Additional evidence for specificity. *Journal of Developmental and Behavioral Pediatrics, 14*, 328–335.

McCauley, E., Feuillan, P., Kushner, H., & Ross, J.L. (2001). Psychosocial development in adolescents with Turner syndrome. *Journal of Developmental and Behavioral Pediatrics, 22*, 360–365.

Meltzer, L., Roditi, B., Houser, R.F., Jr., & Perlman, M. (1998). Perceptions of academic strategies and competence in students with learning disabilities. *Journal of Learning Disabilities, 31*, 437–451.

Molko, N., Cachia, A., Riviere, D., Mangin, J.F., Bruandet, M., Le Bihan, D., et al. (2003). Functional and structural alterations of the intraparietal sulcus in a developmental dyscalculia of genetic origin. *Neuron, 40*, 847–858.

Murphy, M.M., Mazzocco, M.M.M., Gerner, G., & Henry, A.E. (2006). Mathematics learning disability in girls with Turner syndrome or fragile X syndrome. *Brain and Cognition, 61*, 195–210.

Murphy, M.M., & Mazzocco, M.M.M. (in press). Mathematics learning disability in girls with Turner syndrome or fragile X syndrome during late elementary school. *Journal of Learning Disabilities.*

Rieser, P.A., & Underwood, L.E. (1989). *Turner syndrome: A guide for families.*

Rivera, S.M., Menon, V., White, C.D., Glaser, B., & Reiss, A.L. (2002). Functional brain activation during arithmetic processing in females with fragile X syndrome is related to FMR1 protein expression. *Human Brain Mapping, 16*, 206–218.

Roberts, J., Mazzocco, M.M.M., Murphy, M.M., & Hoehn-Saric, R. (2006). *Arousal modulation in fragile X or Turner syndrome.* Manuscript under review.

Ross, J.L., Roeltgen, D., Kushner, H., Wei, F., & Zinn, A.R. (2000). The Turner syndrome-associated neurocognitive phenotype maps to distal Xp. *American Journal of Human Genetics, 67*, 672–681.

Rousseau, F., Heitz, D., Tarleton, J., MacPherson, J., Malmgren, H., Dahl, N., et al. (1994). A multicenter study on genotype-phenotype correlations in the fragile X syndrome, using direct diagnosis with probe StB12.3: The first 2,253 cases. *American Journal of Human Genetics, 55*, 225–237.

Rovet, J., & Netley, C. (1982). Processing deficits in Turner's syndrome. *Developmental Psychology, 18*, 77–94.

Rovet, J.F. (1993). The psychoeducational characteristics of children with Turner syndrome. *Journal of Learning Disabilities, 26*, 333–341.

Rovet, J.F., Szekely, C., & Hockenberry, M.N. (1994). Specific arithmetic calculation deficits in children with Turner syndrome. *Journal of Clinical and Experimental Neuropsychology, 16*, 820–839.

Sävendahl, L., & Davenport, M.L. (2000). Delayed diagnoses of Turner's syndrome: Proposed guidelines for change. *Journal of Pediatrics, 137*, 455–459.

Simon, J.A., Keenan, J.M., Pennington, B.F., Taylor, A.K., & Hagerman, R.J. (2001). Discourse processing in women with fragile X syndrome: Evidence for a deficit establishing coherence. *Cognitive Neuropsychology, 18*, 1–18.

Simon, T.J., Burg, M., & Gothelf, D. (in press). Chromosome 22q11.2 deletion syndrome. In M.M.M. Mazzocco & J.L. Ross (Eds.), *Neurogenetic developmental disorders: Manifestations and identification in childhood.* Cambridge, MA: MIT Press.

Sobesky, W.E., Porter, D., Pennington, B.F., & Hagerman, R.J. (1995). Dimensions of shyness in fragile X females. *Developmental Brain Dysfunction, 8,* 280–292.

Tamm, L., Menon, V., & Reiss, A.L. (2003). Abnormal prefrontal cortex function during response inhibition in Turner syndrome: Functional magnetic resonance imaging evidence. *Biological Psychiatry, 53,* 107–111.

Temple, C.M. (2002). Oral fluency and narrative production in children with Turner's syndrome. *Neuropsychologia, 40,* 1419–1427.

Temple, C.M., & Carney, R. (1996). Reading skills in children with Turner's syndrome: An analysis of hyperplexia. *Cortex, 32,* 335–345.

Temple, C.M., & Carney, R.A. (1993). Intellectual functioning of children with Turner syndrome: A comparison of behavioural phenotypes. *Developmental Medicine and Child Neurology, 35,* 691–698.

Temple, C.M., & Carney, R.A. (1995). Patterns of spatial functioning in Turner's syndrome. *Cortex, 31,* 109–118.

Temple, C.M., Carney, R.A., & Mullarkey, S. (1996). Frontal lobe function and executive skills in children with Turner's syndrome. *Developmental Neuropsychology, 12,* 343–363.

Temple, C.M., & Marriott, A.J. (1998). Arithmetical ability and disability in Turner's Syndrome: A cognitive neuropsychological analysis. *Developmental Neuropsychology, 14,* 47–67.

Vaidya, S.R. (1999). Metacognitive learning strategies for students with learning disabilities. *Education, 12,* 186–189.

Verkerk, A.J., Pieretti, M., Sutcliffe, J.S., Fu, Y.H., Kuhl, D.P., Pizzuti, A., et al. (1991). Identification of a gene (FMR-1) containing a CGG repeat coincident with a breakpoint cluster region exhibiting length variation in fragile X syndrome. *Cell, 65,* 905–914.

Waber, D.P. (1979). Neuropsychological aspects of Turner's syndrome. *Developmental Medicine and Child Neurology, 21,* 58–70.

Chapter 10

Mathematical Disabilities in Congenital and Acquired Neurodevelopmental Disorders

Marcia A. Barnes, Jack M. Fletcher, and Linda Ewing-Cobbs

+ +

Understanding how children acquire mathematical skills and why some children have difficulty with mathematics requires a sustained research effort that builds knowledge across several domains of inquiry, including cognitive development, learning disabilities, and neurobiological factors. The investigation of mathematical processing in children with neurological disorders is a research strategy that has several advantages for understanding mathematical disabilities. This chapter discusses research on math functioning in children with spina bifida myelomeningocele (SBM), a congenital neurodevelopmental disorder, and pediatric traumatic brain injury (TBI), an acquired neurological disorder. Both disorders are associated with significant difficulties in mathematical function.

Individuals with congenital and acquired neurodevelopmental disorders have been studied in order to address different questions about math disabilities, including questions related to neurobehavioral plasticity and vulnerability. We have used SBM in this context to test math disability models that propose relations between visuospatial skills and math because SBM is associated with significant deficits in both of these domains. Because SBM is detected in utero or at birth and is associated with a high rate of math disability at school age, this disorder is also ideal for investigating the emergence of mathematical difficulties, their developmental precursors, and their long-term consequences (Barnes, Smith-Chant, & Landry, 2005; Dennis & Barnes, 2002).

Acquired brain injuries such as pediatric TBI provide a model for studying the effects of early neural injuries on academic skill development that disrupt what are often normal developmental trajectories. TBI affects regions of the brain that are important to the development of information processing speed and executive processes, including inhibitory control and working memory (Diamond, 2002; Konrad, Gauggel, Manz, & Scholl, 2000); TBI is associated with disruptions of the development of these skills (Ewing-Cobbs, Levin, Fletcher, Iovino, & Miner, 1998; Levin et al., 1996, 2002; Willmott, Anderson, & Anderson, 2000). Information processing speed and executive processes are also processes implicated in the development of mathematical ability (Espy et al., 2004; Geary & Hoard, 2005) and disability (Bull & Johnston, 1997; Bull & Scerif, 2001; McLean & Hitch, 1999; Marzocchi, Lucangeli, De Meo, Fini, & Cornoldi, 2002; Passolunghi & Siegel, 2001). Thus, individuals with TBI comprise an interesting population within which to study the interaction of mathematical skills and executive processes and the neural substrates supporting both. Prior to discussing math disorders in SBM and TBI, we briefly describe the nature of these two disorders.

SPINA BIFIDA MYELOMENINGOCELE

Epidemiology

A congenital disorder, SBM falls under the umbrella category of neural tube defects, which include disorders such as anencephaly. Together, SBM and anencephaly, a lethal defect, account for most neural tube defects. Approximately 1–2 per 1,000 births are associated with a neural tube defect, and approximately half of these involve SBM (see Norman, McGillivray, Calloused, Hill, & Poskitt, 1995, for a discussion of neural tube defects). SBM is named for the characteristic spinal lesion (myelomeningocele) seen at birth, representing an open sac though which the spinal cord protrudes. However, there are also significant brain malformations, as well as complications from secondary hydrocephalus, which affect cognitive outcomes.

Pathophysiology

In contrast to TBI, discussions of the pathophysiology of SBM do not revolve around age or severity. Although there is variation in the pattern of dysmorphology, SBM stems from a series of events that begin in the first 30 days of gestation and result in congenital malformations of the spine and brain. The spinal lesion varies in location on the spine and leads to varying orthopedic and urinary complications depending on the level of the lesion (Reigel & Rotenstein, 1994). In the brain, SBM is usually associated with a malformation of the hindbrain and cerebellum (Chiari II malformation) that leads to hydrocephalus, requiring shunting in approximately 80% of children with this condition (Barkovich, 2000). Abnormalities of the corpus callosum are almost always apparent, with about half of the children showing partial dysgenesis that may involve the rostrum, posterior body and splenium, or both (Hannay, Fletcher, & Brandt, 1999). In other cases, thinning (hypoplasia) of part or all of the corpus callosum is apparent, representing the effects of hydrocephalus, which stretches white matter tracts throughout the brain. Hydrocephalus disrupts myelination, destroys gray matter, and reduces overall brain mass (del Bigio, 1993).

General Outcomes

As a consequence of the spinal lesion, children with SBM have problems with ambulation and bladder control depending on the level of the spinal lesion (Reigel & Rothenstein, 1994). Cognitive and motor outcomes vary depending on the specific pattern of central nervous system (CNS) dysmorphology and the severity of hydrocephalus (Fletcher, Brookshire, Bohan, Brandt, & Davidson, 2005). Although there are effects of SBM on intelligence and adaptive behavior, mental retardation occurs in only about 20% of the population. A characteristic pattern often emerges, with strengths in areas that involve verbal skills, such as vocabulary and grammar, rote memory, and word recognition, and weaknesses in pragmatic language, perceptual and memory skills involving representation and construction, and reading comprehension and math. Dennis, Landry, Barnes, and Fletcher (2006) have suggested that these phenotypic differences are not domain specific but represent different examples of strengths involving associative processing and weaknesses involving assembled processes. These differences lead to the domain-specific skill assets and skill deficits associated with SBM. In individual children with SBM, these patterns represent interactions of primary brain malformations, secondary brain insults (hydrocephalus, shunt revisions), and the environment.

TRAUMATIC BRAIN INJURY

Epidemiology

TBI is the most common cause of death and cognitive morbidity in North American children. Although approximately 90% of TBI cases in children are mild injuries, the 10% that are severe are usually associated with significant neurobehavioral deficits. Up to 5% of children with TBI have severe disabilities that persist into adulthood. The primary causes of pediatric TBI include falls, accidents during recreational activities, and motor vehicle accidents, but in infants and preschoolers, abuse is a common cause; in adolescents, automobile accidents predominate as driving is initiated, particularly in males (Kraus, 1995).

Pathophysiology

Most severe TBI cases involve a combination of diffuse and focal injury. The focal component involves contusions, intracerebral hematomas, and extraaxial hematomas. Focal lesions produce behavioral deficits related to direct tissue damage as well as to remote mass effects, such as midline shift, herniation, and compression of brainstem structures. The distribution of acute focal injuries varies with age at injury. Intraparenchymal hemorrhage, subarachnoid hemorrhage, and infarct/edema occur more frequently in infants and preschoolers, especially after accidental or inflicted TBI (Ewing-Cobbs, Prasad, et al., 1998). In older children, focal lesions are common and occur most frequently in the dorsolateral frontal, orbitofrontal, and frontal lobe white matter regions (Levin et al., 1997).

The diffuse component has its origins in acceleration-deceleration motion that deforms the brain, leading to diffuse axonal injury and alterations in neurotransmitter function. Diffuse axonal injury represents widespread microscopic lesions in the white matter (Gennarelli, Thibault, & Graham, 1998), often leading to alterations of consciousness and coma and eventually to atrophy of the white matter (Levin et al., 2000). TBI also leads to the release of excitotoxic neurotransmitters that cause additional widespread neuronal injury and deterioration in cellular functions (Povlishock, 2000). Other secondary injuries can include diffuse brain swelling, which occurs twice as often in children under 16 years than in adults.

General Outcomes

The volume of focal brain lesions, as well as the degree of atrophy, are significant predictors of functional outcome and quality of neuropsychological functioning (Levin et al., 1993, 2001). In severe TBI, residual neurological deficit is apparent in half the cases, but mental retardation and frank aphasia are rare; in preschoolers, even milder injuries lead to significant long-term deficits that can include severe problems in attention and language. Neurobehavioral outcomes vary depending on the pattern of injury but can involve multiple areas of functioning, including intelligence, memory, attention, adaptive behavior, motor function, executive function, and psychiatric domains. Injuries that involve the frontal lobes are particularly associated with executive function and attention deficits. Academic problems involving math and writing are common (Ewing-Cobbs, Levin, & Fletcher, 1998).

MATHEMATICAL DISABILITIES IN SPINA BIFIDA MYELOMENINGOCELE

SBM, like fragile X syndrome, Turner syndrome, and chromosome 22q11.2 deletion syndrome, is associated with elevated risk for problems in mathematics (Barnes et al., 2002; Mazzocco, 1998, 2001; Rovet, Szekely, & Hockenberry, 1994; Simon, Bearden, McDonald-Ginn, & Zackai, 2005; Wills, 1993). SBM is especially relevant to learning disability models because of the high rate of math disability in the absence of reading disability. More than 50% of children with SBM have a math disability, and 29% of school-age children with SBM have a specific math disability, that is, a math disability with no reading disability (Fletcher et al., 2005), which is much higher than the rate in the general population (Kosc, 1974; Shalev, Auerbach, Manor, & Gross-Tsur, 2000). In contrast, fewer than 3% of children with SBM have a specific word reading disability (Fletcher et al., 2005). The uneven development of math and reading decoding skills in children with SBM is especially relevant to math disability models in which the nature of the math disability is hypothesized to vary as a function of comorbid word reading disability (Geary, 1993; Rourke, 1993). Thus, SBM provides a paradigm within which to study proposed subtypes of math disabilities and the core cognitive processes associated with those disabilities.

The presence or absence of a comorbid disability in word reading is central to models of math disability, especially to those that grew out of neuropsychological perspectives on learning disabilities (e.g., Rourke & Finlayson, 1978) and that have their origins in early classification systems for acquired acalculia. Early studies showed that children with both word reading and mathematics disorders have a different *neurocognitive* profile from that of children with a disability in math but not reading (Morrison & Siegel, 1991; Rourke, 1993). Children with comorbid reading and math disabilities are more likely to have deficits in verbal *and* visual working memory (Siegel & Ryan, 1989) and phonological processing (Rourke, 1993; Swanson & Sachse-Lee, 2001), whereas those with specific mathematics disability are more likely to have deficits in visual memory, visuospatial working memory (McLean & Hitch, 1999; Siegel & Ryan, 1989), and visuospatial function (Rourke, 1993; Share, Moffitt, & Silva, 1988). The assumption is that co-occurring deficits in visuospatial processing and math calculations are not accidental; that is, calculation problems in children with specific math disability are proposed to reflect underlying deficits in the visuospatial and nonverbal aspects of number (Geary, 1993; Geary & Hoard, 2005; Rourke, 1993), particularly during the acquisition of calculation skills (Rourke & Conway, 1997).

Although studies of the neurocognitive correlates of different types of learning disabilities are of interest to math disability models, they are not necessarily informative of mathematical processing itself or of the actual role that these neurocognitive skills play in mathematical performance. More recent studies have used the theories and research tools of cognitive and developmental psychology to understand mathematical processing in children with different forms of math disability. These studies investigated both the development of mathematical processes in children with math disabilities and the underlying neurocognitive abilities associated with such processes (e.g., Geary, Hamson, & Hoard, 2000; Geary, Hoard, & Hamson, 1999). These investigations are rooted in a model that proposes subtypes of math calculation disabilities that are associated with distinct patterns of mathematical processing, different neurocognitive correlates, and variable relations to word reading disability (Geary, 1993; Geary & Hoard, 2005). In this model, for example, difficulties in math computation are hypothesized to arise from 1) problems in learning, representing, and retrieving math facts from semantic memory, a subtype hypothesized to be related to reading disability through a common proposed deficit in phonological working memory and phonological processing; 2) difficulties in the acquisition and use of developmentally mature problem-solving strategies or procedures to perform mental or written calculations, a subtype in which the relation to reading is not specified; and 3) difficulties in the spatial representation and manipulation of number information, a less common subtype thought to characterize individuals with specific math impairment but no reading disability.

Research based on this model has found some similarities and some differences in mathematical processing among children with both math and reading disabilities and children with specific math disabilities. Children with comorbid reading and math disabilities have the most pervasive problems in math (Geary et al., 1999; Hanich, Jordan, Kaplan, & Dick, 2001). They have difficulties in math fact retrieval; math concepts, such as place value; word problem solving; and estimation. Children with specific math disability have more restricted deficits: They are slow at retrieving math facts, which suggests imperfect math fact mastery, and they have difficulties in estimation and math concepts such as place value. However, they perform better than do children with comorbid reading and math disabilities in language-related aspects of mathematics, such as counting and solving word problems (Hanich et al., 2001).

Of note is the finding that regardless of word reading skill, children with math disability have problems with math fact mastery (Jordan, Hanich, & Kaplan, 2003a, 2003b), which is somewhat unexpected in light of models that propose direct links between deficits in math fact retrieval and phonological processing (e.g., Geary, 1993). Such findings have led to suggestions that math fact mastery may be related less to phonological processes and more to the manipulation of number along a mental number line (Jordan et al., 2003b). The mental number line is thought to be a semantic representation that captures quantitative relations between numbers in terms of size and distance (Dehaene, 1992; Dehaene, Piazza, Pinel, & Cohen, 2005).

SBM provides a strong test of the relation of specific math disability to visuospatial processing because the disorder is associated with high rates of both math disability (Fletcher et al., 2004, 2005) and visuospatial deficit (Dennis, Fletcher, Rogers, Hetherington, & Francis, 2002; Fletcher et al., 2004, 2005). Fletcher and colleagues (2004, 2005) have shown that some children with SBM have both reading and math disability (approximately 30%, as defined by low achievement), many have specific math disability (approximately 30%), and many have no learning disability (approximately 40%). However, the visuospatial skills of the latter group are weaker than those of children who are typically developing (Barnes et al., 2006).

Next, we describe our investigations of multidigit calculation and the integrity of math fact retrieval skills in SBM and the relation of these calculation skills to visuospatial and phonological processes. We also report on studies that test the relation of visuospatial skills to other aspects of mathematics, such as word problem solving, geometry, and estimation.

Multidigit Calculation in Spina Bifida Myelomeningocele

Calculation skills have been studied in children who are typically developing (e.g., Brown & Burton, 1978; van Lehn, 1982) and in neuropsychological studies of children and adults with brain injuries (Ashcraft, Yamashita, & Aram, 1992; Hartje, 1987) by investigating the types of errors that are made in multidigit arithmetic. In the typical development of multidigit computation, children may make mistakes due to imperfect single-digit arithmetic (e.g., $496 - 248 = 247$), which may be the result of errors in math fact retrieval (i.e., $16 - 8 = 7$). Children also make errors in calculation procedures such as carrying and borrowing as they are learning and consolidating algorithms. For example, in first learning how to subtract, a child might not know how to borrow and so may subtract the smaller from the larger number even when the smaller number is part of the minuend (e.g., $486 - 379 = 113$). A child may learn borrowing procedures but may still have difficulties borrowing from zero. These types of procedural errors are considered to reflect poor conceptual knowledge of the base-10 system (Fuson & Kwon, 1992) and/or problems in the application of subtraction procedures. Van Lehn (1982) distinguished between procedural errors that occur consistently (bugs) and that likely reflect a lack of conceptual and procedural knowledge, and procedural errors that occur only occasionally (slips) and that likely reflect either a lack of consolidation of knowledge or possibly lapses in attention (Barnes et al., 2002). Although not described in the developmental literature, errors due to visuospatial difficulties, such as inversions (reading or writing a 9 for a 6), reversals (15 for 51), crowding of work, neglect of one side of a problem, misalignment of digits in columns, or problems in visual attention and monitoring (e.g., ignoring signs, changing operations part way through a problem), have been the topic of several neuropsychological investigations of dyscalculia (Hartje, 1987; Strang & Rourke, 1985). These three types of errors—math fact, procedural, and visuospatial— which can be discerned in multidigit computation, map on to the subtypes of math disabilities in the model discussed previously.

Although several studies of math in children with SBM report achievement levels in math calculations (Fletcher et al., 1995; Friedrich, Lovejoy, Shaffer, Shurtleff, & Beilke, 1991; Halliwell, Carr, & Pearson, 1980; Shaffer, Friedrich, Shurtleff, & Wolf, 1985; Tuleya-Payne, 1983; Wills, Holmbeck, Dillon, & McLone, 1990), more recent studies have begun to investigate the cognitive processes involved in calculation performance through analysis of calculation errors. The logic behind these studies is that children with SBM should make more errors reflecting difficulties in visuospatial processing or visual attention than children without SBM, and that these types of errors might particularly characterize children with SBM who have specific math disability. These studies used an experimental written subtraction paradigm; unlike multiplication, which is thought to draw heavily on the language system, subtraction is associated with those parietal circuits implicated in the representation of the mental number line (Chochon, Cohen, van de Moortele, & Dehaene, 1999; Simon et al., 2005). Studies of written subtraction in children with SBM have shown that those who have math difficulties as well as problems in visuospatial processing are no more likely than their peers who are typically developing to make visuospatial/visual attention errors (Barnes et al., 2002; Barnes et al., 2006; Ayr, Yeates, & Enrile, 2005). Children with SBM who have both reading and math disabilities do make more math fact errors than children with specific math disability (Barnes et al., 2006), however. Concomitantly, visuospatial errors are not found in children with SBM for other operations such as long division (Barnes et al., 2002), which is also believed to draw heavily on visuospatial abilities (Rourke & Conway, 1997). Furthermore, visuospatial abilities and performance on multidigit calculation are not correlated in children with SBM nor in children who are typically developing (Ayr et al., 2005; Barnes et al., 2002).

It is interesting to note that in our studies of calculation errors in children with SBM (Barnes et al., 2006), all groups with SBM made more slips than did children in control groups considered to be typically developing. Whether this reflects lack of consolidation of computational procedures or attention difficulties is not clear. Attention disorders are common in children with SBM (Burmeister et al., 2005), and there is substantial overlap of attention problems and math difficulties in children without brain injury (Fuchs et al., 2005; Lyon, Fletcher, & Barnes, 2003). Whether and how attention disorders affect mathematical performance in children with and without math disabilities is an area that requires further study.

These studies of errors in multidigit arithmetic have several implications for math disability models. First, the types of visuospatial errors in calculation that have been noted in adults with acquired spatial dyscalculia and, by extension, hypothesized to typify children with specific math disabilities are, in fact, not characteristic of children with SBM who have deficits in both math calculation and visuospatial processing. This holds true even for those children with the most severe visuospatial deficits and even when operations that are purported to draw more heavily on nonverbal, spatial representations, such as subtraction and long division, are used. Furthermore, visuospatial skills were unrelated to multidigit calculation across several studies (see also Cirino, Morris, & Morris, 2002 and Rovet et al., 1994, for similar findings in different populations). These findings are not easily reconcilable with models of math disability that posit a spatial subtype of disability in math calculations for children with no reading disability. Second, consistent with the proposal that math fact retrieval is impaired in children with both reading and math disability, more errors in single-digit arithmetic were observed for the group with SBM with both disabilities.

Math Fact Retrieval in Children with SBM

The mastery of math facts (i.e., the ability to quickly and accurately retrieve answers to single-digit arithmetic problems) may be a foundational math skill important for growth in more complex calculations and perhaps for other domains of mathematics as well. The ability to solve single-digit arithmetic problems develops from counting strategies that change with experience and result, over time, in greater use of memory retrieval (Ashcraft, 1992; Siegler, 1987). Math fact retrieval is considered to be a core deficit in children with some types of math disabilities (Geary, 1993), and recent studies suggest that math fact retrieval is impaired in children with math disabilities regardless of whether there is a comorbid word reading disability (Jordan et al., 2003a, 2003b).

Barnes and colleagues (2006) compared math fact retrieval processes in children who were typically achieving and in children with SBM who had specific mathematics disability, both reading and mathematics disabilities, or no learning disability. This study addressed three questions:

1. Are the mathematical processing deficits in children who have significant perturbations of brain development similar to those in children with math disabilities without such neurological disorder? This comparison

speaks to how well models of math disability can explain findings across populations of children with math disabilities.

2. What is the relation between math fact mastery and more complex mathematical skills, such as multidigit arithmetic?

3. What is the relation between math fact mastery and those cognitive skills hypothesized to be important for the development of math fact retrieval skills, namely phonological abilities (Geary, 1993) and visuo-spatial abilities (Jordan et al., 2003b)?

Findings addressing these questions are presented next. Do children with SBM and math disabilities have difficulties with math fact retrieval? Children with SBM who had math disabilities were less accurate in single-digit arithmetic than children who were typically developing and children with SBM and no math disability. They were more likely to use less-mature counting strategies than the other groups and they were slower even on those problems in which they reported and appeared from observation to be retrieving math facts directly from memory (e.g., just knowing that 3 + 4 = 7 without having to compute the answer through counting strategies). Children with specific math disability had an advantage over those with both reading and math disabilities in that they were more accurate at solving small sum problems (i.e., problems with answers less than 10), which are most reliably retrieved directly from memory and which are hypothesized to draw more strongly on language-based representations (Stanescu-Cosson et al., 2004). This finding is compatible with the hypothesis that children who have comorbid reading and math disabilities lack the verbal working memory skills needed to hold all parts of a problem in memory in order learn the association between addends and answers (Geary, 1993). In all, the findings are in keeping with recent studies of children with math disabilities without neurodevelopmental disorder (e.g., Jordan et al., 2003a, 2003b). Of import, these findings from studies of math fact mastery in children with SBM suggest that regardless of reading status or the presence of significant perturbations of brain development, children with math disabilities have a core deficit in math fact retrieval. The convergence of findings across populations of children imposes constraints on the hypothesized core deficits in math disability models.

Although children with SBM and no learning disability were just as accurate on single-digit arithmetic problems as children who were typically developing, they used direct retrieval less often and were slower on direct retrieval trials. Although well within the average range on a standardized math computations test, their math achievement scores were not as high as those of typically developing children (Barnes et al., 2006). These findings suggest that, like phonological awareness and reading, math fact mastery is a skill that tracks variability in level of overall math computation ability. In other words, deficits in math fact mastery do not simply define math disabilities; math fact mastery is a skill that is normally distributed across children with differing levels of skill in mathematical computation. Models of reading are able to account for both ability and disability because phonological processes can be both core assets and core deficits. It remains to be seen whether math fact mastery plays a similar role in models of math development and disability or whether math fact mastery simply represents an outcome, rather than a cause, of mathematical difficulties.

Is there a relation between math fact mastery and more complex computation? In two studies, one with children who were typically developing from Grades 2 to 8 and one with children with SBM and control groups of children who were typically developing (in Grades 3 to 12), accuracy and speed in single-digit addition were highly predictive of accuracy in multi-digit written subtraction (Barnes et al., 2005; Barnes et al., 2006). This relation held even when single-digit arithmetic was very accurate. Results such as these suggest that the fluency of arithmetic operations at the single-digit level may be important for freeing cognitive resources to learn more complex computation procedures and for accurate performance of complex written calculations (Russell & Ginsburg, 1984).

Is there a relation between phonological skills, visuospatial skills, and math fact mastery? Several hypotheses surround the sources of deficits in math fact mastery, including deficient phonological representations (Geary, 1993); problems in inhibiting closely related math facts in memory (Geary, 2003); slow information processing across cognitive domains, including math (Bull & Johnston, 1997); and difficulties in manipulating nonverbal spatial representations, such as the mental number line (Jordan et al., 2003b). In the study reported here, children with SBM and no math disability actually had better word-reading and phonological skills than did the children who were typically developing, yet they were less skilled in math fact retrieval, suggesting that phonological skills cannot be the most important determinant of math fact mastery. Furthermore, phonological skills and visuospatial skills both accounted for significant but small amounts of variance in single-digit addition accuracy and problem-solving speed. Although these findings do not reveal what the nature of the representation is that underlies math fact mastery, they do suggest that neither phonological nor visuospatial abilities fully explain math fact mastery. More generally, the relation of space and number in both the development of mathematical skills and in the performance of calculation is poorly understood (Nuerk, Willmes, & Fias, 2005).

In our research we have found that fine motor or finger skills, not visuospatial skills, are strongly related to computational abilities in both children with SBM who have fine motor difficulties and in children who are typically developing (Barnes et al., 2005; see also Butterworth, 1999; Fayol, Barrouillet, & Marinthe, 1998). We have also found that fine motor skills, but not visuospatial skills, are related to counting knowledge and counting procedures at age 3, though visuospatial skills are related to matching on the basis of quantity (Barnes et al., 2005). Results such as these suggest that the way in which a skill is learned is important for the way in which it comes to be mentally represented; although math fact mastery appears to be a language-based skill in adults, its developmental course involves the use of finger and verbal counting, which may have implications for some types of mathematical representations.

Visuospatial Skills and Relation to Other Domains of Mathematics in Spina Bifida Myelomeningocele

Although we, and others, have found no evidence for a spatial form of dyscalculia in SBM, arithmetic or computation is only one aspect of mathematics. Research in cognitive neuroscience and cognitive studies in mathematics suggest that visuospatial skills are implicated in aspects of mathematics other than calculation. For example, numerical estimation recruits areas of the brain also involved in visuospatial cognition (Dehaene, Spelke, Pinel, Stanescu, & Tsivkin, 1999). In children who are typically developing, numerical estimation in multidigit addition is related to visuospatial working memory; exact calculation is related to verbal working memory with carrying and to verbal memory span when regrouping is not required (Khemani & Barnes, 2005). Word-problem solving has also been related to visuospatial skill (Geary, 1996), as has geometry (Clements, 1999). In a study of children with hydrocephalus, most with SBM, mathematical skills such as number knowledge (reading numbers, understanding number size, fractions, percents) and calculation were not as impaired as real-world estimation, geometry, and word-problem solving (Barnes et al., 2002). For children with SBM as well as children who are typically developing, visuospatial skills were related to performance on tests of math achievement measuring estimation, geometry, and word problems (Barnes et al., 2002).

In conclusion, SBM represents a congenital disorder in which brain development is impaired almost from the beginning of conception and further affected by secondary injuries involving hydrocephalus and shunting. Studies of math in children with SBM therefore involve brains in which substantial reorganization must occur in order to learn. In contrast, depending on the age of injury, TBI is a disorder in which development typically proceeds normally until the onset of injury. Outcomes vary with age and the amount of skill acquisition that has occurred prior to the injury. In the next section, we summarize studies of math development in children who have sustained TBI at different ages.

MATHEMATICAL SKILLS IN
CHILDREN WITH TRAUMATIC BRAIN INJURY

Studies of mathematical processing in children with TBI are relatively few, and most report overall levels of performance on academic achievement tests. Comparisons based on patterns of reading and math skills are not likely because distinct variations are not dramatically apparent compared with SBM or developmental learning disabilities. Often, the issue with TBI is explaining why day-to-day performance in school is poor despite adequate performance on standardized achievement tests. However, several studies of general math achievement in school-age children have suggested that math calculations are particularly affected by TBI compared with other academic skills such as reading (e.g., Chadwick, Rutter, Shaffer, & Shrout, 1981; Jaffe et al., 1992). Findings from more recent prospective investigations of math after childhood TBI are variable, with some studies reporting recovery of math computations into the average range by at least one year postinjury even in severely injured children (Ayr et al., 2005; Roncadin, Tiley, Ewing-Cobbs, Levin, & Barnes, 2004) and other studies reporting lower math computation scores in children with more severe injuries (Ewing-Cobbs et al., 1998; Taylor et al., 2002). The source of differences in results between these studies is not well understood, but even when the computation skills of children with severe brain injuries recover to age-appropriate levels, these basic skills do not translate into success in mathematics in the classroom. Only a fifth of children with severe TBI were in regular educational placements 2 years after their injury, despite average scores on tests of basic academic skills (Ewing-Cobbs, Levin, Fletcher, et al., 1998), and parent ratings of academic difficulties were typically far in excess of that revealed by scores on tests of basic academic skills (Ewing-Cobbs et al., 2004). It is interesting to note that in one study, although children with severe TBI did not differ from those with mild injuries or children in noninjured control groups on math computations, the group of severely injured children did have difficulty on achievement tests involving applied problem solving (Roncadin et al., 2004).

Relation of Mathematical Skills and Executive Processes

This pattern of results across studies suggests two possible explanations that are not necessarily mutually exclusive. One is that school-age children with TBI might have math disabilities in domains of mathematics other than calculation, which accounts for their poor classroom performance. This hypothesis awaits further validation research on whether there are one or more types of math disabilities (Lyon et al., 2003) as well as more comprehensive studies of mathematical processing in TBI. A second hypothesis is that many children with TBI do not have a primary disability in math computations, but their deficits in other cognitive domains significantly affect math performance.

Certainly, the average scores on tests of math calculations of many children with TBI do not translate into adequate mathematical functioning in the classroom. Academic performance in the classroom is strongly related to the level of competence in social and executive skills, particularly self-management skills (Hinshaw, 1992). Traditional tests of academic achievement often do not require such skills, and they combine problems of multiple types that draw on these skills to differing degrees into a single score (Ginsburg, Klein, & Starkey, 1998). It may be that deficits in processing speed, working memory, inhibitory control, and other executive skills affect these children's classroom performance in several domains of mathematics, including calculation. Findings relevant to this issue are presented below.

Children with TBI have deficits in several cognitive functions, such as working memory, planning, and processing speed (Anderson & Pentland, 1998; Barnes, Dennis, & Wilkinson, 1999; Dennis, Guger, Roncadin, Barnes, & Schachar, 2001; Ewing-Cobbs, Prasad, et al., 1998; Kinsella et al., 1995; Levin et al., 1996, 2002), which are also weak in children with math disabilities. The focus of recent studies on mathematical processing in TBI has been to investigate relations between various cognitive processes and math calculation skills. One such study (Ayr et al., 2005) found relations between performance on standardized or experimental calculation tasks and measures of planning (Tower of London), working memory (Freedom from Distractibility index; Wechsler Intelligence Scale for Children, 3rd edition [WISC-III; Wechsler, 1991]), declarative memory (recall of stories and word pairs), and processing speed (WISC-III Processing Speed Index). These measures, however, did not account for unique variance in math calculations for the TBI group. Two studies that looked at the types of errors made in math calculations found that TBI groups did not differ from control groups in errors purported to be related to executive processes, such as difficulty in switching between operations from one problem to another (Ayr et al., 2005; Roncadin et al., 2004).

Our new studies of math in children with TBI proceed from cognitive models of executive processes and cognitive developmental models of mathematical processing to more directly address questions about the interaction between executive dysfunction and math disabilities after childhood TBI. We propose that math disabilities in TBI are best predicted by brain injury variables that are associated with age at injury and that affect the development of working memory, other executive processes, and processing speed. In combination with core academic skills (such as math computation), these injury-related variables and deficits in executive processes determine the level of more integrative academic skills (such as math problem solving), that are important for classroom performance.

Age and the Effect of TBI on the Development of Math Computations

Hebb (1942) hypothesized that the earlier a brain lesion is sustained, the greater the potential impact on later development because brain injury is likely to adversely affect the acquisition of new skills. Dennis (1988) and Ewing-Cobbs and colleagues (Ewing-Cobbs, Fletcher, Landry, & Levin, 1985) have suggested that skills in a rapid stage of development might be most vulnerable to disruption by brain injury; conversely, skills that were well-consolidated at the time of injury might be more resistant to disruption. This seems to be the case for literacy, as diffuse injuries such as TBI or radiation for acute lymphoblastic leukemia prior to formal school instruction affects the acquisition of word reading skills (Barnes et al., 1999; Ewing-Cobbs et al., 2004; Spiegler & Barnes, 1997). Working memory, inhibitory control, and other executive processes that are implicated in the acquisition of mathematical skills (e.g., Espy et al., 2004) develop rapidly during the preschool and elementary years and are often disrupted by TBI. Thus, young children may be particularly vulnerable to posttraumatic deficits in executive processes and math.

A prospective longitudinal study of academic achievement after TBI has provided some evidence for this hypothesis (Ewing-Cobbs et al., 2004). Growth in math calculations in three groups of children were compared: those who sustained injuries between 5 and 7 years of age (before formal schooling in math or at the beginning of instruction in single-digit calculation and multidigit addition), those injured between 8 and 12 years of age (when multidigit arithmetic skills are being acquired), and those injured between 12 and 15 years of age (after most operations with whole numbers have been learned). Children were followed at six time points from shortly after the injury to 5 years postinjury. Individual growth curve analyses of math calculation scores showed that calculation scores were initially lower for children injured at an older age shortly after injury but that their scores increased more over the follow-up than did those of the younger children. In contrast, there was a deceleration in growth of math computation skills for children with both mild/moderate and severe head injuries who were injured in the preschool and early school years.

To conclude, the study of math in children with TBI reveals several points of interest regarding the understanding of math disabilities. Early diffuse injuries to the brain affect the developmental trajectory of math computation, suggesting that math skills that have yet to be learned or that are in a rapid phase of acquisition may be particularly vulnerable to early brain injury. Other acquired neurological disorders might produce similar effects on mathematical development. In any event, for TBI, a young age at injury appears to be a risk factor for the acquisition of some mathematical skills. Unlike most children who are typically developing and children with math disabilities, performance on math calculation achievement tests does not predict academic success in mathematics for children with TBI. Many children with TBI may not have a primary disability in math calculations. However, their difficulties in mathematics in the classroom are real and are likely mediated by impairments in working memory, other executive processes, and processing speed, which are more directly a consequence of the brain injury itself. Although this explanation of mathematical function applies to TBI, it also raises the question of whether math disabilities are fully captured through current diagnostic schemes applied to other children with suspected learning disorders. We do not mean to suggest that identification of math disabilities ought to include measures of executive processes (Lyon et al., 2003) but rather that the assessment of math for some children may need more evaluation of what is required to perform well in the classroom (Ewing-Cobbs et al., 2004).

GENERAL CONCLUSIONS AND FUTURE DIRECTIONS

In this chapter, we have compared and contrasted mathematics difficulties in children with two different pediatric brain injuries. SBM is a congenital disorder that begins almost at conception and is epitomized in children by disrupted development of math skills and good development of word recognition skills, reflecting a very high rate of impairment in mathematics abilities. Thus, in children with SBM, the development of mathematics occurs in neural systems that have already experienced considerable reorganization. In contrast, TBI represents a pediatric brain injury in which development can be disrupted at any point after birth. In many children, development has proceeded normally and the pattern of impairment reflects the age at which the injury was sustained and its severity. Mathematical skill development is more vulnerable to disruption by significant TBI sustained at a younger age. In children with SBM, math calculation tests are very predictive of achievement in mathematics; but in children with TBI, performance on such tests does not predict academic success. Children with SBM show impairment in a variety of mathematic tasks involving calculation and problem solving. The correlates of these performances are similar to those seen in children with developmental disorders affecting mathematics. In addition, distinctions between children with SBM who are impaired only in math and children with SBM who are impaired in both math and reading are just as relevant as those in the developmental learning disabilities literature. In contrast, children with TBI tend to show performance difficulties in math that are closely linked to executive function deficits, especially in school-age children. Deficits on executive function tasks predict impairment in a variety of areas after severe TBI. In mathematics, these deficits lead to more impairment on problem-solving tasks than on calculation tasks, although day-to-day performance in mathematics is often poor. In general, mathematics impairments in TBI reflect the effects of top-down cognitive processes, whereas in SBM there seems to be greater impairment of basic, or bottom-up, cognitive processes. This is consistent with the pathophysiology of the two disorders: Injury to the frontal lobes is very prominent in determining outcomes in TBI, whereas SBM has much to do with impairment in the posterior brain and cerebellum. Both disorders are associated with significant injury to the white matter that affects overall neural connectivity, but the mechanisms of injury are quite different (diffuse axonal injury versus hydrocephalus, respectively).

Future studies should compare the effects of different brain injuries on mathematics development using similar measures of mathematical processing and math-related cognitive competencies. In addition to SBM and TBI, it would be useful to directly compare mathematics development in children with other neurogenetic disorders, such as fragile X syndrome, Turner syndrome, and velocardiofacial syndrome. The latter disorders are all characterized by relatively sharp impairments in math and better development in word recognition abilities. In addition, evaluating performance on tasks involving math and cognitive processes in relation to direct assessments of the integrity of the brain are encouraged. Within each of these disorders, contemporary functional and structural imaging is beginning to reveal more directly how patterns of brain impairment produce patterns of impairment on academic and cognitive tasks. These types of studies are encouraged, particularly the use of functional imaging assessments, in which a particular math component process can be directly imaged in relation to an assessment of neural functioning and the use of new structural techniques, such as diffusion tensor imaging (see Ewing-Cobbs et al., in press). This latter technique shows particular promise in identifying effects of the injury on discrete white matter pathways, which in turn may better predict academic and cognitive impairments than may traditional voxel-based MRI morphometry. Such studies may well prove illuminating in identifying the neural networks that support skilled and impaired development in mathematic skills, with direct implications for understanding the neural basis for mathematics impairments in children with acquired and developmental learning disabilities.

REFERENCES

Anderson, V., & Pentland, L. (1998). Residual attention deficits following childhood brain injury: Implications for ongoing development. *Neuropsychological Rehabilitation, 8,* 283–300.

Ashcraft, M. (1992). Cognitive arithmetic: A review of data and theory. *Cognition, 44,* 75–106.

Ashcraft, M.H., Yamashita, T.S., & Aram, D.M. (1992). Mathematics performance in left and right brain-lesioned children and adolescents. *Brain and Cognition, 19,* 208–252.

Ayr, L.K., Yeates, K.O., Enrile, B.G. (2005). Arithmetic skills and their cognitive correlates in children with acquired and congenital brain disorder. *Journal of the International Neuropsychological Society, 11,* 249–262.

Barkovich., A.J. (2000). *Pediatric neuroimaging* (3rd ed.). New York: Raven Press.

Barnes, M.A., Dennis, M., & Wilkinson, M. (1999). Reading after closed brain injury in childhood: Effects on accuracy, fluency, and comprehension. *Developmental Neuropsychology, 15,* 1–24.

Barnes, M.A., Pengelly, S., Dennis, M., Wilkinson, M., Rogers, T., & Faulkner, H. (2002). Mathematics skills in good readers with hydrocephalus. *Journal of the International Neuropsychological Society, 8,* 72–82.

Barnes, M.A., Smith-Chant, B., & Landry, S. (2005). Number processing in neurodevelopmental disorders: Spina bifida myelomeningocele. In J.I.D. Campbell (Ed.), *Handbook of Mathematical Cognition* (pp. 299–313). New York: Psychology Press.

Barnes, M.A., Wilkinson, M., Boudousquie, A., Khemani, E., Dennis, M., & Fletcher, J.M. (2006). Arithmetic processing in children with spina bifida: Calculation accuracy, strategy use, and fact retrieval fluency. *Journal of Learning Disabilities, 39,* 174–187.

Brown, J.S., & Burton, R.R. (1978). Diagnostic models for procedural bugs in basic mathematical skills. *Cognitive Science, 2,* 155–192.

Bull, R., & Johnston, R.S. (1997). Children's arithmetic difficulties: Contributions from processing speed, item identification, and short-term memory. *Journal of Experimental Child Psychology, 65,* 1–24.

Bull, R., & Scerif, G. (2001). Executive functioning as a predictor of children's mathematics ability: Inhibition, switching, and working memory. *Developmental Neuropsychology, 19,* 273–293.

Burmeister, R., Hannay, H.J., Fletcher, J.M., Boudousquie, A., & Dennis, M. (2005). Attention problems and executive functions in children with spina bifida and hydrocephalus. *Child Neuropsychology, 11,* 265–284.

Butterworth, B. (1999). *What counts: How every brain is hardwired for math.* New York: Simon & Schuster.

Chadwick, O., Rutter, M., Shaffer, D., & Shrout, P.E. (1981). A prospective study of children with head injuries: Specific cognitive difficulties. *Journal of Clinical Neuropsychology, 3,* 101–120.

Chochon, F., Cohen, L., van de Moortele, P.F., & Dehaene, S. (1999). Differential contributions of the left and right inferior parietal lobules to number processing. *Journal of Cognitive Neuroscience, 11,* 617–630.

Cirino, P.T., Morris, M.K., & Morris, R.D. (2002). Neuropsychological concomitants of calculation skills in college students referred for learning difficulties. *Developmental Neuropsychology, 21,* 201–218.

Clements, D.H. (1999). Geometric and spatial thinking in young children (1999). In J.V. Copley (Ed.), *Mathematics in the early years* (pp. 66–79). Reston, VA: National Council of Teachers of Mathematics.

Dehaene, S. (1992). Varieties of numerical abilities. *Cognition, 44,* 1–42.

Dehaene, S., Piazza, M., Pinel, P., & Cohen, L. (2005). Three parietal circuits for number processing. In J.I.D. Campbell (Ed.), *Handbook of mathematical cognition* (pp. 433–453). New York: Psychology Press.

Dehaene, S., Spelke, E., Pinel, P., Stanescu, R., & Tsivkin, S. (1999). Sources of mathematical thinking: Behavioral and brain-imaging evidence. *Science, 284*(5416), 970–974.

del Bigio, M. (1993). Neuropathological changes caused by hydrocephalus. *Acta Neuropathologica, 18*, 573–585.

Dennis, M. (1988). Language and the young damaged brain. In T. Boll & B.K. Bryant (Eds.), *Clinical neuropsychology and brain function: Research, measurement, and practice: Vol. 7. The master lecture series* (pp. 89–123). Washington, DC: American Psychological Association.

Dennis, M., & Barnes, M.A. (2002). Math and numeracy in young adults with spina bifida and hydrocephalus. *Developmental Neuropsychology, 21*, 141–155.

Dennis, M., Fletcher, J.M., Rogers, T., Hetherington, R., & Francis, D. (2002). Object-based and action-based visual perception in children with spina bifida and hydrocephalus. *Journal of the International Neuropsychological Society, 8*, 95–106.

Dennis, M., Guger, S., Roncadin, C., Barnes, M.A., & Schachar, R. (2001). Attentional-inhibitory control and social-behavioral regulation after childhood closed brain injury: Do biological, developmental, and recovery variables predict outcome? *Journal of the International Neuropsychological Society, 7*, 683–692.

Dennis, M., Landry, S.H., Barnes, M.H., & Fletcher, J.M. (2006). A model of neuro-cognitive function in spina bifida over the lifespan. *Journal of the International Neuropsychological Society, 12*, 285–296.

Diamond, A. (2002). Normal development of prefrontal cortex from birth to young adulthood: Cognitive functions, anatomy, and biochemistry. In D.T. Stuss & R.T. Knight (Eds.), *Frontal lobe function* (pp. 466–503). New York: Oxford University Press.

Espy, K.A., McDiarmid, M.M., Cwik, M.F., Stalets, M.M., Hamby, A., & Senn, T.F. (2004). The contribution of executive functions to emergent mathematic skills in preschool children. *Developmental Neuropsychology, 26*, 465– 486.

Ewing-Cobbs, L., Barnes, M., Fletcher, J., Levin, H.S., Swank, P.R., & Song, J. (2004). Modeling of longitudinal academic achievement scores after pediatric traumatic brain injury. *Developmental Neuropsychology, 25*, 107–134.

Ewing-Cobbs, L., Fletcher, J.M., Landry, S.H., & Levin, H.S. (1985). Language disorders after pediatric brain injury. In J.E. Darby (Ed.), *Speech and Language Evaluation in Neurology: Childhood Disorders* (pp. 97–111). Orlando, FL: Grune & Stratton, Inc.

Ewing-Cobbs, L., Hasan, K., Prasad, M., Kramer, L., & Bachevalier, J. (in press). Relation of corpus callosum diffusion anisotropy and neuropsychological outcomes in twins disconcordant for traumatic brain injury. *American Journal of Neuroradiology.*

Ewing-Cobbs, L., Levin, H.S., & Fletcher, J.M. (1998). Neuropsychological dequeleae following pediatric traumatic brain injury: Advances during the past decade. In M. Yivisaker (Ed.), *Head injury rehabilitation in children and adolescents* (pp. 11–26). San Diego: College Hill.

Ewing-Cobbs, L., Levin, H.S., Fletcher, J.M., Iovino, I., & Miner, M.E. (1998). Academic achievement and academic placement following traumatic brain injury in children and adolescents: A two-year longitudinal study. *Journal of Clinical and Experimental Neuropsychology, 20*, 769–781.

Ewing-Cobbs, L., Prasad, M., Fletcher, J.M., Levin, H.S., Miner, M.E., & Eisenberg, H.M. (1998). Attention after pediatric traumatic brain injury: A multidimensional assessment. *Child Neuropsychology, 4*, 35–48.

Fayol, M., Barrouillet, P., & Marinthe, C. (1998). Predicting arithmetical achievement from neuro-psychological performance: A longitudinal study. *Cognition, 68*, 363–370.

Fletcher, J.M., Brookshire, B.L., Bohan, T.P., Brandt, M.E., & Davidson, K.C. (1995). Early hydrocephalus. In B.P. Rourke (Ed.), *Syndrome of nonverbal learning disabilities: Neurodevelopmental manifestations* (pp. 206–238). New York: Guilford Publications, Inc.

Fletcher, J.M., Copeland, K., Frederick, J., Blaser, S.E., Kramer, L.A., Northrup, H., et al. (2005). Spinal lesion level in spina bifida meningomyelocele: A source of neural and cognitive heterogeneity. *Journal of Neurosurgery, 102,* 268–279.

Fletcher, J.M., Dennis, M., Northrup, H., Barnes, M.A., Hannay, H.J., Landry, S.H., et al. (2004). Spina bifida: Genes, brain, and development. In L.M. Glidden (Ed.), *Handbook of research on mental retardation* (Vol. 28). San Diego: Academic Press.

Friedrich, W.N., Lovejoy, M.C., Shaffer, J., Shurtleff, D.B., & Beilke, R.L. (1991). Cognitive abilities and achievement status of children with myelomeningocele: A contemporary sample. *Journal of Pediatric Psychology, 16,* 423–428.

Fuchs, L.S., Compton, D.L., Fuchs, D., Paulsen, K., Bryant, J.D., & Hamlett, C.L. (2005). The prevention, identification, and cognitive determinants of math difficulty. *Journal of Educational Psychology, 9,* 493–513.

Fuson, K.C., & Kwon, Y. (1992). Korean children's understanding of multidigit addition and subtraction. *Child Development, 63,* 491–506.

Geary, D.C. (1993). Mathematical disabilities: Cognitive, neuropsychological, and genetic components. *Psychological Bulletin, 114,* 345–362.

Geary, D.C. (1996). Sexual selection and sex differences in mathematical abilities. *Behavioral and Brain Sciences, 19,* 229–284.

Geary, D.C. (2003). Learning disabilities in arithmetic: Problem-solving differences and cognitive deficits. In H.L. Swanson, K.R. Harris, & S. Graham (Eds.), *Handbook of learning disabilities.* (pp. 199–212). New York: The Guilford Press.

Geary, D.C., Hamson, C.O., & Hoard, M.K. (2000). Numerical and arithmetical cognition: A longitudinal study of process and concept deficits in children with learning disability. *Journal of Experimental Child Psychology, 77,* 236–263.

Geary, D.C., & Hoard, M.K. (2005). Learning disabilities in arithmetic and mathematics: Theoretical and empirical perspectives. In J.I.D. Campbell (Ed.), *Handbook of mathematical cognition (pp. 253–267).* New York: Psychology Press.

Geary, D.C., Hoard, M.K., & Hamson, C.O. (1999). Numerical and arithmetical cognition: Patterns of functions and deficits in children at risk for a mathematical disability. *Journal of Experimental Child Psychology, 74,* 213–239.

Gennarelli, T.A., Thibault, L.E., & Graham, D.I. (1998). Diffuse axonal injury: An important form of traumatic brain damage. *Neuroscientist, 4,* 202–215.

Ginsburg, H.P., Klein, A., & Starkey, P. (1998). The development of children's mathematical thinking: Connecting research with practice. In W. Damon (Series Ed.) & I.E. Siegel & K.A. Renninger (Vol. Eds.), *Handbook of child psychology: Vol. 4. Child psychology in practice* (5th ed., pp. 401–476). New York: John Wiley & Sons.

Halliwell, M.D., Carr, J.G., & Pearson, A.M. (1980). The intellectual and educational functioning of children with neural tube defects. *Zeitschrift fur Kinderchirurgie, 31,* 375–381.

Hanich, L., Jordan, N., Kaplan, D., & Dick, J. (2001). Performance across different areas of mathematical cognition in children with learning difficulties. *Journal of Educational Psychology, 93,* 615–626.

Hannay, H.J., Fletcher, J.M., & Brandt, M.E. (1999). The role of the corpus callosum in the cognitive development of children with congenital brain malformations. In S.H. Broman & J.M. Fletcher (Eds.), *The changing nervous system: Neurobehavioral consequences of early brain disorders* (pp. 149–171). New York: Oxford University Press.

Hartje, W. (1987). The effect of spatial disorders on arthimetical skills. In G. Deloche & X. Seron (Eds.), *Mathematical disabilities: A cognitive neuropsychological perspective* (pp. 121–135). Mahwah, NJ: Lawrence Erlbaum Associates.

Hebb, D.O. (1942). The effect of early and late brain injury upon test scores, and the nature of normal adult intelligence. *Proceedings of the American Philosophical Society, 85,* 275–292.

Hinshaw, S.P. (1992). Externalizing behavior problems and academic underachievement in childhood and adolescence: Causal relationships and underlying mechanisms. *Psychological Bulletin, 111,* 127–155.

Jaffe, K.M., Fay, G.C., Polissar, N.L., Martin, K.M., Shurtleff, H., Rivara, J.B., et al. (1992). Severity of pediatric traumatic brain injury and early neurobehavioral outcome: A cohort study. *Archives of Physical Medicine and Rehabilitation, 73,* 540–547.

Jordan, N.C., Hanich, L.B., & Kaplan, D. (2003a). A longitudinal study of mathematical competencies in children with specific math difficulties versus children with comorbid mathematics and reading difficulties. *Child Development, 74,* 834–850.

Jordan, N.C., Hanich, L.B., & Kaplan, D. (2003b). Arithmetic fact mastery in young children: A longitudinal investigation. *Journal of Experimental Child Psychology, 85,* 103–119.

Khemani, E. & Barnes, M.A. (2005). Calculation and estimation in typically developing children from grade 3 to 8. *Canadian Psychology, 46,* 219.

Kinsella, G., Prior, M., Sawyer, M., Murtagh, D., Eisenmajer, R., Anderson, V., et al. (1995). Neuropsychological deficit and academic performance in children and adolescents following traumatic brain injury. *Journal of Pediatric Psychology, 20,* 753–767.

Konrad, K., Gauggel, S., Manz, A., & Scholl, M. (2000). Inhibitory control in children with traumatic brain injury (TBI) and children with attention deficit/hyperactivity disorder (ADHD). *Brain Injury, 14,* 859–875.

Kosc, L. (1974). Developmental dyscalculia. *Journal of Learning Disabilities, 7,* 46–59.

Kraus, J.F. (1995). Epidemiological features of brain injury in children: Occurrence, children at risk, causes, and manner of injury, severity, and outcomes. In S.H. Broman & M.E. Michel (Eds.), *Traumatic brain injury in children* (pp. 22–39). New York: Oxford University Press.

Levin, H.S., Benavidez, D.A., Verger-Maestre, K., Perachio, N., Song, J., Mendelsohn, D.B., et al. (2000). Reduction of corpus callosum growth after severe traumatic brain injury in children. *Neurology, 54,* 647–653.

Levin, H.S., Culhane, K.A., Mendelsohn, D., Lilly, M.A., Bruce, D., Fletcher, J.M., et al. (1993). Cognition in relation to magnetic resonance imaging in head-injured children and adolescents. *Archives of Neurology, 50,* 897–908.

Levin, H.S., Fletcher, J.M., Kufera, J.A., Harward, H., Lilly, M.A., Mendelsohn, D., et al. (1996). Dimensions of cognition measured by the Tower of London and other cognitive tasks in head-injured children and adolescents. *Developmental Neuropsychology, 12,* 17–34.

Levin, H.S., Hanten, G., Chang, C., Zhang, L., Schachar, R., Ewing-Cobbs, L., et al. (2002). Working memory after traumatic brain injury in children. *Annals of Neurology, 52,* 82–88.

Levin, H.S., Mendelsohn, D., Lilly, M.A., Yeakley, J., Song, J., Scheibel, R.S., et al. (1997). Magnetic resonance imaging in relation to functional outcome of pediatric closed brain injury: A test of the Ommaya-Gennarelli model. *Neurosurgery, 40,* 432–441.

Levin, H.S., Song, J., Ewing-Cobbs, L., Chapman, S.B., & Mendelsohn, D. (2001). Word fluency in relations to severity of closed brain injury, associated frontal brain lesions, and age at injury in children. *Neuropsychologia, 39,* 122–131.

Lyon, G.R., Fletcher, J.M., & Barnes, M.C. (2003). Learning disabilities. In E.J. Mash and R. Barkley (Eds.), *Child psychopathology* (2nd ed., pp. 520–588). New York: Guilford.

Marzocchi, G.M., Lucangeli, D., De Meo, T., Fini, F., & Cornoldi, C. (2002). The disturbing effect of irrelevant information on arithmetic problem solving in inattentive children. *Developmental Neuropsychology, 21,* 73–92.

Mazzocco, M.M.M. (1998). A process approach to describing mathematics difficulties in girls with Turner syndrome. *Pediatrics, 2,* 492–496.

Mazzocco, M.M.M. (2001). Math learning disability and math LD subtypes: Evidence from studies of Turner syndrome, fragile X syndrome, and neurofibromatosis type 1. *Journal of Learning Disabilities, 34,* 520–533.

McLean, J.F., & Hitch, G.J. (1999). Working memory impairments in children with specific arithmetic learning difficulties. *Journal of Experimental Child Psychology, 74,* 240–260.

Morrison, S.R., & Siegel, L.S. (1991). Learning disabilities: A critical review of definitional and assessment issues. In J.E. Obrzut & G.W. Hynd (Eds.), *Neuropsychological foundation of learning disabilities: A handbook of issues, methods, and practice* (pp. 79–98). New York: Academic Press.

Norman, M.C., McGillivray, B.C., Calloused, D.K., Hill, A., & Poskitt, K.J. (1995). *Congenital malformations of the brain.* New York: Oxford.

Nuerk, H.C., Willmes, K., & Fias, W. (2005). Perspectives on number processing: Editorial. *Psychology Science, 47,* 4–9.

Passolunghi, M.C., & Siegel, L.S. (2001). Short-term memory, working memory, and inhibitory control in children with difficulties in arithmetic problem solving. *Journal of Experimental Child Psychology, 80,* 44–57.

Povlishock, J. (2000). Pathophysiology of neural injury: Therapeutic opportunities and challenges. *Clinical Neurosurgery, 46,* 113–126.

Reigel, D.H., & Rotenstein, D. (1994). Spina bifida. In W.R. Cheek (Ed.), *Pediatric neurosurgery* (3rd ed., pp. 51–76). Philadelphia: W.B. Saunders.

Roncadin, C., Tiley, H., Ewing-Cobbs, L., Levin, H., & Barnes, M.A. (2004). Math skills following childhood closed brain injury. *Journal of the International Neuropsychological Society, 10*(51), 51.

Rourke, B.P. (1993). Arithmetic disabilities, specific and otherwise: A neuropsychological perspective. *Journal of Learning Disabilities, 26,* 214–226.

Rourke, B.P., & Conway, J.A. (1997). Disabilities of arithmetic and mathematical reasoning: Perspectives from neurology and neuropsychology. *Journal of Learning Disabilities, 30,* 34–46.

Rourke, B.P. & Finlayson, M.A.J. (1978). Neuropsychological significanceof variations in patterns of academic performance: Verbal and visual–spatial abilities. *Journal of Abnormal Child Psychology, 6,* 121–133.

Rovet, J., Szekely, C., & Hockenberry, M.N. (1994). Specific arithmetic calculation deficits in children with Turner syndrome. *Journal of Clinical Experimental Neuropsychology, 16,* 820–839.

Russell, R.L., & Ginsburg, H.P. (1984). Cognitive analysis of children's mathematical difficulties. *Cognition and Instruction, 1,* 217–244.

Shaffer, J., Friedrich, W.N., Shurtleff, D.B., & Wolf, L. (1985). Cognitive and achievement status of children with myelomeningocele. *Journal of Pediatric Psychology, 10,* 325–336.

Shalev, R.S., Auerbach, J., Manor, O. & Gross-Tsur, V. (2000). Developmental dyscalculia: Prevalence and prognosis. *European Child and Adolescent Psychiatry, 9,* 58–64.

Share, D.L., Moffitt, T.E., & Silva, P.A. (1988). Factors associated with arithmetic-and-reading disability and specific arithmetic disability. *Journal of Learning Disabilities, 21,* 313–320.

Siegel, L.S., & Ryan, E.B. (1989). The development of working memory in normally achieving and subtypes of learning disabled children. *Child Development, 60,* 973–980.

Siegler, R.S. (1987). The perils of averaging data over strategies: An example from children's addition. *Journal of Experimental Psychology: General, 116,* 250–264.

Simon, T.J., Bearden, C.E., McDonald-Ginn, D.M., & Zackai, E. (2005). Visuospatial and numerical cognitive deficits in children with chromosome 22q11.2 deletion syndrome. *Cortex, 41,* 145–155.

Spiegler, B.J., & Barnes, M.A. (1997). Two different forms of brain injury (ALL & CHI) before the age of 6 disrupt the acquisition of phonological analysis skills in reading. *Journal of the International Neuropsychological Society, 3,* 62.

Stanescu-Cosson, R., Pinel, P., van de Moortele, P.F., Le Bihan, D., Cohen, L., & Daehene, S. (2004). Cerebral bases of calculation processes: Impact of number size on the cerebral circuits for exact and approximate calculation. *Brain, 123,* 2240–2255.

Strang, J.D., & Rourke, B.P., (1985). Arithmetic disability subtypes: The neuropsychological significance of specific arithmetical impairment in childhood. In B.P. Rourke (Ed.), *Neuropsychology of learning disabilities: Essentials of subtype analysis* (pp. 167–183) New York: Guilford Press.

Swanson, H.L., & Sachse-Lee, C. (2001). Mathematical problem solving and working memory in children with learning disabilities: Both executive and phonological processes are important. *Journal of Experimental Child Psychology, 79,* 294–321.

Taylor, H.G., Yeates, K.O., Wade, S.L., Drotar, D., Stancin, T., & Minich, N. (2002). A prospective study of short- and long-term outcomes after traumatic brain injury in children: Behavior and achievement. *Neuropsychology, 16,* 15–27.

Tuleya-Payne, H.D. (1983). Mathematics achievement and cognitive factors in spina bifida children with hydrocephalus. *Dissertation Abstracts International, 44,* 1423a.

van Lehn, K. (1982). Bugs are not enough: Empirical studies of bugs, impasses and repairs in procedural skills. *Journal of Mathematical Behavior, 3,* 3-71.

Wechsler, D. (1991). *Wechsler intelligence scale for children* (3rd ed.). New York: Harcourt Assessment.

Willmott, C., Anderson, V., & Anderson, P. (2000). Attention following pediatric brain injury: A developmental perspective. *Developmental Neuropsychology, 17,* 361–379.

Wills, K.E. (1993). Neuropsychological functioning in children with spina bifida and/or hydrocephalus. *Journal of Clinical Child Psychology, 22,* 247–265.

Wills, K.E., Holmbeck, G.N., Dillon, K., & McLone, D.G. (1990). Intelligence and achievement in children with myelomeningocele. *Journal of Pediatric Psychology, 15,* 161–176.

Chapter 11

Math Performance of Students with ADHD

Cognitive and Behavioral Contributors and Interventions

Sydney S. Zentall

+ +

Attention deficit hyperactivity disorder (ADHD) is a chronic, neuro-behavioral disability with both genetic and environmental etiologies. The diagnosis of ADHD is based on observations and ratings of the major symptoms of hyperactivity/impulsivity and inattention. Usually, however, a diagnosis is warranted only when ADHD is severe enough to impair functioning (typically in learning or socialization tasks). In other words, it is the degree and chronicity of this behavioral symptomology that differentiates it from age-appropriate behavior (e.g., most toddlers and preschoolers show developmentally appropriate active and "inattentive" behavior). Using these criteria of symptoms and impairment, ADHD is identified as the most prevalent disorder in children in the United States, estimated to affect 3%–7% of American children and 5%–10% of children worldwide (American Psychiatric Association, 2000; Faraone, Sergeant, Gillberg, & Bierderman, 2003). Prevalence rates differ for the various subtypes of ADHD: the inattentive subtype (20%–30%), the hyperactive/impulsive subtype (15%), and the combined subtype (50%–75%) (American Psychiatric Association, 2000; Mayes, Calhoun, & Crowell, 2000).

Even though the number of symptoms and degree of impairment vary, the majority of students with ADHD experience attention and behavior difficulties that compromise their academic success. Underachievement in students with ADHD has been documented across the academic areas of reading, spelling, and arithmetic, even when IQ score is taken into account. For example, 30% of students with ADHD fail to achieve at a level predicted by their age or IQ score (Barry, Lyman, & Klinger, 2002; Marshall, Hynd, Handwerk, & Hall, 1997).

This chapter will focus on the performance of students with ADHD in arithmetic. Underachievement in mathematics increases with age in the general population, and for those students diagnosed with attention deficits, the discrepancy between IQ score and math achievement increases with age (Jordan & Hanich, 2003; Nussbaum, Grant, Roman, Poole, & Bigler, 1990). Moreover, higher rates of math learning disabilities are also reported for students with ADHD (31%) than are reported for the general population (6%–7%), and a quarter of students with arithmetic disabilities also have ADHD (Mayes et al., 2000; Shalev et al., 2001). For students identified with the inattentive or the combined subtype of ADHD (i.e., approximately 85% of all students with ADHD, Mayes et al., 2000), inattention has been associated with math difficulties or mathematical learning disabilities (MLD) (e.g., Marshall, 1997; Marshall, Schafer, O'Donnell, Elliott, & Handwerk, 1999). Also, students identified with MLD have been assessed as having problems with attention and organization (Badian & Ghublikian, 1983). This association between attention and mathematics has *not* been found when students with ADHD (or reading disability) were excluded from the samples studied (Shalev et al., 2001). (The issue of ADHD versus learning difficulties and their overlap will be addressed in a later section of this chapter on co-occurring disabilities.)

The relationship between inattention and math performance, specifically in students with ADHD, is intriguing and will be emphasized in the next section, which addresses the cognitive contributors to math performance. Based on an understanding of these contributing factors, this chapter will draw implications for instruction for students with ADHD and report related research on interventions. The empirical findings in this chapter are reported without specifying the definition of ADHD, its severity in study participants, co-occurring conditions, or identified subtypes. Most researchers have not identified the subtypes of ADHD in their study samples, although differences in mathematics have rarely been observed among subtypes. The reader is thus forewarned that the study findings reviewed may be influenced by these nonspecified factors. Some empirical work in this chapter will include greater specification (i.e., those studies with statistical or design controls that lead to more definitive conclusions). For a review that provides a foundation for some of the research presented in this chapter on etiologies and theories, attention, working memory, and academic achievement of children with ADHD, see Zentall (2006).

IMPAIRMENTS IN SUSTAINED ATTENTION AND WORKING MEMORY

Students with ADHD habituate to stimuli more rapidly than do their peers (e.g., Sergeant, Geurts, Huijbregts, Scheres, & Oosterlaan, 2003). Perhaps for this reason, they 1) have difficulty maintaining attention to repetitive stimuli, 2) spend less time rehearsing verbal information unless reinforced at high rates, and 3) demonstrate increased activity and errors, especially during later trials of rote or overly familiar tasks. When students with ADHD attempt to maintain attention and then perform an additional task (e.g., hold information in mind in order to organize or update that information), they demonstrate difficulties with these additional requirements of working memory (e.g., McInnes, Humphries, Hogg-Johnson, & Tannock, 2003). (See Chapter 5 for additional information on working memory). Some of these impairments in students with ADHD have been documented during the performance of laboratory tasks requiring recall of verbal items in a specific order with verbal interference (Kataria, Hall, Wong, & Keys, 1992; Webster, Hall, Brown, & Bolen, 1996) and with memory updating (i.e., recall of recent items in the proper order; Roodenrys, Koloski, & Grainger, 2001).

Working memory might be better termed *working attention* (Kaplan, Crawford, Dewey, & Fisher, 2000; Sergeant et al., 2003) because it involves manipulating information held in mind rather than storing information (memory). Students with ADHD perform adequately on memory tasks. The only documented memory differences between students with ADHD and their classmates have been found where there was verbal interference (e.g., new information) prior to storage (see Zentall, 2006). That is, an interference task changes a sustained attention task to a working memory task and adds a working memory component to a memory task.

The impairment of working memory in students with ADHD appears to be specific to auditory processing (Chang et al., 1999; Jonsdottir, Bouma, Sergeant, & Scherder, 2004). There is evidence that these students perform well with visual formatting that is not embedded with visual distractors, and specifically when they are given opportunities to review cues (Chang et al., 1999), even though students with ADHD have more difficulty recalling sequences of visual cues that change spatial locations than do students without ADHD but with equivalent IQ scores (McInnes et al., 2003). In contrast, impairments in working memory for students with MD have been consistently documented in both visual and verbal areas, both of which are related to their mathematics performance (see Geary, Hoard, Byrd-Craven, & DeSoto, 2004; Keeler & Swanson, 2001).

Failure to Sustain Attention Affects
Computational Performance

For students with ADHD, difficulties sustaining attention during repetitive tasks could contribute to their failure to overlearn or automatize basic computational skills. In fact, research in this area more often reports group differences in math facts than in problem solving, with at least one study reporting worse performance for students with ADHD on math facts than on applied word problems (Marshall et al., 1999). Furthermore, performance on rote math calculations elicits responses, such as more activity and errors over time and greater within-session variability, that are similar to those observed during other sustained attention tasks (Bennett, Zentall, Giorgetti-Borucki, & French, 2006; Lee & Zentall, 2002; Zentall & Smith, 1993). Evidence showing that these impairments persist over time for students with ADHD (e.g., Zentall & Smith, 1993) as well as for students with MLD (in contrast to time-limited difficulties with procedural skill, such as counting strategies, Geary, 1994), indicate that deficits in fact retrieval are not just a lag in acquisition.

Although most students with ADHD experience chronic difficulties with math fact performance, the nature of this difficulty does change with age. For example, Mariani and Barkley (1997) found clinic-referred preschool children with ADHD to be less accurate in mathematics than preschoolers without ADHD, and another study found that elementary students with ADHD also performed less accurately than did children in comparison groups (Zentall, Smith, Lee, & Wieczorek, 1994). In contrast, by the middle school years, accuracy is no longer a sensitive measure of ADHD; only fluency continues to differentiate students with ADHD from comparison participants. Impairments in fluency have been demonstrated in second- through eighth-grade students with ADHD (with and without aggression), using paper- and computer-presented tasks, even with performance scores adjusted for IQ score and for the slower typing speed of youth with ADHD (Zentall, 1990; Zentall & Smith, 1993; Zentall et al., 1994). Ackerman, Anhalt, Dykman, and Holcomb (1986) reported that out of all learned automatic skills (e.g., naming speed, number computations, writing speed), only number computations had *not* become automatized for students with attention disorders (with and without hyperactivity) relative to comparisons matched in age, and with IQ statistically partialed out.

Students with MLD are also slower in math fact performance tasks than their peers who are typical learners (Cawley, Parmar, Foley, Salmon, & Roy, 2001; for review, see Gersten, Jordan, & Flojo, 2005). Differences between students with ADHD and those with other impairments have been documented only in addition facts, such that students with learning disabilities (LD) and those with both ADHD and aggression demonstrate the most severe problems in timed addition facts, followed by students with ADHD only, and then by students without ADHD (Zentall, 1990; Zentall & Smith, 1993).

Working Attention Affects Computational Performance

Holding information in mind while ignoring external stimulation is required for the performance of mental math (Carver, 1979).

> "The child not only has to store the verbal form of the problem, but to retrieve and apply learned mathematical rules or to make on-line mathematical calculations. At the same time he or she may also have to store intermediate products of calculations." (Pickering & Gathercole, 2004, p. 404)

On a similar but simpler task, such as verbally reordering a sequence of digits backwards, students with ADHD and MLD have performed worse than students who were typical learners (e.g., Passolunghi, Marzocchi, & Fiorillo, 2005). In the classroom, working memory impairments can be observed during math performance that involves multiple steps. In fact, Bryant, Bryant, and Hammill (2000) found teacher ratings of students' performance on multistep problems to be the single strongest predictor of math achievement for students with LD (from an original pool of about 30 math behaviors, such as *makes borrowing errors* and *disregards decimals,* that were associated with math LD). Holding multiple steps in mind could also be implicated in procedural skill errors, which have accounted for 84% of the variance associated with the complexity of addition problems for students with MLD (Geary, 1994; Geary et al., 2004).

Working Attention Affects Word Problem Performance

Students with ADHD have demonstrated difficulties in math word problems specifically associated with different operations in single-action word problems and mixed actions in same-operation word problems (i.e., working memory requirements) (Zentall, 1990). That is, they do not differ from comparison adolescents in the performance of single-action word problems with a single operation (when controlling for group-assessed reading achievement, cognitive skills, etc.; Zentall, 1990). Using more precise control with computers, we hypothesized that elementary students with attention disorders would have greater difficulty than students in a comparison group in terms of holding the question in mind while processing relevant problem information (Zentall et al., 1994). To test this, we assigned an unknown variable to the beginning (? + b = c), middle (a + ? = c), or end (a + b = ?) of a problem. In other words, we changed the order of information with no change in information or vocabulary. The group differences associated with holding the unknown in the first and second positions (i.e., working memory requirements) were no longer found when verbal cognitive ability was statistically controlled. In other words, group differences in math word problems are often related to working memory requirements.

In contrast, Passolunghi & Pazzagliab (2004) found that working memory skills are proficient in children who are typical learners, who could recall text information, solve word problems, and perform computations. Even though working memory skills are proficient in typical learners, the number of words and computations in a word problem have accounted for 87% of the variance in word problem difficulty for typical fifth graders (for review, see Geary, 1994, p. 97).

Differences in the type of working memory impairments (primarily verbal for students with ADHD and verbal plus visual for students with MLD) could explain differential findings from studies that assess the effects of verbal versus visual irrelevant information and verbal versus visual working memory impairments. For instance, Passolunghi et al. (2005) found that students with ADHD solved, recalled, and used information from problems with irrelevant verbal information "that greatly enriched the surface representation of the problem" *less* frequently than students with MLD; however, students with ADHD solved problems with irrelevant numeric information *more* frequently than did students with MLD (Passolunghi et al., 2005, p. 747). (Students in comparison groups solved more problems with both types of nonrelevant information than either group with disabilities.) Also, performance gains on the Raven's Standard Progressive Matrices (Raven, 1965) produced by attentional cuing are greatest for those students with ADHD with poor working memory of word sequences, in contrast to students with LD, whose gains due to attentional cuing are associated with poor working memory of object sequences (Cherkes-Julkowski, Stolzenberg, & Segal, 1991).

Failure to hold information in mind could also lead to secondary outcomes during the performance of verbal comprehension tasks, such as word problem performance. For instance, an inability to hold information in mind associated with ADHD could contribute to findings that students with ADHD respond more rapidly to stimuli than their peers (e.g., Banaschewski et al., 2003) and to spend less time considering alternative solutions (e.g., Cohen, Weiss, & Minde, 1972). Tant and Douglas (1982) gave students with and without ADHD pictures of letters, flowers, and numbers that varied along several dimensions (e.g., size, position) in a visual concept task that required holding multiple dimensions in mind. Students with ADHD asked a larger proportion of questions about single dimensions (e.g., size only) than students with reading disability (RD) matched in verbal IQ score. During the performance of communication tasks, students with ADHD also requested fewer cues, especially when getting more information also meant receiving additional interpersonal or instructional delay time. As has been found for math problem solving, verbal problem solving is *not* an impaired skill for students with ADHD when there are few requirements for working memory or delayed responding (Barry et al., 2002; Zentall, Kuester, & Craig, 2006).

Co-occurring Disabilities and Associated Attention and IQ Impairments

Building on the previously described overlap between groups of students with ADHD and MLD, this section addresses the extent of overlap between ADHD and RD and among reading, math, and inattention.

Learning Disability Overlap   In a study of 241 students with ADHD, approximately 9% (having a mean full-scale IQ score of 100) had RD, 26% were average readers, and 15% achieved higher scores that predicted by IQ score (the remaining half could not be classified based on the strict criteria for group assignment) (Halperin, Gittelman, Klein, & Rudel, 1984). For students with ADHD and co-occurring RD, poorer cognitive skills (verbal memory and IQ) have been documented relative to matched groups of individuals with ADHD without RD (Jordan & Hanich, 2003; McGee, Williams, Moffitt, & Anderson, 1989; Willcutt et al., 2001). These cognitive skill impairments have outcomes in receptive language; Pisecco, Baker, Silva, and Brooke (2001) found that receptive language problems for 3- to 5-year-old children with comorbid ADHD and RD or with RD were greater only than for young children with ADHD only, who did not differ from students in comparison groups. The 3- to 5-year-olds with ADHD and RD in that study also exhibited more disruptive behavior disorders than did children with ADHD only.

Children with both ADHD and RD, with their associated cognitive, language, and disruptive behavioral difficulties, represent a relatively small percentage of children with ADHD. However, the overlap of ADHD with milder forms of RD or with MLD, as previously described, is more common. Some of this overlap can be explained by difficulties with reading and the association between reading and math performance. Generally, the failure to develop basic skills of decoding (i.e., recognizing words) can restrict encoding (i.e., understanding the meaning of words, sentences, and paragraphs), which detracts from the comprehension of math word problems, especially for younger children. The association between reading and math difficulties, which is examined in greater detail in Chapter 6, is relevant because researchers have sometimes failed to control for possible reading problems in students with ADHD when assessing performance on math story problems. In such cases, it is possible that reading ability confounds findings on math word problems. For students with ADHD (without RD), true differences relative to comparison students with LD have been found in reading comprehension (but not in word-attack skill) (Cherkes-Julkowski & Stolzenberg, 1991; Nussbaum et al., 1990).

The overlap between ADHD and LD is so common that "some have questioned the nature and direction of the relationship" (Pisecco et al., 2001, p. 98; for review, see Pennington, 1991, pp. 87–90). Rather than either of these disabilities causing the other, the association between them may be mediated by a third variable, inattention, which characterizes both students with LD and those with ADHD (Merrell & Tymms, 2001; Zentall, 2005). For example, in one study, 66% of seventh and eighth graders with LD and 100% of those with ADHD were characterized by inattention and impulsivity (Zentall, 2006). Although there was overlap in the attentional characteristics of the two groups, there were also differences in the severity of inattention. That is, attention problems (assessed as a discrepancy from IQ score) are more severe for students with ADHD than for students with LD (Mayes et al., 2000). Of course, the largest discrepancy between IQ and inattention is typically found in the comorbid group, who exhibit more severe learning problems than children with LD only and more severe attention problems than those with ADHD only.

Differences between children with ADHD or LD may be attributed to the primacy of attentional difficulties. That is, task difficulty may be a necessary condition to document inattention in students with LD (in the specific tasks and subject areas related their learning disability). Their greater initial effort or history of failure may leave them less able to sustain attention. Similarly, students with or without disabilities but with lower IQ scores allocate more time off task during math problem-solving tasks (Zentall, 1990). The inattention of students with ADHD can also be engendered by task difficulty (e.g., requirements for rapid processing, visual search of embedded contexts), especially early in performance. However, evidence indicates that easy or boring tasks also produce inattention (albeit later in performance)—as does no task at all. Thus, task difficulty is *not* a necessary condition for inattention in students with ADHD.

Cotugno (1987) found that students with LD (with and without ADHD) were slower in attention selectivity than students who were typical learners, with students who had co-occurring disabilities confining their visual scans to even smaller areas than students with LD only. Unfortunately, students with "pure" ADHD were not assessed in this study, so the author could only conclude that the difficulty associated with ADHD, above and beyond the effects of LD, was an inability to stay focused on relevant cues while ignoring peripheral distractions (i.e., an attentional bias toward salient information). Related evidence has similarly documented that students with ADHD show poorer performance and shorter visual fixations on detailed, complex pictures (e.g., embedded figures) than peers, even though they adequately search pictures for global information or themes and adequately perform tasks requiring perception of the whole (Gestalt closure) (Kalff et al., 2002; Karatekin & Asarnow, 1999; Pennington & Ozonoff, 1996). What makes selective attention difficult for students with ADHD is the need to ignore irrelevant information in a complex field (Cooley & Morris, 1990). This is more difficult for these students when the irrelevant information is new or salient, because that type of information is more attention captivating (Kimberg, D'Esposito, & Farah, 1997).

In sum, ADHD, MLD, and LD each contribute independently and interactively to attention selectivity in the following ways:

1. Students with ADHD work at a faster rate, have shorter visual scans of detailed visual information, and attend to (i.e., are distracted by) non-relevant task-overlapping verbal or visual information, although they show good attention to global cues.

2. Students with MLD attend to (i.e., are distracted by) nonrelevant numerical information.

3. Students with LD or co-occurring ADHD/LD work at a slower rate and have a narrower focus.

These differences in selective attention appear to be more a cause of under-achievement than a consequence of it. At the very least, the relationship between inattention and learning differences is bidirectional, depending on the type of attention assessed. That is, selective inattention decreases academic performance, especially for students with ADHD, and difficulty with or an unwillingness to perform certain academic tasks decreases attention to task, especially for students with learning difficulties.

Low IQ Score Overlap Statistical control of IQ is important in the assessment of word problem performance, even when students' IQ scores fall within a normal range. Although the overall distribution of the IQ scores of students with ADHD is normal (Kaplan et al., 2000), samples of students with ADHD may have lower IQ scores (e.g., older students [Nussbaum et al., 1990], students from clinical samples [Leung & Connolly, 1998], and students taking IQ tests that include subtests of digit span or mental math). Controlling for possible differences in IQ score may be especially important when making comparisons among disability groups. That is, artifacts in a selected sample can bring out spurious group differences in math problem solving (e.g., after adjusting the math applications subtest by IQ score, only students with LD performed worse than both the ADHD and comparison groups, which did not differ from each other; Zentall, 1990).

Controlling for IQ score or mental age can also reveal true impairments in math word problems between students with and without ADHD, such as problems with concepts (e.g., distance, money) (Zentall et al., 1994). Controlling for mental age has similarly revealed that youth with mental disabilities experience difficulty with math problems involving distance (e.g., miles run) and time (e.g., hours worked) but not with problems involving concrete objects (e.g., pens, candy) (Judd & Bilsky, 1989). Students with MLD, unlike students with equivalent IQ scores who do not have MLD, also show difficulty with the concepts of weight and measurement (i.e., not solvable by counting concrete objects) (Derr, 1985). These difficulties with nonverbal concepts are not explained by impairments in verbal working memory or low IQ score.

Even though IQ score plays a role in word-problem performance, its role appears to be minimal in computation performance. An experimental study in this area by Kirby and Becker (1988) tested the hypothesis that lower level skill performance might be regulated by higher level strategy implementation. Addition and subtraction equations (e.g., $2 + 7 = 8$) were presented on a computer monitor, and students who were typical learners were asked to indicate whether the equation was true or false. Four subtasks were measured: 1) recognizing numbers, 2) selecting the appropriate operation, 3) performing addition or subtraction operations, and 4) selecting the correct answer—true or false. Because the assessed time to encode numbers and to select a strategy contributed minimally to the overall time assessed, these researchers concluded that the cognitive aspects of computation were minor and that learning problems in math were associated with slowed execution of operations.

EDUCATIONAL IMPLICATIONS AND TARGETED INTERVENTIONS

Given the math problems of many students with ADHD and the probability of co-occurring math disabilities, it is understandable that these students (similar to students with LD) have lowered academic self-concept. Self-evaluation of academic capability determines subsequent motivation and skill acquisition (for review, see Schunk, 1996). When children see themselves as less intelligent and attribute their failure to unalterable factors, such as "being stupid," they have lower expectations for future success and respond to failure with decreased effort (e.g., Licht & Dweck, 1984). In particular, Stipek and MacIver (1989) showed that math performance can be used as a basis for self-judging intellectual ability. Students with ADHD could be characterized by these low self-perceptions because they report more frustration in response to failure than comparison students and show less effort and persistence even in the absence of group differences in age or IQ score (Milich, 1994; Milich & Okazaki, 1991).

Learning failure in mathematics can also be understood by analyzing the interaction of the student characteristics discussed above and the instructional context. Quality of instruction is a key factor in mathematics success, especially for students with disabilities. Traditional learning contexts involve teacher lecture and student independent work. For example, in general education, 70%–90% of the time is spent working out of a textbook, with limited teacher input or communication with other students (Armbruster & Anderson, 1988; Woodward, Monroe, & Baxter, 2001). In special education resource rooms, approximately one third of instructional time is devoted to mathematics (Carpenter, 1985), with independent work and the use of memorized strategies typically occurring during this part of the school day (Woodward et al., 2001). Most of this time is devoted to remedial work in fluency.

Targeting Math-Fact Fluency

Performance of math facts has been a consistent and significant predictor of math problem solving for students in comparison groups as well as for students with LD and ADHD (Muth, 1984; Zentall, 1990; Zentall & Smith, 1992). According to Gagne (1983), if computations were mastered to an automatic level, students would be able to direct attention to the complex aspects of math problem solving. Although some would disagree about the centrality of fluency in story problem performance, a thorough review of this disagreement is beyond the scope of this chapter. Nevertheless, it is an important issue in the field: 1) most intervention work emphasizes fluency, 2) researchers recommend providing students with tutoring in computations, and 3) texts focus on computations to be practiced by paper-and-pencil learning activities (Cawley & Parmar, 1990) or practiced in a more meaningful fashion (Kirby & Becker, 1988). Interventions used in the standard curriculum include computers, peers, and self-monitoring.

Computers can provide a meaningful and stimulating context for students to practice computations. During computer game activities, more sustained attention and reduced impulsivity have been reported for students with ADHD (but not for students in comparison groups) than in standard computerized tasks (Ford, Poe, & Cox, 1993; Shaw, Grayson, & Lewis, 2005). These effects are even more pronounced during competitive computer games with peers (Ford et al., 1993). These findings support implications derived from motivational work by Carlson, Booth, Shin, and Canu (2002), who suggested that games with public recognition of performance could be especially important for students with the hyperactive/impulsive subtype of ADHD. Also, students with ADHD can be taught to self-monitor and self-graph to improve sustained attention (for a review, see Reid, Trout, & Schartz, 2005).

Computer work can improve not only the attention but also the performance of students with LD and ADHD more than written seatwork. Kleiman, Humphrey, and Lindsay (1981) found that students with ADHD completed more math facts while using computers than while doing seatwork. Three students with co-morbid ADHD and LD completed slightly more math facts correctly per minute among using computers (Ota & Du-

Paul, 2002). When more novelty was added to computer drill work (e.g., a game format with immediate feedback, points earned and traded for a video game) in comparison with seatwork, improved math-fact fluency was documented for three students with ADHD (Mautone, DuPaul, & Jitendra, 2005). Furthermore, improvements were observed in basic math skills when peers serve as tutors, from 22% during baseline to 82% during peer interventions (in single-subject designs; DuPaul & Eckert, 1998; DuPaul & Henningson, 1993). Scripted, classwide peer tutoring has also been used to improve math accuracy and on-task attention (improvements were found for approximately half of the students with ADHD; DuPaul, Ervin, Hook, & McGoey, 1998).

Improved math accuracy and productivity were also achieved using self-monitoring in self-contained special education classes for three students with ADHD and LD (Shimabukuro, Prater, Jenkins, & Edelen-Smith, 1999). These techniques have been less effective in general education classes, even with points exchanged for rewards (the procedures had to be modified with additional cues, changed methods of self-recording for the one child with ADHD; McDougall & Brady, 1998). However, video self-monitoring (i.e., daily viewing of 3 minutes of the students' own on-task math performance) improved attention and math production—sustained in a 4-month follow-up—for four students with ADHD (Woltersdorf, 1992).

Computer-, peer-, and self-monitoring interventions are typically presented with incentives and are designed to improve attention and math fluency and accuracy for students with ADHD. Most of these provide immediate gains; video self-monitoring may provide longer-term benefits. However, even when students with mild disabilities have achieved a high level of accuracy on single-digit problems, generalizing to multidigit problems has not been achieved (see Cawley et al., 2001), nor has improved fluency led to the use of more sophisticated mathematics strategies (Hasselbring, 1985). In fact, impairments in math problem solving could be exacerbated by instructional approaches that primarily focus on memorizing a fixed body of information (e.g., math facts, vocabulary, procedural requirements). Because students with MD show only 1 year of growth for every 2 to 3 years of schooling (Cawley et al., 2001) and impairments in retrieval fluency (and math concepts) persist for both LD and ADHD groups, practice to achieve fluency does not appear to be sufficient.

One alternative to targeting children's fluency/accuracy impairments is to adapt the learning context, for instance, by adding educationally relevant or nonrelevant stimulation to the task or ambient environment. Increased external stimulation has improved simple math performance in the same way that it has improved other types of repetitive task performance. For example, according to Hallam and Price (1998, p. 90), music added to the background increased the accuracy rate of math facts for children with behavior problems, especially for those with high levels of "stimulus-seeking and over-activity, closely resembling the 'hyperactivity syndrome.'" Students with ADHD attempt more and/or complete more facts correctly in the presence of music playing in the background than of silence (or with speech) (Abikoff, Courtney, Szeibel, & Koplewicz, 1996; Scott, 1970) (In fact, overlapping conversations decrease math fact accuracy relative to low levels of noise [Zentall & Shaw, 1980]). Students with ADHD also attempt more problems and/or are more accurate when color, movement, or both are added to math facts relative to low-stimulation conditions (Hall & Zentall, 2000; Lee & Asplen, 2005; Lee & Zentall, 2002). Similarly, choice about type of feedback to be received during a computer task of 240 simple addition facts versus no choice of feedback has produced behavioral gains (Bennett et al., 2006). These immediate, positive effects of task and environmental stimulation have *not* been found for comparison students and have not been assessed for students with LD.

The beneficial effects of external stimulation parallel the immediate benefits derived from low doses of psychostimulant medication relative to placebo (i.e., in that there are an increased number of math facts attempted, number of responses correct, number of responses correct per minute, and number of self-corrected errors) (Douglas, Barr, O'Neill, & Britton, 1986; for review, see Lindsay, Tomazic, Levine, & Accardo, 1999). Parallel outcomes suggest that added biochemical or environmental/task stimulation increases arousal sufficiently to improve attention, which is necessary for optimal performance on rote or repetitive tasks.

Targeting Selective Attention

Selective attention is required to identify relevant information within a complex task. Students with ADHD selectively attend to stimulation (color, movement, aggression themes) and have difficulty ignoring attractive but irrelevant information. When added visual stimulation is placed within complex tasks, it can lead students with ADHD astray *or* help them perform optimally, depending on the placement of that stimulation. Using color to direct attention to relevant information, for example, has been demonstrated to improve the performance of elementary and secondary students in spelling, art, and handwriting (see Zentall, 2005). In these studies, color normalized performance (i.e., equivalent to matched peers) or produced responses that were better for students with ADHD than those of matched comparisons.

Although this research shows that attention can be directed, the generality of focusing attention on relevant information has not been assessed within math word problems. One study assessed three students with ADHD, whose accuracy on word problems improved after selective attention training on visual perceptual tasks and math operations (with added self-monitoring and teacher reinforcement) (Cameron & Robinson, 1980). The lack of additional evidence may account for reports that only about 10% of special educators and 3% of secondary educators use color coding (e.g., for different steps within multiple-step problems) (Maccini & Gagnon, 2006).

Targeting Working Memory

Information (irrelevant or relevant) added to math problems increases working memory requirements. Perhaps for this reason, problems with mixed actions, mixed operations, and mixed order of operations require working memory. Although research can assess the contribution of added information and statistically control for poor working memory, these curriculum factors still contribute to math problem-solving performance and achievement. It is, therefore, important to reduce the amount of verbal information, especially early in instruction, or design interventions to help students with MLD and ADHD attend to and hold relevant information over time. Interesting content can facilitate recall. For this reason real-world problems could be useful, as long as problem length was restricted. Also beneficial to students are problems involving divergent thinking, such as those that call for describing relationships among quantities using text, tables, or graphs; explaining why something that appears to be true is or is not; and justifying and predicting the advantages of one procedure or solution over others (e.g., Lesh & Doerr, 1998).

Assistive technology (e.g., calculators) can be used to reduce working-memory load. Zentall (2006) recalled how calculators made a difference in students she studied:

> "For example, one child could perform math as long as he had a calculator in his hands. . . . So, each math class assignment and test that did not allow a calculator he failed, even though he could perform his independent work." (2006, p. 248)

Maccini and Gagnon (2006) found that calculators are allowed for students with mild disabilities during multiple-step problems by approximately half of the special educators and only 36% of secondary educators.

Alternatively, increasing students' level of arousal could help them sustain attention and hold information in mind. For example, requiring students to make additional verbal and motor responses increases their overall level of stimulation. Verbal exchanges can be accomplished in small-group settings or in teams to supplement regular instruction (Bryant & Rivera, 1995). In small groups, students can externalize their thinking (metacognition). Typical learners appear to be more successful problem solvers when they take turns explaining why answers are correct (Siegler, 2000). Self-verbalizations may also be useful for students with ADHD, who tend to be more accurate when asked to verbalize story problems before writing answers than when only writing answers (Lovitt & Curtis, 1968). Teaching students with ADHD to use verbal mediators can be useful, as long as those verbalizations do not involve complex language that must be held in mind (e.g., using the letters *www* for cuing the words *who, what,* and *where* to focus attention on the necessary components of written language; Reid & Lienemann, 2006). The externalized thinking of children can also help teachers. Peterson, Carpenter, and Fennema (1989) found that teachers' knowledge of problem-solving skills, derived from questioning each student about his or her other methods for solving problems, was a better predictor of achievement gains than teachers' knowledge of math strategies. Brief, vigorous exercise (of approximately 5 minutes in length, but not 10) has also led to better problem solving for students with and without ADHD (Molloy, 1989).

Overall, these findings are consistent with self-reports from students with ADHD, who prefer to work with other students and with teachers and to stand and move more during math problem solving in their general education classrooms (through social, physical, and cognitive engagement) (Zentall & Smith, 1992).

Targeting Math Concept Development

Failure to develop an understanding of math concepts (e.g., number, distance, time, money, conservation) is not explained by poor verbal IQ score or working memory. It is known that individuals who focus on the deeper structure of problems have better conceptual knowledge and procedural skill to apply to novel problems (Hiebert & Wearne, 1986; Jonassen, 2003). Focusing attention on underlying features has been examined by asking typical learners to identify problems within a set that were different from model problems (Low & Over, 1989) or that could be solved similarly to the model problems (Hardiman, Dufresne, & Mestre, 1989). In each of these studies, the initial ability to categorize problems correlated significantly with performance.

However, students with ADHD have difficulty categorizing. In one study, they differed from comparison students in the recall of words only when the words were uncategorized but performed equivalently when using a precategorized list (Voelker, Carter, Sprague, Gdowski, & Lachar, 1989). Building on these findings, we instructed students with and without ADHD to initially sort (categorize) word problems conceptually (e.g., by distance, time) (Kercood, Zentall, & Lee, 2004). We found that the probability of using concepts in math word problems was higher for students with category instruction than for those students who sorted without category instruction; however, we did not find that sorting differentially improved the performance of students with ADHD (i.e., both groups improved).

An alternative type of category is schema (i.e., a common underlying structure in word problems). Schema can facilitate conceptual understanding of mathematical relations and reduce complex language through the use of mathematical equations (Hegarty & Kozhevnikov, 1999). The use of schema is likely to be differentially beneficial for students with ADHD, who have difficulty with the requirements of working memory and perform better with global than detailed information. In focusing students' attention to schema, it is important to deemphasize surface features (e.g., identifying or calculating mathematical operations). Evidence for mathematical schema as a way to improve word-problem performance comes from single-subject and group research with students with LD and mild cognitive disabilities (e.g., Fuchs et al., 2004; Neef, Nelles, Iwata, & Page, 2003; Xin, Jitendra, & Deatline-Buchman, 2005). Unfortunately, the instructional protocols in these studies require considerable teacher training and time and have not been assessed with students with ADHD.

CONCLUSIONS

This chapter describes the math performance of students with ADHD and the underlying contributors to that performance that are similar to and different from students with LD. Both groups have chronic impairments in 1) math concepts, which are not fully explained by group differences in verbal IQ score, working memory, or reading comprehension; and 2) reduced fluency of fact retrieval not explained by lower IQ score or slower physical responding. These similarities between LD and ADHD populations are explained in the overlap between attention and working memory and the importance of these variables to math.

Attention is a critical factor in math performance and achievement. Students with ADHD scan detailed information in less time, which contributes to careless errors in aligning numbers, attending to calculation signs, carrying numbers in addition, and canceling numbers in subtraction (i.e., characterizing about 42% of students with MLD; Badian, 1983). See Figure 11.1 and relationship A, denoted by an arrow from *selective attention* to the amount/kind of information (e.g., visual complexity) in problems to *accuracy of fact retrieval*.

Figure 11.1 represents a summary of the research reviewed in this chapter. As reviewed earlier, sustained attention to repetitive stimuli is required to overlearn math facts; thus failure to practice or benefit from repeated exposure may contribute to the slower retrieval of math facts and

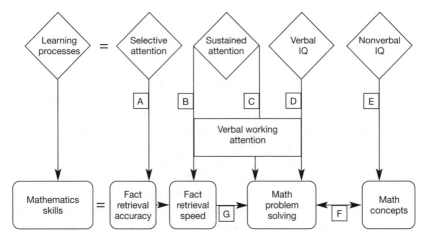

Figure 11.1. Factors contributing to the arithmetic performance of students with attention deficit hyperactivity disorder (ADHD).

to the greater *within-session* performance variability of students with ADHD. See Figure 11.1 and relationship B between *sustained attention* and *fact retrieval speed.* Students with LD perform more slowly in addition facts than do students with ADHD, who in turn perform more slowly than do typical learners. For students with LD, problems with short-term memory could also be implicated in their poorer fact retrieval and *day-to-day* performance variability (not charted in Figure 11.1). However, short-term memory problems do not characterize students with ADHD unless there is verbal interference (e.g., new salient verbal information) prior to storage.

Because it is difficult for students with ADHD to sustain attention, it is also more difficult for them to hold information in mind in order to manipulate it. See Figure 11.1 and relationship C between *sustained attention* and *math problem solving* that is mediated by *verbal working memory.* Impairments in attention also characterize students with LD but usually only in their area(s) of academic disability (e.g., math, reading). Research will continue to document impairments in working memory as a contributor to 1) math and reading difficulties (e.g., in manipulating and storing letters, simple math answers, and math steps (Hecht, Torgesen, Wagner, & Rashotte, 2000), and 2) the poor language production and sequencing documented for students with ADHD (Braun et al., 2004; Zentall, 1988).

Verbal IQ score also contributes to math problem solving (see Figure 11.1, illustrated by relationship D). When statistical controls for verbal IQ score (or reading comprehension) are used, the remaining, true impairments for students with ADHD are math concepts. Math concept performance may be associated with nonverbal IQ score. See Figure 11.1 and the presumed relationship E between *nonverbal IQ* and *math concepts*, denoted by a dotted line, and the bidirectional relationship F between *math concepts* and *problem solving*. More research is needed to replicate and more clearly define students' difficulties with math concepts (i.e., before combining disability groups in research). The development of number concept is being conducted in research with typical learners (Jordan, Kaplan, Olah, & Locuniak, 2006).

Educators have tended to focus on the development of fact retrieval and procedural strategies for students with MLD because of the relationship between *fact retrieval* and *math problem solving* (shown as relationship G in Figure 11.1) and because of the greater number of studies and educational strategies addressing these problems. However, evidence reported in this chapter indicates that increasing accuracy with single-digit problems does not improve accuracy on multidigit problems, nor does improving fluency lead to the use of more sophisticated strategies. Thus, fluency training may be less important than interventions for working memory, especially during early learning. This was suggested by Geary (1994), who found that poor working memory is associated with the use of finger counting as a problem-solving strategy for first-grade children (but not for third or fifth graders). Initial failure to hold multiple dimensions in working memory could lead to a delay in the acquisition of advanced strategies.

Evidence from this review further suggests emphasizing concept development and problem solving. That is, students with ADHD may perform better on applied problems than on fact retrieval, indicating that difficulties with computation do not preclude math problem solving. Even so, accommodations can be made available for tasks involving math fact fluency (e.g., using color, background nonvocal music, computers, games) to enhance the effective stimulation or arousal needed for sustained attention. A foundation for the relationship among arousal, attention, working memory, and the academic performance of students with ADHD has been provided elsewhere (Zentall, 2005, 2006; Zentall & Zentall, 1983).

Psychostimulant medication can also improve the math fact performance of students with ADHD, but it does not improve higher level skills such as concept development or the comprehension of math, reading, or language tasks (e.g., Swanson, McBurnett, Christian, & Wigal, 1995). However, placing color strategically on relevant dimensions could be used to direct attention, decrease working memory requirements, and improve multiple-step problem performance. Finally, interventions for problem solving in a meaningful peer context could reduce a widening achievement gap; students with ADHD need less emphasis on memorizing and convergent solutions and more emphasis on math and its communicative and persuasive possibilities.

REFERENCES

Abikoff, H., Courtney, M.E., Szeibel, P.J., & Koplewicz, H.S. (1996). The effects of auditory stimulation on the arithmetic performance of children with ADHD and nondisabled children. *Journal of Learning Disabilities, 29,* 238–246.

Ackerman, P.T., Anhalt, J.M., Dykman, R.A., & Holcomb, P.J. (1986). Effortful processing deficits in children with reading and/or attention disorders. *Brain and Cognition, 5,* 22–40.

American Psychiatric Association (2000). *Diagnostic and statistical manual of mental disorders* (4th ed.). Washington, DC: Author.

Armbruster, B.B., & Anderson, T.H. (1988). On selecting "considerate" content area textbooks. *Remedial and Special Education, 9,* 47–52.

Badian, N.A. (1983). Dyscalculia and nonverbal disorders of learning. In H.R. Myklebust (Ed.), *Progress in learning disabilities* (Vol. 5, pp. 235–264). New York: Stratton.

Badian, N.A., & Ghublikian, M. (1983). The personal-social characteristics of children with poor mathematical computation skills. *Journal of Learning Disabilities, 16,* 154–157.

Banaschewski, T., Brandeis, D., Heinrich, H., Albrecht, B., Brunner, E., & Rothenberger, A. (2003). Association of ADHD and conduct disorder—Brain electrical evidence for the existence of a distinct subtype. *Journal of Child Psychology and Psychiatry, 44,* 356–376.

Barry, T.D., Lyman, R.D., & Klinger, L.G. (2002). Academic underachievement and attention-deficit/hyperactivity disorder: The negative impact of symptom severity on school performance. *Journal of School Psychology, 40,* 259–283.

Bennett, D.E., Zentall, S.S., Giorgetti-Borucki, K., & French, B.F. (2006). The effects of computer-administered choice on students with and without characteristics of attention deficit hyperactivity disorder. *Behavioral Disorders, 31,* 187–201.

Braun, C.M.J., Godbout, L., Desbiens, C., Daigneault, K., Lussier, F., & Hamel-Hebert, I. (2004). Mental genesis of scripts in adolescents with attention deficit/hyperactivity disorder. *Child Neuropsychology, 10,* 280–296.

Bryant, B., & Rivera, D. (1995). *Using assistive technology to facilitate cooperative learning.* (ERIC Document Reproduction Service No. ED 380975).

Bryant, D.P., Bryant, B.R., & Hammill, D.D. (2000). Characteristic behaviors of students with LD who have teacher-identified math weaknesses. *Journal of Learning Disabilities, 33,* 168–177.

Cameron, M.I., & Robinson, V.M.J. (1980). Effects of cognitive training on academic and on-task behavior of hyperactive children. *Journal of Abnormal Child Psychology, 8,* 405–420.

Carlson, C.L., Booth, J.E., Shin, M., & Canu, W.H. (2002). Parent-, teacher-, and self-rated motivational styles and ADHD subtypes. *Journal of Learning Disabilities, 35,* 104–113.

Carpenter, R.L. (1985). Mathematics instruction in resource rooms: Instruction time and teacher competence. *Learning Disability Quarterly, 8,* 95–100.

Carver, C.S. (1979). A cybernetic model of self-attention processes. *Journal of Personality and Social Psychology, 37,* 1251–1281.

Cawley, J., Parmar, R., Foley, T.E., Salmon, S., & Roy, S. (2001). Arithmetic performance of students: Implications for standards and programming. *Exceptional Children, 67,* 311–328.

Cawley, J.F., & Parmar, R.S. (1990). Issues in mathematics curriculum for handicapped students. *Academic Therapy, 25,* 507–521.

Chang, H.T., Klorman, R., Shaywitz, S.E., Fletcher, J.M., Marchione, K.E., Holahan, J.M., et al. (1999). Paired-associate learning in attention-deficit/hyperactivity disorder as a function of hyperactivity-impulsivity and oppositional defiant disorder. *Journal of Abnormal Child Psychology, 27*, 237–245.

Cherkes-Julkowski, M., & Stolzenberg, J. (1991). The learning disability of attention deficit disorder. *Learning Disabilities: A Multidisciplinary Journal, 2*, 8–15.

Cherkes-Julkowski, M., Stolzenberg, J., & Segal, L. (1991). Prompted cognitive testing as a diagnostic compensation for attentional deficits: The Raven Standard Progressive Matrices and attention deficit disorder. *Learning Disabilities, 2*, 1–7.

Cohen, N.J., Weiss, G., & Minde, K. (1972). Cognitive styles in adolescents previously diagnosed as hyperactive. *Journal of Child Psychology and Psychiatry, 13*, 203–209.

Cooley, E.L., & Morris, R.D. (1990). Attention in children: A neuropsychologically based model of assessment. *Developmental Neuropsychology, 6*, 239–274.

Cotugno, A.J. (1987). Cognitive control functioning in hyperactive and nonhyperactive learning disabled children. *Journal of Learning Disabilities, 20*, 563–567.

Derr, A.M. (1985). Conservation and mathematics achievement in the learning disabled child. *Journal of Learning Disabilities, 18*, 333–336.

Douglas, V.I., Barr, R.G., O'Neill, M.E., & Britton, B.G. (1986). Short-term effects of methylphenidate on the cognitive learning and academic performance of children with attention deficit disorder in the laboratory and the classroom. *Journal of Child Psychology and Psychiatry, 27*, 191–212.

DuPaul, G.J., & Eckert, T.J. (1998). Academic interventions for students with attention-deficit/hyperactivity disorder: A review of the literature. *Reading and Writing Quarterly, 14*, 59–82.

DuPaul, G.J., Ervin, R.A., Hook, C.L., & McGoey, K.E. (1998). Peer tutoring for children with attention deficit hyperactivity disorder: Effects on classroom behavior and academic performance. *Journal of Applied Behavior Analysis, 31*, 579–592.

DuPaul, G.J., & Henningson, P.N. (1993). Peer tutoring effects on the classroom performance of children with attention deficit hyperactivity disorder. *School Psychology Review, 22*, 134–143.

Faraone, S.V., Sergeant, J., Gillberg, C., & Bierderman, J. (2003). The worldwide prevalence of ADHD: Is it an American condition? *World Psychiatry, 2*, 104–113.

Ford, M.J., Poe, V., & Cox, J. (1993). Attending behaviors of ADHD children in math and reading using various types of software. *Journal of Computing in Childhood Education, 4*, 183–196.

Fuchs, L.S., Fuchs, D., Prentice, K., Hamlett, C.L., Finelli, R., & Courey, S.J. (2004). Enhancing mathematical problem solving among third-grade students with schema-based instruction. *Journal of Educational Psychology, 96*, 635–647.

Gagne, R.M. (1983). Some issues in the psychology of mathematics instruction. *Journal for Research in Mathematics Education, 14*, 275–282.

Geary, D.C. (1994). *Children's mathematical development.* Washington, DC: American Psychological Association.

Geary, D.C., Hoard, M.K., Byrd-Craven, J., & DeSoto, M.C. (2004). Strategy choices in simple and complex addition: Contributions of working memory and counting knowledge for children with mathematical disability. *Journal of Experimental Child Psychology, 88*, 121–151.

Gersten, R., Jordan, N.C., & Flojo, J.R. (2005). Early identification and interventions for students with math difficulties. *Journal of Learning Disabilities, 38*, 293–304.

Hall, A.M. & Zentall, S.S. (2000). Homework stations and the completion of math. *Journal of Behavioral Education, 10*, 123–137.

Hallam, S., & Price, J. (1998). Can the use of background music improve the behavior and academic performance of children with emotional and behavioral difficulties? *British Journal of Special Education, 25,* 88–91.

Halperin, J.M., Gittelman, R., Klein, D.F., & Rudel, R.G. (1984). Reading-disabled hyperactive children: A distinct subgroup of attention deficit disorder with hyperactivity? *Journal of Abnormal Child Psychology, 12,* 1–14.

Hardiman, P.T., Dufresne, R.J., & Mestre, J.P. (1989). The relation between problem categorization and problem solving among novices and experts. *Memory & Cognition, 17,* 627–638.

Hasselbring, T.S. (1985). Microcomputer applications to instruction. In E.A. Polloway, J.S. Payne, J.R. Patton, & R.A. Payne (Eds.), *Strategies for teaching retarded students* (3rd ed., pp. 154–175). Columbus, OH: Charles E. Merrill.

Hecht, S.A., Torgesen, J.K., Wagner, R.K., & Rashotte, C.A. (2000). The relations between phonological processing abilities and emerging individual differences in mathematical computation skills: A longitudinal study from second to fifth grades. *Journal of Experimental Child Psychology, 79,* 191–227.

Hegarty, M., & Kozhevnikov, M. (1999). Types of visual-spatial representations and mathematical problem solving. *Journal of Educational Psychology, 91,* 684–689.

Hiebert, J., & Wearne, D. (1986). Procedures over concepts: The acquisition of decimal number knowledge. In J. Hiebert (Ed.), *Conceptual and procedural knowledge: The case of mathematics* (pp. 199–223). Mahwah, NJ: Lawrence Erlbaum Associates.

Jonassen, D.H. (2003). Designing research-based instruction for story problems. *Educational Psychology Review, 15,* 267–296.

Jonsdottir, S., Bouma, A., Sergeant, J.A., & Scherder, E.J.A. (2004). Effects of transcutaneous electrical nerve stimulation (TENS) on cognition, behavior, and the rest-activity rhythm in children with attention deficit hyperactivity disorder, combined type. *Neurorehabilitation and Neural Repair, 18,* 212–221.

Jordan, N.C., & Hanich, L.B. (2003). Characteristics of children with moderate mathematical deficiencies: A longitudinal perspective. *Learning Disabilities Research, 18,* 213–221.

Jordan, N.C., Kaplan, D., Olah, L. N., & Locuniak, M.N. (2006). Number sense growth in kindergarten: A longitudinal investigation of children at risk for mathematics difficulties. *Child Development, 77,* 153–175.

Judd, T.P., & Bilsky, L.H. (1989). Comprehension and memory in the solution of verbal arithmetic problems by mentally retarded and nonretarded individuals. *Journal of Educational Psychology, 81,* 541–546.

Kalff, A.C., Hendriksen, J.G.M., Kroes, M., Vles, J.S.H., Steyaert, J., Feron, F.J.M., et al. (2002). Neurocognitive performance of 5- and 6-year-old children who met criteria for attention deficit/hyperactivity disorder at 18 months follow-up: Results from a prospective population study. *Journal of Abnormal Child Psychology, 30,* 589–598.

Kaplan, B.J., Crawford, S.G., Dewey, D.M., & Fisher, G.C. (2000). The IQs of children with ADHD are normally distributed. *Journal of Learning Disabilities, 33,* 425–432.

Karatekin, C., & Asarnow, R.F. (1999). Exploratory eye movements to pictures in childhood-onset schizophrenic and attention-deficit/hyperactivity disorder (ADHD). *Journal of Abnormal Child Psychology, 27,* 35–49.

Kataria, S., Hall, W.C., Wong, M.M., & Keys, F.G. (1992). Learning styles of LD and NLD ADHD children. *Journal of Clinical Psychology, 48,* 371–378.

Keeler, M.L., & Swanson, H.L. (2001). Does strategy knowledge influence working memory in children with mathematics disabilities? *Journal of Learning Disabilities, 34,* 418–434.

Kercood, S., Zentall, S.S., & Lee, D.L. (2004). Focusing attention to deep structure in math problems: Effects on elementary education students with and without attentional deficits. *Learning and Individual Differences, 14,* 91–105.

Kimberg, D.Y., D'Esposito, M., & Farah, M.J. (1997). Cognitive functions in the prefrontal cortex working memory and executive control. *Current Directions in Psychological Science, 6,* 185–192.

Kirby, J.R., & Becker, L.D. (1988). Cognitive components of learning problems in arithmetic. *Remedial and Special Education, 9,* 7–15, 27.

Kleiman, G., Humphrey, M., & Lindsay, P.H. (1981). Microcomputers and hyperactive children. *Creative Computing, 7,* 93–94.

Lee, D.L., & Asplen, J. (2005). Using color to increase the math persistence of children with co-occurring learning disabilities and attentional deficits. *Learning Disabilities: A Multidisciplinary Journal, 13,* 55–60.

Lee, D.L., & Zentall, S.S. (2002). The effects of visual stimulation on the mathematics performance of children with attention deficit/hyperactivity disorder. *Behavioral Disorders, 27,* 278–288.

Lesh, R., & Doerr, H. (1998). Symbolizing, communicating, and mathematizing: Key components of models and modeling. In P. Cobb & E. Yackel (Eds.), *Symbolizing, communicating, and mathematizing.* Mahwah, NJ: Lawrence Erlbaum.

Leung, P.W.L., & Connolly, K.J. (1998). Do hyperactive children have motor organization and/or execution deficits? *Developmental Medicine and Child Neurology, 40,* 600–607.

Licht, B.G., & Dweck, C.S. (1984). Determinant of academic achievement—The interaction of children's achievement orientations with skill area. *Developmental Psychology, 20,* 628–636.

Lindsay, R.L., Tomazic, T., Levine, M.D., & Accardo, P.J. (1999). Impact of attentional dysfunction in dyscalculia. *Developmental Medicine and Child Neurology, 41,* 639–642.

Lovitt, T., & Curtis, K. (1968). Effects of manipulating an antecedent event on mathematics response rate. *Journal of Applied Behavior Analysis, 1,* 329–333.

Low, R., & Over, R. (1989). Detection of missing and irrelevant information within algebraic story problems. *British Journal of Educational Psychology, 59,* 296–305.

Maccini, P., & Gagnon, J.C. (2006). Mathematics instructional practices and assessment accommodations by secondary special and general educators. *Exceptional Children, 72,* 217–234.

Mariani, M.A., & Barkley, R.A. (1997). Neuropsychological and academic functioning in preschool boys with attention deficit hyperactivity disorder. *Developmental Neuropsychology, 13,* 111–119.

Marshall, R.M., Hynd, G.W., Handwerk, M.J., & Hall, J. (1997). Academic underachievement in ADHD subtypes. *Journal of Learning Disabilities, 30,* 635–642.

Marshall, R.M., Schafer, V.A., O'Donnell, L., Elliott, J., & Handwerk, M.J. (1999). Arithmetic disabilities and ADD subtypes: Implications for DSM-IV. *Journal of Learning Disabilities, 32,* 239–247.

Mautone, J.A., DuPaul, G.J., & Jitendra, A.K. (2005). The effects of computer-assisted instruction on mathematics performance and classroom behavior of children with ADHD. *Journal of Attention Disorders, 9,* 290–300.

Mayes, S.W., Calhoun, S.L., & Crowell, E.W. (2000). Learning disabilities and ADHD: Overlapping spectrum disorders. *Journal of Learning Disabilities, 33,* 417–424.

McDougall, D., & Brady, M.P. (1998). Initiating and fading self-management interventions to increase math fluency in general education classes. *Exceptional Children, 64,* 151–167.

McGee, R., Williams, S., Moffitt, T., & Anderson, J. (1989). A comparison of 13-year-old boys with attention deficit and/or reading disorder on neuropsychological measures. *Journal of Abnormal Child Psychology, 17,* 37–53.

McInnes, A., Humphries, T., Hogg-Johnson, S., & Tannock, R. (2003). Listening comprehension and working memory are impaired in children with ADHD irrespective of language development. *Journal of Abnormal Child Psychology, 31,* 427–433.

Merrell, C., & Tymms, P.B. (2001). Inattention, hyperactivity and impulsiveness: Their impact on academic progress and achievement. *British Journal of Educational Psychology, 71,* 43–56.

Milich, R. (1994). The response of children with ADHD to failure: If at first you don't succeed, do you try, try again? *School Psychology Review, 23,* 11–28.

Milich, R., & Okazaki, M. (1991). An examination of learned helplessness among attention-deficit hyperactivity disordered boys. *Journal of Abnormal Child Psychology, 19,* 607–623.

Molloy, G.N. (1989). Chemicals, exercise and hyperactivity: A short report. *International Journal of Disability, 36,* 57–61.

Muth, K.D. (1984). Solving arithmetic word-problems—role of reading and computational skills. *Journal of Educational Psychology, 76,* 205–210.

Neef, N.A., Nelles, D.E., Iwata, B.A., & Page, T.J. (2003). Analysis of precurrent skills in solving mathematics story problems. *Journal of Applied Behavior Analysis, 36,* 21–33.

Nussbaum, N.L., Grant, M.L., Roman, M.J., Poole, J.H., & Bigler, E. (1990). Attention deficit hyperactivity disorder and the mediating effect of age on academic and behavioral variables. *Developmental Behavioral Pediatrics, 11,* 22–26.

Ota, K.R., & DuPaul, G.J. (2002). Task engagement and mathematics performance in children with attention deficit hyperactivity disorder: Effects of supplemental computer instruction. *School Psychology Quarterly, 17,* 242–257.

Passolunghi, M.C., Marzocchi, G.M., & Fiorillo, F. (2005). Selective effect of inhibition of literal or numerical irrelevant information in children with attention deficit hyperactivity disorder (ADHD) on arithmetic learning disorder (ALD). *Developmental Neuropsychology, 28,* 731–753.

Passolunghi, M.C., & Pazzagliab, F. (2004). Individual differences in memory updating in relation to arithmetic problem solving. *Learning and Individual Differences, 14,* 219–230.

Pennington, B.F. (1991). *Diagnosing learning disorders: A neuropsychological framework.* New York: Guilford Press.

Pennington, B.F., & Ozonoff, S. (1996). Executive functions and developmental psychopathology. *Journal of Child Psychology and Psychiatry, 37,* 51–87.

Peterson, P.L., Carpenter, T., & Fennema, E. (1989). Teachers' knowledge of students' knowledge in mathematics problem solving: Correlational and case analyses. *Journal of Educational Psychology, 81,* 558–569.

Pickering, S.J., & Gathercole, S.E. (2004). Distinctive working memory profiles in children with special needs. *Educational Psychology, 24,* 393–408.

Pisecco, S., Baker, D.B., Silva, P.A., & Brooke, M. (2001). Boys with reading disabilities and/or ADHD: Distinctions in early childhood. *Journal of Learning Disabilities, 34,* 98–106.

Raven, J. (1965). *Raven's Colored and Standard Progressive Matrices.* San Antonio, TX: Harcourt Assessment.

Reid, R., & Lienemann, T.O. (2006). Self-regulated strategy development for written expression with students with attention deficit hyperactivity disorder. *Exceptional Children, 73,* 53–68.

Reid, R., Trout, A.L., & Schartz, M. (2005). Self-regulation interventions for children with attention deficit hyperactivity disorder. *Exceptional Children, 71,* 361–377.

Roodenrys, S., Koloski, N., & Grainger, J. (2001). Working memory function on attention deficit hyperactivity disordered and reading disabled children. *British Journal of Developmental Psychology, 19,* 325–337.

Schunk, D.H. (1996). Goal and self-evaluative influences during children's cognitive skill learning. *American Educational Research Journal, 33,* 359–382.

Scott, T.J. (1970). The use of music to reduce hyperactivity in children. *American Journal of Orthopsychiatry, 40,* 677–680.

Sergeant, J.A., Geurts, H., Huijbregts, S., Scheres, A., & Oosterlaan, J. (2003). The top and bottom of ADHD: A neuropsychological perspective. *Neuroscience and Biobehavioral Review, 27,* 583–592.

Shalev, R.S., Manor, O., Kerem, B., Ayali, M., Badichi, N., Friedlander, Y., et al. (2001). Developmental dyscalculia is a familial learning disability. *Journal of Learning Disabilities, 60,* 973–980.

Shaw, R., Grayson, A., & Lewis, V. (2005). Inhibition, ADHD, and computer games: The inhibitory performance of children with ADHD on computerized tasks and games. *Journal of Attention Disorders, 8,* 160–168.

Shimabukuro, P., Prater, M.A., Jenkins, A., & Edelen-Smith, P. (1999). The effects of self-monitoring of academic performance of students with learning disabilities and ADD/ADHD. *Education and Treatment of Children, 22,* 1–10.

Siegler, R.S. (2000). The rebirth of children's learning. *Child Development, 71,* 26–35.

Stipek, D., & MacIver, D. (1989). Developmental changes in children's assessment of intellectual competence. *Child Development, 60,* 521–538.

Swanson, J.M., McBurnett, K., Christian, D.L., & Wigal, T. (1995). Stimulant medication and treatment of children with ADHD. In T.H. Ollendick & R.J. Prinz (Eds.), *Advances in clinical child psychology* (Vol. 17, pp. 265–322). New York: Kluwer Academic/Plenum.

Tant, J.L., & Douglas, V.I. (1982). Problem solving in hyperactive, normal and reading-disabled boys. *Journal of Abnormal Child Psychology, 10,* 285–306.

Voelker, S.L., Carter, R.A., Sprague, D.J., Gdowski, J.M., & Lachar, D. (1989). Developmental trends in memory and metamemory in children with attention deficit disorder. *Journal of Pediatric Psychology, 14,* 75–88.

Webster, E.R., Hall, W.C., Brown, B.M., & Bolen, M.L. (1996). Memory modality differences in children with attention deficit hyperactivity disorder with and without learning disabilities. *Psychology in the Schools, 33,* 193–201.

Willcutt, E.G., Pennington, B.F., Boada, R., Ogline, J.S., Tunich, R.A., Chhabildas, N.A., et al. (2001). A comparison of the cognitive deficits in reading disability and attention-deficit/hyperactivity disorder. *Journal of Abnormal Psychology, 110,* 157–172.

Woltersdorf, M.A. (1992). Videotape self-modeling in the treatment of attention-deficit hyperactivity disorder. *Child and Family Behavior Therapy, 14,* 53–73.

Woodward, J., Monroe, K., & Baxter, J. (2001). Enhancing student achievement on performance assessments in mathematics. *Learning Disability Quarterly, 24,* 33–46.

Xin, Y.P., Jitendra, A.K., & Deatline-Buchman, A. (2005). Effects of mathematical word problem-solving instruction on middle school students with learning problems. *Journal of Special Education, 39,* 181–192.

Zentall, S.S. (1988). Production deficiencies in elicited language but not in spontaneous verbalizations of hyperactive children. *Journal of Abnormal Child Psychology, 16,* 657–673.

Zentall, S.S. (1990). Fact-retrieval automatization and math problem solving by learning disabled, attention-disordered, and normal adolescents. *Journal of Educational Psychology, 82,* 856–865.

Zentall, S.S. (2005). Theory- and evidence-based strategies for children with attentional problems. *Psychology in the Schools, 42,* 821–836.

Zentall, S.S. (2006). *ADHD and education: Foundations, characteristics, methods, and collaboration.* Upper Saddle River, NJ: Prentice Hall.

Zentall, S.S., Kuester, D.A., & Craig, B. (2006). *Behavior and goals of students with and without ADHD during cooperative problem solving.* Manuscript submitted for publication.

Zentall, S.S., & Shaw, J.H. (1980). Effects of classroom noise on performance and activity of second-grade hyperactive and control children. *Journal of Educational Psychology, 72,* 830–840.

Zentall, S.S., & Smith, Y.N. (1992). Assessment and validation of the learning and behavioral style preferences of hyperactive and comparison children. *Learning and Individual Differences, 4,* 25–41.

Zentall, S.S., & Smith, Y.N. (1993). Mathematical performance and behavior of children with hyperactivity with and without coexisting aggression. *Behavior Research and Therapy, 31,* 701–710.

Zentall, S.S., Smith, Y.N., Lee, Y.B., & Wieczorek, C. (1994). Mathematical outcomes of attention-deficit hyperactivity disorder. *Journal of Learning Disabilities, 27,* 510–519.

Zentall, S.S., & Zentall, T.R. (1983). Optimal stimulation: A model of disordered activity and performance in normal and deviant children. *Psychological Bulletin, 94,* 446–471.

Chapter 12

Neuropsychological Case Studies on Arithmetic Processing

Laura Zamarian, Alex López-Rolón, and Margarete Delazer

+ +

Dyscalculia may arise early in an individual's development or may be acquired as a result of a stroke, a tumor, or head trauma or as a consequence of dementia. Performing simple tasks, such as solving 5 + 4 or 4 × 8, writing the number *101*, estimating the number of dots in a set, or counting backwards from 10 may become impossible for individuals with acquired dyscalculia.

Since the beginning of the 20th century it has been well-known that brain lesions, in particular left posterior lesions, can cause specific patterns of dyscalculia (e.g., Berger, 1926; Henschen, 1919, 1920; Lewandowsky & Stadelman, 1908), a finding that has been consistently reported in later studies (e.g., Grafman, Passafiume, Faglioni, & Boller, 1982; Hecaen, Angelergues, & Houllier, 1961). Neuropsychologists actively examine and report cases of individuals who have experienced brain damage because these cases offer unique insight into cognitive processes that underlie various kinds of numerical and arithmetic knowledge. The study of individual cases is generally known in neuropsychology as the single-case approach.

Such single-case studies are based on the observation of double dissociations in the performance of individuals with neuropsychological disorders. *Double dissociation,* which describes an important concept in neuropsychology, in general refers to the existence of contrasting patterns of impairment in two people or two groups of people. For example, individual 1 and individual 2, who have different brain disorders, both perform task A and task B, which assess different cognitive functions. In a typical double dissociation, individual 1 has no problems performing task A but does very poorly at task B. The opposite is true for individual 2, who performs task B well but struggles with task A. Double dissociations help neuropsychologists conclude that someone's performance is impaired not because a given task is particularly difficult but because the tasks (in this example, tasks A and B) assess two independent functions, which may be affected differently by the individuals' disorders.

Single-case studies are also based on the assumptions of functional modularity of cognitive processes (i.e., the functions of cognitive processes are located in dissociable modules or systems in the mind) and of uniformity of functional architecture across people (i.e., functions are essentially similar across people and are consequently comparable) (e.g., Shallice, 1979, 1988).

The single-case approach in neuropsychological research on number processing has proven to be extremely fruitful. It has provided the basis for the development of cognitive as well as anatomical models of number processing, which in turn constitute the theoretical framework for the precise diagnosis of acquired calculation deficits and the development of appropriate rehabilitation designs. Systematic case studies from the 1980s[1] onwards, in particular, have provided insight into cognitive number processing mechanisms.

In this chapter we review some of the most important single-case studies on the cognitive processes involved in simple arithmetic, which are potentially relevant to the development of cognitive models. We specifically discuss findings that have shed light on arithmetic fact knowledge, conceptual knowledge, and procedural skills, as well as on the role of approximate processing.

ARITHMETIC FACTS

Definition

Although there is no agreement among researchers as to which problems should be considered "arithmetic facts," the term usually refers to one-digit problems (addition, multiplication, subtraction, possibly division; e.g., $2 + 4; 3 \times 5; 6 - 3; 8 \div 2$) that do not require further computational processes or strategies to be solved but can be directly retrieved from long-term memory, as can other semantic knowledge (e.g., Ashcraft, 1992, 1995; Campbell, 1995; McCloskey, Caramazza, & Basili, 1985). McCloskey (1992), for example, distinguishes between three subsets of single-digit problems in multiplication: 0s problems (all problems involving 0 as an operand),

---

[1]A review on the contribution of earlier studies is given in Chapter 1 of this volume.

1s problems (all problems involving 1 as an operand), and 2–9 problems (2 × 2 through 9 × 9). Whereas the first two subsets of problems (involving 0 or 1) are thought to be answered by accessing a stored rule (e.g., "all multiplications with 0 as an operand have the solution 0"), problems in the last subset are labeled *arithmetic facts*. According to McCloskey, arithmetic facts are stored as individual memory representations. This assumption of long-term storage and automatic retrieval of all single-digit multiplication problems from 2 × 2 to 9 × 9 contrasts with recent reports on the frequent use of backup strategies even in healthy adults (LeFevre, Bisanz, et al., 1996; LeFevre, Sadesky, & Bisanz, 1996). An alternative proposal comes from Dehaene and Cohen's (1995) model in which only multiplication and some very simple addition problems are thought to be retrieved automatically, whereas backup strategies are used for the less-rehearsed subtraction, more complex addition (with sums larger than 10), and division problems.

Authors fail to agree on whether simple division problems are stored facts or whether they are answered by procedural strategies. Cipolotti and de Lacy Costello (1995) have argued for a long-term semantic storage of division problems, whereas other studies (Hittmair-Delazer, Semenza, & Denes, 1994; see also Delazer, Domahs, Lochy, Karner, Benke, & Poewe, 2004; Girelli, Delazer, Semenza, & Denes, 1996) have adopted the view that division problems are mostly answered by making reference to the corresponding multiplication problems. There is no doubt, however, that considerable interindividual differences, such as age, educational level, and daily practice, greatly influence the knowledge of arithmetic facts and the automaticity of retrieval.

Mental Representations of Arithmetic Facts

Two influential models of numerical processing have been proposed, both based on the observation of individuals' behaviors. The first is a purely cognitive model by McCloskey and colleagues (e.g., McCloskey et al., 1985; McCloskey, 1992); the other is a neurocognitive model by Dehaene and colleagues (e.g., Dehaene, 1992; Dehaene & Cohen, 1995, 1997). There are other, alternative proposals, such as the preferred-entry hypothesis (Noël & Seron, 1993, 1995).

According to McCloskey and colleagues (1985; see also McCloskey, 1992; McCloskey, Aliminosa, & Sokol, 1991; McCloskey, Harley, & Sokol, 1991; McCloskey, Sokol, & Goodman, 1986; Sokol & McCloskey, 1991; Sokol, McCloskey, & Cohen, 1989; Sokol, McCloskey, Cohen, & Aliminosa, 1991), a central semantic system is accessed in all calculation processes independently from the input format (see Figure 12.1). All number formats (spoken number words, written number words, Arabic digits) are converted into

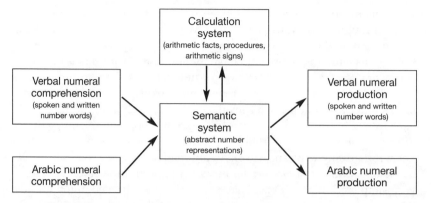

Figure 12.1. Schematic representation of McCloskey's cognitive model of numerical processing, in which a central semantic system is accessed in all calculation processes independent from the input format. (McCloskey, Caramazza, & Basili [1985].)

abstract representations that specify the magnitude of the number and serve as input and output for the calculation system (consisting of an arithmetic fact component, procedural knowledge, and the processing of arithmetic signs). A number of single-case studies have provided evidence supporting the concept of such modality independent calculation systems. For example, in one study, an individual referred to as PS[2] (Sokol et al., 1991; Sokol & McCloskey, 1991) was tested extensively on multiplication in three stimulus formats (Arabic numerals, number words, and dot arrays). When each possible combination of presentation and response format was tested (e.g., presentation of dots, response in Arabic digits), PS's error rate was found to be unaffected by stimulus or response format. This result supports the hypothesis that arithmetic fact retrieval is mediated by internal numerical representations that are independent of the format in which problems are presented or responses are given. However, as Sokol and colleagues (1991) noted, this particular result obtained from PS does not necessarily support the claim that numerical representations are abstract. The additional claim of abstract representations is supported by the specific type of errors observed, that is, operand errors (e.g., $7 \times 6 = 48$), which typically reflect numerical similarity rather than phonological similarity.

An alternative to McCloskey and colleagues's model has been advanced by Dehaene and Cohen (1995, 1997; Dehaene, 1992; see also Dehaene, Molko, Cohen, & Wilson, 2004; Dehaene, Piazza, Pinel, & Cohen, 2003) (see Figure 12.2). They suggest a triple-code model of number processing comprising a visual Arabic number code (thought to mediate digital input and

---

[2]Individuals in neuropsycholocial case studies will henceforth be referred to with initials only in this chapter.

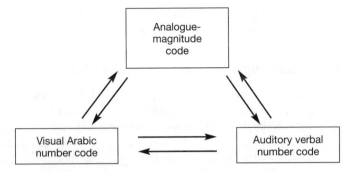

Figure 12.2. Schematic representation of the triple-code model of number processing (e.g., Dehaene, 1992).

output, multidigit operations, and parity judgments), an auditory verbal code (which represents numbers as syntactically organized sequences of words and mediates verbal input and output, counting, and memorized arithmetic facts), and an analogue magnitude code (which represents the quantity associated with a number as local distribution of activation on an oriented number line and underlies number comparison, approximate calculation, estimations, and subitizing[3]). The model postulates that a direct, asemantic verbal route is used for overlearned calculations (in particular, for multiplication problems and small additions) and that an indirect, semantic route is employed in answering simple calculation problems when no verbal association is available (typically with subtraction problems). This indirect route requires access to the analogue-magnitutde (quantity) code.

The preferred-entry code hypothesis proposed by Noël and Seron (1993, 1995) stresses individual differences among subjects. As they observed in neuropsychological case studies, subjects may prefer a particular code in order to access number meaning and to perform numerical tasks. Some subjects prefer a verbal entry code (as did those described by Noël & Seron, 1993, 1995), others a visual entry code. If the transcoding from a specific notation (e.g., Arabic) to the preferred-entry code (e.g., verbal) is impaired, all numerical tasks (i.e., number comparison or calculation) presented in this notation (e.g., Arabic) will be impaired.

Calculation models differ considerably in their assumptions concerning the representation format of arithmetic facts. They disagree as to whether facts are stored as verbal sequences or as abstract memory representations. As a consequence, they also differ in their explanations of typical effects observed in acquired dyscalculia. One of the most commonly observed

---

[3]The term *subitizing* refers to the ability to rapidly assess the numerosity of small samples of items (up to three or four items) without counting (e.g., Dehaene & Cohen, 1994; Mandler & Shebo, 1982).

effects is the dissociation between different kinds of operations (e.g., Berger, 1926; Lewandowsky & Stadelmann, 1908; Singer & Low, 1933).

Dissociations Among Operations and Language Abilities

McCloskey, Aliminosa, and colleagues (1991) tested 12 individuals with dyscalculia and found that for all 12, performance was consistently worse on multiplication tasks than for addition and subtraction; for some, subtraction was worse than addition. One might assume from this that multiplication is simply more difficult than subtraction and addition, and that the pattern of preserved and impaired performance reflects differences among operations in premorbid strength of the stored facts. Within this framework, multiplication would be more difficult than subtraction, and subtraction more difficult than addition. However, various patterns of selectively preserved and selectively impaired operations have been observed, and a simple operation-difficulty effect cannot account for the results. Impaired multiplication tables with better or entirely preserved addition and/or subtraction have been repeatedly reported (e.g., Delazer et al., 2004; Hittmair-Delazer et al., 1994; van Harskamp & Cipolotti, 2001), and the reverse dissociation has been observed as well (Dehaene & Cohen, 1997; Delazer & Benke, 1997; Delazer, Karner, Zamarian, Donnemiller, & Benke, 2006; Singer & Low, 1933; van Harskamp & Cipolotti, 2001). Furthermore, subtraction has occasionally been found to be better preserved than multiplication and addition (Dagenbach & McCloskey, 1992; McNeil & Warrington, 1994; Pesenti, Seron, & van der Linden, 1994). The opposite dissociation, selectively impaired subtraction, was reported by van Harskamp and Cipolotti (2001). Van Harskamp and Cipolotti (2001) also observed a case of selectively impaired addition, but in contrast to other cases, this individual (FS) made predominantly operation errors, producing in most cases the "correct" multiplication result to the addition operands (e.g., 2 + 3 = 6). Thus, the problem in the case of FS may have been an incorrect choice of operation or the insufficient inhibition of multiplication rather than poor addition itself (Dehaene et al., 2003).

Neuropsychological models propose divergent explanations to account for these operation-specific deficits. Dagenbach and McCloskey (1992) suggested that dissociations between operations result from a selective damage to segregated memory networks specific for each operation. A different interpretation was proposed by Dehaene and Cohen (1995), who emphasised the different processing levels employed in answering the four basic operations. Though multiplication and very simple addition are taught systematically and depend heavily on rote-verbal memory, subtraction, more complex addition, and division are not taught systematically and require backup strategies and semantic manipulation of numerical quantities. Thus, patterns of selectively preserved and selectively disrupted operations are thought to reflect problems in specific levels of processing components rather than selective damage to stored representations. Accordingly, a disruption of memory representations should result in a severe deficit in multiplication but not in subtraction. A problem in executing backup strategies or in quantitative processing, on the other side, should lead to problems in subtraction and division but not in the overlearned multiplication tables (see Dehaene & Cohen, 1995). Since the operations are thought to differ in the representation format (multiplication and simple addition processed in verbal-auditory code; subtraction processed in analogue-magnitude code) as well as in the complexity of processing, patterns of modality- and operation-specific deficits have been predicted (Dehaene & Cohen, 1997).

Some case studies indeed show an association between intact language and preserved multiplication (e.g., Dehaene & Cohen, 1997; Delazer & Benke, 1997). An individual (HR) with posterior cortical atrophy showed excellent verbal intelligence (e.g., in vocabulary tests or in completing proverbs) but severe numerical deficits (Delazer et al., 2006). HR preserved multiplication tables (as well as other overlearned verbal sequences) but failed in all tasks that required access to quantity meaning or understanding of arithmetic operations. For example, HR was able to provide the answer for 7 × 8 but was unable to give the answer for 7 – 3 or to name the midpoint between 5 and 9.

Other cases do not show a systematic association between good language skills and multiplication. Delazer and colleagues (2004) reported that HGM, who suffered from an idiopathic progressive calcification of the basal ganglia, showed impairments in multiplication and division but had intact language abilities, number comprehension, and approximate processing. This case study suggests that retrieval of multiplication facts relies not only on verbal skills but on other abilities as well. Also, Whalen and colleagues (Whalen, McCloskey, Lindemann, & Bouton, 2002) argued against a purely language-based account of fact retrieval. Their participants (KSR, JM) successfully retrieved answers to simple arithmetic problems from memory even when they were unable to generate the phonological representation of either the problem itself or the answer. Thus, retrieval based on a purely phonological representation of arithmetic facts is unlikely. In sum, although there are in general systematic correlations between language and calculation, single neuropsychological cases point to a relative autonomy of both domains. Very likely, dissociations between language and calculation skills (and between arithmetic operations) are related to the depth of processing of arithmetic problems. For example, an individual may have preserved language skills and be able to recite the multiplication tables but have no understanding of the underlying arithmetic operation (e.g., Delazer et al., 2006). In this case, multiplication is recited just as the days of the week or a simple poem would be. Language may support the numerical system by verbal associations, for example, by counting rhymes or table rhymes (Kashiwagi, Kashiwagi, & Hasegawa, 1987). Impaired language would thus also affect to some extent the numerical system, making it less efficient without the verbal support. Exceptions to this frequent association, however, show that good language skills alone are not a sufficient precondition for intact fact retrieval (Delazer et al., 2004). Other cognitive components contribute to it as well, such as working memory and fast sequencing.

Errors in Simple Arithmetic

Some stable effects have been observed in simple arithmetic, namely, that neither reaction times nor error rates are randomly distributed over problems. Problems involving large operands (e.g., 9 × 8 or 8 × 7), in general, yield longer reaction times and higher error rates than problems involving small numbers (e.g., 2 × 3). However, size of the operands (and of the result) is not the only determining factor, and performance across problems can vary considerably across individuals (McCloskey, Aliminosa, et al., 1991). The individual error pattern of people with dyscalculia, however, may be highly consistent; for example, some problems may always (or mostly) be answered correctly, whereas other problems are never answered correctly. This non-uniform pattern of impairment (i.e., selective disruptions to some but not all arithmetic problems) has theoretical implications as well. Mc-Closkey, Harley, and colleagues (1991) argued that the non-uniformity of impairment is best accommodated by models postulating distinct representations for each fact (some facts being intact, some facts being impaired), whereas an extensive overlap of internal problem representations seems less plausible.

In fact, retrieval errors are highly systematic. In multiplication, a large proportion of such errors involve multiples of one of the operands, such as in 5 × 4 = 24 (e.g., Campbell & Graham, 1985; Siegler, 1988; Sokol et al., 1991). These *operand errors* are, for the most part, close to the correct result; and they differ by a maximum of +/− two operands. For example, 8 × 7 = 48 differs from the correct result (8 × 7 = 56) by one operand (Campbell & Graham, 1985; McCloskey, 1992). Operand errors are also the most frequent error type in individuals with acalculia. However, error patterns may differ across individuals. Individuals with dyscalculia may also show a high incidence of *close-miss errors* (5 × 6 = 31) (Girelli et al., 1996) or *non-table errors* (3 × 4 = 37; i.e., numbers that are not part of any multiplication table). Interestingly, such highly implausible error types may disappear during remediation in favor of more plausible operand errors (Domahs, Bartha, & Delazer, 2003; Girelli et al., 1996). There is also evidence of *cross-operation errors* (e.g., Grafman, Kampen, Rosenberg, Salazar, & Boller, 1989; van Harskamp & Cipolotti, 2001)—correct multiplication results stated for addition problems, or vice versa (e.g., 3 + 4 = 12, 2 × 5 = 7). In healthy subjects, cross-operation errors have been interpreted in terms of highly interrelated representations for multiplication and addition (e.g., Miller, Perlmutter, & Keating, 1984). In individuals with neuropsychological disorders, such errors may be related to failure in the choice of the correct operation as well as to problems in inhibiting the interference derived from the related operation (Dehaene et al., 2003; McNeil & Burgess, 2002).

Problems involving 0 or 1 as operands are thought to be solved by the application of a general rule rather than by memory retrieval (e.g., McCloskey, 1992). Double dissociations have been observed between rule-based and fact-based problems in individuals with neuropsychological disorders (e.g., McCloskey, Aliminosa, et al., 1991). Typically, rule-based problems show consistent error patterns. All problems of one type (e.g., N × 0) are answered by the same wrong algorithm (e.g., N × 0 = N).[4] Although a single rule is more frequently applied to all problems, dissociations between n × 0 and 0 × n problems have also been observed within single cases (McCloskey, Aliminosa, et al., 1991; see also Pesenti, Deeporter, & Seron, 2000, for an example of the 0 rule in addition). A dissociation between rule-based problems within the same operation has also been reported for division. For example, HGM (Delazer et al., 2004) consistently answered both N:N problems (100% correct) and N:1 problems (100% false) with 1. The authors suggested that difficulties in monitoring the correctness and plausibility of the answers played a critical role in the disruption of rule knowledge in this individual.

PROCEDURAL KNOWLEDGE

In multidigit problems (e.g., 34 × 25), calculation involves access to simple arithmetic facts (4 × 5, 3 × 5, 4 × 2, 3 × 2) as well as to procedures that specify the sequence of steps to be carried out (e.g., McCloskey, 1992). Neuropsychological data (e.g., McCloskey, Aliminosa, et al., 1991; Sokol et al., 1991; Warrington, 1982) as well as developmental studies (e.g., Temple, 1991) provide strong evidence that arithmetic facts and procedures are functionally independent components of the calculation system and may dissociate in both directions. It has also been suggested that procedural and conceptual knowledge (i.e., the understanding of arithmetic operations and principles) may dissociate. In fact, it has been shown that preserved subprocedures in multidigit calculation are not necessarily supported by conceptual knowledge (Girelli & Delazer, 1996; see also McCloskey, Aliminosa, et al., 1991). The reverse dissociation, intact conceptual knowledge in the

---

[4]The notation $N \times 0$ refers to all the multiplicative problems involving 0, regardless of the order of the operands (e.g., $0 \times 4, 4 \times 0$). The notations $0 \times n$ and $n \times 0$ refer, respectively, to problems in which 0 is the first operand (0×4) or the second operand (4×0).

context of deficient procedural knowledge, has been reported as well (Cappelletti, Butterworth, & Kopelman, 2001; see also Cappelletti, Kopelman, Morton, & Butterworth, 2005).

Selective deficits in calculation procedures have been reported in a number of single-case studies. McCloskey and colleagues (1985), for instance, described the difficulties encountered by four individuals in multidigit calculation. These individuals had problems either in handling the carrying and borrowing procedures or in aligning intermediate results properly. Of import, deficits in arithmetical procedures were found to be specific for the single operations. Thus, McCloskey and colleagues suggested that in the calculation system, procedures may be represented autonomously for each basic operation. Girelli and Delazer (1996) described MT, with a left parietal lesion, who was able to perform single-digit addition and subtraction, but was severely impaired in multidigit subtraction. His error pattern was highly consistent across problems (subtraction of the smaller digit from the larger digit irrespective of position). The authors argued that such errors resulted from the application of an erroneous algorithm. These results have been replicated in a recent case study by Sandrini, Miozzo, Cotelli, and Cappa (2003).

In Semenza, Miceli, and Girelli's (1997) developmental case study, MM showed serious difficulties with written multidigit multiplication, although access to multiplication facts was preserved. Performance on multidigit addition and subtraction was relatively intact (92% and 90% of the presented problems were correct, respectively). MM experienced greater difficulties in more complex problems and with the final steps of complex algorithms. Semenza and colleagues suggested that the procedural deficit was due to the inability to monitor the sequence of steps specified in the procedure rather than to distorted procedural knowledge. Similarly, Benke, Delazer, Bartha, and Auer (2003) attributed individuals' difficulties in calculation procedures to deficits in sequential processing (i.e., in executing a complex, multistep procedure) caused by basal ganglia lesions. Thus, multidigit calculation has often been found to be impaired in individuals with a dysfunction of frontal lobes or related structures (e.g., Lucchelli & De Renzi, 1993). Recently, McNeil and Burgess (2002) described an individual we will refer to as SR, with probable Alzheimer's disease and selective deficits with arithmetical procedures. SR had preserved arithmetic fact knowledge for all four basic operations, good number processing skills, good number comprehension, and intact general numerical knowledge. In contrast, performance on multidigit problems, fractions, and decimals was dramatically impaired. SR's difficulties involved confusion and misapplication of a variety of procedures rather than an inability to perform calculations. As suggested by the authors, an impairment with task-switching would account for the discrepancy between relatively preserved addition and subtraction and strongly impaired multiplication and division multidigit calculations.

Multidigit multiplication and division require switching between different operations (e.g., multiplying the operands and then adding the partial products in multiplication), whereas addition and subtraction do not. Although this may have been applicable to SR, this hypothesis could not be further tested in this subject.

In sum, deficits in written multidigit calculation are frequently observed in individuals with acquired brain lesions. Deficits have been classified into two different types. In the first, difficulties arise because of deficits in the retrieval and/or storage of arithmetical procedures in long-term memory. In the second, difficulties are attributed to impaired monitoring and sequencing of complex procedures.

CONCEPTUAL KNOWLEDGE

Arithmetic processing is not only based on the retrieval of stored arithmetic facts or the execution of procedural steps but also on conceptual knowledge—that is, the understanding of arithmetic operations and principles. Neuropsychological case studies have evidenced double dissociations between conceptual knowledge and arithmetic fact retrieval. For instance, some individuals have shown severe deficits in fact retrieval while exhibiting excellent conceptual knowledge (Hittmair-Delazer et al., 1994; Hittmair-Delazer, Sailer, & Benke, 1995); some of the subjects have exhibited severe deficits in conceptual knowledge with partially preserved fact knowledge (Delazer & Benke, 1997). It has also been suggested that procedural and conceptual knowledge may dissociate (Cappelletti et al., 2001, 2005; Girelli & Delazer, 1996).

A fruitful approach to assessing conceptual knowledge is the analysis of backup procedures in the case of failed fact retrieval. Healthy subjects use a variety of strategies even for simple arithmetic problems such as addition (LeFevre, Sadesky, et al., 1996) and multiplication (LeFevre, Bisanz, et al., 1996). The use of backup strategies has been repeatedly described in individuals with dyscalculia as well (McCloskey et al., 1985; Sokol & McCloskey, 1991). For example, an individual we refer to as IE (Sokol et al., 1989, 1991; Sokol & McCloskey, 1991) was able to work out addition and multiplication problems that she could not solve by fact retrieval. For example, she split the addition problem 9 + 2 into 9 + (1 + 1), then into (9 + 1) + 1 to arrive at the correct answer of 11.

The most extensive analysis on backup strategies to date was performed on BE, a 45-year-old accountant who suffered a cerebral embolism affecting the left basal ganglia. This left him with a right hemiparesis and a nonfluent aphasia (Hittmair-Delazer et al., 1994). Except for the easiest ones, (including the table of 2 and some problems with 3, 4, and 5 as operands) BE had lost a great many memorized multiplication facts, as well as most division facts. Of interest, BE developed highly elaborated and flexible strategies to overcome his deficit with multiplication and division and showed excellent understanding of arithmetical principles. The results of this study suggest that conceptual knowledge and fact knowledge are supported by separate cognitive mechanisms (see also Hittmair-Delazer et al., 1995; McCloskey et al., 1985; Sokol et al., 1989; Sokol & McCloskey, 1991; Warrington, 1982). This assumption is also supported by case studies that report partially preserved fact knowledge with impaired conceptual knowledge (Dehaene & Cohen, 1997; Delazer & Benke, 1997; Delazer et al., 2004). For example, HGM (Delazer et al., 2004) could answer simple subtraction and addition problems but failed in all tasks tapping conceptual and procedural knowledge. He was not able to develop backup strategies or to recognize and apply arithmetical principles. He even failed to recognize the relation between multiplication and division problems. This case, along with others (e.g., Delazer & Benke, 1997), underlies the separate implementation of fact knowledge and conceptual knowledge.

Those involved in neuropsychological case studies have also argued that procedural and conceptual knowledge represent distinct types of knowledge. It has been repeatedly reported that individuals with dyscalculia may apply procedures or part of procedures correctly without understanding the underlying numerical operations (e.g., Girelli & Delazer, 1996). Thus, correct procedures are not always grounded on conceptual understanding of the single steps performed. Some have also reported that intact conceptual knowledge may be associated with severe procedural deficits. Cappelletti and colleagues (2001; see also Cappelletti et al., 2005) described IH as having semantic dementia, a progressive cortical degeneration that mainly affects the temporal lobes and selectively impairs semantic memory (e.g., word meanings and concepts). IH's progressive impairment with retrieval of multiplication facts and application of the standard procedure in the solution of multidigit multiplication was compensated for by the use of laborious, spontaneously devised noncanonical algorithms. For example, IH solved the problem 23 x 35 as $(35 \times 10) + (35 \times 10) + (35 \times 3) = 350 + 350 + 105 = 805$, adapting the associative principle to 2-digit $\times$ 2-digit multiplication problems. IH clearly demonstrated flexible and skilled conceptual understanding of arithmetic despite severe impairment of non-arithmetic conceptual knowledge.

In conclusion, neuropsychological case reports provide good evidence for separate representations of fact knowledge, procedural knowledge, and conceptual knowledge. Although evidence is convincing that these types of knowledge are selectively vulnerable to brain damage and functionally independent, it should be noted that the different types of knowledge benefit from each other. For example, good conceptual knowledge allows the targeted selection and efficient application of calculation procedures, and a rich lexicon of stored facts supports insight into the relations of different number combinations, and leads to a better conceptual understanding in the number domain. Fact knowledge and procedural knowledge are also less error prone and more flexible when supported by conceptual knowledge (Resnick, 1982).

While some evidence for the relationship between fact knowledge, procedural knowledge, and conceptual knowledge has been accumulated, less is known about the relationship between quantity knowledge and conceptual knowledge. The assessment of quantity knowledge is typically composed of the evaluation of distance effects in number comparison,[5] subitizing tasks, estimation tasks, and approximate calculation tasks (e.g., Lemer, Dehaene, Spelke, & Cohen, 2003). These tasks are believed to rely on access to an internal quantity code (e.g., Dehaene & Cohen, 1995). Few studies have assessed conceptual knowledge and quantity processing in detail (e.g., Delazer & Benke, 1997; Delazer et al., 2004). In the few cases where both abilities (quantity processing and conceptual processing) were at least partially assessed, dissociations were only found between preserved quantity processing and impaired conceptual knowledge (e.g., Delazer & Benke, 1997). One might also speculate that intact quantity processing and intact comprehension of the number concept is a precondition for intact conceptual knowledge (Delazer & Butterworth, 1997).

EXACT AND APPROXIMATE CALCULATION

Cognitive estimation is a pervasive part of daily life and consists simply of giving an appropriate answer when an exact solution is not readily available (e.g., Brand, Kessler, Kalbe, Ruediger, & Behrendt, 2000). Numerical quantity is among the many dimensions generally estimated. In fact, the ability to estimate or approximate the value of a set of items is considered part of an evolutionary heritage and the basis of humans' ability to calculate exact values (Dehaene, 1997). Evidence from neuropsychological patient studies consistently suggests that approximation and exact calculation are indeed supported by distinct, dissociable brain systems and that both parietal lobes play a central role in numerical quantity processing (e.g., Dehaene & Cohen, 1997; Lemer et al., 2003).

DRC (Warrington, 1982), a medical doctor suffering from a left hematoma in the left parietal and occipital lobes, had difficulties solving even the most basic addition, subtraction, and multiplication problems. For example, his reply to the problem 5+7 was "about 13." He complained that he was no longer able to solve automatically simple calculations and had to make use of laborious and slow counting strategies. However, his performance in

---

[5]Response times and error rates systematically increase as the distance between two numbers decreases (first reported by Moyer & Landauer, 1967).

other numerical tasks was normal or near normal. For example, in addition to being able to clearly define arithmetic operations, he could give the approximate solution of simple and complex arithmetic problems. Furthermore, his cognitive estimation skills of size and number, as well as his ability to judge the numerosity of arrays of dots, were intact. DRC's case study has been particularly influential in the field of mathematical cognition because it was the first comprehensive quantitative report of such a distinct dissociation between exact and approximate arithmetic calculation.

Dehaene and Cohen (1991) examined NAU, a middle-aged executive salesperson. A computerized axial tomography (CAT) scan revealed a large reduction of density in the temporal, parietal, and occipital lobes, affecting most of the posterior half of the left hemisphere. NAU showed a profound deficit in exact calculation, but his ability to approximate was preserved. For instance, NAU consistently realized that a calculation such as $2 + 2 = 9$ was incorrect, but he considered as correct such calculations as $2 + 2 = 5$ or offered 3 as the answer to $2 + 2$, regardless of the problem presentation modality. NAU's numerical deficits also involved common numerical facts such as the number of days in a month, the number of minutes in a quarter of an hour, and the number of seasons in a year. His answers, although incorrect half of the time, were always approximately correct. For instance, he could say that a year consisted of 350 days or that an hour had 50 minutes. Therefore, NAU seemed to have spared analogue representations for approximate quantities, but his exact number processing skills were extremely impaired. Based on NAU's case, Dehaene and Cohen (1991) suggested that in healthy subjects exact and approximate number processing are not components or different stages of a single unitary system but distinct and dissociable processing routes. In other words, one route allows the representation, memory, and calculation of exact numbers using symbolic notation (e.g., Arabic digits), whereas the other route permits for approximate computations using an analogue representation of quantities. The role of these two routes or systems for exact and approximate number processing and calculation appears to be difficult to specify, because they are thought to work simultaneously and in coordination with each other. However, the existence of two routes can account for the impairments in individuals such as NAU and DRC.

Another important study that revealed a double dissociation between approximation and exact calculation involved the systematic examination of two individuals with acalculia (BRI and LEC) by Lemer and colleagues (2003). Their findings support the assumption that human arithmetic is underpinned by the integration of two separate and dissociable systems: a verbal system for number words and a non-symbolic representation system of approximate quantities. BRI had semantic dementia with reduced metabolism mainly in the left hemisphere of her brain. LEC had a focal lesion in the left parietal lobe. BRI and LEC showed contrasting patterns of performance on approximate and exact number-processing tasks as well as in arithmetic operations and numerical quantity processing. BRI was more impaired in exact than in approximate calculation, whereas the opposite was true for LEC. The latter admitted that she was utterly unable to approximate and had to calculate the correct answer in the approximation tasks. The experimental investigation on BRI and LEC yielded evidence for a double dissociation between multiplication and subtraction as well. BRI, who had a verbal deficit, was impaired in multiplication but relatively preserved in subtraction, whereas LEC, who had difficulties with quantity tasks, performed poorly in subtraction but was less impaired in multiplication. This seems to support the view that verbal abilities mediate the processing of multiplication, which relies on verbally stored tables, whereas subtraction relies more on quantity processing. Furthermore, Lemer and colleagues found a double dissociation in the processing of non-symbolic stimuli consisting of arrays of squares displayed on a computer screen. BRI could normally subitize (i.e., recognize 1 to 3 squares), but his performance on tasks involving counting numerosities outside the subitizing range was impaired. LEC was very slow at counting but could count as accurately as individuals in a control group. LEC had to count each item presented even when stimuli were within the subitizing range. This result refutes the idea that subitizing is part of a single continuum of counting difficulty. Finally, BRI and LEC had to compare or compute an approximate addition of numbers between 11 and 99, either with two arrays of dots or with 2-digit Arabic numerals. LEC's performance on these tasks was consistently poor, indicating a numerical quantity-related deficit, whereas BRI had an unimpaired performance, suggesting no numerical quantity-related deficit. The cases of BRI and LEC support the view that numerical abilities may be based on the integration of a symbolic system (verbal or Arabic) and a non-symbolic system of approximate quantities, which are dissociable.

DISCUSSION

Neuropsychological case studies provide clear evidence that in adults, different types of knowledge contribute to arithmetic processing. These types of knowledge are selectively vulnerable to brain degeneration or acquired brain lesions and are functionally independent. Double dissociations have been described between fact knowledge and procedural knowledge, between fact knowledge and conceptual knowledge, and between procedural knowledge and conceptual knowledge. There is also evidence of a double dissociation between exact and approximate number knowledge. Though evidence from case studies suggests that these different components are separately implemented in the human brain, they benefit from their linking.

Fact knowledge is only meaningful when supported by conceptual knowledge and is very often compensated for by procedural backup strategies. Procedures are less error prone when effectively supported by conceptual knowledge. Conceptual knowledge is more advantageous when more memory-based facts and procedures can be used. Exact fact knowledge is more efficiently processed when estimation abilities and approximate knowledge of number are available. Approximation is also essential in checking the plausibility of a result obtained by exact calculation. Although the cognitive architecture of number processing seems to be modularly organized, the cooperation of different types of knowledge leads to meaningful and efficient processing.

Regarding the numerical abilities of children, one should be cautious not to draw too-simple parallels between adults' and children's cognitive architecture. As has been shown in developmental literature, different types of knowledge influence one another during the acquisition of arithmetic abilities. On the one hand, progress in one component may be advantageous for the development of another component. On the other hand, newly acquired knowledge may cause interference (e.g., Miller & Paredes, 1990).

In conclusion, neuropsychological studies with adults show that different types of knowledge are involved in number processing and that they benefit from their linking. For example, fact knowledge not supported by conceptual knowledge is meaningless and cannot be applied successfully. This is certainly also true for children; therefore, all types of knowledge should be considered in teaching environments and encouraged to gradually evolve over the years.

REFERENCES

Ashcraft, M.H. (1992). Cognitive arithmetic: A review of data and theory. *Cognition, 44,* 75–106.

Ashcraft, M.H. (1995). Cognitive psychology and simple arithmetic: A review and summary of new directions. *Mathematical Cognition, 1,* 3–34.

Benke, T., Delazer, M., Bartha, L., & Auer, A. (2003). Basal ganglia lesions and the theory of fronto-subcortical loops: Neuropsychological findings in two patients with left caudate lesions. *Neurocase, 9,* 70–85.

Berger, H. (1926). Über Rechenstörungen bei Herderkrankungen des Großhirns [Calculation disorders in focal lesions of the brain]. *Archiv für Psychiatrie und Nervenkrankheiten, 78,* 238–263.

Brand, M., Kessler, J., Kalbe, E., Ruediger M., & Behrendt, J. (2000). How long is a fly? A test for cognitive estimation in patients with probable Alzheimer's disease. *Neurobiology of Aging, 21,* 233.

Campbell, J.I.D. (1995). Mechanisms of simple addition and multiplication: A modified network-interference theory and simulation. *Mathematical Cognition, 1,* 121–165.

Campbell, J.I.D., & Graham, D.J. (1985). Mental multiplication skills: Structures, process and acquisition. *Canadian Journal of Psychology, 39,* 338–366.

Cappelletti, M., Butterworth, B., & Kopelman, M.D. (2001). Spared numerical abilities in a case of semantic dementia. *Neuropsychologia, 39,* 1224–1239.

Cappelletti, M., Kopelman, M.D., Morton, J., & Butterworth, B. (2005). Dissociations in numerical abilities revealed by progressive cognitive decline in a patient with semantic dementia. *Cognitive Neuropsychology, 22*(7), 771–793.

Cipolotti, L., & de Lacy Costello, A. (1995). Selective impairment for simple division. *Cortex, 31,* 433–449.

Dagenbach, D., & McCloskey, M. (1992). The organisation of arithmetic facts in memory: Evidence from a brain-damaged patient. *Brain and Cognition, 20,* 345–366.

Dehaene, S. (1992). Varieties of numerical abilities. *Cognition, 44,* 1–42.

Dehaene, S. (1997). *The number sense.* New York: Oxford University Press.

Dehaene, S., & Cohen, L. (1991). Two mental calculation systems: A case study of severe acalculia with preserved approximation. *Neuropsychologia, 29,* 1045–1054.

Dehaene, S., & Cohen, L. (1994). Dissociable mechanisms of subitizing and counting: Neuropsychological evidence from simultagnosic patients. *Journal of Experimental Psychology: Human Perception and Performance, 20,* 958–975.

Dehaene, S., & Cohen, L. (1995). Towards an anatomical and functional model of number processing. *Mathematical Cognition, 1,* 83–120.

Dehaene, S., & Cohen, L. (1997). Cerebral pathways for calculation: Double dissociation between rote verbal and quantitative knowledge of arithmetic. *Cortex, 33,* 219–250.

Dehaene, S., Molko, N., Cohen, L., & Wilson, A.J. (2004). Arithmetic and the brain. *Current Opinion in Neurobiology, 14,* 218–224.

Dehaene, S., Piazza, M., Pinel, P., & Cohen, L. (2003). Three parietal circuits for number processing. *Cognitive Neuropsychology, 20,* 487–506.

Delazer, M., & Benke, T. (1997). Arithmetic facts without meaning. *Cortex, 33,* 697–710.

Delazer, M., & Butterworth, B. (1997). A dissociations of number meanings. *Cognitive Neuropsychology, 14,* 613–636.

Delazer, M., Domahs, F., Lochy, A., Karner, E., Benke, T., & Poewe, W. (2004). Number processing and basal ganglia dysfunction: A single case study. *Neuropsychologia, 42,* 926–938.

Delazer, M., Karner, E., Zamarian, L., Donnemiller, E., & Benke, T. (2006). Number processing in posterior cortical atrophy—A neuropsychological case study. *Neuropsychologia, 44*(1), 36–51.

Domahs, F., Bartha, L., & Delazer, M. (2003). Rehabilitation of arithmetic abilities: Different intervention strategies for multiplication. *Brain and Language, 87,* 165–166.

Girelli, L., & Delazer, M. (1996). Subtraction bags in an acalculic patient. *Cortex, 32,* 547–555.

Girelli, L., Delazer, M., Semenza, C., & Denes, G. (1996). The representation of arithmetical facts: Evidence from two rehabilitation studies. *Cortex, 32,* 49–66.

Grafman, J., Kampen, D., Rosenberg, J., Salazar, A.M., & Boller, F. (1989). The progressive breakdown of number processing and calculation ability: A case study. *Cortex, 25,* 121–133.

Grafman, J., Passafiume, D., Faglioni, P., & Boller, F. (1982). Calculation disturbances in adults with focal hemispheric damage. *Cortex, 18,* 37–50.

Hecaen, H., Angelergues, T., & Houiller, S. (1961). Les varietes cliniques des acalculies au cours des lesions retroronlandiques The clinical varieties of acalculias during petrocolaudic lesions: Statistical approach to the problem. *Revue Neurologique, 105,* 85–103.

Henschen, S.E. (1919). Über Sprach-, Musik-, und Rechenmechanismen und ihre Lokalisationen im Großhirn Language, music, and calculation mechanisms, and their localizations in the brain. *Zeitschrift für die gesamte Neurologie und Psychiatrie, 52,* 273–298.

Henschen, S.E. (1920). *Klinische und anatomische Beiträge zur Pathologie des Gehirns* Clinical and anatomical contributions regarding brain pathology *(Vol. 5).* Stockholm: Nordiska Bokhandeln.

Hittmair-Delazer, M., Sailer, U., & Benke, T. (1995). Impaired arithmetic facts but intact conceptual knowledge—Single-case study of dyscalculia. *Cortex, 31,* 139–147.

Hittmair-Delazer, M., Semenza, C., & Denes, G. (1994). Concepts and facts in calculation. *Brain, 117,* 715–728.

Kashiwagi, A., Kashiwagi, T., & Hasegawa, T. (1987). Improvement of deficits in mnemonic rhyme for multiplication in Japanese aphasics. *Neuropsychologia, 25,* 443–447.

LeFevre, J., Bisanz, J., Daley, K., Buffone, L., Greenham, St., & Sadesky, G. (1996). Multiple routes to solution of single-digit multiplication problems. *Journal of Experimental Psychology: General, 125,* 284–306.

LeFevre, J., Sadesky, G., & Bisanz, J. (1996). Selection of procedures in mental addition: Reassessing the problem-size effect in adults. *Journal of Experimental Psychology: Learning, Memory, and Cognition, 22,* 216–230.

Lemer, C., Dehaene, S., Spelke, E., & Cohen, L. (2003). Approximate quantities and exact number words: Dissociable systems. *Neuropsychologia, 41,* 1942–1958.

Lewandowsky, M., & Stadelmann, E. (1908). Über einen bemerkenswerten Fall von Hirnblutung und über Rechenstörungen bei Herderkrankung des Gehirns A special case of hemoragic insult and calculation disorders in focal brain lesions. *Journal für Psychologie und Neurologie, 11,* 249–265.

Lucchelli, F., & De Renzi, E. (1993). Primary dyscalculia after a medial frontal lesion of the left hemisphere. *Journal of Neurology, Neurosurgery and Psychiatry, 56,* 304–307.

Mandler, G., & Shebo, B.J. (1982). Subitizing: An analysis of its component processing. *Journal of Experimental Psychology: General, 111,* 1–22.

McCloskey, M. (1992). Cognitive mechanisms in numerical processing: Evidence from acquired dyscalculia. *Cognition, 44,* 107–157.

McCloskey, M., Aliminosa, D., & Sokol, S.M. (1991). Facts, rules, and procedures in normal calculation: Evidence from multiple single-patient studies of impaired arithmetic fact retrieval. *Brain and Cognition, 17,* 154–203.

McCloskey, M., Caramazza, A., & Basili, A.G. (1985). Cognitive mechanisms in number processing and calculation: Evidence from dyscalculia. *Brain and Cognition, 4,* 171–196.

McCloskey, M., Harley, W., & Sokol, S.M. (1991). Models of arithmetic fact retrieval: An evaluation in light of findings from normal and brain-damaged subjects. *Journal of Experimental Psychology: Learning, Memory, and Cognition, 17,* 377–397.

McCloskey, M., Sokol, S.M, & Goodman, R.A. (1986). Cognitive processes in verbal-number production: Inferences from the performance of brain-damaged subjects. *Journal of Experimental Psychology: General, 115,* 307–330.

McNeil, J.E., & Burgess, P.W. (2002). The selective impairment of arithmetical procedures. *Cortex, 38,* 569–587.

McNeil, J.E., & Warrington, E.K. (1994). A dissociation between addition and subtraction within written calculation. *Neuropsychologia, 32,* 717–728.

Miller, K.F., & Paredes, D.R. (1990). Starting to add worse: Effects of learning to multiply on children's addition. *Cognition, 37,* 213–242.

Miller, K.F., Perlmutter, M., & Keating, D. (1984). Cognitive arithmetic: Comparison of operations. *Journal of Experimental Psychology: Learning, Memory, and Cognition, 10,* 46–60.

Moyer, R.S., & Landauer, T.K. (1967). Time required for judgements of numerical inequality. *Nature, 215,* 1519–1520.

Noël, M.P., & Seron, X. (1993). Arabic number reading deficit: A single case study or when 236 is read (2306) and judged superior to 1258. *Cognitive Neuropsychology, 10,* 317–339.

Noël, M.P., & Seron, X. (1995). Lexicalization errors in writing Arabic numerals. *Brain and Cognition, 29,* 151–179.

Pesenti, M., Deeporter, N., & Seron, X. (2000). Noncommutability of the N+0 arithmetical rule: A case study of dissociated impairment. *Cortex, 36,* 445–454.

Pesenti, M., Seron, X., & van der Linden, M. (1994). Selective impairment as evidence for mental organisation of arithmetical facts: BB, a case of preserved subtraction? *Cortex, 30,* 661–671.

Resnick, L.B. (1982). Syntax and semantics in learning to subtract. In T.P. Carpenter, J.M. Moser, & T.H. Romberg (Eds.), *Addition and subtraction: A cognitive perspective.* Hillsdale, NJ: Lawrence Erlbaum Associates.

Sandrini, M., Miozzo, A., Cotelli, M., & Cappa, S.F. (2003). The residual calculation abilities of a patient with severe aphasia: Evidence for a selective deficit of subtraction procedures. *Cortex, 39,* 85–96.

Semenza, C., Miceli, L., & Girelli, L. (1997). A deficit for arithmetical procedures: Lack of knowledge or lack of monitoring? *Cortex, 33,* 483–498.

Shallice, T. (1979). Case study approach in neuropsychological research. *Journal of Clinical Neuropsychology, 1,* 183–211.

Shallice, T. (1988). *From neuropsychology to mental structure.* New York: Cambridge University Press.

Siegler, R. (1988). Strategy choice procedures and the development of multiplication skill. *Journal of Experimental Psychology: General, 117,* 258–275.

Singer, H.D., & Low, A.A. (1933). Acalculia (Henschen): A clinical study. *Archives of Neurology and Psychiatry, 29,* 476–498.

Sokol, S.M., & McCloskey, M. (1991). Cognitive mechanisms in calculation. In R. Sternberg & P.A. Frensch (Eds.), *Complex problem solving: Principles and mechanisms* (pp. 85–116). Mahwah, NJ: Lawrence Erlbaum Associates.

Sokol, S.M., McCloskey, M., & Cohen, N.J. (1989). Cognitive representations of arithmetic knowledge: Evidence from acquired dyscalculia. In A.F. Bennett & K.M. McConkie (Eds.), *Cognition in individual and social contexts* (pp. 577–591). Amsterdam: Elsevier.

Sokol, S.M., McCloskey, M., Cohen, N.J., & Aliminosa, D. (1991). Cognitive representations and processes in arithmetic: Inferences from the performance of brain-damaged patients. *Journal of Experimental Psychology: Learning, Memory, and Cognition, 17,* 355–376.

Temple, C. (1991). Procedural dyscalculia and number facts dyscalculia: Double dissociation in developmental dyscalculia. *Cognitive Neuropsychology, 8,* 155–176.

Van Harskamp, N.J., & Cipolotti, L. (2001). Selective impairments for addition, subtraction and multiplication: Implications for the organisation of arithmetical facts. *Cortex, 37,* 363–388.

Warrington, E.K. (1982). The fractionation of arithmetical skills: A single case study. *The Quarterly Journal of Experimental Psychology, 34A,* 31–51.

Whalen, J., McCloskey, M., Lindemann, M., & Bouton, G. (2002). Representing arithmetic table facts in memory: Evidence from acquired impairments. *Cognitive Neuropsychology, 19,* 505–522.

Neuropsychological Factors

Rebecca Bull

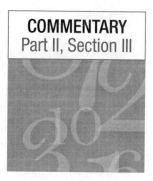

The chapters presented in this section of the book have addressed selected developmental disorders for which a math disability is one of the primary cognitive sequelae (i.e., a consequence or result of the disorder). These include specific language impairment (SLI), Turner syndrome, fragile X, spina bifida myelomeningocele (SBM), attention-deficit/hyperactivity disorder (ADHD), acquired impairments in adults, and traumatic brain injury (TBI) in children. Each chapter has highlighted current findings regarding the role of retrieval skills, working memory/executive control, and visuospatial skills in the math performance of individuals with the disorder in question, and the authors have considered whether the disorder is representative of a potential mathematical learning disability (MLD) subtype. In this commentary I attempt to pull together the findings from these populations to address potential MLD subtypes and highlight a number of issues that need to be considered to make further progress toward understanding the numerical and cognitive underpinnings of MLD.

VISUOSPATIAL AND NONVERBAL NUMERICAL SKILLS

One of the identified subtypes of MLD includes those individuals believed to have impairments in visuospatial skills (Geary, 1993). Visuospatial skills may have a negative impact on an individual's math skills at various levels—number inversions and reversal; misalignment of column digits; problems in visual attention and monitoring, such as ignoring signs or changing operation partway through completion of a problem; and acquiring concepts of borrowing and carrying. Other aspects of nonverbal numerical processing, such as estimation, magnitude comparison, and generation of mental number lines, are also considered to be in this subtype, although it is not clear whether such skills interact with or develop independently from other forms of visuospatial reasoning (Dehaene, 1997). Studies of individuals with SLI or other populations in which language impairments are known to occur (e.g., fragile X) allow interesting questions to be asked about the importance of language in mathematical cognition. Furthermore, by contrasting such populations with those known to have intact language skills but impaired visuospatial skills (e.g., Turner syndrome), it may be possible to distinguish more clearly those aspects of number development that are constrained by language from those constrained by nonverbal abilities.

Evidence from studies of both acquired (see Dehaene, Spelke, Pinel, Stanescu, & Tsivkin, 1999; Zamarian et al., this volume) and developmental disorders (e.g., Donlan, this volume) suggests that certain aspects of numerical understanding, for example, numerosity and magnitude judgments and approximation, are independent of language and are associated with distinct neuroanatomical substrates. Such skills have been described within the realm of a rudimentary number sense that is present without explicit instruction (see Berch, 2005; Dehaene, 1997) and provides the foundational structure for elementary numerical abilities (e.g., Geary, 1995; Jordan, Kaplan, Olah, & Locuniak, 2006; Mazzocco, 2005). As children learn the sequence of number words, they are able to map this more exact system to their nonverbal representations of quantity, allowing them to accurately enumerate arrays of objects. It has been argued that an impaired nonverbal representation of approximate magnitude may constrain typical development of exact number abilities across time (Ansari & Karmiloff-Smith, 2002). An inaccurate representaion or even one that lacks clarity may lead to difficulty in establishing robust links between Arabic numerals and their associated semantic information, leading to difficulties with estimation and magnitude comparison (akin to the notion of assembled processing discussed in relation to performance impairments of those with SBM—see Dennis, Landry, Barnes, & Fletcher, 2006). It may also lead to more variability between the boundaries of different magnitudes along the mental number line (see Rubinsten & Henik, 2005, for such evidence in developmental dyscalculia). Indeed, Jordan, Hanich, and Kaplan (2003) speculated that weaknesses in spatial representations of numerical magnitude—in particular, difficulties manipulating visual representations on a number line—are particularly influential during the early acquisition of calculation skills and may underpin the retrieval impairments observed in many populations with MLD.

Of the populations reported in the chapters reviewed here, several show impairments in visual and/or spatial functioning and nonverbal numerical processing. Individuals with Turner syndrome have more widespread impairments in both visual and spatial cognition. However, visuospatial skills are not predictive of math performance in individuals with Turner syndrome, and their basic number sense is intact. Those with fragile X syndrome show a more specific impairment in spatial cognition (Mazzocco, Bhatia, & Lesniak-Karpiak, 2006) that is predictive of their mathematical performance, and there is clear evidence of difficulties in number sense skills, particularly in making magnitude and mental number line judgments. There are also visuospatial strengths and weaknesses in those with SBM (strength in visual perception and weakness in spatial representation—see Dennis et al., 2006). Although Barnes, Fletcher, and Ewing-Cobbs (Chapter 10, this volume) find that these skills are not predictive of arithmetic performance, visuospatial skills may be a significant predictor of performance on more complex mathematical problems (e.g., estimation, geometry, and word problems) for both children with SBM and typically developing children (Barnes et al., 2002).

How can we account for apparent inconsistent findings (particularly between fragile X and Turner syndrome) concerning the relationship between visuospatial/nonverbal skills and math abilities? The different patterns of results may be explained by considering the relative strengths evident in individuals with these impairments. Those with Turner syndrome have relatively intact language skills, and indeed show no impairments on simple arithmetic problems that are thought to be solved by rote verbal memory (e.g., multiplication and simple addition; Bruandet, Molko, Cohen, & Dehaene, 2004). This is also true of those with SBM, for which there is a high incidence of specific MLD with relatively intact reading and language skills. Therefore, poor visuospatial skills may only predict MLD when an alternative representational basis (verbal) for number cannot be easily utilized, for example, when there are corresponding language problems or when poor number sense limits the association of nonverbal representations to the verbal number system.

PROCEDURAL SKILLS AND COUNTING STRATEGIES

For many children with MLD, one of the early signs of mathematical difficulties manifests itself as a procedural impairment in counting and arithmetic strategy use and in difficulties executing or monitoring the various stages of more complex problem solving (e.g., borrowing and carrying). Such difficulties are typically accounted for by deficient representation and manipulation of numerical information within the language system, for example, production, storage, and monitoring of number words and counting. Immature or error-prone counting creates fewer situations for practice of arithmetical procedures and number combinations, and frequent counting errors may result in difficulty establishing strong representations of number combinations in long-term memory. Alternatively, individuals may be able to correctly apply the procedures necessary in complex problem solving, but impairments in executive control lead to difficulties in sequencing and monitoring complex procedures (discussed in many of the chapters in this section). Finally, recent findings also indicate that many tasks that deal with exact symbolic numerosities automatically activate nonsymbolic number representations of the type discussed in the previous section (e.g., Barth, Kanwisher, & Spelke, 2003), so a deficient number sense may also account for procedural impairments.

Donlan's work (Chapter 8, this volume) shows that although children with SLI do not have difficulties with early number concepts (showing typical number line effects such as symbolic distance effects) and are as capable as peers who are typically developing in comparing multidigit numbers (Donlan & Gourlay, 1999), procedural impairments associated with counting are particularly problematic for further math development. These procedural impairments, in particular production of the number-word sequence, in children with SLI have been accounted for by clear impairments in phonological processing and storage, although it should be noted that these children also show impairments in executive and visuospatial functioning (Cowan, Donlan, Newton, & Lloyd, 2005). With an impairment in the language representations supporting numerical skills, individual differences in visuospatial and nonverbal representations may be an important predictor of developing mathematical competencies. Indeed, Donlan's NumberTalk study showed that number sequence production, transcoding, and basic calculation were uniquely predicted by language and working memory, as might be expected, but with nonverbal reasoning also making a unique contribution to predicting these skills. Poor conceptual knowledge (e.g., lack of understanding of counting principles, associativity, and commutativity) has also been proposed as a contributor to delays in more sophisticated counting procedures. Through the use of a novel technique (Martian maths), Donlan (Chapter 8) also showed that despite an early procedural impairment in production of the counting sequence, children with SLI had intact conceptual understanding of arithmetical principles, suggesting no direct link between language and number concepts or between procedural and conceptual knowledge in arithmetic. This is supported by dissociations between conceptual and procedural knowledge in studies of acquired mathematical difficulties (see Zamarian et al., this volume).

Individuals with fragile X display difficulty with applied counting and understanding of counting principles but are good at rote counting. The difficulties were accounted for by both visual and spatial recall related to detection of counting errors. When the difficulty of tasks is increased (e.g., an extra step may be added to increase the working memory load), individuals with fragile X fail to show an increase in brain activation that is evidenced in populations of individuals who are typically developing, suggesting a working memory rather than a visuospatial impairment per se (I will return to this issue later). Turner syndrome is also characterized by the use of immature counting strategies and procedural errors in arithmetic problem solving. These procedural difficulties appear to be independent of the visuospatial problems evidenced in Turner syndrome and so may be predicted by individual differences in language-based aspects of numerical processing.

SEMANTIC/ASSOCIATIVE IMPAIRMENTS AND FACT RETRIEVAL

The other, more persistent (and often defining), impairment typically observed in children with MLD is the inability to store and retrieve number combinations from long-term memory. Suggested sources of this impairment in math fact mastery include a general semantic/associative impairment; deficient phonological representations (Geary, 1993); problems inhibiting closely related math facts in memory (Deheane, Spelke, Pinel, Stanescu, & Tsivkin, 2003; Geary, 2004); slow information processing across cognitive domains, including math (Bull & Johnston, 1997); and difficulties in manipulating nonverbal spatial representations, such as the mental number line (Jordan et al., 2003). There is also evidence of this core deficit in individuals with SLI, ADHD, SBM, and Turner syndrome, and it is particularly evident in individuals within these populations who show comorbid language difficulties. Findings from acquired MLD also suggest that impaired language can account for impairments in fact retrieval, although a number of exceptions to this association show that good language alone is not a sufficient precondition for intact fact retrieval (Delazer et al., 2004) because other cognitive components contribute to such difficulties. In virtually all populations, this fact retrieval impairment manifests itself in the form of slow and unpredictable response times. Lack of automaticity, indicated by impaired retrieval, also means that limited cognitive resources (present in many individuals within these populations) are directed toward the use of often slow and inefficient counting strategies and away from the more complex aspects of mathematical processing.

So far I have said little about either pediatric TBI or ADHD. Both groups show a primary deficit in executive functioning (depending on the age of acquired injury in TBI), which is likely to affect all aspects of learning at both a cognitive and behavioral level regardless of mathematical content. For children with TBI or ADHD, the core mathematical difficulties appear to be the lack of or unsystematic retrieval of number combinations due to working memory, attentional, and inhibitory impairments (although number sense has not been systematically examined in these populations). In Chapter 11, Zentall argues that for those with ADHD, lack of computational fluency may arise from an inability to stay focused on repetitive tasks, with less time spent rehearsing arithmetic combinations and more variability in the answers produced. Those with ADHD also have difficulty selectively attending to and inhibiting irrelevant information on cognitive tasks, which results in difficulty holding information in working memory as more information than is necessary is processed and held in limited capacity stores. That MLD is not a primary disorder in ADHD is also supported by the fact that under certain environmental conditions, those with ADHD do not show significant arithmetical difficulties.

COMPLEX MATHEMATICS AND COMPLEX COGNITION

Mazzocco, Murphy, and McCloskey (Chapter 9, this volume) note that one of the main challenges in understanding the links between cognition and mathematics lies in the complexity of mathematics and the cognitive correlates themselves. Consideration of findings from multiple studies with such a wide range of populations is difficult given differences in the selection criteria and the measures used to classify children as having specific MLD as opposed to more general learning difficulties. Clearly, the relationships between cognition, math, and language will be heavily influenced by the chosen methods of assessment. The research on MLD in the special populations reported in these chapters highlights a critical move to administering tests of numerical understanding that are more sensitive than standardized achievement measures. The aim of such efforts is to examine discrete aspects of numerical understanding rather than to obtain an overall mathematics score, which, depending on its emphasis, may over- or underestimate actual mathematical achievement. This in-depth approach can reveal mathematical strengths as well as weaknesses and will help in understanding the interdependencies of various aspects of mathematical functioning. It is also important to bear in mind that mathematics is not a static skill; that is, the nature of mathematical skills changes dramatically as children enter later school grades, and findings presented by Ayr, Yeates, and Enrile (2005) show a clear interaction between age and predictors of mathematical ability. So far there is little understanding of how the nature of the relationship between cognitive competencies and math changes across development (although see Holmes & Adams, 2006, for a discussion of the possible changing roles of visuospatial and phonological processes with increasing age and mathematical experience). Also, researchers still shy away from trying to pinpoint the cognitive skills supporting complex tasks like geometry and algebra.[1] Coming to grips with the complex interactions between developing numerical skills, developing cognitive competencies, and the protracted development of attentional control skills may only be achievable

---

[1]Lee, Ng, Ng, & Peh (2006) have begun examining the breakdown of algebraic tasks into the constituent parts necessary for successful solution, such as identifying the relevant information and the knowns and unknowns within that information, translating that information into an appropriate procedure, and being able to accurately compute the final answer. It appears thus far that each aspect of understanding may be predicted by different cognitive processes.

through the use of longitudinal studies, which would also allow a separating out of transitory delays in numerical understanding from true mathematical learning disabilities that remain stable over time.

Numerous studies in the MLD literature, including many of those reported in the chapters in this book, underscore the central role of executive, attentional, and working memory skills in various aspects of mathematical understanding. Research that aims to specify the lower level cognitive skills needed for accurate performance on complex cognitive tasks can help further the understanding of what it is within these broadly defined processes that is necessary for mathematical learning. For example, recent studies emphasize tasks that can be used across a wide age range to assess finer grained executive function skills and to help clarify the age at which critical periods of development in certain EF skills occur (Davidson, Amso, Anderson, & Diamond, 2006; Huizinga, Dolan, & van der Molen, 2006). Research studies conducted by van der Sluis, de Jong, and ver der Leij (2004) make use of tasks that allow for the control of individual differences in nonexecutive processing (e.g., speed of naming stimuli involved in the task), resulting in "purer" measures of the executive skills of interest. Research by Cowan and colleagues (e.g., Cowan, Saults, & Elliott, 2002) examines the processes underlying age-related changes in working memory, including changes in processing speed, strategy use, and rate of decay of information. It is difficult to capture the construct of complex cognitive processes by only using one measure, and the use of multiple measures for each construct being considered will help to identify the shared variance of those tasks and tease apart the contributions of theoretically and statistically defined constructs, such as working memory updating, inhibition, and shifting ability (Espy et al., 2004).

Finally, a number of studies (e.g., Holmes & Adams, 2006; Kyttala, Aunio, Lehto, Van Luit, & Hautamaki, 2003; McLean & Hitch, 1999), including some of those presented in these chapters, have underscored the importance of visuospatial skills in many aspects of mathematics; but here again, many of the tasks are highly attention demanding, making it difficult to pinpoint the precise links among visual, spatial, and attentional skills and mathematics. Indeed, Mazzocco and colleagues (Chapter 9, this volume) note that problems on visuospatial tasks shown by individuals with fragile X or Turner syndrome may be due to the attentional/executive demands, particularly when these populations also show executive function impairments. After finding that disruption to visuospatial resources is particularly detrimental to the arithmetic performance of young children (McKenzie, Bull, & Gray, 2003), my colleagues and I have taken a step back to examine tasks that selectively measure visuospatial skills and also vary in their attentional demands necessary for task completion. Only with a better grasp of the cognition tapped by such tasks can there be a clearer understanding of their specific role in developing mathematical competencies. This would seem to be particularly pertinent when dealing with populations with diverse cognitive impairments.

DEVELOPMENTAL VERSUS ACQUIRED DISORDERS OF MATHEMATICAL DIFFICULTIES

A body of evidence from adults with neuropsychological disorders and from brain imaging studies reveals dissociations in the brain regions involved in numerical versus language tasks. It also shows dissociations within the realm of numerical processing itself, for example, between reading and writing numbers versus comparing numerosities. Such findings offer a unique insight into cognitive processes that underlie various kinds of numerical and arithmetic knowledge and into the potential neural systems that may contribute to the procedural, conceptual, and fact retrieval impairments of children with MLD. Thus, they could offer guidance in trying to pinpoint the difficulties shown by those with developmental disorders. However, the development of individuals with genetic disorders is different from embryogenesis onwards, making it likely that mechanisms underlying numerical skills in such disorders are different from the mechanisms underlying impaired numerical skills in adults with neuropsychological disorders who have followed a typical developmental trajectory (Karmiloff-Smith, 1998; Paterson, Girelli, Butterworth, & Karmiloff-Smith, 2006). Therefore, accounting for commonalities is difficult, and the patterns of disorders and dissociations of skills observed may be very different. For example, in populations with MLD who are typically developing and those with neurodevelopmental disorders who show MLD, procedural and fact retrieval impairments almost invariably go hand in hand. Procedural counting difficulties and use of inefficient counting strategies lead to weak representations of number facts in long-term memory and subsequent retrieval impairments. However, in acquired disorders there is evidence of impaired fact knowledge in the presence of intact procedural knowledge.

Although certain aspects of numerical skill are dissociated in fully matured adult functioning, it clearly cannot be said that those skills will be dissociated during development. Zamarian, López-Rolón, and Delazer (Chapter 12, this volume) themselves acknowledge that even though certain skills may be dissociated, only an integration of all aspects of mathematical knowledge will result in efficient problem solving. Therefore, it is not enough to just consider the end outcome. Just because individuals in two different populations show similar levels of understanding in particular numerical domains does not mean that they arrived at that understanding following the same developmental route (e.g., see Paterson et al., 2006, for studies of individuals with Williams syndrome and Down syndrome). A good example of this is provided in a study of individuals with Turner syndrome by Kesler, Menon, and Reiss (2006). Participants were asked to complete both two- and three-operand arithmetic calculation. On the three-operand task, control participants showed increased activation in brain regions supporting executive processes, reflecting an increase in attentional effort compared with the two-operand task. In contrast, participants with Turner syndrome recruited brain regions responsible for both executive and language processing. Kesler et al. argued that individuals with Turner syndrome may demonstrate superior language skills and thus may approach difficult arithmetic tasks by drawing on these cognitive strengths. In-depth analysis of the skills shown by such populations will help to address questions regarding the development of alternative strategies in numerical understanding, as has been the case in studies of language development in developmental disorders (e.g., Karmiloff-Smith et al., 1997).

A middle ground can be found here. What about acquired impairments in a developmental population? Barnes and colleagues (Chapter 10, this volume) note that while traumatic brain injury at different points in development yields differences in the diffusion of brain damage, in the majority of children focal lesions will be apparent in the frontal cortex with damage to executive resources such as inhibition and working memory—skills that are critical to math development in typically developing children. Outcomes will vary with age and the amount of skill acquisition prior to injury (i.e., the point at which a typical developmental trajectory is arrested). It would be intriguing to know how the development of math skills in these individuals compares with atypical trajectories from birth (e.g., in SBM in which brain development is disturbed almost from the beginning of conception and then further affected by secondary injuries) and to arrested mature skills in adulthood. Such comparisons would provide valuable information regarding the lower level numerical skills needed to support higher, complex forms of mathematical knowledge.

EDUCATIONAL OPPORTUNITIES

Information gained from studies identifying the dissociations in numerical skills and their supporting cognitive competencies, as well as from those which highlight the cognitive and numerical strengths (as well as weaknesses) within these populations, may provide pointers for bypassing some of the evident processing difficulties. I have already briefly mentioned work cited by Zentall (Chapter 11, this volume) showing that under certain environmental conditions and with certain modifications to stimuli used in mathematical tasks, individuals with ADHD with severe limitations in executive functioning can perform well in mathematics. So, the question is whether the cognitive difficulties present in these populations represent unavoidable obstacles. For example, in populations in which language difficulties may limit development of math skills through a verbal route, is it possible to play to the individuals' processing strengths, such as using nonverbal techniques to study quantity processing in children with SLI (Chapter 8, this volume) or assessing numerical skills through visuospatial means in individuals who are deaf (Zafarty, Nunes, & Bryant, 2004; Nunes & Moreno, 2002) or who have fragile X syndrome (Murphy, Mazzocco, Gerner, & Henry, 2006)?

Studies of typical mathematical development reveal that executive functioning, including inhibition and updating of information in working memory, represents a critical cognitive underpinning of numerical skills across a broad age range (e.g., Bull & Scerif, 2001; Espy et al., 2004). Furthermore, in many of the populations discussed within the chapters reviewed here, there is evidence of working memory and/or executive functioning difficulties. What can be done to support or circumvent these difficulties? Can teaching be structured to offer more external support that may reduce the demands on working memory (e.g., should children be allowed to use a calculator as a memory aid to reduce memory load?), minimize switching between arithmetical tasks and concepts, or lessen the amount of distracting information contained within teaching materials? Many of the techniques for encouraging focused and sustained attention highlighted by Zentall (Chapter 11, this volume) have not been examined in children with MLD who are typically developing.

Donlan (Chapter 8, this volume) also makes an important point about separating out what he refers to as primary deficits versus secondary deficits that may arise due to limited educational access. Math curricula tend to become differentiated for such special populations, and it is not known how this affects the ongoing development of mathematical skills. Zentall (Chapter 11, this volume) also discusses academic self-concept, expectations for future success, and the likelihood that students will respond with decreased efforts when they begin to recognize their difficulties with math. A number of the chapters also underscore the important interactions between cognitive and affective processing. Mazzocco and colleagues (Chapter 9, this volume) discuss the effects of anxiety and negative attitudes on cognitive processes, and there is extensive literature examining the effects of mood and emotion on cognition generally, including the ability to think flexibly and imaginatively and the ability to stay focused on tasks. Should we resist testing under timed conditions, which may raise anxiety levels in certain individuals and result in performance being underestimated? Where math anxiety may divert limited resources away from cognitive processing, its effects could be particularly pronounced in individuals whose cognitive resources are somewhat limited at the outset (see Chapter 15 for a more thorough treatment of such issues). The main question to consider is whether math difficulties are being further compounded by the methods, procedures, and environments in which such skills are taught and assessed.

CONCLUSIONS

Findings from both developmental and acquired disorders of MLD appear to suggest that basic numerical skills are underpinned by the integration of two separate and dissociable systems, namely, a verbal system for number words that allows for the representation, memory, and calculation of exact numbers using symbolic notation; and a nonsymbolic representational system of approximate quantities that allow for skills such as estimation. Although these may be independent systems supported by neurologically distinct parts of the brain, information from both systems needs to be integrated to provide the most complete understanding of number and to allow for flexible methods of problem solving. Those with a specific impairment in math do fit well with Geary's definition of a visual-spatial subtype (see Geary, 2004). Such individuals may be able to use the intact language route as the main support for developing mathematical competencies, and as such, show less severe forms of mathematical difficulty compared with those who also have impaired language and verbal functioning.

In terms of the difficulties observed in procedural and conceptual understanding and fact retrieval in these populations, again there is clear overlap with the procedural and semantic subtypes described by Geary (2004), with similar cognitive underpinnings identified, particularly difficulties with phonological memory and executive control (including attention and inhibition). Although acquired MLD dissociations provide evidence that many of these aspects of arithmetical processing are separately implemented in the human brain, they benefit from their linkages, and this is particularly so in children who are in the process of acquiring, practicing, strengthening, and integrating these skills. Borrowing the words of Zamarian and colleagues (Chapter 12, this volume), because I myself could not have put it better,

> Fact knowledge is only meaningful when supported by conceptual knowledge and is very often compensated for by procedural backup strategies. Procedures are less error prone when effectively supported by conceptual knowledge. Conceptual knowledge is more advantageous when more memory-based facts and procedures can be used. Exact fact knowledge is more efficiently processed when estimation abilities and approximate knowledge of number are available. Approximation is also essential in checking the plausibility of a result obtained by exact calculation. Although the cognitive architecture of number processing seems to be modularly organized, the cooperation of different types of knowledge leads to meaningful and efficient processing.

Within each of these disorders, functional and structural imaging are beginning to reveal more directly how patterns of brain impairment produce patterns of impairment on academic and cognitive tasks. Likewise, comparisons across functioning in acquired and developmental disorders may tell more about the different developmental trajectories that mathematical learning (particularly arithmetical skills) may take. However, it is also important to more carefully address numerical skills occurring prior to and beyond arithmetical skills. More studies are now paying attention to the informal nonverbal numerical skills acquired (or innately present) early in development and what can be done to encourage the linkage between nonverbal and symbolic numerical representations (e.g., Siegler & Booth, 2004). However, knowledge of later developing mathematical skills and their numerical and cognitive underpinnings is still woefully inadequate. Continued cross-syndrome comparisons may be instrumental in clarifying the relationships among mathematical performance, language, cognitive ability, and specific cognitive processes, such as visuospatial ability, and the changing nature of these relationships across development.

REFERENCES

Ansari, D., & Karmiloff-Smith, A. (2002). Atypical trajectories of number development: A neuroconstructivist perspective. *Trends in Cognitive Sciences, 6*, 511–516.

Ayr, L.K., Yeates, K.O., & Enrile, B.G. (2005). Arithmetic skills and their cognitive correlates in children with acquired and congenital brain disorder. *Journal of the International Neuropsychological Society, 11*, 249–262.

Barnes, M.A., Pengelly, S., Dennis, M., Wilkinson, M., Rogers, T., & Faulkner, H. (2002). Mathematics skills in good readers with hydrocephalus. *Journal of the International Neuropsychological Society, 8*, 72–82.

Barth, H., Kanwisher, N., & Spelke, E. (2003). The construction of large number representation in adults. *Cognition, 86*, 201–221.

Berch, D.B. (2005). Making sense of number sense: Implications for children with mathematical disabilities. *Journal of Learning Disabilities, 38*, 333–339.

Bruandet, M., Molko, N., Cohen, L., & Dehaene, S. (2004). A cognitive characterization of dyscalculia in Turner syndrome. *Neuropsychologia, 42*, 288–298.

Bull, R., & Johnston, R.S. (1997). Children's arithmetical difficulties: Contributions from processing speed, item identification, and short-term memory. *Journal of Experimental Child Psychology, 65*, 1–24.

Bull, R., & Scerif, G. (2001). Executive functioning as a predictor of children's mathematics ability: Inhibition, switching, and working memory. *Developmental Neuropsychology, 19*, 273–293.

Cowan, N., Saults, J.S., & Elliott, E.M. (2002). The search for what is fundamental in the development of working memory. *Advances in Child Development and Behavior, 29*, 1–29.

Cowan, R., Donlan, C., Newton, E.J., & Lloyd, D. (2005). Number skills and knowledge in children with specific language impairment. *Journal of Educational Psychology, 97*, 732–744.

Davidson, M.C., Amso, D., Anderson, L.C., & Diamond, A. (2006). Development of cognitive control and executive functions from 4 to 13 years: Evidence from manipulations of memory, inhibition, and task switching. *Neuropsychologia, 44,* 2037–2078.

Dehaene, S. (1997). *The number sense: How the mind creates mathematics.* New York: Oxford University Press.

Dehaene, S., Piazza, M., Pinel, P., & Cohen, L. (2003). Three parietal circuits for number processing. *Cognitive Neuropsychology, 20,* 487–506.

Dehaene, S., Spelke, E., Pinel, P., Stanescu, R., & Tsivkin, S. (1999). Sources of mathematical thinking: Behavioural and brain imaging evidence. *Science, 284,* 970–973.

Delazer, M., Domahs, F., Lochy, A., Karner, E., Benke, T., & Poewe, W. (2004). Number processing and basal ganglia dysfunction: A single case study. *Neuropsychologia, 42,* 926–938.

Dennis, M., Landry, S.H., Barnes, M., & Fletcher, J.M. (2006). A model of neurocognitive function in spina bifida over the life span. *Journal of the International Neuropsychological Society, 12,* 285–296.

Donlan, C., & Gourlay, S. (1999). The importance of nonverbal skills in the acquisition of place-value knowledge: Evidence from normally-developing and language-impaired children. *British Journal of Developmental Psychology, 17,* 1–19.

Espy, K.A., McDiarmid, M.M., Cwik, M.F., Stalets, M.M., Hamby, A., & Senn, T.F. (2004). The contribution of executive functions to emergent mathematic skills in preschool children. *Developmental Neuropsychology, 26,* 465–486.

Geary, D.C. (1993). Mathematical disabilities: Cognitive, neuropsychological, and genetic components. *Psychological Bulletin, 114,* 345–362.

Geary, D.C. (1995). Reflections on evolution and culture in children's cognition: Implications for mathematical development and instruction. *The American Psychologist, 50,* 24–37.

Geary, D.C. (2004). Mathematics and learning disabilities. *Journal of Learning Disabilities, 37,* 4–15.

Holmes, J., & Adams, J.W. (2006). Working memory and children's mathematical skills: Implications for mathematical development and mathematics curricula. *Educational Psychology, 26,* 339–366.

Huizinga, M., Dolan, C.V., & van der Molen, M.W. (2006). Age-related change in executive function: Developmental trends and a latent variable analysis. *Neuropsychologia, 44,* 2017–2036.

Jordan, N.C., Hanich, L.B., & Kaplan, D. (2003). A longitudinal study of mathematical competencies in children with specific math difficulties versus children with comorbid mathematics and reading difficulties. *Child Development, 74,* 834–850.

Jordan, N.C., Kaplan, D., Olah, L.N., & Locuniak, M.N. (2006). Number sense growth in kindergarten: A longitudinal investigation of children at risk for mathematics difficulties. *Child Development, 77,* 153–175.

Karmiloff-Smith, A. (1998). Development itself is the key to understanding developmental disorders. *Trends in Cognitive Sciences, 2,* 389–398.

Karmiloff-Smith, A., Grant, J., Berthoud, I., Davies, M., Howlin, P., & Udwin, O. (1997). Language and Williams syndrome: How intact is "intact"? *Child Development, 68,* 246–262

Kesler, S.R., Menon, V., & Reiss, A.L. (2006). Neurofunctional differences associated with arithmetic processing in Turner syndrome. *Cerebral Cortex, 16,* 849–856.

Kyttala, M., Aunio, P., Lehto, J.E., Van Luit, J., & Hautamaki, J. (2003). Visuospatial working memory and early numeracy. *Educational and Child Psychology, 20,* 65–76.

Lee, K., Ng, E.L., Ng, S.F., & Peh, S. (2006). *Individual differences in algebraic problem solving: The roles of executive functions.* Paper presented at the Fourth International Conference on Memory, Sydney, Australia.

Mazzocco, M.M.M. (2005). Challenges in identifying target skills for math disability screening and intervention. *Journal of Learning Disabilities, 38,* 318–323.

Mazzocco, M.M.M., Bhatia, N.S., & Lesniak-Karpiak, K. (2006). Visuospatial skills and their association with math performance in girls with fragile X or Turner syndrome. *Child Neuropsychology, 12,* 87–110.

McKenzie, B., Bull, R., & Gray, C. (2003). The effects of visual-spatial and phonological disruption on children's arithmetical skills. *Educational and Child Psychology, 20,* 93–108.

McLean, J.F., & Hitch, G.J. (1999). Working memory impairments in children with specific arithmetic learning difficulties. *Journal of Experimental Child Psychology, 74,* 240–260.

Murphy, M.M., Mazzocco, M.M.M., Gerner, G., & Henry, A.E. (2006). Mathematics learning disability in girls with Turner syndrome or fragile X syndrome. *Brain and Cognition, 61,* 195–210.

Nunes, T., & Moreno, C. (2002). An intervention program to promote deaf pupil's achievement in numeracy. *Journal of Deaf Studies and Deaf Education, 7,* 120–133.

Paterson, S.J., Girelli, L., Butterworth, B., & Karmiloff-Smith, A. (2006). Are numerical impairments syndrome specific? Evidence from Williams syndrome and Down's syndrome. *Journal of Child Psychology and Psychiatry, 47,* 190–204.

Rubinsten, O., & Henik, A. (2005). Automatic activation of internal magnitudes: A study of developmental dyscalculia. *Neuropsychology, 19,* 641–648.

Siegler, R.S., & Booth, J. (2004). Development of numerical estimation in young children. *Child Development, 75,* 428–444.

van der Sluis, S., de Jong, P.F., & van der Leij, A. (2004). Inhibition and shifting in children with learning deficits in arithmetic and reading. *Journal of Experimental Child Psychology, 87,* 239–266.

Zarfaty, Y., Nunes, T., & Bryant, P. (2004). The performance of young deaf children in spatial and temporal number tasks. *Journal of Deaf Studies and Deaf Education, 9,* 315–326.

Neurobiological and Genetic Substrates

"How can you shorten the subject? That stern struggle with the multiplication table, for many people not yet ended in victory, how can you make it less? Square root, as obdurate as a hardwood stump in a pasture nothing but years of effort can extract it. You can't hurry the process. Or pass from arithmetic to algebra; you can't shoulder your way past quadratic equations or ripple through the binomial theorem. Instead, the other way; your feet are impeded in the tangled growth, your pace slackens, you sink and fall somewhere near the binomial theorem with the calculus in sight on the horizon. So died, for each of us, still bravely fighting, our mathematical training; except for a set of people called 'mathematicians'—born so . . ."
—Stephen Leacock

As discussed in Chapter 2, mathematical learning disability (MLD) is defined in part as a biologically based disorder. The chapters in Section IV attempt to explore what this means at two levels: the neurobiological and the genetic. For example, one might ask the following questions: Are there distinct neural circuits dedicated to the acquisition and processing of quantitative and numerical information? Do genetic factors play an important role in the development of specific regions of the brain that subserve basic numerical processing? Could this kind of knowledge help us diagnose and eventually remediate MLD? Definitive answers to such questions are not currently available, as research of this type is in its earliest stages. Nevertheless, it is important to examine contemporary approaches in cognitive neuroscience as well as in quantitative and molecular genetics, and learn of the potential progress that can be made by virtue of recent technological advances in these fields.

Over the past several years, a number of neuroimaging studies have provided some important insights into regions of the brain that appear to be recruited when adults without MLD engage in quantitative and arithmetic processing. These findings are establishing a foundation for future investigations of the neuroanatomical substrates of deficits in mathematical cognition. In Chapter 13, Simon and Rivera describe the cognitive neuroscientific approach to the study of mathematical thinking, focusing particularly on the use of functional magnetic resonance imaging (fMRI) and event-related potentials (ERP). These authors also explain the advantages of using such methods as compared with the assessment of individuals with actual brain damage or the study of simulated brain damage in healthy adults. Furthermore, findings from some recent neuroimaging studies of children who are typically achieving are reviewed. Finally, the authors discuss the potential value of this kind of research for informing both the diagnosis and remediation of mathematical learning disabilities.

In Chapter 14, Petrill and Plomin describe recent research on both the genetic and environmental origins of mathematics ability and disability, providing a mini-tutorial on the quantitative genetics approach—including the meaning of concepts such as heritability, shared family environment, and nonshared environment. After discussing what we have learned thus far about math skills from the comparatively limited number of studies using univariate genetic analytic methods, these authors present some recent data from a multivariate project involving the testing of a large and representative sample of twins. They point out that this kind of approach can reveal important information regarding the degree to which mathematics skills correlate with other skills such as reading and general cognition. Petrill and Plomin then discuss the potential benefits of using a molecular genetics approach, such as identifying genes that are specific to math. They conclude by emphasizing that the indication thus far of substantial genetic influences on mathematics ability and disability should *not* be taken to signify that the environment is of comparatively little importance, because the impact of genes on mathematics skills does not occur in isolation from environmental factors. Finally, they point out that knowledge of genetic effects on variation in math ability may eventually make it possible to assess a child's risk of developing math difficulties before they begin to arise.

REFERENCE

Leacock, S. (1988). In H. Eves, *Return to mathematical circles*, Boston: Prindle, Weber, & Schmidt.

Chapter 13

Neuroanatomical Approaches to the Study of Mathematical Ability and Disability

Tony J. Simon and Susan M. Rivera

+ +

Our goal in this chapter is to describe the cognitive neuroscience approach to the study of numerical and mathematical ability and disability and to demonstrate its potential value for informing both the diagnosis and remediation of impairments. To begin, we compare the cognitive neuroscience approach to others that have been used, emphasizing that as all methods have both strengths and weaknesses, their suitability for different kinds of studies depends on the objectives of the research. Our focus here is on studies that have attempted to identify the areas of the human brain involved with numerical thinking and how those brain regions relate to the processes used by a person carrying out a task.

Behavioral studies of children's math performance, such as those that describe children's use of everyday mathematics (see Pellegrini & Stanic, 1993), or their ability to perform arithmetic operations such as counting and calculating (e.g., Canobi, Reeve, & Pattison, 2002; Fuson, 1992), have provided a wealth of information about the typical and atypical development of math ability. This approach, however, is primarily descriptive in nature

This work was supported in part by National Institutes of Health (NIH) grants (HD46159 and HD42974) to Tony J. Simon, and by an investigator-initiated grant from the M.I.N.D. Institute to Susan M. Rivera. We are indebted to Kami Koldewyn and Zhongle Wu for their assistance with Figure 13.1.

and does not significantly advance our understanding of the specific thinking processes underlying these abilities, or how and where they are implemented in terms of the neuroanatomy of the brain.

Standardized tests involve giving specific problems to a child to work through and then comparing his or her performance with that of a large, normative sample of children. Such tests are enormously useful for determining appropriate or inappropriate developmental progress and for assessing and reporting outcomes (e.g., in evaluating the effectiveness of various interventions). Also, standardized tests are frequently used very effectively as measurement tools in a range of clinical research studies (e.g., Murphy, Mazzocco, Gerner, & Henry, 2006). Much like behavioral studies, however, these tools typically provide us with little specificity about the precise cognitive processes a child is employing to achieve a given level of performance.

Cognitive experiments (e.g., Geary & Wiley, 1991; Siegler & Booth, 2004) are designed to assess very specific aspects of math ability in a given domain. As a result, they are much more able to explicitly delineate the cognitive processes that groups of children carry out; yet, they give only very broad and somewhat speculative ideas as to how these processes are actually related to specific brain regions or circuits. When used in conjunction with information about brain structure and function, however, such experiments provide a critical component of cognitive neuroscience research. The major goal of such investigations is the explication of structure–function relationships between the mental computations carried out in the mind and the neuroanatomical structures of the brain that support those computations. Of course, gaining information about brain structure and function has historically been the most challenging problem for researchers, and recent advances have been crucial to the development of cognitive neuroscientific methods.

Lesion studies provided many of the first important insights into how changes in the brain can alter specific functions of the mind. Individuals, usually adults, who have experienced damage, disease, or injury to the brain, have been studied in an attempt to understand the relationship between alterations to brain tissue and the resulting changes in behavior and/or abilities. This research method essentially began with the famous case of Phineas Gage, who suffered frontal lobe damage when a tamping iron pierced his skull in a railroad construction accident in 1848. The damage was assumed to be related to his resulting personality changes, which led Gage's acquaintances to the impression that "he was no longer Gage" (see Damasio, Grabowski, Frank, Galaburda, & Damasio, 1994). Since that time, the field of clinical brain research has become highly sophisticated and has produced many important insights (Roman et al., 2003; Semenza et al., 2006; Tohgi et al., 1995; Verstichel & Masson, 2003). However, although brain injury can now be accurately characterized using modern imaging

methods, neural changes, even those resulting from specific surgical procedures, are rarely localized to specific anatomical structures or functional
circuits. This makes it hard to draw the kind of precise structure–function
inferences that are important to nonclinical, basic research questions.

Technological advances, including the development of brain imaging
methods such as functional Magnetic Resonance Imaging (fMRI) and event-
related potentials (ERP), have brought researchers closer than ever to the
goal of localizing brain function for specific cognitive processes. These two
methods detect two fundamentally different physiological phenomena associated with brain activity. ERPs are averages of the electrical activity arising from the firing of neurons that are time-locked to particular stimulus
presentations. They rely on electroencephalography (EEG), the continuous
recording of brain electrical activity measured by electrodes placed on the
scalp surface (for more details, see Luck, 2005). The transmission of electrical potentials during ERP recording is virtually instantaneous, with measurable activity occurring within milliseconds from the presentation of a stimulus. Thus, the temporal resolution of the ERP is excellent. Nevertheless,
the spatial resolution of scalp-recorded electrical potentials is notoriously
imprecise, and it cannot be assumed that the neural generators of a given
electrical signal are located directly under the scalp area of the electrode
recording the signal.

In contrast to ERPs, the fMRI method measures a blood-oxygenation-
level-dependent (BOLD) response and is based on the proposition that when
brain areas become active, they increase their blood flow disproportionately to metabolic need, resulting in a net increase in tissue oxygenation
(see Fox, Raichle, Mintun, & Dence, 1988). Highly oxygenated areas of the
brain have a stronger MR signal than less oxygenated regions. It is this signal increase that is detected by a computer analysis of the image data and
then represented as color-coded "activation maps" (for more details, see
Buxton, 2002). This resultant signal increase, however, is not instantaneous,
and its peak is thought to occur as late as 5 to 6 seconds after the actual neuronal activity that generated the blood flow changes. Thus, while fMRI provides excellent spatial localization in the millimeter range, its temporal resolution falls far short of that provided by the ERP method. In response to
this tradeoff, some cutting-edge studies have been able to combine both
techniques in the same scanning session to optimize spatiotemporal resolution. Of course, it should be noted that neither of these techniques creates
a direct measure of neuronal activity. ERPs are a remote measurement of the
electric potential generated by neuronal activity, whereas fMRI measures
the changes in blood oxygenation that result from neuronal activity.

Both of these imaging methods have been shown to hold some promise for studies of mathematical thinking. Although attempts have been made
to use ERPs for the purposes of localization of function (Montgomery,

Montgomery, & Guisado, 1992), more often the research goals have been geared toward parsing mathematical thinking into its constituent components (e.g., in delineating the differences in brain function between processing incongruous versus correct arithmetic results) or to ascertain what strategies subjects were using during arithmetic processing by looking for ERP signatures consistent with one type of thinking versus another (El Yagoubi, Lemaire, & Besson, 2005; Galfano, Mazza, Angrilli, & Umilta, 2004; Iguchi & Hashimoto, 2000; Pauli et al., 1994; Szucs & Csepe, 2005; Wang, Kong, Tang, Zhuang, & Li, 2000). Other studies have used fMRI to investigate the neuroanatomical bases of numerical processing, and many of those studies will be reviewed below.

Before we begin to examine the research using brain imaging techniques, it is useful to ask the following: In what specific ways do these techniques add to the findings from studies using the other methods? One is that, as mentioned above, the use of noninvasive imaging techniques has allowed for a much more precise localization of function in the brain than is possible with neuropsychological, behavioral, or lesion studies. Thus, these techniques allow questions about both precisely where and when maturational changes occur in the brain and how these changes relate to the development of cognitive abilities. Another advantage of using brain imaging techniques becomes clear when one considers that behavioral performance is an index of what might be referred to as an "output state." For example, looking at an individual's performance on a given arithmetic task as the sole determinant of his or her numerical ability might mean missing an important part of the cognitive processing as well as the developmental picture. Individuals can arrive at the same answer to a problem whether or not they are using the same underlying mental processing algorithms and brain circuitry to do so. Therefore, the methods that exemplify cognitive neuroscience allow a deeper understanding of precisely which mental processing and brain activity patterns, combine to produce an output state. In other words, when asking questions about the neural substrates for accomplishing a given skill in either typical or atypical development, there is a significant value added with the use of brain imaging techniques, especially when they are combined with cognitive processing experiments, as is typical of most cognitive neuroscience research programs. As we begin to describe studies in which neural activation in various brain regions has been detected, consult Figure 13.1 for information pertaining to the precise locations of these neuroanatomical subtrates.

STUDIES OF ACTUAL AND SIMULATED BRAIN INJURY

Much of the knowledge about how the brain processes numerical stimuli initially came from lesion studies. Most of the documented lesions were the

1. Supplementary Motor Area
2. Superior Frontal Gyrus
3. Superior Frontal Gyrus (medial aspect)
4. Middle Frontal Gyrus
5. Precuneus
6. Angular Gyrus
7. Supramarginal Gyrus
8. Cuneus
9. Middle Occipital Gyrus
10. Inferior Frontal Gyrus (w/out triangularis
    or orbital aspects)
11. Fusiform Gyrus
12. Anterior Cingulate
13. Posterior Cingulate
14. Insula
15. Intraparietal sulcus
16. Horizontal segment of the intraparietal sulcus (HIPS)

Brain Surface View

a: back
b: bottom
c: front
d: top
e: left

Orthogonal Slice View

f: coronal (y = −46)
g: axial (z = 28)
h: sagital (x = −32)
i: coronal (y = 6)
j: axial (z = 8)
k: sagital (x = −2)

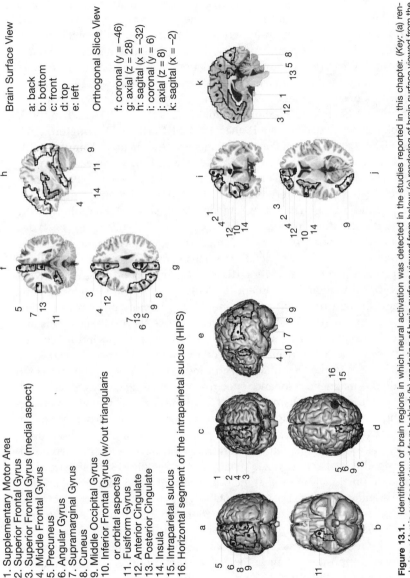

Figure 13.1. Identification of brain regions in which neural activation was detected in the studies reported in this chapter. (*Key:* (a) rendering of brain surface viewed from behind; (b) rendering of brain surface viewed from below; (c) rendering of brain surface viewed from the front; (d) rendering of brain surface viewed from above; (e) rendering of brain surface viewed from the left; (f) posterior region brain slice viewed from behind; (g) superior region brain slice viewed from above; (h) lateral region brain slice viewed from the left; (i) anterior region brain slice viewed from the front; (j) inferior region brain slice viewed from above; (k) medial region brain slice viewed from the left.)

result of stroke or some other brain insult or injury process and so occurred predominantly in middle-aged to older adults (see Chapter 12 for a detailed discussion of single case studies). Thus, the information gathered was largely restricted to impairments in numerical processing that emerged long after full acquisition of numerical and mathematical knowledge and procedures had taken place. A typical finding was that acalculia, the impaired ability to perform arithmetic calculations, resulted from damage to the parietal cortex, usually in the left hemisphere (Benson & Weir, 1972; Cohen, Dehaene, Chochon, Lehericy, & Naccache, 2000; Dehaene, 1997; Dehaene & Cohen, 1991; Grafman, Passafiume, Faglioni, & Boller, 1982; Henschen, 1920; Lampl, Eshel, Gilad, & Sarova-Pinhas, 1994; McCarthy & Warrington, 1988; Rosselli & Ardila, 1989; Takayama, Sugishita, Akiguchi, & Kimura, 1994; Tohgi et al., 1995; Warrington, 1982; Whalen, McCloskey, Lesser, & Gordon, 1997). In addition, lesions to prefrontal (Fasotti, Eling, & Bremer, 1992), frontoparietal (Cipolotti, Butterworth, & Denes, 1991), and subcortical structures, including the thalamus (Ojemann, 1974), showed associations with impaired calculation. In an early report, Cipolotti and colleagues (1991) described the case of a woman who demonstrated the Gerstmann syndrome after damage to her left parietal lobe. This syndrome is characterized by four primary symptoms: writing disability (agraphia or dysgraphia), disability for calculation or arithmetic (acalculia or dyscalculia), an inability to distinguish right from left, and an inability to identify one's own fingers (finger agnosia). In particular, her acalculia was so serious that she was unable to comprehend any number above 4. A less dramatic and much less typical example comes from the case of an 18-year-old male who showed some features of the Gerstmann syndrome, particularly a developmental acalculia. A magnetic resonance spectroscopy imaging study showed that he had reduced metabolism in the left temporal/parietal region, involving the angular gyrus (Levy, Reis, & Grafman, 1999). So, the early impression was that the inferior parietal lobe, especially involving the left angular gyrus, was an important neuroanatomical substrate for adult mathematical thinking. It was also recognized that this brain region was likely part of an extended functional circuit that includes prefrontal and subcortical areas.

A significant number of studies of individuals with spatial neglect have revealed further details about the relationship between numerical processing and the typically developing brain. Spatial neglect is defined as a "clinical syndrome in which patients are unaware of entire sectors of space on the side opposite to their lesion [. . . that] is produced by a lateralized disruption of spatial attention and representation" (Chatterjee, 2002). For example, Vuilleumier, Ortigue, and Brugger (2004) studied 14 adults with right hemisphere damage, half of whom showed left-sided spatial neglect and half of whom showed no spatial neglect, and 7 individuals considered healthy controls. To investigate numerical function, they used a standard numerical distance effect task, which generally involves the participant deciding whether a presented single-digit number (from 1 to 9) is greater or smaller than a remembered or visually presented standard. Difficulty in this task increases as the "numerical distance" between the target number and the standard decreases. In contrast to the comparison groups (individuals from nonneglect and healthy control groups), individuals with left neglect showed a unique handicap in responding to numbers that were smaller than the standard and immediately to the "left" of the standard (i.e., as represented along a mental number line). Interestingly, they showed this effect for the number 4 but not for 6 when the standard was 5; then, when the standard was changed to 7, they showed the same effect for the numbers 5 and 6. This result demonstrated the importance of spatial attention and cognitive processes to some noncomputational aspects of numerical cognition.

A similar study of four individuals with unilateral left spatial neglect resulting from right parietal lesions found that they systematically misstated the midpoint number (i.e., misidentified the spatial center point) between two aurally perceived numbers, with increasing inaccuracy as the distance between the two numbers increased (Zorzi, Priftis, & Umilta, 2002). Small intervals produced significant leftward shifts (e.g., the midpoint between 11 and 13 was given as 10), and large intervals produced rightward shifts (e.g., the midpoint between 11 and 19 was given as 17). This pattern of results was found despite the individuals' intact numerical and arithmetical abilities, whereas neither healthy participants nor individuals with injury to the right brain but without spatial neglect exhibited such errors. Clearly, damage to inferior parietal areas impairs the processing of spatial as well as numerical information and points to an important relationship between the two.

One concern about drawing strong inferences from studies of brain function following injury such as stroke is that the damage is unlikely to be precise in terms of localization to only a specific cortical structure or region or to its connections to other structures or regions that could potentially affect the functioning of the target region. Furthermore, adults with sufficiently serious health problems who have experienced a stroke may not be the ideal model from which to draw inferences about structure–function mappings in other populations. This is especially true when children constitute the group of interest. Thus, it is particularly interesting to consider the results of studies using transcranial magnetic stimulation (TMS), which is a method of temporarily and noninvasively "deactivating" fairly precise areas of cortex to examine the effects on resulting function. To date, this has typically been carried out with healthy young adult participants, so although differences are still likely to exist between these participants and children, these differences are likely to be less significant than is true for older individuals with stroke.

One such study by Göbel and colleagues (Göbel, Calabria, Farne, & Rossetti, 2006) actually showed that the effect reported by Vuilleumier and colleagues (2004) could be transiently induced in healthy adults by simulating left-sided neglect. Using repetitive transcranial magnetic stimulation (rTMS), researchers temporarily deactivated the left and right posterior parietal sites (angular gyrus and posterior supramarginal gyrus) and medial occipital cortex. Before stimulation, the participants' error in the numerical bisection task varied with interval size, just as with Zorzi and colleagues's (2002) participants. However, error was significantly increased by rTMS over right posterior parietal cortex and shifted in the rightward direction (consistent with Zorzi et al.'s findings, as the intervals were large and varied from 16 to 64). A nonsignificant effect was found in the same direction for left parietal stimulation, but no effect was found on bisection error.

To summarize, these results show that adults who have achieved typically developed levels of numerical and arithmetical ability experience significant impairments in that domain when areas of the posterior parietal lobes are damaged or deactivated by rTMS. The posterior parietal areas implicated by most of these reports are the angular and supramarginal gyri. Some studies have also indicated that impairments can occur when either the left or right parietal areas are affected, although the effects are not identical. Researchers naturally concluded that, at least in adults, the posterior parietal lobes are critical brain regions for numerically related processing, especially when the tasks involved retain some of the spatial characteristics associated with more approximate numerical reasoning (such as magnitude comparison). The neglect studies also implicate spatial attention processes as an important component of numerical cognition. The weakness of these studies, from the standpoint of researchers whose goal is to accurately localize numerical functioning in the brains of typically developing adults, is their low spatial resolution (but see Chapter 12 for a discussion of insights gained on a wide range of numerical processes from neuropsychological case studies). Brain injury is never restricted to specific anatomical structures or circuits. Furthermore, although rTMS can be applied accurately to specific areas of the scalp, its effect has far less than pinpoint accuracy. Thus, in the 1990s, many researchers turned to the emerging technology of fMRI to gain much more accuracy in their attempt to localize numerical and arithmetical functioning in typically developing adults.

THE NEUROIMAGING CORRELATES
OF NUMERICAL PROCESSING IN ADULTS

Although space limitations prevent us from reviewing the now considerable number of functional neuroimaging studies of numerical processing, we will start by presenting perhaps the predominant view of the neural circuitry involved. Then we will summarize several studies that augment or complement that view in one way or another.

Dehaene, Piazza, Pinel, and Cohen (2003) presented evidence from neuroimaging and neuropsychological (i.e., primarily individuals with lesions) studies in support of what they described as a "tentative model" for three parietal circuits on which number processing depends in adults who are typically developing. Despite their use of the term *parietal circuits,* each of the three components mentioned is actually a rather distinct anatomical structure. We will address other brain areas that appear to form circuits in tandem with these regions later in this section. The horizontal segment of the intraparietal sulcus (or HIPS) is the landmark that separates the superior and inferior sections of the parietal lobe. The reference known as *Gray's Anatomy* (Lewis, 1924) states that

> From about the middle of the postcentral sulcus, or from the upper end of its inferior ramus, the horizontal portion of the intraparietal sulcus is carried backward and slightly upward on the parietal lobe, and is prolonged, under the name of the occipital ramus, on to the occipital lobe, where it divides into two parts, which form nearly a right angle with the main stem and constitute the transverse occipital sulcus. (pp. 828–829)

Dehaene and colleagues proposed that "a nonverbal representation of numerical quantity, perhaps analogous to a spatial map or 'number line' is present in the HIPS of both hemispheres" (2003, p. 489). They presented evidence that the HIPS is active when mental arithmetic requires a quantitative representation of numbers and when a comparative operation, such as is called upon by magnitude comparison or numerical distance effect tasks, is required. They also suggested that the HIPS is domain specific for numbers but indicated that it is not yet clear whether the HIPS "is strictly specific for numbers or whether it extends to other categories that have a strong spatial or serial component (e.g., the alphabet, days, months, spatial prepositions)" (p. 492).

The left angular gyrus (AG), located below and behind the HIPS in the posterior parietal lobe, is identified by Dehaene and colleagues (2003) as the locus of a very different kind of numerical processing. They stated that

> The left AG does not seem to be concerned with quantity processing, but shows increasingly greater activation as tasks put greater requirement on verbal processing. We therefore propose that this region is part of the language system, and contributes to number processing only inasmuch as some arithmetic operations, such as multiplication, make particularly strong demands on a verbal coding of numbers. (2003, p. 494)

Finally, Dehaene and colleagues (2003) suggested that an area of the posterior superior parietal lobe (PSPL) behind the HIPS and above and more medial than the left angular gyrus is involved in number comparison, approximation, subtraction, and counting. This area also appears to be more active when a participant carries out two operations during a calculation rather than a single one. The authors indicated that this area is not specific to the number domain. They explained that the PSPL is involved in these tasks because "it also plays a central role in a variety of visuospatial tasks including hand reaching, grasping, eye and/or attention orienting, mental rotation, and spatial working memory" (p. 498). It should be noted that Dehaene and colleagues (2003) were careful to limit their claims about the specificity of these regions for numerical processing to the HIPS only. Although their hypothesis appears to minimize the impact of development and experience by assuming "an initial prespecialization of the brain circuits that will ultimately support high-level arithmetic in adults" (p. 499), the authors indicated that "much of the human capacity for number processing [within the parietal lobe] relies on representations and processes that are not specific to the number domain" (p. 501). This at least leaves open the possibility implied by the lesion studies that spatial and attentional processes may not just be important components of fully developed numerical and mathematical cognition but may even be necessary precursor abilities. Such a view has been advanced by one of us (TJS) elsewhere (Simon, 1997, 1999).

Obviously, the three regions identified by Dehaene and colleagues (2003) are not the only brain areas that are consistently found to activate when typically developing adults engage in a range of numerical processing tasks. What follows is a very brief review of brain activations that show some degree of consistency for different kinds of tasks. Given the short history of neuroimaging studies in this domain, far too few studies have yet taken place for a definitive set of "typical adult numerical brain circuits" and their variants in special populations to have been identified. Except where specified, activations will refer to those found in young, healthy adults.

Perhaps the largest set of studies has employed magnitude comparison or numerical distance effect tasks, like those described earlier, to explore the neuroanatomy of numerical processing. Pinel and colleagues (Pinel, Dehaene, Riviere, & LeBihan, 2001; Pinel et al., 1999) not only reported parietal activations like those already described in response to such a task but they also found them to be part of a large, distributed network that "included visual and motor cortical areas as well as prefrontal and anterior cingulate cortices" (1999, p. 1477). Visual cortex is situated primarily in the occipital lobes, the most posterior lobe of the cerebral cortex, and is comprised of Brodmann's areas 17, 18, and 19. Motor cortex is the region of cerebral cortex that is situated in the most posterior part of the frontal lobe, just in front of the central sulcus, which divides frontal and parietal cortical areas. It is comprised of the primary motor cortex (Brodmann's area 4) and the lateral and medial premotor or supplementary motor cortex (Brodmann's area 6). These researchers took their studies a step further by carrying out fMRI and ERP experiments to enable a more precise examination of the location and timing of brain activity during different processing stages of a magnitude comparison task. Their main finding was that varying numerical distance produced most activation change "in the bilateral parietal lobes, in the banks of the intraparietal sulcus, and in the precuneus, with small additional effects in the posterior cingulate cortex and middle temporal region" (Pinel et al., 2001, p. 1022). The intraparietal and precuneus areas appear to map rather closely onto the aforementioned HIPS and PSPL regions, respectively.

Turconi and her collaborators (Turconi, Jemel, Rossion, & Seron, 2004) used ERPs to compare processing on a magnitude comparison task with two tasks in which order (i.e., before or after the target in a list rather than smaller or greater magnitude) was the dimension of interest. They found that all three tasks were associated with neural activity in electrodes sited in the temporal, occipital, and parietal regions, and they also found activity in medial frontal regions. The distance effect task produced bilateral parietal activations that were more left biased when judging *magnitude* using numbers and more right biased when judging *order* using numbers. The control task of judging order using letters inverted the polarity of the ERP signal but still showed a bilateral parietal effect that was more pronounced in the left hemisphere.

Fulbright and colleagues (Fulbright, Manson, Skudlarski, Lacadie, & Gore, 2003) carried out an fMRI task that also required order judgments, either in terms of alphabetic location, position in the number line, or relative physical size of shapes. They also created "near" and "far" trials as in most distance effect studies. All three order tasks produced intraparietal sulcus activations. These were bilateral in all cases except for the physical size task, in which the left IPS activations did not reach the statistical threshold. Comparing near to far trials showed that the more difficult near trials activated inferior frontal regions for all three tasks, with the left supramarginal gyrus being the only parietal activation for numbers. Interestingly, the intraparietal sulcus was activated for near trials more than far only for physical size judgments.

Several studies have combined fMRI investigations of numerical magnitude comparison tasks with judgments made on other physical characteristics of the stimuli. Cohen-Kadosh and collaborators (Cohen-Kadosh et al., 2005) compared activations for comparisons based on number, physical size, and luminance, showing

> Activation of a widespread cortical network that was highly similar for all the comparisons. Clusters of activation included the bilateral occipitotemporal and occipitoparietal pathways, IPS, FEF, SMA, IFG, insula and the sensorimotor areas. There was more activation in the right temporal lobe than the left, whereas the angular gyrus was more activated on the left than on the right. (pp. 1243–1244)

(IPS is the intraparietal sulcus; FEF, SMA, and IFG are the frontal lobe areas of the frontal eye fields, supplementary motor areas, and the inferior frontal gyrus, respectively). Much of this network is similar to the extended one described earlier from Pinel et al.'s 2001 study. Although the intraparietal sulcus was activated by all three kinds of comparisons, the authors concluded that there was a specific area of the left IPS (and right temporal lobe) that was associated with the numerical distance effect.

A very similar study by Pinel and colleagues (Pinel, Piazza, LeBihan, & Dehaene, 2004) also required participants to compare physical size (with numbers and letters) and luminance as well as numerals. Numerical comparisons activated the HIPS area bilaterally as well as the left precentral gyrus, whereas the other comparisons activated different networks, each involving some part of the intraparietal sulcus (though not usually the HIPS). There was little overlap with Cohen-Kadosh and colleagues' (2005) activations for these other tasks. Despite the similarity of the judgments involved, these findings may have been due to great differences in the stimuli and task demands.

Overall, these studies appear to support the evidence for posterior parietal involvement in numerical processing, although not exactly in the same way as specified by Dehaene and colleagues (2003). These activation studies also introduce evidence of some prefrontal and temporal region involvement, as was indicated by the lesion literature. Finally, they also suggest that the posterior parietal activations observed are not necessarily domain specific and limited only to numerical cognition.

Of course, the tasks of judging numerical order or relative magnitude are only two of the numerically relevant tasks that adults might undertake. Several studies have addressed other aspects of numerically relevant processing. Using positron emission tomography (PET), Sathian and colleagues (1999) examined counting as well as visual search. Though subitizing (the rapid and accurate detection and enumeration of one to three objects) was most strongly associated with the middle occipital gyrus, counting activated a large fronto-parieto-cerebellar network that included the cerebellar vermis (the central or wormlike structure that separates the two hemispheres of the cerebellum), middle occipital regions, the right inferior frontal gyrus, and bilateral intraparietal sulcus areas. Similar middle occipital and intraparietal activations were found by Piazza and colleagues (Piazza, Mechelli, Butterworth, & Price, 2002) using fMRI, especially when six to nine randomly placed dots were presented. These studies contribute a further link between space and number processing. This is because counting of visually presented objects, which usually requires the use of spatial search and working memory processes, appears to also involve prefrontal along with similar posterior parietal regions to those seen in the magnitude comparison tasks.

Some studies have looked directly at activations associated with arithmetic itself. Dehaene and colleagues (Dehaene, Spelke, Pinel, Stanescu, & Tsivkin, 1999) examined the differences in brain activations when individuals chose an exact answer to computations (such as 4 + 5 = either 9 or 7) compared with when they selected the best approximate, or most plausible, answer (such as 4 + 5 = either 8 or 3). The latter task, which resembles a magnitude comparison judgment, activated the left and right intraparietal sulcus in the region of the HIPS along with the right superior parietal cortex and left prefrontal areas among others. The authors ascribe this activation pattern to the spatial nature of this version of the numerical task. Conversely, the exact calculation task, which the authors claim is based on well-established linguistic representations and processes, mainly activated a left inferior frontal region associated with verbal association tasks. This latter task also produced some parietal activations, including the left (and right) angular gyri and precuneus along with the left cingulate and right middle temporal areas, just below the inferior parietal supramarginal area. An associated ERP study produced signals consistent with the fMRI activations.

There seems to be rather less consensus concerning the brain regions involved in mental arithmetic. In a study with addition problems using Arabic numerals or canonical (i.e., dice-like) dot patterns, Venkatraman and colleagues (Venkatraman, Ansari, & Chee, 2005) found no differences between exact and approximate versions of their addition task and no significant activation in left hemisphere language areas for the exact addition task. In all cases, activations were produced bilaterally in the anterior IPS (in the same region as the HIPS) as well as the left posterior IPS and left precentral gyrus when compared with a control task that presented single examples of stimuli identical to those in each addition task. Those stimuli were chosen to control for the assumed automatic activation of magnitude-related areas of the parietal lobes in response to the viewing of any numbers and thus to isolate areas associated with mental addition. In addition, most tasks activated medial frontal gyrus, dorsolateral prefrontal cortex, insula, and fusiform gyrus. So the specifics of task design appear to affect the activations that are observed quite strongly in studies of mental arithmetic. This is presumably because they directly affect the representations and processes required for each different set of conditions.

Kong and colleagues (2005) studied much more complex, exact computation by using large magnitude addition and subtraction tasks whose products would not be readily available for retrieval from memory. The left posterior IPS, close to the area reported by Venkatraman and colleagues (2005), was activated for all computations along with the left inferior frontal gyrus, left superior parietal and precuneus regions, and the right inferior parietal lobe in the area of the supramarginal gyrus. When the more complex problems (involving borrowing and carrying) were compared with the simpler (not involving borrowing and carrying) ones, the left posterior IPS and left inferior frontal gyrus activations were accompanied by activity in the bilateral medial frontal and anterior cingulate cortex. Similar to Venkatraman and colleagues's study, all tasks activated the left insula along with the left occipital gyrus and medial frontal gyrus/cingulate cortex, and most tasks activated the left fusiform and right insula.

Menon and colleagues (Menon, Rivera, White, Eliez, et al., 2000; Menon, Rivera, White, Glover, & Reiss, 2000) examined the relative contributions of prefrontal and parietal regions to components of arithmetical processing. In their studies, participants were asked to indicate whether the given result for an arithmetic equation was correct or incorrect. Researchers manipulated complexity in terms of the number of operands a problem contained; they also manipulated difficulty in terms of the solution time available. Two-operand tasks were of the form $1 + 2 = 3$; three-operand tasks were of the form $6 - 3 + 5 = 7$. Problems were presented either quickly (one every 3 seconds) or slowly (one every 6 seconds) during the fMRI scanning experiment. Because college-age adults solved the slow (6-second), easy (two-operand) problems fairly effortlessly, there were no significant activations during those trials. All of the other trial types activated a network rather similar to the other arithmetic studies: the inferior frontal gyrus, medial frontal gyrus, supramarginal and angular gyri in the inferior parietal lobe, and the presupplementary motor area. Because the task design involved one manipulation of difficulty that did not involve calculation (rate) and one that did (number of operands), it was possible to dissociate the relative neural contributions of these two factors. In response to an increase in rate (i.e., going from slow to fast presentation), frontal activity was observed—specifically in the left insula and the basal operculum of the orbitofrontal gyrus. The orbitofrontal cortex lies on the base of the frontal cortex in its most anterior segment, above the eyes or orbits. In response to an increase in the number of operands to be calculated (i.e., going from two to three), posterior parietal activity was observed, namely, the left and right angular gyrus. This dissociation served to pinpoint the areas responsible for arithmetic computation independent of other processing demands. Of note, in a follow-up experiment, the same authors showed that the only difference that discriminated a subset of the participants who produced 100% correct performance in the fast, difficult condition from those who made at least one error was significantly lower activation in the left angular gyrus. This is consistent with Dehaene and colleagues's (2003) claim that, in adults, this area typically activates for tasks such as mental arithmetic, and it suggests that the amount of activation may be positively correlated with the difficulty of the task for the participant.

A similar but much more intensive study of the effects of complexity on several types of numerical calculation tasks, and similarly structured but nonnumerical reasoning tasks, was carried out by Gruber and colleagues (Gruber, Indefrey, Steinmetz, & Kleinschmidt, 2001). Despite the much greater numerical magnitude of the values used in this study than those used in the Menon and colleagues's studies (Menon, Rivera, White, Eliez, et al., 2000; Menon, Rivera, White, Glover, et al., 2000), all tasks, including the nonnumerical ones, nonetheless activated a very similar network of areas. Gruber and colleagues reported that their "five conditions showed a similar left-dominant, bilateral prefrontal, premotor and parietal response pattern" (p. 353). The main areas included the inferior frontal sulcus and gyrus, premotor cortex (the medial part of which overlaps with the supplementary motor area), the posterior intraparietal sulcus and adjacent inferior and superior parietal cortex, and the presupplementary motor area extending into the anterior cingulate cortex. Like Menon and colleagues's findings, the authors reported a particular focus of activity in the left angular gyrus associated with numerical calculation. Gruber et al. found a strong association between activations in the medial posterior parietal region and the easier tasks, but the harder tasks tended to activate left inferior, prefrontal cortex adjacent to the anterior inferior frontal sulcus and the anterior cingulate cortex.

A study by Delazer and colleagues (Delazer et al., 2003) took calculation a step further and trained healthy adults to carry out complex multiplication problems. They also increased the complexity in a series of conditions. Compared with a control number-matching condition, problems that required just fact retrieval activated a network rather similar to the ones described above in response to arithmetical tasks. This network comprised the bilateral posterior intraparietal sulcus and adjoining left angular gyrus; left superior, bilateral middle, and inferior frontal gyri; left precentral sulcus; insular cortex; and anterior cingulate and bilateral cerebellum. Moving from relatively easy fact retrieval problems to hard, novel, or untrained multiplication problems also produced bilateral activations in the posterior intraparietal sulcus, inferior frontal gyrus, and cerebellum. Left hemisphere activations of the superior frontal gyrus and cuneus were seen, along with activations of the right hemisphere fusiform and medial frontal gyrus. The difference between the hardest task (the untrained multiplication problems) and the more familiar trained multiplication problems was seen only in the left hemisphere. The less difficult problems activated posterior IPS, inferior parietal and sylvian fissure regions, lingual gyrus, and the inferior frontal gyrus more than did the more difficult problems. Conversely, the main effect of maximum difficulty was seen in activations of the left angular gyrus, inferior frontal, and anterior cingulate gyrus, along with bilateral paracentral and cerebellar hemisphere.

So the circuits involved in typical adults' processing of exact and approximate arithmetic remain rather less clear than for magnitude comparison tasks. However, this is not necessarily cause for concern. Instead, it demonstrates a central tenet of cognitive neuroscience studies: that *subtle changes in task requirements will have specific effects on the representational and processing demands of the subject, and these will be directly observable in terms of distinct activation patterns.* Overall, however, the brain does seem to rely on a complex and extensive set of prefrontal, cingulate, insular, parietal, and temporal regions depending on the nature and complexity of the task and the processes required of the participant. Clearly, an extensive program of cognitive neuroscience investigation is needed in order to specify the different processes associated with the wide range of numerical processes in which most adults engage and the neuroanatomical substrates with which they are associated.

NEUROIMAGING STUDIES OF NUMERICAL PROCESSING IN CHILDREN

As with the lesion studies, most of what we know about the neuroanatomical correlates of numerical processing from neuroimaging studies has been garnered from investigations carried out with adult participants. This means that the pathways to typical and atypical development of numerical cognition and the necessary and sufficient building block competencies remain largely unstudied. It also means that the current consensus of the neurocognitive basis of function in this domain, as described previously, is likely to be skewed by the omission of developmental studies. However, brain imaging studies of mathematical reasoning have recently begun to be conducted with children only (Rivera, Reiss, Eckert, & Menon, 2005) and with both children and adults (Kawashima et al., 2004). Rivera and colleagues (2005) conducted fMRI with participants ranging in age from 9 to 18 years who performed a simple two-operand addition and subtraction task, for which accuracy was comparable across age. The study revealed both increases and decreases in activation with age, suggesting disparate levels and trajectories of functional maturation in particular brain regions. Although older children reached similar levels of accuracy on these simple problems to younger children, they presumably exhibited a more efficient recruitment of neural resources to do so. Accordingly, they demonstrated more activation in left parietal areas that have been consistently implicated in mental arithmetic processing, including the supramarginal gyrus and adjoining intraparietal sulcus. Older subjects also demonstrated more activation in the left lateral occipital-temporal cortex, an area thought to be important for visual word and symbol recognition (Cohen & Dehaene, 2004; Hart, Kraut, Kremen, Soher, & Gordon, 2000; Kronbichler et al., 2004; Price & Devlin, 2003, 2004). By contrast, younger subjects showed greater activation in the prefrontal cortex, including the dorsolateral and ventrolateral prefrontal cortex and anterior cingulate. Taken together, these findings suggest a process of increased functional specialization of the left posterior parietal cortex with age, with decreased dependence on working memory and attentional resources.

SUMMARY AND DISCUSSION

In this chapter, we have reviewed evidence from several sources that have been used to establish an understanding of the neuroanatomical correlates of numerical and mathematical thinking. Studies of adults who have experienced brain injury or who have had certain brain regions temporarily deactivated with transcranial magnetic stimulation indicate that posterior parietal areas are strongly associated with numerical competence. These studies also point to a relationship between spatial and numerical cognition, especially when magnitude comparison tasks are used. Various brain imaging methodologies (such as PET, fMRI, and ERP) have indicated that even those tasks tend to activate an extensive neural network involving the frontal and parietal lobes as well as some subcortical structures and the cerebellum. Studies of arithmetic show that different variants of this neural network become active depending on the precise details of the task requirements presented to the participant. This undoubtedly reflects the fact that different representations and processes are required by each task variant, and those differences involve different neural substrates for their implementation. The diversity of neural activity reported in response to the different tasks is clear evidence that the relationship between cognitive processes and neural substrates can be investigated and understood to a very high level of detail. Nonetheless, that encouraging interpretation does point to several shortcomings with the current state of this scientific enterprise.

One such weakness is that current understanding of how activity in the brain relates to mental processes associated with numerical and mathematical thinking does not provide a definitive picture of how domain specific that activity is. To an extent, this issue will be addressed when more developmental studies of the foundational competencies of mathematical cognition and studies of atypical development of numerical abilities are carried out. However, different views still remain and have yet to be reconciled. One position is that there are no initially domain-specific number areas in the brain and that neural circuits involved in the early development of object and spatial cognition, including spatial attention, form the foundation of the network that supports later mathematical ability (e.g., Simon, 1997). Another view suggests much more prespecification of a neuroanatomy for numerical processing. In this view, the horizontal section of the intraparietal sulcus (HIPS) has been advanced as a candidate for a domain-specific numerical processing region. Dehaene and colleagues stated "At least two of the three parietal circuits that we have described . . . are thought to be associated with broader functions than mere calculation" (2003, p. 501). The remaining HIPS area is, they claim, "a more plausible candidate for domain specificity," though they prefer the term "number-essential."

However, the HIPS region is also reliably activated in adults by many nonnumerical functions that might form the foundation for the construction of domain-specific numerical processing. In an fMRI experiment, Wojciulik and Kanwisher (1999) looked for overlap activation in multiple tasks (AOMT) involving spatial attention and object processing. None of the tasks was numerical in nature. The most reliable areas of AOMT were in the intraparietal sulcus, with most participants activating a region that Wojciulik and Kanwisher referred to as anterior intraparietal sulcus (AIPS). The location of this region and the volume of activated tissue indicate strong overlap with Dehaene and colleagues's HIPS region. Another, even more reliably activated part of the IPS was the one at the junction of the transverse occipital sulcus (IPTO), leading to Wojciulik and Kanwisher's conclusion that "IPTO and AIPS . . . may be part of a more extensive network of overlapping activations that span much of IPS and SPL" (1999, p. 750). This means that both the HIPS and superior parietal "numerical circuits" described by Dehaene and colleagues (2003) would be included in these regions. Shuman and Kanwisher (2004) even directly tested the numerical domain specificity claim for HIPS by using nonsymbolic stimuli to test for numerical versus nonnumerical judgments and for difficulty effects. They concluded that their experiments "failed to support the hypothesis that the human parietal lobe contains the neural instantiation of a domain specific mechanism for representing abstract numerical magnitude" (p. 7).

Another shortcoming of the current body of evidence is that almost all of the neuroanatomical studies of numerical cognition have been carried out on adults. This is perfectly understandable in a historical context. It is likely, however, that the impression left by these studies of a single "neuroanatomy of mathematical ability" is a false one. If subtle changes in representation and processing are related to significant changes in neural activations, then the neural activation seen in children who are typically developing (i.e., who are in the fluid state of still acquiring numerical and mathematical knowledge and skills) might be quite different from that reported in typically developed adults, who have crystallized that ability. The neural activity associated with those processes used by children who are not developing typically in the acquisition of numerical competence will likely be characteristically different from both of those groups. Thus, it is safest to assume for now that there will be different neuroanatomical correlates associated with the varieties of numerical abilities that individuals have at different points in the lifespan. Considerable research is clearly needed in order to specify those different patterns.

The activation of brain regions detected in adults in response to numerical tasks should not necessarily lead one to assume that those circuits are hardwired into the brain and prespecified as the basis of numerical processing. To adopt such a view would lead to the further inference that numerical and mathematical disability necessarily arises from lesions to or dysfunctions in those specific circuits. Indeed, as Johnson and colleagues (Johnson, Halit, Grice, & Karmiloff-Smith, 2002) suggested, those two assumptions are inappropriate for understanding typical and atypical neural development in any domain. The former, or "static," assumption is that brain–behavior relationships are fixed and that the age at which individuals are studied in order to determine that relationship is unimportant. The latter, or "deficit," assumption refers to the unidirectional inference that "damage to specific neural substrates both causes and explains the behavioral deficits observed in developmental disorders" (p. 525).

Despite this critique, the assumptions just described remain widespread and are implied by Landerl and colleagues's (Landerl, Bevan, & Butterworth, 2004) statement that "neuropsychological evidence indicates that numerical processing is localized to the parietal lobes bilaterally, in particular the intra-parietal sulcus (Dehaene et al., 2003), and is independent of other abilities. Developmental dyscalculia is likely to be the result of the failure of these brain areas to develop normally, whether because of injury or because of genetic factors" (p. 121). Obviously, a greater understanding of these issues is needed and will likely emerge only when extensive developmental studies of typical and atypical numerical and mathematical cognitive development have been carried out using experimental and neuroimaging methods. The results of such a program of research are likely to provide deep insights into the cognitive and neuroanatomical bases of numerical and mathematical disability that will help us to understand and ultimately remediate or even prevent such outcomes from occurring.

REFERENCES

Benson, D.F., & Weir, W.F. (1972). Acalculia: Acquired anarithmetia. *Cortex, 8*(4), 465–472.

Buxton, R. (2002). *Introduction to functional magnetic resonance imaging: Principles and techniques.* New York: Cambridge University Press.

Canobi, K.H., Reeve, R.A., & Pattison, P.E. (2002). Young children's understanding of addition concepts. *Educational Psychology, 22*(5), 513–532.

Chatterjee, A. (2002). Neglect: A disorder of spatial attention. In M. D'Esposito (Ed.), *Neurological foundations of cognitive neuroscience* (pp. 1–26). Cambridge, MA: MIT Press.

Cipolotti, L., Butterworth, B., & Denes, G. (1991). A specific deficit for numbers in a case of dense acalculia. *Brain, 114,* 2619–2637.

Cohen, L., & Dehaene, S. (2004). Specialization within the ventral stream: The case for the visual word form area. *NeuroImage, 22*(1), 466–476.

Cohen, L., Dehaene, S., Chochon, F., Lehericy, S., & Naccache, L. (2000). Language and calculation within the parietal lobe: A combined cognitive, anatomical and fMRI study. *Neuropsychologia, 38*(10), 1426–1440.

Cohen-Kadosh, R., Henik, A., Rubinsten, O., Mohr, H., Dori, H., van de Ven, V., et al. (2005). Are numbers special? The comparison systems of the human brain investigated by fMRI. *Neuropsychologia, 43*(9), 1238–1248.

Damasio, H., Grabowski, T., Frank, R., Galaburda, A.M., & Damasio, A.R. (1994). The return of Phineas Gage: Clues about the brain from the skull of a famous patient. *Science, 264*(5162), 1102–1105.

Dehaene, S. (1997). *The number sense: How the mind creates mathematics.* New York: Oxford University Press.

Dehaene, S., & Cohen, L. (1991). Two mental calculation systems: A case study of severe acalculia with preserved approximation. *Neuropsychologia, 29*(11), 1045–1054.

Dehaene, S., Piazza, M., Pinel, P., & Cohen, L. (2003). Three parietal circuits for number processing. *Cognitive Neuropsychology, 20*, 487–506.

Dehaene, S., Spelke, E.S., Pinel, P., Stanescu, R., & Tsivkin, S. (1999). Sources of mathematical thinking: Behavioral and brain imaging evidence. *Science, 284*, 970–974.

Delazer, M., Domahs, F., Bartha, L., Brenneis, C., Lochy, A., Trieb, T., et al. (2003). Learning complex arithmetic—An fMRI study. *Cognitive Brain Research, 18*(1), 76–88.

El Yagoubi, R., Lemaire, P., & Besson, M. (2005). Effects of aging on arithmetic problem-solving: An event-related brain potential study. *Journal of Cognitive Neuroscience, 17*(1), 37–50.

Fasotti, L., Eling, P.A., & Bremer, J.J. (1992). The internal representation of arithmetical word problem sentences: Frontal and posterior-injured patients compared. *Brain and Cognition, 20*(2), 245–263.

Fox, P.T., Raichle, M.E., Mintun, M.A., & Dence, C. (1988). Nonoxidative glucose consumption during focal physiologic neural activity. *Science, 241*(4864), 462–464.

Fulbright, R.K., Manson, S.C., Skudlarski, P., Lacadie, C.M., & Gore, J.C. (2003). Quantity determination and the distance effect with letters, numbers, and shapes: A functional MR imaging study of number processing. *American Journal of Neuroradiology, 24*(2), 193–200.

Fuson, K.C. (1992). Research on whole number addition and subtraction. In D.A. Grouws (Ed.), *Handbook of research on mathematics teaching and learning* (pp. 243–275). New York: Macmillan.

Galfano, G., Mazza, V., Angrilli, A., & Umilta, C. (2004). Electrophysiological correlates of stimulus-driven multiplication facts retrieval. *Neuropsychologia, 42*(10), 1370–1382.

Geary, D.C., & Wiley, J.G. (1991). Cognitive addition: Strategy choice and speed-of-processing differences in young and elderly adults. *Psychology and Aging, 6*(3), 474–483.

Göbel, S.M., Calabria, M., Farne, A., & Rossetti, Y. (2006). Parietal rTMS distorts the mental number line: Simulating 'spatial' neglect in healthy subjects. *Neuropsychologia, 44*(6), 860–868.

Grafman, J., Passafiume, D., Faglioni, P., & Boller, F. (1982). Calculation disturbances in adults with focal hemispheric damage. *Cortex, 18*(1), 37–49.

Gruber, O., Indefrey, P., Steinmetz, H., & Kleinschmidt, A. (2001). Dissociating neural correlates of cognitive components in mental calculation. *Cerebral Cortex, 11*(4), 350–359.

Hart, J., Jr., Kraut, M.A., Kremen, S., Soher, B., & Gordon, B. (2000). Neural substrates of orthographic lexical access as demonstrated by functional brain imaging. *Neuropsychiatry, Neuropsychology, & Behavioral Neurology, 13*(1), 1–7.

Henschen, S. (1920). *Klinische und anatomische beitraege sur pathologie des Gehirns* (Vol. 5). Stockholm: Nordiska Bokhandeln.

Iguchi, Y., & Hashimoto, I. (2000). Sequential information processing during a mental arithmetic is reflected in the time course of event-related brain potentials. *Clinical Neurophysiology, 111*(2), 204–213.

Johnson, M.H., Halit, H., Grice, S.J., & Karmiloff-Smith, A. (2002). Neuroimaging of typical and atypical development: A perspective from multiple levels of analysis. *Developmental Psychopathology, 14*(3), 521–536.

Kawashima, R., Taira, M., Okita, K., Inoue, K., Tajima, N., Yoshida, H., et al. (2004). A functional MRI study of simple arithmetic—A comparison between children and adults. *Cognitive Brain Research, 18*(3), 227–233.

Kong, J., Wang, C., Kwong, K., Vangel, M., Chua, E., & Gollub, R. (2005). The neural substrate of arithmetic operations and procedure complexity. *Cognitive Brain Research, 22*(3), 397–405.

Kronbichler, M., Hutzler, F., Wimmer, H., Mair, A., Staffen, W., & Ladurner, G. (2004). The visual word form area and the frequency with which words are encountered: Evidence from a parametric fMRI study. *NeuroImage, 21*(3), 946–953.

Lampl, Y., Eshel, Y., Gilad, R., & Sarova-Pinhas, I. (1994). Selective acalculia with sparing of the subtraction process in a patient with left parietotemporal hemorrhage. *Neurology, 44*(9), 1759–1761.

Landerl, K., Bevan, A., & Butterworth, B. (2004). Developmental dyscalculia and basic numerical capacities: A study of 8–9-year-old students. *Cognition, 93*(2), 99–125.

Levy, L.M., Reis, I.L., & Grafman, J. (1999). Metabolic abnormalities detected by ^{1}H-MRS in dyscalculia and dysgraphia. *Neurology, 53,* 639–641.

Lewis, W.H. (1924). *Anatomy of the human body by Henry Gray* (21st ed.). Philadelphia & New York: Lea & Febiger.

Luck, S. (2005). *An introduction to the event-related potential technique.* Cambridge, MA: MIT Press.

McCarthy, R.A., & Warrington, E.K. (1988). Evidence for modality-specific meaning systems in the brain. *Nature, 334*(6181), 428–430.

Menon, V., Rivera, S.M., White, C.D., Eliez, S., Glover, G.H., & Reiss, A.L. (2000). Functional optimization of arithmetic processing in perfect performers. *Cognitive Brain Research, 9*(3), 343–345.

Menon, V., Rivera, S.M., White, C.D., Glover, G.H., & Reiss, A.L. (2000). Dissociating prefrontal and parietal cortex activation during arithmetic processing. *NeuroImage, 12,* 357–365.

Montgomery, R.W., Montgomery, L.D., & Guisado, R. (1992). Cortical localization of cognitive function by regression of performance on event-related potentials. *Aviation, Space, and Environmental Medicine, 63*(10), 919–924.

Murphy, M.M., Mazzocco, M.M.M., Gerner, G., & Henry, A.E. (2006). Mathematics learning disability in girls with Turner syndrome or fragile X syndrome. *Brain and Cognition, 61*(2), 195–210.

Ojemann, G.A. (1974). Mental arithmetic during human thalamic stimulation. *Neuropsychologia, 12*(1), 1–10.

Pauli, P., Lutzenberger, W., Rau, H., Birbaumer, N., Rickard, T.C., Yaroush, R.A., et al. (1994). Brain potentials during mental arithmetic: Effects of extensive practice and problem difficulty. *Cognitive Brain Research, 2*(1), 21–29.

Pellegrini, A.D., & Stanic, G.M.A. (1993). Locating children's mathematical competence: Application of the developmental niche. *Journal of Applied Developmental Psychology, 14*(4), 501–520.

Piazza, M., Mechelli, A., Butterworth, B., & Price, C.J. (2002). Are subitizing and counting implemented as separate or functionally overlapping processes? *NeuroImage, 15*(2), 435–446.

Pinel, P., Dehaene, S., Riviere, D., & LeBihan, D. (2001). Modulation of parietal activation by semantic distance in a number comparison task. *NeuroImage, 14*(5), 1013–1026.

Pinel, P., Le Clec'H, G., van de Moortele, P., Naccache, L., Le Bihan, D., & Dehaene, S. (1999). Event-related fMRI analysis of the cerebral circuit for number comparison. *Neuroreport, 10*(7), 1473–1479.

Pinel, P., Piazza, M., LeBihan, D., & Dehaene, S. (2004). Distributed and overlapping cerebral representations of number, size, and luminance during comparative judgments. *Neuron, 41*(6), 983–993.

Price, C.J., & Devlin, J.T. (2003). The myth of the visual word form area. *NeuroImage, 19*(3), 473–481.

Price, C.J., & Devlin, J.T. (2004). The pro and cons of labelling a left occipitotemporal region: "the visual word form area." *NeuroImage, 22*(1), 477–479.

Rivera, S.M., Reiss, A.L., Eckert, M.A., & Menon, V. (2005). Developmental changes in mental arithmetic: Evidence for increased functional specialization in the left inferior parietal cortex. *Cerebral Cortex, 15*(11), 1779–1790.

Roman, F., Salgado-Pineda, P., Bartres-Faz, D., Sanchez-Navarro, J.P., Martinez-Lage, J., Lopez-Hernandez, F., et al. (2003). Neuropsychological deficits in a child with a left penetrating brain injury. *Brain Injury, 17*(8), 695–700.

Rosselli, M., & Ardila, A. (1989). Calculation deficits in patients with right and left hemisphere damage. *Neuropsychologia, 27*(5), 607–617.

Sathian, K., Simon, T.J., Peterson, S., Patel, G.A., Hoffman, J.M., & Grafton, S.T. (1999). Neural evidence linking visual object enumeration and attention. *Journal of Cognitive Neuroscience, 11*(1), 36–51.

Semenza, C., Delazer, M., Bertella, L., Grana, A., Mori, I., Conti, F.M., et al. (2006). Is math lateralised on the same side as language? Right hemisphere aphasia and mathematical abilities. *Neuroscience Letters, 406*(3), 285–288.

Shuman, M., & Kanwisher, N. (2004). Numerical magnitude in the human parietal lobe; tests of representational generality and domain specificity. *Neuron, 44*(3), 557–569.

Siegler, R.S., & Booth, J.L. (2004). Development of numerical estimation in young children. *Child Development, 75*(2), 428–444.

Simon, T.J. (1997). Reconceptualizing the origins of number knowledge: A "non-numerical" approach. *Cognitive Development, 12,* 349–372.

Simon, T.J. (1999). The foundations of numerical thinking in a brain without numbers. *Trends in Cognitive Sciences, 3*(10), 363–365.

Szucs, D., & Csepe, V. (2005). The effect of numerical distance and stimulus probability on ERP components elicited by numerical incongruencies in mental addition. *Cognitive Brain Research, 22*(2), 289–300.

Takayama, Y., Sugishita, M., Akiguchi, I., & Kimura, J. (1994). Isolated acalculia due to left parietal lesion. *Archives of Neurology, 51*(3), 286–291.

Tohgi, H., Saitoh, K., Takahashi, S., Takahashi, H., Utsugisawa, K., Yonezawa, H., et al. (1995). Agraphia and acalculia after a left prefrontal (F1, F2) infarction. *Journal of Neurology, Neurosurgery, & Psychiatry, 58*(5), 629–632.

Turconi, E., Jemel, B., Rossion, B., & Seron, X. (2004). Electrophysiological evidence for differential processing of numerical quantity and order in humans. *Cognitive Brain Research, 21*(1), 22–38.

Venkatraman, V., Ansari, D., & Chee, M.W. (2005). Neural correlates of symbolic and non-symbolic arithmetic. *Neuropsychologia, 43*(5), 744–753.

Verstichel, P., & Masson, C. (2003). ["Progressive acalculia": A variety of focal degenerative atrophy affecting number processing.] *Revue Neurologique (Paris), 159*(4), 413–420.

Vuilleumier, P., Ortigue, S., & Brugger, P. (2004). The number space and neglect. *Cortex, 40*(2), 399–410.

Wang, Y., Kong, J., Tang, X., Zhuang, D., & Li, S. (2000). Event-related potential N270 is elicited by mental conflict processing in human brain. *Neuroscience Letters, 293*(1), 17–20.

Warrington, E.K. (1982). The fractionation of arithmetical skills: A single case study. *Quarterly Journal of Experimental Psychology [A], 34*(Pt 1), 31–51.

Whalen, J., McCloskey, M., Lesser, R.P., & Gordon, B. (1997). Localizing arithmetic processes in the brain: Evidence from a transient deficit during cortical stimulation. *Journal of Cognitive Neuroscience, 9*(3), 409–417.

Wojciulik, E., & Kanwisher, N. (1999). The generality of parietal involvement in visual attention. *Neuron, 23*(4), 747–764.

Zorzi, M., Priftis, K., & Umilta, C. (2002). Brain damage: Neglect disrupts the mental number line. *Nature, 417*(6885), 138–139.

Chapter 14

Quantitative Genetics and Mathematical Abilities/Disabilities

Stephen A. Petrill and Robert Plomin

+ +

I t is widely recognized that there is a pressing need to increase the knowledge base about mathematics development, especially about the more complex and abstract aspects of mathematics and its relationship to other areas of academic achievement and cognitive development. At least 5% of school children have mathematical disabilities (Geary, 2004), and these seem especially intractable. An important step toward understanding the origins of individual differences in mathematics learning is to investigate its genetic and environmental underpinnings.

In this chapter we will describe the emerging literature examining the genetic and environmental etiology of mathematics ability, the links between mathematics ability and disability, and the relationship between math, reading, and other cognitive skills. We will also describe the implications of these findings for future mathematics research in quantitative genetics, molecular genetics, and neuroscience.

UNIVARIATE GENETIC AND ENVIRONMENTAL ANALYSIS OF INDIVIDUAL DIFFERENCES IN MATHEMATICS PERFORMANCE

Although studies have demonstrated that genetic disorders such as Williams syndrome are associated with particular deficits in math performance (e.g., Paterson, Brown, Gsödl, Johnson, & Karmiloff-Smith, 1999), the vast ma-

This chapter is supported by a grant (HD46167) from the National Institute of Child Health and Development/Institute of Educational Sciences (NICHD/IES).

jority of children with math disabilities have no known genetic or environmental etiology. More generally, because math performance is a normally distributed behavioral phenotype, the genes and environments that influence math skills may also be functioning throughout the range of ability (Plomin & Kovas, 2005). Univariate quantitative genetic methods serve as an important first step in examining the magnitude of genetic and environmental influences on individual differences in math performance. This method assumes that individual differences in a measured trait (such as mathematics) may be divided into genetic and environmental components of variance by examining family members who vary in their degree of genetic relatedness. For example, identical, also called monozygotic or M2, twins are genetically identical, whereas fraternal twins share 50% of the same genes, on average. If identical, also called dizygotic or D2 twins are more similar in mathematics performance than fraternal twins, then the increased phenotypic resemblance for identical twins is attributed to their greater genetic similarity (Plomin, DeFries, McClearn, & McGuffin, 2001). Heritability (h^2) quantifies "how much" individual differences on an outcome measure (such as mathematics) are influenced by genetic differences. A heritability of .50 means that 50% of the differences in a given outcome are due to genetic differences. It is important to stress that $h^2 = .50$ means that 50% of the differences in a group of people may be attributable to genetic differences. It does not mean that 50% of a particular person's mathematical performance is determined by genes.

In addition to genetics, the quantitative genetic approach also estimates the proportion of variance in an outcome that is due to the shared family environment (also called the "common environment," or c^2). Shared environment is defined as anything that family members have in common beyond their genetic similarity. Shared environmental influences can occur inside the home (e.g., same parents) or outside the home (same school); they can be biological (similar exposure to teratogens in the womb) or behavioral (similar exposure to math concepts).

Finally, quantitative genetic methods may be used to quantify the proportion of variance due to nonshared environment (or e^2), which includes any nongenetic factor that makes family members different. For example, siblings growing up in the same home do not necessarily have the same parental, peer, or educational experiences. It is important to note that nonshared environment also contains error of measurement.

This relatively straightforward univariate approach has led to important discoveries in the domains of general cognitive ability and reading. Most notably, research has moved away from arguments of nature versus nurture toward a more balanced acceptance of the role of both nature and nurture. Unfortunately, unlike research on general cognitive ability and reading, only a handful of genetic studies examine mathematics. Moreover, the findings of these studies yield widely varying estimates of heritability, from $h^2 = .20$ (Thompson, Detterman, & Plomin, 1991; Wadsworth, DeFries, Fulker, & Plomin, 1995) to .40 (Loehlin & Nichols, 1976) to .60 (Husén, 1959; Oliver et al., 2004) to .90 (Alarcón, Knopik, & DeFries, 2000). Estimates of the importance of shared environmental influences also differ greatly in these studies.

Such variability in results is not surprising given differences in sampling and measurement. For example, Thompson and colleagues (1991) examined mathematics performance in a U.S.-based sample of 9- to 13-year-old twin pairs using tester-administered psychometric tests. Oliver and colleagues (2004) employed teacher assessments of math performance based on UK National Curriculum criteria in 7-year-old UK twin pairs, and Alarcón and colleagues (2000) used a latent factor of math performance derived from U.S. twin pairs of a wide age range (8–20 years) selected for reading problems. Another likely factor in the diversity of results is sample size, because estimates of heritability and shared environment have wide confidence intervals—the sample sizes in these studies varied from a few hundred to several thousand pairs of twins.

Given wide differences in study designs, only broad conclusions can be drawn: Genetic influences are generally significant and there is also some evidence for shared environmental effects. Thus, as for general cognitive ability and reading, the importance of both nature and nurture should serve as a working hypothesis.

UNIVARIATE GENETIC AND
ENVIRONMENTAL ANALYSIS OF MATHEMATICS DISABILITY

Quantitative genetic methods may also be used to examine the genetic and environmental etiology of groups selected for extreme low math performance. A traditional method is to use twin concordance, which treats disability and ability as dichotomous. A cutoff is used to define disability (e.g., standardized math score below 2 standard deviations [SD]). If identical twin pairs are both more likely to fall below the cutoff than are fraternal twins, genetic influences are implicated.

Another method of examining math disability combines the analysis of disability and individual differences in ability. DeFries and Fulker (1985, 1988) developed a regression-based approach called DF analysis that measures the quantitative distribution of a behavioral trait while allowing for selection based on that trait. As shown in Figure 14.1, a group of probands, defined as case twins who fall below a certain threshold of math performance, are compared with their co-twins on mean quantitative trait scores. The issue is the extent to which the mean of these co-twins approaches the mean of their selected proband siblings compared with the mean of the un-

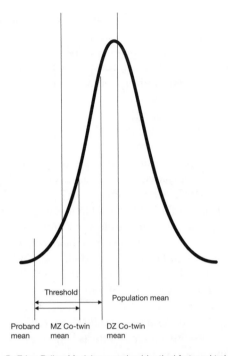

Figure 14.1. DeFries-Fulker Model comparing identical fraternal twin probands selected for math disability with their co-twin siblings.

selected population. In other words, assuming a trait with a population mean of 100, if the mean math performance score of the proband group is 70, then greater familial resemblance is implied if the co-twin group mean is 80 as opposed to 95. By comparing family members of varying genetic relatedness, it is possible to estimate genetic and environmental effects. For example, if the mean of identical co-twins is closer to the proband mean than is the mean of fraternal co-twins, genetic influences are implied. The statistic that measures this effect is called group heritability (h_g^2) because it indexes the extent to which the mean difference between the probands and the population can be attributed to genetic factors. Put another way, h_g^2 estimates the extent to which genetics explains why a group of children has a mean level of math performance below the population mean. This is in contrast to heritability (h_g^2), which refers to the genetic differences in individuals across the entire range of ability. Group shared environmental influences (c_g^2) are indicated to the extent that MZ co-twin means are closer to the proband mean than expected on the basis of group heritability. Group nonshared environmental influences (and error) are implied to the extent that the MZ co-twin mean approaches the mean of the unselected population. As a result, DF analyses typically report only h_g^2 and c_g^2 are estimates.

DF analysis may be used to address two important questions concerning the etiology of the extremes in this case, low math performance, as they compare to the unselected population. First, DF analyses may be used to quantify and test the statistical significance of genetic and environmental influences on the extremes. Second, DF analysis also provides a way to compare the etiology of the extremes to the etiology of normal variation in the unselected population—for example, by comparing DF group heritability for a selected extreme group to individual differences in heritability for the normal distribution. On the one hand, discontinuity is implied if the genetic etiology of the extremes is different from that of the unselected sample. On the other hand, if the genetic etiology of the extremes is similar in magnitude to that of the unselected sample, this is consistent with the hypothesis that genes that affect the extremes constitute the lower tail of normally distributed genetic effects that operate across the range of ability. Finding that genetic effects at the extremes are similar in magnitude to those across the entire range of ability does not prove that the same genes are involved. A definitive test of continuity of effects from the extremes to normal variation will come when specific genes associated with math are identified and can be used to investigate the extent to which such genes are associated with ability as well as disability. The same logic applies for the shared environment. In the case of mathematics, the continuity or discontinuity of genetic and environmental effects has important implications. For example, if there is continuity, the genes and environments that affect math disability would be expected to be normally distributed and important across the entire range of math performance.

Only two published studies have examined this issue in mathematics. Alarcón, DeFries, Light, and Pennington (1997) examined 40 identical and 23 same-sex fraternal twin pairs ages 8 to 20 years in which one or both twins in a family were 1.5 *SD* below the mean on the Wide Range Achievement Test–Revised (WRAT-R) arithmetic score (Jastak & Wilkinson, 1984). Group heritability was $h^2 = .38$, suggesting that approximately 40% of the mean difference between the low math group and the unselected population was due to genetic differences between the two groups. This estimate falls in the middle of the range of heritability estimates in unselected samples ($h^2 = .20-.90$, as described previously). The second study (Oliver et al., 2004), conducted as part of our univariate analysis of teacher-rated math

Table 14.1.   Genetic and shared environmental estimates for children below the 15th percentile in math performance and normal variation in an unselected sample (*Source:* Oliver et al., 2004).

Variable	< 15th percentile		Unselected sample	
	h_g^2	c_g^2	h^2	c^2
Using and applying number	.69	.00	.61	.10
Numbers	.62	.04	.63	.06
Shapes, space, and measures	.54	.15	.65	.09
Composite	.65	.07	.66	.09

Note: n twin pairs: >165 MZ and >184 DZ for lowest 15%; >1044 MZ and >957 same-sex DZ for unselected sample. h_g^2 = group heritabilities; c_g^2 = group shared environmental estimates; h^2 = individual differences heritabilities; c^2 = shared environmental estimates.

across the range of ability described above, made a more systematic comparison of genetic and environmental influences in low versus unselected math performance using a sample of 2,178 pairs of 7-year-old twins. Low math groups were formed, defined as those whose performance was at or below the 15th percentile of teacher ratings of UK National Curriculum criteria, yielding 370 pairs of selected twins for analysis. As shown in Table 14.1, Oliver and colleagues found that the genetic and shared environmental etiology of low math performance was nearly identical to that of the unselected population.

Taken together, these two studies provide initial evidence that the etiology of low math performance may be influenced by the same set of genetic and environmental factors that influence the entire range of math performance. This finding is consistent with studies examining ability and disability in reading and general cognitive skills. In general, with the exception of adults 80 years and older (Petrill et al., 2001), h^2 is similar in magnitude to h_g^2 (Petrill et al., 1997; Petrill et al., 1998; Plomin, 2001; Plomin & Thompson, 1993; Spinath, Harlaar, Ronald, & Plomin, 2004) irrespective of sample differences. Early analyses of reading from Colorado data (DeFries & Alarcón, 1996) suggested that the h_g^2 of reading disability was less than the h^2 of reading ability, but as the sample size increased, the difference between these estimates converged (Fisher & DeFries, 2002).

MULTIVARIATE GENETIC ANALYSIS

Although univariate genetic analyses are an important first step toward understanding the origins of mathematics ability and disability, a multivariate perspective provides important insight into the overlap and independence among different aspects of mathematics ability as well as the covariance between mathematics ability and other skills, such as reading and general cognitive skills. Multivariate genetic methods investigate the genetic and environmental contributions to the covariance between disorders and dimensions rather than analyze the variance of each trait separately (Martin & Eaves, 1977). The analyses produce three genetic statistics: *bivariate heritability, genetic correlation,* and *unique genetic influence* (Plomin & DeFries, 1979). Just as heritability indicates the proportion of variance that can be attributed to genetic factors, *bivariate heritability* refers to the proportion of the phenotypic covariance that can be attributed to genetic covariance. Similar to the formula used for Pearson correlations, bivariate heritability equals the covariance due to genetics divided by the square root of the product of the variances for each measure. The *genetic correlation* represents the extent of genetic overlap between the traits regardless of their heritability. In this case, genetic correlation is equal to the covariance due to genetics divided by the square root of the product of the heritabilities (the genetic variance). A concrete way of thinking about the genetic correlation is that it indicates the probability that a gene associated with one trait will also be associated with another trait. *Unique genetic influence* is genetic influence independent from other traits (genetic specificity).

Multivariate genetic research conducted to date on academic achievement indicates that different types of achievement (e.g., mathematics and reading) correlate highly and that academic achievement correlates substantially with general cognitive ability. Early multivariate genetic analyses found substantial genetic overlap between different types of academic achievement (Plomin & DeFries, 1979). The first multivariate genetic analysis of academic achievement and general cognitive ability also found substantial genetic overlap between these domains (Thompson et al., 1991), a finding replicated in subsequent studies (see Petrill & Wilkerson, 2000). For example, the Colorado twin studies have suggested substantial genetic overlap between mathematics and reading (Knopik, Alarcón, & DeFries, 1997) and between mathematics and general cognitive ability (Alarcón et al., 2000; Light, DeFries, & Olson, 1998). All of this work focused on variation within the normal range, but one small study of mathematics disability involving twins also reported substantial genetic mediation of comorbidity between mathematics disability and reading disability (Knopik et al., 1997).

Although substantial genetic overlap among mathematics, reading, and general cognitive ability calls into question the specificity of mathematics, most of the research also leaves room for some specificity. In our own work, we examined 2875 pairs of twins who were assessed by their teachers for mathematics and reading at 7 years and tested for general cognitive ability (Kovas, Harlaar, Petrill, & Plomin, 2005). Our findings suggested that 31% of the variance in mathematics was accounted for by genes shared with both general cognitive ability and reading, 13% was accounted for by genes shared with reading but independent from general cognitive ability, and 24% was accounted for by genes specific to math. The remaining variance in math was accounted for by shared environmental influences associated with reading (5%) and shared environmental influences specific to math (4%), as well as nonshared environmental influences shared with reading (4%) and specific to math (20%, including error).

SUMMARY OF THE EXISTING LITERATURE

Four conclusions may be drawn from the meager but emerging quantitative genetic literature on mathematics. First, genetic influences—and to a lesser extent, shared environmental influences—appear to be important to individual differences in math performance. Second, the magnitude of genetic and environmental influences of low math performance appear to be similar to those that operate across the range of math ability, suggesting that math disability is at the end of a continuum of math skills. Third, results suggest that, while roughly two thirds of the variance in math ability is influenced by genes shared with reading and general cognitive ability, a third of the variance in mathematics is influenced by genes specific to math. Finally, the results for math are consistent with findings related to other complex cognitive outcomes, most notably general cognitive ability and reading ability. We hypothesize that mathematics, like reading and general cognitive ability, is best characterized by the generalist genes hypothesis, which states that genetic influences are largely shared across different measures of cognitive functioning (Plomin & Kovas, 2005). As shown in Figure 14.2, the correlation between mathematics and reading, for example, is largely influenced by genetic factors. In contrast, the discontinuity between reading and math skills is influenced by independent genetic effects but also by independent environmental influences.

If this hypothesis continues to be supported by quantitative genetic studies, theories of mathematics ability and disability must encompass the possibility that the substantial phenotypic correlation among mathematics, reading, and general cognitive ability (e.g., Hecht, Torgesen, Wagner, & Rashotte, 2001; Jordan & Montani, 1997) is not only rooted in environmental influences (e.g., common instruction methods) but also due to genetic factors. These findings amplify Fletcher's (2005) suggestion that in order to study math difficulties, it may be necessary to examine math skills associated with reading ability. On the other hand, the quantitative genetic evidence also points to the importance of math performance separate from reading skills. This is consistent with neurobiological evidence suggesting some degree of independence in brain-based correlates of math performance (e.g., Dehaene, 1996; Dehaene & Cohen, 1995). Although there is substantial overlap in the biological pathways that influence reading, mathe-

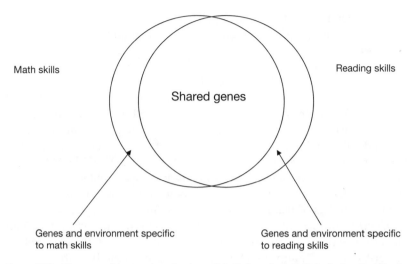

Figure 14.2. The generalist genes hypothesis predicts that most genes that affect math skills also affect other learning skills, such as reading (Plomin & Kovas, 2005).

matics, and general cognitive ability, independent biological pathways specific to math may also be present.

GOALS FOR FUTURE QUANTITATIVE GENETIC STUDIES

Despite these initial findings, much is still unknown about mathematics from a quantitative genetic perspective. First, quantitative genetic studies have been confined to measures of overall math performance and have not systematically examined the genetic and environmental mechanisms responsible for overlap and independence among components of mathematics. If genetic overlap is high, then there is evidence for a set of genetically mediated processes important for all math skills. If there is genetic independence, then the distinction, for example, between computational and problem-solving skills is the result of different genetically mediated processes. As those in the field of mathematics work to identify the central skill or set of skills that underlie individual differences in math performance (Chiappe, 2005), quantitative genetic studies could serve an important role in understanding the etiology of these skills and how they overlap with and are independent from the skills associated with reading and general cognitive ability.

Again, the reading literature offers important insight into what one might expect when examining math and math disability. Beginning with Olson, Gillis, Rack, DeFries, and Fulker (1991), researchers began to demonstrate that genetic influences on general reading ability are also important for components of reading ability, such as phonological awareness and decoding, reading comprehension, spelling, orthographic knowledge, and rapid automatized naming (see Compton, Davis, DeFries, Gayan, & Olson, 2001; Gayan & Olson, 2001, 2003; Knopik, Alarcón, & DeFries, 1998; Olson, Forsberg, & Wise, 1994; Olson et al., 1991).

Another central goal of the mathematics literature is to give insight into the pathways through which mathematics abilities and disabilities develop. In particular, recent work provides mixed evidence concerning the longitudinal stability of math performance (e.g., Geary, Hamson, & Hoard, 2000; Jordan & Hanich, 2003; Mazzocco & Meyers, 2003; Shalev, Manor, & Gross-Tsur, 2005). Although at the time this book was published, no longitudinal quantitative genetic studies of mathematics could be found in the literature, studies of reading and general cognitive ability are instructive. First, genetic influences on reading skills may become more important with age, at the expense of the shared environment (Byrne et al., 2002; Petrill, Deater-Deckard, Thompson, DeThorne, et al., in press). If confirmed, this result would be similar to the strong evidence in the general cognitive ability literature that heritability increases with the age of the sample from $h^2 =$ .20 in infancy to .40 in childhood to .80 in adulthood, at the expense of the shared environment, which declines to zero by adolescence. Nonshared environmental influences, including error, are generally stable at approximately .20 across the lifespan (e.g., McCartney, Harris, & Bernieri, 1990; McGue, Bouchard, Iacono, & Lykken, 1993; Plomin, Fulker, Corley, & DeFries, 1997). Moreover, longitudinal research on general cognitive ability suggests that the age-to-age correlation between measures of general cognitive ability across age becomes increasingly mediated by genetics (Bartels, Rietveld, van Baal, & Boomsma, 2002; Petrill et al., 2004). Shared environmental contributions to the covariance across age are also important in early childhood but are ultimately nonsignificant by adolescence. In the context of reading, recent studies focusing on twins ages 5 to 8 years have suggested not only substantial genetic and shared environmental contributions to the correlation among reading skills across age but also evidence for independent genetic (related to rapid naming) and shared environmental effects (related to phonological awareness) at later ages (see Byrne et al., 2005; Petrill, Deater-Deckard, Thompson, Schatschneider, et al., in press). Finally, other quantitative genetic studies have utilized latent growth curve and multilevel modeling procedures to test more explicitly genetic and environmental influences on change (e.g., McArdle, 1986; McArdle, Prescott, Hamagami, & Horn, 1998; McGue & Christensen, 2002; Neale & McArdle, 2000; Reynolds, Finkel, Gatz, & Pedersen, 2002). These studies have suggested that genetic influences are primarily responsible for the intercept (mean level of performance), whereas nongenetic influences are implicated in slope (degree of change).

GOALS FOR FUTURE MOLECULAR GENETIC STUDIES

No molecular genetic research has been reported on mathematics other than a few studies of mathematical disabilities in individuals with genetic disorders such as fragile X or Turner syndrome (Bruandet, Molko, Cohen, & Dehaene, 2004; Molko et al., 2003). In contrast, reading has been a prime target for molecular genetic research since the 1980s, in part because a solid quantitative genetic foundation had been established for reading ability and disability and in part for the historical reason that reading disability was the first complex behavioral trait for which linkage was reported with DNA markers (Fisher & DeFries, 2002).

Similarly, quantitative genetic research provides a rationale for molecular genetic research on mathematics ability and disability: There appear to be genetic influences on mathematics ability that operate across the range of ability. Moreover, given that genes associated with math skills are highly correlated with reading and general cognitive ability, a sensible first step is to examine whether markers associated with reading and general cognitive ability are also associated with math skills. In particular, eight major linkage regions have been reported for reading (Grigorenko, 2005), and associations for cognitive ability have been reported for several genes (Plomin, Kennedy, & Craig, in press). In addition, the first linkage studies for general cognitive ability have reported some positive results (Dick et al., 2005; Posthuma et al., 2005). Given the generalist genes hypothesis, we hypothesize that if the genes responsible for these linkages are found, some of these genes are also likely to be related to mathematics.

Moreover, molecular genetic research is also needed to identify the genes that are specific to math. Microarrays that genotype hundreds of thousands of potential DNA differences (using single nucleotide polymorphisms, or SNPs; see Syvanen, 2005) are revolutionizing quantitative trait locus (QTL) research by making it possible to conduct genome-wide association scans (Carlson, Eberle, Kruglyak, & Nickerson, 2004; Hirschhorn & Daly, 2005). This advance also raises problems, such as the need to balance false positive and false negative effects when testing hundreds of thousands of SNPs (Thomas, Haile, & Duggan, 2005), especially in the search for QTLs of small effect size. Both false positives and false negatives are equally problematic. False positives lead to wasted effort on markers that are ultimately uninformative, and false negatives result in promising markers being left unstudied. One way to greatly reduce the amount of genotyping for large samples is to pool DNA from many individuals into groups, such as cases versus controls or groups low versus high on a quantitative trait (Norton, Williams, O'Donovan, & Owen, 2004; Sham, Bader, Craig, O'Donovan, & Owen, 2002). DNA pooling is best viewed as a tool to screen large numbers of SNPs for large samples in order to nominate a small number of candidate markers that can then be confirmed with individual genotyping. This approach method has been applied in a multistage design using a microarray that genotypes 10,000 SNPs; it identified four SNPs associated with general cognitive ability in a sample of 6,000 children (Butcher et al., 2004). A microarray that genotypes 500,000 SNPs is now commercially available (Affymetrix 500K GeneChip), which will greatly increase the effect size of such QTL sets. Through this process, it may be possible to detect some of the QTLs responsible for the high heritability of math disability and ability.

SUMMARY AND IMPLICATIONS

Several important conclusions can be drawn from the published literature on mathematics. First, quantitative genetic studies point to the importance of genetic *variability* to individual differences in mathematics. It is highly unlikely that this genetic variability is due to one gene or a handful of genes that "cause" math disability. Instead, as with most complex traits, this genetic variability is likely the aggregation of numerous individual genes, each having a small, individual effect on math performance. Second, mathematics, reading, and general cognitive ability do not exist in genetic isolation from one another. Thus, on the one hand, it is to be expected that many DNA markers will be common across different kinds of developmental disability. On the other hand, given evidence for genetic specificity in mathematics, it is also likely that other DNA markers are specific to math skills.

Another important implication involves gene–environment processes. The heritability of mathematics is significant to the extent that MZ twins are more similar than DZ twins. This difference in similarity may reflect direct genetic effects but also may reflect greater MZ similarity in the environmental experiences associated with math skills (see Plomin & Bergeman, 1991, for a more general discussion). For example, because MZ twins are more likely to have more similar math skills than DZ twins, they may also be more likely to seek out or be provided with more similar environments. This leads us to perhaps the most important point—that the presence of substantial genetic influences on math and math disability does not imply genetic determinism or relegate the environment to a secondary role. Genes do not turn on and cause a child to develop math skills in isolation from environmental experiences. However, understanding why children with math problems experience certain environments must also be examined in the context of genetic influences on math performance; in some cases, genes related to math may alter the probability of coming into contact with environments that are helpful or harmful to math skills. Genetically sensitive designs are essential to the systematic study of how genes and environments work together to influence individual differences in math performance. Most important, understanding the genetic effects on normally occurring variation in math and related outcomes may ultimately facilitate efforts to estimate a particular child's risk of developing math difficulties before those difficulties develop.

REFERENCES

Alarcón, M., DeFries, J.C., Light, J.G., & Pennington, B.F. (1997). A twin study of mathematics disability. *Journal of Learning Disabilities, 30,* 617–623.

Alarcón, M., Knopik, V.S., & DeFries, J.C. (2000). Covariation of mathematics achievement and general cognitive ability in twins. *Journal of School Psychology, 38,* 63–77.

Bartels, M., Rietveld, M.J.H., van Baal, G.C.M., & Boomsma, D.I. (2002). Genetic and environmental influences on the development of intelligence. *Behavior Genetics, 32*(3), 237–249.

Bruandet, M., Molko, N., Cohen, L., & Dehaene, S. (2004). A cognitive characterization of dyscalculia in Turner syndrome. *Neuropsychologia, 42,* 288–298.

Butcher, L.M., Meaburn, E., Liu, L., Hill, L., Al-Chalabi, A., Plomin, R., et al. (2004). Genotyping pooled DNA on microarrays: A systematic genome screen of thousands of SNPs in large samples to detect QTLs for complex traits. *Behavior Genetics, 34,* 549–55.

Byrne, B., Delaland, C., Fielding-Barnsley, R., Quain, P., Samuelsson, S., Hoien, T., et al. (2002). Longitudinal twin study of early reading development in three countries: Preliminary results. *Annals of Dyslexia, 52,* 49–74.

Byrne, B., Wadsworth, S., Corley, R., Samuelsson, S., Quain, P., DeFries, J.C., et al. (2005). Longitudinal twin study of early literacy development: Preschool and kindergarten phases. *Scientific Studies of Reading, 9*(3), 219–236.

Carlson, C.S., Eberle, M.A., Kruglyak, L., & Nickerson, D.A. (2004). Mapping complex disease loci in whole-genome association studies. *Nature, 429,* 446–452.

Chiappe, P. (2005). How reading research can inform mathematics difficulties: The search for the core deficit. *Journal of Learning Disabilities, 38*(4), 313–317.

Compton, D.L., Davis, C.J., DeFries, J.C., Gayan, J., & Olson, R.K. (2001). Genetic and environmental influences on reading and RAN: An overview of results from the Colorado Twin Study. In M. Wolf (Ed.), *Conference proceedings of the Dyslexia Research Foundation Conference in Extraordinary Brain Series: Time, fluency, and developmental dyslexia* (pp. 277–303). Baltimore: York Press.

DeFries, J.C., & Alarcón, M. (1996). Genetics of specific reading disability. *Mental Retardation and Developmental Disabilities Research Reviews, 2*(1), 39–47.

DeFries, J.C., & Fulker, D.W. (1985). Multiple regression analysis on twin data. *Behavior Genetics, 15,* 467–473.

DeFries, J.C., & Fulker, D.W. (1988). Multiple regression analysis of twin data: Etiology of deviant scores versus individual differences. *Acta Geneticae Medicae et Gemellologicae, 37,* 205–216.

Dehaene, S. (1996). The organization of brain activations in number comparisons: Event-related potentials and the additive factors methods. *Journal of Cognitive Neuroscience, 8,* 47–68.

Dehaene, S., & Cohen, L. (1995). Towards an anatomical and functional model of number processing. *Mathematical Cognition, 1,* 83–120.

Dick, D.M., Aliev, F., Bierut, L., Goate, A., Rice, J., Hinrichs, A., et al. (2005). Linkage analyses of IQ in the Collaborative Study on the Genetics of Alcoholism (COGA) sample. *Behavior Genetics, 36*(1), 77–86.

Fisher, S.E., & DeFries, J.C. (2002). Developmental dyslexia: Genetic dissection of a complex cognitive trait. *Nature Reviews Neuroscience, 3*, 767–780.

Fletcher, J.M. (2005). Predicting math outcomes: Reading predictors and comorbidity. *Journal of Learning Disabilities, 38*(4), 308–312.

Gayan, J., & Olson, R.K. (2001). Genetic and environmental influences on orthographic and phonological skills in children with reading disabilities. *Developmental Neuropsychology, 20* (2), 487–511.

Gayan, J., & Olson, R.K. (2003). Genetic and environmental influences on individual differences in printed word recognition. *Journal of Experimental Child Psychology, 84*, 97–123.

Geary, D.C. (2004). Mathematics and learning disability. *Journal of Learning Disabilities, 37*(1), 4–15.

Geary, D.C., Hamson, C.O., & Hoard, M. K. (2000). Numerical and arithmetical cognition: A longitudinal study of process and concept deficits in children with learning disability. *Journal of Experimental Child Psychology, 77*, 236–263.

Grigorenko, E.L. (2005). A conservative meta-analysis of linkage and linkage-association studies of developmental dyslexia. *Scientific Studies of Reading, 9*(3), 285–316.

Hecht, S.A., Torgesen, J.K., Wagner, R.K., & Rashotte, C.A. (2001). The relations between phonological processing abilities and emerging individual differences in mathematical computational skills: A longitudinal study from second to fifth grades. *Journal of Experimental Child Psychology, 79*(2), 192–227.

Hirschhorn, J.N., & Daly, M.J. (2005). Genome-wide association studies for common diseases and complex traits. *Nature Reviews Genetics, 6*, 108.

Husén, T. (1959). *Psychological twin research.* Stockholm: Almqvist & Wiksell.

Jastak, M., & Wilkinson, G. (1984). *Wide Range Achievement Test—Revised.* Wilmington, DE: Jastak Associates.

Jordan, N.C., & Hanich, L.B. (2003). Characteristics of children with moderate math deficiencies: A longitudinal perspective. *Learning Disabilities Research and Practice, 18*(4), 213–221.

Jordan, N.C., & Montani, T.O. (1997). Cognitive arithmetic and problem solving: A comparison of children with specific and general mathematics difficulties. *Journal of Learning Disabilities, 30*(6), 624–634.

Knopik, V.S., Alarcón, M., & DeFries, J.C. (1997). Comorbidity of mathematics and reading deficits: Evidence for a genetic etiology. *Behavior Genetics, 27*, 447–453.

Knopik, V.S., Alarcón, M., & DeFries, J.C. (1998). Common and specific gender influences on individual differences in reading performance: A twin study. *Personality and Individual Differences, 25*(2), 269–277.

Kovas, Y., Harlaar, N., Petrill, S.A., & Plomin, R. (2005). 'Generalist genes' and mathematics in 7-year-old twins. *Intelligence, 33*, 473–489.

Light, J.G., DeFries, J.C., & Olson, R.K. (1998). Multivariate behavioural genetic analysis of achievement and cognitive measures in reading-disabled and control twin pairs. *Human Biology, 70*, 215–237.

Loehlin, J.C., & Nichols, R.C. (1976). *Heredity, environment, and personality: A study of 850 sets of twins.* Austin: University of Texas.

Martin, N.G., & Eaves, L.J. (1977). The genetical analysis of covariance structure. *Heredity, 38*, 79–95.

Mazzocco, M.M.M., & Myers, G.F. (2003). Complexities in identifying and defining mathematics learning disability in the primary school-age years. *Annals of Dyslexia, 53*, 218–253.

McArdle, J.J. (1986). Latent variable growth within behavior genetic models. *Behavior Genetics, 16*(1), 163–200.

McArdle, J.J., Prescott, C.A., Hamagami, F., & Horn, J.L. (1998). A contemporary method for developmental-genetic analyses of age changes in intellectual abilities. *Developmental Neuropsychology, 14*(1), 69–114.

McCartney, K., Harris, M.J., & Bernieri, F. (1990). Growing up and growing apart: A developmental meta-analysis of twin studies. *Psychological Bulletin, 107,* 226–237.

McGue, M., Bouchard, T.J., Jr., Iacono, W.G., & Lykken, D.T. (1993). Behavioral genetics of cognitive ability: A lifespan perspective. In R. Plomin & G.E. McClearn (Eds.), *Nature, nurture, and psychology.* Washington, DC: American Psychological Association.

McGue, M., & Christensen, K. (2002). The heritability of level and rate-of-change in cognitive functioning in Danish twins aged 70 years and older. *Experimental Aging Research, 28(4),* 435–451.

Molko, N., Cachia, A., Riviere, D., Mangin, J.F., Bruandet, M., Le Bihan, D., et al. (2003). Functional and structural alterations of the intraparietal sulcus in a developmental dyscalculia of genetic origin. *Neuron, 40,* 847–858.

Neale, M.C., & McArdle, J.J. (2000). Structured latent growth curves for twin data. *Twin Research, 3,* 165–177.

Norton, N., Williams, N.M., O'Donovan, M.C., & Owen, M.J. (2004). DNA pooling as a tool for large-scale association studies in complex traits. *Annals of Medicine, 36,* 146–152.

Oliver, B., Harlaar, N., Hayiou-Thomas, M.E., Kovas, Y., Walker, S.O., Petrill, S.A., et al. (2004). A twin study of teacher-reported mathematics performance and low performance in 7-year-olds. *Journal of Educational Psychology, 96,* 504–517.

Olson, R.K., Forsberg, H., & Wise, B. (1994). Genes, environment, and the development of orthographic skills. In V.W. Berninger (Ed.), *The varieties of orthographic knowledge I: Theoretical and developmental issues* (pp. 27–71). Dordrecht, The Netherlands: Kluwer Academic Publishers.

Olson, R.K., Gillis, J.J., Rack, J.P., DeFries, J.C., & Fulker, D.W. (1991). Confirmatory factor analysis of word recognition and process measures in the Colorado Reading Project. *Reading and Writing, 3,* 235–248.

Paterson, S.J., Brown, J.H., Gsödl, M.K., Johnson, M.H., & Karmiloff-Smith, A. (1999). Cognitive modularity and genetic disorders. *Science, 286*(5448), 2355–2358.

Petrill, S.A., Deater-Deckard, K., Thompson, L.A., DeThorne, L.S., Schatschneider, C., & Vandenbergh, D.J. (in press). Reading skills in early readers: Genetic and shared environmental influences. *Journal of Learning Disabilities.*

Petrill, S.A., Deater-Deckard, K., Thompson, L.A., Schatschneider, C., & DeThorne, L.S. (in press). Longitudinal genetic analysis of early reading: The Western Reserve Reading Project. *Reading and Writing.*

Petrill, S.A., Johansson, B., Pedersen, N.L., Berg, S., Plomin, R., Ahern, F., et al. (2001). Low cognitive functioning in nondemented 80+-year-old twins is not heritable. *Intelligence, 29,* 75–83.

Petrill, S.A., Lipton, P.A., Hewitt, J.K., Cherny, S.S., Plomin, R., Corley, R., et al. (2004). Genetic and environmental contributions to general cognitive ability through the first 16 years of life. *Developmental Psychology, 40,* 805–812.

Petrill, S.A., Saudino, K.J., Cherny, S.S., Emde, R.N., Fulker, D.W., Hewitt, J.K., et al. (1998). Exploring the genetic and environmental etiology of high general cognitive ability in 14 to 36 month-old twins. *Child Development, 69,* 68–74.

Petrill, S.A., Saudino, K.J., Cherny, S.S., Emde, R.N., Hewitt, J.K., Fulker, D.W., et al. (1997). Exploring the genetic etiology of low general cognitive ability from 14 to 36 months. *Developmental Psychology, 33,* 544–548.

Petrill, S.A., & Wilkerson, B. (2000). Intelligence and achievement: A behavioral genetic perspective. *Educational Psychology Review, 12,* 195–199.

Plomin, R. (2001). Genetic factors contributing to learning and language delays and disabilities. *Child and Adolescent Psychiatric Clinics of North America, 10,* 259–277.

Plomin, R., & Bergeman, C.S. (1991). The nature of nurture: Genetic influence on "environmental" measures. *Behavioral and Brain Sciences, 14*(3), 373–427.

Plomin, R., & DeFries, J.C. (1979). Multivariate behavioral genetic analysis of twin data on scholastic abilities. *Behavior Genetics, 9,* 505–517.

Plomin, R., DeFries, J.C., McClearn, G.E., & McGuffin, P. (2001). *Behavior genetics* (4th ed.). New York: Worth.

Plomin, R., Fulker, D.W., Corley, R., & DeFries, J.C. (1997). Nature, nurture, and cognitive development from 1 to 16 years: A parent-offspring adoption study. *Psychological Science, 8*(6), 442–447.

Plomin, R., Kennedy, J.K.J., & Craig, I.W. (in press). The quest for quantitative trait loci associated with intelligence. *Intelligence.*

Plomin, R., & Kovas, Y. (2005). Generalist genes and learning disabilities. *Psychological Bulletin, 131*(4), 592–617.

Plomin, R., & Thompson, L.A. (1993). Genetics and high cognitive ability. In *Ciba Foundation Symposium: 178. The origins and development of high ability* (pp. 67–84). Oxford, England: John Wiley & Sons.

Posthuma, D., Luciano, M., Geus, E.J., Wright, M.J., Slagboom, P.E., Montgomery, G.W., et al. (2005). A genomewide scan for intelligence identifies quantitative trait loci on 2q and 6p. *American Journal of Human Genetics, 77*(2), 318–326.

Reynolds, C.A., Finkel, D., Gatz, M., & Pedersen, N.L. (2002). Sources of influence on rate of cognitive change over time in Swedish twins: An application of latent growth. *Experimental Aging Research, 28*(4), 407–433.

Shalev, R.S., Manor, O., & Gross-Tsur, V. (2005). Developmental dyscalculia: A prospective six-year follow-up. *Developmental Medicine and Child Neurology, 47,* 121–125.

Sham, P., Bader, J.S., Craig, I., O'Donovan, M., & Owen, M. (2002). DNA pooling: A tool for large-scale association studies. *Nature Review Genetics, 3,* 862–871.

Spinath, F.M., Harlaar, N., Ronald, A., & Plomin, R. (2004). Substantial genetic influence on mild mental impairment in early childhood. *American Journal on Mental Retardation, 109*(1), 34–43.

Syvanen, A.C. (2005). Toward genome-wide SNP genotyping. *Nature Genetics, 37,* S5–10.

Thomas, D.C., Haile, R.W., & Duggan, D. (2005). Recent developments in genome-wide association scans: A workshop summary and review. *American Journal of Human Genetics, 77,* 337–345.

Thompson, L.A., Detterman, D.K., & Plomin, R. (1991). Associations between cognitive abilities and scholastic achievement: Genetic overlap but environmental differences. *Psychological Science, 2,* 158–165.

Wadsworth, S.J., DeFries, J.C., Fulker, D.W., & Plomin, R. (1995). Covariation among measures of cognitive ability and academic achievement in the Colorado Adoption Project: Sibling analysis. *Personality and Individual Differences, 18,* 63–73.

Part III

Additional Influences on Math Difficulties

"I do hate sums. There is no greater mistake than to call arithmetic an exact science. There are permutations and aberrations discernible to minds entirely noble like mine; subtle variations which ordinary accountants fail to discover; hidden laws of number which it requires a mind like mine to perceive. For instance, if you add a sum from the bottom up, and then from the top down, the result is always different."
— Mrs. LaTouche

variety of factors can moderate if not mediate the successful learning of mathematical concepts and skills. These include math anxiety, motivation, gender, and cultural factors, among others. The two chapters in this section examine these topics in detail, provide appraisals of the research literature in each of these areas, examine alternative explanations for some of the findings, propose directions for future research, and discuss the implications of this research for understanding how best to ameliorate math performance that might otherwise be negatively affected by some of these factors.

In Chapter 15, Ashcraft, Krause, and Hopko examine the construct of math anxiety, which they define as the negative emotional reaction experienced by some individuals when put in situations that require mathematical reasoning or problem solving. These feelings of tension, apprehension, or fear can in turn impair mathematical performance. As these authors point out, this anxiety is aroused not only in academic settings when one is learning math or taking a math test but also at home and in other everyday settings (e.g., when trying to balance a checkbook). In their review of the relevant research, these authors point out that we still know comparatively little about the antecedents of math anxiety, and that our limited knowledge in this regard constrains efforts to improve of our understanding of this problem. How can one measure math anxiety? Currently, researchers assess it by means of a questionnaire in which participants rate their perceived level of anxiety in everyday situations, such as taking a math test or trying to figure out if they have been overcharged on their restaurant bill. Past research using such measures has demonstrated that students with high math anxiety take fewer math courses, earn lower grades in the classes they do take, and demonstrate lower math achievement and aptitude than do their counterparts with low math anxiety. Based on their own research, Ashcraft and colleagues estimate that approximately 17% of the population can be classified as high in math anxiety. These authors conclude that although math anxiety does not qualify as the same kind of disability factor as some of the other syndromes and disorders described elsewhere in this volume, it does appear to function like a genuine math learning disability in that its manifestation includes poor math achievement, at least under certain circumstances.

In Chapter 16, Royer and Walles examine the influences of gender, ethnicity, and motivation on math performance. With respect to the role of gender, these authors point out that although the evidence shows negligible mean differences in math test performance in elementary and secondary school students, there are differences in the variability of test performance, with males performing better than females at the upper end of the distribution but worse than females at the lower end. Furthermore, Royer and Walles indicate that, according to the research literature, the math grades of females exceed those of males from elementary school right through the college years. After discussing research on the topic of math performance in various ethnic groups, these authors review evidence showing that White students consistently outperform Black and Hispanic or Latino/Latina students on national math achievement tests during the elementary and secondary school years, but they also note that the gap between ethnic groups has been declining since the 1970s. They then examine various potential explanations of this shrinking gap, focusing particularly on changes in mathematics course-taking patterns. Royer and Walles also review the shifting patterns in math-related motivational disposition and self-esteem as children progress in school, finding not only that these changes are complex but also that the degree of change in these patterns varies as a function of both gender and ethnicity. Finally, these authors call for research aimed at sorting out some of the conflicting explanations for the variations in mathematics performance that have been associated with gender, ethnicity, and shifting patterns of motivation and self-esteem.

REFERENCE

LaTouche, Mrs. (1924). *Mathematical Gazette, 12.*

Chapter 15

Is Math Anxiety a Mathematical Learning Disability?

Mark H. Ashcraft, Jeremy A. Krause, and Derek R. Hopko

+ +

I n this chapter we address the topic of math anxiety, the negative emotional reaction some people experience when placed in situations that require mathematical reasoning or problem solving. We review the research in this area, focusing on the personal, educational, and cognitive consequences of math anxiety. We also discuss some of the gaps in the literature, especially in the understanding of precursors and etiological factors related to math anxiety and how this lack of knowledge limits efforts to understand math anxiety better. We conclude by posing the question of whether the accumulated evidence about math anxiety justifies its inclusion in the list of genuine mathematical learning disabilities that are discussed throughout this book.

A BRIEF REVIEW OF MATH ANXIETY RESEARCH

Math anxiety is typically defined as a negative emotional reaction to math and to situations in which math reasoning or problem solving must be performed. In a foundational paper on the topic, Richardson and Suinn described it as ". . . a feeling of tension and anxiety that interferes with the manipulation of numbers and the solving of mathematical problems in a wide variety of ordinary life and academic situations" (1972, p. 551). Math anxiety reactions vary from mild states described as apprehension or dislike

We wish to thank Christopher Kearney for several useful conversations about social anxiety and possible etiological factors.

to genuine fear or dread (McLeod, 1994). In fact, some have argued that math anxiety fits the classic definition of a phobia (e.g., Faust, 1992), in that it is a state anxiety reaction, shows elevated cognitive or physiological arousal, and is a stimulus- and situation-specific learned fear.

This anxiety is aroused in both everyday and academic settings, disrupting activities such as balancing one's checkbook or figuring change, studying or learning math, and taking a classroom or standardized math test. Math anxiety reactions are often on display in educational settings. Indeed, one of the earliest papers on the topic was an anecdotal report by Gough (1954), who noted that several of her female students exhibited emotional difficulties with math and were in fact failing their math course despite normal academic progress in other areas. These reactions are occasionally on display even in lab experiments on seemingly simple, elementary school math tasks (e.g., Ashcraft, 2002).

The first important empirical paper on math anxiety was by Dreger and Aiken (1957) on "number anxiety" among college students. The paper was important for several reasons. Dreger and Aiken were apparently the first researchers to conduct a genuine empirical investigation of the topic. Their review mentioned psychoanalytic viewpoints, in which "failure in arithmetic may be related to maternal overprotection" (e.g., Klein, 1949), and the generally accepted notion that emotional factors may disrupt mastery of mathematics (e.g., Schonell, 1937). They also noted, however, that "almost no controlled research has been attempted in the realm of emotional problems associated with arithmetic and mathematics" (p. 344).

A major contribution of this paper, an obvious step in retrospect, concerned the assessment of math anxiety. Dreger and Aiken added three questions about emotional reactions to math to the Taylor Manifest Anxiety Scale (e.g., "Many times when I see a math problem I just 'freeze up'"; Taylor, 1953). This was apparently the first attempt, however limited, to introduce standardized assessment into the study of math anxiety.

The most prominent subsequent development in the math anxiety literature was the publication of Richardson and Suinn's (1972) Mathematics Anxiety Rating Scale (MARS), the first full-length assessment tool for math anxiety. The MARS was a 98-item test in which subjects rated (from 1, *not at all*, to 5, *very much*) how anxious they would feel in a variety of academic and everyday math situations, such as opening a math textbook or figuring a restaurant bill they think was miscalculated. An individual's score on the MARS was simply the sum of the ratings across all 98 items; scores thus ranged from 98 to 490.

The MARS immediately became the test of choice in math anxiety research because of the wide range of relevant situations it tested and the reassuring psychometric data presented; for instance, the 2-week test–retest reliability of the test was .85 (e.g., Brush, 1978). As an example of its popularity, in two important meta-analyses providing the most comprehensive summaries of what was known about math anxiety—one considering only research with pre-college samples (Ma, 1999) and one also including college samples (Hembree, 1990)—well over half of the analyzed studies used either the MARS or MARS-A, a revised version suitable for adolescents.

Subsequent research has used either the original MARS or one of its descendants. For example, in our work (e.g., Ashcraft & Kirk, 2001) we have used an abbreviated, 25-item version of the MARS (which we termed the sMARS, for shortened MARS), developed by Alexander and Martray (1989). The test has a more sensible scoring procedure than the original MARS (e.g., total scores range from 0 to 100), and it does not appear to sacrifice reliability for the gains in efficiency in administration. Hopko, Mahadevan, Bare, and Hunt (2003) have published an even shorter test, the 9-item Abbreviated Math Anxiety Scale (AMAS). The test has a 2-week test–retest reliability of .85 and a substantial correlation with the MARS and sMARS. Hopko and colleagues's factor analysis revealed two underlying factors, *learning math anxiety* and *math evaluation anxiety,* which together accounted for 70% of the overall variance in test scores. Given its high reliability and a known factor structure, the AMAS would appear to be the best current test for assessing math anxiety. In passing, we note that the question we always ask our subjects ("On a scale from 1 to 10, how math anxious are you?") has correlated between .40 and .85 with their sMARS scores. Apparently, one does not need to probe too deeply to discover a person's math anxiety status. Likewise, in our culture, it is deemed perfectly acceptable to confess openly—and certainly in a research setting—that one is math anxious.

THE PREVALENCE OF MATH ANXIETY

Rather surprisingly, no research that we are aware of has ventured to make claims about how math anxious an individual must be before being designated as "high math anxious." In our own research, we have adopted a purely statistical definition of high math anxiety: individuals whose math anxiety scores are at least one standard deviation (*SD*) above the mean (and our low-math-anxious groups are composed of individuals whose scores are at least one *SD* below the mean). Under the assumption that math anxiety scores are normally distributed, this definition means that roughly 17% of the population is high math anxious. Note, however, that even individuals who fall into our medium anxiety group, within the range defined as the mean +/−.5 *SD*, display performance differences compared with those in the low anxiety group. Unfortunately, the field lacks additional research that examines cutoff scores with respect to, for example, *Diagnostic and Statistical Manual of Mental Disorders, Fourth Edition (DSM-IV-TR)* (American Psychiatric Association, 2000), criteria for disorders.

THE CORRELATES OF MATH ANXIETY: PERSONAL AND EDUCATIONAL CONSEQUENCES

The hypotheses that have occupied the majority of researchers in the field of math anxiety were well articulated in the original Dreger and Aiken (1957) paper. It is actually rather remarkable how focused the first empirical study in the area was on what are still viewed as central questions to the field and how its results have been replicated and upheld, without serious modifications, for such a long period of time. Dreger and Aiken hypothesized, first, that math anxiety was conceptually distinct from general anxiety, predicting that math anxiety would overlap only partially with general anxiety. Second, they suggested that math anxiety was not an intellectual factor but an emotional one. As such, they predicted that math anxiety would not be systematically related to general intelligence once the contribution of quantitative scores was removed from IQ scores. Third, they proposed that math anxiety would be a disruptive factor in students' academic performance in math coursework.

By the time of Hembree's (1990) meta-analysis, fully 151 studies had tested some or all of these three primary predictions (see also Ma, 1999). Table 15.1, expanded from Ashcraft and Ridley (2005), is organized around Dreger and Aiken's three primary hypotheses and summarizes some of the more important findings in the literature. These are discussed next.

Hypothesis I: Math Anxiety Is Separate From General Anxiety

Section I of Table 15.1 shows the average correlations between math anxiety (as measured by the MARS) and scores on other anxiety assessments. Based on this evidence, it seems clear that Dreger and Aiken's prediction that math anxiety is distinct from general anxiety has been repeatedly and consistently supported; the average correlation between math anxiety and general anxiety is .35 (there are apparently no published data on the incidence of comorbidity), and .38 between math and trait anxiety. The most strongly related (.52) form of anxiety is test anxiety, another situation-specific, state anxiety reaction.

Early debates in the literature about math anxiety's status as a distinct construct eventually faded in the face of such evidence. For instance, in one research program that examined whether math anxiety was distinct from general anxiety (Dew, Galassi, & Galassi, 1983), correlations between math anxiety and other forms of anxiety were in the range shown in Sec-

Table 15.1. Selected correlations with math anxiety

Correlation with MARS[a]	r
I. Measures of anxiety	
Test anxiety	.52
General anxiety	.35
Trait anxiety	.38
State anxiety	.42
AMAS[b]	.85
Rated math anxiety[c]	.81
II. Measures of intelligence/aptitude	
IQ score	−.17
Verbal aptitude/achievement (pre-college)	−.06
III. Measures of math achievement	
Math achievement (pre-college)	−.34
Math achievement (college)	−.31
High school math grades	−.30
College math grades	−.27
IV. Measures of math attitudes	
Enjoyment of math (pre-college)	−.75
Enjoyment of math (college)	−.47
Rated enjoyment[c] (college only)	−.74
Self-confidence in math (pre-college)	−.82
Self-confidence in math (college)	−.65
Motivation	−.64
Usefulness of math	−.37
Math teachers	−.46
Computers	−.32
V. Measures of avoidance	
Extent of high school math	−.31
Number of high school math courses[c]	−.45
Intent to enroll in more math (college)	−.32

Sources: All other correlations from Hembree, 1990, pp. 38–40.
[a]Mathematics Anxiety Rating Scale (Richardson & Suinn, 1972, p. 181).
[b]Abbreviated Math Anxiety Scale (Hopko, Mahadevan, Bare, & Hunt, 2003).
[c]Ashcraft & Kirk, 2001, p. 233.

tion I of Table 15.1. In contrast, they found correlations among several different measures of math anxiety ranging from .50 to .80; in Hopko and colleagues (2003), the AMAS measure correlated .85 with the MARS. Based on this evidence, Hembree commented that even for the most highly correlated test anxiety factor, "only 37 percent of one construct's variance is predictable from the variance of the other" (1990, p. 45), compared with shared variance among the math anxiety measures of up to 72%. In other words, fully two thirds of the variance in math anxiety is unexplained by test anxiety, the most strongly correlated form of anxiety. In contrast, fully two thirds of the variance among different math anxiety assessments is shared.

Hypothesis II: Math Anxiety Is Not Related to Intelligence

Section II of Table 15.1 shows the correlations between math anxiety and measures of intelligence. The telling result is the weak correlation between math anxiety and overall IQ scores (-.17), which decreases to a nonsignificant (-.06) relationship when the math sections are deleted from the IQ assessments, that is, when verbal achievement or aptitude scores are correlated with the MARS. Even Dreger and Aiken (1957), who found the same relationship, noted that this result rules out the simplest etiological explanation for math anxiety, low intelligence. Standard definitions of learning disabilities have often relied on just such discrepancies, of course—for example, the discrepancy between a student's aptitude or achievement in math and either reading or some more general aptitude/achievement (but see Chapter 2). In contrast, it should be noted that test anxiety may share a much stronger relationship with performance IQ score as measured by the Wechsler Adult Intelligence Scale-III (WAIS-III) (Wechsler, 1991). In regression analyses that assessed the relations of test, math, state, and trait anxiety to IQ score, only test anxiety was found to be a significant predictor of performance on the letter–number sequencing and digit-span subtests of the WAIS-III (Hopko, Armento, & Hunt, 2005).

Hypothesis III: Highly Math Anxious Individuals Will Score Poorly on Math Tests

Dreger and Aiken (1957) collected their large sample data ($n = 704$) from a freshman-level university math class. Grades in the course correlated −.44 with number anxiety (−.51 for a group of 40 participants who were tested in a follow-up study). Section III of Table 15.1 shows that the correlations between math anxiety and a variety of performance measures, including class grades and standardized tests, were generally lower than these values in Dreger and Aiken's study, but certainly they show the same general relationship. As students' math anxiety increases, there is a significant tendency for high school and college math grades to decline and for scores on standardized tests of math achievement to be lower, as well (e.g., Betz, 1978; but see the section to follow on the difficult issue of testing math achievement among math-anxious individuals).

Attitudes About Math and Avoidance of Math

Section IV of Table 15.1 shows correlations between math anxiety and various tests examining attitudes about math. Although the relationships are not particularly surprising, they are worrisome in terms of personal and educational attainment. In general, individuals with higher levels of math anxiety express more negative attitudes about math and report both lower enjoyment of math and lower self-confidence in math. As Section V of Table 15.1 shows, comparable relationships can be found between math anxiety and measures of math avoidance, in particular avoidance of math in school. For example, math anxiety correlates −.31 with the extent of enrollment in high school math and −.32 with the intent to enroll in college math.

When considered in light of the correlations between math anxiety and grades or achievement scores, this evidence leads to a particularly poor prognosis. Higher levels of math anxiety are accompanied by poorer attitudes about math and poorer attitudes about one's own ability to learn math. Higher levels of math anxiety are also accompanied by lower grades in math classes, lower intent to enroll in math classes, and in fact, lower incidence of enrollment. In short, math-anxious individuals take fewer math classes and perform more poorly in the classes they do take. A straightforward deduction, then, is that high-math-anxious individuals learn less math, that their mastery of math is lower than that of their low-anxious peers. These relationships are all correlational and so, of course, do not permit straightforward conclusions regarding causation. Nonetheless, given the elective nature of much of the high school and college math curriculum, it does seem very likely that poor attitudes about math, including views about its usefulness, play an important role in students' self-regulated exposure to math. Putting it simply, if one dislikes math and feels that one is poor at math, then one probably does not enroll in math beyond basic graduation requirements.

Several researchers have characterized this general pattern as depicting avoidance, certainly a characteristic of many phobias. In short, because graduation requirements permit it, highly math anxious individuals avoid math. The overall pattern is captured well by Fennema's (1989) Autonomous Learning Behavior model, in which external influences play a strong role in shaping one's internal attitudes. For example, people may accept or endorse stereotyped beliefs about women and math or general cultural attitudes that math is hard, somewhat optional, and a matter of skill rather than persistence and effort. Such attitudes, along with internal influences like low self-confidence in math, have an impact on an individual's autonomous learning behaviors, such as spending additional time on homework, asking questions in math class, and deciding to take additional math courses. These behaviors—or rather, their absence—then affect one's ultimate performance in terms of lower mastery. The term *avoidance* captures the outcomes quite well: Highly math anxious individuals avoid math and math settings when possible and avoid commitment to the setting when the setting itself (such as a required class) cannot be avoided.

Gender Effects in Math and Math Anxiety

Conventional wisdom, as Ashcraft and Ridley (2005) noted, suggests that there are strong effects of gender on math and math anxiety. Furthermore, a widespread view is that math is a male-dominated field—again, a view based on conventional wisdom. Despite the popularity of these views, the empirical evidence for them is quite mixed and inconsistent (see Geary, 1994, for a review). As an example, although "everyone knows" that males outperform females on math tasks, there are very few consistent or strong gender effects in the literature (Hyde, 2005). Girls often perform better than boys in basic arithmetic studies (Hyde, Fennema, & Lamon, 1990; Royer, Tronsky, Chan, Jackson, & Marchant, 1999), although in industrialized societies, boys do tend to show an advantage on math achievement tests. Gender effects favoring males tend to be stronger in studies that test more select groups of subjects, for instance, mathematically gifted children (Benbow, Lubinski, Shea, & Eftekhari-Sanjani, 2000) or college students (Hyde, Fennema, Ryan, Frost, & Hopp, 1990). In our work with several surveys of math attitudes, participants of neither gender agreed with the stereotypical view that math is a male-dominated subject (Ashcraft & Kirk, 2001), although this may have been due to participants' reluctance to endorse such views.

Indeed, recent patterns of enrollments and graduation suggest that if the stereotypical views were correct at some point in history—for example, the gender differentials in math enrollments and selection of math and science fields for college majors (e.g., Dick & Rallis, 1991)—they no longer are. National Science Foundation data show that females now earn 50% of bachelor's degrees in science and engineering and 47% of natural science and mathematics bachelor's degrees; they make up 48% of graduate students in the natural, behavioral, and social sciences (cf. 34% 20 years ago; see Mervis, 2003).

Thus, a curious paradox exists. Although it is no longer the case that females represent a small minority of enrollments in math and science, prevailing attitudes and stereotypes hold that females are especially poor at math, seek less exposure to math and science, and avoid degree and career paths that involve math. Females themselves may be especially prone to holding such attitudes. In several studies, researchers have investigated "stereotype threat" effects among females. In such studies, participants are told first that they will be completing a math test for the study, and second, that the females will probably do more poorly on the test than the males. With the stereotype threat thus aroused, females in fact demonstrate depressed levels of performance on the math task (e.g., Beilock, Rydell, McConnell, & Carr, 2003; similar effects have been found with racial stereotypes). The obvious interpretation is that females' performance suffers because the stereotype matches their own attitudes and beliefs.

The literature on gender and math anxiety also leads to mixed conclusions. In our own work, females are often overrepresented in the high-math-anxious group and underrepresented in the low anxious group, with groups being defined statistically as described earlier (e.g., Ashcraft & Faust, 1994; Faust, Ashcraft, & Fleck, 1996). Hembree's (1990) data indicated that females scored a nearly constant 20 points higher in math anxiety scores than males from sixth grade through college. He remarked, however, that "the higher levels do not seem to translate into more depressed performance or to greater mathematics avoidance" (p. 45). On the other hand, Ma (1999) found a statistically significant but trivially small gender effect on the relationship between math anxiety and achievement.

THE CONFOUND BETWEEN MATH ANXIETY AND ACHIEVEMENT

The negative relationship between math anxiety and math achievement, the −.34 correlation for grades 5 through 12, for example, is deceptively plausible in our view. That is, it makes perfectly good sense that math achievement scores would be inversely related to math anxiety, based on avoiding math courses and getting lower grades in the courses that are taken. This would surely set the stage for lower math achievement scores. The "deceptive" part, however, is that the relationship between math anxiety and achievement is considerably more complex than the correlation suggests and is considerably more troublesome for researchers than is often recognized.

To begin with, it must be the case that math anxiety along with poor attitudes about math will influence a student's learning in math class because both anxiety and attitudes will influence factors like attention, motivation, and diligence. This may also mean that individuals with high math anxiety learn less in class, because they experience the negative effects of math anxiety during class.

A plausible alternative hypothesis is that the math anxiety reaction is most disruptive during testing or other high-pressure situations. This hypothesis does not deny the role of attitudes in the attention, motivation, and diligence aspects of learning classroom math, of course. It does suggest, however, that the online math anxiety reaction is significantly disruptive only when there is pressure either to perform well, as in achievement testing, or to perform under pressure, for example, under time or social pressure or both.

As Ashcraft and Ridley (2005) noted, this explanation extends to the testing of achievement as well, another one of the complexities involved in the "higher anxiety, lower achievement" relationship. The simple conclusion about math anxiety and achievement—that one is lower when the other is higher—ignores the very real likelihood that the observed achievement scores themselves are depressed by the math anxiety aroused by the test itself. After all, achievement or aptitude testing is usually high-stakes testing, and almost invariably performed under time pressure. It would actually be quite unusual for such a testing situation *not* to arouse math anxiety. (See the section to follow on cognitive consequences.)

Consistent with such an explanation, Hembree (1990) reported that interventions shown to be effective in reducing math anxiety were also accompanied by significant improvements in math achievement scores, bringing individuals up to levels approaching those of low anxiety individuals. Because the interventions did not include instruction in math per se, one can only conclude that the original low achievement scores were anxiety-induced underestimates of participants' true math achievement.

A final complexity in the math anxiety–math achievement relationship involves the actual math content under consideration. The simple interpretation is that the relationship is universal, that it affects all levels and types of math. This is a common understanding of the negative correlation between anxiety and achievement. We encountered this in our early experimental work when testing college adults on two-column addition performance (Ashcraft & Faust, 1994). We found significant anxiety group differences, with slower reaction times and higher error rates for the high-math-anxiety group, especially when carrying was involved. Critics argued that the effect was just as (or more) easily interpreted as a competence or achievement effect because lower math achievement is typical of high-math-anxious individuals.

In response, we demonstrated in two ways that the confound between math anxiety and competence/achievement was not universal. First, we tested participants on the same math content as had been used in the laboratory task, but in paper-and-pencil format with no time pressure. We found equivalent performance across the anxiety groups (e.g., Faust et al., 1996), illustrating that with the more leisurely written form of testing, even the high anxious participants had the basic knowledge necessary to perform well in the timed laboratory task. Second, we administered a standard test of math achievement, the Wide Range Achievement Test-Revised (WRAT-3; Jastak Associates, 1993) to a large sample of undergraduates. After finding the typical correlation between participants' math anxiety scores and their scores on the WRAT-3, we then scored the WRAT-3 on a line-by-line basis, taking advantage of the structure of the test itself (line-by-line increases in the difficulty of the math content). Only the later lines on the test, with problems involving fractions, long division, unknowns, and so forth, showed differences varying with math anxiety. The earlier lines, the ones testing the whole-number arithmetic that we had used in our laboratory tasks, showed no anxiety effects at all; in fact, all groups were at the ceiling in terms of accuracy on these problems.

Clearly, the negative relationship between math anxiety and math achievement or competence is not universal, that is, math anxiety does not affect all levels of math content. Just as clearly, it remains difficult to disentangle anxiety and competence effects as the math content grows more and more difficult.

COGNITIVE CONSEQUENCES OF MATH ANXIETY

We began investigating the possible effects of math anxiety on cognition (Ashcraft & Faust, 1994; Faust et al., 1996) by using the laboratory tasks and manipulations that were typical of the general mathematical cognition literature. Four results bear mentioning here. First, we found the benchmark "problem size effect," an increase in latencies and errors as problems grow larger (Zbrodoff & Logan, 2005), but this effect did not differ across math anxiety groups in simple addition or multiplication. Responses to incorrect problems in the true/false task did show math anxiety effects, however. When the proposed (but wrong) answer deviated more from the correct answer, for instance, $9 + 7 = 39$ versus $9 + 7 = 18$, participants typically responded more rapidly and with fewer errors, based on the lower plausibility of such answers (Zbrodoff & Logan, 1990). The higher math anxiety groups, however, actually showed *higher* error rates as the proposed answer deviated more from the correct one, as if $9 + 7 = 39$ did not seem particularly implausible. This suggests that the notion of number sense (Dehaene, 1997) might be weak or lacking in those individuals with higher levels of math anxiety.

Third, high-math-anxious individuals often traded accuracy for speed in our tasks; that is, they performed quite rapidly on simple problems but usually at the cost of considerably higher errors. We termed this *local avoidance*, comparable with the global avoidance of math courses and so forth that high-math-anxious individuals show; by speeding through the experiment, these individuals minimized the time they had to spend doing math. Finally, we found that higher levels of math anxiety were associated with considerably slower performance and less accuracy on two-column problems, especially when the arithmetic processes involved carrying or borrowing.

We hypothesized that this final result could be attributed to the involvement of working memory in problem solving. According to this view, two-column problems involve not only retrieval from memory for the individual sums or differences but also carrying, borrowing, rule application, and keeping track of processes necessitated by the larger problems. Such processes are recognized as being considerably slower than simple memory retrieval and considerably more demanding (e.g., Seyler, Kirk, & Ashcraft, 2003), and in fact have long been considered as being highly dependent on working memory (see LeFevre, DeStefano, Coleman, & Shanahan, 2005, for a review). Thus, we developed the hypothesis that highly math anxious individuals showed slower and less-accurate performance on these problems because of a disruption in their working memory processes.

This is not to say that low working memory capacity is necessarily a characteristic of high-math-anxious individuals, although—as we outline below—this might be one of several potential risk factors. Instead, we have pursued a somewhat different hypothesis based on Eysenck's (1992) treatment of cognition and anxiety. Eysenck claims that anxiety disrupts ongoing cognitive processes to the degree that those processes rely on working memory. In this view, anxious individuals devote at least some portion of their working memory to their own anxiety reaction, their worry, intrusive thoughts, concerns over performance evaluation, and the like. The result of this is that working memory is doing two things at once: attending to the cognitive process under investigation and monitoring the anxiety reaction. When the cognitive process demands additional working memory resources, say, because of increased task difficulty, resources are insufficient to support the cognitive processing simultaneously with self-monitoring of the anxiety. We have merely extended this explanation to the specific situation of math-anxious individuals doing math.

Our clearest test of this hypothesis supported the prediction completely. Ashcraft and Kirk (2001) gave participants two-column addition problems, half of them requiring carrying, in a dual-task setting that required holding and then reporting a working memory load (random letters) concurrently with solving the addition problems. When the memory load was heavy (six random letters), errors increased substantially and especially so for problems that required carrying. This pattern was apparent in all three groups, but was especially dramatic in the group with high math-anxiety. In other words, in a task that places heavy demands on working memory, and while performing problems that require considerable working memory resources, the highly math anxious were at a particular disadvantage—they were already consuming some working memory resources with their anxiety reaction, leaving working memory seriously depleted for the arithmetic and memory load tasks. (See Beilock et al., 2003, for similar results using the stereotype threat paradigm.)

This research is based on the idea that working memory contains a finite pool of mental resources that are necessary for difficult cognitive processing (e.g., Baddeley, 1986). A second approach to working memory is also prominent in research, one that views working memory as a system that maintains focus on a task and permits the individual to resist or avoid interference or inhibit attentional responses. As an example, Kane and Engle (2003) found that individuals with low working memory span showed greater interference in the classic Stroop task (in which a word like *RED* is printed in green ink, with instructions to name the ink color). Math anxiety may be functionally the same as low working memory span when anxiety is aroused. For instance, Hopko, McNeil, Gleason, and Rabalais (2002) tested a numerical version of the Stroop task (e.g., one that shows a display of three 4s and asking subjects to say how many digits are on the screen). They found an elevated interference effect among high-math-anxious individuals. We are currently exploring this result further to see how widespread it is across several versions of the regular and numerical versions of the Stroop task.

THE ETIOLOGY OF MATH ANXIETY: SOME PREDICTIONS

Little is known about the onset of math anxiety, and even less is known about the factors that either predispose one toward or cause math anxiety. With only a handful of exceptions (e.g., Gierl & Bisanz, 1995), the bulk of the research on the development of math anxiety has tested school children beginning in the sixth grade. Hembree's analysis showed an increase of approximately 30 points on the MARS from grades 6 to 10 in math anxiety level, followed by a modest decline up through college levels; the pattern was approximately the same for males and females, although females scored roughly 20 points higher in math anxiety at every grade. Regardless of whether math anxiety begins earlier than sixth grade, then, it increases significantly during adolescence and declines only a small amount thereafter.

A surprising number of our subjects across the years have made one of two observations about their own math anxiety. First, a fair number have singled out one particular branch of mathematics—often algebra—as the one that causes them the greatest difficulty. Algebra is often introduced in the middle school years or later, making it difficult to know whether the critical factor is the math content or the age at which that content is introduced. Second, our subjects remark that math anxiety started to be a problem when they were asked to do math in front of the class, such as solving a problem on the blackboard. Such a remark suggests that there may be social reasons behind math anxiety, that is, the embarrassment of revealing one's lack of understanding in front of peers or of being criticized publicly by the teacher.

Although not focusing directly on the topic of math anxiety, a provocative study reports on the consequences of different teaching styles in math classes. Turner and colleagues (2002) documented patterns of student avoidance in math classes that resulted from teachers who conveyed a high demand for correctness but provided little or no cognitive or motivational support during class; for instance, "he often showed annoyance when students gave wrong answers. . . . He held them responsible for their lack of understanding" (p. 102). These researchers concluded that students with such teachers may feel "vulnerable to public displays of incompetence" (p. 101), based on the pattern of avoidance researchers observed, such as students not seeking help with homework or avoiding eye contact with the teacher during class. We speculate that students with such teachers would be more prone to developing math anxiety than those with supportive teachers who provide explanations and maintain motivation.

Math anxiety may be considered a performance-based anxiety disorder (Hopko, McNeil, Zvolensky, & Eifert, 2001), a condition that is functionally similar to anxiety disorders that include social phobia (Newman, Hofmann, Trabert, Roth, & Taylor, 1994) and test anxiety (Mueller, Elser, & Rollack, 1993). This group of anxiety disorders is characterized by anxious responding that presumably is a function of aversive conditioning experiences, social learning processes, the development of maladaptive cognitive schemata, skill deficits, or some combination of these factors. Anxious responding is perceived as occurring in the immediate context of a performance-based setting or possibly in anticipation of having to perform and the potential negative evaluation associated with this behavior.

Defining features of performance-based anxiety disorders generally include 1) *physiological hyperarousal,* elicited in performance-based contexts; 2) *negative cognitions* (e.g., excessive fear of negative evaluation) that occur prior to, during, or following performance; 3) *escape and/or avoidance* of performance-related situations (Faust et al., 1996; Rapee, Sanderson, & Barlow, 1988); and, 4) when an individual cannot avoid or escape, *performance deficits,* which are conceptualized as a function of anxiety-related responding and/or associated skill deficits (Hopko et al., 2001). Although these conditions are not categorized based on performance-related criteria in the *DSM-IV-TR* (American Psychiatric Association, 2000), they represent significant and prevalent clinical problems and frequently co-occur with other disorders (Hembree, 1990; Kessler et al., 1994).

Given the lack of direct information about the etiology of math anxiety, we conclude with several plausible predictions for the development or onset of math anxiety. Based on the conceptualization of math anxiety as a performance-based anxiety disorder, and consistent with an earlier theoretical formulation on etiological factors (Hopko et al., 2001), we believe that multiple pathways may result in the experience of math anxiety and associated performance deficits. Based on the framework highlighted in Figure 15.1, we predict the following:

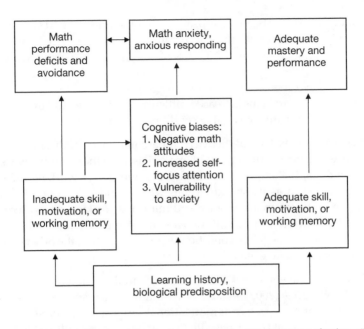

Figure 15.1. A proposed framework for situating math anxiety within the context of various etiological, developmental, and educational factors.

1. Math-anxious responding is a product of some combination of both distal and proximal learning experiences (via social learning and aversive conditioning), biological predisposition toward anxiety (Barlow, 2002), decreased computational skill at more advanced levels of math, cognitive biases that included negative attitudes toward math (Fennema, 1989), increased rumination or self-focused attention, and working memory deficits. Furthermore, the relation between math anxiety and math performance is multifaceted. First, math performance deficits and avoidance may largely be a product of anxious responding, whereby poor performance is directly related to anxiety-related interference insofar as negative cognitions consume available processing resources (i.e., interference models; Eysenck & Calvo, 1992; Sarason, 1984). Second, deficient skill levels may increase the probability of becoming anxious, leading to math performance deficits and avoidance behaviors (i.e., deficit models; Greeno, 1991; Tobias, 1985). Finally, skill deficits may negatively affect performance independent of anxiety level. In contrast, skillful performance on math-related tasks would involve adequate skills, minimal cognitive biases and decreased anxiety, and adequate motivation and approach (rather than avoidance) behavior.

2. Math anxiety will begin to appear in school settings around sixth grade. This is somewhat later than is customarily found for social anxiety or specific phobias (mean of 7.3 years of age and 6.3, respectively, according to Costello, Egger, & Angold, 2004) but would coincide with the increase in difficulty of the math curriculum at the close of the elementary school years. This increased difficulty level also would presumably allow for more direct aversive conditioning experiences.

3. Math anxiety will be particularly apparent among children who experience academic difficulties with math. Based on the cognitive work we have done, this might include students with lower working memory capacity, such as those individuals who would have more difficulty doing multistep math because of diminished working memory capacity. Alternatively, these skill deficits might increase the likelihood of experiencing a negative conditioning event and thus, the onset of math anxiety or a more generalized social phobia.

4. Students who encounter teachers similar to those described in Turner and colleagues (2002)—teachers with a high demand for correctness and little or no cognitive or motivational support during class—should be particularly at risk, especially those who are more vulnerable to performance-based anxiety (e.g., those with lower self-esteem, those with biological vulnerabilities or family history of performance-based anxiety, and those more likely to be emotionally affected by a harsh teaching style). Based on Turner and colleagues's results, we predict a straightforward, positive relationship—the more teacher-induced avoidance, the greater the math anxiety. It seems obvious that students who experience such negative teachers are more likely to avoid advanced math to a greater degree than those who experience more supportive teachers.

5. Because society tolerates such poor attitudes about math and individuals' math mastery (see Chapter 16), and because the *required* curriculum later in high school and college is minimal, we suggest that the general math avoidance seen among math-anxious individuals permits those who develop math anxiety to maintain that response pattern via the process of negative reinforcement. In this circumstance, math-related activities and environments are avoided to reduce physiological and cognitive manifestations of anxiety. Situations that might result in math success are not experienced, thus preventing extinction of the anxiety response.

6. In general, when math-anxious individuals do engage in math-related behavior, an inverse relationship should be evident between math achievement and task complexity. For less complex tasks, skill deficits will be less consequential in eliciting anxious responding and associ-

ated performance deficits. Evaluative concerns also would be less pronounced in such a circumstance. For more advanced math topics, however, we would expect math-anxious individuals to show decreased achievement, largely because of increased performance demands, associated increases in anxiety, and the greater potential for negative evaluation (Eysenck, 1992).

IS MATH ANXIETY A MATHEMATICAL LEARNING DISABILITY?

Math anxiety is related to deliberate avoidance of math, certainly of the math curriculum in high school and college, and also of career paths that rely on math achievement and skill. It compromises people's mastery of math—at least as measured by in-class and standardized tests—to a significant degree. It is associated with poor attitudes concerning math as well as poor self-attitudes, such as low self-esteem with regard to math abilities. It also interferes with math performance, certainly on standardized tests of math achievement but also in laboratory tasks with relatively simple problems like two-column addition.

We do not argue that math anxiety is the same kind of disability factor as some of the other conditions and patterns described in other chapters in this book (although the possibility of comorbidity with those conditions and patterns is worth exploring). Nor do we insist on a discrepancy-based definition of disabilities, which might classify math anxiety as a learning disability. But in some important functional ways, math anxiety does seem to operate like a genuine math learning disability, insofar as the outward manifestation includes poor math achievement under certain circumstances. What may differ are the fundamental performance abilities on very basic tests of numerosity.

Regardless of whether math anxiety is considered a disability or merely a difficulty, consider the following: If we maintain our statistical cutoff for high math anxiety at one *SD* above the mean, roughly 17% of the population would be labeled as high math anxious. Even if we found performance differences only at this level or above, this definition suggests that nearly one fifth of the population experiences high math anxiety. What other syndrome, condition, or circumstance discussed in this book is as widespread and as disruptive—possibly even for a lifetime—as math anxiety, with one fifth of the population at risk? We believe the answer to that question may be "none."

REFERENCES

Alexander, L., & Martray, C. (1989). The development of an abbreviated version of the Mathematics Anxiety Rating Scale. *Measurement and Evaluation in Counseling and Development, 22,* 143–150.

American Psychiatric Association. (2000). *Diagnostic and statistical manual of mental disorders* (4th ed.). Washington, DC: Author.

Ashcraft, M.H. (2002). Math anxiety: Personal, educational, and cognitive consequences. *Current Directions in Psychological Science, 11,* 181–185.

Ashcraft, M.H., & Faust, M.W. (1994). Mathematics anxiety and mental arithmetic performance: An exploratory investigation. *Cognition and Emotion, 8,* 97–125.

Ashcraft, M.H., & Kirk, E.P. (2001). The relationships among working memory, math anxiety, and performance. *Journal of Experimental Psychology: General, 130,* 224–237.

Ashcraft, M.H. & Ridley, K.S. (2005). Math anxiety and its cognitive consequences: A tutorial review. In J.I.D. Campbell (Ed.), *Handbook of mathematical cognition* (pp. 315–327). New York: Psychology Press.

Baddeley, A. (1986). *Working memory.* Oxford: Clarendon Press.

Barlow, D.H. (2002). *Anxiety and its disorders: The nature and treatment of anxiety and panic* (2nd ed.). New York: Guilford Press.

Beilock, S.L., Rydell, R.J., McConnell, A.R., & Carr, T.H. (2003). *Stereotype threat: Is it a threat on working memory capacity?* Manuscript submitted for publication.

Benbow, C.P., Lubinski, D., Shea, D.L., & Eftekhari-Sanjani, H. (2000). Sex differences in mathematical reasoning ability at age 13: Their status 20 years later. *Psychological Science, 11,* 474–479.

Betz, N.E. (1978). Prevalence, distribution, and correlates of math anxiety in college students. *Journal of Counseling Psychology, 25,* 441–448.

Brush, L.R. (1978). A validation study of the Mathematics Anxiety Rating Scale (MARS). *Educational and Psychological Measurement, 38,* 484–489.

Costello, E.G., Egger, H.L., & Angold, A. (2004). Developmental epidemiology of anxiety disorders. In T.H. Ollendick & J.S. Meoch (Eds.), *Phobic and anxiety disorders in children and adolescents: A clinician's guide to effective psychosocial and pharmacological interventions* (pp. 61–91). New York: Oxford University Press.

Dehaene, S. (1997). *The number sense: How the mind creates mathematics.* New York: Oxford University Press.

Dew, K.M.H., Galassi, J.P., & Galassi, M.D. (1983). Mathematics anxiety: Some basic issues. *Journal of Counseling Psychology, 30,* 443–446.

Dick, T.P., & Rallis, S.F. (1991). Factors and influences on high school students' career choices. *Journal for Research in Mathematics Education, 22,* 281–292.

Dreger, R.M., & Aiken, L.R. (1957). The identification of number anxiety in a college population. *Journal of Educational Psychology, 48,* 344–351.

Eysenck, M.W. (1992). *Anxiety: The cognitive perspective.* Mahwah, NJ: Lawrence Erlbaum Associates.

Eysenck, M.W., & Calvo, M.G. (1992). Anxiety and performance: The processing efficiency theory. *Cognition and Emotion, 6,* 409–434.

Faust, M.W. (1992). *Analysis of physiological reactivity in mathematics anxiety.* Unpublished doctoral dissertation, Bowling Green State University, Ohio.

Faust, M.W., Ashcraft, M.H., & Fleck, D.E. (1996). Mathematics anxiety effects in simple and complex addition. *Mathematical Cognition, 2,* 25–62.

Fennema, E. (1989). The study of affect and mathematics: A proposed generic model for research. In D.B. McLeod & V.M Adams (Eds.), *Affect and mathematical problem solving: A new perspective* (pp. 205–219). New York: Springer-Verlag.

Geary, D.C. (1994). *Children's mathematical development: Research and practical applications.* Washington, DC: American Psychological Association.

Gierl, M.J., & Bisanz, J. (1995). Anxieties and attitudes related to mathematics in grades 3 and 6. *Journal of Experimental Education, 63,* 139–158.

Gough, M.F. (1954). Mathemaphobia: Causes and treatments. *Clearing House, 28,* 290–294.

Greeno, J.G. (1991). Number sense as situated knowing in a conceptual domain. *Journal for Research in Mathematics Education, 22,* 170–218.

Hembree, R. (1990). The nature, effects, and relief of mathematics anxiety. *Journal for Research in Mathematics Education, 21,* 33–46.

Hopko, D.R., Armento, M.E.A., & Hunt, M.K. (2005). Attentional task aptitude and performance anxiety. *International Journal of Stress Management, 12,* 425–436.

Hopko, D.R., Mahadevan, R., Bare, R.L., & Hunt, M.A. (2003). The Abbreviated Math Anxiety Scale (AMAS): Construction, validity, and reliability. *Assessment, 10,* 178–182.

Hopko, D.R., McNeil, D.W., Gleason, P.J., & Rabalais, A.E. (2002). The emotional Stroop paradigm: Performance as a function of stimulus properties and self-reported mathematics anxiety. *Cognitive Therapy and Research, 26,* 157–166.

Hopko, D.R., McNeil, D.W., Zvolensky, M.J., & Eifert, G.H. (2001). The relation between anxiety and skill in performance-based anxiety disorders: A behavioral formulation of social phobia. *Behavior Therapy, 32,* 185–207.

Hyde, J.S. (2005). The gender similarities hypothesis. *American Psychologist, 60,* 581–592.

Hyde, J.S., Fennema, E., & Lamon, S.J. (1990). Gender differences in mathematics performance: A meta-analysis. *Psychological Bulletin, 107,* 139–155.

Hyde, J.S., Fennema, E., Ryan, M., Frost, L.A., & Hopp, C. (1990). Gender comparisons of mathematics attitudes and affect. *Psychology of Women Quarterly, 14,* 299–324.

Jastak Associates. (1993). *The Wide Range Achievement Test-Rev. 3.* Wilmington, DE: Jastak Associates.

Kane, M.J., & Engle, R.W. (2003). Working-memory capacity and the control of attention: The contributions of goal neglect, response competition and task set to Stroop interference. *Journal of Experimental Psychology: General, 132,* 47–70.

Kessler, R.C., McGonagle, K.A., Zhao, S., Nelson, B., Hughes, M., Eshleman, S., et al. (1994). Lifetime and 12-month prevalence of DSM-III-R psychiatric disorders in the United States. *Archives of General Psychiatry, 51,* 8–19.

Klein, E. (1949). Psychoanalytic aspects of school problems. In A. Freud, H. Hartmann, & E. Kris (Eds.), *Psychoanalytic study of the child* (Vols. III–IV, pp. 369–390). New York: International Universities Press.

LeFevre, J., DeStefano, D., Coleman, B., & Shanahan, T. (2005). Mathematical cognition and working memory. In J.I.D. Campbell (Ed.), *Handbook of mathematical cognition* (pp. 361–377). New York: Psychology Press.

Ma, X. (1999). A meta-analysis of the relationship between anxiety toward mathematics and achievement in mathematics. *Journal for Research in Mathematics Education, 30,* 520–541.

McLeod, D.B. (1994). Research on affect and mathematics learning in the JRME: 1970 to the present. *Journal for Research in Mathematics Education, 25,* 637–647.

Mervis, J. (2003). Down for the count? *Science, 300,* 1070–1074.

Mueller, J.H., Elser, M.J., & Rollack, D.N. (1993). Test anxiety and implicit memory. *Bulletin of the Psychonomic Society, 31,* 531–533.

Newman, M.G., Hofmann, S.G., Trabert, W., Roth, W.T., & Taylor, C.B. (1994). Does behavioral treatment of social phobia lead to cognitive changes? *Behavior Therapy, 25,* 503–517.

Rapee, R.M., Sanderson, W.C., & Barlow, D.H. (1988). Social phobia features across the DSM-III-R anxiety disorders. *Journal of Psychopathology and Behavioral Assessment, 10,* 287–299.

Richardson, F.C., & Suinn, R.M. (1972). The Mathematics Anxiety Rating Scale. *Journal of Counseling Psychology, 19,* 551–554.

Royer, J.M., Tronsky, L.N., Chan, Y., Jackson, S.J., & Marchant, H. III (1999). Math-fact retrieval as the cognitive mechanism underlying gender differences in math test performance. *Contemporary Educational Psychology, 24,* 181–266.

Sarason, I.G. (1984). Stress, anxiety, and cognitive interference: Reactions to tests. *Journal of Personality and Social Psychology, 46,* 929–938.

Schonell, F.J. (1937). *Diagnosis of individual difficulties in arithmetic.* Edinburgh: Oliver & Boyd.

Seyler, D.J., Kirk, E.P., & Ashcraft, M.H. (2003). Elementary subtraction. *Journal of Experimental Psychology: Learning, Memory, and Cognition, 29,* 1339–1352.

Taylor, J.A. (1953). A personality scale of manifest anxiety. *The Journal of Abnormal and Social Psychology, 48,* 285–29

Tobias, S. (1985). Test anxiety: Interference, defective skills, and cognitive capacity. *Educational Psychologist, 20,* 135–142.

Turner, J.C., Midgley, C., Meyer, D.K., Gheen, M., Anderman, E.M., Kang, Y., et al. (2002). The classroom environment and students' reports of avoidance strategies in mathematics: A multimethod study. *Journal of Educational Psychology, 94,* 88–106.

Wechsler, D. (1991). *Wechsler Adult Intelligence Scale–III.* San Antonio, TX: Harcourt Assessment.

Zbrodoff, N.J., & Logan, G.D. (1990). On the relation between production and verification tasks in the psychology of simple arithmetic. *Journal of Experimental Psychology: Learning, Memory, and Cognition, 16,* 83–97.

Zbrodoff, N.J., & Logan, G.D. (2005). What everyone finds: The problem-size effect. In J.I.D. Campbell (Ed.), *Handbook of mathematical cognition* (pp. 331–345). New York: Psychology Press.

Chapter 16

Influences of Gender, Ethnicity, and Motivation on Mathematical Performance

James M. Royer and Rena Walles

+ +

Most research on mathematical learning disabilities (MLD) has focused on the cognitive processing dysfunctions that underlie the mathematics difficulties exhibited by children with MLD. However, fundamental aspects of cognition are not the only contributors to poor mathematics performance, particularly in cases in which poor mathematics achievement may mimic MLD despite the lack of any cognitive dysfunction. Noncognitive factors, including gender, ethnicity, and motivation, may also affect achievement in mathematics. In this chapter we examine how these factors influence math performance and how they seem to be intertwined among some students who exhibit poor math performance. A major challenge for future research will be to try to disentangle the pattern of relationships in order to determine whether these noncognitive factors themselves affect math achievement or whether they are part of a complex pattern of interaction effects.

The chapter begins with an examination of gender differences in math performance. The literature shows that minimal mean differences in math test performance have been found between elementary and secondary school students. There are, however, differences in the variability of test performance; males at the higher end of the distribution perform better than do females, whereas at the lower end of the distribution, females perform better than do males (Hyde, Fennema, & Lamon, 1990; Willingham & Cole, 1997). The literature also shows a persistent advantage in math grades for females from elementary school to college (Kimball, 1989).

The next topic examined in the chapter is the math performance of ethnic groups. The literature shows consistent advantages for White students over Black and Hispanic students during the elementary and secondary school years, although the gap between ethnic groups has reduced over time. One possible explanation for changes in test performance is that they are associated with changes in patterns of math course taking. The data relevant to this hypothesis are examined in the section on ethnic differences in math performance.

The third topic examined in the chapter is the shifting patterns of motivation and math self-esteem as children move through the school system. As noted, changes in math motivation and self-esteem are complex and appear to interact with both gender and ethnicity.

The final section of the chapter briefly reviews some of the explanations for the patterns of performance examined in the earlier sections of the chapter. It also proposes research needed to sort out some of the conflicting explanations for variations in math performance associated with gender, ethnicity, and shifting patterns of motivation and self-esteem.

GENDER DIFFERENCES IN MATH TEST PERFORMANCE

The literature on gender differences in math performance shows an interesting and puzzling mix of differences. It demonstrates that there is no clear or consistent pattern of specific gender differences over time.

General Population Differences in Elementary and Secondary Students

According to much of the research and literature to date, males and females do not differ greatly in terms of math performance either during the elementary or secondary school years. When gender differences in math performance do emerge, the research is both difficult to interpret and of considerable importance: On the one hand, these differences may contribute to males pursuing math-intensive careers with greater frequency than females; on the other hand, these differences may contribute to higher incidences for dropout for males than for females, for example.

The general findings of the Long-Term Trends in Mathematics National Assessment of Educational Progress (NAEP) indicate that differences between boys and girls at all age levels were relatively small from 1973 to 2004, although there were some pattern changes during these years. Specifically, at ages 9 and 13, girls outperformed boys in 1973 by 2 points (at each age), but by 2004 boys were outperforming girls by 3 points. Among 17-year-olds, males consistently outperformed females to a small extent, with the gap decreasing from 8 points in 1973 to 3 points in 2004 (Perie, Moran, & Lutkus, 2005).

The conclusion that there are minimal differences between male and female math test performance in the elementary and secondary school years was reinforced in Willingham and Cole's (1997) exhaustive review of gender differences in test performance. They reviewed data from nine test batteries given to children in the elementary and secondary grades. These batteries included achievement tests used with students in kindergarten through eighth grade (e.g., the Iowa Test of Basic Skills, the Stanford Achievement Tests), two different forms of the National Assessment of Educational Progress, and the four-test battery included as part of the National Longitudinal Study of 1988. Willingham and Cole found a slight female advantage in tests of computational ability in the lower grades. One common way to examine differences between groups is to use d units (mean for males minus mean for females divided by the within-sexes standard deviation). Cohen (1988) described d differences of 0.2 as small effects, differences of 0.5 as medium effects, and differences of 0.8 as large effects. Willingham and Cole reported differences between males and females in computation performance of $d = -0.06$ (the negative score reflects that females scored higher than males). In higher elementary and secondary grades, in which the test emphasis was on math concepts and problem solving, a small advantage was often found for males as the complexity of the content increased.

Hyde, Fennema, and Lamon's (1990) meta-analysis of 100 studies involving more than 3 million participants reached similar conclusions. They found that math comparisons between males and females from the general population slightly favored females ($d = -0.05$), although the pattern of differences did change as a function of grade. In the elementary ($d = -0.06$) and middle school years ($d = -0.22$), females outperformed males on math tests by a small margin, but males tended to outperform females in the high school years, again by only a small margin ($d = 0.20$).

The research cited here typically involved cross-sectional data. Longitudinal data have also been found consistent with the conclusion that males and females in elementary and secondary school have similar math test performance. Lachance and Mazzocco (2006) followed more than 200 students from kindergarten to grade 3. Over the course of the study, they administered IQ tests, tests of cognitive ability (e.g., spatial cognition assessments), reading tests, and several different math tests, with many of the measures repeated annually over the 4-year period. The general finding was that boys and girls differed only minimally in their development of math skills. Moreover, detailed analyses indicated that boys and girls were equally likely to score both low and high on the indices of math ability, and rates of growth in these skills were also comparable.

Unlike the longitudinal study reported previously, which found minimal sex differences in math test variability, Willingham and Cole (1997) have reported differences in variability. They found that males displayed greater variability than females on virtually all standardized tests, including math tests. Both male and female test score distributions typically approximate a normal curve, and males and females show approximately the same mean performance. One implication of the larger variability for males is that they tend to exhibit higher scores than females at the higher end of the distribution, and lower scores than females at the lower end of the distribution. The next section of the chapter examines this implication.

Gender Differences in Math in High and Low Select Populations

The general finding in the literature is that the more select (at the higher end of the test score distribution) the population, the greater the tendency for males to outperform females on college entrance math tests. The gap between males and females on the SAT math test (SAT-M) has remained between 30 and 40 points for over 30 years (Lagenfield, 1997). The ACT Assessment (ACT) test shows a similar, though smaller, gap. More advanced tests have also shown a trend favoring male performance. Langenfeld (1997), for example, reported that the gap between males and females on the math section of the Graduate Record Examinations (GRE) was 80 points, favoring males. This finding is somewhat misleading because males are more likely than females to apply to graduate programs requiring high-level math skills, but even when males and females are equated with respect to program of study, there is a male advantage. Langenfeld (1997) reported that, averaged across 11 intended fields of study, the advantage for males on the GRE-M was 40 points ($d = 0.35$).

A male advantage in math test performance has also been present in other select populations. Hyde and colleagues (1990) reported moderate gender differences ($d = 0.54$) in the highly select group of students involved in the Study of Mathematically Precocious Youth (SMPY). Stanley (1994) reported a similar gap ($d = 0.44$) on the math section of the Secondary School Admission Test, administered to more than 8,000 students participating in the Johns Hopkins University Center for Talented Youth.

These data from Hyde and colleagues (1990) and Stanley (1994) document one aspect of the implication of greater variability of male test scores: a tendency for males to outperform females on math tests at the higher end of the test score distribution. There are also data supporting the second part of the implication that females outperform males at the lower end of the distribution. Barbaresi, Katusic, Colligan, Weaver, and Jacobsen (2005) examined medical records, educational achievement data, and IQ scores for every child born in the Rochester, Minnesota, area ($N = 5,718$) from 1976 to 1982. Their sample mimicked the demographic characteristics of the Rochester area, which was 96% White and predominantly middle class. Barbaresi and colleagues used three separate procedures to identify children with MLD. Two of the procedures were based on a discrepancy between IQ and achievement test scores; the third identified children with MLD as having low math achievement and at least a low average IQ score. All three procedures identified more males with MLD than females. The two discrepancy procedures identified twice as many males with MLD as females (7.8% vs. 3.9%, respectively, and 13.2% vs. 6.2%, respectively), and the low achievement procedure identified 16.7% of the males and 10.8% of the females as having MLD.

Gender Differences in Other Aspects of Math Performance

The previous text indicated that there are minimal differences between males and females in overall math test performance but that there are differences at the extremes of the distribution of test performance. Other indices of math performance also show gender differences. Kimball's (1989) review of the math achievement literature reported that during the junior high (now often referred to as *middle school*) and high school years, girls receive better grades than do boys in specific courses and in overall mathematics grade point average. This finding of female superiority in terms of math grades has also been reported at the college level, even when males and females are equated on factors such as SAT-M performance and the specific math class in which they are enrolled (Bridgeman & Lewis, 1996; Wainer & Stienberg, 1992).

Royer and his colleagues (Royer, Tronsky, Chan, Jackson, & Marchant, 1999) reported another gender difference in math that appears to play a role in math test performance. They measured the speed of math fact retrieval (e.g., $5 + 4 = \_\_\_\_$) for students in Grades 1–8 and in college. At all grades for which math test data were available, speed of math fact retrieval was a significant predictor of math test performance, and greater variability was found in the male distribution of math fact retrieval speed than in the female distribution. This gender difference in the variability of retrieval speed mimicked group differences in the variability of math test performance; at the higher end of the male and female distributions, males were faster than females, whereas at the lower end of the distribution, females were faster than males.

ETHNIC DIFFERENCES IN MATHEMATICS PERFORMANCE

The previous section examined variation in patterns of math performance as a function of student gender. A second source of differences in math performance is student ethnicity. The patterns of math performance associated with ethnicity are somewhat clearer than those associated with gender differences, although as will be seen, some puzzling findings exist in the literature. In general, White students display better math performance than their minority counterparts. However, there have been changes in the pattern of differences, and the causes of the changes are not apparent.

Our focus on ethnicity will only involve examinations of the mathematics performance of White, Black, and Hispanic students. It should also be noted that ethnicity often serves as a proxy for socioeconomic status, and many of the differences among ethnic groups that we examine may well be associated with socioeconomic status.

NAEP Comparisons in Math Between
White Students and Black and Hispanic Students

Long-term trend NAEP data show a considerable gap between the math performance of White students and Black and Hispanic students at all age levels (favoring White students); however, the gap decreased from 1973 to 2004. The gap for 9-year-old White and Black students dropped from 35 points in 1973 to 23 points in 2004. There were comparable changes in 13-year-olds (from 46 to 27 points) and 17-year-olds (from 40 to 28 points) (Perie et al., 2005).

Similar changes occurred in the gap between White and Hispanic students, although that gap has generally been smaller than the gap between White and Black students. Among 9-year-old White and Hispanic students, the gap was 23 points in 1973 and 18 points in 2004. Again, similar changes occurred among 13-year-olds (from 35 to 23 points) and 17-year-olds (from 33 to 24 points). In the case of both comparisons, the pooled standard deviation (*SD*) was approximately 30; thus, the gap between the groups ranged from approximately 1.2 *SD* units to 0.8 *SD* units (Perie et al., 2005).

Lee (2002) has pointed out that the emphasis on the overall reduction of the White–minority math gap (particularly the gap between White and Black students) from 1973 to 2004 ignores another trend in the data. A general shrinkage occurred in the gap from 1973 to 1990, followed by a trend toward an increase in the gap among 13- and 17-year-olds from 1990 to 2004. This trend toward an increasing gap between 1990 and 2004 is relevant to an evaluation of the impact of changes in course-taking patterns, discussed in the next section.

PATTERNS IN MATHEMATICS COURSE TAKING

One hypothesis that could be advanced about changing patterns of math test performance is that these patterns are related to changing patterns of math course taking. That is, improvement in the performance of Black and Hispanic students on NAEP tests from 1973 to 1990 may have been mediated by an increase in math course taking as students proceeded through the school years. A similar, related hypothesis could be advanced regarding gender differences. That is, the reason females have not closed the gap with males on SAT-M performance may be that they have not taken as many high-level math courses as their male counterparts. This could also contribute to a disinclination on the part of females to pursue math-intensive careers. The section that follows provides evidence relevant to evaluating the course-taking hypothesis.

Data available through the National Center for Educational Statistics for 1986 to 2004 showed an increased enrollment in higher level math courses among all students at ages 13 and 17 (U.S. Department of Education, Institute of Education Sciences, 2007). At the same time, a particularly striking drop occurred in the number of 13-year-old students taking basic mathematics courses (from 61% in 1986 to 33% in 2004) and a large increase in the number of students taking first-year algebra (from 16% to 29%). Comparable changes were evident in the 17-year-old group, with the percentage of students taking pre-algebra or lower-level math course dropping from 20% to 4% and the percentage of students taking Algebra 2 increasing from 37% to 53%. The percentage of 17-year-old students taking calculus also increased over this time period (from 6% to 17%).

These changes in course-taking patterns were not restricted to White students. Figure 16.1 shows the changes in White and minority student math enrollments for 17-year-old students from 1978 to 2004. The graphs show a very encouraging pattern of change over this period, with Hispanic students enrolling nearly as frequently as White students in Algebra 2 in 2004 and Black students actually enrolling more frequently than Whites in Algebra 2. Although minority students still did not enroll in calculus classes as frequently as did White students, both Black and Hispanic students increased their enrollment in calculus classes to a considerable extent during this time period (U.S. Department of Education, Institute of Education Sciences, 2007).

The patterns of math course taking of males and females have shifted, as well. The data in Figure 16.2 are from a random sampling of 10% of the students taking the ACT exam in 1987 and 1997. As these data indicate, a larger proportion of males than females took higher level math courses in 1987, but in 1997 females were taking all math courses except calculus and trigonometry with greater frequency than males. Riegle-Crumb's (2005) analysis of a large national data set also confirmed that males and females were taking higher level high school math courses with comparable frequency. In fact, her data indicated that White and Black females were taking calculus and pre-calculus before leaving high school with greater frequency than were White and Black males (McLure, 1998).

The Relationship Between Course-Taking Patterns and Math Test Performance

As the data on course-taking patterns would suggest, there does not seem to be a clear relationship between shifts in course-taking patterns and changes in patterns of math test performance. First, although the general increase in math course taking from 1978 to 2004 for Black students is consistent with

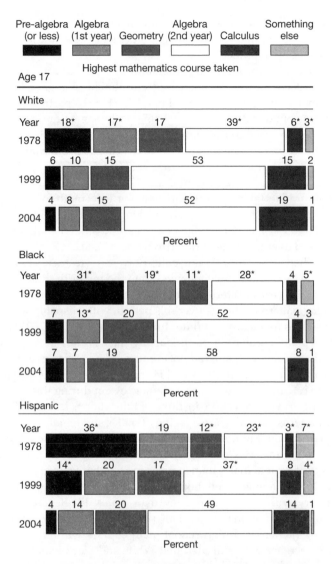

Figure 16.1. Patterns of mathematics course taking for White, African American, and Hispanic students from 1978 to 2004. (National Center for Education Statistics, U.S. Department of Education) * Indicates values that are significantly different from the values in 2004.

a general reduction in the NAEP math gap between White and Black students, course-taking changes continued to occur throughout the entire period from 1978 to 2004 (with students taking more advanced courses) while the math gap between White and Black students diminished over time until approximately 1990 and thereafter increased over time.

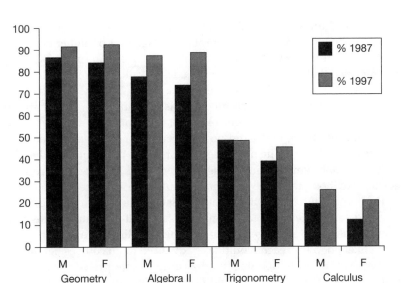

Figure 16.2. Percentage of male and female college-bound students taking high school math courses, 1987 and 1997 (*Source:* McLure, 1998).

No clear relationship was found, as well, between course-taking patterns and differences between males and females on math tests. The data from the ACT surveys and from Riegle-Crumb's (2005) analysis of data from a national survey indicated that females have made gains, and perhaps even surpassed, their male counterparts in math course taking during high school. However, there was only a very small change in NAEP math performance over that time period, and there has been virtually no change in the male–female SAT-M gap since the mid 1960s.

One possible explanation for the lack of a direct connection between course taking patterns and course performance is that the "yield" for advanced course taking is different for White and Black students and for male and female students. Riegle-Crumb (2005) examined longitudinal course-taking patterns for more than 7,000 students who attended one of 69 schools during the 1990s, using data administered through the National Longitudinal Study of Adolescent Health (Add Health). Riegle-Crumb evaluated two research questions in her analyses. First, given that White and minority students begin high school at the same level in the math course sequence, were minority students subsequently given the same returns (advancement through the course sequence) as White students, and did returns vary as a function of gender? Second, are academic grades a factor in explaining why students who start at a comparable position in the math sequence do not end high school in equivalent positions?

Riegle-Crumb's (2005) initial set of descriptive analyses indicated that male and female White students enrolled in Algebra 1 or higher in Grade 9 with greater frequency (76%) than did their Black counterparts (60%). She also reported that White students enrolled in calculus or pre-calculus (40%) with greater frequency than did their Black peers (24%) by the end of high school. Riegle-Crumb then reported results relevant to her two central research questions. First, after controlling for relevant background variables, she found that Black males did not proceed as far in the math course sequence as did their White male peers. That is, if a White male and a Black male were both enrolled in an Algebra 1 class as freshmen, there was a greater likelihood that the White male would take advanced math courses by the end of high school than that the Black male would. This result did not hold for White and Black females. That is, if a White female and a Black female both took Algebra 1 as freshmen, no difference could be found in the likelihood that each would take advanced math courses before leaving high school. Although this finding could be interpreted as suggesting that many females (both White and Black) pursue advanced math courses, the likelihood of doing so is the same in both groups of females because few females in either group pursue advanced math courses, relative to their male counterparts.

Riegle-Crumb's (2005) second research question addressed the issue of whether failure to proceed with high-level math courses was related to one's grade in Algebra 1. She found that Black males received lower "return" from good grades than did their White peers. A Black male who received the same grade as a White male in Algebra 1 was less likely to take high-level math courses than his White male counterpart.

The Algebra 1 grade analysis for White and Black females showed results somewhat different than those for White and Black males. Both White and Black males declined to pursue higher level math courses if they received a low grade in Algebra I. However, in the female analyses, the relationship between Algebra 1 grades and advanced math course taking was greater for White females than it was for Black females. Riegle-Crumb (2005) suggested that this result meant that Black females were more resilient to the impact of academic difficulties and discouragement than their White female counterparts and took advanced courses even when their grade in Algebra 1 would not have predicted it.

As explained, some changes have occurred in the gap between White and Black students on NAEP math tests, although the trend is inconsistent with early reductions in that the gap between White and Black students is reversing and has become larger in the past 15 years. With respect to male–female comparisons, the performance of boys and girls on NAEP tests has been very similar between the mid-1970s and 2007, when this book was published, but the fairly substantial gender gap on SAT-M tests has remained constant over the same interval. Finally, the data reviewed in the previous section suggest that changes in math test performance have not been mediated by changes in patterns of math course taking. Enrollment in math courses by both minority groups and females has steadily increased over a long time period, but changes in math test performance have not followed these changes in course-taking patterns.

We now turn to an issue relevant to the somewhat puzzling pattern of data that we have examined thus far. Specifically, how do minority students and females view their mathematical competence, and do those self-concept judgments change as a function of advancement through the school years?

MOTIVATION AND SELF-ESTEEM PATTERNS REGARDING MATHEMATICS

One of the central themes of developmental research on motivational and self-esteem patterns regarding mathematics is that there is a striking shift in mathematics-related motivational patterns and self-esteem patterns for many children as they transition from elementary school to middle school, junior high school, or high school. These patterns are particularly apparent for minorities and females. The next few sections of the chapter will describe these changes.

General Shifts from Intrinsic to Extrinsic Motivation

Susan Harter (e.g., 1981, 1986, 1990, 1996) has examined the extent to which a child's motivation to learn is driven by intrinsic or extrinsic motivation. Intrinsic motivation is defined as learning motivated by one's own interest in the subject material and by curiosity and preference for challenge; extrinsic motivation is driven by a desire to obtain grades, win teacher approval, avoid censure, and meet the external demands of the school system (Harter, 1996). Harter's research has shown a systematic grade-related shift from an intrinsic motivational orientation in Grade 3 to an extrinsic motivational orientation in Grade 9. This shift has also been reported by other researchers (e.g., Eccles & Midgley, 1988, 1990).

Harter's research has generally been conducted in the Denver, Colorado, area, where students transition from elementary school into middle school after Grade 5. Harter (1981) showed that changes in preference for challenging academic work, curiosity and interest in schoolwork, and the development of an attitude of independent mastery of schoolwork were more pronounced after the transition to middle school than before.

General Shifts in Math Motivation and Self-Image Associated with Transitioning out of Elementary School

Jacquelynne Eccles and her colleagues conducted a research program on developmental motivational patterns, and their research complements Har-

ter's research described above. Midgley, Feldlaufer, and Eccles (1989) conducted a study of more than 3,000 students from 15 school systems in
Michigan. The students were largely from lower- to upper-middle-class
homes, and there were relatively few minority students. Midgley and colleagues focused on student's attitudes toward math and English across
grades 5–12. In particular, they were interested in the perceived value of
math and English, students' self-concept of math and English ability, and
the perceived difficulty of math and English. There was little change in the
attitudinal variables from the earliest grades to the later grades for English,
but grade differences were found for math. Specifically, the perceived value
of math and students' self-concept of math ability showed a drop as students transitioned from elementary school to junior high or middle school.
In addition, there was a sharp rise in the perceived difficulty of math from
Grade 6 to Grade 7. These trends generally persisted through to Grade 12,
with perceived value of math and math self-concept steadily declining and
perceived difficulty of math steadily increasing to grade 12.

Motivation and Self-Image Shifts for Minorities and Females

There is some evidence that the grade-related shifts for all students described
above are especially evident among minority groups and females. Catsambis
(1994) reported a study using the National Educational Longitudinal Study
of 1988 (NELS:88) data, which involved a national probability sample of
24,500 Grade-8 students (U.S. Department of Education Sciences, National
Center for Education Statistics, 2007). The students were initially studied in
1988 and studied a second time in 1990, when they were in Grade 10. Of particular interest for this chapter is Catsambis's findings regarding math
achievement (measured by standardized math tests), math grades, and math
attitudes for males and females from White, Black, and Hispanic groups.

Catsambis (1994) found that changes in math self-concept among females seemed to be disassociated from actual indicators of math performance. Grade-8 females in three ethnic groups (White, Black, and Hispanics)
were similar to their male counterparts in math test performance, were generally better than their male counterparts in math grades, and were taking
higher level math courses with greater frequency than their male counterparts (data consistent with the ACT data reported in the previous section).
Despite these objective indicators of performance, females from all three
ethnic groups tended to report less interest in math-intensive careers than
their male peers, and they showed less inclination to respond positively to
statements about looking forward to math classes. They did, however, report that they tended to work hard in math classes with greater frequency
than was reported by male peers.

Catsambis (1994) followed the NELS:88 sample to Grade 10 and found
some interesting shifts, particularly in the objective indicators of math per-

formance. Similar to the Grade-8 data, no differences were found in math achievement test performance for white male and female students in grade 10. However, unlike the Grade-8 data, Grade-10 Black and Hispanic females significantly outscored their male counterparts on math tests. There were even more striking differences between Grade 8 and Grade 10 students in math grades. In Grade 8, White and Hispanic females received significantly higher grades than their male counterparts. However, in Grade 10, White males received significantly higher math grades than their female class- mates, and the previous advantage for Hispanic females was no longer sig- nificant. (Other researchers, however, have found evidence that females' grade advantage over males extends through high school [Kimball, 1989; Willingham & Cole, 1997].)

Attitudes about math among females in Grade 10 in all three ethnic groups were even more negative than they had been in Grade 8. Whereas there were some nonsignificant differences between attitudinal and self- esteem statements in the Grade 8-data set, by Grade 10 the view of females toward mathematics appeared to have taken a significant downturn rela- tive to their male counterparts.

EXPLANATIONS FOR THE PATTERNS OF DIFFERENCES

The question of why females perform as well as males on standardized tests in elementary and secondary school but do not perform as well as males on university entrance exams has received an enormous amount of atten- tion (e.g., Gallagher & Kaufman, 2005; Geary, 1996; Royer & Garofoli, 2005; Royer, et al., 1999; Wilder, 1997; Willingham & Cole, 1997). A detailed dis- cussion of this topic is beyond the scope of this chapter, but a brief review of some of the hypotheses will be given along with references for examin- ing the topic in more depth. It should be mentioned that, whereas the gap between select (high-end) males and females on college admission tests has attracted considerable research interest, far less attention has been paid to the question of why males at the low end of the distribution have poorer math achievement than their female counterparts.

The most frequently mentioned hypothesis for the male–female gap on tests such as the SAT-M is that males have a biological advantage on tasks involving mathematics (e.g., Geary, 1996). The cognitive mechanism most often mentioned that provides this biological advantage is spatial cognition ability, which is hypothesized to have a genetic basis. Males have often been shown to have better spatial cognition abilities than females (in some tasks), and spatial cognition ability has been shown to be a significant predictor of math test performance (Geary, 1996; Royer et al., 1999).

A second popular hypothesis involves different socialization patterns (e.g., Beal, 1994). This hypothesis suggests that girls are treated (socialized) in a manner that leads them to believe that they are less talented in math than are boys and that it is "unfeminine" to have an active interest in math and to pursue a math-intensive career.

Yet another hypothesis is that cognitive mechanisms such as fast math fact retrieval (for which males are faster than females) provide males with an advantage on math tests but not on math activities associated with classroom work (Royer et al., 1999).

Finally, some researchers have posited that male advantages on high-end math tests are associated with a mix of all of the above factors (e.g., Wilder, 1997). See Gallagher and Kaufman (2005) for a detailed discussion of all of these views.

An enormous amount of research has also been devoted to identifying the underlying causes of achievement gaps between White and minority students (e.g., Balfanz, 2000; Jenks & Phillips, 1998; Lee, 2002; Slaughter-Defoe, 1997). One of the most widely discussed factors is inequality in educational opportunities. Specifically, minority students are hypothesized to have less access to educational opportunities, both in the home and in the classroom (e.g., Ikpa, 2004; Lee, 2004). For example, minority students are typically of a lower socioeconomic status (SES), which is associated with having fewer books in the home and lower parental education level; these two factors have been associated with poorer academic performance (Crane, 1996; Hedges & Nowell, 1998; Orr, 2003). Inequality within the school manifests itself in a variety of ways, including poorer quality of teaching (Kober, 2001), economically and socially segregated schools (Ikpa, 2004), and the damaging effects of negative racial stereotypes (Sadowski, 2001).

The achievement gap between White and minority students, which is influenced primarily by a difference in socioeconomic status, may thus be exacerbated by the diminished academic expectations of minority parents (Birenbaum & Nasser, 2006). Although the achievement gap may be most evident as students approach their high school years, the problem likely begins much earlier. Coley (2002) discussed ethnic differences in school readiness, specifically that many White children begin kindergarten with a much higher level of proficiency than their minority counterparts. Identification of children at risk, in combination with effective intervention programs, may help to eliminate the achievement gap.

Although no real consensus has been reached concerning the specific combination of factors contributing to the ethnic achievement gap in math, the lines of research mentioned above have advanced our knowledge. Future research should serve to increase the number of children who are identified as at risk for academic failure, pinpoint the causes of the current ethnic achievement gap, and form the basis of effective interventions.

Despite improvements in math test performance, changes in course-taking patterns, and advantages in course grades, minority and female students have not increased their performance on math college entrance examinations relative to White males, and they are underrepresented in math-intensive career paths (Betz, 1997; Jordan & Plank, 2000; Oakes, 1990). Why? One hypothesis is that motivational and self-esteem issues may to some extent mitigate the positive changes in these areas. These negative motivational and self-esteem issues seem to have the largest impact on female and minority students.

Eccles (1997) suggested several reasons for the shifting motivational patterns that affect all students. One is that with many teachers in middle and junior high school instructing as many as 150 students at a time, teachers may not have the knowledge, time, or personal commitment to help students who may be struggling or who may need encouragement to succeed. Another factor is that junior high school teachers may be more subject to stereotyping the adolescents they work with. Eccles suggested that adolescents are generally perceived as difficult to work with; indeed, many junior high teachers she studied agreed with the statement that adolescents were overwhelmed with hormones and incapable of learning in this particular period. Other researchers have suggested that the implicit expectations known as *stereotype threat* may play a substantial role in the reduced interest that females show in math performance and math-intensive career paths (Davies & Spencer, 2005).

Balfanz (2000) has provided a more qualitative view of some of the causes of failure and low motivation among students, focusing in particular on urban public schools. He described largely minority schools as paying little attention to what he called "the technical core of schooling." This core consists of common curricula and instructional materials across grades and communication between teachers so that they know what students have been exposed to in earlier grades and can begin where students left off in the previous grade. The urban schools Balfanz studied rarely had this focus, and as a result, limited time was spent on moving students forward.

NEEDED FUTURE RESEARCH

The research summarized in this chapter merely brushes the surface of a complex topic. There is some evidence indicating that certain cognitive differences may contribute to the lower math performance of minority students and may cause females to be disinclined to pursue mathematics beyond high school. These cognitive differences may be associated with socioeconomic or other cultural influences, and, for gender differences, may also be influenced by biology. In addition, students experience certain motivational changes that exacerbate performance differences and that contribute to lowered math self-esteem and lowered willingness to choose math-intensive career paths. Much is known about these topics separately, and many educators and experts know of targeted interventions that can separately change math achievement patterns and shift motivational indicators. What is not known as much is how to package both cognitive and motivational interventions targeted at the critical middle and junior high school years, that will bring about sustained change in both math achievement and inclination to pursue math-oriented careers. This research would probably entail much more than combining a set of attractive educational procedures with a set of motivational procedures that have a track record in previous research. Rather, it would probably need to consist of a systematic, long-term program that investigates how to combine both educational and cognitive interventions with motivational interventions. This kind of research program could ultimately result in classroom instruction that not only improves math performance but also makes students feel good about their achievement and eager to pursue future math activity.

REFERENCES

Balfanz, R. (2000). Why do so many urban public school students demonstrate so little academic achievement? In M.G. Sanders (Ed.), *Schooling students placed at risk* (pp. 37–64). Mahwah, NJ: Lawrence Erlbaum Associates.

Barbaresi, W.J., Katusic, S.K., Colligan, R.C., Weaver, A.L., & Jacobsen, S.J. (2005). Math learning disorder: Incidence in a population-based birth cohort, 1976–82, Rochester, Minn. *Ambulatory Pediatrics, 5*, 281–289.

Beal, C.R. (1994). *Boys and girls: The development of gender roles.* New York: McGraw-Hill.

Betz, N. (1997). What stops women and minorities from choosing majors in science and engineering? In D. Johnson (Ed.), *Minorities and girls in school* (pp. 105–140). Thousand Oaks, CA: Sage Publications.

Birenbaum, M., & Nasser, F. (2006). Ethnic and gender differences in mathematics achievement and in dispositions toward the study of mathematics. *Learning and Instruction, 16,* 26–40.

Bridgeman, B., & Lewis, C. (1996). Gender differences in college mathematics grades and SAT-M scores: A reanalysis of Wainer and Steinberg. *Journal of Educational Measurement, 33,* 257–270.

Catsambis, S. (1994). The path to math: Gender and racial-ethnic differences in mathematics participation from middle school to high school. *Sociology of Education, 67,* 199–215.

Cohen, J. (1988). *Statistical power for the behavioral sciences* (2nd ed.). Mahwah, NJ: Lawrence Erlbaum Associates.

Coley, R. (2002). *An uneven start: Indicators of inequality in school readiness. Policy information report.* Princeton, NJ: Educational Testing Service.

Crane, J. (1996). Effects of home environment, SES, and maternal test scores on mathematics achievement. *Journal of Educational Research, 89,* 305–314.

Davies, P.G., & Spencer, S.J. (2005). The gender-gap artifact: Women's underperformance in quantitative domains through the lens of stereotype threat. In A.M. Gallagher & J.C. Kaufman (Eds.), *Gender differences in mathematics* (pp. 172–188). New York: Cambridge University Press.

Eccles, J.S. (1997). User-friendly science and mathematics: Can it interest girls and minorities in breaking through the middle school wall? In D. Johnson (Ed.), *Minorities and girls in school* (pp. 65–104). Thousand Oaks, CA: Sage Publications.

Eccles, J.S., & Midgley, C. (1988). Stage–environment fit: Developmentally appropriate classrooms for young adolescents. In R.E. Ames & C. Ames (Eds.), *Research on motivation in education, goals and cognition: Vol. 3* (pp. 139–186). San Diego: Academic Press.

Eccles, J.S., & Midgley, C. (1990). Changes in academic motivation and self-perceptions during early adolescence. In R. Montemayor, G.R. Adams, & T.P. Gullotta (Eds.), *Advances in adolescent development: From childhood to adolescence. Vol. 2.* (pp. 134–155). Thousand Oaks, CA: Sage Publications.

Gallagher, A.M., & Kaufman, J.C. (2005). *Gender differences in mathematics.* New York: Cambridge University Press.

Geary, D.C. (1996). Sexual selection and sex differences in mathematical abilities. *Behavioral and Brain Sciences, 19,* 229–247.

Harter, S. (1981). A new self-report scale of intrinsic versus extrinsic orientation in the classroom: Motivational and informational components. *Developmental Psychology, 17,* 300–312.

Harter, S. (1986). Processes underlying the construction, maintenance, and enhancement of the self-concept in children. In J. Suls & A.G. Greenwald (Eds.), *Psychological perspectives on the self: Vol. 3* (pp. 137–181). Mahwah, NJ: Lawrence Erlbaum Associates.

Harter, S. (1990). Self and identity development. In S.S. Feldman & G.R. Elliott (Eds.), *At the threshold: The developing adolescent* (pp. 352–387). Cambridge, MA: Harvard University Press.

Harter, S. (1996). Teacher and classroom influences on scholastic motivation, self esteem, and level of voice in adolescents. In J. Juvonen & K. Wentzel (Eds.), *Social motivation: Understanding children's school adjustment.* New York: Cambridge University Press.

Hedges, L., & Nowell, A. (1998). African American-White test score convergence since 1965. In C. Jencks and M. Phillips (Eds.), *The African American–White test score gap* (pp. 149–181). Washington, DC: Brookings Institute Press.

Hyde, J.S., Fennema, E., & Lamon, S.J. (1990). Gender differences in mathematics performance: A meta-analysis. *Psychological Bulletin, 107,* 139–155.

Ikpa, V. (2004). Leaving children behind: The racial/ethnic achievement gap. *Research for Educational Reform, 9,* 3–13.

Institute of Education Sciences, National Center for Education Statistics. *National Education Longitudinal Study of 1988.*

Jenks, C., & Phillips, M. (Eds.). (1998). *The African American–White score gap.* Washington, DC: Brookings Institution Press.

Jordan, W.J., & Plank, S.B. (2000). Talent loss among high-achieving poor students. In M.G. Sanders (Ed.), *Schooling students placed at risk* (pp. 83–108). Mahwah, NJ: Larence Erlbaum Associates.

Kimball, M.M. (1989). A new perspective on women's math achievement. *Psychological Bulletin, 105,* 198–214.

Kober, N. (2001). *It takes more than testing: Closing the achievement gap.* Washington, DC: Center on Education Policy.

Lachance, J., & Mazzocco, M.M.M. (in press). A longitudinal study of sex differences in math and spatial skills in primary school age children. *Learning and Individual Differences*.

Langenfeld, T.E. (1997). Test fairness: Internal and external investigations of gender bias in mathematics testing. *Educational Measurement: Issues and Practice, 16,* 20–26.

Lee, J. (2002). Racial and ethnic achievement gap trends: Reversing the progress toward equity? *Educational Researcher, 31,* 3–12.

Lee, J. (2004). Multiple facets of inequity in racial and ethnic achievement gaps. *Peabody Journal of Education, 79,* 51–73.

McLure, G.T. (1998). Are America's students taking more science and mathematics course work? ACT Research, Information Brief 98–2. Retrieved Jan. 24, 2007, from http://www.act.org/research/briefs/98–2.html

Midgley, C., Feldlaufer, H., & Eccles, J. (1989). Student/teacher relations and attitudes toward mathematics before and after the transition to junior high school. *Child Development, 60,* 98–1992.

National Center for Education Statistics, U.S. Department of Education. (2007). Trends in mathematics course-taking at age 17 by race/ethnicity. Retrieved Jan. 11, 2007, from http://nces.ed.gov/nationsreportcard/ltt/results2004/exp-math-race17.asp

Oakes, J. (1990). Opportunities, achievement and choice: Women and minority students in science and mathematics. *Review of Educational Research, 16,* 153–222.

Orr, A. (2003). African American–White differences in achievement: The importance of wealth. *Sociology of Education, 76,* 281–304.

Perie, M. Moran, R., & Lutkus, A.D. (2005). *NAEP 2004 trends in academic progress: Three decades of student performance in reading and mathematics* (NCES 2005–464). U.S. Department of Education, Institute of Education Sciences, National Center for Education Statistics. Washington, DC: Government Printing Office.

Riegle-Crumb, C. (2005). *The path through math: Course sequences and academic performance at the intersection of race/ethnicity and gender* (PRC Working Paper Series 2004–2005. No. 04-05-09). The University of Texas at Austin, Population Research Center.

Royer, J.M., & Garofoli, L. (2005). Cognitive contributions to sex differences in math performance. In A.M. Gallagher & J.C. Kaufman (Eds.), *Gender differences in mathematics* (pp. 99–120). New York: Cambridge University Press.

Royer, J.M., Tronsky, L.N., Chan, Y., Jackson, S.J., & Marchant, H. (1999). Math-fact retrieval as the cognitive mechanism underlying sex differences in math test performance. *Contemporary Educational Psychology, 24,* 181–266.

Sadowski, M. (2001). Closing the achievement gap requires multiple solutions. Cambridge, MA: *Harvard Education Letter*.

Slaughter-Defoe, D.T. (1997). Ethnicity, poverty, and children's educability: A developmental perspective. In D. Johnson (Ed.), *Minorities and girls in school: Effects on achievement and performance* (pp. 37–64). Thousand Oaks, CA: Sage Publications.

Stanley, J.S. (1994). Gender differences for able elementary school students on above-grade-level ability and achievement tests. In N. Colangelo, S.G. Assouline, & D.L. Ambroson (Eds.), *Talent development Vol. 2: Proceedings from the 1993 Henry B. and Jocelyn Wallace National Research Symposium of Talent Development*. Vandalia, OH: Ohio Psychological Press.

U.S. Department of Education, Institute of Education Sciences, National Center for Education Statistics. (2007). National Assessment of Educational Progress (NAEP), selected years, 1978–2004, Long-term trend mathematics assessments.

Wainer, H., & Steinberg, L.S. (1992). Sex differences in the performance on the mathematics section of the Scholastic Aptitude Test: A bidirectional validity study. *Harvard Educational Review, 62,* 323–336.

Wilder, G.Z. (1997). Antecedents of gender differences. In W.W. Willingham and L.M. Johnson (Eds.), *Supplement to gender and fair assessment.* Princeton, NJ: Educational Testing Service.

Willingham, W.W., & Cole, N.S. (1997). *Gender and fair assessment.* Mahwah, NJ: Lawrence Erlbaum Associates.

Yan, W., & Lin, Q. (2005). Parent involvement and mathematics achievement: Contrast across racial and ethnic groups. *The Journal of Educational Research, 99,* 116–127.

Instructional Interventions

*"We had the best of educations . . . Reeling and Writhing,
of course, to begin with, and then the different branches
of arithmetic: ambition, distraction, uglification, and derision."*
— Lewis Carroll

While Sections I–V have examined the nature and origins of mathematical difficulties and disabilities, the three chapters in this final section treat more applied issues, including intervention programs for young children at risk for developing mathematical learning disabilities and difficulties, instructional interventions for improving math problem-solving skills in the early elementary grades, and how the lack of quantitative understanding and skills can put adults with dyscalculia at a serious disadvantage in the home and community, as well as in the workplace.

In Chapter 17, Griffin defines mathematics and math knowledge as a set of conceptual relationships among the separate worlds of real quantities, counting numbers, and formal symbols. She goes on to describe several intervention programs aimed primarily at young children who are at risk for developing mathematical disabilities and difficulties. In particular, she focuses on her own Number Worlds program, describing a core group of its theoretically based instructional principles that have been translated into a set of teaching strategies, which she argues can also be used to improve math learning and achievement for children who are typically achieving. Griffin provides evidence that children from an urban, low socioeconomic status (SES) community who were exposed to this program in their first 3 years of schooling surmounted the considerable disadvantages they began with relative to a normative group of peers from a more affluent community. She concludes that this program provides an effective intervention for children at risk of developing mathematical learning difficulties.

Fuchs and Fuchs begin Chapter 18 on instructional interventions by examining the construct of mathematical problem solving (MPS), and conclude that not only can MPS be distinguished from calculation skill but also that strategies for solving word problems need to be taught explicitly. After reviewing three of their intervention studies, these authors conclude that 8- to 9-year-old students with and without disabilities can benefit from MPS instruction, even when they possess immature calculation skills. Moreover, they conclude that in order for students (children with and without math disabilities) to transfer their MPS skills from familiar to novel problems, they must receive explicit instruction to enhance their awareness of the relationships between these sets of problems.

In Chapter 19, McCloskey challenges the notion that individuals with dyscalculia should not find themselves at a disadvantage in adult life unless they were to pursue a career in a field that requires some knowledge of mathematics (e.g., accounting). Rather, he argues that quantitative skills and understanding are needed in many facets of everyday adult life, including in the home (e.g., managing one's finances) and the community, in addition to the workplace. To support his position, he provides anecdotal evidence in the form of testimonials from adults with dyscalculia. He also points out that not only teachers but also friends, relatives, and employers frequently fail to comprehend or accept the idea that an individual can experience a selective quantitative disability. He concludes that additional research needs to be conducted on the difficulties encountered by adults with dyscalculia in their attempts to cope with the quantitative demands they face in everyday life, as well as on ways to reduce these difficulties.

Ginsburg and Pappas review the chapters in this section by organizing their commentary around five instructional goals: prevention, reforms for improving the educational system, remediation, preparation for the workforce and everyday life, and encouragement of students so that they focus on *current* mathematical activities (instead of solely on worrying about preparing for the future). They argue that instruction should include efforts to stimulate and challenge students to go beyond the projected limits of their expected learning trajectories. Furthermore, these authors contend that although hands-on activities are crucial for young children, teachers need to focus on the use of concrete materials for promoting mathematical learning rather than just for purposes of play. Ginsburg and Pappas also propose that mathematics learning should involve some degree of creativity, flights of imagination, and just plain enjoyment. Finally, they suggest that teachers ought to be sensitive to the learning needs of children from different cultural and social groups.

REFERENCE

Carroll, L. (2002). *Alice's adventures in Wonderland*. New York: Modern Library. (Original work published 1865)

Chapter 17

Early Intervention for Children at Risk of Developing Mathematical Learning Difficulties

Sharon Griffin

+ +

R esearch that has accumulated in the field of cognitive science over the past 20 years has allowed "early intervention" to be conceptualized in a much more focused way than was possible in the 1960s, when the Head Start program was launched. Because of this research, detailed portraits now exist of the manner in which children construct knowledge of quantity (Starkey, 1992), number (Gelman & Gallistel, 1978; Ginsburg, Klein, & Starkey, 1998; Griffin & Case, 1997; Siegler & Robinson, 1982), and geometry (Clements, Wilson, & Sarama, 2004) over the early and middle childhood years. These developmental progressions (or *learning trajectories,* as they are sometimes called) permit a much more precise specification of the math concepts and skills that are needed to ensure successful learning in school than was possible at the beginning of the Head Start program. The new knowledge base also includes assessment tools, often linked to the developmental progressions, which permit gaps in children's early learning and foundational knowledge to be identified and addressed. Finally, a number of factors that facilitate learning, for children and adults alike, have been

The research reported in this chapter was made possible by the generous support of the James S. McDonnell Foundation. The author gratefully acknowledges this support as well as the contributions of all of the teachers and children who have used the Number Worlds program in various stages of development, and who have helped shape its final form.

identified in recent years (see Donovan, Bransford, & Pellegrino, 1999, for a summary of this research), providing a rich framework for the design of effective instruction.

With all this new knowledge, one might expect that early childhood education and intervention programs, which until recently have been produced almost exclusively by commercial publishing houses in the United States, would be considerably more effective than they were 20 years ago. However, the facts suggest that this expectation has not yet been met. In spite of early warning signals that appeared in the 1980s and 1990s in international and national comparisons of children's mathematics achievement, U.S. children are still lagging behind their peers in Japan, Korea, China, and several other developed societies as early as kindergarten (Ginsburg et al., 1997; Starkey et al., 1999; Stigler, Lee, & Stevenson, 1990). Within the United States, the socioeconomic achievement gap that was identified in the mid-1980s (Entwistle & Alexander, 1990) persists, with children from low-income homes underperforming their middle-income peers by a considerable margin throughout the elementary and high school years and as early as the prekindergarten years (Griffin, Case, & Siegler, 1994; Starkey & Klein, 2000).

This grim picture inspired a number of developmental and educational psychologists to join the educational arena in the 1990s and, using their knowledge of cognitive science, to attempt to develop early mathematics intervention (or prevention) programs that would be more effective than those available from commercial publishing houses. In this chapter, I describe seven such programs, giving a disproportionate amount of space to one program, Number Worlds (Griffin, 2007), in order to provide an illustrative example of the nature of a theory- and research-based mathematics intervention program and the sorts of learning gains one can expect from such a program.

In the following sections, I briefly describe the manner in which math competence develops across the preschool and middle childhood years and the theoretical framework, central conceptual structure theory (Case & Okamoto, 1996), which made it possible to chart this progression and to identify the knowledge that is central to success in school math at several age levels. An assessment tool, the Number Knowledge Test (Griffin & Case, 1997), which can be used to measure a child's progress along this developmental progression, is mentioned next. I then discuss research findings demonstrating that many children living in low-income communities in the United States and Canada start school with a developmental lag of approximately 1–2 years in the math knowledge needed for successful learning of mathematics in Grade 1 and, consequently, are at risk of developing mathematical learning difficulties.

The body of this chapter is devoted to a description of a core set of instructional principles that underlie the Number Worlds program. I attempt in this chapter to generalize these principles and to present a set of teaching

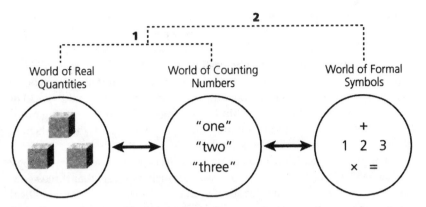

Figure 17.1. Core image of mathematics showing the three worlds of mathematics represented by three circles: the world of real quantities that exist in space and time, the world of counting numbers and iconic symbols (e.g., spoken language), and the world of formal symbols (e.g., written numerals and operation signs). Dotted line *1* marks the integration of the first two worlds in children's thought. Dotted line *2* marks the integration of the third world with the first two worlds.

strategies that can be used to enhance math learning and achievement for a broad range of children, including children who are typically developing as well as those with specific or general developmental lags and/or learning disabilities. Six other early mathematics intervention programs that were developed by members of the same general research community are also briefly described, and the common and distinctive features of all seven programs are highlighted. Finally, highlights from the evaluation studies that have been conducted to assess the effectiveness of the Number Worlds program are presented.

Before I began the curriculum development work that is mentioned in the preceding paragraph, I created a model that helped me define the discipline of mathematics and knowledge needed to master this discipline. This model, which was inspired by Robbie Case,[1] (personal communication, 1988), served as an excellent tool as I proceeded through each stage of this work, and I use it repeatedly in this chapter to illustrate the ways in which the various features of this work—from theory building to the creation of a model for describing the development of number knowledge to the creation of an intervention program to teach this knowledge—are interconnected.

CORE IMAGE OF MATHEMATICS

As illustrated in Figure 17.1, the discipline of mathematics is composed of three worlds: the world of real quantities that exist in space and time, the world of counting numbers and iconic symbols (e.g., spoken language), and the world of formal symbols (e.g., written numerals and operation

---

[1] Principal architect of central conceptual structure theory and an eminent cognitive developmental theorist.

signs). Math competence rests, fundamentally, on the construction of a rich set of conceptual relationships among these worlds. Readers may ask, "Why three worlds, instead of two?" The world of formal symbols and the world of real quantities are obvious choices in any model of mathematics if one considers the fact that the symbol system, which is dominant in everyone's image of mathematics, has no meaning without its referents in the world of real quantities. The reasoning behind including the world of counting numbers in this model and giving it equal status with the other two worlds may be less obvious. Two bodies of knowledge support this choice.

The first comes from pioneering work in cognitive neuropsychology (Dehaene, 1997; Dehaene & Cohen, 1995), which suggests that three separate regions of the brain are implicated in even the simplest mathematical problem-solving tasks, such as determining whether a given number is bigger or smaller than 5. These regions are the visual center of the brain (the occipital lobe), where symbolic material is processed; the verbal center of the brain (the left temporal lobe), where verbal material is processed; and the spatial center of the brain (the parietal lobe), where spatial material and judgments of relative size are processed (see Chapter 13 for a more detailed explication of these ideas). As can be seen, these centers map directly onto the three worlds defined in the model. The second body of knowledge comes from research in cognitive developmental psychology, which is described in the following section. As will become apparent, for the construction of mathematical knowledge as opposed to the use of this knowledge for everyday problem solving, the middle world—the world of counting numbers—may be the most important world of all.

THE DEVELOPMENT OF MATHEMATICAL KNOWLEDGE

Well before the world of formal symbols is within most children's ken, they learn the counting words: "one-two-three" or "one-two-three-four-five." Knowledge of the verbal counting words grows systematically over the preschool years, and by the age of 4–5 years, most children have constructed an *initial counting schema* (Gelman, 1978; Griffin & Case, 1997). This schema enables them to reliably count a small set of objects and determine how many there are. Children's knowledge of the world of real quantities grows systematically over this period as well, supported to a large extent by opportunities to explore the physical and spatial world and the availability of a mentor (a parent or guide) who makes aspects of this world (e.g., variables of height, length, weight) salient to children by naming them (e.g., "big," "little," "heavy," "light"). By the ages of 4–5 years, most children have also constructed a *global quantity schema* (Griffin & Case, 1997; Starkey, 1992), which enables them to say, for example, which of two sets is bigger or smaller, longer or shorter, or heavier or lighter.

Although children can count by the ages of 4–5 years, it is not until the ages of 5–6 years that children spontaneously use their knowledge of counting to make quantity estimates. The most compelling evidence for this robust finding comes from studies using Siegler and Robinson's (1982) balance beam task. When presented with two stacks of weights that differ in number but that look similar in visual appearance, children below the ages of 5–6 will typically rely on visual appearance alone and predict that the beam will balance. Even when this judgment is refuted by the beam's action, most children at this age do not consider counting the weights to see if one stack might be larger (of greater quantity) and therefore heavier than the other. Children above this age level, who have linked their knowledge of counting with their knowledge of quantity and who can thus appreciate what the counting words can tell them about the quantitative world, choose to count automatically, even when their eyes tell them that the weights on each side of the beam are identical. The cognitive transition that is illustrated in this example, and that is indicated by the dotted line marked 1 in Figure 17.1, marks a major transition in children's thought. When children have achieved this transition, they have constructed what is called a *central conceptual structure for number* (Griffin, 2002; Griffin & Case, 1997; Griffin, Case, & Siegler, 1994). This enables them to use the counting numbers alone, in the absence of countable objects, to make sense of a range of quantitative situations (e.g., to tell you how many you would have if you had four of something and someone gave you three more).

When the counting numbers acquire meaning by being solidly linked to the quantitative world, children are ready to make sense of the world of formal symbols. In a very real sense, this symbolic world acquires meaning for children through its connections to the interconnected worlds of counting numbers and real quantities, as illustrated in the dotted line marked 2 in Figure 17.1. The counting numbers, which many children have used from the age of 2 years and onward, thus provide the intermediary link through which the symbolic world becomes connected to the world of real quantities. Without the set of connections specified in the dotted lines in the figure, the world of formal symbols can remain forever mysterious and devoid of any real meaning.

As development proceeds, children's central conceptual structure for number becomes differentiated around the ages of 7–8 years into a bidimensional structure, which allows them to solve quantitative problems that vary along two dimensions (e.g., tens and ones in the area of school math; dollars and cents in the area of money; hours and minutes in the area of time). Children's central conceptual structure is further differentiated and elaborated around the ages of 9–10 years, allowing them to handle triple-digit numbers and problems involving a trade-off between two quantitative dimensions (Griffin, 2002; Griffin & Case, 1997). As should be apparent, the major scaffolding for development across the elementary school years is constructed around the age of 5 years. If this scaffold is weak or non-existent, a child will lack not only a firm conceptual foundation on which to build higher order understandings but also an ability to make sense of the instruction that is provided in school and that is designed to teach these higher order understandings. The emotional consequences of this situation—a dislike of school math, a lack of confidence in one's ability to do math—will be familiar to all readers of this book.

ASSESSING NUMBER KNOWLEDGE

The developmental progression that is outlined in the previous section describes the manner in which a typical child in developed societies (i.e., a child who typically succeeds in school math) constructs mathematical knowledge. A test to measure this knowledge at four age levels—4, 6, 8, and 10 years old—was developed in the mid-1980s (Griffin & Case, 1997; Griffin, Case, & Sandieson, 1992). This instrument, the Number Knowledge Test (Griffin, 2002, 2005a), has been refined, subjected to developmental scaling techniques, evaluated, and used extensively. Chronological age equivalents for raw scores on this test allow teachers and clinicians to determine a developmental age score for children and, thus, to assess the extent to which a developmental delay might be present. The test is also a reliable predictor of success in school math, as indicated in findings presented later in this chapter. The Number Knowledge Test is published elsewhere (see Griffin, 2002, 2005a) and is readily available (www.clarku.edu/numberworlds). As suggested in the introduction, research studies conducted over a number of years in several low-income communities across the United States and Canada suggest that large numbers of children (more than 50% in some populations) fail the 5- to 6-year-old level of this test at the end of kindergarten and start first grade without the knowledge needed for successful learning of arithmetic in school (Griffin & Case, 1997; Griffin et al., 1995; Griffin et al., 1994).

THE NUMBER WORLDS INTERVENTION PROGRAM

The Number Worlds program (Griffin, 2007) was developed to teach the knowledge needed for success in school math at several successive age and grade levels from preschool through Grade 6. The major objective of the program is to ensure that children acquire the central conceptual understandings that are expected for particular age and grade levels, on the basis of the theory and research just described. A second focus is to ensure that children acquire the content knowledge specified in *Principles and Standards for School Mathematics* (National Council of Teachers of Mathematics, 2000).

The rate at which children are expected to acquire this knowledge is determined by their capabilities, and the entire program is sequenced to allow children to start at a level they are comfortable with and to proceed at a pace that is manageable for them. The goal is to allow children to consolidate one level of knowledge before moving on to the next level of cognitive challenges, and thus to ensure that at each level, children acquire a solid foundation of mathematical knowledge on which to build higher level understandings.

The first four levels of the Number Worlds program, for prekindergarten through Grade 2, were developed and systematically evaluated between 1988 and 2000. Various aspects of these grade-level programs, which were designed to prevent school failure rather than to intervene after failure has occurred, are described in detail in several different publications (Griffin, 2002, 2003, 2004a, 2004b, 2004c, 2005a; Griffin et al., 1994). To give readers a flavor of the prekindergarten–Grade 6 series, a core set of the instructional principles that was used to create the program and to further define program objectives is presented next in the bulleted list. In the following section, a subset of these principles is translated into a more general set of teaching strategies that can be used, with or without the Number Worlds program, to foster successful learning of mathematics in school.

- Teach specific math concepts and skills—ones that are foundational for later learning.

- Expose children to the major ways number is represented and talked about in modern cultures.

- Ensure that children acquire the rich set of interconnected knowledge that underlies number sense.

- Lead children through a developmental sequence that conforms to the natural developmental progression.

- Provide hands-on games and activities that encourage children to construct their own mathematical meanings.

- Provide plenty of opportunity for children to communicate mathematically, both orally and in writing.

- Ensure that activities capture children's emotions and imaginations as well as their minds.

- Ensure that activities are appropriate for children from a wide range of social and cultural backgrounds.

TEACHING STRATEGIES TO HELP CHILDREN LEARN

As was implied in the previous section, an instructional principle determines the general and specific goals of a curriculum as well as the entire set of teaching materials that is created to address these goals. This includes the learning activities that are developed; the manipulative materials that are created or selected to accompany these activities; and the directions that are provided for teachers to specify the manner in which each activity, as well as the program as a whole, should be taught. If the instructional principles that are selected for program development are based on solid research in the learning sciences (see, for example, Donovan & Bransford, 2005), as was the case for the Number Worlds program and for the six other programs that are described later in this chapter, and if all components of the program are carefully aligned with these principles, implementation of the program should be smooth and learning gains should be significant. Although there is substantial evidence, presented later in this chapter, to suggest that the latter expectation is warranted, extensive experience has indicated that implementation of the Number Worlds program, indeed of any new and innovative curriculum, is not nearly as smooth as originally anticipated.

Teachers frequently personalize any curriculum they are using to suit their own teaching style and priorities as well as the needs and interests of their students. This is a teacher's right and also a teacher's responsibility. The most carefully crafted set of teacher directions is thus often adapted, either consciously or unconsciously, in ways that can enhance the learning goals of the program or undermine them. Acquainting teachers with the goals of a program and its underlying instructional principles is clearly not sufficient to enable teachers to use the program in the intended manner. Rather, what is needed is the articulation of a general set of teaching strategies that define the instructional principles in operational terms and that make elements of effective practice salient for teachers. In this section, I describe five such strategies.

The strategies presented here are closely linked to the model presented in Figure 17.1. They are also described in more general terms than is typical in the teacher education literature to give teachers a general instructional framework that they can use to guide their minute-to-minute classroom decisions. Finally, for each strategy presented, I also describe the pitfalls that teachers may encounter in their attempts to interpret and use it.

Strategy 1: Begin Instruction in the World of Real Quantities

For each math concept taught, begin instruction in the world of real quantities. Stay in this world long enough to allow students to construct a good intuitive understanding of the quantities and/or quantity transformations that underlie the concept.

To appreciate the importance of this strategy, answer the following questions:

1.   Which is bigger, 7 or 9?

2.   Which is bigger, $\frac{5}{8}$ or $\frac{3}{5}$?

Most adults can answer the first question in a split second without any hesitation whatsoever. The second question is much more challenging, and many college seniors not only are unable to answer it with any certainty after reflecting for several minutes but also are unable to recall a procedure, such as converting fractions to decimals, that could be used to compute an answer. The root of this problem may be traced to the fact that, in all their years of formal schooling, many students have not been exposed to real quantities that would give rational numbers meaning. Without this exposure, which is amply provided for whole numbers in most early mathematics programs, it is difficult for many students to describe what a fraction is, let alone determine its relative size.

In the Number Worlds program, children are immersed in the world of real quantities in every lesson. Although the Warm-Up section of each lesson is typically devoted to the development of computational fluency (i.e., counting skills and mental math skills), the Whole Class and Small Group games that follow the Warm-Up provide hands-on opportunities for children to use a variety of physical props (e.g., game boards, people pawns that represent students on the board, dice, counting chips, number cards, base 10 blocks) to explore learning contexts that are often spatial in nature. By moving around or along a game board, for example, and by following the rules of the game, children encounter or create quantity displays, which they must deal with in some fashion to achieve the goals of the game. Through their own activity, therefore, children can construct a rich set of intuitive understandings of the quantities they are exposed to in the game and the quantity transactions they are enacting. The social nature of these small- or large-group activities enhances the learning possibilities that they provide.

As one example, in the Secret Number Game, four children take turns rolling a die and putting that many Lite-Brite pegs along their own number line pegboard. On each turn, children use pegs of a different color to indicate the quantity rolled on that turn. When all children have had two or three turns, they pause to discuss where they are and how they got there. This discussion typically reveals that you can get to 7, for example, in a variety of ways (e.g., by rolling 4 and 3, or 3 and 4, or 6 and 1, or 2 and 5, etc.). It also reveals that a child who is on 8 has one more peg than a child who is on 7 and is one number higher up on the pegboard. Similarly, a child who is on 6 has one fewer peg than a child who is on 7 and is one number lower on the pegboard. Through conversations such as these, which are informed by the visuospatial displays in front of them, children build up a rich intuitive understanding of the additive composition of numbers, of the commutative property of addition, and of the addition facts. Play continues until one child reaches the end of the pegboard at number 25. At this point, a secret number, which the teacher has hidden in an envelope, is drawn and the child who has landed on this number during game play is the winner of the game. The need to prove that the child actually landed on this number necessitates that the child describe the quantities he or she rolled to get there, which provides another opportunity for the child to attend to addition facts and to properties of the addition operation.

Because children love the games and are happy to dwell in this world for as long as they are permitted, one would think that the program provides a fail-safe way to ensure that teaching strategy 1 is implemented. This is not necessarily the case. In the Secret Number Game, for example, more than one well-meaning first-grade teacher has decided to enhance the activity by requiring that each child keep a written record of each quantity rolled before placing pegs on the board. The task of creating such a record consumes all of each child's attention and energy and essentially aborts the purpose of the game. While one child is laboriously recording the quantity rolled, the next child, tired of waiting, usually takes his or her turn and the game becomes a mechanical exercise of rolling the die and writing on a piece of paper, rather than a social journey during which children can attend to one another's progress on the number line and compare the routes they took to get there. There is a place for such record keeping in the program (i.e., when children have built up solid, intuitive understandings of the quantities involved and can communicate these orally with ease), but it is not during the early phases of playing this game.

When one considers Stigler and Hiebert's (1999) finding that math teaching in the United States typically starts in the symbolic world (i.e., with formal definitions and explanations) and proceeds to practice with or exploration of the concepts just defined, it is easy to see why teachers who alter activities believe that they are enhancing them. This is the model that they have been exposed to throughout their own learning history, and this is the model that makes sense to them. Asking teachers to reverse this model and to use the model that is typical of schooling in Asian countries (Stigler & Hiebert, 1999) and that is recommended in this chapter and in the Number Worlds program is asking quite a lot.

Although teachers of young children uniformly endorse the use of manipulative materials, in classroom after classroom, I have observed first- and second-grade teachers who were using a variety of more traditional mathematics programs. These teachers were asking their students to use the materials to illustrate formal mathematical expressions that were written on the board, rather than use them to build up an understanding of the concepts underlying these formal expressions. If children do not understand the symbols, it is difficult if not impossible for them to use objects to illustrate them. If they do understand the symbolic expressions, the task of illustrating them with objects is an empty activity. For children who are good in math, these instructional flaws may waste time, but they are not harmful. However, for students with learning difficulties, these flaws present one more opportunity for them to feel "dumb" in math ("I can't even use manipulatives!") and one more missed opportunity for them to gain some useful knowledge.

Strategy 2: Provide Ample Opportunities for Oral Language

Provide ample opportunity for students to use oral language to process the information obtained in the world of real quantities and to make sense of it. Stay in the world of counting numbers long enough to ensure that students can fluently describe the quantity transactions they have been enacting.

This strategy is illustrated in part in the preceding section, in the emphasis placed on oral discussion during game play. The instructional principle underlying this strategy has been called *integration of implicit and explicit knowledge* in previous publications (e.g., Griffin & Case, 1997) and has been operationalized in the Number Worlds program as follows: The activities encourage children to build up representations that involve a strong global/spatial component and help them to move back and forth between these intuitive representations and representations that are more explicit and that involve a strong verbal component. Most of the activities included in the Number Worlds program not only encourage this mental activity but also require it in the way the games are structured and in the way the lesson plans for the teacher are scripted. However, in spite of this careful scaffolding, this is the one aspect of the Number Worlds program that is most often aborted or abbreviated.

In the Secret Number Game, for example, teachers are often tempted to skip over or abbreviate the discussion part of the activity—the crucial sense-making component of the lesson—for a variety of reasons. They want students to finish the game quickly so they can move on to another subject that is also required in the early elementary school curriculum; they want to avoid conversations among children that can get loud and noisy and disturb other groups of children; they believe that talking about quantities and using the counting numbers to do so is a preschool activity that has little value in an elementary mathematics classroom; or they believe that the real focus of mathematics teaching should be on the formal symbol system and teaching children how to use this system. It is easy to see where these beliefs come from and why a teacher might be motivated to shortchange this component of a lesson. However, if one considers how mathematical knowledge is constructed, as illustrated in Figure 17.1 and described in a previous section, it is also easy to see how such an action can abort the knowledge-construction process. Some children may be capable of making these connections on their own. For children with learning difficulties and for children who lack a rich experiential base in the world of real quantities and the world of counting numbers, the oral sense-making component of a lesson might the most important component of all.

Strategy 3: Gradually and Systematically Introduce Students to the World of Formal Symbols

Gradually and systematically, introduce students to the tools they need to record their understandings in the world of formal symbols. Make this task meaningful by providing contexts in which it makes sense to create a formal record.

Although the Number Worlds program is firmly grounded in a neo-Piagetian constructivist theory (see Griffin & Case, 1997), it does not assume, as do some constructivist approaches, that the understandings children acquire through their own hands-on activities will enable them to make sense of formal algorithms and use the formal symbol system with ease. Rather, as suggested in this strategy and in information processing models of learning (see Ginsburg, Klein, & Starkey, 1998, for a review of these models), it is assumed that children need a carefully crafted set of opportunities to learn how to translate the understandings they have gained in the first two worlds into a set of skills and understandings that will enable them to navigate smoothly and efficiently in the symbolic world. These opportunities are built into the Number Worlds program, from Grade 1 onwards, by requiring children to create written records of their actions during game play (e.g., by writing a series of addition and/or subtraction equations) to serve some purpose that is built into the game (e.g., to provide formal proof that they landed on the secret number during game play; to provide a set of directions that another student can use to recreate their moves). In these situations, frequent feedback on the adequacy and efficiency of the formal record is always provided by the peer group or the teacher, and opportunities to discuss alternate record-keeping strategies are built into every lesson. Consistent with the constructivist philosophy, the task of creating these records is often presented to children as a problem, and their input is solicited on the best way to solve it.

The background knowledge and skills that teachers bring to the classroom usually enable them to implement this strategy with relative ease, and several teachers have enhanced the program by creating record-keeping forms that make potential errors in the record-keeping process (e.g., forgetting to record the sum of the previous turn as the first addend for a new turn) salient for children. When the use of the formal symbol system has a purpose and when it is closely linked to children's own activity in the world of real quantities, children are better able to appreciate the meaning of each element in this system and note obvious errors in their use of it. Having repeated opportunities to engage in this activity in a variety of contexts and for a variety of purposes also helps children become fluent at interpreting and creating a wide variety of formal expressions.

Strategy 4: Start at Students' Level of Understanding and Teach Concepts in the Order Naturally Acquired

In selecting concepts to teach, start at students' current level of understanding and teach concepts in the order in which they are naturally acquired rather than the order suggested by a top-down analysis of mathematical concepts.

In addition to implementing a knowledge-construction progression that is natural for children in the way each individual concept is taught, as suggested by strategies 1 to 3 above, the concepts taught in the program as a whole should also be carefully sequenced, within and across grade levels, to recapitulate the natural developmental progression. Although the Number Worlds program gives teachers a lot of flexibility in the activities used on any particular day, the difficulty levels that have been assigned to each activity on the basis of extensive developmental research help teachers to select learning pathways through the program that allow each child to build systematically on his or her current knowledge. For this reason, teachers using the Number Worlds program generally have little difficulty implementing strategy 4.

For teachers using other programs that are not as carefully linked to the developmental research base, implementing this strategy can be a major challenge. Many commercial mathematics programs, for example, mandate that telling time to the hour and minute be taught in Grade 1, a full year before most children become capable of handling the conceptual demands (i.e., interpreting and relating two quantitative dimensions) of such a task. Similarly, these programs often require children to solve double-digit arithmetic problems (with the same set of conceptual demands) at the same grade level and/or require use of the formal symbol system in kindergarten, before children have consolidated the central conceptual understandings that would make this task meaningful. When I visit classrooms to supervise preservice teachers and these lessons are in progress, the classroom teachers often tell me, "I know this is developmentally inappropriate and I know the children can't handle this lesson, but I have to teach it. It's in the curriculum." As is true for other instructional flaws mentioned in previous sections, children who typically do well in school math are not seriously hurt by being exposed to some material they are not yet ready to handle. For children with learning difficulties and/or developmental delays, these instructional flaws undermine an already shaky confidence in their ability to make sense of numerical information, and such practices can have more serious, long-term consequences.

Stragegy 5: Let Students Use Natural Strategies but Expose Them to Other Problem-Solving Strategies

Let students use strategies that are natural for them as long as they need these strategies; at the same time, expose them to a range of other effective problem-solving strategies.

Because the use of strategies that are natural for children (e.g., using fingers to count) is not only encouraged in the Number Worlds program but also actively taught to children who do not spontaneously use them on their own, implementing this strategy is not a problem for Number Worlds' teachers once they overcome a common, initial reluctance to consider these strategies acceptable. Most children (and adults too!) use their fingers to count and to solve any computation problem that cannot easily be handled in their heads, and they abandon the use of this strategy as soon as it is no longer needed. In spite of this fact, many teachers continue to believe that using fingers to count is harmful to children (e.g., it might prevent them from acquiring mental math proficiency or from memorizing the basic facts) and should be discouraged, if not explicitly forbidden. Similarly, many commercial curricula mandate that children use subtraction to solve a host of arithmetic problems (e.g., missing addend problems and compare word problems that ask, for example, how many more one set has than another) when a substantial research base (see Case & Bereiter, 1982) has shown that children represent these problems as addition problems for many years (e.g., from the ages of 6 to about 9) and use addition spontaneously to solve them. As is true for the other strategies recommended in this chapter, depriving children of the opportunity to use a strategy that comes naturally and that will help them make sense of mathematical situations does a huge disservice to all children. For children with learning difficulties, this is perhaps the cruelest blow of all.

OTHER RESEARCH-BASED MATHEMATICS INTERVENTION PROGRAMS

Six other early mathematics programs that have been developed can be characterized, individually, by a set of distinctive features that were shaped by the authors' research interests, their areas of research expertise within the field of mathematics, and their perspectives on the nature of mathematical learning. These include 1) Mathematics Recovery (Wright, Stewart, Stafford, & Cain, 1998), a one-on-one intervention program specifically designed for first graders who are below average in arithmetic; 2) Building

Blocks (Sarama & Clements, 2004), a technology-based program designed to teach geometry and to foster spatial sense; 3) 'Round the Rug Math (Casey, 2004), a language-based program designed to foster spatial sense; 4) Big Math for Little Kids (Greenes, Ginsburg, & Balfanz, 2004), a comprehensive program designed to encourage the exploration of complex ideas; 5) Helping Children Think Mathematically (Baroody, 1998), a broad-based, comprehensive program with a particular focus on arithmetic; and 6) the Berkeley Math Readiness Curriculum (Klein & Starkey, 2004), also a broad-based comprehensive program. Like Number Worlds, which was designed to teach number sense, each of these programs is more extensive than the distinctive features characterization might suggest.

As noted, two of the programs were specifically designed to teach spatial sense, and they are unique in giving priority to an area of mathematics that is often neglected in early childhood programs. One of these, Building Blocks, uses computers as the primary teaching/learning tool; the other, 'Round the Rug Math, uses a storytelling format. These differences in instructional format may make each of these programs more effective for particular groups of students whose natural talents and inclinations lead them to favor one format as opposed to the other. Although all of these programs are grounded in recent research on how children think, learn, and remember, Mathematics Recovery and Number Worlds are distinct in being grounded in a particular theory of cognitive development (Steffe's social constructivist model and Central Conceptual Theory, respectively), which, in each case, is used to define the particular mathematics knowledge that the program was designed to teach and the way the knowledge objectives are sequenced within the program. By contrast, Big Math for Little Kids, although it is informed by the developmental progressions that have been charted in the literature, encourages children to break the bounds of these progressions and to construct complex mathematical ideas that are often not achieved until an older age. Finally, to a greater extent than the other programs, four of the programs (Big Math for Little Kids, 'Round the Rug Math, Building Blocks, and Number Worlds) incorporate the newest design feature to be added to the list of instructional principles identified in the cognitive science literature: a set of narratives, icons, and other devices to ensure that the learning activities children are exposed to engage their imagination and emotions as well as their minds.

Although each of these programs is unique in terms of the specific math knowledge that is taught and the specific instructional technology that was recruited or developed to teach this knowledge, the seven programs described in this chapter share a set of common features. Given that they were all informed by the same knowledge base, these commonalities are not surprising. All the programs seek to support and enhance children's mathematical development, as opposed to teaching a limited set of skills. All provide a developmentally sensitive curriculum that is, at the same time, sensitive to the needs of individual learners. All, with the possible exception of Math Recovery, provide an inquiry-based approach to learning, with plenty of encouragement for prediction, explanation, mathematical communication, multiple ways of representing number and quantity, and the use of multiple problem-solving strategies.

Because all of the programs mentioned in this section are newer than Number Worlds, they have not yet been subjected to the extensive evaluation research that has been conducted for Number Worlds and that is described in the following section. Controlled studies to assess learning gains are in progress for Building Blocks and have been reported for the Berkeley Math Readiness Project. For the latter project, the results showed that intervention significantly enhanced the informal math knowledge of both middle-income and low-income groups, and that both of these groups exhibited better math knowledge than the comparison group (Klein & Starkey, 2004). Pre–post learning gains for Math Recovery show that 69% of a large group of first graders (n = 91) who were 1 or more years below average at the start of first grade exceeded curricular expectations at the end of the school year (Wright et al., 1998). 'Round the Rug Math was tested under two conditions, with findings suggesting that using a story context to teach spatial skills is more effective than presenting the same content in a decontextualized form (Casey, 2004). Note that this finding provides convergent support for the model of mathematics that was presented at the beginning of this chapter, which suggests that the world of oral language is a crucial component in children's mathematics learning. Finally, for all programs, results of formal and/or extensive informal assessments indicated substantial growth in mathematical knowledge, demonstrating the effectiveness of instruction that is grounded in cognitive science theory and research.

NUMBER WORLDS EVALUATION FINDINGS

Although the Number Worlds program has not always been implemented in the intended manner, the resources it provides to address program objectives and to implement the teaching strategies described earlier are rich enough to ensure that these objectives are met, to a greater or lesser extent, by all teachers using the program. In this section I present three sets of findings to illustrate the sorts of learning this approach makes possible. All of the findings come from a longitudinal study that followed three groups of children for a 3-year period, from the beginning of kindergarten to the end of grade 2.

The Number Worlds group (n = 54 at the beginning of kindergarten) attended neighborhood schools in a low socioeconomic status (SES) community in an urban center with high rates of crime and drug use. Although these children had not yet been diagnosed with any learning disabilities, school records showed that the majority lived in single-parent homes and several were born with addictive drugs in their system. A control group ($n = 48$), matched as closely as possible for SES and ethnicity, attended neighborhood schools in an adjoining community, and a normative group ($n = 78$) attended an award-winning magnet school serving more affluent communities in the broader city. The Number Worlds group received the Number Worlds program in their classrooms for the entire period; the control group and the normative group received a variety of other commercially available mathematics programs that had been selected by their schools over the same time period.

Changes in Number Knowledge over a 3-Year Period

Figure 17.2 shows children's performance on the Number Knowledge Test at the beginning of kindergarten, at the end of kindergarten, and at the end of Grades 1 and 2. On the basis of the theory described in this chapter, a developmental level score of 0.0 is expected for 4-year-olds, a score of 1.0 for 6-year-olds, and a score of 2.0 for 8-year-olds. As the figure suggests, the performance of the normative group is consistent with developmental expectations at each time period. By contrast, both the Number Worlds group and the control group started kindergarten at a distinct disadvantage compared with the normative group, demonstrating a developmental delay of

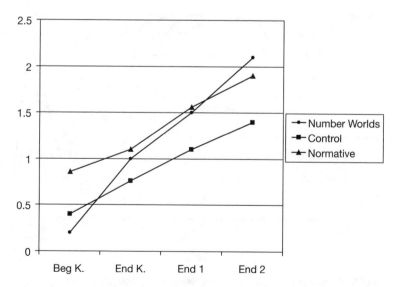

Figure 17.2. Mean developmental level scores on Number Knowledge Test at four time periods.

1½ to 2 years in conceptual knowledge of number. Whereas this discrepancy remained constant for the control group as they progressed through the first 3 years of school, the discrepancy vanished for the Number Worlds group by the end of kindergarten. At the end of Grades 1 and 2, the performance of the Number Worlds group was indistinguishable from the performance of the normative group and was higher, in absolute terms, at the end of Grade 2. These findings suggest that the Number Worlds program was remarkably successful is doing what it was designed to do to: enabling children who start school at a considerable disadvantage to their peer group to acquire the central conceptual understandings of number that are expected for their age and grade levels.

Computational Skills at the End of Grade 1

Although the Number Worlds program exposed children systematically to the world of mathematical symbols, it did so in an innovative fashion. Traditional worksheets, for example, were never used. It was of interest, therefore, to see how well children who had been exposed to this program would do on more traditional tests of procedural knowledge. To assess this, Stigler, Lee, and Stevenson's (1990) Computation Test was administered to all children in the sample at the end of Grade 1. Figure 17.3 shows the perform-

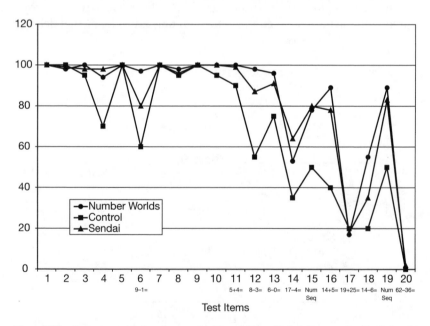

Figure 17.3. Percentage of first graders passing items 1–20 on Stigler's Computation Test in Sendai (Stigler's norms) and Worcester (Number Worlds and Control samples).

ance of the Number Worlds group, the control group, and Stigler et al.'s Japanese sample on the first 20 items of this test (i.e., the items created for the first-grade level). As the figure suggests, the performance of the Number Worlds group was commensurate with the performance of their Japanese peers on every item of this test. By contrast, the performance of the control group was significantly lower on several items, as well as on the test as a whole, and this discrepancy was most apparent on the subtraction questions. These findings provide strong evidence that children who received the Number Worlds program had acquired a solid base of procedural knowledge that they could deploy in a flexible fashion (i.e., to solve novel problems).

Performance on Three Transfer Tests at the End of Grade 2

To assess broader transfer to domains of knowledge and problem formats that had not been taught in the Number Worlds program, a Time test, a Money test, and a Formal Notation test were administered to all children in the sample at the end of grade 2. Note that time problems and money problems had been carefully avoided in the material presented at each grade

Table 17.1. Percent of students passing selected items from three transfer tests at the end of Grade 2

Test items	Intervention (n = 28) %	Control (n = 21) %	Normative (n = 31) %
Time Test:			
Which is longer: 1 hour and 50 minutes or 2 hours and 1 minute?	93	48	83
If I wait 30 minutes and another 30 minutes, how long altogether (in hours) will I wait?	93	43	70
It's 3:00 now. What time will it be in 2 hours?	85	33	68
Money Test:			
Show a dime plus 6 cents: How much do I have altogether?	96	52	67
Which is closer to 19 cents: A quarter or a dime?	93	43	63
This candy costs 7 cents. If I pay 10 cents, how much do I get back?	85	38	60
Formal Notation Test:			
23 $+ 36$	86	48	81
87 $- 54$	86	24	58
$3 \times 5 =$	71	0	35

level to ensure that these tests would provide valid measures of transfer. Table 17.1 shows the performance of the three groups included in the sample on selected items from these tests. As was the case for the other data sets described above, the Number Worlds group outperformed the control group on each of these tests. They also compared favorably to the normative group on all items included in these tests. These findings suggest that the understandings acquired by the Number Worlds children had a wide range of applicability, enabling them to keep pace with and/or outperform more advantaged children who had been explicitly taught time-telling and money-handling skills in their regular classroom instruction.

CONCLUSION

In this chapter, mathematics and mathematical knowledge have been defined as a set of conceptual relationships among three worlds: the world of real quantities, the world of counting numbers, and the world of formal symbols. The model that was presented to illustrate this definition—three interconnected circles—was also used to describe the manner in which this set of conceptual relationships is constructed, between the ages of 2 and 10 years, and the teaching strategies that can and should be used to facilitate this knowledge-construction process. Although young children are capable of constructing a lot of mathematical knowledge on their own, many young children fail to construct enough of this knowledge to profit from the instruction that is offered in school, either because they lack opportunities to do so or because of a variety of general or specific learning disabilities. For these children, the kind of instruction they receive in school is critical, especially in the early years before disenchantment with mathematics and feelings of inadequacy set in. As suggested by the research findings presented in the previous section, this instruction can determine the shape and course of their mathematical journey.

The children who were exposed to a mathematics program, Number Worlds, which was explicitly built to teach the set of conceptual relationships specified in the model, experienced a good measure of success in their first 3 years of schooling. By contrast, children who started school at a similar disadvantage and who received a variety of other mathematics programs (i.e., the control group) experienced a lot of failure, as indicated in the results reported in this chapter. Additional research findings reported elsewhere (see Griffin & Case, 1996; Griffin, Case, & Siegler, 1994) indicate that the effects of the Number Worlds program last for 1 full year beyond exposure to the program, and anecdotal information suggests that the number of children who are required to repeat a grade or who are referred for special education services because of mathematical difficulties in school is significantly reduced in classrooms using the Number Worlds curriculum.

Taken together, these findings suggest that the Number Worlds program provides an effective intervention for children at risk of developing mathematical learning difficulties.

In closing, it is worth asking: What are the elements of the Number Worlds approach that contributed to its success? The answer to this question, which is amply provided in this chapter, can be summarized by suggesting that the crucial elements are extremely simple ones: (a) Teach knowledge that is central to children's understanding of the domain, and (b) present material in a manner that is consistent with children's sense-making capabilities. The success of the Number Worlds curriculum and of the other research-based early mathematics programs mentioned in this chapter provides evidence that an approach to mathematics teaching that is based on cognitive science can go a long way toward preventing school failure in mathematics for the group of children most at risk for this failure: children who start school with developmental lags in number knowledge and/or with general or specific learning disabilities.

Thanks to a new national mandate for research-based curricula, commercial publishing houses are now seeking out programs that are solidly grounded in the research base, and all of the programs described in this chapter are now, or soon will be, commercially available. This will permit a much broader distribution of this set of programs and make it possible to assess the relative effectiveness of each for particular mathematical learning goals, particular groups of students, and particular intervention contexts (e.g., whole-class, small-group, and individual instruction). This is a promising avenue for future research.

REFERENCES

Baroody, A.J., with Coslick, R.T. (1998). *Fostering children's mathematical power: An investigative approach to K-8 mathematics instruction.* Mahwah, NJ: Lawrence Erlbaum Associates.

Case, R., & Bereiter, C. (1982, June). *From behaviorism to cognitive behaviorism to cognitive developmental theory: Steps in the evolution of instructional design.* Paper presented at the Conference for Educational Technology in the 80s, Caracas, Venezuela.

Case, R., & Okamoto, Y. (1996). The role of central conceptual structures in the development of children's thought. *Monographs of the Society for Research in Child Development, 61,* (Serial No. 246).

Casey, B. (2004). Mathematics problem-solving adventures: A language-arts-based supplementary series for early childhood that focuses on spatial sense. In D.H. Clements, J. Sarama, & A. DiBiase (Eds.), *Engaging young children in mathematics: Standards for early childhood mathematics education* (pp. 377–389). Mahwah, NJ: Lawrence Erlbaum Associates.

Clements, D., Wilson, D., & Sarama, J. (2004). Young children's composition of geometric figures: A learning trajectory. *Mathematical Thinking and Learning, 6(2),* 163–184.

Dehaene, S. (1997). *The number sense.* New York: Oxford University Press.

Dehaene, S., & Cohen, L. (1995). Towards an anatomical and functional model of number processing. *Mathematical Cognition, 1,* 83–120.

Donovan, S., Bransford, J., & Pellegrino, J. (1999). *How people learn.* Washington, DC: National Academies Press.

Donovan, S., & Bransford, J. (2005). *How students learn: History, mathematics, and science in the classroom.* Washington, DC: National Academies Press.

Entwistle, D., & Alexander, K. (1990). Beginning school math competence: Minority and majority comparisons. *Child Development, 61,* 454–471.

Gelman, R. (1978). Children's counting: What does and does not develop. In R.S. Siegler (Ed.), *Children's thinking: What develops* (pp. 213–242). Mahwah, NJ: Lawrence Erlbaum Associates.

Gelman, R., & Gallistel, C. (1978). *The child's understanding of number.* Cambridge, MA: Harvard University Press.

Ginsburg, H., Klein, A., & Starkey, P. (1998). The development of children's mathematical thinking: Connecting research with practice. In W. Damon, I.E. Siegel, & K.A. Renninger (Eds.), *Handbook of child psychology: Vol. 4. Child psychology in practice* (5th ed., pp. 401–476). New York: John Wiley & Sons.

Ginsburg, H., Choi, Y., Lopez, L., Netley, R., & Chi, C.-Y. (1997). Happy birthday to you: The early mathematics thinking of Asian, South American and U.S. children. In T. Nunez & P. Bryant (Eds.). *Learning and teaching mathematics: An international perspective* (pp. 1–45). Mahwah, NJ: Lawrence Erlbaum Associates.

Greenes, C., Ginsburg, H.P., & Balfanz, R. (2004). Big math for little kids. *Early Childhood Research Quarterly, 19,* 159–166.

Griffin, S. (2002). The development of math competence in the preschool and early school years: Cognitive foundations and instructional strategies. In J. Royer (Ed.), *Mathematical cognition* (pp. 1–32). Greenwich, CT: Information Age Publishing.

Griffin, S. (2003, February). Laying the foundations for computational fluency in early childhood. *Teaching Children Mathematics, 306–309.* Reston, VA: National Council of Teachers of Mathematics.

Griffin, S. (2004a).Teaching number sense. *Educational Leadership, 61*(6), 39–42.

Griffin, S. (2004b). Building number sense with Number Worlds. *Early Childhood Research Quarterly, 19,* 173–180.

Griffin, S. (2004c). Number Worlds: A research-based mathematics program for young children. In D.H. Clements, J. Sarama, & A. DiBiase (Eds.), *Engaging young children in mathematics: Standards for early childhood mathematics education* (pp. 325–342). Mahwah, NJ: Lawrence Erlbaum Associates.

Griffin, S. (2005a). Fostering the development of whole number sense: Teaching mathematics in the primary grades. In J. Bransford & S. Donovan (Eds.), *How students learn: A targeted report for teachers* (pp. 250–302). Washington, DC: National Academies Press.

Griffin, S. (2005b). Contributions of central conceptual structure theory to education. In A. Demetriou & A. Raftopoulos (Eds.), *Cognitive developmental change: Models, methods, and measurement* (pp. 264–295). Cambridge: Cambridge University Press.

Griffin, S. (2007). *Number Worlds: A mathematics intervention program for grades prek-6.* Columbus, OH: SRA/McGraw-Hill.

Griffin, S., & Case, R. (1996). Evaluating the breadth and depth of training effects when central conceptual structures are taught. In R. Case & Y. Okamoto (Eds.), the role of central conceptual structures in the development of children's thought. *Monographs of the Society for Research in Child Development, 61*(1–2), 83–102.

Griffin, S., & Case, R. (1997). Re-thinking the primary school math curriculum: An approach based on cognitive science. *Issues in Education, 4*(1), 1–51.

Griffin, S., Case, R., & Capodilupo, A. (1995). Teaching for understanding: The importance of central conceptual structures in the elementary mathematics curriculum. In A. McKeough, I. Lupert, & A. Marini (Eds.), *Teaching for transfer: Fostering generalization in learning* (pp. 121–151). Mahwah, NJ: Lawrence Erlbaum Associates.

Griffin, S., Case, R., & Sandieson, R. (1992). Synchrony and asynchrony in the acquisition of children's everyday mathematical knowledge. In R. Case (Ed.), *The mind's staircase: Exploring the conceptual underpinnings of children's thought and knowledge* (pp. 75–97). Mahwah, NJ: Lawrence Erlbaum Associates.

Griffin, S., Case, R., & Siegler, R. (1994). Rightstart: Providing the central conceptual prerequisites for first formal learning of arithmetic to students at-risk for school failure. In K. McGilly (Ed.), *Classroom lessons: Integrating cognitive theory and classroom practice* (pp. 24–49). Cambridge, MA: Bradford Books, MIT Press.

Klein, A., & Starkey, P. (2004). Fostering preschool children's mathematical knowledge: Findings from the Berkeley math readiness project. In D.H. Clements, J. Sarama, & A. DiBiase (Eds.), *Engaging young children in mathematics: Standards for early childhood mathematics education* (pp. 343–360). Mahwah, NJ: Lawrence Erlbaum Associates.

National Council of Teachers of Mathematics. (2000). *Principles and standards for school mathematics.* Reston, VA: Author.

Okamoto, Y., & Case, R. (1996). Exploring the microstructure of children's conceptual structures in the domain of number. In R. Case & Y. Okamoto (Eds.), The role of central conceptual structures in the development of children's thought. *Monographs of the Society for Research in Child Development, 61* (Serial No. 246).

Sarama, J., & Clements, D.H. (2004). Building Blocks for early childhood mathematics. *Early Childhood Research Quarterly, 19,* 181–189.

Siegler, R.S., & Robinson, M. (1982). The development of numerical understanding. In H.W. Reese & L.P. Lipsitt (Eds.), *Advances in child development and behavior.* New York: Academic Press.

Starkey, P. (1992). The early development of numerical reasoning. *Cognition and Instruction, 4,* 93–126.

Starkey, P., & Klein, A. (2000). Fostering parental support for children's mathematical development: An intervention with Head Start families. *Early Education and Development, 11,* 659–680.

Starkey, P., Klein, A., Chang, I., Dong, Q., Pang, L., & Zhou, Y. (1999). *Environmental supports for young children's mathematical development in China and the United States.* Paper presented at the biennial meeting of the Society for Research in Child Development, Albuquerque, NM.

Stigler, J., & Hiebert, J. (1999). *The teaching gap.* New York: The Free Press.

Stigler, J.W., Lee, S.Y., & Stevenson, H.W. (1990). Mathematical knowledge of Japanese, Chinese, and American elementary school children. *Monographs of the National Council of Teachers of Mathematics.*

Wright, R.J., Stewart, R., Stafford, A., & Cain, R. (1998). Assessing and documenting student knowledge and progress in early mathematics. In S.B. Berenson, K.L. Dawkins, M. Blanton, W. N. Coulombe, J. Kolb, K. Norton, & L. Stiff (Eds.), *Proceedings of the Twentieth Annual Meeting of Mathematics Education, 1,* 211–216.

Chapter 18

Mathematical Problem Solving

Instructional Intervention

Lynn S. Fuchs and Douglas Fuchs

+ +

Important work on mathematical learning disability (MLD) has been accomplished since the early 1990s. This body of work describes the arithmetic difficulties of students with MLD and demonstrates how cognitive abilities are associated with the development of arithmetic skill (see Geary, 1993). The literature has focused predominantly on the acquisition of number combinations (e.g., arithmetic facts with one-digit operands, such as $3 + 5$; $9 - 2$; 3×2), with some attention to procedural skill (e.g., multidigit operations that involve application of algorithms, such as $24 + 39$; $102 - 47$; 25×32). The research shows, for example, that students with MLD manifest greater difficulty with counting than do students without MLD (e.g., Geary, 1990; Geary et al., 1992) and that they persist with immature backup strategies. It is not surprising, then, that students with MLD fail to make the shift to memory-based retrieval for deriving number combinations (Fleishner, Garnett, & Shepherd, 1982; Geary, Widaman, Little, & Cormier, 1987; Goldman, Pellegrino, & Mertz, 1988). In fact, when children with MLD do retrieve answers from memory, they commit more errors and manifest unsystematic retrieval speeds more than younger, academically typical counterparts (e.g., Geary, 1990; Geary & Brown, 1991; Gross-Tsur et al., 1996; Ostad, 1997).

This research was supported in part by grants (#1RO1 HD46154 and Core Grant HD15052) from the National Institute of Child Health and Human Development (NICHD) to Vanderbilt University. Statements do not reflect agency position or policy, and no official endorsement should be inferred.

Although these and other findings about calculation skill are important, less systematic inquiry has been aimed at mathematical problem solving (MPS). When MPS has been studied (e.g., Jordan & Hanich, 2000), it has been confined largely to one-step word problems involving number combination answers (e.g., "José has 3 nickels. Ben gives him 4 more. How many nickels does José have now?"). This research shows, for example, that students who experience difficulty with math and reading (as opposed to math deficits alone) have more difficulty with these simple word problems (e.g., Hanich, Jordan, Kaplan, & Dick, 2001; Jordan & Hanich, 2000). This may be due to a different pattern of underlying deficits in the cognitive abilities associated with comorbidity, to the working memory load created in processing the language demands of word problems (when students cannot access that language by reading), or perhaps to the more severe deficits these students experience with number combinations.

In any case, these simple word problems, which constitute the primary focus of research on MPS disability, are relegated to the first- and second-grade curriculum and fail to represent the kinds of MPS situations found in the real world. Complex MPS incorporates multiple sources of contextual realism. These sources of contextual realism may, for example, come from the inclusion of irrelevant information in the problem narrative, the need to consult other sources to find information required for problem solution, and the combination of problem types that necessitate multistep calculation solutions (e.g., "John worked 3 days at the gas station to earn $32. At the supermarket, he bought 2 sandwiches. Each sandwich cost $3. How much did he have left to spend later that day at the ball game?").

Given the more prominent role complex MPS plays as grade level increases and in the real world, the lack of sustained research on complex MPS is unfortunate. Over the past 5 years, therefore, we have initiated a program of research designed to increase understanding about MPS and improve student MPS performance in its simple as well as its more complex forms. In this chapter, which focuses on instructional intervention to improve complex MPS performance, we begin by providing background information on MPS, including a brief discussion about what contributes to difficulty with MPS and whether MPS is an ability that is distinct from calculation skill. We then describe our program of intervention research on complex MPS with third-grade students.

We emphasize that our work on MPS instructional intervention represents only one approach; we focus primarily (but not exclusively) on helping students sort out the complexities of problem narratives and the situations in which the mathematics is embedded. Other perspectives seek to deepen students' grasp of mathematics; still other methods rely on metacognitive instruction, which emphasizes general organizational and planning strategies for approaching MPS problems.

BACKGROUND INFORMATION ON MPS

The major (but not only) distinction between calculation and MPS is the addition of linguistic information, which requires children to construct a problem model. Whereas a calculation problem is already set up for solution, a word problem requires students to use the text to identify what information is missing, construct the number sentence, and derive the calculation problem for finding the missing number. Although this transparent difference would seem to alter the nature of the task, few studies have examined whether calculation and MPS skills actually constitute a single ability or are separate dimensions of mathematics competence.

One strategy for gaining insight into this issue is to explore whether the cognitive abilities underlying these aspects of math performance are the same or different. Three large-scale studies provide the basis for such insight. Studying 353 first, second, and third graders, Swanson and Beebe-Frankenberger (2004) identified working memory as an ability that contributed to strong performance in both these areas of math. Some unique cognitive abilities for each area, however, also emerged as important: phonological processing for calculation and fluid intelligence and short-term memory for simple word problems. Fuchs, Fuchs, Compton, et al. (2006) also examined the concurrent cognitive correlates of calculation versus simple word problems, this time controlling for the role of arithmetic skill in simple word problems among 312 third graders. Teacher ratings of attentive behavior were identified as an ability common to both skill areas, but the remaining abilities differed: for calculation, phonological decoding and processing speed were important; for simple word problems, nonverbal problem solving, concept formation, sight word efficiency, and language were important.

The third study (Fuchs et al., 2005) used beginning-of-the-year cognitive abilities to predict the development of skill across first grade among 272 children. Results again suggested some common and some unique patterns of cognitive abilities. The common predictors were working memory and ratings of attentive behavior. The unique predictors were phonological processing for calculation and nonverbal problem solving for simple word problems.

Across these studies, some findings recur; others are idiosyncratic. The results do indicate that some abilities underlying these areas of skill are unique. This provides the basis for hypothesizing that these two aspects of math performance may be distinct areas of competence. Consequently, Schatschneider, Fuchs, Fuchs, and Hamlett (2005) sought to address this question more directly. We assessed a representative sample of 634 third graders on three measures of calculation and four measures of MPS. Analyses showed that children who were strong on the calculation measures were not necessarily the same students who were strong on MPS. A two-factor model that differentiates calculation from MPS was better in accounting for the data. Moreover, in a series of analyses, we controlled for various skills and abilities thought to underlie MPS: reasoning, word identification and listening comprehension, and working memory. Regardless of the combination of abilities we controlled for, the 2-factor model, which preserved calculation skill and MPS skill as separate constructs, was dramatically superior to a 1-factor model. In addition, this study provided insight into how difficulty in one of these areas of math may depart from difficulty in the other by identifying students at the low end of the distribution on calculation and/or on MPS (designating them calculation and/or MPS disabled) and examining patterns of overlap. Findings suggested key differences in the cognitive abilities between these groups of students. Moreover, students who experienced difficulty with MPS with or without calculation problems were disproportionately from low socioeconomic backgrounds compared with students who experienced only calculation deficits. This suggests the possibility that language or math experience in the home may exacerbate a predisposition toward MPS disability. In any case, the literature on MPS is small, and it is hardly definitive. Additional work needs to be conducted to refine and corroborate results. Nevertheless, the body of work conducted to date does suggest that MPS may be distinct from calculation skill and that strategies for solving word problems need to be taught explicitly.

So, what may contribute to the differentiation between MPS and calculation skill? As already mentioned, the most transparent distinction between calculation and MPS problems is the addition of linguistic information, which requires children to construct a problem model. It is not surprising therefore that the manner in which problems are worded, including the length, the grammatical and semantic complexity, and the order of statements, helps determine the difficulty of the problem (e.g., Briars & Larkin, 1984; Helwig, Rosek-Toedesco, Tindal, Heath, & Almond, 1999).

Difficulty also increases as problems require more than one calculation step and are embedded in contextually realistic situations, with longer narratives or irrelevant information. Say, for example, that a student masters the problem type for calculating multiple quantities at a given price (e.g., "Fiona orders 3 new shirts. Each shirt costs $10. How much does she spend on shirts?"). In school, the student has been taught a solution strategy for this problem type and has practiced that solution strategy on multiple problems. Now consider two problems. Both incorporate the problem type for calculating multiple quantities at a given price, and both are novel (i.e., the student has never seen them before). The first problem simply states, "John bought 2 sandwiches. Each sandwich cost $3. How much did he spend?" This problem narrative, although including a novel cover story (i.e., the story features in the problem narratives), is highly similar to the problem narratives the student has practiced in school, and this similarity makes it relatively easy for the student to recognize that the novel problem belongs to the specific problem type for calculating multiple quantities at a given price. By contrast, the second problem, "John worked 3 days at the gas station to earn $32. At the supermarket, he bought 2 sandwiches. Each sandwich cost $3. How much did he have left to spend later that day at the ball game?" is longer, adds irrelevant information ("worked 3 days at the gas station"), and incorporates an extra step (computing how much was left). Each of these features increases the difficulty of recognizing this novel problem as belonging to the problem type for calculating multiple quantities at a given price and, therefore, increases the difficulty of finding the answer.

In fact, the addition of irrelevant information or an extra step increases difficulty more for students with MLD than for their peers who are typically developing. With a cross-sectional sample of students in Grades 3–8, Parmar, Cawley, and Frazita (1996) showed that the inclusion of irrelevant information in addition problems produced a similar drop in accuracy for third graders with and without learning disabilities or behavior disorders; however, by eighth grade, the drop associated with the inclusion of irrelevant information was twice as large for students with disabilities as for students without disabilities. A similar but more dramatic pattern emerged when an extra step was required for problem solution. This illustrates how students who are typically achieving gradually develop greater capacity to transfer the MPS skills they learn in school (i.e., to attack complex novel problems) better than do students with disabilities.

Russell and Ginsburg (1984) provided additional insight into the MPS performance of students with MLD. They compared fourth graders with MLD to typical third and fourth graders on one-step word problems portraying realistic situations, varying the complexity of semantic structures and manipulating the inclusion of irrelevant information. Students with MLD performed similarly to typical third and fourth graders on simple addition problems involving two or three addends, with nearly 100% of students in all three groups demonstrating mastery. When irrelevant information was incorporated into a simple three-addend problem, however, the performance of MLD students deteriorated more than that of typical third and fourth quarters. In a similar way, when a subtraction problem became more semantically complex, the performance of MLD students deteriorated more dramatically than the performance of either comparison group. This work suggests that students with MLD may approach MPS in a relatively inflexible way; irrelevant information makes problems for which solution strategies have been learned seem confusing and novel.

It is unfortunate, therefore, that school instruction does little to vary the nature or complexity of narratives of math word problems and fails to provide students with explicit strategies for connecting longer narratives, which contain irrelevant information and/or extra steps, to the problem types they have learned. In our intervention research program, by contrast, we have sought to explicitly teach relatively young children (third graders) about the complexities associated with transferring their MPS skill to novel problems that incorporate more contextually realistic situations, with irrelevant information, extra steps, and longer narratives. In the rest of this chapter, we summarize our intervention research program on MPS. We begin by describing the theoretical underpinnings of our intervention methods, summarizing similarly conceptualized intervention research, and explaining how our research expands on those earlier studies. Following this is a description of three intervention studies designed to enhance MPS performance. We conclude with some recommendations for practice and future research.

MPS INSTRUCTIONAL INTERVENTION: CONCEPTUAL UNDERPINNINGS

MPS can be addressed from different theoretical perspectives. In our work, we have conceptualized MPS as a transfer challenge, which requires students to apply knowledge, skills, and strategies to novel problems (cf. Bransford & Schwartz, 1999; Mayer, Quilici, & Moreno, 1999). Schema theory has provided the framework for conceptualizing how MPS is achieved. This theory postulates that MPS occurs when students develop schemas for grouping problems into types that require the same solution (Chi, Feltovich, & Glaser, 1981; Gick & Holyoak, 1980; Mayer, 1992; Quilici & Mayer, 1996). The broader the schema, the greater the probability that students will recognize connections between familiar and novel problems and know when to apply the solution methods they have mastered (Gick & Holyoak, 1983). When this happens, transfer and MPS occur.

To promote the MPS of primary-grade children with math disability, we have relied on schema construction theory in designing an intervention that explicitly teaches transfer. As conceptualized by Cooper and Sweller (1987), three variables contribute to MPS transfer. Students must 1) master rules for problem solution, 2) develop categories for sorting problems that require similar solutions, and 3) be aware that novel problems are related to previously solved problems. Research has substantiated the importance of the first variable (e.g., Sweller & Cooper, 1985). As students master problem-solution rules, they allocate less working memory to the details of the solution and instead devote cognitive resources to identifying connections between novel and familiar problems and to planning work.

Regarding the second variable, which is central to the role schemas play in transfer, Cooper and Sweller (1987) questioned eighth graders as they worked novel algebra problems. Responses were coded in terms of whether statements reflected schemas (e.g., when faced with a new problem, students reported thinking about how an earlier problem had been solved).

Results showed that schemas strongly influenced performance on problems that fell within the boundaries of those schemas, but that students' schemas were disappointingly narrow. The challenge in effecting the transfer involved in MPS, of course, is to help learners develop broad schemas.

With respect to Cooper and Sweller's (1987) third variable, prior work has revealed the importance of triggering awareness of the connections between training and transfer tasks. Research (Asch, 1969; Catrambone & Holyoak, 1989; Gick & Holyoak, 1980; Keane, 1988; Ross, 1989) has shown that performance increases when participants are cued to anticipate similarities across tasks. To achieve the transfer involved in MPS, however, it is necessary to go beyond cueing by an external agent. Methods are needed to activate independent searches for connections between novel and familiar tasks.

MPS INSTRUCTIONAL INTERVENTION: PRIOR RESEARCH

Unfortunately, schema induction has proven difficult to achieve (e.g., Bransford & Schwartz, 1999; Cooper & Sweller, 1987; Mayer et al., 1999). Some work has examined how examples can be used to induce schemas. Quilici and Mayer (1996), for example, demonstrated that college students who independently studied statistics problems grouped by problem type (*t* test versus chi square versus correlation) sorted subsequent problems on the basis of problem type rather than on the substance of the cover stories, more so than did students who studied without examples. They also showed that schema induction was strengthened through the use of examples that emphasized the problem type over the cover story. Of interest, the pattern was stronger for students of lower ability, who may have tended to focus more on cover stories than did peers of higher ability unless primed to do otherwise. (Among these college students, low ability was operationalized as a mathematics SAT score below 575, a definition with limited application to the school-age population.) In related work with elementary school children, Chen (1999) examined how the variability of sample problems facilitated not only schema induction but also problem–solution accuracy and its relation to schema development. Older children (10- to 12-year-olds) were more successful than were younger children (8- to 9-year-olds) at extracting schemas from the sample problems and at solving subsequent problems.

As Quilici and Mayer's (1996) and Chen's (1999) studies illustrate, important questions remain about how to promote MPS among low-performing and younger students. Both studies, as is the case for much of the research on schema induction, relied on single-session interventions without explicit instruction to prompt students' schema construction. As Quilici and Mayer concluded, further study is warranted to examine whether explicit instruction and structured practice in schema-inducing activities, rather than independent study of examples, might strengthen effects.

Some research has explored the potential of teacher-directed schema-inducing instruction as a method for promoting MPS. In a small-group tutoring study conducted with students in Grades 2–6 who were low achieving, Jitendra and colleagues (1998) tested a two-step intervention that combined schema-induction methods with the use of diagrams. In the first step, designed to induce schemas, students categorized an arithmetic word problem as a change, group, or compare-problem type; in the second step, students used a diagram representing the relevant problem type to assist in problem solution. Effects were statistically significant. Results suggest the potential for schema construction theory to guide the development of teacher-directed instruction on MPS but do not provide the basis for separating the effects of schema-induction methods from the use of diagrams. So, in the first study presented below, our goal was to pinpoint the effects of schema-based instruction for promoting MPS.

THREE ILLUSTRATIVE INSTRUCTIONAL INTERVENTION STUDIES

In this section we summarize three studies in our research program on MPS intervention (see Table 18.1). (For additional studies in this research program, see Fuchs, Fuchs, Finelli, et al., 2006; Fuchs, Fuchs, Finelli, et al., 2004; Fuchs, Fuchs, Prentice, et al., 2004.) In all three studies, regardless of intervention condition, all students used the same basal text and district curriculum. Also, we selected four problem types from the district curriculum on which to focus our intervention and outcome measures. This ensured that the control groups had instruction relevant to the study outcomes.

Study 1: The Potential of Schema-Based Instruction

The first study examined the potential for whole-class instruction rooted in schema-based theory to effect better MPS outcomes.

Question and Study Groups   Our research question involved pinpointing the effects of schema-based instruction. Fuchs and colleagues (2003a) randomly assigned 24 third-grade classes to four conditions for 16 weeks of intervention. Six classrooms were assigned to a *control session* (Group 1), representing conventional classroom MPS instruction. The other three conditions involved experimenter-designed instruction, which was explicit, incorporated worked examples (i.e., already solved problems, which the teacher explained) and dyadic practice (i.e., in pairs of students), and involved two to three sessions per week. Six classrooms were randomly assigned to 32 sessions of *problem–solution rules instruction* (Group 2), without any explicit attempt to broaden schemas. Another six classrooms were

Table 18.1. Summary of three mathematical problem-solving (MPS) instructional intervention studies in third grade

Reference	Conditions	Results			Findings for students with mathematical learning disability (MLD)
		Immediate transfer	Near transfer	Far transfer	
Fuchs et al. (2003b)	1. Control (teacher-designed) 2. Problem–solution rules 3. Shortened problem–solution rules + schema-based instruction 4. Full problem–solution rules + schema-based instruction	4, 2 > 3 > 1	4, 3 > 2 > 1	4, 3 > 2 = 1	On immediate transfer, percentage of nonresponders was 20 for condition 2, 60 for condition 3; 9 for condition 4. On near transfer, respective figures were 60, 60, and 18; on far transfer, 20, 80, 16. This shows the need for helping students develop a strong foundation in problem–solution methods prior to teaching for transfer.
Fuchs et al. (2003a)	1. Control (teacher-designed) 2. Full problem–solution rules + schema-based instruction 3. Full problem–solution rules + schema-based instruction + self-regulated learning strategies	3 > 2 > 1	High-achieving: 3 > 2 > 1 Average and low-achieving: 3 = 2 > 1	3 > 1	On immediate transfer, 3 = 2 > 1; on near transfer, 3 > 1; on far transfer, 3 > 1.
Fuchs et al. (2002)	1. Control (teacher-designed) 2. Schema-based tutoring 3. Computer-assisted practice on far transfer measures 4. Schema-based tutoring + computer-assisted practice on far transfer measure	4 = 2 > 3 = 1	4 = 3 = 2 > 1	Not significant. Percentage of nonresponders: 20 for conditions 2 and 4; 62 for condition 3.	Entire sample had MLD.

assigned to *schema-based instruction with shortened problem-solution instruc-tion* (Group 3). To add 10 sessions on schema-based transfer instruction for Group 3 while maintaining a total of 32 sessions, we shortened the number of sessions on problem–solution rules. With schema-based instruction, teachers first taught the concept of transfer. Then, teachers taught four transfer features that change a problem without altering its type or solu-tion. That is, a familiar problem type might be formatted so that the prob-lem looks novel, might use unfamiliar vocabulary, might pose a different question, or might represent a small part of a bigger problem. Also, teach-ers reminded students to search novel problems for transfer features in order to identify familiar problem types and apply the solutions they knew. Finally, to test the power of the full intervention, another six classrooms were assigned to *experimenter-designed schema-based instruction with full problem-solution instruction* (Group 4). This condition incorporated the full set of 32 sessions of teacher-directed instruction on problem-solution rules plus the 10 sessions of schema instruction for a total of 42 sessions.

Results Results supported the usefulness of the experimenter-designed problem–solution instruction. On the immediate-transfer test, which re-quired students to solve problems when cover stories constituted the only source of novelty, the two groups that received more of the experimenter-designed problem–solution intervention improved significantly and sub-stantially more than the group that received less of the experimenter-designed problem–solution intervention (and also more than the control group). In addition, on the near-transfer test, in which problems incorpo-rated greater novelty, all three experimental conditions again improved sig-nificantly and substantially more than the control group.

More important, results also supported the efficacy of the schema-based instruction. On the near-transfer test, dramatically superior growth occurred for students who received schema-based instruction compared with students who did not receive schema-based instruction. The most convincing measure of learning, however, was the far-transfer test, our real-world MPS measure that posed questions with the greatest degree of nov-elty: an unfamiliar cover story, simultaneous manipulation of all four trans-fer features taught, inclusion of irrelevant information, and incorporation of additional problem structures and content taught in the district's curricu-lum. On this far-transfer, both groups that received schema-based transfer instruction improved impressively more than did the control group. By con-trast, the problem–solution condition, which did not receive the schema-based transfer intervention, did not outgrow the control group.

We also examined interactions between study condition and the math-ematics grade-level status with which students began the study. We found no significant interaction, indicating that effects were not mediated by stu-dents' prior achievement histories. This is notable in light of previous work indicating that transfer is more difficult to effect among low-achieving students (Cooper & Sweller, 1987; Fuchs, Fuchs, Karns, Hamlett, & Katzaroff, 1999; Mayer, 1998; Woodward & Baxter, 1997).

What about the effects for students with MLD? Among these children, effects were least evident for the combined condition that incorporated only the partial set of problem-solution lessons. This underscores the need to develop a strong foundation in problem-solution rules in order for instruction designed to promote transfer to work. For the other conditions, which incorporated the full set of lessons designed to teach problem–solution methods, findings were encouraging for students with MLD and illustrate how worked examples and peer mediation are effective in helping students with MLD master problem–solution rules.

As problems became increasingly novel compared with those practiced during instruction, however, the discrepancy of effects between students with and without MLD grew. For near transfer, the effect for students with MLD, although moderate, was dramatically lower than for typical students. And on far transfer, in which the problem situation approximated real-world MPS, there was no reliable effect for students with MLD, whereas students who were typically achieving clearly had transferred their knowledge to the real-life MPS situation.

Study 2: The Contribution of Self-Regulated Learning Strategies

From the first study, we realized the need to strengthen the power of the intervention to address the needs of students with MLD. Our next step in the research program, therefore, was to add an instructional component to boost the power of the intervention, a component that relied on self-regulated learning strategies (e.g., Graham & Harris, 1997). We then examined the separate contribution of self-regulation to the combined intervention package.

Purpose and Study Groups The practice of incorporating self-regulated learning strategies within MPS intervention made conceptual sense because MPS requires metacognition (i.e., decision-making processes that regulate the selection of various forms of knowledge; Zimmerman, 1989). Also, metacognition is a critical process for self-regulation; self-regulated learners set goals for themselves, monitor their progress, and evaluate their performance (cf. Zimmerman, 1990).

We were also interested in whether the contribution of self-regulated learning strategies would vary as a function of students' achievement histories. This seemed plausible, because early work showed that children with cognitive deficiencies experienced difficulty in determining how well they used strategies (Borkowski & Buechel, 1983) and failed to make accurate competency assessments (Licht & Kistner, 1986). As Schunk (1996) suggested, because average and high achievers assess their progress more reliably than remedial students, self-regulated learning strategies effects may be weaker for low achievers.

So, in Study 2, Fuchs and colleagues (2003b) employed an experimental design to separate the effects of self-regulated learning strategies, including goal setting and self-evaluation, on MPS for third-grade children with varying achievement histories. We investigated the effects using the same MPS measures as in Study 1, but we also included measures of self-regulated learning processes. Intervention duration again was 16 weeks, and all three conditions, including the control condition, focused on the same four problem types and incorporated a 3-week researcher-designed introductory unit on basic problem-solving strategies (e.g., making sure answers make sense; lining up numbers from text to perform math operations; checking computation; labeling work with words, monetary signs, and mathematics symbols).

The three conditions were as follows. First, we employed a control group, as in Study 1, to reflect conventional classroom instruction on mathematical problems. Our second condition was identical to Study 1's Group 4: it included 42 sessions of problem-solution and schema-based instruction. In the third condition, we incorporated lessons on six self-regulated learning strategies into the 42 sessions of problem-solution and schema-based instruction. With the first strategy, after students completed an independent problem during each session, they *scored their independent problem* using an answer key. The second strategy was for students to *chart their daily scores* on thermometers. At the beginning of the next session, students used the third strategy, *inspecting those thermometers* and *setting a goal to beat their highest score on that day's independent problem.*The fourth strategy was for students to *score homework* with an answer key. In the fifth strategy, at the beginning of each session students *reported examples of how they had transferred the unit's problem structure to another part of the school day or outside of school.* The sixth strategy involved a *class graph,* on which the teacher recorded the number of students who had submitted homework and the number of pairs reporting a transfer event. Self-regulated learning strategies thus incorporated goal setting and self-assessment referenced to the content of instructional sessions, including problem-solution rules instruction and transfer instruction.

Results   Results strengthened previous findings (Fuchs et al., 2003a) by showing that MPS is enhanced with schema-based instruction. On the immediate and near-transfer MPS measures, students who received schema-based instruction improved reliably more than those in the control group; effects were large and similar to those reported in Study 1. On far transfer, however, effects did not reliably favor schema-based instruction over the control group, as Fuchs and colleagues (2003a) had found, even though the effects were moderate to large.

By contrast, across the three transfer measures, the combination of the schema-based instruction and self-regulated learning strategies promoted reliably stronger improvement compared with the control group, with very large effect size. So, whereas the schema-based transfer instruction alone failed to promote reliable effects on the far-transfer measure (the most novel, and therefore truest, measure of MPS), the combination of schema-based transfer and self-regulated learning strategies succeeded.

In addition, findings for the measures of self-regulated processes indicated that the explanation for the superior effect of the combined intervention may reside with self-regulated learning strategies. On questions assessing self-efficacy, goal orientation, self-monitoring, and effort, students in the combined intervention scored better than did those in the schema-based instruction condition without self-regulated learning strategies (and better than did those in the control group). Self-regulated learning strategies may have provided the mechanism by which the effects of the combined intervention were realized.

Students with MLD in both intervention groups grew comparably on immediate transfer and improved more than did the control group, and those effects were large. Moreover, effects for the combined intervention on the near- and far-transfer measures, with greater novelty, were statistically significant, with notably large effect sizes. So, even for students in this lowest-achieving group—who may experience difficulty with setting realistic goals (Robbins & Harway, 1977; Tollefson, Tracy, Johnsen, Buenning, & Farmer, 1982) and monitoring performance accurately (e.g., Borkowski & Buechel, 1983; Licht & Kistner, 1986)—self-regulated learning strategies, combined with schema-based instruction, appear promising.

Study 3: Delivering Schema-Based Transfer Instruction in Small Groups

Another strategy for strengthening the effects of schema-based instruction is to intensify instruction by relying on small-group tutoring. Fuchs, Fuchs, Hamlett, and Appleton (2002) examined the effectiveness of schema-based instruction for students with MLD when schema-based instruction was conducted in groups of two to four students. The lessons were identical to those used in Study 1's Group 4: schema-based instruction with the full set of problem-solution instruction sessions (without self-regulated learning strategies).

Study Groups To create a stringent test of efficacy, we assessed the contribution of this intervention to computer-assisted practice, in which students actually had intensive, guided, direct practice on alternate forms of the study's far-transfer task. Students were randomly assigned to schema-based transfer tutoring (or not) and to computer-assisted far-transfer task practice (or not). This created four conditions: schema-based transfer tutoring, computer-assisted far-transfer task practice, schema-based transfer tutoring plus computer-assisted far-transfer task practice, and control. Students in all conditions received the same math curriculum from which the four problem types had been selected.

Six special education teachers nominated 62 students who had standard scores above 89 on an individually administered intelligence test and who were reported by their teachers as having MLD. We administered to these students a test of computational fluency to identify 40 students who scored at least 1.5 standard deviations (*SD*) below a regional normative sample. Stratifying so that each condition was represented approximately equally for each teacher, we randomly assigned students, with 10 students in each of four conditions. The composition/characteristics of the groups were comparable in terms of factors related to gender, free/reduced lunch status, race, and problematic classroom behavior and on computational fluency, math applications, and arithmetic story problems.

Results   Results showed that schema-based transfer tutoring differentially promoted MPS growth among students with MLD. Of note, this growth was manifested on the full range of measures, although the effects on the real-world far-transfer measure were smaller. On the immediate-transfer and near-transfer measures, tutoring produced statistically significant improvement compared with the control condition and the computer-assisted practice condition. On the immediate-transfer measure, effect sizes comparing the tutoring condition and the control group exceeded 2 *SD* and were in the same range as those documented in the study for students who were typically achieving (Fuchs et al., 2003a). On the near-transfer measure, effects were reliable and large, nearly double those for students with MLD when lessons were delivered to the whole class (Fuchs et al., 2003a).

In addition, although results for the far-transfer measure were not statistically significant, the effects approximated those associated with the computer-assisted far-transfer practice condition, even though this contrast group spent all of its experimental time practicing problems analogous to the far-transfer task. Moreover, the effect for students with MLD when lessons were delivered in small groups was substantially larger than the effect for students with MLD when lessons were delivered to the whole class. Across the three transfer tasks, therefore, results supported the value of small-group instruction (Elbaum, Vaughn, Hughes, & Moody, 2000), where opportunities to respond, to seek clarification, and to obtain guided feedback are substantially greater than during whole-class instruction.

This study provides the basis for some optimism and caution. On the one hand, results documented the efficacy of explicit instruction on problem solutions and schema-based instruction when instruction is delivered in small groups. Effects paralleled findings for students with MLD when the MPS program was delivered in large-class format (Fuchs et al., 2003a). As documented by Fuchs and colleagues, the effectiveness of the schema-based transfer program resides in both components. That is, instruction on rules for problem solution explains growth on the immediate-transfer measure; the schema-based instruction component explains growth on the near- and far-transfer measures. This study therefore extends previous work by documenting effects on MPS, a curricular area that has received relatively little attention, especially for students with MLD, and where previous work has indicated that outcomes are difficult to effect.

CONCLUSIONS

These three studies illustrate our research program on MPS intervention. On the basis of this research, we draw three conclusions about how to enhance MPS. First, students as young as 8 or 9 years old with or without MLD can profit from MPS instruction, even when their calculation skills are still immature. This should encourage primary-grade teachers to include a focus on MPS while continuing to teach foundational math skills.

Second, a strong base in problem-solution rule is necessary within MPS instruction. This means that children must master problem-solution methods on problems with low transfer demands (i.e., identically worded problems that only vary cover stories).

Third, there is a need for explicit instruction on transfer, designed to increase students' awareness of the connections between novel and familiar problems. Toward that end, we relied on schema-construction theory to build our intervention. The three experiments presented here illustrate the efficacy of such explicit, schema-based instruction for promoting transfer among typical students; effects were substantial on the range of transfer measures. Moreover, our studies show that this approach also promotes improvement for students with MLD. Of course, among students with MLD, results are more impressive and reliable for near-transfer measures than for far-transfer measures. Additional work is required to identify strategies for increasing the magnitude and range of MPS effects. In our subsequent studies within this research program, we continue to examine the effects of additional strategies.

In terms of future research, we offer five directions. First, future research can pose important questions about the mechanisms by which schema-based instruction effects MPS competence. Second, with respect to service delivery, it seems timely, in light of the popularity of multitiered instructional systems and response-to-intervention as a basis for identifying learning disabilities (e.g., Vaughn & Fuchs, 2003), to explore tiers of whole-class and small-group tutoring arrangements for MPS. Third, a direction future studies need to take is to examine how combinations of instructional components, in addition to self-regulated learning strategies, promote MPS. Fourth, given evidence that MPS represents a productive instructional target for children as young as third grade, it seems important to test the possibility of extending a schema-based instructional paradigm to include younger children. Fifth and finally, it seems potentially instructive to study the cognitive features associated with poor response to otherwise effective MPS instruction. This final research extension should link to previous work on the cognitive abilities underlying MPS (e.g., Fuchs, Fuchs, Compton, et al., 2006; Fuchs et al., 2005; Swanson & Beebee-Frankenberger, 2004). This could help researchers identify other features of effective MPS instruction and lead to the development of measures to screen children for earlier intervention. We are currently pursuing these directions.

REFERENCES

Asch, S.E. (1969). A reformulation of the problem of associations. *American Psychologist, 24*, 92–102.

Borkowski, J.G., & Buechel, F.P. (1983). Learning and memory strategies in the mentally retarded. In M. Pressley & J.R. Levin (Eds.), *Cognitive strategy research: Psychological foundations* (pp. 103–128). New York: Springer-Verlag.

Bransford, J.D., & Schwartz, D.L. (1999). Rethinking transfer: A simple proposal with multiple implications. In A. Iran-Nejad & P .D. Pearson (Eds.), *Review of research in education* (pp. 61–100). Washington, DC: American Educational Research Association.

Briars, D.J., & Larkin, J.H. (1984). An integrated model of skill in solving elementary word problems. *Cognition and Instruction, 1*, 245–296.

Catrambone, R., & Holyoak, K.J. (1989). Overcoming contextual limitations on problem-solving transfer. *Journal of Experimental Psychology: Learning, Memory, and Cognition, 15*, 1127–1156.

Chen, Z. (1999). Schema induction in children's analogical problem solving. *Journal of Educational Psychology, 91*, 703–715.

Chi, M.T.H., Feltovich, P.J., & Glaser, R. (1981). Categorization and representation of physics problems by experts and novices. *Cognitive Science, 5*, 121–152.

Cooper, G., & Sweller, J. (1987). Effects of schema acquisition and rule automation on MPS transfer. *Journal of Educational Psychology, 79*, 347–362.

Elbaum, B., Vaughn, S., Hughes, M.T., & Moody, S.W. (2000). How effective are one-to-one tutoring programs in reading for elementary students at risk for reading failure? A meta-analysis of the intervention research. *Journal of Educational Psychology, 92*, 605–619.

Fleishner, J.E., Garnett, K., & Shepherd, M.J. (1982). Proficiency in arithmetic basic fact computation of learning disabled and nondisabled children. *Focus on Learning Problems in Mathematics, 4*, 47–56.

Fuchs, L.S., Compton, D.L., Fuchs, D., Paulsen, K., Bryant, J.D., & Hamlett, C.L. (2005). The prevention, identification, and cognitive determinants of math difficulty. *Journal of Educational Psychology, 97*, 493–513.

Fuchs, L.S., Fuchs, D., Compton, D.L., Powell, S.R., Seethaler, P.M., Capizzi, A.M., et al. (2006). The cognitive correlates of third-grade skill in arithmetic, algorithmic computation, and word problems. *Journal of Educational Psychology*.

Fuchs, L.S., Fuchs, D., Finelli, R., Courey, S.J., & Hamlett, C.L. (2004). Expanding schema-based transfer instruction to help third graders solve real-life mathematical problems. *American Educational Research Journal, 41*, 419–445.

Fuchs, L.S., Fuchs, D., Finelli, R., Courey, S.J., Hamlett, C.L., Sones, E.M., et al. (2006). Teaching third graders about real-life mathematical problem solving: A randomized controlled study. *Elementary School Journal, 106,* 293–312.

Fuchs, L.S., Fuchs, D., Hamlett, C.L., & Appleton, A.C. (2002). Explicitly teaching for transfer in small groups: Effects on the mathematical problem-solving performance of students with mathematics disabilities. *Learning Disability Research and Practice, 17,* 90–106.

Fuchs, L.S., Fuchs, D., Karns, K., Hamlett, C.L., & Katzaroff, M. (1999). Mathematics performance assessment in the classroom: Effects on teacher planning and student learning. *American Educational Research Journal, 36,* 609–646.

Fuchs, L.S., Fuchs, D., Prentice, K., Burch, M., Hamlett, C.L., Owen, R., et al. (2003a). Enhancing third-grade students' mathematical problem solving with self-regulated learning strategies. *Journal of Educational Psychology, 95,* 306–315.

Fuchs, L.S., Fuchs, D., Prentice, K., Burch, M., Hamlett, C.L., Owen, R., et al. (2003b). Explicitly teaching for transfer: Effects on third-grade students' mathematical problem solving. *Journal of Educational Psychology, 95,* 293–304.

Fuchs, L.S., Fuchs, D., Prentice, K., Hamlett, C.L., Finelli, R., & Courey, S.J. (2004). Enhancing mathematical problem solving among third-grade students with schema-based instruction. *Journal of Educational Psychology, 96,* 635–647.

Geary, D.C. (1990). A componential analysis of an early learning deficit in mathematics. *Journal of Experimental Child Psychology, 49,* 363–383.

Geary, D.C. (1993). Mathematical disabilities: Cognitive, neuropsychological, and genetic components. *Psychological Bulletin, 114,* 345–362.

Geary, D.C., Bow-Thomas, C.C., & Yao, Y. (1992). Counting knowledge and skill in cognitive addition: A comparison of normal and mathematically disabled children. *Journal of Experimental Child Psychology, 54,* 372–391.

Geary, D.C., & Brown, S.C (1991). Cognitive addition: Strategy choice and speed-of-processing differences in gifted, normal, and mathematically disabled children. *Developmental Psychology, 27,* 398–406.

Geary, D.C., Widaman, K.F., Little, T.D., & Cormier, P. (1987). Cognitive addition: Comparison of learning disabled and academically normal elementary school children. *Cognitive Development, 2,* 249–269.

Gick, M.L., & Holyoak, K.J. (1980). Analogical problem solving. *Cognitive Psychologist, 12,* 306–355.

Gick, M.L., & Holyoak, K.J. (1983). Schema induction and analogical transfer. *Cognitive Psychology, 15,* 1–38.

Goldman, S.R., Pellegrino, J.W., & Mertz, D.L. (1988). Extended practice of addition facts: Strategy changes in learning-disabled students. *Cognition and Instruction, 5,* 223–265.

Graham, S., & Harris, K.R. (1997). Self-regulation and writing: Where do we go from here? *Contemporary Educational Psychology, 22,* 102–114.

Gross-Tsur, V., Manor, O., & Shalev, R.S. (1996). Developmental dyscalculia: Prevalence and demographic features. *Developmental Medicine and Child Neurology, 37,* 906–914.

Gross-Tsur, V., Manor, O., & Shalev, R.S. (1996). Developmental dyscalculia: Prevalence and demographic features. *Developmental Medicine and Child Neurology, 38,* 25–33.

Hanich, L.B., Jordan, N.C., Kaplan, D., & Dick, J. (2001). Performance across different areas of mathematical cognition in children with learning difficulties. *Journal of Educational Psychology, 93,* 615–626.

Helwig, R., Rosek-Toedesco, M.S., Tindal, G., Heath, B., & Almond, P.J. (1999). Reading as an access to mathematics problem solving on multiple-choice tests for sixth-grade students. *Journal of Educational Research, 93,* 113–125.

Jitendra, A.K., Griffin, C.C., McGoey, K., Gardill, M.C., Bhat, P., & Riley, T. (1998). Effects of mathematical word problem solving by students at risk or with mild disabilities. *Journal of Educational Research, 91*, 345–355.

Jordan, N.C., & Hanich, L.B. (2000). Mathematical thinking in second-grade children with different forms of LD. *Journal of Learning Disabilities, 33*, 567–578.

Keane, M. (1988). *Analogical problem solving.* Chichester, England: Ellis Horwood.

Licht, B.G., & Kistner, J.A. (1986). Motivational problems of learning-disabled children: Individual differences and their implications for treatment. In J.K. Torgesen & B.W.L. Wong (Eds.), *Psychological and educational perspectives on learning disabilities* (pp. 225–255). Orlando, FL: Academic Press.

Mayer, D.P. (1998). Do new teaching standards undermine performance on old tests? *Educational Evaluation and Policy Analysis, 15*, 1–16.

Mayer, R.E. (1992). *Thinking, problem solving, cognition* (2nd ed.). New York: Freeman.

Mayer, R.E., Quilici, J.L., & Moreno, R. (1999). What is learned in an after-school computer club? *Journal of Educational Computing Research, 20*, 223–235.

Ostad, S.A. (1997). Developmental differences in addition strategies: A comparison of mathematically disabled and mathematically normal children. *British Journal of Educational Psychology, 67*, 345–357.

Parmar, R.S., Cawley, J.F., & Frazita, R.R. (1996). Word problem-solving by students with and without mild disabilities. *Exceptional Children, 62*, 415–429.

Quilici, J.L., & Mayer, R.E. (1996). Role of examples in how students learn to categorize statistics word problems. *Journal of Educational Psychology, 88*, 144–161.

Robbins, R.L., & Harway, N.I. (1977). Goal setting and reactions to success and failure in children with learning disabilities. *Journal of Learning Disabilities, 10*, 356–362.

Ross, B.H. (1989). Distinguishing types of superficial similarities: Different effects on the access and use of earlier problems. *Journal of Experimental Psychology: Learning, Memory, and Cognition, 15*, 456–468.

Russell, R.L., & Ginsburg, H.P. (1984). Cognitive analysis of children's mathematical difficulties. *Cognition and Instruction, 1*, 217–244.

Schatschneider, C., Fuchs, L.S., Fuchs, D., & Hamlett, C.L. (2005). Math *problem solving at third grade: A distinct form of mathematical cognition?* Unpublished raw data.

Schunk, D.H. (1996). Goal and self-evaluative influences during children's cognitive skill learning. *American Educational Research Journal, 33*, 359–382.

Swanson, H.L., & Beebe-Frankenberger, M. (2004). The relationship between working memory and mathematical problem solving in children at risk and not at risk for serious math difficulties. *Journal of Educational Psychology, 96*, 471–491.

Sweller, J., & Cooper, G.A. (1985). The use of worked examples as a substitute for problem solving in learning algebra. *Cognition and Instruction, 2*, 59–89.

Tollefson, N., Tracy, D.B., Johnsen, E.P., Buenning, M., & Farmer, A.W. (1982, March). *Teaching learning disabled adolescents to set realistic goals.* Paper presented at the annual meeting of the American Educational Research Association, New York.

Vaughn, S.R., & Fuchs, L.S. (2003). Redefining learning disabilities as inadequate response to treatment: Rationale and assumptions. *Learning Disabilities Research and Practice, 18*, 137–146.

Woodward, J., & Baxter, J. (1997). The effects of an innovative approach to mathematics on academically low-achieving students in inclusive settings. *Exceptional Children, 63*, 373–388.

Zimmerman, B.J. (1989). A social cognitive view of self-regulated academic learning. *Journal of Educational Psychology, 81*, 329–339.

Zimmerman, B.J. (1990). Self-regulated learning and academic achievement: An overview. *Educational Psychologist, 25*, 3–18.

Chapter 19

Quantitative Literacy and Developmental Dyscalculias

Michael McCloskey

> *For as long as I can remember, numbers have not been my friend.*
> — Jess Blackburn

+ +

D evelopmental dyslexia is widely recognized as a significant disability; individuals who have reading and/or writing disabilities are obviously at a serious disadvantage in a society inundated with written material. As a consequence, enormous effort has been directed toward understanding, diagnosing, and treating developmental reading deficits. Developmental dyscalculias (developmental difficulties or disabilities involving quantitative concepts, information, or processes) have received far less attention.[1] This state of affairs can probably be traced in part to the widely held belief that in contrast to reading and writing skills, quantitative skills are not especially important in adult life. From the standpoint of this belief, some might discount the significance of developmental dyscalculias on grounds such as the following:

The author thanks Uyen Le, Michèle M.M. Mazzocco, and Daniel B. Berch for their helpful comments.

[1]I use the term *dyscalculia* rather than *math learning disability* in an effort to avoid creating the impression that the disabilities under discussion are limited to traditional school mathematics. Unfortunately, *dyscalculia* is not an ideal term either (as it might be taken to imply difficulty only with calculations), so it is worth emphasizing that in my usage the term encompasses difficulty or deficit in any form of quantitative skill. Also, I use the plural form *dyscalculias* as a reminder that developmental dyscalculia (like developmental dyslexia) is not a unitary disorder but can take a variety of forms (e.g., impaired number sense, difficulty memorizing arithmetic facts, difficulty learning or carrying out sequences of steps in quantitative problem solving, difficulty with the spatial concepts implicated in many quantitative tasks, and so forth).

Children with developmental dyscalculias will struggle in math classes at school. However, once out of school, dyscalculia is not a significant problem, because math is just not that important in adult life. Most of us never use the algebra or geometry we learned (or at least encountered) in math class, and if we need to do arithmetic we can always use a calculator. A person with dyscalculia would probably not be able to pursue a career in mathematics or accounting, but otherwise would not be significantly disadvantaged.

In this chapter I argue that this point of view is seriously misguided. I begin by discussing the concept of quantitative literacy, showing that quantitative concepts and information are pervasive in adult life, and that a broad range of quantitative skills are needed to handle these concepts and information effectively. Furthermore, I argue that the ability to meet the quantitative demands of everyday life is not merely desirable but in fact crucial, especially in two facets of adult life: work and tasks dealing with money. On the basis of these points, I contend that developmental dyscalculias may cause very significant difficulties in adult life. Although systematic research directly relevant to this contention is remarkably sparse, I discuss several findings suggesting that individuals with poor quantitative skills are disadvantaged in adult life. I also offer anecdotal evidence from the writings of adults with dyscalculias. I conclude that more attention should be directed toward improved understanding of the developmental dyscalculias, especially with respect to their effects in adulthood.

QUANTITATIVE LITERACY

More and more frequently, discussions surrounding the abilities needed by adults to function adequately in the workplace, home, and community have emphasized quantitative knowledge and skills (referred to collectively as *quantitative literacy*) (e.g., Curry, Schmitt, & Waldron, 1996; Gal, van Groenestijn, Manly, Schmitt, & Tout, 2005; Secretary's Commission on Achieving Necessary Skills, 1991; Steen, 1997, 2001b; White & Dillow, 2005). One indication of the importance attached to quantitative abilities is that quantitative literacy is a major component in both of the large-scale literacy assessments administered to American adults—the National Assessment of Adult Literacy (NAAL) and the international Adult Literacy and Lifeskills survey (ALL). The NAAL measures prose, document, and quantitative literacy (see, e.g., White & Dillow, 2005); the ALL survey focuses on prose and document literacy, numeracy,[2] and analytical reasoning/problem solving (e.g., see Murray, Clermont, & Binkley, 2005).

---

[2]The terms *quantitative literacy* and *numeracy* are usually, although not always, synonymous. *Numeracy* as defined for purposes of the ALL survey corresponds closely to what I mean by *quantitative literacy*. In the NAAL, this is defined somewhat more narrowly, but the document literacy category covers many of the additional skills (e.g., graph interpretation skills) included in broader definitions.

In this section I provide a brief introduction to the notion of quantitative literacy, with the aim of characterizing the spectrum of quantitative information, knowledge, and skills implicated in daily life. I first survey briefly the categories of knowledge and information that fall within the scope of quantitative literacy, and then describe the skills needed for dealing with the information and concepts. (For more detailed discussions see Curry et al., 1996; Dossey, 1997; Gal et al., 2005; and Steen, 2001a, among others).

A point worth emphasizing at the outset is that quantitative literacy is not the same as proficiency at school mathematics. The concept of quantitative literacy focuses on the quantitative knowledge and skills adults need in everyday life (including work, home, and community settings). Accordingly, school-based competencies, such as the ability to solve equations via the quadratic formula, or the ability to prove theorems in geometry, would not fall within the scope of quantitative literacy. In this regard the quantitative literacy concept is narrower than that of proficiency in school mathematics. In other respects, however, the quantitative literacy concept is arguably the broader of the two. For one thing, quantitative literacy encompasses information, concepts, and skills that are not typically thought of as traditional school mathematics subject areas—for example, the ability to interpret charts, graphs, diagrams, and maps, or the ability to appreciate the sources of uncertainty in economic forecasts. (Topics such as these may be covered in math classes, but they are not what people ordinarily have in mind when they think about math skills.) Also, the quantitative literacy concept emphasizes the ability to apply quantitative knowledge and skills to real-world situations, an ability that is not always a major focus in school math instruction.

QUANTITATIVE DOMAINS

Several schemes have been proposed for categorizing the types of knowledge and information falling within the scope of quantitative literacy (e.g., Australian Association of Mathematics Teachers, 1996; Curry et al., 1996; Dossey, 1997; Gal et al., 2005; Steen, 2001a). Although the schemes differ in some respects, all reflect the view that adults must deal with a broad range of quantitative information and concepts in daily life. For purposes of illustration I describe briefly the scheme proposed by Gal and colleagues (2005) in their conceptual framework for assessing numeracy in the Adult Literacy and Lifeskills survey. Gal and colleagues specify five quantitative domains: quantity and number; dimension and shape; pattern, functions, and relationships; data and chance; and change.

Quantity and Number

According to Gal and colleagues (2005), quantity refers to the basic concepts and information involved in quantifying the world around us, using such measures as area, volume, temperature, humidity, population, or profit. Number is central to quantification, and includes whole numbers, fractions, decimals, percentages, ratios, and so forth. Quantity and number concepts are involved in virtually all everyday quantitative tasks, including time and money management.

Dimension and Shape

In the Gal and colleagues (2005) system, dimension refers to spatial dimensions and related concepts, such as perimeter, direction, and location. Shape applies to objects ranging from buildings to knots to snowflakes, and also includes abstract entities of more than three dimensions. Information and concepts in the dimension and shape domain are important for everyday tasks ranging from reading maps to determining how much paint is needed to cover a room.

Pattern, Functions, and Relationships

Pattern has to do with systematic variation over space or time, and includes patterns in music, nature, traffic, and so forth. Functions and relationships concern how variables are related to one another—for example, how home heating costs vary with the thermostat setting, or how blood pressure is related to weight.

Data and Chance

According to Gal and colleagues (2005), data covers topics such as variability, sampling, error, and prediction, as well as data collection and data display. Chance encompasses probability, random events, and related statistical methods. Information and concepts in the data and chance domain are important in such tasks as estimating the amount of money needed for retirement, deciding whether to buy a lottery ticket, and evaluating the rhetoric of political candidates about the economy.

Change

This quantitative domain has to do with describing how the world varies over time. Examples include growth in savings with compound interest, changes in prices over time, or changes in carbon dioxide levels in the atmosphere. Important concepts include rate of change and distinctions among additive, multiplicative, and exponential patterns of change.

QUANTITATIVE SKILLS

To cope with the various forms of quantitative information and tasks encountered in daily life, adults need a variety of skills (e.g., Curry et al., 1996; Gal et al., 2005; Steen, 2001a). I discuss some of the more important classes of skills next.

Number Sense

Number sense, the most fundamental quantitative skill, may be described as a basic understanding of quantity and number, forms of numerical representation (e.g., base-10 notation, fractions, percentages), and simple numerical operations (e.g., addition, multiplication). Number sense is implicated in virtually any quantitative task, from deciding whether a price is reasonable to interpreting statistical information about the risks associated with a medical treatment (e.g., Curry et al., 1996; Steen, 2001a).

Calculation Skills

Calculation skills are those required for performing basic arithmetic operations—addition, subtraction, multiplication, division—on numbers in various forms (e.g., whole numbers, decimals). Calculation skills are required in many work- and home-related tasks (e.g., preparing a bid for a construction job, totaling the prices on a purchase order, determining the amount of carpeting needed to cover a floor, subtracting the amount of a check from the current checking account balance to obtain the new balance).

Numerical Estimation Skills

Many everyday quantitative tasks do not require (or do not lend themselves to) precise answers. Examples include estimating expenses in various categories (e.g., food, clothing) when preparing a home budget, or estimating the time needed to complete a multistep task at work. The ability to estimate is also important for assessing the reasonableness of exact answers obtained by calculation. Numerical estimation draws on number sense and calculation skills, but it also requires additional skills (e.g., the ability to round precise numerical values). Furthermore, as emphasized by Siegler and Booth (2005), estimation often involves not the execution of fixed procedures (such as those involved in performing a calculation) but rather the flexible application of numerical and mathematical knowledge to meet the demands of particular estimation tasks. According to some authors, estimation skills are among the quantitative skills adults use most frequently (e.g., Curry et al., 1996; Patton, Cronin, Bassett, & Koppel, 1997; Siegler & Booth, 2005).

Measurement Skills

These are the skills involved in performing and interpreting measurements of attributes such as length, area, volume, thickness, temperature, or duration (e.g., Dossey, 1997). Many work- and home-related tasks (e.g., construction, landscaping, cooking, sewing) rely heavily on measurement skills.

Quantitative Representation Skills

Representational skills are those required for creating and interpreting representations of quantitative information and relationships—graphs, charts, equations, and the like (e.g., Steen, 2001a). These representations are ubiquitous in business settings (e.g., graphs of company statistics such as sales, expenses, or job-related injuries), in the news media (e.g., stock market reports, depictions of survey results), and elsewhere.

Computer Skills

Computer skills are increasingly important for handling quantitative information, both at home and at work. In the white-collar workplace, spreadsheet programs and other software applications are used for maintaining financial records, inventories, and so forth. Even low-skill jobs, however, may involve the use of a computer for processing quantitative data. For example, assembly-line workers may be required to enter quality control data into a computer system and interpret analyses generated as output (e.g., see Curry et al., 1996). In the home, online banking, shopping, and bill paying, as well as financial management and tax preparation software, require at least basic computer skills.

Quantitative Communication Skills

The ability to communicate about quantitative concepts and information is a significant aspect of quantitative literacy, especially in work environments (e.g., Curry et al., 1996). Communication skills are important not only at the management level in business but also in most jobs that involve contact with customers or clients. For example, real estate agents must be able to communicate clearly with clients about square footage, interest rates, and closing costs; a company sales representative must be able to communicate about prices, discounts, and delivery schedules.

Skills for Relating Real-World Situations to Quantitative Concepts

An essential but difficult-to-characterize set of skills are those required for applying quantitative concepts to real-world situations (e.g., Curry et al., 1996; Steen, 2001a). The skills discussed in the preceding sections are of little value if one cannot apply these skills in everyday life. For example, excellent calculation and measurement skills are of little use in determining how much paint will be needed to cover a room if one does not realize that the surface area of the walls needs to be computed, and that the area of a wall may be determined by measuring height and width and multiplying these values. Similarly, an abstract understanding of probability and chance is not helpful in deciding whether to buy a daily lottery ticket or play roulette in a casino unless one applies this knowledge to determine that the expected value of the activity is negative.

THE IMPORTANCE OF QUANTITATIVE LITERACY

The preceding discussion strongly suggests that quantitative skills are useful in everyday life. But are these skills truly necessary? Put another way, can individuals with poor quantitative skills get along with few significant difficulties in daily life, or might they encounter more serious problems? Two general points can be made in response to these questions. First, because quantitative concepts and information are involved in many facets of home, work, and community life, individuals with poor quantitative skills are likely to experience at least some difficulty in a variety of circumstances. Second, poor quantitative skills are likely to pose very significant problems in two critical components of adult life: work and dealing with money.

Work

Recognition is growing of the importance of quantitative skills for success in the workplace (e.g., Bynner & Parsons, 1997; Coben, 2003; Murnane, Willett, & Levy, 1995; Patton et al., 1997; Secretary's Commission on Achieving Necessary Skills, 1991). In 1991 the U.S. Secretary of Labor's Commission on Achieving Necessary Skills (SCANS) published an influential report on the skills American citizens would need to succeed in the 21st century workplace (Secretary's Commission on Achieving Necessary Skills, 1991). The report's executive summary emphasizes the importance of quantitative skills:

> **Mathematics** and **computational skills** will also be essential. Virtually all employees will be required to maintain records, estimate results, use

spreadsheets, or apply statistical process controls as they negotiate, identify trends, or suggest new courses of action. Most of us will not leave our mathematics behind us in school. Instead, we will find ourselves using it on the job, for example, to:

- Reconcile differences between inventory and financial records;

- Estimate discounts on the spot while negotiating sales;

- Use spreadsheet programs to monitor expenditures;

- Employ statistical process control procedures to check quality; and

- Project resource needs over the next planning period.

(p. ix, emphasis in original)

The SCANS report defines five sets of basic skills, including arithmetic/mathematics ("performs basic computations and approaches practical problems by choosing appropriately from a variety of mathematical techniques"). These skills, the report emphasizes, are crucial not just for managerial or professional jobs but for almost every job: "The basic skills are the irreducible minimum for anyone who wants to get even a low-skill job" (p. 14).

Several recent studies have reported correlational results showing a relationship between quantitative skills and success in the workplace (e.g., Bynner, 1998; Bynner & Parsons, 1997; Murnane et al., 1995). For example, Murnane and colleagues analyzed results from two longitudinal surveys of American high school students and found that the score on a math test administered in the last year of high school was positively correlated with wages at age 24. Although firm causal conclusions cannot be drawn from these correlational studies, the findings are consistent with the contention that quantitative skills are important for success in the workplace.

This contention finds further support in the results of a project carried out by the Adult Numeracy Practitioners Network (ANPN) (Curry et al., 1996). As part of their effort to catalogue the knowledge and skills that constitute quantitative literacy, the ANPN convened focus groups of teachers, employers, adult learners, and other stakeholders to discuss the quantitative skills that were needed in the workplace and in other aspects of life. Describing the results, Curry and colleagues stated:

> No matter what the occupation, employers and employees furnished many examples of how critical number is in their lines of work:
> An automotive parts plant manager from New England ticked off aspects of number proficiency needed in his workplace. The workers are usually on a forklift making some quick calculations such as knowing how many boxes of filters to load if a dealer orders 100 and there are a dozen per box. . . .
> A learner states, "Everyday at work I use math. I'm a cashier and gas station attendant without a cash register. Therefore I have to figure out

change on my own and if people get the wrong change back, they become highly upset and critical." (1996, p. 37)

As another example, the ANPN report discussed quality control in manufacturing, noting that many companies use statistical control processes to monitor their production lines. According to the report, the front-line employees are often required to collect and interpret the necessary data and therefore need an understanding of charts as well as some grasp of concepts in probability, sampling, and statistics. Finally, the report made clear that quantitative skills are especially important for those who own or manage small businesses:

> As a business man in a community, I use math everyday to run my business. Without it, my business would come to a standstill. I use it [for] controlling my inventory, receivables, payables, and accounting. It is probably the most important aspect to understand to run my business. Without having any math skills, it would probably be impossible to run my business. (Curry et al.,1996, p. 19)

Money

The ability to deal competently with money is crucial in adult life. Money-related decisions and activities occur frequently and are often highly important in one's personal life (as well as in many jobs). Examples include the following:

- Counting change
- Judging whether a price is reasonable
- Deciding whether one can afford to buy an item
- Paying bills
- Managing a credit card account
- Keeping financial records
- Developing a monthly budget
- Understanding interest on a car loan or mortgage
- Preparing an income tax return
- Making investment decisions
- Planning financially for retirement

Quantitative skills, especially number sense, calculation skills, and estimation skills, are obviously essential for dealing with these and other financial matters (e.g., Coben, 2003; Patton et al., 1997; Secretary's Commission on Achieving Necessary Skills, 1991).

Although this discussion has emphasized the role of quantitative literacy in the realms of work and money, quantitative skills are important in many other facets of life as well. For example, Schwartz, Woloshin, and Welch (2005) found that scores on a numeracy measure were positively correlated with adults' ability to interpret the sorts of real-world medical statistics routinely encountered in drug advertisements, news reports, and physicians' conversations with patients about medical risks; and Patton and colleagues (1997) provided an extensive catalog of real-world tasks that draw on math skills. The conclusion seems clear: Quantitative literacy is not merely useful but, in fact, vital for success in 21st century life.

THE CONSEQUENCES OF DEVELOPMENTAL DYSCALCULIA

Given the importance of quantitative literacy, one would expect individuals who have developmental quantitative impairments to encounter significant difficulties not only in school but also in adult life. Although I am not aware of any systematic research on life outcomes for individuals with developmental dyscalculias, a wealth of anecdotal evidence suggests that individuals with such disabilities do indeed experience serious negative consequences. In the following discussion I draw on several sources to illustrate the practical and emotional difficulties encountered by people with developmental dyscalculias during their schooling and subsequently in adult life.

School

Two recent articles present autobiographical accounts of childhood and adult experiences with developmental dyscalculia: Jess Blackburn's account of her difficulties with numbers on the Dyscalculia and Dyslexia Interest Group (DDIG) web site (http://ddig.lboro.ac.uk/), and Gaby Roughneen's discussion of her dyscalculia in *Reality* magazine. Both authors described extremely negative experiences with math in school. For example, Jess Blackburn wrote this:

> I've never been good with numbers, but, being articulate and an excellent reader, it was dismissed as me being lazy or disruptive. . . . From the age of 6 when I stood stuttering and red-faced, yet again unable to recite my 3 times table and the class genius was invited to smugly recite his 13 times tables immediately after to show how easy it was, I thought something wasn't right. Not only was it not right, it wasn't ruddy fair. Hot tears would run down my cheeks and I'd creep away feeling stupid, angry, miserable and very, very alone. . . .

Gaby Roughneen's (2006, p. 10) account is strikingly similar:

I knew I was in trouble in Second Class when I was eight years old. I watched the others get the right answers but I never could. . . . When called on for an answer, if the teacher had given me a moment to explain, I could have told her not to waste her time, that I didn't have and never would have the answer she wanted. All I could do was take a shot at it and then wait for the backwash. It came in accusations of laziness, inattention, and lack of interest. I was punished and humiliated. . . . My hatred of school set in.

Anyone who has worked with children suffering from developmental math disabilities can testify that experiences such as these are, unfortunately, not yet a thing of the past.

Money

Individuals with developmental dyscalculia often have serious difficulty dealing with money in all its manifestations, and they suffer serious anxiety about financial matters. Participants of the Dyscalculia Forum, a web-based discussion group (http://www.dyscalculiaforum.com), frequently discuss money-related issues. (In the following quotations I have left unaltered the informal vocabulary, syntax, and punctuation characteristic of such discussion groups.)

Does anybody have a way to make money feel real?! Like in my head I know its valuable, but when it comes to keeping to a budget, or planning ahead, I CANNOT do it . . . nor can i pay bills on time etc. I dont know what i will do if my mom ever stops helping me with it!!! I dunno . . . i have cash, and it disapears, and I couldnt tell ya where it goes. Its very frustrating . . . in fact this is one of the things that cinched the dyscalculia diagnosis for me . . . (Dyscalculia Forum participant)

I . . . have anxiety attacks about money, whether it's trying to sort out my finances (and not just because there are none but because I can't grasp how to DO it) so I get very very anxious when dealing with a bank, or a company I've to pay money to, etc. To the extent that after an encounter (even checking my bank balance when I know there's money there) I feel very tearful and upset. (Dyscalculia Forum participant)

Similarly, in a master's thesis on developmental dyscalculia, Renee Newman (1998) quoted an e-mail she received:

I have absolutely no sense of money whatsoever. It makes me so nervous, that if I have any cash at all, I immediately go spend it, usually on clothes because there are several lovely dress shops around my bank. That really makes for a problem when I realize that I went to the bank in order to go pay the power bill. I do not and cannot ever have a bank account because checks make no sense to me and I just write them willy-nilly regardless of my balance. (I am not an irresponsible person at all—just can't handle numbers.) (p. 15)

Jess Blackburn, in her article *Damn the Three Times Table,* described her financial difficulties succinctly and with humor: "My bank manager makes his living out of the vortex which is my overdraft; the swine."

Work

As one might expect, individuals with developmental dyscalculias encounter a variety of problems in the workplace. Jess Blackburn wrote the following: "Work is incredibly difficult as I've lost jobs because I can't count properly. It somehow implies untrustworthiness if someone doesn't want to handle money or avoids using figures."

Also attesting to the workplace problems arising from poor quantitative skills are quotations from the focus group participants in the Adult Numeracy Practitioners Network study (Curry et al., 1996) and from the participants in the Dyscalculia Forum (http://www.dyscalculiaforum.com):

> "Dairy Queen wouldn't hire me because I couldn't make change in my head. I couldn't give the answers in an oral quiz to making change questions." (Curry et al., 1996, p. 63)

> "I worked for Nabisco. As a mixer you had to know the correct scale and formulas. I kept messing up. I lost my job. It doesn't look too good on the record. If you don't know math you can't succeed." (Curry et al., 1996, p. 63)

> The only time I break out into a cold sweat is when a potential client asks me for a quote on an editing project (I do freelance English language proofreading/editing). I always have to tell them I'll get back to them in a couple of hours. That's how long it takes me to multiply the number of pages by the fee that I plan to charge! I always seem to get a wrong total each time, even using a calculator. Often I e-mail a colleague and ask him/her what he/she would charge, and then take it from there. (Dyscalculia Forum participant)

> I won't even be able to keep a job as a waiter or in a supermarket even if my life would depend on it! (Dyscalculia Forum participant)

> I am currently in the process of QUITTING a job because of their incessant need to make me feel like a second-class citizen because of my inability to handle financial paperwork. (i'm a graphic artist with 17 years experience . . .) . . . This company is willing to let me go due to my inability to file PAPERWORK. (i took a client who spent NOTHING with them and turned them into their 3rd biggest client), yet the fact that i can't file the right papers is paramount to them). But, i HAVE to leave. EVERY DAY i would breathe my way through a panic attack. Every day i would feel as if i was dying, my heart convulsing and aching in my chest. (Dyscalculia Forum participant)

Note that many of these examples involve difficulty not in occupations that obviously have a strong quantitative or mathematical component, but in jobs that one would not immediately think of as demanding quantitative skills.

Social Life

Surprisingly, quantitative deficiencies can even cause problems in social life, as described by two participants in the Dyscalculia Forum:

> I miss out on a lot of fun stuff with my friends—poker night, mostly, and casino outings, too—because playing cards nearly makes me black out from anxiety. It's pretty scary being the only dyscalculic I know, especially because not even my fiancé really understands. (Dyscalculia Forum participant)

> I have panic attacks, not very often, but I definitely get them when i'm confronted with anything mathematical. If I'm in a party and someone suggests a card game, I might get one of those dreaded attacks! (Dyscalculia Forum participant)

Lack of Understanding

As some of the previous quotations illustrate, the difficulties experienced by individuals with developmental dyscalculias are often exacerbated by the failure of teachers, employers, friends, and relatives to understand or accept the notion of a selective quantitative disability. Gaby Roughneen (2006) made the point clearly:

> People usually react in one of three ways when I tell them I don't understand what they're talking about in maths: they simply don't believe me, or they come up with their ideas as to how I should go about studying maths, or they just dismiss it.

In her article on the Dyscalculia and Dyslexia Interest Group web site (http://ddig.lboro.ac.uk), Jess Blackburn pointed out that whereas dyslexia has gained some measure of public awareness and understanding, dyscalculia has not.

> Dyscalculia is where dyslexia was 20 years ago and it needs to be brought into the public domain. The misery and frustration that goes with dyscalculia is so unnecessary and I predict that once it becomes better known, there will be a tidal wave of people all desperate to share their experiences. Some will burn with shame at their memories, others will be angry or upset, but they will all feel, as I did, the wonderful relief that goes with knowing it wasn't their fault.

CONCLUDING REMARKS

Developmental dyscalculias constitute a significant societal problem. Quantitative literacy is crucial for success in 21st century life, and individuals with impaired quantitative skills are therefore at a serious disadvantage, perhaps most notably in the workplace and in managing their finances. Given especially that developmental dyscalculias are far from rare (e.g., see Barbaresi, Katusic, Colligan, Weaver, & Jacobsen, 2005, for a discussion), this class of learning disability deserves considerably more attention from researchers, practitioners, and policy makers. In addition to basic research on the cognitive and neural dysfunctions underlying the various forms of developmental dyscalculia, there needs to be a better understanding of 1) the quantitative demands adults face in the workplace, home, and community; 2) the difficulties encountered by adults with developmental dyscalculias as they attempt to navigate these demands; and 3) methods (educational, technological, legal, etc.) that could potentially ameliorate the difficulties.

REFERENCES

Australian Association of Mathematics Teachers. (1996). *Mathematical knowledge and understanding for effective participation in Australian society.* Adelaide, South Australia: Author.

Barbaresi, W.J., Katusic, S.K., Colligan, R.C., Weaver, A.L., & Jacobsen, S.J. (2005). Math learning disorder: Incidence in a population-based birth cohort, 1976–82, Rochester, Minn. *Ambulatory Pediatrics, 5,* 281–289.

Blackburn, J. (n.d.). *Damn the three times table.* Retrieved September 7, 2006, from Dyscalculia and Dyslexia Interest Group web site: http://ddig.lboro.ac.uk/documents/Jess_dyscalculia.doc

Bynner, J. (1998). Education and family components of identity in the transition from school to work. *International Journal of Behavioral Development, 22,* 29–53.

Bynner, J., & Parsons, S. (1997). *Does numeracy matter? Evidence from the National Child Development Study on the impact of poor numeracy on adult life.* London: Basic Skills Agency.

Coben, D. (2003). *Adult numeracy: Review of research and related literature.* London: National Research and Development Centre for Adult Literacy and Numeracy.

Curry, D., Schmitt, M.J., & Waldron, S. (1996). *A framework for adult numeracy standards: The mathematical skills and abilities adults need to be equipped for the future.* Retrieved from http:/www.literacynet.org/ann/framework.html, Adult Numeracy Network.

Dossey, J.A. (1997). Defining and measuring quantitative literacy. In L.A.Steen (Ed.), *Why numbers count* (pp. 173–186). New York: College Entrance Examination Board.

Gal, I., van Groenestijn, M., Manly, M., Schmitt, M.J., & Tout, D. (2005). Adult numeracy and its assessment in the ALL survey: A conceptual framework and pilot results. In T.S. Murray, Y. Clermont, & M. Binkley (Eds.), *Measuring adult literacy and life skills: New frameworks for assessment* (pp. 137–191). Ottawa, Canada: Statistics Canada.

Murnane, R.J., Willett, J.B., & Levy, F. (1995). *The growing importance of cognitive skills in wage determination* (Rep. No. 5076). Cambridge, MA: National Bureau of Economic Research.

Murray, T.S., Clermont, Y., & Binkley, M. (2005). *Measuring adult literacy and life skills: New frameworks for assessment.* Ottawa, Canada: Statistics Canada.

Newman, R.M. (1998). *The dyscalculia syndrome: A master's thesis.* Philadelphia: LaSalle University.

Patton, J.R., Cronin, M.E., Bassett, D.S., & Koppel, A.E. (1997). A life skills approach to mathematics instruction: Preparing students with learning disabilities for the real-life math demands of adulthood. *Journal of Learning Disabilities, 30,* 178–187.

Roughneen, G. (2006). Dyscalculia—I can't do sums! *Reality, 71,* 10–12.

Schwartz, L.M., Woloshin, S., & Welch, H.G. (2005). Can patients interpret health information? An assessment of the medical data interpretation test. *Medical Decision Making, 25,* 290–300.

Secretary's Commission on Achieving Necessary Skills. (1991). *What work requires of schools: A SCANS report for America 2000.* Washington, DC: United States Department of Labor.

Siegler, R.S. & Booth, J.L. (2005). Development of numerical estimation: A review. In J.I.D.Campbell (Ed.), *Handbook of mathematical cognition* (pp. 197–212). New York: Psychology Press.

Steen, L.A. (Ed.). (1997). *Why numbers count: Quantitative literacy for tomorrow's America.* New York: College Entrance Examination Board.

Steen, L.A. (2001a). The case for quantitative literacy. In L.A. Steen (Ed.), *Mathematics and democracy: The case for quantitative literacy* (pp. 1–22). Princeton, NJ: Woodrow Wilson National Fellowship Foundation.

Steen, L.A. (Ed.). (2001b). *Mathematics and democracy: The case for quantitative literacy.* Princeton, NJ: Woodrow Wilson National Fellowship Foundation.

White, S., & Dillow, S. (2005). *Key concepts and features of the 2003 National Assessment of Adult Literacy.* Washington, DC: National Center for Education Statistics.

COMMENTARY
Part III, Section VI

Instructional Interventions and Quantitative Literacy

Herbert P. Ginsburg and Sandra Pappas

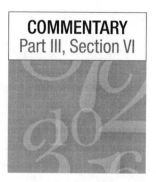

The chapters in Section VI suggest a discussion of basic issues concerning the goals, strategies, content, and methods of intervention for mitigating math learning difficulties, as well as barriers to successful remediation. After reviewing these issues, we conclude with a few words on the contributions and limitations of research providing the foundations for intervention.

WHERE ARE WE NOW?

It is abundantly clear that many people exhibit difficulties in learning mathematics. In one sense, the United States as a whole suffers from underachievement in mathematics. Children in the United States generally perform relatively poorly in international comparisons (Mullis et al., 2000). Moreover, the difficulty is strongly linked to disadvantage: Minority children from low-income families perform more poorly in mathematics (and other subjects) than do their peers from middle-income families (Denton & West, 2002). And some U.S. citizens (a relatively small proportion of children, but a significant number of individuals in general) have genuine learning disabilities that affect their ability to perform well in mathematics.

WHAT SHOULD BE OUR GOALS?

In order to improve the mathematical skills and knowledge of citizens in the United States and elsewhere, we and the authors of these chapters would like readers to consider five goals: prevention, reform, remediation, preparation, and carpe diem.

Prevention

As in many other academic areas, prevention is the key, at least for the vast majority of children. In Chapter 17, Griffin frames the problem nicely, arguing for the development of early mathematics intervention (or prevention) programs and for the application of instructional principles "that can be used to enhance math learning and achievement for a broad range of children, including children who are typically developing as well as those with specific or general developmental lags and/or a learning disabilities." From this perspective (Bowman, Donovan, & Burns, 2001), the most effective strategy for improving achievement and reducing the incidence of learning difficulties is to provide early childhood mathematics education to the broad population of young children, especially minority children from low-income homes who lack the opportunities to develop informal and formal mathematical knowledge and who are at risk of school failure and of attending failing schools (Lee & Burkham, 2002).

Reform

What about those already in the educational system? Obviously, it is essential to improve what our schools currently do. We need exciting new programs of the sort exemplified by the work of Fuchs and Fuchs in Chapter 18 on word problems. But much more is required than specific programs, as valuable as they may be. The system as a whole needs major reform. For example, the development and quality of U.S. textbooks leave a great deal to be desired (The Thomas B. Fordham Institute, 2004).

Remediation

For some children who have genuine learning disabilities, neither prevention nor general reform may be sufficient, and special remedial efforts are needed. In Chapter 18, Fuchs and Fuchs provide a promising example of this approach. They employ special interventions designed to promote self-regulation and metacognition in students with mathematical learning disabilities (MLD) who have difficulty in applying their successful problem-solving methods to novel, more complex tasks (i.e., far transfer).

Preparation

In Chapter 19, McCloskey describes an impressive variety of mathematical skills that adults need to meet the demands of everyday life. These include number sense (e.g., for determining whether a price is reasonable); estimation (e.g., for determining about how much time is needed to complete several tasks); the ability to understand symbolic representations (e.g., for understanding stock market reports or graphs); computer skills (e.g., for entering quality control data into a computer system); and applying quantitative (mathematical) concepts to everyday situations (e.g., for applying knowledge of probability to health-related risks). Of course, these skills are more than strictly "quantitative." They include " . . . the ability to interpret charts, graphs, diagrams, and maps, or the ability to appreciate the sources of uncertainty in economic forecasts." Also central are concepts of "dimension and shape; pattern, functions, and relationships; data and chance."

One of these skills—applying concepts—deserves particular emphasis. Several reports (National Education Goals Panel, 1997; Secretary's Commission on Achieving Necessary Skills, 1991) and mathematicians with experience in industry (e.g., Pollak, 1987) stress the importance of applying mathematical knowledge to complex, real-life problems that go far beyond the kind of anemic and dreary word problems prevalent in textbooks today. The challenge for researchers such as Fuchs and Fuchs is to extend their paradigm to genuinely challenging problem situations.

McCloskey uses fascinating anecdotal data to show how adults with developmental dyscalculia experience great difficulty in coping with the quantitative demands of everyday life as described above—dealing with money, with work, and even with social life (for example, playing cards). But the difficulty is not limited to those with dyscalculia. In our complex economy, U.S. workers generally need to improve their mathematics literacy.

The goal of preparing students for the workforce requires that we broaden the content of the mathematics curriculum. In a sense it is true that a good deal of the mathematics children learn in school really is useless and outmoded. In the age of rapid technological advances, we need to go beyond the straight edge and compass to learn such topics as modeling, application, statistics, and the habits of mind needed for flexible and creative application.

Here's a conjecture: Broadening the mathematics curriculum to make it more relevant and useful will reduce learning difficulties, at least some of which are caused or at least exacerbated by a dull and irrelevant educational experience. Computer programs that simulate workplace experiences involving complex problem solving (Ferrari, Taylor, & VanLehn, 1999) can excite students and produce high levels of achievement, even in children of low socioeconomic status who struggle with mathematics (Duffy, Farr, Greene, & Mikulecky, 2001). It's very possible that programs such as these can even be beneficial to children who have actual learning disabilities. By engaging in challenging problems and group work, children with learning disabilities may capitalize on their real talents (Cole & Traupmann, 1981) rather than focusing on their impairments.

Carpe Diem

In Latin, *carpe diem* means "seize the day." An exaggerated focus on the future can be self-defeating. It entails the danger of ignoring and even spoiling the present and thereby ultimately limiting what can be accomplished in the future. As philosopher and educational theorist John Dewey (who advocated pragmatism and "learning by doing") put it:

> What, then, is the true meaning of preparation in the educational scheme? In the first place, it means that a person, young or old, gets out of his present experience all that there is in it for him at the time in which he has it. When preparation is made the controlling end, then the potentialities of the present are sacrificed to a suppositious future. When this happens, the actual preparation for the future is missed or distorted (1938, p. 49).

The message is simple. We need to help students learn and enjoy as much as they can in the present. In Chapter 17, Griffin maintains that we should "ensure that activities capture children's emotions and imaginations as well as their minds." This may well contribute to enhanced motivation to learn mathematics and serve to diminish the negative feelings often associated with the subject. Clearly, then, one of the goals should be to encourage and foster students' *current* mathematical activities and to avoid having them (and their educators) perpetually worry about that uncertain future (and economic system).

WHAT SHOULD WE TEACH?

There is widespread agreement that beginning in the early years, children should be exposed to a broad range of mathematical content (National Association for the Education of Young Children and National Council of Teachers of Mathematics, 2002). As mentioned, children need to learn not only about number ("numeracy") but also about shape, space, measurement, and pattern. Efforts at "prevention" need to be broad ranging. Similarly, as we have seen, McCloskey argues that to prepare for work and adult life, students in the higher grades need to learn a broad variety of material, ranging from map reading to understanding uncertainties in investments.

Content coverage should be not only broad but deep. As Griffin points out, teaching specific, foundational content knowledge, or "focal points" (NCTM, 2006), should be basic to the enterprise of mathematics education, even at the preschool and kindergarten levels. Furthermore, consensus now exists that foundational knowledge of this type must include mathematics concepts as well as basic facts and procedures (Kilpatrick, Swafford, & Findell, 2001). So, if we are to prevent difficulties and prepare students for the future, even the youngest children should study foundational material from a broad range of topics, and older students should do the same. Fuchs and Fuchs advocate teaching not only content but also important modes of thought: understanding the basic structure of problems and how some changes are relevant and others are not, setting goals for problem solving, making sure answers make sense, checking one's work, explaining work to peers, and evaluating one's performance. Their research reinforces the point that one goal of mathematics education is to promote mathematical *thinking* and *communication*, not just the mastery of skills and concepts. And as we have seen, this kind of intervention may be especially useful for students with MLD and MD.

HOW SHOULD WE TEACH?

If students need to learn foundational concepts in a broad array of areas, as well as sound mathematical thinking, metacognition, and language, how should we teach? Psychological frameworks can provide a good starting point. Griffin begins Chapter 17 by presenting a model of mathematics learning supported both by cognitive neuropsychology (Dehaene, 1997) and cognitive developmental research (Case & Okamoto, 1996). The essence is that fruitful mathematics learning involves children's integration of the real world of quantity with their informal counting system and the formal system of mathematical symbolism. "The counting numbers, which many children have used from the age of 2 and older, thus provide the intermediary link through which the symbolic world becomes connected to the world of real quantities." Although this model is perhaps limited (for example, it may not work well with geometry, where the counting numbers are less relevant), it shares a key idea with other models (e.g., Baroody, 1987; Ginsburg, 2006; Resnick, 1992) that draw on Piaget's (1977) and Dewey's (1976) central insight, namely that meaningful and effective education involves a guided integration of what children bring to the task (their informal knowledge) and the wisdom of the culture (what is taught in school, or at least should be). The general model leads Griffin to create tasks that immerse children in the world of number, draw on their prior knowledge, and attempt to transform it into a more mature and formal form.

In Chapter 18, Fuchs and Fuchs base their approach on a related cognitive model, schema theory, which stresses the understanding of the basic structure of problems and their variant and invariant features. This approach stresses helping students to understand the connections among classes of problems—a key form of sense making in mathematics. As noted earlier, the hope is that the model and instructional interventions will soon be extended to problems more genuine and challenging than the typical textbook word problem.

Of course, a single principle—whether it involves the integration of various areas of knowledge or schema theory—is not enough. In her chapter, Griffin also relies on general cognitive principles useful for learning at any age level (Bransford, Brown, & Cocking, 1998). These principles, which are said to apply to any early mathematics program, include the following:

- Align instruction with the natural developmental progression of mathematical thinking.

- Provide hands-on games and activities that can encourage children to construct meaning.

- Encourage communication in spoken language and writing.

- Ensure that activities capture children's emotions and imaginations.

- Create activities appropriate for children from different cultural and social backgrounds.

We have several comments on these excellent points. First, developmental research does indeed provide guidelines for the introduction of mathematical content. Research has identified typical "trajectories" (Clements, Sarama, & DiBiase, 2004) through which children's mathematical thinking naturally progresses. Clearly, instruction should take the trajectories into account. At the same time, we believe, curriculum developers should not treat them as setting final and absolute limits on what children can learn. Most research from which trajectories derive involves examination of children's current abilities and does not necessarily explore what children *can* do under stimulating conditions. As both Papert (1980) and Vygotsky (1978) pointed out, children may be more capable than we expect, and we can only learn about their true abilities if we challenge them and test them under deliberately atypical conditions.

Second, the use of hands-on activities is crucial, especially for young children. At the same time, all teachers need to understand (as some unfortunately fail to) that the purpose of hands-on activities is not to foster play with the concrete materials themselves but to promote mathematical learning (Kamii, Lewis, & Kirkland, 2001). This is clearly one area where teachers can subvert a developer's good intentions.

Third, the stress on written and verbal communication is commendable. As mentioned previously, metacognition is key. Also, as we have suggested elsewhere (Pappas, Ginsburg, & Jiang, 2003), children from low-income homes may have particular difficulty with putting their thoughts into words, a characteristic that may lead teachers to think of them as less intelligent than they really are and therefore to provide these children with less than optimal instruction.

Fourth, cognitive theorists seldom talk about capturing children's emotions and imaginations, but they should follow Griffin's example. It is vital for children to enjoy mathematical learning (some even love it or can learn to love it) and to respond to it in imaginative ways. We sometimes forget that mathematics learning is not all about learning necessary skills for future economic prosperity but also should involve some degree of creativity and whimsy.

Finally, it is necessary to be sensitive to the learning needs of children from different cultural and social groups. One example involves Mexican American families. Velez-Ibanez and Greenberg (1992) describe "funds of knowledge" in these families that can be drawn on to create effective mathematics learning opportunities for the children in those families. At the same time, one must also recognize that many mathematical abilities and interests are universal, so that most children will be interested in whatever (interesting) mathematical tasks are created for them.

THE REAL WORLD GETS IN THE WAY

In Chapter 17, Griffin shows that the availability of carefully designed, research-based materials does not guarantee their successful application. In the real world, implementation of a curriculum is fraught with difficulties. There are several reasons for this. One is that teachers must be able to adapt any curriculum to their own style of teaching. "This is a teacher's right as well as a teacher's responsibility," she states. However legitimate and desirable, adaptations of a core idea are hard to manage (Cole & Distributed Literacy Consortium, 2006). They require what philosopher William James called the "intermediary inventive mind" of the teacher (1958, pp. 23–24). Yet inventiveness is not overly abundant.

Another source of difficulty is that teachers may misinterpret basic principles. For example, one key principle is to immerse the children in the world of real quantities. But Griffin shows how some teachers subvert the idea by introducing formulas prematurely. Another key principle is to help students integrate implicit and explicit knowledge. But teachers often ignore the integration and stress the formal. Griffin also makes the valuable point that some teacher practices that fall short of the mark may not harm children who are on track but may be particularly damaging for those who are not.

The roadblocks we have described are not isolated examples. Research has established that many teachers lack fundamental mathematical knowledge (Ball & Bass, 2000); that instruction in American preschools is of poor quality, especially for children from low-income homes (Lee & Burkham, 2002; Pianta et al., 2005); and that instruction in the United States seems to focus more on procedures than on concepts that can make procedures meaningful (Stigler & Perry, 1990). We have already reviewed shortcomings in textbooks. It is perhaps not an exaggeration to maintain that the biggest risk factor in learning problems—especially for minority children from low-income homes—is the educational system itself.

A FINAL POINT ON PRIDE AND MODESTY

Griffin's chapter begins by pointing out something that researchers should be proud of, namely that since the 1980s and 1990s, cognitive research on the development of mathematical thinking has not only grown by leaps and bounds but has also made substantial progress. The research community has provided a good conceptual foundation for thinking about problems of learning difficulty and disability (Gersten, Jordan, & Flojo, 2005; Jordan, Hanich, & Uberti, 2003); the theoretical basis for sound methods of assessment, for example, the Number Knowledge Test (Griffin & Case, 1997) and the TEMA-3 (Ginsburg & Baroody, 2003); and also the underpinnings of several curricula and programs (as represented in the work of Griffin and Fuchs and Fuchs). The research has even influenced the content of television shows such as *Sesame Street* and *Blue's Clues* (Fisch, 2004). "Basic" cognitive research on the apparently esoteric subject of young children's mathematical thinking has proven to be of great practical value.

Furthermore, as we have seen, Griffin proposes that basic psychological principles of instruction are of supreme importance. She argues, "an instructional principle determines the general and specific goals of a curriculum as well as the entire set of teaching materials that is created to address these goals" (Chapter 17). Although we concur that instructional principles can and should guide curriculum development, we do not agree that they should fully determine it. In our view, this places too great a burden on instructional principles and those who create them. Principles need to be supplemented by strong doses of creativity, whimsy, and fun. The cognitive principle may specify that immersing children in the world of real quantities stimulates learning, but the curriculum developer can implement it in many ways, some more engaging than others. Creating attractive materials is perhaps more the province of the artist or even the classroom teacher than of the research psychologist. As Shakespeare's Hamlet noted to his friend and fellow student (an educational research scholar) from Wittenberg University, "There are more things in heaven and earth, Horatio, than are dreamt of in your philosophy" (Act 1, Scene 5).

REFERENCES

Ball, D.L., & Bass, H. (2000). Interweaving content and pedagogy in teaching and learning to teach: Knowing and using mathematics. In J. Boaler (Ed.), *Multiple perspectives on the teaching and learning of mathematics* (pp. 83–104). Stamford, CT: Ablex.

Baroody, A.J. (1987). *Children's mathematical thinking: A developmental framework for preschool, primary, and special education teachers.* New York: Teachers College Press.

Bowman, B.T., Donovan, M.S., & Burns, M.S. (Eds.). (2001). *Eager to learn: Educating our preschoolers.* Washington, DC: National Academies Press.

Bransford, J.D., Brown, A.L., & Cocking, R.R. (Eds.). (1998). *How people learn: Brain, mind, experience, and school.* Washington, DC: National Academies Press.

Case, R., & Okamoto, Y. (1996). The role of central conceptual structures in the development of children's thought. *Monographs of the Society for Research in Child Development, 61*(1–2, Serial No. 246).

Clements, D.H., Sarama, J., & DiBiase, A.-M. (Eds.). (2004). *Engaging young children in mathematics: Standards for early childhood mathematics education.* Mahwah, NJ: Lawrence Erlbaum Associates.

Cole, M., & Distributed Literacy Consortium. (2006). *The Fifth Dimension: An after-school program built on diversity.* New York: Russell Sage Foundation.

Cole, M., & Traupmann, K. (1981). Comparative cognitive research: Learning from a learning disabled child. In W.A. Collins (Ed.), *The Minnesota Symposia on Child Psychology, Vol. 14* (pp. 125–154). Mahwah, NJ: Lawrence Erlbaum Associates.

Dehaene, S. (1997). *The number sense: How the mind creates mathematics.* Oxford, UK: Oxford University Press.

Denton, K., & West, J. (2002). *Children's reading and mathematics achievement in kindergarten and first grade.* Washington, DC: National Center for Education Statistics.

Dewey, J. (1938). *Experience and education.* New York: Collier Books.

Dewey, J. (1976). The child and the curriculum. In J.A. Boydston (Ed.), *John Dewey: The middle works, 1899–1924: Vol. 2. 1902–1903* (pp. 273–291). Carbondale: Southern Illinois University Press.

Duffy, T., Farr, R., Greene, E., & Mikulecky, L. (2001). *A study examining an innovative classroom program: Distance education, accountability, and problem solving: Preliminary final report.* New York: The Andrew W. Mellon Foundation.

Ferrari, M., Taylor, R., & VanLehn, K. (1999). Adapting work simulations for schools. *Journal of Educational Computing Research, 21*(1), 25–53.

Fisch, S.M. (2004). *Children's learning from educational television: Sesame Street and beyond.* Mahwah, NJ: Laurence Erlbaum Associates.

Gersten, R., Jordan, N.C., & Flojo, J.R. (2005). Early identification and interventions for students with mathematics difficulties. *Journal of Learning Disabilities, 38*(4), 293–304.

Ginsburg, H.P. (2006). Mathematical play and playful mathematics: A guide for early education. In D. Singer, R.M. Golinkoff, & K. Hirsh-Pasek (Eds.), *Play = learning: How play motivates and enhances children's cognitive and social-emotional growth* (pp. 145–165). New York: Oxford University Press.

Ginsburg, H.P., & Baroody, A.J. (2003). *The test of early mathematics ability* (3rd ed.). Austin, TX: PRO-ED.

Griffin, S., & Case, R. (1997). Rethinking the primary school math curriculum: An approach based on cognitive science. *Issues in Education, 3,* 1–49.

James, W. (1958). *Talks to teachers on psychology and to students on some of life's ideals.* New York: W.W. Norton & Company.

Jordan, N.C., Hanich, L.B., & Uberti, H Z. (2003). Mathematical thinking and learning difficulties. In A.J. Baroody & A. Dowker (Eds.), *The development of arithmetic concepts and skills: Constructing adaptive expertise* (pp. 359–383). Mahwah, NJ: Lawrence Erlbaum Associates.

Kamii, C., Lewis, B.A., & Kirkland, L. (2001). Manipulatives: When are they useful? *The Journal of Mathematical Behavior, 20* (1), 21–31.

Kilpatrick, J., Swafford, J., & Findell, B. (Eds.). (2001). *Adding it up: Helping children learn mathematics.* Washington, DC: National Academies Press.

Lee, V.E., & Burkham, D.T. (2002). *Inequality at the starting gate: Social background differences in achievement as children begin school.* Washington, DC: Economic Policy Institute.

Mullis, I.V.S., Martin, M.O., Gonzalez, D.L., Gregory, K.D., Garden, R.A., & O'Connor, K.M. (2000). *TIMSS 1999 International Mathematics Report: Findings from IEA's repeat of the Third International Mathematics and Science Study at the eighth grade.* Boston: International Study Center, Boston College.

National Association for the Education of Young Children and National Council of Teachers of Mathematics. (2002). Position statement. *Early childhood mathematics: Promoting good beginnings*. Retrieved from http://www.naeyc.org/about/positions/psmath.asp

National Council of Teachers of Mathematics. (2006). *Curriculum focal points for pre-kindergarten through grade 8 mathematics: A quest for coherence*. Reston, VA: Author.

National Education Goals Panel. (1997). *The national education goals report: Mathematics and science achievement for the 21st century*. Washington, DC: Author.

Papert, S. (1980). *Mindstorms: Children, computers, and powerful ideas*. New York: Basic Books.

Pappas, S., Ginsburg, H.P., & Jiang, M. (2003). SES differences in young children's metacognition in the context of mathematical problem solving. *Cognitive Development, 18*(3), 431–450.

Piaget, J. (1977). Comments on mathematical education. In H.E. Gruber & J.J. Voneche (Eds.), *The essential Piaget* (pp. 726–732). New York: Basic Books.

Pianta, R.C., Howes, C., Burchinal, M., Bryant, D.M., Clifford, D., Early, D., et al. (2005). Features of pre-kindergarten programs, classrooms, and teachers: Do they predict observed class-room quality and child-teacher interactions? *Applied Developmental Science, 93*(3), 144–159.

Pollak, H.O. (1987). Cognitive science and mathematics education: A mathematician's perspective. In A.H. Schoenfeld (Ed.), *Cognitive science and mathematics education* (pp. 253–264). Mahwah, NJ: Lawrence Erlbaum Associates.

Resnick, L.B. (1992). From protoquantities to operators: Building mathematical competence on a foundation of everyday knowledge. In G. Leinhardt, R. Putnam, & R.A. Hattrup (Eds.), *Analysis of arithmetic for mathematics teaching* (pp. 373–429). Mahwah, NJ: Lawrence Erlbaum Associates.

Secretary's Commission on Achieving Necessary Skills. (1991). *What work requires of schools: A SCANS report for America 2000*. Washington, DC: United States Department of Labor.

Stigler, J.W., & Perry, M. (1990). Mathematics learning in Japanese, Chinese, and American classrooms. In J.W. Stigler, R.A. Shweder, & G. Herdt (Eds.), *Cultural psychology: Essays on comparative human development* (pp. 328–353). New York: Cambridge University Press.

The Thomas B. Fordham Institute. (2004). *The mad, mad world of textbook adoption*. Washington, DC: Author.

Velez-Ibanez, C.G., & Greenberg, J.B. (1992). Formation and transformation of funds of knowledge among U.S.-Mexican households. *Anthropology and Education Quarterly, 23*(4), 313–335.

Vygotsky, L.S. (1978). *Mind in society: The development of higher psychological processes*. Cambridge, MA: Harvard University Press.

Index

Page references followed by *f* indicate figures; those followed by *t* indicate tables; those followed by *n* indicate footnotes.